BRITISH ECONOMIC GROWTH

1688-1959

TRENDS AND STRUCTURE

BY

PHYLLIS DEANE

AND

W. A. COLE

Department of Applied Economics
University of Cambridge

SECOND EDITION

CAMBRIDGE UNIVERSITY PRESS

CAMBRIDGE

LONDON   NEW YORK   NEW ROCHELLE

MELBOURNE   SYDNEY

Published by the Press Syndicate of the University of Cambridge
The Pitt Building, Trumpington Street, Cambridge CB2 1RP
32 East 57th Street, New York, NY 10022, USA
296 Beaconsfield Parade, Middle Park, Melbourne 3206, Australia

Library of Congress catalogue card number: 67-21956

ISBN 0 521 04801 X hard covers
ISBN 0 521 09569 7 paperback

First published 1962
Reprinted 1964
Second edition 1967
First paperback edition 1969
Reprinted 1978 1980

First printed in Great Britain by
Spottiswoode Ballantyne & Co. Ltd, London and Colchester
Reprinted in Great Britain at the
University Press, Cambridge

CONTENTS

List of Tables   *page* vii

List of Figures   xi

Preface to the Second Edition   xiii

Preface to the First Edition   xvii

Chapter I   Taking the Long View of British Economic Growth

1	The starting-point	1
2	Broad trends in population growth	5
3	The value of money	12
4	The wages of labour	18
5	The changing relationship with the rest of the world	28
6	The vantage of the nineteen-fifties	38

Chapter II   The Eighteenth-Century Origins of Economic Growth

1	The evidence of the trade statistics	41
2	The course of industrial change	50
3	The role of agriculture	62
4	Trends in total and per capita real output	75
5	The mechanics of eighteenth-century growth	82

Chapter III   Industrialisation and Population Change in the Eighteenth and Early Nineteenth Centuries

1	The changing distribution of population	99
2	Migration and natural increase	106
3	Changes in birth and death rates	122

Chapter IV   Changes in the Industrial Distribution of the Labour Force and Employment Incomes in the Nineteenth and Twentieth Centuries

1	The evidence of the census returns	137
2	The changing distribution of the labour force 1801–1951	141
3	The industrial distribution of incomes from employment 1801–1951	148

Chapter V   The Changing Structure of National Product

1   Structure of national product in the eighteenth century   155
2   The structure of industry at the beginning of the nine-
     teenth century   158
3   The period of industrialisation   164
4   Industrial structure in the twentieth century   173
5   Two and a half centuries of industrial change   179

Chapter VI   The Growth of the Nineteenth-Century Staples

1   The textile industries   182
2   The mining industry   214
3   The iron industry   221
4   The transport industry   229

Chapter VII   Long-term Trends in the Factor Composition of
                   National Income

1   Incomes from employment since the First World War   243
2   Incomes from employment before the First World War   245
3   Employment incomes before 1860   248
4   Conclusions   255

Chapter VIII   Long-term Trends in Capital Formation

1   Changes in the rate of capital formation   259
2   Changes in the structure of the national capital   269

Chapter IX   British Economic Growth in Retrospect: A
                   Summary of Conclusions

1   Long-term trends in national income   278
2   The role of population in economic growth   285
3   Changes in industrial structure   290
4   Long-term changes in factor shares   299
5   Changes in the rate of capital formation   303
6   Long-term trends in the volume of international trade   309
7   Twentieth-century trends   312

Appendix 1   Statistics of eighteenth-century trade   315

Appendix 2   Note on incomes assessed to tax in the Napoleonic
                   Wars   323

Appendix 3   United Kingdom national income tables   329

Literature   336

Index   345

LIST OF TABLES

1	The social accounts of England and Wales in 1688	page 2
2	Estimates of population in the eighteenth century	6
3	The growth of population in the United Kingdom	8
4	Net gain or loss by migration in England, 1841–1911	10
5	Indices of eighteenth-century money wages in building	19
6	The course of money wages 1790–1860	23
7	Money wages and real wages 1850–1906	25
8	The rate of growth of international trade	29
9	The changing pattern of British commodity exports 1830–1950	31
10	The pattern of imports into the United Kingdom 1840–1950	33
11	The balance of payments of the United Kingdom 1816–1913	36
12	The balance of payments of the United Kingdom 1907–1938	37
13	Comparison of the official value of eighteenth century foreign trade with estimates of the value at constant 1796–8 prices	44
14	Eighteenth-century foreign trade	48
15	Selected indicators of eighteenth-century industrial growth	51
16	Selected eighteenth-century exports	59
17	Estimates of corn output in England and Wales in the eighteenth century	65
18	Indicators of eighteenth-century meat production	72
19	Index numbers of eighteenth-century real output	78
20	Estimated annual percentage rates of growth of eighteenth-century real output	80
21	Eighteenth-century price relatives: imports and exports	84
22	Geographical distribution of eighteenth-century foreign trade	87
23	Index numbers of the price of wheat in relation to the prices of producer and other consumer goods	91
24	Estimated population of England and Wales by counties 1701–1831	103
25	Migration and natural increase 1701–1831	108
26	Average annual rates of migration and natural increase 1701–1830	115
27	Migration and natural increase by regions	118
28	Average regional birth and death rates, 1701–1830	127
29	Average county birth rate and death rates, 1701–1830	131
30	Estimated percentage distribution of the British Labour force, 1801–1951	142
31	Estimated industrial distribution of the British Labour force 1801–1951	143

32 Distribution of the labour force in manufacturing industry 1891–1951 *page* 146

33 Distribution of the occupied population of the United Kingdom   147

34 The industrial distribution of British wages and salaries 1801–1858   152

35 The structure of national product before the industrial revolution   156

36 The structure of British national product at the beginning of the nineteenth century   161

37 The industrial distribution of the national income of Great Britain   166

38 Nineteenth-century rates of growth in the real product of Great Britain   170

39 Nineteenth-century rates of growth in the average real product of Great Britain   172

40 The industrial distribution of the national income of Great Britain in the first quarter of the twentieth century   175

41 Distribution of the gross national product of the United Kingdom 1924–55   178

42 Estimates of cotton-industry output, 1760–1816   185

43 Development of the cotton manufacture of the United Kingdom, 1819–1907   187

44 Age and sex distribution of cotton operatives, 1835–1907   190

45 Capital equipment of the cotton industry, 1819–1903   191

46 Estimates of sheep and wool output in the first half of the nineteenth century: derived from contemporary sources   195

47 The growth of the United Kingdom woollen industry, 1805–1908   196

48 Spindles and looms in the woollen industry, 1840–1904   200

49 The output of the United Kingdom linen industry, 1770–1907   204

50 Estimated output of the jute industry, 1870–1907   207

51 The nineteenth-century silk industry   210

52 Net output of the principal textile industries of the United Kingdom, 1770–1870   212

53 Index of the growth in real net output for textiles, 1770–1870   213

54 Nineteenth-century coal output   216

55 Estimated distribution of coal in the United Kingdom   219

56 Growth of the iron and steel industry, 1805–1907   225

57 Share of the iron industry in the national product of Great Britain, 1805–1907   226

58 Numbers of blast furnaces, 1806–1910   228

59 United Kingdom railway investment, 1800–46   231

60 The growth of the railway industry 1845–60   232

61 Development of the railway industry in the second half of the nineteenth century   233

62 The growth of the United Kingdom shipping industry *page* 234

63 National income and incomes from employment, United Kingdom, 1920–59 244

64 The components of United Kingdom employment incomes 1920–58 245

65 The distribution of United Kingdom national income, 1860–1959 247

66 Distribution of the occupied population by industrial status, 1911–51 248

67 Industrial composition of United Kingdom wages and salaries, 1901–56 257

68 The disposition of resources in the United Kingdom, 1860–1959 266

69 Gross capital formation deflated by an index of money wages 269

70 The structure of the national capital of Great Britain, 1798–1927 271

71 The national capital, 1865–1933. Estimated by the income method 274

72 The national product of Great Britain in the nineteenth century 282

73 Nineteenth-century rates of growth in British real formation 283

74 United Kingdom rates of growth 1855–1959 284

75 Rates of growth of population, 1701–1931 288

76 The structure of British national product 291

77 The rate of growth of United Kingdom industrial production 297

78 The share of agriculture in United Kingdom national income 1867–1934 298

79 Twentieth century industrial structure in the United Kingdom 299

80 Estimates of the distribution of income by factor shares 301

81 Changes in the reproducible national capital of Great Britain, 1832–1933 306

82 Trends in United Kingdom capital formation, 1860–1959 308

83 Growth in volume of international trade and national income in the nineteenth century 311

84 Ratios of the real to the official values of selected imports, re-exports and exports, 1796–8 317

85 Official values of eighteenth-century foreign trade 319

86 Woollen exports 1697–1708 322

87 Gross incomes assessed to tax 1800–14 325

88 Schedule A assessments, 1806–14 327

89 Estimated national income of Great Britain 1801 and 1811 328

90 The growth of national income 1855–1959 329

91 The disposition of gross national product at market prices, 1860–1959 332

92 Three approaches to an estimate of United Kingdom G.N.P. 335

LIST OF FIGURES

1   Eighteenth-century foreign trade   *page* 46

2   The growth of foreign trade   49

3   Printed goods charged with duty, 1713–98   54

4   The growth of eighteenth-century real output   81

5   Average annual rates of natural increase, 1701–1800   116

6   Births, deaths and populations, by regions, 1701–1831   126

7   The long-term trend in British prices, 1661–1959   *pullout at end of book*

PREFACE TO THE SECOND EDITION

SINCE the first edition of this book went to press in 1961 there have been two developments encouraging us to re-think this first attempt to establish the main quantitative features of British economic growth since 1688. The first was the publication of certain new, more definitive, research results where we had made shift with very rough estimates. The second was the appearance of some thoughtful and stimulating reviews which cast doubt on some of our less convincing judgments and hypotheses.

Neither the new researches nor the critical comments so far published have yet touched more than limited sections of the very wide field that we have tried to cover in this book. So this is not the time for a major revision. But we have taken the opportunity of a new printing to correct the errors of which we have now been made aware, to re-write some passages where the argument seemed to be unnecessarily obscure or incomplete, and to replace some rough estimates with figures based on deeper research.

The main substantive changes that have been made in this edition are as follows: (1) In Chapter VI our estimates of capital investment in the railway and cotton industries respectively (pp. 229–34 and pp. 190–2) have been radically revised on the basis of Dr Mitchell's and Dr Blaug's researches.[1] (2) In Chapter IX we have modified our conclusion on the influence of structural change on the rate of U.K. economic growth towards the end of the nineteenth century (pp. 299–300) in the light of calculations made by Professor Ashworth.[2] (3) At the end of Appendix 3 we have now included a rough reconciliation of our various national income estimates. In addition, of course, there are consequent additions to the bibliography on pp. 336–343, but we have made no attempt to expand the latter so as to include all the relevant new material published since 1961: it may be worth repeating here (since it seems to have escaped the notice of some of our critics) that the list of items included in the bibliography is not an exhaustive list of works consulted in the course of this inquiry but an alphabetical list of books, pamphlets and articles specifically referred to in text or footnote.

Apart from these changes and from a number of minor amendments designed to correct errors or clear up obscurities and misconceptions

---

[1] B. R. Mitchell, 'The Coming of the Railway and United Kingdom Economic Growth' *Journal of Economic History*, September 1964. M. Blaug, 'The Productivity of Capital in the Lancashire Cotton Industry during the Nineteenth Century', *Economic History Review* 1961.

[2] W. Ashworth, 'Changes in Industrial Structure', *Yorkshire Bulletin of Economic and Social Research*, 1965.

pointed out by our readers we have left our main estimates and conclusions unaltered. This is not because we are inclined to shrug off the criticism to which this book has been subjected by some of its more serious reviewers. It is because they have not, in our view, advanced the argument, even where their doubts have been most impressive.

Essentially the criticisms have been of three main kinds. First there have been those who are dubious of the basic methodology of our approach and who suspect that attempts to analyse the origins and causes of economic growth through the media of national income aggregates run the risk of obscuring the significant factors, because the experience of a pre-industrial economy does not fit naturally into the conventional national income matrix.[1] The risk is real enough but it is necessary to take it. It is not possible to study economic growth without some sort of quantitative yardstick to indicate the timing, directions and pace of economic change at the national level. Hence it is important to make the statistical bases of our judgments as explicit and as systematic as possible (even if this serves only to reveal the extent of our ignorance) rather than to mask it in a cloud of quantitative generalities or partial quantities or qualitative indicators. If the national income approach is too narrow it is necessary to suggest practical ways of supplementing it with a broader vision, not to abandon it.

Secondly, there have been criticisms of the statistical bases of our estimates. In particular, for example, the estimates of the growth of eighteenth-century output in Table 19 (p. 78) have come under fire. We have lamented the inadequacies of our statistical raw material at such length already that it scarcely seems necessary to do more than agree wholeheartedly with this criticism. As far as the estimates in Table 19 are concerned, however, it may be worth repeating that they are put forward as 'a set of hypotheses about the causes of eighteenth-century growth rather than a set of conclusions.' We could have developed a more complex set of estimates by embodying more series and making more adjustments (e.g. for factors like the cattle plague or for smuggling). In practice, however, we found that the refinements and adjustments which it was open to us to make with the material at our disposal were so inconclusive and arbitrary, and so unimportant in their effect on the rates of growth which it was our objective to calculate, that it was not worth complicating the picture by including them. Readers who use the estimates in Table 19—estimates which were deliberately based on a representative rather than an exhaustive collection of series—can see clearly the limited range and the implications of their tools and will beware accordingly.

Similarly, we would accept the criticisms of the price indices which have been used to deflate our nineteenth-century income or output estimates in trying to measure rates of growth. When considering the

[1] Cf. A. H. John, *Kyklos* 1964, p. 280, 'All in all, it is difficult to avoid the conclusion that aggregates may well darken counsel in the studies of economies other than the very modern.'

differing rates of growth derived from different deflators, however, it is salutary to recall that there is not one answer to the question 'what was the rate of growth of the economy over a particular period of time?' There are several valid answers, each dependent on the implied value system adopted, i.e. on the weights attached to particular prices. This is not to deny that the inadequacy of our price data was the most significant gap of all in the statistics we had at our disposal. But even had we all the price quotations we wanted we should still find that the deflation of a national product table designed, say, for purposes of productivity analysis would suggest a different rate of growth to the deflation of a national expenditure table in which the object was to draw welfare conclusions: and of course in either case we should find that in a long period of rapid economic change a deflator based on the weights appropriate to an early year in a series would generally give an appreciably higher rate of growth than one based on a late year in the series.

Finally, and most commonly, there were the critics who pointed out that the evidence we presented in support of some of our cherished hypotheses were open to alternative explanations.[1] This point was often made, and with justice, in relation to our argument that the crucial beginnings of economic growth can be dated from the 1740's rather than the 1780's. Of course this is true and some of the alternative hypotheses advanced by our reviewers seemed to us forceful and plausible. Were we to write this book again today we might be tempted to take our stand on somewhat different ground, notably, for example, on the role of foreign trade in eighteenth-century growth. As it is, the alternative hypotheses, being supported, as yet, by no better basis of data than our own, remain interesting alternatives. A major revision of this book will become necessary when new data become available as a result of new research. Till then there seems no reason to tear up the temporary building blocks we have laid down here.

November 1966.   P. D.
                                                                   W. A. C.

---

[1] Cf. Donald Whitehead, *Business Archives and History*, 1964, and J. F. Wright, *Economic History Review*, 1965.

PREFACE TO THE FIRST EDITION

THE object of the inquiry which gave rise to this volume was to establish the main quantitative features of the British economy over as long a period as the available statistics would permit. It is the first attempt of its kind to tell the story of British economic development in quantitative terms, but it is not likely to be the last for two reasons. One of these is the current interest in the theory of economic growth. Growth is essentially a quantitative concept and it is not possible to test or to assess the validity of existing theories of economic growth, partial though they are, without a knowledge of the chronology and relative dimensions of the factors at work in specific cases. In this connection the experience of the first country to undergo an industrial revolution is of special interest, both because it was the first and because it permits the longest time-perspective.

The second main reason why this study is not likely to be the last of its kind is that so many of its results have turned out to be tentative and questionable. What it led to was not a set of definitive conclusions but a collection of what seemed to us to be consistent (though by no means exhaustive) hypotheses. The statistical data proved to be both more numerous and more incomplete than we had expected. While we have reasonable confidence that we have discerned the main features of the growth process and that our measurements, though rough, are generally of the right order of magnitude, the details of the picture are extremely doubtful; and it is the details that may be crucial in suggesting the causal connections of the process. Moreover, for the earlier part of the period of over two and a half centuries which we have tried to cover, the statistics were too incomplete to permit systematic estimates of the main aggregates. For most of the eighteenth century our quantitative conclusions are heavily dependent on our interpretation of qualitative evidence. Our results for the nineteenth century are based on a small part of the evidence available in parliamentary papers and other contemporary documents. We have made little use of the immense statistical resources of the twentieth century except to use the readily available material to bring the main features of the story up to date. We started out with the intention of covering the whole of the United Kingdom, but in the event this proved too much for us. Most of the eighteenth-century material in this book relates to England and Wales, and most of the nineteenth-century material to Great Britain.

We have tried, by constant criticism of our own interpretations and estimates and of the data on which they are based, to emphasise their weaknesses and to indicate the directions in which they might be improved. This preoccupation with the data has resulted in a certain lack of balance in the shape of the volume, which is reflected in the unequal length of the chapters. A brief treatment of a particular topic may be justified by our confidence in the results and their underlying data; or it may be an indication that we have not been able to do any original work on the topic and have preferred to state our conclusions without elaborate discussion of bases which are obviously crude or have been fully discussed in another source. Conversely, a lengthy description of problems and methods of inquiry leading up to a particular conclusion may represent a detailed description of new estimates and interpretations, or a recapitulation of well-known arguments, designed to reveal their inconsistencies and inadequacies as well as their strength as bases for familiar conclusions.

This persistent scepticism may also have lent a certain inconclusiveness to the results without ensuring their freedom from the obstinate blind spots affecting most investigators who try to organise incomplete records into a coherent story. It would be a pity if we seemed to doubt those aspects of our conclusions in which we have reasonable confidence. On the other hand, we believe that the compilers of estimates which are not subject to conclusive empirical check should be their own severest critics. Once such estimates reach the sanctity of print the incentive to question them is much reduced. It is essential to keep them under continuous critical review.

The plan of the volume is as follows. The first chapter represents an attempt to put into long-term perspective certain important concomitants of economic growth which are discussed incidentally or in greater detail in later chapters but whose general trend it is convenient to outline in advance of the detailed discussions. Chapter II, on the eighteenth-century origins of economic growth, attempts to deduce from eighteenth-century statistics a plausible chronology of the beginnings of rapid economic growth in each of the major sectors of the economy and an assessment of the progress achieved by the English economy as a whole in the course of the century. In view of the importance of the role of population in the early stages of the industrial revolution, chapter III considers separately the published evidence on the timing and economic significance of changes in the English birth rate, death rate, and internal distribution of the population.

For the nineteenth and twentieth centuries our attention has been mainly concentrated on the task of measuring changes in the industrial structure. Before the first censuses of production the main source of evidence on industrial structure was the decennial census of population which began in 1801. Chapter IV uses the evidence of the census returns to measure the changing industrial distribution of the population, and, largely with the aid of Bowley's and Wood's collections of wage and salary data, to arrive at estimates of incomes from employment at decade intervals from 1801 to 1911. Chapter V combines these estimates of employment incomes analysed by industry with census of production data and national income estimates to calculate the changing structure of national product from 1801 to 1955. These calculations are necessarily confined to a somewhat broad industry grouping (at any rate until 1907 when the first census of production was taken) and to bench-mark years. Chapter VI estimates in greater detail, and for a more continuous time-period, changes in the nineteenth-century rate of growth of some of the major individual industries. Chapters VII and VIII summarise briefly the readily available evidence on two other aspects of long-term economic growth—the shifts in the distribution of incomes among factors of production and the changes in the rates and patterns of capital formation. Finally, in chapter IX we have tried to summarise the findings of the inquiry by considering the main features of British economic growth over a period of about two and a half centuries.

Most of the statistics which are printed in this volume are processed data. In view of the highly subjective character of much of this processing and of the scope for differences in interpretation of the raw material, we should feel obliged to reprint a much larger proportion of the original series underlying our estimates were it not for the fact that they will be largely reprinted elsewhere. Dr Mitchell has prepared an abstract of historical statistics for Great Britain, which will contain the basic series that we have found of most use in this study, and is being published as a companion volume. The trade statistics compiled by Mrs Schumpeter, on which much of the argument of Chapter II is based, have been published in a volume which is edited by Professor T. S. Ashton. We are grateful to Professor Ashton for allowing us to photograph and use these statistics in advance of publication at an early stage of our inquiry.

The inquiry into the economic growth of the United Kingdom of which this study and the abstract of historical statistics are the joint products, was carried out at the University of Cambridge Department of Applied Economics with the aid of a grant from the Committee on Economic Growth of the Social Science Research Council. We are glad to have this opportunity to express our gratitude to the Committee on Economic Growth which provided the original grant and generously extended it to enable us to complete this book and the abstract of historical statistics. We are indebted to many economists and economic historians for advice and assistance at various stages of our investigation, but we should like in particular to express our thanks to Professor J. R. N. Stone, Professor T. S. Ashton, Mr Charles Wilson and Mr David Joslin, who were on the advisory committee which launched the project, and to Mr Kenneth Berrill, whose constructive criticism indicated some of the obscurities and weaknesses of the penultimate draft. To Professor Simon Kuznets, who initiated the inquiry as one of a series of similar studies in different countries, we are immensely indebted for inspiration, encouragement and example at all stages of the investigation.

Finally, we want to acknowledge the patient collaboration of those members of the Department of Applied Economics who helped us with this book, and in particular to thank Mrs Lilian Silk who did much of the typing, Mrs Verna Drake who carried out most of the tedious and tricky calculations involved in processing eighteenth-century statistics, and Mr Gilbert Warren who drew all the graphs.

P. D.
W. A. C.

CHAPTER I

TAKING THE LONG VIEW OF BRITISH ECONOMIC GROWTH

I. THE STARTING-POINT

THE period we propose to take into consideration in this volume begins with the Glorious Revolution of 1688 and ends in the 1950's. The starting-point was imposed by the nature of the data available. To this period belong the first regularly compiled statistics of English overseas trade, the first acceptable population estimate and the first systematic contemporary estimate of national income and expenditure.

Unfortunately it was not the beginning of a new era in economic statistics. More than a century passed before the administrative records yielded as good a basis for a quantitative analysis of the English economy as they had at the time of Gregory King. In their completeness and internal consistency his estimates remained unique until the twentieth century. But their usefulness is somewhat reduced by their isolation, by the fact that there are no independent statistics for the pre-industrial period which are adequate to check or confirm or compare with the overall picture given by King.

They are valuable nevertheless, if only as a precise statement of the dimensions which a well-informed contemporary attributed to the English economy at the end of the seventeenth century. From King's manuscripts and working sheets and from the contemporary sources in which his data were analysed it is possible to construct an outline set of social accounts for England and Wales *circa* 1688.[1] Except that his definition of a household was such as to net out the incomes of domestics and that he distinguished no corporate sector, he provided all the information required for a set of accounts. Probably the omission of a corporate sector was unimportant. The total paid-up capital of British joint-stock companies was not much more than half a million pounds at this period.[2] The omission of the incomes of domestics is more serious if we want to make comparisons with later periods, and a rough estimate (itself based on King's figures) was necessary to complete the picture. The resulting set of accounts is summarised in Table 1.

The picture presented by King's estimates was of an economy dominated by the economic activities of the household sector. We may

---

[1] A detailed discussion of the sources and methods involved in setting up these accounts is given in Phyllis Deane, 'The Implications of Early National Income Estimates for the Measurement of Long-Term Economic Growth in the United Kingdom', *Economic Development and Cultural Change* (November 1955).

[2] W. R. Scott, *The Constitution and Finance of English, Scottish and Irish Joint Stock Companies* (1911), vol. I, p. 325, and vol. III, pp. 461 *et seq.*

Table 1. *The social accounts of England and Wales in 1688* (in £m.)

I. NATIONAL PRODUCT AND EXPENDITURE

1. Indirect taxes			4. Consumption of goods and services (10)	46·0
(a) Central government (20)	2·1		5. Government expenditure on goods and services (17)	2·4
(b) Local government (21)	0·7		6. Domestic capital formation (24)	1·7
2. National income at factor cost (14)	48·0		7. Exports (29)	5·1
			8. Less imports (31)	−4·4
3. National product at market prices	50·8		9. Expenditure on national product	50·8

II. PERSONAL INCOME AND EXPENDITURE

10. Consumption by persons (4)			14. Incomes (2)	
(a) Food	20·0		(a) Rents	13·0
(b) Drink	1·3		(b) Wages and salaries	17·7
(c) Rent	2·5		(c) Cottagers and paupers	2·6
(d) Clothing	10·4		(d) Profits, interest and other mixed incomes	14·7
(e) Domestic service	4·5			
(f) Other goods and services	7·3			
11. Direct taxes (22)	0·2		15. Transfers to poor (18)	0·6
12. Saving (27)	2·4			
13. Total personal expenditure	48·6		16. Total personal incomes	48·6

III. GOVERNMENT INCOME AND EXPENDITURE

17. Expenditure on goods and services (5)			20. Customs and excise duties (1a)	2·1
(a) Central government	2·3		21. Poor rate (1b)	0·7
(b) Local government	0·1		22. Hearth money (11)	0·2
18. Poor-relief (15)	0·6			
19. Total government expenditure	3·0		23. Total government income	3·0

IV. CAPITAL ACCOUNT

24. Domestic investment (6)	1·7		27. Private saving (12)	2·4
25. Foreign lending (32)	0·7			
26. Payments on capital account	2·4		28. Receipts on capital account	2·4

V. REST OF THE WORLD ACCOUNT

29. Exports (7)			31. Imports (8)	
(a) Merchandise f.o.b.	4·3		(a) Merchandise f.o.b.	4·0
(b) Shipping services	0·8		(b) Shipping services	0·4
			32. Foreign lending (25)	0·7
30. Total receipts from abroad	5·1		33. Total payments abroad	5·1

Sources and notes: Two Tracts by Gregory King, edited by George E. Barnett (1936); Charles Davenant, *Works*. For more detailed reference to sources see Deane, *Economic Development and Cultural Change* (1955), *op. cit.* Some items were estimated by us—in particular item 10 (*e*), incomes of domestics—and there was an element of estimate in the breakdown between food and drink (based on King's 1695 estimates) and in the breakdown of local government expenditure on poor-relief and other goods and services.

The factor incomes distinguished under item 14 are classified arbitrarily. Wages and salaries, for example, include the incomes of persons in offices, clergymen, persons in science and the liberal arts, artisans and craftsmen, labouring people and outservants, naval and military officers, common seamen and soldiers. It is evident that not all these represent incomes from employment. Conversely some of the 'shopkeepers and tradesmen' and nobility which we have included with mixed incomes were probably not self-employed.

presume that he framed his estimates in net rather than gross terms, after making what allowance he could for capital consumption. Government expenditure then accounted for only about 5½ per cent of net national product at market prices and capital formation for less than 5 per cent. About 10 per cent of the value of national product represented receipts from abroad. The corporate sector was in its infancy and its share in the nation's product apparently negligible. On the other hand, the subsistence sector—which bulks so large in twentieth-century pre-industrial economies—seems also to have been of minor importance. If there were any producers who got the greater part of their incomes from subsistence activity they must have fallen within the category of 'cottagers and paupers' which, according to King's estimates, accounted for under 5½ per cent of national income and nearly a quarter of total population. A century or so later when Colquhoun drew up what was intended to be a comparable list of incomes for England and Wales the subsistence producer seems to have disappeared, for he distinguishes no cottager class as such.[1]

King's classification of the population was in terms of social rather than economic groups and it is doubtful whether the economy was sufficiently specialised to permit a meaningful occupational or industrial analysis. An attempt to put an economic interpretation on his categories suggests that between 70 and 80 per cent of the occupied population was primarily engaged in agriculture, though of course many of them must have pursued secondary occupations in industry and trade. The strictly rural population (the inhabitants of the villages and hamlets) accounted for about three-quarters of the total, and London with its spreading suburbs outside the walls for about 10 per cent.

The average level of annual income suggested by King's estimates is of less than £9 per head of the population. Currently (1959) it is roughly £365 per head of a population which is eight times as large. If we take the available price indices as a measure of the change in the value of money over this period of nearly two and three-quarter centuries we can deduce that average real incomes have multiplied by a factor of about seven. The change in content, however, has been such that no meaningful comparison can be made in these terms.

The broad features of the industrial revolution which transformed this predominantly rural, family-based economy into its present form are well known. What is still obscure is the chronology and dimensions of the process and their causal connections. To explore the relations between shifts in economic structure and variations in the rate of economic growth we need to know a great deal more than we now do about the pattern and momentum of change. When and how, for example, did the industrial revolution effectively begin, and what was its connection with the changes in population or in the volume of overseas trade? What was the precise mechanism whereby

[1] P. Colquhoun, *Treatise on Indigence* (1806).

industrialisation led to a rising level of real incomes, and how, or to what extent, was the rise maintained after industrialisation was virtually complete? Basically what we need in order to come to grips with questions such as these are comparable statistics of national income and its major constituents. It was the object of the research project of which this book is the outcome to compile and interpret long-term national-income statistics, or approximations thereto, for the whole of the period of the British industrial revolution and its aftermath.

The data problems have dominated the inquiry. Contemporary national-income estimates proved to be both rare and difficult to interpret, while retrospective estimates can be constructed only on dangerously inadequate foundations. The difficulties multiply as we go back in time. For the eighteenth century we must draw what conclusions we can from a handful of incomplete statistics and a mass of qualitative information or contemporary guesswork of dubious significance. Hence the results of our researches for the period in which the industrial revolution originated (analysed in chapter II) do not find expression in terms of direct national-income estimates. They are no more than first guesses at trends and rates of progress and significant components. Even the population statistics are so incomplete and so intriguing in their implications for the beginnings of British economic growth that we chose (in chapter III) to discuss the bases of our hypotheses in some detail.

Direct estimates of national income require at least a rudimentary framework of overall statistics of economic activity or output or income and it is not until the nineteenth-century population census and income-tax returns become available that they are feasible. Even so, the early returns are too sketchy or incomplete to justify annual estimates and we have confined ourselves to bench-mark estimates for the first half-century. Using these crudely constructed aggregates as a frame of reference it is possible to examine the structural aspects of British economic change, and we have concentrated on three of these—industrial structure, factor distribution of incomes, and capital formation.

A summary of the findings of the inquiry is contained in chapter IX. These are broad and tentative conclusions which depend for their validity on the methods adopted to reach them. They require constant checking against other sources of evidence. Hence most of this book is taken up with detailed discussion of quantitative and qualitative materials for particular sectors of the economy and of the interpretations we have chosen to place on inadequate material. In the hope of making the route less laborious and perplexing for the reader who prefers to appreciate the scope and directions of the research before considering its problems it may be useful, by way of introduction, to sketch certain preliminary guide lines. By describing the broad background trends in population, value of money, wages and international trade, we seek to indicate some general directions for the economy over the very long period.

2. BROAD TRENDS IN POPULATION GROWTH

One of the most striking manifestations of the expansion of the United Kingdom economy in the modern period was an unprecedented growth of population. The origins of this movement are somewhat obscure. There was no full census of population in Great Britain before 1801 or in Ireland before 1821 and no attempt was made to collect age data at the censuses until 1821. Hence the population figures for the eighteenth century are imprecise. Although there are enough data available to provide reasonable estimates of the broad trends involved, the specific turning-points cannot be located and the character and causes of the initial changes are still a matter of controversy.[1]

For England and Wales estimates are generally based on the returns of baptisms, burials and marriages, at decade intervals, which Rickman collected from the keepers of the parish records. These were published in the Parish Register Abstracts of the 1801 census and amended in the 1811 census and have given rise to several series of plausible estimates of total population, the differences between the series being a consequence of each author's assumptions concerning the completeness of the data and the appropriate conversion coefficients.[2] Table 2 selects Brownlee's estimates for England and Wales, but for the other sets of estimates the orders of magnitude are similar, which is not surprising in view of the fact that they derive from the same raw material.[3] For Scotland there were a census taken by Webster in 1755 and Sir John Sinclair's estimates for the last decade of the century based on his *Statistical Account*. For Ireland K. H. Connell made estimates based on his own interpretation of the contemporary estimates and of the hearth tax returns. Estimates for Scotland and Ireland are thus based on even scantier evidence than the English figures and not much can be said about relative rates of growth for the different parts of the

---

[1] See, for example, the two articles by T. H. Marshall reprinted in *Essays in Economic History*, edited by E. H. Carus-Wilson (1954); H. J. Habakkuk, 'English Population in the Eighteenth Century', *Economic History Review*, December 1953; and Thomas McKeown and R. G. Brown, 'Medical Evidence Related to English Population Changes in the Eighteenth Century', *Population Studies*, November 1955.

[2] *Sessional Papers 1843*, vol. XXII, for Rickman's results, and *S.P. 1853*, vol. LXXXVIII, for Farr's interpretation of them in the introduction to the 1851 census. For later discussions and interpretations of Rickman's data see especially E. C. K. Gonner, 'The Population of England in the Eighteenth Century', *Journal of the Royal Statistical Society*, vol. LXXVI (February 1913); John Brownlee, 'History of the Birth and Death Rates in England and Wales, taken as a whole from 1570 to the present time', *Public Health*, June and July 1916; and T. H. Marshall, 'The Population Problem during the Industrial Revolution: a Note on the Present State of the Controversy', *Economic History I* (1929), reprinted in *Essays in Economic History*, edited by E. M. Carus-Wilson (1954).

[3] Differences of this order appear for example in three of the most plausible series:

	Farr	Gonner	Brownlee
1701	6·122	5·800	5·826
1751	6·336	6·320	6·140
1801	9·139	9·156	9·156

See Brownlee, *op. cit.* p. 228, for a table setting out the differences between several different series.

United Kingdom in the eighteenth century. As orders of magnitude, however, the Scottish and Irish totals given in Table 2 are probably acceptable.

Table 2. *Estimates of population in the eighteenth century*

(in millions)

	England and Wales	Scotland	Ireland	United Kingdom
1701	5·826	1·040	2·540	9·406
1711	5·981	—	2·765	—
1721	6·001	—	—	—
1731	5·947	—	3·015	—
1741	5·926	—	—	—
1751	6·140	1·250	3·125	10·515
1761	6·569	—	—	—
1771	7·052	—	3·530	—
1781	7·531	—	4·048	—
1791	8·247	1·500	4·753	14·500
1801	9·156	1·599	5·216	15·972

Sources: The estimates for England and Wales are those calculated by Brownlee on the basis of the burial and baptism series compiled by Rickman. Brownlee, *op. cit.* p. 228. Those for Ireland are based on Connell's estimates (interpolating or extrapolating his figures for 1687, 1712, 1754, 1767, and 1772 to give estimates for the years selected above); see Kenneth H. Connell, *The Population of Ireland 1750–1845* (1950), p. 25. Figures for Scotland are based on those given by Sir John Sinclair, *Analysis of the Statistical Account of Scotland* (1825), p. 149.

The estimates for England and Wales suggest that the population stagnated for the first four decades of the century although there may have been short sub-periods of more or less sharp increase or decrease within this period. Taking the century as a whole it appears that there were two periods in the eighteenth century in which the rate of population growth tended to accelerate, one from 1740 to 1760 and the other from 1780 onwards.[1] The former upsurge is interesting in that it marked the beginning of an entirely new trend in population —a sustained increase.[2] The latter was stronger and continued at an increasing rate into the nineteenth century. Between 1781 and 1811 the increase for England and Wales was of the order of 38 per cent, and over the sixty years between 1771 and 1831 the population practically doubled. In Scotland the rate of increase may have been a little smaller: in Ireland it may have been considerably larger.

No satisfactory explanation has yet been adduced for the population growth which began around the middle of the eighteenth century and reached its peak in the second decade of the nineteenth.[3] It is generally assumed to have been the consequence of a rapidly falling death rate

[1] Cf. T. H. Marshall, 'The Population of England and Wales from the Industrial Revolution to the World War', reprinted from *Econ. Hist. Rev.* (1935), reprinted in *Essays in Economic History, op. cit.* p. 331.

[2] It is a question of course whether the point of departure was the acceleration of the 1740's (which was not of itself stronger than many earlier spurts) or the increase and maintenance of a higher rate of growth in the 1750's and 1760's.

[3] It is discussed more fully in chapter III, see below, pp. 122–135.

and more particularly of a fall in the infantile death rate.[1] This in its turn used to be ascribed to the progress of medicine rather than to any appreciable change in economic conditions. But the evidence for medical progress is vague and inconclusive and the explanation has been questioned by medical historians.[2] Whatever the operative cause of the change in the population trend the fact of the change is undeniable. It is reasonably certain that the rate of growth of English population accelerated markedly somewhere about the middle of the eighteenth century, and that for Great Britain this was the beginning of a trend which, though it failed to maintain its early nineteenth-century peak, never again deteriorated to the prolonged stagnation or absolute decline which was common enough in the earlier periods of British history.

Associated with this increase in total population there was a marked rise in the proportion of the population living in urban areas. At the beginning of the eighteenth century London had more than half a million inhabitants and Edinburgh perhaps 35,000, but only two other towns had more than 20,000—they were Bristol and Norwich. Apart from Birmingham and Glasgow with between 10,000 and 15,000 inhabitants each, it does not seem that there were any other towns with populations exceeding 10,000. At most we may doubt whether the population living in concentrations of 5,000 or more amounted to as much as 13 per cent of the population of Great Britain. By the middle of the century this proportion may have risen to between 15 and 16 per cent of the national total and by 1801 to about 25 per cent. If anything the metropolis may have grown rather more slowly than the provincial towns, but it still accounted for between 9 and 10 per cent of the total at the end of the eighteenth century.

We are still dealing with 'orders of magnitude' of course. Figures of urban populations in pre-census years though numerous are frequently unreliable. The evidence suggests, however, that in the first half of the eighteenth century the fastest-growing towns were Liverpool —the centre for the West India trade—and Birmingham—the centre for the metal industries. The former is estimated to have roughly trebled in population in the first four decades and to have increased more than fivefold between then and the end of the century.[3] Birmingham is estimated to have increased some four and a half times between

---

[1] The case for an increase in the birth rate has also been plausibly argued. See H. J. Habakkuk, *op. cit.*

[2] Compare, T. H. Marshall's statement, *op. cit.* p. 334, that there is 'little evidence of anything that could be called an economic cause of this improvement in health', with the view of two medical historians that 'whether we accept the birth rate or the death rate as the most important influence on the rise of population, the conclusion that [economic] conditions improved in the late eighteenth century must follow rejection of effectiveness of medical effort'. McKeown and Brown, *op. cit.* p. 141. More recently it has been argued that one medical advance of the period—inoculation against smallpox—did have a significant effect on mortality rates. See P. E. Razzell, 'Population Change in Eighteenth Century England. A Reinterpretation.' *Econ. Hist. Rev.* Vol. XVIII (1965).

[3] See, for example, the estimates given by Matthew Gregson, *Portfolio of Fragments Relative to the History and Antiquities of the County Palatine and the Duchy of Lancaster* (London, 1817), and James Wheeler, *Manchester, its Political, Social and Commercial History* (London, 1836), p. 146.

1675 and 1760 and to have doubled between then and 1801.[1] In the last thirty years of the century Manchester (with Salford) seems to have grown faster than any other English town. Between 1773 and 1801 its population is estimated to have more than trebled.[2] But Glasgow, another cotton capital, presumably grew nearly as fast as Manchester. Between 1763 and 1801 its population roughly trebled.[3] It is true that all these towns had passed the 20,000 level by 1760, but London was still the home of approximately four out of five residents in the large towns of Great Britain. By 1801 not many more than half of those living in towns of over 20,000 inhabitants lived in London.[4]

The upsurge that began in the 1780's led to a doubling of the population of the United Kingdom by 1841 (i.e. within about sixty years) and an increase that was nearly fourfold in 150 years. Table 3 gives a broad view of the growth of population over this period of one and a half centuries. But these overall figures cloak sharply divergent trends in the population history of Ireland and that of Great Britain, a divergence which reflects totally different patterns of economic change in the two areas concerned and which underlines the import-

Table 3. *The growth of population in the United Kingdom*

(millions of persons)

	Great Britain	Ireland	United Kingdom
1781	8·900	4·100	13·000
1791	9·700	4·800	14·500
1801	10·686	5·216	15·902
1811	12·147	5·956	18·103
1821	14·206	6·802	21·007
1831	16·368	7·767	24·135
1841	18·551	8·200	26·751
1851	20·879	6·514	27·393
1861	23·189	5·788	28·977
1871	26·158	5·398	31·556
1881	29·789	5·146	34·934
1891	33·122	4·680	37·802
1901	37·093	4·446	41·538
1911	40·918	4·381	45·299
1921	42·814	4·354	47·168
1931	44·831	4·176	49·007

Sources: Registrar-General's estimates for middle of each year from 1801 onwards. See, for example, *S.P. 1886*, vol. XVII, for U.K. to 1871; *S.P. 1914–16*, vol. IX, for U.K. 1881–1911; *S.P. 1894*, vol. XXV, for Ireland to 1881, and so on. Figures for 1921 and 1931 include Eire. For source of estimates for earlier years see note to Table 2. There is a small discrepancy in the estimates for 1801 in these two tables due to the fact that we have accepted Brownlee's series for the eighteenth century and the Registrar-General's for the nineteenth century.

[1] Conrad Gill, *History of Birmingham*, vol. I (1951), p. 56.
[2] James Wheeler, *op. cit.*
[3] Robert Chapman, *The Topographical Picture of Glasgow in its Ancient and Modern State* (London, 1820).
[4] Using Welton's estimates of the population of the major urban areas in 1801 based on a rather careful analysis of the boundaries and populations returned at the census. Thomas Welton, 'On the Distribution of Population in England and Wales and its Progress in the Period of Ninety Years from 1801 to 1891', *J. Roy. Statist. Soc.*, vol. XLIII (1900).

ance of considering Ireland separately throughout the period. By 1931 the population of Great Britain had increased some fivefold, whereas the population figure for Ireland was near enough to the 1781 estimate to be well within the margin of error of the latter.

In effect the Irish population had risen and then fallen during the course of the nineteenth century. This fall was a direct consequence of the potato famine, and the preceding rise has also been attributed to the potato. By 1841 the Irish population, like the British population, had roughly doubled in six decades.[1] It reached its all-time peak in 1845–6 when there were about 8·3 million people in Ireland which then accounted for about 30 per cent of the population of the United Kingdom. Then the process was reversed and the population, which fell by a quarter in the twenty years after the disaster, was not much more than half its 1845 level by the early nineteen-thirties.

The overall similarity of the population trends in Ireland and Great Britain before the potato famine should not be allowed to obscure important differences in the character of the growth process for the two areas. Population data for Ireland are unsatisfactory before the first census in 1821 but there is no evidence that a marked urbanisation of the population was taking place. The increase in population seems to have been due largely, if not entirely, to the limitless opportunities for family expansion which were provided by the culture of the potato.[2] Hence whereas by 1841 more than a third of the population of England and Wales was living in towns of over 20,000 inhabitants, less than 8 per cent of the population of Ireland were living in towns no more than half that size.[3] This was a level of urbanisation below that of early eighteenth-century England and Wales.

In Great Britain on the other hand, and in England and Wales in particular, the nineteenth-century increase in population seems to have been positively associated with the increasing economic opportunities which were being provided in the urban areas, and urbanisation of the population accordingly accelerated. There may have been, in the late eighteenth and early nineteenth century, some 'swarming' of population in the agricultural areas of England and Wales which was similar to that taking place in Ireland. The figures of baptisms and burials and of poor-relief in the agricultural counties suggest that the rural

[1] This is based on Connell's estimate for 1781 (see note to Table 2) and the Registrar-General's estimates for 1801 onwards. Other estimates suggest a much larger rise for the period 1781–1801, but they are based on the traditional evidence of contemporary estimates and do not seem very well founded.

[2] 'The dominating position the potato had come to occupy by the end of the eighteenth century in the diet of the countryman throughout Ireland meant that the expense his children put him to for food was slight: nor did their clothing or schooling commit him to appreciable outlay. Children, then, absorbed little of the family resources but early in life made a contribution to their expansion.' Kenneth H. Connell, *op. cit.* p. 15. The Irish population problem may also owe something to the land tenure system. See R. D. Edwards and T. D. Williams, *The Great Famine, Studies in Irish History*, New York, 1957.

[3] T. W. Grimshaw, 'A Statistical Survey of Ireland', *Journal of the Statistical Society of Ireland*, Part 68 (1888), p. 335, gives the numbers in towns of 10,000 and over at 621,000 in 1841, or 7·6 per cent of the population, rising to 815,000 in 1881, or about 15·8 per cent of the population.

areas were increasing almost as rapidly as the manufacturing districts in the last two decades of the eighteenth century. In the first two decades of the nineteenth century, rural districts and small towns (as defined by Price Williams in a paper read to the London Statistical Society in 1880) increased their joint population at a rate which was not far short of the rate for the country as a whole.[1] Analysis of the speed and characteristics of British urbanisation is complicated, however, by the problems of defining urban boundaries. Areas that were rural at the beginning of the century were suburban before the end of it. Changes in the boundaries of registration districts as between one census and another further diminish the accuracy of the calculations. Whatever quantitative conclusions are drawn must depend heavily on the groupings that are adopted.

According to Cairncross's calculations the English towns gained by net migration a population of nearly 3 million inhabitants in the last six decades of the nineteenth century. Except in the decade of the eighties, when there was heavy net emigration, the towns absorbed more than half a million persons per decade. London itself accounted for nearly a quarter of a million per decade. In 1841 the population of the rural districts as defined by Cairncross formed 39 per cent of the total for the country: by 1911 it formed no more than 19 per cent. But in spite of this enormous movement from the countryside to the towns the population of the rural areas was higher in 1911 than in 1841.[2] Table 4 summarises the movements of English population in terms of these calculations.

Table 4. *Net Gain* (+) *or loss* (−) *by migration in England, 1841–1911*

(in thousands)

	London	Other towns	Colliery districts	Rural areas	Total England (net external migration)
1841–1851	+274	+386	+ 82	−443	+294
1851–1861	+244	+272	+103	−743	−122
1861–1871	+262	+271	+ 91	−683	− 60
1871–1881	+307	+297	+ 84	−837	−148
1881–1891	+169	− 31	+ 90	−845	−617
1891–1901	+226	+294	+ 85	−660	− 54
1901–1911	−232	− 89	+114	−295	−502

Source: This is a summary of the results given on p. 70 of Cairncross, *op. cit.*

For the first eighty years of the nineteenth century the movement from the countryside to the towns was strong and steady. The influx into the towns reached its peak in the forties when it was inflated by the

[1] R. Price Williams, 'On the Increase of Population in England and Wales', *Journal of the Statistical Society*, vol. XLIII (1880), pp. 462–96. See also the additional tables printed in the discussion as a note to Sir R. W. Rawson's remarks on pp. 500–1.
[2] A. K. Cairncross, *Home and Foreign Investment 1870–1913* (Cambridge, 1953), pp. 65–83.

Irish exodus.[1] It was high throughout the middle four decades of the century. In the last two decades of the century, however, a change in the pattern of internal migration was evident in the population records. It seems as though the urbanisation which was particularly associated with the process of industrialisation had been completed. From then on, although there was still plenty of movement from one area to another, it could no longer be described in terms of the traditional drift to the towns but was explained by changes in the relative prosperity or depression of particular regions. The shifts between industrial areas or between home and overseas became more important factors in the situation than the movement between town and country. Thus even in the 1890's, when the urban areas again absorbed a net migration of more than half a million, it is significant that the southern towns took nearly four times as many migrants as the northern towns and that this was very largely due to the increased prosperity of London and its satellites relatively to the northern industrial areas.

In the twentieth century there has been some movement out of the urban areas into the rural areas as overcrowded populations have spilled across town borders. The period immediately before the First World War, for example, was characterised by an increase in the rate of growth of population of the agricultural counties and a reduction of the rate of growth of the industrial counties. This was shown to be due to 'mining, manufacturing and residential development which had resulted from the proximity of urban areas and the overspilling of populations from expanding towns into the surrounding districts.'[2]

In sum, therefore, although the population of Great Britain has not ceased to grow or to shift, the revolutionary changes in its size and distribution which were associated with the Industrial Revolution had spent their force before the beginning of the twentieth century. Over the past five decades the overall picture has been one of slow growth and stability with little prospect of any striking change.

The Irish population history of this period has of course been totally different. It never recovered from the disaster of the eighteen-forties, and in spite of a rising standard of living which has been estimated to have increased faster than that of Great Britain,[3] it has continued to decline or stagnate for the past century. The causes of the decline seem to have been low fertility, a delayed age of marriage and a high propensity to emigrate.[4] But whatever its causes, it represents one of

---

[1] 'By 1881 there were about one-ninth as many Irish in England and Wales as there were in Ireland itself, and in Liverpool one in eight of the population was Irish born.' Mary P. Newton and James R. Jeffery, 'Internal Migration', General Register Office *Studies on Medical and Population Subjects*, No. 5 (H.M.S.O., 1951), p. 10.

[2] Newton and Jeffery, *op. cit.* p. 11.

[3] R. C. Geary, 'The Future Population of Saorstat Eireann, and Some Observations on Population Statistics', *Journal of the Statistical and Social Inquiry Society of Ireland*, 1935–6, pp. 24–5, 30.

[4] Cf. Geary, *ibid.* p. 25: 'There is nothing in the statistics inconsistent with the view that the great exodus of 1845–54 in placing a vast Irish population across the Atlantic and the Irish Sea, which created a powerful magnetic field in which millions of Irish were irresistibly

the most remarkable population trends recorded for any modern community.[1]

3. THE VALUE OF MONEY

Much of the quantitative material presented in this book is expressed in current values, and long-period comparisons of these data are subject to the qualifications introduced by changes in the value of money. As part of the background to their interpretation, therefore, it may be useful to review the general level of prices for the whole period under consideration. This raises two kinds of problems, the conceptual and the practical.

The conceptual problems are peculiarly intractable for the earlier part of our period. In an integrated market economy where there is a high degree of interdependence of prices and transactions it is possible to regard the average of all price changes as a useful, if imprecise, reflection of changes in the value of money. For eighteenth-century England in which it took ten to twelve days to travel from London to Edinburgh,[2] when the price of coal might vary from under 15s. a chaldron to over £3 a chaldron according to the distance from the pits,[3] and the wages of a building craftsman from 2s. to 3s. a day in different counties, there is no form of general price index which would reflect changes in the value of money for the economy as a whole. Each region had its own price history and its own set of price relationships. Even if we knew enough about regional prices to construct a national average it is doubtful what meaning we could attribute to the result.

On the other hand it is certain that there were important changes in the purchasing power of money during the latter part of the eighteenth century and that these changes were reflected in prices. By the 1790's —probably by the 1760's—the majority of prices had developed an upward trend. Until after the Napoleonic Wars, however, possibly until the beginning of the railway age, the movements of individual prices are so divergent and so variable as between different regions of the country that the attempt to measure the changes in terms of a general price index is a highly dubious procedure.

The data problems are also formidable. There are a number of more or less general price indices available for varying periods within this broad span of over two and a half centuries. But for most of it, certainly for the whole of the period before the First World War, there is no index number which is based on a sufficiently broad selection of quotations

drawn from their native country, was the fount and origin of Irish emigration and depopulation.'

[1] It is interesting to note the divergence in the population histories of Northern Ireland and the Irish Republic. In the thirty years 1921–51 the former increased in population by about 9 per cent while the latter declined by about 4½ per cent.

[2] W. T. Jackman, *The Development of Transportation in Modern England*, vol. 1 (1916), p. 335, states that 'In 1754 the journey between London and Edinburgh required ten days in summer and twelve days in winter'.

[3] According to the replies received by Arthur Young to his circular letter of 1795. *Annals of Agriculture*, vol. XXIV (1795).

or an adequate system of weights to approximate a reliable average. Hence although these incomplete measures may suggest the direction of the main secular trends they do not give enough information to establish the turning-points or to measure the amplitude of the fluctuations.

For the eighteenth century a number of price series are given in Lord Beveridge's volume on prices and wages in the mercantile era.[1] These were compiled from the accounts of institutions (mainly schools and hospitals) and government departments. They have been used by Elizabeth Gilboy and Elizabeth Schumpeter as bases for weighted and unweighted general indices of prices covering the whole of the eighteenth century.[2] The main fault of all these institutional series if we want to use them as indications of changes in market price levels is that they are contract prices. This means not only that they tend to lag behind open market prices in their response to changes in demand and supply conditions, but also that they tend, probably more than other kinds of price quotations, to mask quality changes behind a customary price. Winchester College, for example, paid 120s. a piece for cloth from 1612 to 1791, and similar long runs at constant prices were recorded by other institutions. Indeed, the only important non-food items for which these institutional prices seemed to move fairly freely throughout the century were candles and coal.

Now it may be true that in the pre-industrial economy, for which technical change was rare and discontinuous, the prices of goods not subject to harvest fluctuations or similar violent disturbances in the supply conditions were less variable from one decade to another than the prices of similar goods in an industrialised economy. It is easy to believe that where economic change was limited to the effects of such non-economic factors as the weather, wars or epidemics the prices of goods in relatively elastic supply and demand could freeze for long periods of time. But the evidence for the eighteenth century does not support a hypothesis of unrelieved stagnation and it is possible that true prices of goods subject to contract were less constant than the records would suggest. There was plenty of scope for variation in quality and even in quantity in a period when standards of measurement were characteristically imprecise. Hence the absence of a marked secular trend in the price indices available for the first half of the eighteenth century may be partly attributable to the nature of the institutional data.[3]

[1] Sir William Beveridge, *Prices and Wages in England from the Twelfth to the Nineteenth Century*, vol. 1 (London, 1939).

[2] E. W. Gilboy, 'The Cost of Living and Real Wages in Eighteenth Century England', *Review of Economic Statistics*, vol. xviii, No. 2 (August 1936); E. B. Schumpeter, 'English Prices and Public Finance 1660–1822', *Review of Economic Statistics*, vol. xx, No. 1 (February 1938).

[3] The use of price currents instead of institutional records would alter the picture considerably for the non-food series: but then the price-current quotations tended to be confined to commodities whose prices were abnormally unstable.

The dashed line in Fig. 7 combines (by arithmetic average) the Gilboy-Schumpeter indices for consumer goods (inclusive of cereals) and producers' goods.[1] In the first half of the century there seems to have been a tendency for prices to decline slightly. Possibly the institutional series have turned this index into a somewhat muted indicator of a positive rise in the value of money but we have found no evidence from other sources of a more marked downward price trend during this period. After the middle of the eighteenth century (possibly even a little before mid-century) the index suggests a tendency for the price level to rise, and the increase accelerated markedly in the 1770's and early 1780's.[2] In the last decade of the century the cumulative effects of a rapidly rising population, a succession of poor harvests and an expensive war had introduced violent inflationary disturbances into the price system and carried all general indices to unprecedented levels.

These disturbances, combined with the fact that none of the general price indices is entirely satisfactory, make it extraordinarily difficult to assess the changes in the value of money in the first quarter of the nineteenth century. With the exception of the Schumpeter series (which does not include producers' goods after 1800–1) most of the indices available for this period are unweighted averages of wholesale prices and are heavily influenced by commodities which tended to be peculiarly vulnerable to the trade dislocations and harvest crises of the Napoleonic Wars.[3] To some extent this bias is inevitable, whatever the weighting system, for it was the vulnerable prices which contemporaries chose to publish regularly. But it means that indices based on these quotations tend to exaggerate the movements in the general price level.

From our point of view the best general price index currently available for this period is the index compiled by Gayer, Rostow and Schwartz.[4] It is superior mainly because it is carefully weighted, because it is based on a relatively large number of quotations and because it includes import duties. Its main deficiency lies in its exclusion of manufactured goods and of services, including rent. The dotted line in Fig. 7 traces the annual course of this index for the

[1] See the pull-out graph at the end of this volume. The basic indices (given in Schumpeter, *Review of Economic Statistics, op. cit.*) are simple unweighted arithmetic means of price relatives for 31 consumers goods (including 9 cereals and 4 animal products) and 12 producers' goods (all from Admiralty Accounts, including 5 for domestic building materials).
[2] The rise was noted by contemporaries in the 1760's and 1770's. See, for example, Arthur Young, *Political Arithmetic* (1774), p. 37. 'But let any person reflect on the rise of prices during the last sixteen years: let them name one article, in the common course of purchase and sale, which has not been considerably advanced.'
[3] A useful critique of the best known price indices available for the period 1790–1850 is contained in Part III of the study by Gayer, Rostow and Schwartz, *The Growth and Fluctuations of the British Economy, 1790–1850* (2 vols., Oxford, 1953), pp. 459–528.
[4] *Ibid.* pp. 461–85. See the dotted line in Fig. 7. There are two sub-indices—domestic products (26 commodities) and imports (52 commodities) and a general index in which the domestic products account for nearly three-quarters of the total weight and domestic foodstuffs (wheat, oats, mutton and beef) for about 50 per cent.

period 1790–1850.[1] It shows a steep erratic climb during the war to a peak in 1813 followed by a rapid decline to near pre-war levels in the second quarter of the century, and a fluctuating but still unmistakeable decline to a low point in 1850.[2]

That there was a marked secular decline in the price level, beginning before the wars ended and continuing until mid-century, seems to be reflected in all the price series. The problem is to say when the decline started and to measure the change in the price level between the end of the eighteenth century and the middle of the nineteenth. This presumably is the change which can be more or less directly associated with the main process of industrialisation.[3]

The Gayer-Rostow-Schwartz index, which is essentially an index of the wholesale price of raw materials and foodstuffs, cannot be expected to reflect, except indirectly, the price fall attributable to improvements in industrial productivity. *A priori* we should expect it to understate the decline after the wars. In so far as the decline in industrial prices became an important factor before the end of the wars, we should also expect the index to overstate the wartime peak and possibly to place it in the wrong year.[4]

Supplementary price data which might confirm or correct these hypotheses are not available, however. There is a well-known price series for cotton yarn (originally given in evidence to a Parliamentary Commission) which suggests that the selling price of coarse cotton yarn fell by two-thirds between 1799 and 1812 and that of fine yarn by about 29 per cent.[5] But the weaving and finishing branches of the industry were still very little affected by technological progress and it is possible to over-emphasise the absolute importance of cotton in the economy. More significant perhaps is the fact that the total declared value of British exports ceased to rise at a faster rate than the corresponding official value in 1803 when declared values were nearly double the official values. Thereafter the gap between the two narrowed so rapidly that by 1820 declared values had fallen below official values. For cotton manufactures the declared values fell below official values in 1815.

In view of the inconclusiveness of the price indices for this period it is of some interest also to take into account an intelligent contemporary assessment of the wartime inflation. Joseph Lowe's estimates of taxable

---

[1] The original series is a monthly index of wholesale prices (including import duties) which we have converted to annual averages.

[2] The decline was interrupted by sharp cyclical peaks, characterised by financial crises, in 1825, 1836, 1839–40 and 1847. The trough in the early 1850's appears (from the Sauerbeck index, for example) to have occurred in 1852.

[3] By 1851 about a third of the occupied population was engaged in the manufacturing group of industries. This proportion was not exceeded until after the First World War. See below, Table 31.

[4] The peak of the Gayer-Rostow-Schwartz total index was reached in 1813, but for the domestic price index it was 1812 and for the import price index 1814. See Gayer, Rostow and Schwartz, *op. cit.* pp. 509–12, for a discussion on the problem of the peak.

[5] This series is quoted in T. Ellison, *The Cotton Trade of Great Britain* (1886), p. 55.

income at real and current prices suggest a price level *circa* 1813–14 at 62 per cent above the pre-war (1792) level, falling *circa* 1822 to about 24 per cent above.[1] This compares with the Gayer-Rostow-Schwartz peak of more than 90 per cent above the 1792 level and a post-war trough (in 1822) which was roughly equivalent to the 1792 value. Lowe's view of the wartime fluctuation seems to have been much less emphatic than the price indices would suggest.

Between 1815 (when prices were already 9 per cent below the average of the war years) and 1850, the Gayer-Rostow-Schwartz index shows a fall of 43 per cent. This fall was arrested in the third quarter of the century and was resumed in the fourth quarter. The heavy solid line in Fig. 7, giving Rousseaux' unweighted index of all prices, illustrates this in a downward trend which characterised most of the nineteenth century. It is doubtful whether it was more than a pause. Most of the indices available for this period are unweighted aggregates of wholesale prices for commodities which were particularly vulnerable to unsettled conditions in overseas markets and it is probably that the peaks in the Rousseaux series for the third quarter exaggerate the peaks in the general price level.[2]

The price decline in the fourth quarter of the nineteenth century is quite marked in all the indices. It seems to have turned into a rise in the last decade, and the rising trend was still apparent up to the outbreak of the First World War. The average index value for the years 1901–13 was about 7 per cent above the average level for the years 1887–99. The effect of a major war, of course, was to reduce the value of money very rapidly, and by 1920 when the Ministry of Labour index of retail prices reached its peak the price level was apparently about two and a half times the 1913 level. After this peak prices fell sharply but at the lowest point of the inter-war period they were still 40 per cent above the 1913 level. A second World war initiated a new inflationary rise which continued into the post-war period. Between 1938 and 1955 the Ministry of Labour index of retail prices again increased some two and a half times.[3]

In sum, the available price indices provide an unsatisfactory reflection of changes in the purchasing power of money. They are seriously incomplete in that important categories of product are omitted. They are crude in that unsophisticated quantity units are employed and quality changes badly reflected. For most of the eighteenth century they are unreliable as measures of what they purport to measure because they include contract prices which are not comparable through

---

[1] Joseph Lowe, *The Present State of England* (1882). See Deane, *Econ. Hist. Rev.* (1956), *op. cit.*, for discussion of Lowe's estimates.

[2] In terms of the Rousseaux index the average for the period 1851–75 inclusive was nearly 5 per cent above the average for the period 1826–50 inclusive. However, if Wood's index of retail prices (1850–1902) is linked to the Gayer-Rostow-Schwartz index (1790–1850) the impression that there was a generally higher level of prices in the third quarter, as compared with the second, is less striking. See George H. Wood, 'Real Wages and the Standard of Comfort since 1850', *J. Roy. Statist. Soc.*, vol. LXXII (March 1909).

[3] The C.S.O. index of market prices of consumers' expenditure shows a similar increase.

time.[1] It is difficult to assess the effects of all these factors on the indices, but it seems likely that they understate the degree of change through most of the eighteenth century, that they overstate the fall in the value of money during the Napoleonic Wars, and that the margins of error are too wide to permit year-by-year comparisons. At best they can be relied upon to indicate directions of change, but not the specific turning-points, and to permit rough comparisons of broad trends over long sub-periods. Wide margins of error attach to all real-product comparisons or rate-of-growth estimates based on deflation of current value data for individual years by any of the pre- Second World War price indices.

Within their limits, however, the existing price indices can be taken as one reflection of the long-term trends in the value of money. Fig. 7 attempts to give shape to this view by stringing them roughly together over a period of three centuries. It suggests the following broad conclusions:

1. Following an apparent decline between the Restoration and the Glorious Revolution no significant trend can be deduced from the evidence for the first half of the eighteenth century. Perhaps the beginnings of an upward trend in prices can be traced to the 1750's. It was quite definite by the 1770's, and the prices of the 1790's must have averaged more than a third above those of the first decade of the century. By then, however, they were being driven up by wartime inflation. Each of the three major wars of the past two centuries has been characterised by a marked downward shift in the value of money. At the peak of the Napoleonic Wars inflation prices may have been double what they had been fifty years earlier, though the limited range of the underlying price data probably exaggerated the rise.

2. If we exclude the disturbed period of the Napoleonic Wars and their aftermath, however, it is evident that the industrial revolution— once it gathered momentum—was associated with a tendency for the value of money to increase. Between 1822 and 1851, for example, both low points on the index, prices dropped about 20 per cent. This trend was temporarily arrested by the gold discoveries which resulted in 'a marked upward heave of general prices' in the 1850's and 1860's.[2] Prices then resumed their downward drift until the 1890's, and by 1895 they were a further 20 per cent below the 1851 level. Then began the rising trend which characterised the two decades before the First World War.

3. For those accustomed to the twentieth-century trends, however, the most striking implication of the earlier price data is the relative stability of the value of money. For almost the whole of the period

---

[1] It is only fair to add that the price series shown in Lord Beveridge's volume on *Prices and Wages in England*, which constitute the bases of the Schumpeter indices, have been deliberately and expertly processed to render them as comparable as possible. Not all observers would agree with us that the excessive rigidity of some of the series throws doubt on their validity.

[2] J. H. Clapham, *An Economic History of Modern Britain*, vol. II (1932), p. 338.

between the French wars and the First World War the price index lay between 70 per cent and 120 per cent of the 1913 level. Indeed, if we exclude the French wars and their immediate aftermath we can trace the index back to the Restoration without finding an annual reading which was more than a third above or below the 1913 level. The twentieth-century experience has been of an altogether different kind. Since 1913 the retail price index has more than doubled, almost halved, and nearly trebled again. By 1959 retail prices were about four and a half times their level in 1913 and about seven times the low point of 1895.

4. THE WAGES OF LABOUR

Given the significant regional differences in population trends and commodity prices in pre-industrial Britain the price of labour may be expected to show corresponding variations. The published wage data available for the eighteenth century are scattered, incomplete and discontinuous, but they leave no doubt of their geographical significance. The outstanding characteristic of eighteenth-century wage history was the existence of wide regional variations in both levels and trends. The fact that these regional variations existed and also that they narrowed markedly in the course of the eighteenth century are important aspects of the early stages of British economic growth. Without a great deal more research at the regional level, however, it is not possible to do more than guess at the main features of this story.

The most thorough attempt so far to exploit English eighteenth-century wage material was made by Dr Gilboy in a study published in 1934.[1] It was confined largely to wages in agriculture and the building-trades and it covered only the London area and a number of counties in the North and West of England. These are important limitations if we want to generalise. But three features emerge convincingly from this study. The first is the wide variation in wage rates as between one region and another. The second is the contraction of regional differentials in the course of the century. The third is the existence of certain general tendencies affecting all regions.

These features are illustrated in Table 5. We have summarised, averaged and reduced to index form (with some interpolation) the series of daily wage rates for the building trades which Dr Gilboy selected as representative of the movement of wages in London, the metropolitan area round London, the West and the North.

The attempt to deduce general tendencies from these series suggests that wage levels changed comparatively little in the course of the eighteenth century but that the changes which did occur took place at the beginning and the end of the period. Thus the century can be divided into three fairly well defined and roughly equal periods. In the first third the wages of labourers in London and Lancashire, and of

[1] Elizabeth W. Gilboy, *Wages in Eighteenth Century England*, Harvard Economic Series 45 (1934).

Table 5. *Indices of eighteenth-century money wages in building*

(1770 = 100)

Daily	London labourers	Kent labourers	Oxford-shire labourers	Lancashire labourers	London craftsmen	Kent craftsmen	Oxford-shire craftsmen	Lancashire craftsmen	General average
1770	24·5d.	18·5d.	(14·0)d.	18·0d.	36·67d.	27·5d.	24·0d.	24·0d.	—d.
1700–4	85·9	97·3	100·0[1]	46·4	83·6	94·2	83·3[1]	50·1[1]	81·7
1705–9	90·3	97·4	100·0[1]	50·7	88·9	94·2	83·3[1]	59·6	83·4
1710–4	90·4	97·3	100·0[1]	52·8[1]	90·5	94·2	83·3	54·2	83·4
1715–9	89·8	97·3	100·0	52·8	91·1	95·5	83·3[1]	50·1[1]	83·1
1720–4	90·8[1]	97·3	100·0	63·9[1]	94·5[1]	100·2	88·9[1]	75·0[1]	88·4
1725–9	89·8	97·3	100·0	61·1[1]	92·7	103·6	88·9[1]	75·0[1]	87·4
1730–4	93·1	97·3	100·0[1]	65·3	94·9	98·9	(88·9)	66·7[1]	87·6
1735–9	96·9	97·3	100·0[1]	66·7[1]	96·9	98·7	100·0[1]	(66·7)	89·5
1740–4	96·1	97·3	97·6[1]	66·7	96·3	98·2	95·8[1]	75·0[1]	88·7
1745–9	96·9	97·3	97·1	66·0	95·9	98·2	98·4	67·4[1]	88·0
1750–4	98·2	97·3	98·6	66·7[1]	97·1	98·2	95·0	75·0[1]	89·1
1755–9	98·0	97·3	100·0	61·1[1]	98·2	98·2	100·0	75·0[1]	88·3
1760–4	98·8	97·3	100·0	75·9[1]	98·6	98·9	100·0	83·3[1]	92·5
1765–9	100·0	95·7	100·0	100·0	100·0	99·5	100·0	100·0[1]	99·4
1770–4	100·0	104·1	106·0[1]	97·8	100·0	102·5	100·0	100·0	101·3
1775–9	99·0	115·4	114·3[1]	100·0[1]	100·5	111·5	116·7[1]	93·8[1]	106·2
1780–4	102·0	116·5	114·3[1]	100·0	105·1	112·7	104·2[1]	100·0	106·6
1785–9	102·0[1]	116·2	(114·3)	109·4	104·5	113·5	(108·3)	105·4	109·6
1790–4	—	120·3	114·3[1]	115·6	—	120·0	—	127·5	—
1795–9	—	124·9			—	128·2			—

Source: Based on the median wage quotations given by E. W. Gilboy, *Wages in the Eighteenth Century England* (1934), Appendix II. Figures are averages of five annual quotations in most cases: but interpolations are given in brackets and averages involving fewer than four yearly quotations are noted by superior figure 1. The figures at the head of each column indicate the daily wage rates in pence in the base year.

skilled workers in all four districts, rose while in Oxford and Kent they remained stationary. In the second period, from the mid-thirties until the sixties, the wages of both craftsmen and labourers showed very little tendency to change in any of the four districts. Finally, in the last third of the century every one of the series represented in the table shows an upward trend, though the rate of increase varied considerably from region to region: for the London labourers the increase was almost negligible before 1787 when the series came to an end.

An interesting feature of these results is that the series for labourers provide clearer evidence of regional differences than the series for craftsmen.[1] It may be plausibly argued that the wages of craftsmen depend largely on the demand for their particular skill, whereas the wages of unskilled labour tend to reflect more directly conditions in the labour market as a whole. If the stimulus towards rising wages is attributed to the development of industry and trade it is not surprising that those areas in which labourers' wages were relatively inflexible during the early part of the century were the primarily agricultural areas and that the upward trend was most marked in Lancashire.

In calculating a rough general average of money wages for the purposes of Table 5 we have given double weight to the labourers' series.[2] But it should be noted that so long as we confine our attention to the regions covered by Dr Gilboy's study it does not matter much

---

[1] Dr Gilboy emphasises in this connection the difficulty of eliminating qualitative variations from the craftsmen's series. *Op. cit.* pp. 223–4.

[2] We weighted the average by the regional population figures, which means that the northern region becomes a progressively more important factor for the later years of the century.

what weight we attach to the craftsmen in relation to the labourers, since the averages of both series suggest broadly similar trends. The differences must be regarded as well within the margin of error of the statistics. In any case, until the wage data for other parts of England, and in particular the Midlands and East Anglia, have been as systematically compiled, conclusions suggested by a study of three or four districts must be regarded as tentative. All that we can say at present is that the evidence on other areas currently available in published sources does not appear to conflict with the broad outlines suggested by Table 5.

Bowley's figures of agricultural earnings, for example, suggest much the same conclusions, both as regards the regional variations and the overall trend. The average agricultural wage apparently increased by something like 25 per cent between the late 1760's and 1795, although it seems likely that most of the advance took place after 1790 for which the Gilboy series are very thin.[1] The rise was most marked in the Yorkshire Ridings, Lancashire, Northumberland and Staffordshire, where the increase exceeded 50 per cent: but over a very large part of eastern, midland and southern England in the second half of the century, agricultural wages seem to have been in a state of relative stagnation similar to that which characterised the London building-trades during this period.

Bowley's estimates were based on the copious wage quotations made by Young, Eden and other late eighteenth-century writers. For earlier periods the published evidence is more scrappy and inconclusive.[2] For what it is worth, it suggests that the stability which characterised labourers' wage rates in the south-west and the district round London in the early part of the century may well have been typical of conditions in the southern rural areas as a whole, but that in the Midlands as in London itself and the North a definite advance took place. Nevertheless the evidence for other districts and industries would not modify the general implication of the Gilboy data that changes in the general level of wages during the first six decades or so were comparatively small. The scattered indications of wages for the coal and iron industries, for example, or for the Cornish mines, suggest that in all three cases wages were relatively static at the beginning of the century and then rose at a gradually accelerating pace towards the end[3]: in none of these industries does there seem to have been any significant increase in wages between 1740 and 1760.

An attempt was made to deduce the implications for real wages by

[1] The averages calculated by Bowley and used here were unweighted, but it is unlikely that weighting the county figures by population would make a significant difference to the final result.

[2] See E. Lipson, *Economic History of England*, vol. III (1947 ed.), pp. 256–63, 516–19; also R. K. Kelsall, *Wage Regulation under the Statute of Artificers* (1938), Appendix I, pp. 111–19; and Thorold Rogers, *History of Agriculture and Prices in England* (7 vols., 1866–1902).

[3] See T. S. Ashton and J. Sykes, *The Coal Industry of the Eighteenth Century* (1929); T. S. Ashton, *Iron and Steel in the Industrial Revolution* (1924); A. K. H. Jenkin, *The Cornish Miner* (1927).

deflating the series in Table 5 by the Gilboy cost-of-living index. The deficiencies in the underlying price data are such that the results are exceedingly crude.[1] The trends they suggest are marked enough to warrant some comment, however. Up to about 1760 money wage rates appeared to be comparatively stable and tended on the whole to move in the opposite direction to prices. In consequence the real wages of both craftsmen and labourers in all regions moved in the same direction, though at widely differing rates. After a period of uncertainty in the first two decades real wages rose in all four districts in the twenties and thirties by amounts ranging from 10 per cent in the case of labourers in the southern rural districts to 45 per cent or more for both labourers and craftsmen in the North. In the forties and fifties, however, the trend was generally downward, until by 1760 the gains registered in the earlier decades by workers in the rural South (but not in London and the North) had apparently been wiped out. After 1760 the regional trends diverged more widely. In the South of England real wages continued to fall, though the downward movement was temporarily checked (and in some cases reversed) about 1780. But in the North real wages seemed to rise again in the sixties and to continue rising until the last decade of the century.

On balance this evidence suggests that the purchasing power of an average day's wage for workers in the building-trades changed little in the last forty years of the eighteenth century: if anything the trend may have been slightly downwards. Much the same impression is derived from Bowley's figures of agricultural wages. As we have already noted, between the late sixties and 1795 the average wage rose by about 25 per cent, but in the same period the cost of living increased, on a conservative estimate, by something like 30 per cent. In ten counties which by 1801 had a combined population of 2·8 millions real wages were maintained or increased. But in eighteen others with a population of just over 3 millions real wages fell. If we compare the overall position at the end of the century with that at the beginning it would appear that the purchasing power of an average day's wages was about the same although regional differences had been considerably reduced. In the South of England real wages were generally lower than in 1700, but in the North they had risen by 50 or 60 per cent.

Finally it must be stressed that the trends described should not be taken as measures of the eighteenth-century changes in earnings or the standard of living. In the first place, wages not only in agriculture but also in many industrial occupations, including building, were frequently supplemented by payments in kind. It may well be that such payments became less common in the course of the century but there is no firm information on the subject. Secondly, the statistics we have

---

[1] The price data were heavily weighted by contract prices and they take no account of regional variations. However, it may be noted that for grain prices, which were an important component of the cost-of-living index, the contracts involved were short-term and the regional variations were generally small.

used make no allowance for variations in the regularity of employment
or the number of hours worked. The complaints of contemporaries,
particularly common in the early part of the century, about the
'idleness' of the labouring poor suggest that wage-earners may have
been more concerned to maintain a traditional standard of life than to
improve their lot. The number of wage-earners who were entirely
dependent on employment income for their livelihood was in any case
relatively small. As industry developed, however, and the range of
cheap manufactures expanded, it is probable that both the opportunity
and desire for regular employment increased. So too did the necessity.
For as the population grew and shifted towards the towns the percentage of pure wage-earners increased. By the beginning of the nineteenth
century the number of English wage-earners who voluntarily worked
an average of less than six days in the week must have been negligible.

For the nineteenth century there is a vast amount of miscellaneous
material in average wages and wage rates. This was thoroughly worked
over by Bowley and Wood, in the twenty years or so before the First
World War. It would still be possible to strengthen and fill out their
results with raw material relating to other years and other industries,
but it seems unlikely that the additional data would modify the long-
term trends which emerge from their studies.

Bowley's first attempts to measure long-term changes in wage rates
were described in his paper for the 1898 meeting of the British Association.[1] He went back to 1840, i.e. to a period 'rich in wage statistics
and in literature on the condition of the working-classes',[2] and he
constructed indices for eight industries—cotton, wool, building, mining,
iron, shipping (sailors), printing (compositors) and agriculture (England
only)—for eleven years in the period 1840–91. At the following meeting
of the British Association, Wood produced a companion paper which
dealt with the course of money wages between 1790 and 1860.[3] Wood,
who had been working independently of Bowley, had approached the
material somewhat differently. He analysed the data by towns or
districts instead of by industries and thus included a wider variety of
data than Bowley was able to cover in his indices. Nevertheless, their
results for the period of overlap were encouragingly similar.[4]

This was the prelude to a fruitful collaboration.[5] The estimates

[1] A. L. Bowley, 'Comparison of the Changes in Wages in France, the United States and
the United Kingdom from 1840 to 1891', *The Economic Journal*, vol. VIII (1898).

[2] *Ibid.* p. 476.

[3] G. H. Wood, 'The Course of Average Wages between 1790 and 1860', *The Economic
Journal*, vol. IX (1899).

[4] 'Comparison of those results with those of Mr Bowley over the period 1840–60 shows
that average variations in wages in the large industries are very nearly representative of the
whole and that when enough data are used the method of arrangement and the use of
weighted or unweighted averages make very little difference to the result.' *Ibid.* pp. 591–2.

[5] See the series of articles on 'The Statistics of Wages in the United Kingdom during the
past Hundred Years', published in the *Journal of the Royal Statistical Society* between 1898 and
1910. Parts I–IV, Agricultural Wages, *J. Roy. Statist. Soc.*, 1898 and 1899; Part V, Printers,
J. Roy. Statist. Soc., 1899; Parts VI–VIII, Building Trades, *J. Roy. Statist. Soc.*, 1900–1;
Part IX, Woollen and Worsted Trades, *J. Roy. Statist. Soc.*, 1902; Parts X–XIV, Engineering

which Bowley presented to the British Association in 1898 were destined to be superseded by later investigations, but Wood's 1899 series still has considerable interest as an indicator of the movements of non-agricultural money wages in the period before 1840. The industry studies are sketchy for this early period and the number of series which it is possible to carry back more or less continuously to 1790 is small. It is also progressively more difficult to weight them for changes in the structure of employment in periods before the first occupation census.[1] If we must operate with unweighted averages, it seems advisable to use Wood's original method with its relatively large number of direct observations rather than to generalise from the few industry series for which early data exist in sufficient quantity and quality.[2]

Accordingly Table 6 is based on Wood's estimates of the movements

Table 6. *The course of money wages 1790–1860*

(1840 = 100)

	Great Britain	Ireland
1790	70	107
1795	82	115
1800	95	125
1805	109	139
1810	124	139
1816	117	136
1820	110	122
1824	105	120
1831	101	114
1840	100	100
1845	98	100
1850	100	100
1855	117	129
1860	115	134

Note on the sources: The index for Great Britain is a weighted average of Wood's general unweighted index of average money wages in towns of the United Kingdom (*Economic Journal*, 1899) and Bowley's indices of average agricultural earnings in England-and-Wales and Scotland respectively (combined according to his weights. *J. Roy. Statist. Soc.*, 1899.) No attempt has been made to extract the Irish components from Wood's United Kingdom index in constructing our Great Britain index because they were not sufficiently different or weighty to affect the result.

The index for Ireland is an average of Wood's index of average money wages in Dublin and Bowley's index of average agricultural earnings (allowing for unemployment) in Ireland. The average is again weighted in accordance with our estimates of the proportions employed in agricultural and non-agricultural occupations.

---

and Shipbuilding, *J. Roy. Statist. Soc.*, 1905–6; Parts XV–XVIII, Cotton, *J. Roy. Statist. Soc.*, 1910. In addition the authors published various more general articles embodying the results of their wage studies during this period.

[1] The first attempt to record occupational data for the whole population was made in connection with the 1841 Census of Population.

[2] Cf. Bowley's comment in his 1898 British Association paper, *op. cit.* p. 481: 'We may be left in doubt as to the wages in a particular trade for certain years to a quite considerable percentage so that we cannot in reality give a satisfactory history of that trade: but when we come to combine the figures with those of other industries for the same year the greatest possible effect on the average is remarkably small.' When the number of industries is small these 'considerable percentage' errors can have a seriously disturbing effect on the index.

in average money wages in different towns of the United Kingdom and on Bowley's estimates of the changes in average agricultural earnings in England and Wales, Scotland and Ireland respectively. The general averages for both Great Britain and Ireland have been weighted by our estimates of the relative importance of agricultural and non-agricultural occupations in the labour force at each period considered. The Irish index should be treated with considerable reserve since it is based on the assumption that Dublin money wages reflected the movements in all non-agricultural wages for Ireland. For all its crudeness, however, it offers a more acceptable estimate of the course of money wages in Ireland—which at this period accounted for nearly a third of the population of the United Kingdom—than any index of British or U.K. wages as a whole.[1]

Within the two decades 1790–1810, the evidence suggests that money wages had risen by roughly 75 per cent in Great Britain and about 30 per cent in Ireland. Whether the 1810 level represented the peak we do not know. Probably it was not far from the peak, and in any case the data are too incomplete to permit precise measurement.[2] That there was an unprecedentedly rapid rise and then a decline seems indisputable, however. The decline may have begun before the wars ended. It was certainly accelerated by demobilisation and the drop in government expenditure. Apparently money wages in general never fell back to pre-war levels in Great Britain but they were back to the level of the first few years of the century by the eighteen-twenties. Then they seem to have settled, with relatively minor fluctuations, until mid-century. In Ireland, where the wartime rise had been moderate, the decline seems to have been at roughly the same rate as in Great Britain until the disasters of the eighteen-forties carried wages to levels that were lower than those of the late eighteenth century. The recovery in the eighteen-fifties appears steeper in Ireland than in Great Britain, partly because the fall had been to famine levels and partly because it precipitated a shift from heavily depressed agricultural areas into less heavily depressed non-agricultural employments. In any case it should be remembered that the Irish figures purport to allow for unemployment, and in so far as they do, may be expected to fluctuate more widely than the corresponding British figures.

For the second half of the century wage data are available for a larger number of industries and it is possible to weight the industry averages by employment proportions. Wood's estimates of changes in money and real wages for the period 1850–1906 are an average of the movements for fourteen separate industries (distinguishing agriculture

---

[1] It should be stressed that in parts of Scotland or Wales the divergences from the trends for Great Britain as a whole were no doubt as marked as was the case for Ireland.

[2] The possibility that the data are overweighted by abnormally high quotations should not be overlooked. There is always the danger that what finds its way into wage or price records is the abnormal rather than the normal observation. The inflation may not have been so universally severe as the records imply.

in England, Scotland and Ireland) weighted by employment.[1] Again it would be possible to refine the results by introducing data for other industries, but again it is doubtful whether the new material would appreciably alter the broad outlines.

Table 7. *Money wages and real wages 1850–1906*

(1850 = 100)

	United Kingdom average money wages	United Kingdom average real wages (adjusted for unemployment)
1850	100	100
1855	116	94
1860	114	105
1866	132	117
1871	137	125
1874	155	136
1877	152	132
1880	147	132
1883	150	142
1886	148	142
1891	162	166
1896	162	177
1900	179	184
1906	181	194

Source: G. H. Wood, *op. cit., J. Roy. Statist. Soc.,* 1909. The industries included in these averages are agriculture, building, printing, engineering, shipbuilding, coal, iron, cotton, wool, worsted, gas and furniture.

Table 7 gives Wood's estimates of average money wages for the average operative and also his index of real wages which has been deflated by an index of retail prices and adjusted for unemployment. It is unfortunately not possible to extract the Irish components from Wood's series but they assume a steadily diminishing importance in the aggregate in the second half of the century. It would appear that a steep rise in money wages, steeper than at any comparable period since the wartime inflation over the turn of the century, took place in the third quarter. It was not sustained however, and the rise flattened out to less than 5 per cent in the period 1874–96.

Real wages followed a somewhat different course. Neither Wood nor Bowley attempted to push their estimates of real wages back to the beginning of the century; but if we deflate the results in Table 6 with the Gayer-Rostow-Schwartz wholesale price index[2] we find an improvement in real wages of about 25 per cent between 1800 and 1824

[1] G. H. Wood, 'Real Wages and the Standard of Comfort since 1850', *J. Roy. Statist. Soc.,* vol. LXXII (March 1909). Bowley and Wood published a variety of successive approximations to a general wage index during the years of their closest collaboration but this seems to have been their latest covering the years back to 1850. For 1880 onwards later estimates are in A. L. Bowley, *Wages and Incomes since 1860* (Cambridge, 1937).

[2] A. D. Gayer, W. W. Rostow and A. J. Schwartz, *The Growth and Fluctuation of the British Economy 1790–1850,* vol. I, p. 468.

and over 40 per cent between 1824 and 1850. These are very rough calculations and make no allowance for unemployment, but when related to the later and better index compiled by Wood (Table 7) the results suggest a positive increase in real wages in the first quarter of the century which accelerated in the second quarter and continued at a high (though probably decelerating) rate up to the end of the century. If we carry the estimates on into the twentieth century we find that in the twenty-five years before 1914 the increase in real wages was not much more than 10 per cent compared with about 35 per cent between 1874 and 1900 and about 36 per cent between 1850 and 1874.[1]

Examination of the results for individual industries reveals some interesting variations. The cotton industry starts from a very high level at the beginning of the nineteenth century, fluctuates around this high level for most of the war period and then dips abruptly so that by the eighteen-thirties money wages appear to have sunk to about half the levels prevailing at the beginning of the century. These are Wood's estimates for all workers.[2] The decline in the case of handloom weavers was much greater—from a weekly wage of about 20s. a week to not much more than 6s. a week in the eighteen-thirties. Meanwhile there was an increase in the labour force of the industry from roughly a quarter of a million persons at the beginning of the century to about 425,000 in 1830. The improvement in earnings came slowly at first as a large pocket of technological unemployment was gradually liquidated. Between 1831 and 1847 the labour force of the industry fell by about 23 per cent and the average money wage improved by about 15 per cent. After this the labour force began to grow again and wages rose faster than ever before if we exclude the halcyon days at the end of the eighteenth century. 'From 1850 no industry shows so great a proportionate advance.'[3]

A somewhat similar picture emerges for the woollen and worsted industries. Starting from a high level near the beginning of the century average money wages dipped after the war and rose again in the second quarter, though recovery was somewhat later than in the case of cotton. The engineering, shipbuilding, and building industries seem to have lagged behind in the post-war inflation and to have had a happier wage history thereafter. In money terms these industries regained their wartime peaks by the eighteen-forties. If we take into account the post-war fall in prices we may conclude that engineers, shipbuilders and builders enjoyed a marked increase in real wages throughout the century with the exception of its first ten to fifteen years.

---

[1] Bowley, *Wages and Income since 1860*, p. 30. Bowley's calculations give a higher increase in the last quarter of the nineteenth century than do Wood's, so that his results would intensify the contrast.

[2] G. H. Wood, 'The Statistics of Wages in the Nineteenth Century, Part XIX, The Cotton Industry', *J. Roy. Statist. Soc.*, vol. LXXIII (June 1910), pp. 598–9.

[3] *Ibid.* p. 617, Wood attributes this to 'its extensive collective bargaining, its high proportion of piecework, and its encouragement of higher efficiency both in operative and machine'.

Agriculture went its own way and its wage trends were of considerable importance in the national total during the first half-century. In England the wartime increase in money wages was of the order of 100 per cent between 1790 and 1810 according to Bowley.[1] It was less spectacular in Scotland, and still less so in Ireland, but Bowley's indices for the United Kingdom as a whole suggest an increase in average money wages of over 70 per cent in the war period. The post-war decline was of the order of 30 per cent in England and 40 per cent for Ireland—the bottom being reached in the late forties. The rise in the second half of the century was commensurate with the rise in the national average for all industries.

It is not surprising therefore that there has been considerable controversy concerning the trends in working-class standards of living during the first half of the nineteenth century and little dispute over its improvement in the second half. More important than scarcity of data in creating obscurity for the early period were the widely varying wage histories of different industries. The fact that cotton, the major British manufacturing industry, which employed over 400,000 persons in 1831 when the total British labour force was probably less than $7\frac{1}{2}$ million persons, experienced such a disastrous fall in money wages in the post-war period was enough in itself to justify the view that industrialisation was not necessarily synonymous with progress in welfare. Taken over all industries the national average of money wages was declining or stagnant for most of the period between Waterloo and 1860. If we have concluded that real wages rose on the average it is only because the price data suggest strongly that the increase in the value of money outweighed the fall in money wages.[2] The conclusion is still tentative because the price data are incomplete and because we are unable to assess the relative weight of the burden of unemployment in the post-war years. In some years it may have been large enough to outweigh the effects of the fall in prices. In some industries or occupations, average standards of living clearly fell during the post-war period and did not begin to recover until the eighteen-forties.

In sum, therefore, this attempt to interpret nineteenth-century wage indices in terms of working-class standards of living suggests that there was a negligible improvement in the Napoleonic war years, an upward trend in the immediate post-war years (though this may have been outweighed by post-war unemployment), an unprecedentedly rapid improvement in the second quarter (which might also be modified on the basis of unemployment data) and an indisputable rise in the third and fourth quarters. This had begun to lose speed before the century

[1] *Op. cit., J. Roy. Statist. Soc.*, 1899.

[2] Any overall price index points to the same conclusion. Cf. E. J. Hobsbawm, 'The British Standard of Living, 1790–1850', *Econ. Hist. Rev.*, 1957: 'It is not too much to say that Clapham's version of the "optimistic" view stood or fell by Silberling.' The other statistics which have been taken into account in this perennial debate about the trends in British standards of living after the Napoleonic Wars are too indirect or too incomplete to be conclusive.

ended. If anything there seems to have been a tendency for real wages to decline in the decade or so before the First World War.

The twentieth-century trends are broken by two world wars. In the inter-war period money wages were falling less rapidly than prices so that real wages improved. The high incidence of unemployment, however, reduced the impact of rising real wages on overall standards of living. In the period of full employment which followed the Second World War wage rates have risen rapidly—less strongly than prices at first, more strongly in recent years.

5. THE CHANGING RELATIONSHIP WITH THE REST OF THE WORLD

(a) The growth of international trade

There is no question of the importance of international trade to the British economy throughout the period of two and a half centuries under consideration in this book, nor of the fact that it grew very substantially in the course of that period. The existence of overseas markets for manufactured British goods and the possibility of tapping overseas supplies of raw materials and staple foods were strategically important factors in the process of industrialisation at all stages. By the end of the nineteenth century the British economy was heavily dependent on world markets, and the rate and pattern of British economic growth was largely conditioned by the responses of producers and consumers in the rest of the world.

The growth in the importance of foreign trade can be illustrated by measuring its value against national income. In the absence of current trade values (and indeed of adequate national income estimates) for the eighteenth century it is difficult to trace this comparison through the early stages of the industrial revolution. Such as they are, the data suggest a substantial increase in the importance of the overseas markets to British producers. Exports valued at constant prices increased roughly fivefold in the course of the eighteenth century[1] while for national income the corresponding increase was probably less than threefold.[2] Gregory King's figures imply that domestic exports of merchandise for England and Wales were only between 5 and 6 per cent of national income in 1688.[3] By the beginning of the nineteenth century, and probably in the last decade or two of the eighteenth century, domestic merchandise exports were in the region of 14 per

---

[1] This is so whether we use the official values based largely on 1697 prices (when the increase between 1702–3 and 1797–8 works out at 398 per cent) or use 1796–8 prices (which suggest an increase of 421 per cent over the same period).

[2] For a discussion of contemporary estimates of eighteenth-century national income see below, pp. 155–8.

[3] For King's estimates of foreign trade values see his pamphlet 'Of the Naval Trade of England anno 1688', reprinted by George Barnett, *op. cit.*; see especially, p. 65. According to a modern investigator, however, King's trade statistics are 'hardly credible; he sets import trade in 1688, at the end, he says, of eleven prosperous years, at . . . not much more than the London import alone of 1669.' Ralph Davis, 'English Foreign Trade 1660–1700', *Econ. Hist. Rev.*, 1954, p. 155.

cent of national income. But this was a period in which internat
trade was certainly increasing faster than national income. The
of domestic exports for most of the first half of the nineteenth cer___,
was between 9 and 11 per cent, except during the late twenties and
early thirties when it would appear that the growth of the home
market outstripped that of the foreign market.

In these terms, the peak was reached for domestic exports in the early
1870's, when they averaged roughly 23 per cent of national income,
and for imports in the early 1880's at a level of roughly 36 per cent of
the national income. It was in the 1880's in the period of the 'Great
Depression' that the rising tide of British exports was seriously challenged by foreign competition. Thereafter the proportion of British
output marketed abroad fluctuated and fell. Domestic exports (averaged over quinquennia) ranged between about 15 per cent and about
21 per cent of national income in the half-century before the First
World War. The demand for imports was less elastic, however, and
after falling from a peak of 36 per cent in the early 1880's they fluctuated within the narrower limits of between 29 per cent and 32 per cent
of national income up to 1914.

During the inter-war period British merchandise exports faced intensified difficulties. Although they amounted to about 17 per cent of
national income at the end of the nineteen-twenties they had fallen to
10 per cent in the late thirties and recovered to 20 per cent again in the
nineteen-fifties. Meanwhile imports, restricted by protection and no
longer supported by the invisible transactions which had compensated
for a weakening commodity trade in the pre-war period, dropped to
new low levels.

The changes in the rate of growth of British international trade
through the past two and a half centuries are illustrated more directly
in Table 8, which shows annual long-term rates of growth in the

Table 8. *The rate of growth of international trade*

Compound rates per cent per annum in volumes (decade averages) of domestic exports plus
retained imports

England and Wales	%	United Kingdom	%
1700–30	1·2	1801–31	2·7
1710–40	1·0	1811–41	3·4
1720–50	1·1	1821–51	4·4
1730–60	1·5	1831–61	4·5
1740–70	1·9	1841–71	4·6
1750–80	1·1	1851–81	4·1
		1861–91	3·4
Great Britain		1870–1900	2·9
		1880–1910	2·5
1760–90	1·8	1904–34	—
1770–1800	2·3	1924–54	1·0

Sources: For eighteenth-century basic figures see Table 85, pp. 319–21 below. Nineteenth-century rates based on Imlah's index of the volume of net imports + domestic
exports. See A. H. Imlah, *Economic Elements* in the *Pax Britannica* (1958). Decade averages
centre on years specified.

aggregate volume of domestic exports and retained imports over a successive series of thirty-year periods.

During the first half of the eighteenth century the volume of international trade seems to have expanded at a rate of not much more than 1 per cent per annum. In view of the stagnation of population over most of the first half of the eighteenth century, expansion at an annual rate of a little over 1 per cent represented a fairly substantial rate of progress for a pre-industrial economy. There was some acceleration in mid-century, which was temporarily checked by the American War of Independence and resumed at the end of the century. Over the last quarter of the eighteenth century and the turn of the next century the annual rate of growth was near $2\frac{1}{2}$ per cent per annum.

The peak seems to have been achieved in the third quarter of the nineteenth century, though for the whole of the period 1821–81 the average long-term rate of growth exceeded 4 per cent per annum. By the turn of the twentieth century, i.e. over the three decades before the First World War, the rate was down to about $2\frac{1}{2}$ per cent per annum. In the next thirty-year period (ending in the 1930's) there was a slight absolute decline in the volume of trade: and in the last period (ending in the 1950's) the rate was back to 1 per cent per annum, which—in the light of a population growth of about $\frac{1}{2}$ per cent per annum and a growth in average real incomes of nearly $1\frac{1}{2}$ per cent—is a very low rate of expansion indeed.

(b) The Composition of Merchandise Trade

These shifts in the relative importance and rates of growth of British external trade were associated with variations in the commodity pattern of exports. At the beginning of the eighteenth century, as at its end, the most important British export was manufactured woollen goods. But whereas in 1699–1701 the woollen manufacture provided more than two-thirds of the value of domestic exports, in 1796–8 it accounted for only 27 per cent.[1] In the intervening century there had been a steady broadening of the base of the British economy. Since British exports were largely exports of manufactured goods the widening of the range of British manufactures associated with the beginnings of industrialisation was particularly strongly reflected in the export trade. There were significant increases in the share of other textiles such as cotton, linen and silk and also in the share of the metal industries such as copper, brass and iron manufactures.

During the first quarter of the nineteenth century the British economy was dominated by the sudden rise of the cotton industry. As far as the export trade was concerned the most spectacular change took place during the Napoleonic Wars. At the end of the eighteenth century,

[1] Figures for 1699–1701 are an average of three years for England and Wales, as extracted by Ralph Davis; see 'English Foreign Trade, 1660–1700', *Econ. Hist. Rev.*, second series, vol. VII (December 1954), p. 165. They are not declared values but are reasonably close to current values. Figures for 1796–8 are from Irving's return, dated March 1800, ('Commercial Accounts of Great Britain and Ireland', *S.P. 1800*, Vol. XLIX) giving total declared value of British exports to all ports (including Ireland).

woollens were still twice the value of cotton exports. By the end of the Napoleonic Wars (on an average of the three years 1814–16) cottons were twice the value of woollen exports and accounted for about 40 per cent of the declared value of all British exports.[1] They reached their peak of relative importance in 1830 when they accounted for more than half of the value of all domestic exports.

In effect, by the 1830's nearly three-quarters of all British exports were provided by the textile and dress industries. Since the turn of the century the volume of domestic exports had roughly quadrupled and most of this increase was a reflection of the industrial revolution in textiles.[2] By contrast the rise in importance of the iron and steel industries (including hardware and cutlery), which increased their share of exports from about 6 per cent in 1814–16 to about 10 per cent in 1830, was of relatively modest significance.

Table 9. *The changing pattern of British commodity exports 1830–1950*

Principal exports as a percentage of total domestic exports of the United Kingdom

	1830	1850	1870	1890	1910	1930	1950
Cotton yarn and manufactures	50·8	39·6	35·8	28·2	24·4	15·3	7·3
Woollen yarn and manufactures	12·7	14·1	13·4	9·8	8·7	6·5	6·5
Linen yarn and manufactures	5·4	6·8	4·8	2·5	—	—	0·9
Silk*	1·4	1·5	0·7	1·0	0·5	0·3	2·3
Apparel	2·0	1·3	1·1	1·9	2·9	3·5	1·6
Iron and steel manufactures†	10·2	12·3	14·2	14·5	11·4	10·3	9·5
Machinery	0·5	0·8	1·5	3·0	6·8	8·2	14·3
Coal, coke, etc.	0·5	1·8	2·8	7·2	8·7	8·6	5·3
Earthenware and glass	2·2	1·7	1·3	1·3	1·0	2·1	2·5
Vehicles‡	—	—	1·1	3·5	3·8	9·0	18·6
Chemicals	—	0·5	0·6	2·2	4·3	3·8	5·0
Electrical apparatus	—	—	—	—	—	2·1	3·9

* Including artificial silk.
† Including hardwares and cutlery.
‡ Carriages, wagons, ships, cars, cycles, aircraft.

Sources: Statistical Abstracts *and* Trade and Navigation Accounts.

Table 9 illustrates the diversification of the pattern of British exports in the course of the following twelve decades. The process seemed to gather momentum in the nineteenth century and to be most rapid in the twentieth. The rate of transformation in the second quarter of the twentieth century is notable. Cotton began to decline in relative importance before the middle of the nineteenth century when the other textile industries, slower to mechanise, were still increasing their share. The textile and dress industries continued to provide more than half of

[1] *Sessional Papers, 1817,* vol. xiv. It was in 1815 that the 'declared' values of cotton exports first dropped below their 'official' values.

[2] In 1800 the 'official' value of British exports was £22·8 m.: by 1840 it had reached £102·7 m. This is a crude measure of volume, being based on seventeenth-century price weights, but it gives some idea of the order of magnitude of the change.

the value of British exports until the late 1870's. Even at the turn of the century cotton still accounted for roughly a quarter of the value of all domestic exports. Iron and steel manufactures were then beginning to lose ground in external trade, but coal and coke were increasing their share, and so, more slowly, were a variety of other industries which were destined to assume significance in the mid-twentieth century. It was not until the three decades following the First World War, when cotton exports halved and vehicles and machinery doubled their respective shares, when artificial silk multiplied the share of the silk industry by a factor of more than six, and when coal exports reduced their share and chemicals raised theirs by about a third, that the export trade was radically transformed.

Analysis of the commodity distribution of imports in the eighteenth and early nineteenth centuries is complicated by the fact that imports continued to be entered at their 'official' values up to 1854. While these may give some indication of the direction of changes in volume, the price structure had changed so much that they are quite unreliable as measures of the composition of the import trade. At the beginning of the eighteenth century rather more than a third of the value of imports fell into the raw-materials category (largely textile materials, yarns and dyes), just under a third were food, drink and tobacco items, and just under a third again were manufactured goods (again largely textiles).[1] A substantial proportion of all imports (probably at least 30 per cent) were re-exported, however, and when we extract these the results suggest that more than 40 per cent of all retained imports were raw materials, and under 30 per cent were attributable either to food, drink and tobacco imports or to manufactured goods respectively.

By 1840 (which is the earliest year for which there are official estimates of the current values of imports) the textile industry dominated the import trade almost as much as the export trade.[2] About 30 per cent of the value of all imports was attributable to textile, raw or semi-manufactured materials exclusive of dyes, bleaches, etc. Manufactured imports were of negligible importance. Food, drink and tobacco imports were almost 40 per cent of the total. By this time goods intended for re-export were a relatively unimportant proportion (under 10 per cent) of all imports.[3] The next century brought considerable changes in the pattern, as is shown by Table 10.

Three features of this table are worth noting. The first is the great importance of raw-material imports in the middle decades of the century. British industrialisation was based on foreign supplies of raw material. The second is the growth of food imports between 1860 and 1880. By the late 1870's about 37 per cent of British consumption of cereals, about half of the cheese and butter and about 20 per cent of

[1] Ralph Davis, *op. cit.* p. 164. Figures are for the average of three years 1699–1701.
[2] Estimates made by the Board of Trade and published in *Sessional Papers, 1863*, vol. LXVI.
[3] Imlah's estimates give total imports £91·2 m. in 1840 and re-exports (which include British merchants' profits) at £10·0 m. Imlah, *op. cit.* p. 38.

Table 10. *The pattern of imports into the United Kingdom 1840–1950*

Current values as percentage of total imports

	Food, drink and tobacco	Raw material and semi-manufactured goods	Manufactured and miscellaneous goods
1840[1]	39·7	56·6	3·7
1860[1]	38·1	56·5	5·5
1880[2]	44·1	38·6	17·3
1900[3]	42·1	32·9	25·0
1910[3]	38·0	38·5	23·5
1930[3]	45·5	24·0	29·4
1950[3]	39·5	38·2	22·3

Sources: 1 Computed real values by the Board of Trade. *S.P. 1863*, vol. LXVI.
2 Our analysis of the trade returns in *Statistical Abstracts*. There is an unallocated item of 6 per cent which may not all be attributable to manufactured goods.
3 From *Statistical Abstracts*.

the meat were imported.[1] The exodus from agriculture was accelerating and supplies of cheap food were becoming available in bulk from the New World. This was the period of the 'great specialisation', the heyday of free trade. Domestic exports were equivalent to about a fifth of the total national income (and total imports to more than a third), and the volume of British international trade was growing at the remarkable pace of more than 4½ per cent per annum. Moreover, Britain dominated world trade. The British share of the world export trade in manufactures was probably more than 40 per cent in 1854 and more than 38 per cent in 1880.

The third notable feature of Table 10 is the growth in the value of manufactured goods imported into the United Kingdom in the latter part of the nineteenth century. The free-trade policy which had drawn cheap food from the Americas was now attracting manufactures from the newly industrialising, protected countries of Europe. By the twentieth century manufactured goods were generally responsible for between 20 and 30 per cent of the value of British imports. At the turn of the century the British share of the world export trade in manufactures was down to 28 per cent. But world trade was still growing. More significant still was the subsequent fall in a stagnant or declining quantum of world trade to a share of 20 per cent in 1929. By 1954 the British share was under 16 per cent and the American share was 26 per cent.[2]

(c) The balance of payments

The trade in merchandise accounts for only a part of the transactions entering into the British balance of payments. For most of the period

[1] For a discussion of the growth of food imports in this period see Stephen Bourne, *Trade Population and Food* (1880). These proportions are from James Caird, *The Landed Interest and its Supply of Food* (1879).

[2] For these percentages see W. Arthur Lewis, 'International Competition in Manufactures', *American Economic Review, Papers and Proceedings*, May 1957, p. 579.

since 1688 the trade in services was an important source of income. Unfortunately there is little information on the invisible trade before the second half of the nineteenth century and the data are imprecise even for the early twentieth century.

It would appear that a passive balance of merchandise trade has been a characteristic feature of British trade for more than two and a half centuries. King's estimates for 1688[1] suggest a value for imports (c.i.f.) of over £7·1 m. and for exports (f.o.b.) of about £4·3 m. (including gold and specie in each case). The balance of about £2·8 m. was more than covered by English receipts from freight, commission and profits, etc., on foreign trade which King estimated at about £3·5 m. A net foreign investment of about £0·7 m. represented about 1½ per cent of national income.

Probably Englishmen continued to invest comparable amounts in the colonial areas for much of the eighteenth century. It is significant that the eighteenth-century trade expansion was almost entirely due to the growth of colonial trade. The heavily protected markets of Europe inhibited expansion in that direction. The European share in British trade declined from about 82 per cent of domestic exports and 62 per cent of all imports in 1700–1 to about 21 per cent of exports and 29 per cent of imports in 1797–8. It was the American market (including the valuable West Indies) which provided the greatest scope for growth. It took 10 per cent of English domestic exports in 1700–1, 37 per cent in 1772–3 and about 57 per cent in 1797–8; it provided 20 per cent of imports (including goods for re-export) in 1700–1, 36 per cent in 1772–3 and about 31 per cent in 1797–8. By comparison the Eastern market expanded only moderately—from 3 per cent of English domestic exports in 1700–1 to 9 per cent in 1772–3 and 1797–8, and from 13 per cent of imports (including goods for re-export) in 1700–1 to 24 per cent in 1797–8.

By the end of the eighteenth century it is reasonable to suppose that the income generated by these colonial investments was substantial. When Pitt made his calculations of income-tax yield he estimated the annual British income from property abroad at about £5 m. and attributed another £12 m. to 'profits on foreign trade and shipping'.[2] On the other hand, there were probably some balancing flows of income from Britain to its creditors in Europe—interest on national debt for example—and there is evidence of a flight from the English funds after the end of the American War of Independence.[3]

Whether or not the net income and capital which Britain obtained

---

[1] Reprinted in George Barnett, *op. cit.* p. 74.

[2] Pitt's estimates are discussed in Deane, 'The Implications of Early National Income Estimates, etc.', *op. cit.* pp. 26–9.

[3] George Grenville estimated in 1768 that national debt interest payment to foreigners amounted to £1·560 m.: in 1783 Sinclair estimated that the flow amounted to under £1 m. See Alice Carter, 'Dutch Investment 1738–1800', *Economica*, vol. xx (November 1953), for a discussion of these and other contemporary estimates of foreign investment in the English funds.

from overseas sources in the second half of the eighteenth century was absolutely and directly important as a source of finance for the industrial revolution it is impossible to say, without detailed research into the records of private companies and public institutions. It is probable, for example, that the aggregate wealth of the 'nabobs' was greatly exaggerated.[1] On the other hand, it is possible that, even if the sums involved were not large in comparison to the national income, their strategic importance in the acceleration of technical progress at the end of the century may have been considerable. Their existence may help to explain the sudden, rapidly dominant, development of what was virtually a new industry and, moreover, an industry dependent on imported raw materials. Indirectly if not directly, the extraordinarily rapid diversion of resources into the cotton textile industry must have owed something to the British trading connection. A century of experience in developing overseas markets and of normal, if un-spectacular, net profits on these enterprises provided the kind of environment which was conducive to new investment in the mass manufacture of commodities saleable overseas. Profits and incomes which had been earned in overseas enterprises could readily be ploughed back into the import of raw materials and the manufacture of finished goods for export. In effect, we do not have to suppose that the overall rate of saving increased or that additional capital became available from overseas sources in the crucial last decades of the eighteenth century, only that capital (and particularly trading capital) which had hitherto been spread over a variety of only moderately profitable industries came to be more and more concentrated on an industry which enjoyed decreasing costs and expansible markets.

Various authors have calculated the components of the British balance of payments before the First World War. The most recent and reliable estimates are those made by Professor Imlah. Table 11 summarises these. Perhaps their most striking implication is the rise in the importance of the invisible items in British international trade during the second half of the nineteenth century. Even in Gregory King's day the invisibles were by no means negligible in this country's balance of payments. But during most of the first six decades of the nineteenth century net receipts from invisibles accounted for between 25 and 30 per cent of all receipts from the rest of the world. During the four decades before the First World War they were running at an average level of 35 to 40 per cent of total receipts from abroad. The re-export trade, however, declined in relative importance during the nineteenth century. After reaching a peak amounting to perhaps 18 per cent of total receipts from abroad at the end of the eighteenth century—and a still higher though short-lived peak in the last few years of the Napoleonic Wars—it dropped to an average of about 11 or 12 per cent at at the close of the nineteenth century.

[1] See, for example, James M. Holzman, *The Nabobs in England* (New York, 1926). A study of the returned Anglo-Indian.

Table 11. *The balance of payments of the United Kingdom 1816–1913*

Annual averages in £m. All figures have been rounded

	(1)	(2)	(3)	(4)	(5)	(6)	(7)
	Balance of visible trade	Net shipping earnings	Profits, interest, dividends	Insurance, brokerage, commissions	Emigrants, tourists, smugglers, government, all other	Balance of invisible trade	Net balance
1816–20	−11	+10	+ 8	+3	−3	+18	+ 7
1821–25	− 8	+ 9	+ 9	+2	−2	+18	+10
1826–30	−15	+ 8	+ 9	+2	−3	+17	+ 3
1831–35	−13	+ 5	+11	+3	−4	+19	+ 6
1836–40	−23	+11	+15	+4	−4	+26	+ 3
1841–45	−19	+12	+15	+4	−5	+25	+ 6
1846–50	−26	+14	+18	+4	−6	+30	+ 5
1851–55	−33	+19	+24	+6	−8	+41	+ 8
1856–60	−34	+26	+33	+8	−8	+60	+26
1861–65	−59	+34	+44	+11	−8	+81	+22
1866–70	−65	+45	+57	+13	−9	+106	+41
1871–75	−64	+51	+83	+16	−12	+139	+75
1876–80	−124	+54	+88	+16	− 9	+149	+25
1881–85	− 99	+60	+96	+16	−11	+161	+61
1886–90	− 89	+57	+115	+15	−11	+177	+88
1891–95	−134	+57	+124	+15	−10	+186	+52
1896–1900	−159	+62	+132	+16	−11	+199	+40
1901–05	−177	+71	+149	+18	−13	+226	+49
1906–10	−144	+89	+196	+22	−18	+290	+146
1911–13	−140	+100	+241	+27	−22	+346	+206

Source: Imlah, *op. cit.* pp. 70–5.

If we accept the last column of Table 11 as a rough measure of the volume of British foreign investment it appears that it was not until the second half of the nineteenth century—beginning in the late 1850's—that the outward flow of capital became of sustained importance in the balance of payments. Even so it fluctuated fairly widely. It reached its peak outflow at an annual average of about 6½ per cent of the national income in the late 1880's and again in the decade before the First World War. It slackened appreciably in the late 1870's and in the decade covering the turn of the century when it fell to between 2 and 2½ per cent. The usual interpretation that much of Britain's late-nineteenth-century and early-twentieth-century investment abroad was financed by reinvesting profits and interest earned in past investments abroad seems plausible enough in the light of the figures in column 3 of Table 11. Certainly after the first quarter of the century, profits, interest and dividends estimated to have been received from abroad were more than adequate to cover the estimated new investments abroad. In the second quarter of the century up to the mid-1850's they may have been large enough to finance a significant proportion of the new capital formation at home. Thereafter it is possible that more than half of their total value on the average was ploughed back into new foreign investments.

In effect, therefore, up to the beginning of the First World War the

United Kingdom's earnings from its foreign assets were more than sufficient to finance the passive balance of merchandise trade, while net shipping and other earnings from the sale of services were still growing steadily. There are no balance-of-payments data for the period of the First World War but we can assume that there was net liquidation of foreign assets. Table 12 extends the balance-of-payments figures into the post-war period on the basis of the Board of Trade estimates published annually from 1923 onwards. These are broadly comparable with the Imlah estimates in Table 11.

Table 12. *The balance of payments of the United Kingdom 1907–38*

Annual averages in £m.

	Balance of visible trade[4]	Net shipping earnings	Net interest, etc.	Net other (commissions, grants, government, etc.)	Balance of invisible trade	Net balance available for foreign investment
1907–10–13[1]	−153	+ 90	+185	+35	+310	+157
1920–24[3]	−258	+178	+199	+42	+419	+161
1925–29[3]	−398	+128	+268	+85	+481	+ 83
1930–34[3]	−328	+ 78	+174	+49	+301	− 27
1935–38[2]	−356	+ 96	+199	+37	+332	− 24

Sources: Board of Trade estimates published annually in the *Board of Trade Journal* using latest estimates available in each case. Thus the 1907–23 estimates are those published in the January 1924 issue of the *Journal*, vol. 112, the 1923 estimates are those published in the 1925 *Journal*, vol. 114, and so on. The 1936–7–8 estimates are those published in the *Journal* for February 1939, vol. 142.

Notes on the estimates: 1 Average of the three years mentioned.
                        2 Four-year average.
                        3 Five-year average.
                        4 Excess of exports valued f.o.b. over imports valued c.i.f.

The data for the inter-war period reflect a radical change in Britain's position *vis-à-vis* the rest of the world. This may have been partly due to a loss of foreign property incomes due to the reduction of overseas assets in financing the First World War, but it seems to have been largely attributable to a failure to expand exports of goods and services in step with the rising volume of imports. The outflow of capital had begun to decline in the 1920's. In the course of the depression of the thirties it had changed direction and become an inflow rather than an outflow. The Second World War accelerated the process of liquidation of United Kingdom foreign assets. During the seven years 1939–45 the balance of visible trade[1] averaged £754 m. per annum: the net foreign disinvestment averaged £678 m., equivalent to nearly 10 per cent of net national income annually.

In the first post-war quinquennium (1946–50) the rate of disinvestment was still running at an annual average of £409 m. The flow was eventually reversed in the 1950's, but the enormous disinvestment of the war and immediate post-war years had completely changed the

[1] Exclusive of the trade in munitions, for which no figures are available. See C.S.O., *Statistical Digest of the War* (H.M.S.O., 1951), for the wartime figures used in this paragraph.

United Kingdom's position in the world economy. It was no longer possible for her to rely on past accumulations of wealth to compensate for the consequences of declines in productivity or in competitive power or of adverse movements in the terms of trade. Current output was once again the most important factor determining the level of current earnings on rest of the world account.

6. THE VANTAGE OF THE NINETEEN-FIFTIES

When Gregory King calculated the national income of England and Wales at the end of the seventeenth century and provided the present volume with a starting-point, this country had apparently achieved a higher level of material welfare than any other country in the world except Holland.[1] It is unlikely, however, that the gap between it and the rest of the world was large or indeed that there had been much improvement in average English standards of living since the fifteenth century though population may have doubled and conditions of life have been better as well as worse for the inhabitants of England and Wales since the Wars of the Roses.[2] King lived in a world in which economic change, outside the cataclysms produced by famines and epidemics, was generally small, slow and easily reversed.

In the past two and a half centuries, however, the change has been spectacular. The British population of the 1950's, grown seven times more dense, enjoyed a material output eight times as large and infinitely more varied. The economy which King could describe in terms of a list of families distinguished by social or economic status had become a complex system of impersonal economic relations. The typical unit of economic activity was not the household but the firm; nearly a fifth of gross national product accrued to corporate enterprise and about two-thirds to employed persons. Most important of all, economic growth—though variable and capable of being halted and reversed by major wars—has become the normal state of affairs in Britain, most of Europe and their overseas descendants in North America and Australasia. In some of these countries the British level of economic wellbeing has been excelled—notably in the United States, where output per worker in the 1950's was estimated to be near twice that of the corresponding ratio in the United Kingdom.[3]

The course of British economic growth over the two hundred and

---

[1] King, *op. cit.* p. 55, put Dutch average incomes at slightly above and the French average about 20 per cent below English incomes per head in 1688.

[2] Cf. E. H. Phelps Brown, *The Growth of British Industrial Relations* (1959), p. 2. 'The fifteenth century, for all the Wars of the Roses, had been a high plateau of economic prosperity; we know that the wage of a mason or a carpenter then would buy him as much of the basic materials of consumption as his successors in the same crafts were fetching around 1880, and it is very probable that this material well-being was general.'

[3] In *A Comparison of National Output and Productivity of the United Kingdom and the United States*, by Deborah Paige and Gottfried Bombach (O.E.E.C., Paris, 1959), it is estimated (p. 25) that U.S. output per worker in 1957 was 218 per cent of the U.K. average when the comparison is weighted by U.K. prices and 177 per cent at U.S. prices.

seventy years covering this transformation has been neither uniform nor inevitable. The changes in the quality and structure of output, in the movements of people and capital and in the character of the international economy have varied through time in direction as well as scope. But there have been certain regularities and certain areas of uniformity. From the beginning to end of this story, for example, the British people have depended for their standard of living largely on their ability to sell their products in overseas markets. There is a sense, to take another example, in which the British economy of the 1870's represents essentially the same universe, the same accounting unit, as it were, as that of the 1950's, though both are so different from that of the 1690's as to make direct comparison of little interest.

It needs no research to show that the economy of this country as at the mid-twentieth century was different altogether from that of the end of the seventeenth century. Much of the economic change which produced this result is a matter of quality rather than quantity and we shall have little to say about the qualitative factors. Changes in the content of economic welfare or in the motives of economic behaviour or in the mechanism of economic organisation are at least as significant conditions of economic progress as changes in the volume and structure of economic activity. There are advantages, however, in focusing on the quantitative story at this stage. The first is that establishing the dimensions of economic change is an essential prelude to systematic exploration of its causes. The second is that for any period of time or any sector of the economy the problem of measurement raises a congeries of related problems which it is instructive to consider together. The third is that it is easier to assess the regularities, the turning-points and the shifts of pace or of emphasis if they are seen in the perspective given by a framework which is as consistent and as well articulated as the data will permit.

CHAPTER II

THE EIGHTEENTH-CENTURY ORIGINS OF ECONOMIC GROWTH

IT used to be held that in contrast with the slow pace of economic change in other periods, the decades after 1760 brought with them a far-reaching and comparatively sudden transformation in both the organisation of industry and the scale of output which amounted to an industrial revolution. Since the publication of Arnold Toynbee's *Lectures on the Industrial Revolution* in 1884, the discoveries of 'industrial revolutions' in practically every century from the thirteenth to the twentieth, and the extension of the boundaries of the classical revolution backwards and forwards in time,[1] have certainly deprived the concept of some of its significance. But it has never been seriously denied that there was some acceleration in the tempo of economic change in eighteenth-century Britain. Moreover, the contemporary interest in economic growth has tended to encourage a return to something like the classical view of the changes which occurred during that period. For although there is plenty of evidence of economic *change* in other places at other times, it is clear that for most of human history the pace of economic *progress*—whatever meaning we may attach to that somewhat elusive term—has been painfully slow, and it is only since the eighteenth century that the regular expansion of the total output of goods and services, in both absolute and per capita terms, has become characteristic of the economic order.

In recent years, the tendency has been to bring the date of the decisive turning-point forward from 1760, and such widely differing scholars as Professors Nef, Ashton and Rostow are apparently agreed that it may be located in the 1780's.[2] So far, however, there has been no systematic attempt to exploit the available statistical evidence in order to confirm or refute this view. Nor do we have any clear idea of the magnitude of changes in the rate of growth, and how it compares with developments earlier in the century, although some writers have pointed to evidence of marked economic expansion as early as 1750.[3] It is true that Professor Hoffmann has tried to measure the growth of British industry in the course of the last two and a half centuries, and

[1] For a recent discussion of these and their significance, see D. C. Coleman, 'Industrial Growth and Industrial Revolutions', *Economica*, new series, vol. XXIII (1956), pp. 1–22.

[2] J. U. Nef, 'The Industrial Revolution Reconsidered', *Journal of Economic History*, vol. III (1943); T. S. Ashton, *An Economic History of England: The Eighteenth Century* (1955), p. 125; W. W. Rostow, 'The Take-Off into Self-sustained Growth', *Economic Journal*, vol. LXVI (1956), pp. 25–48.

[3] A. J. Youngson, *Possibilities of Economic Progress* (Cambridge, 1959), pp. 114–17. See also J. D. Chambers, 'The Vale of Trent, 1670–1800', *Econ. Hist. Rev.*, Supplement No. 3 (1957).

his findings apparently support the view 'that the change in the rate of production which occurred about 1780 was so definite that it clearly marks an epoch in the evolution of Britain's industrial economy'.[1] But, for the eighteenth century at least, Hoffmann's index is too narrowly based to be conclusive.[2] Moreover, an index of industrial production for a pre-industrial economy is an indicator of developments in a small sector. It tells us nothing about the growth of output as a whole or its relation to changes in the size of the population.

We attempted first to make use of contemporary estimates of the national income to illuminate this problem.[3] These estimates proved too few and scattered to cast much light on the detailed chronology of change. But, somewhat surprisingly, they suggested that the acceleration in the rate of economic growth in the latter part of the eighteenth century was much less marked than most recent discussion implies, and that in per capita terms the last quarter of the century may even have witnessed the loss of some of the modest gains achieved in earlier decades. In this chapter, therefore, we propose to consider how far the other statistical evidence available enables us to trace the early stages of economic growth more completely or more conclusively. Unfortunately, there is no quantitative information on the growth of service industries in the eighteenth century, and the data we have on industry and agriculture are seriously defective. In the first three sections, therefore, we shall examine the indicators which are available in an attempt to make an assessment—albeit somewhat subjective— of the probable direction and magnitude of the changes in industry and agriculture during the period. We shall then consider what deductions can be drawn from this material about the growth of output as a whole, and its relationship to changes in the size of the population. Finally, in section 5, we shall attempt to offer a tentative explanation of the pattern of growth which emerges.

I. THE EVIDENCE OF THE TRADE STATISTICS

The only statistical series we possess which relates to most of the major branches of British industry in the eighteenth century is that for foreign trade. The interpretation of these records is fraught with difficulties and, as they stand, the totals of imports and exports cannot be regarded as a reliable guide to the growth of the industrial economy. On the

---

[1] W. G. Hoffmann, *British Industry, 1700–1950*, translated by W. O. Henderson and W. H. Chaloner (Oxford, 1955), p. 32.

[2] See the reviews by Phyllis Deane, *Economic Journal*, vol. LXVI (1956), pp. 493–500; J. F. Wright, *J. Econ. Hist.*, vol. XVI (1956), pp. 356–64; W. A. Cole, *Econ. Hist. Rev.*, second series, vol. XI (1958), pp. 309–15.

[3] Phyllis Deane, 'The Implications of Early National Income Estimates for the Measurement of Long-Term Economic Growth in the United Kingdom', *Economic Development and Cultural Change*, vol. IV (1955), pp. 3–38; 'The Industrial Revolution and Economic Growth: The Evidence of Early British National Income Estimates', *ibid.*, vol. V (1957), pp. 159–74. See also below, chapter V, where we summarise our conclusions about the contemporary national income estimates for the eighteenth century.

other hand, it is clear that in the eighteenth century a substantial proportion of Britain's total industrial output was sent overseas— possibly as much as a third, though the proportion varied[1]—and since exports of manufactures accounted for roughly 85 per cent of the total value of domestic exports even at the beginning of the century,[2] a study of the trade figures in conjunction with other indicators should enable us to form some impression of the speed and direction of industrial change. Hitherto, however, they have been relatively neglected, and until recently we have not even had a series which distinguishes re-exports of foreign and colonial produce from exports of British goods.[3] No doubt, this is mainly because from the eighteenth century onwards serious criticisms have been made of the reliability of the figures.[4] These do not imply that the statistics are worthless, but it is evident that they require careful sifting before analytical use can be made of them.

Detailed annual accounts of the quantity and value of imports and exports were kept for each year from 1697 onwards, and in the first few years an attempt was made to value the goods at current prices. In the case of exports, the basis of valuation roughly corresponds with that in use today, but in the case of imports, the goods were not valued on a c.i.f. basis, but at 'first cost', i.e. at the estimated prices in the country of origin. After the first few years the practice of revising the rates of valuation in accordance with changes in market prices was gradually abandoned. Occasional changes were made in the import rates during the first two decades of the eighteenth century, but thereafter they tended to become stereotyped. The re-export rates, on the other hand, seem to have become ossified in this way at the very beginning of the eighteenth century. Similarly, the rates for most exports, except woollens, were not amended after 1703, and after a wholesale revision of the woollen rates in 1709, they, too, remained unaltered. Not all goods were valued at official rates: some, notably a large number of East India goods, were entered 'at value' on the declaration of the merchants concerned. Even so, some of the more

---

[1] This figure, which relates to the latter part of the century, is based on a comparison of the export figures with the data contained in contemporary national income estimates and with the estimates by Sir F. M. Eden of the gross value of industrial output, which are printed in D. Macpherson, *Annals of Commerce*, vol. IV (1805), pp. 458–60. Elsewhere, Macpherson quotes an estimate by an unknown author to the effect that home consumption was thirty-two times as much as exports to foreign countries. (*Ibid.*, vol. III, p. 340, cited by Ashton, *An Economic History of England: The Eighteenth Century*, p. 63.) This is clearly an overestimate and probably refers to the estimates of the consumption and exports of *grain* in the early part of the century which were made by Charles Smith in his *Three Tracts on the Corn Trade and Corn Laws* (1766).

[2] See Ralph Davis, 'English Foreign Trade, 1660–1700', *Econ. Hist. Rev.*, second series, vol. VII (1954), pp. 150–66. Most of the remainder were products of the extractive industries, although exports of grain were also of some importance in the early part of the century.

[3] There are several published sources for the figures of gross imports and total exports. Of these, the best is probably the series for England and Wales compiled by the late Mrs Schumpeter. See E. B. Schumpeter, *English Overseas Trade Statistics, 1697–1808* (1960).

[4] For a detailed discussion of these criticisms, see G. N. Clark, *Guide to English Commercial Statistics 1696–1782* (1938).

important of these, such as tea, gradually came in practice to be entered at fixed rates.

Thus we have a series which is for the most part, but not exclusively, at constant prices. As a matter of fact, even the official rates never became completely immutable, and very occasionally changes were made in the rates for individual commodities. These variations were in practice not important enough to make much difference to the figures of total imports and exports, and we propose, therefore, to treat the aggregates as rough indices of changes in the volume of trade, at any rate from 1709 onwards.[1] Before 1709 we have substituted estimates of the value of woollen exports at the 1709 rates of valuation, and the adjusted figures for total exports calculated on this basis will be used throughout the discussion which follows.[2]

It has sometimes been argued that we are not justified in treating the official values as a volume index, since changes in the price *structure* may have been so large in the course of the eighteenth century as to make a series weighted with the prices of *circa* 1700 highly unreliable. It is possible to apply a limited check to this view, despite our comparative ignorance of eighteenth-century price movements. At the end of the century, contemporaries became increasingly aware of the divergence between the official values and market prices, and a number of attempts were made to estimate the real value of trade at current prices. The most detailed were those made for the years 1796–8 by the Inspector General of Imports and Exports, Thomas Irving.[3] Irving's estimates were very detailed, and a comparison of the prices he used for imports and re-exports with those quoted for the period in Tooke's *History of Prices* suggests that they were also remarkably accurate. Accordingly, with his figures as a basis, we have calculated the value of foreign trade for a number of selected years throughout the century at constant 1796–8 prices. The methods employed in the construction of these estimates are described in an appendix to this volume, but the figures obtained are set out in Table 13, side by side with the corresponding totals for the same years of the official values of trade. By comparing the corresponding index numbers it is possible to appreciate the extent of the bias introduced into the two series by weighting with prices at the beginning and end of the century respectively.

The comparison suggests that, in the case of exports, the official values give us a more reliable picture of long-term changes in the volume of trade than has sometimes been imagined; and over the last thirty years of the century, in particular, when the official values might

---

[1] Records of Scotland's overseas trade were not kept until 1755, and when they were, many commodities were valued at different rates from the English. Fortunately, the differences are in many cases small, and since Scottish trade was only a fraction of English (about 5 per cent in 1755), the effect on the aggregates for Great Britain as a whole can safely be ignored.

[2] The detailed annual statistics of imports, exports and re-exports, which we have extracted from the trade records, are presented in Appendix I.

[3] 'Commercial Accounts of Great Britain and Ireland', *S.P. 1800*, vol. XLIX, (981).

Table 13. *Comparison of the official value of eighteenth-century foreign trade with estimates of the value at constant 1796–8 prices*

	Exports				Imports				Re-Exports			
	Official value (£000)	Index	At 1796–8 prices (£000)	Index	Official value (£000)	Index	At 1796–8 prices (£000)	Index	Official value (£000)	Index	At 1796–8 prices (£000)	Index
England												
1702–3	3,509	36	5,497	34	4,269	34	9,127	37				
1722–3	5,009	51	6,886	43	6,442	52	12,577	51				
1742–3	6,481	67	9,627	60	7,335	59	14,823	61				
1752–3	8,479	87	11,988	74	8,257	66	16,237	66				
1762–3	9,461	97	14,079	87	10,034	81	18,908	77				
1772–3	9,739	100	16,116	100	12,432	100	24,426	100				
Great Britain												
1772–3	10,196	100	17,298	100	13,595	100	26,915	100	6,930	100	9,252	100
1780–1	8,218	81	13,903	80	12,219	80	20,404	76	4,248	61	5,545	60
1789–90	14,351	141	23,981	139	18,476	136	36,610	136	5,380	78	7,370	80
1797–8	18,288	179	30,751	178	24,436	180	43,077	160	12,967	187	12,472	135

have been most misleading, the movement of the two series is almost identical. The divergence between the import indices is somewhat more marked, largely because of the enormous increase in imports of goods such as tea and coffee which were much cheaper at the end of the century than at the beginning. But even here the two series move in much the same way for most of the period. We have not been able to extend our estimates of re-exports at 1796–8 prices back beyond 1772, since figures for re-exports broken down by commodities are not readily available for the early part of the century. But it seems probable that if it were possible to complete the re-export series it would lead to much the same conclusions as the import series. In the last decade of the century, however, there is a sharp divergence between the two series for re-exports, the official figures showing a much greater increase than the calculated figures at 1796–8 prices. This is primarily due to the rapid expansion of re-exports of coffee, mainly to the German market, in the 1790's. Coffee was officially valued at £14. 10s. per cwt. on re-export, and whereas in the early seventies it had constituted 12–13 per cent of total re-exports, by 1796–8 the proportion had risen as high as 38 per cent. Irving, on the other hand, reckoned that at the latter date the actual re-export price of coffee averaged £6. 12s. 3d., and that it contributed only 19 per cent of total re-exports at current prices. With this qualification, however, the comparison does suggest that we are justified in regarding the official values as a rough index of secular changes in the volume of trade.[1]

A more serious difficulty concerns the defects in the quantity figures on which the estimates of value were based. It is generally agreed that the physical quantities recorded in the statistics are as accurate as eighteenth-century officialdom could make them. But the figures cannot, of course, make any allowance for fraudulent entries at the customs, nor for the substantial proportion of trade which did not pass through the customs at all. We know that in the eighteenth century traffic in

[1] It is much less certain that the same is true of short term movements. The figures for imports at 1796–8 prices, for example, seem to be much more sensitive to the effects of war in the latter part of the century than the official values.

contraband was an important economic activity, although attempts to measure it cannot be much more than guesswork. Fortunately, the export trade was little affected by smuggling, since for most of the century British manufactures were exempt from the payment of export duties. But in the case of heavily taxed imports such as tea, tobacco and foreign spirits the illicit traffic may well have been more important than the legal trade. It has been argued elsewhere[1] that smuggling probably rose to a peak in the thirties and early forties, and then declined until the end of the Seven Years War (1756–63). Thereafter, it rose again, reaching its highest point during the American War of Independence (1775–83); but with Pitt's reform of the customs and the reduction and simplification of the tariffs in the early eighties, the smugglers suffered a reverse from which they never completely recovered before the advent of free trade in the nineteenth century rendered their activities largely superfluous. It is possible that, during the American Revolution, the annual imports of all kinds of smuggled goods averaged £2–£3 m., or anything up to 25 per cent of the official value of legal imports. This is a maximum estimate, and it may be that the position was not as bad as these figures suggest. But if we need not completely discount the evidence of the official trade figures, it would certainly be wise to recognise that they constitute an inexact guide to the trade in certain classes of imported goods, and hence to changes in the volume of imports and re-exports as a whole.

With these reservations in mind, let us glance briefly at the main developments in the field of foreign trade which are revealed by the statistics. According to the traditional view, there was a slow but persistent growth of foreign trade from the beginning of the eighteenth century, marked, however, by frequent oscillations due mainly to the effect of wars, and then a 'giddy ascent' of both imports and exports in the last two decades of the century.[2] This account was, of course, based upon series which did not distinguish exports and re-exports, and which, owing to the changes in the rates of valuation, tended to overstate the relative level of exports at the beginning of the century. Moreover, in his graphic illustration of the process, Mantoux employed an arithmetic vertical scale which, as we know, is liable to give a misleading impression of rates of growth. If, on the other hand, we take our revised series, distinguishing exports and re-exports, and, at the same time, plot the figures as growth curves, as we have done in Fig. 1, the picture appears in a rather different light. These curves do not conflict with Mantoux's picture of rapid expansion after 1780, but they do suggest other notable movements in the course of the century.

At first sight, the most rapid advance in the last two decades seems to have occurred in the re-export trade. It should be noted, however, that re-exports had entered a period of sustained growth in the midfifties and that the sudden upsurge at the end of the century followed

[1] W. A. Cole, 'Trends in Eighteenth-Century Smuggling', *Econ. Hist. Rev.*, second series, vol. x (1958), pp. 395–410.
[2] P. Mantoux, *The Industrial Revolution in the Eighteenth Century* (1928), pp. 103–5.

a particularly severe fall in the volume of trade during the American War of Independence (1775–83). Moreover, this advance became spectacular only in the 1790's and, as we suggested earlier, there are good reasons for believing that the official values of trade exaggerate

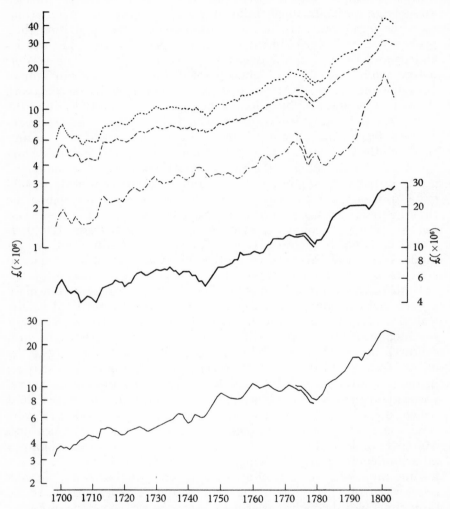

Fig. 1. Eighteenth-century foreign trade (three-yearly moving averages): .... imports (c.i.f.); ---- imports (first cost); —·—·—· re-exports; ———— net imports; ———— exports.

the real growth of re-exports during this period, While it may be true, therefore, that growth was slightly more rapid in the recovery of the late eighties and nineties, it is doubtful whether the overall rate of increase between 1775 and 1800 was as great as it had been in the third quarter of the century.

More significant from our present point of view—since we are primarily interested in the relationship between foreign trade and the growth of the home economy—is the import curve. In this case, it is clear that the period of rapid growth starts, not in the 1780's, but in the mid-forties, and the expansion at the end of the century represents little more than a return to a movement initiated a generation before, after the disastrous interlude of the American War. True, the expansion of legal imports after 1745 was slow at first, and may have been due in part to a temporary decline in smuggling. But, by the 1760's at least, the import trade had certainly entered a phase of rapid and sustained growth which gathered increasing momentum as the century wore on. In contrast, growth in the first half of the eighteenth century had been both slow and uneven. Between 1699/1701 and the mid-forties imports increased by less than a fifth, and even if we assumed that at the latter date illegal imports amounted to as much as £2 m. each year, the increase would still be little more than a half. In the latter part of the century, on the other hand, English imports roughly trebled. Clearly, the years 1745–60 constitute a landmark in the history of this branch of trade.

Unfortunately, there are no reliable statistics of the volume of imports actually retained for consumption at home. Since imports were valued at first cost, and re-exports at prices inclusive of insurance, freight, merchant's profit, and sometimes duty, the figures of net imports obtained by deducting re-exports from gross imports may be misleading. We have therefore attempted to estimate the value of imports inclusive of insurance and freight on the basis of the re-export rates of valuation, less an appropriate deduction for merchant's profit. These estimates are described in more detail in Appendix I, but the figures of net imports, derived from them and the official values of re-exports, form the basis of the curve of net imports which is shown in Fig. 2. The absolute levels of net imports calculated in this way are not very different from those of gross imports valued at first cost, and though there are significant differences in their rates of growth, the long-period trends of the two series are roughly similar. In the early part of the century the increase in net imports was even smaller than that of gross imports. After 1745, on the other hand, net imports grew much faster than gross imports, although, as we might expect, in the 1790's the rate of growth of net imports was substantially reduced. Thus it would seem that the increase in Britain's retained imports was even greater in the second half of the century than the figures of gross imports imply.

The history of exports is quite different. Here it is undoubtedly true that the growth of trade between 1780 and 1800 was both more rapid and certainly more sustained than in any previous period. Before 1780, on the other hand, the outstanding feature of the export curve— like the import curve before 1745—is its uneven character. If we examine its behaviour over the century as a whole, it is possible to distinguish five fairly distinct periods of alternating growth and decline.

The first is a period of steady expansion from the beginning of the century up to about 1715, followed by fifteen years of uncertainty and stagnation. Recovery starts around 1730, although there was a temporary setback at the outbreak of the War of the Austrian Succession, and it was not until the mid-forties that growth again becomes rapid. Between 1745 and 1760, the advance was almost as spectacular, if not nearly as regular, as in the years after 1780. But it was not maintained, and there followed nearly a quarter of a century of stagnation and decline before the final upsurge at the end of the century.

Table 14. *Eighteenth Century Foreign Trade*

(Annual averages in £000)

	Net imports	Domestic exports	Imports + Exports
England			
1697–1704	4,989	3,507	8,496
1700–1709	4,805	3,961	8,766
1706–1715	4,612	4,557	9,169
1710–1719	5,167	4,775	9,942
1715–1724	5,803	4,835	10,638
1720–1729	6,296	4,937	11,233
1725–1734	6,834	5,243	12,077
1730–1739	7,041	5,858	12,899
1735–1744	6,535	6,075	12,610
1740–1749	6,227	6,556	12,783
1745–1754	7,007	7,961	14,968
1750–1759	8,257	8,750	17,007
1755–1764	9,272	9,622	18,894
1760–1769	10,637	10,043	20,680
1765–1774	11,890	9,843	21,733
1770–1779	11,811	9,287	21,098
1775–1784	11,769	8,689	20,458
Great Britain			
1775–1784	12,477	9,246	21,723
1780–1789	15,760	10,889	26,649
1785–1794	19,529	14,205	33,734
1790–1799	21,192	17,697	38,889
1795–1804	24,306	21,933	46,239

Sources: See text and Appendix I.

Much of the difference between the growth of the two major branches of commerce can probably be attributed to the effect of variations in the terms of trade. In the detailed table of trade statistics in the appendix we give an index of the gross barter terms of trade for the eighteenth century which has been obtained by dividing an index of the volume of exports by the corresponding index of net imports. This illustrates the close association between the terms of trade and the highly irregular growth of exports to which we have referred. Throughout the century, periods of expansion in the export trade tended to coincide with an adverse movement of the terms of trade and periods of stagnation with a favourable movement. Moreover, it will be observed that until 1745 the volume of imports and exports tended to move in opposite directions, and even in the latter part of the century their rates of growth were very different. There were, in fact, only two periods of any importance when imports and exports rose together, the first from 1745 to 1760, and the second from 1780 to the end of the century. For this reason, it would be unwise to attempt to generalise about short-term trends in the growth of commerce as a whole on the basis of the individual series alone. The combined totals of net imports and domestic exports, illustrated by Fig. 2 and the data summarised in Table 14, suggest, however, that there were two significant turning-points in the history of trade in the eighteenth century, rather than one as Mantoux suggested.

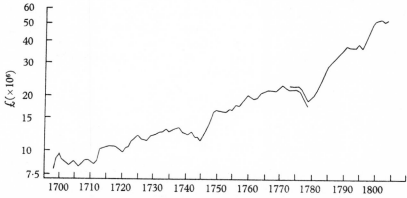

Fig. 2. The growth of foreign trade (net imports and domestic exports: three-yearly moving averages).

In the first forty-five years, after a sharp depression during the War of the Spanish Succession (1702–13), and a rapid post-war recovery, growth was relatively slow. Then followed a period of much more rapid expansion, which started about 1745 and apparently faded away in the sixties and early seventies, before the disastrous interlude of the American War of Independence and the final, dramatic acceleration in the last twenty years of the century. Between 1700 and 1745 the volume of net imports and domestic exports increased by only 0·5 per cent per annum, and even up to the peak reached immediately before the War of the Austrian Succession (1739–48) the average rate of growth was only 0·8 per cent. From 1745 to 1771, on the other hand, it rose to 2·8 per cent, reaching 3·9 per cent in the years 1745–60, and averaging 1·7 per cent over the whole of the period 1737 to 1771. Finally, in the great upsurge of trade between 1779 and 1802, the annual rate of increase was no less than 4·9 per cent, and even over the period 1771–1802 it averaged 2·6 per cent, despite the collapse of trade during the American War.[1]

---

[1] The measurements are between averages of three years centring on the years specified. The years 1699–1701 were chosen as the base period, because trade appears to have been exceptionally depressed during the years immediately before and after. A modern student

These figures cannot, of course, do more than indicate the approximate rate of advance. The upward bias in the official values of re-exports is greater than in the import series, however, and for this reason the trends revealed by our estimates of net imports for the latter part of the century are almost identical with those suggested by the corresponding series at 1796–8 prices.[1] On the other hand, it should be remembered that smuggling probably declined from 1745 to 1760 and again in the last twenty years of the century, and it seems likely that our estimates may somewhat overstate the rate of growth during those periods. Conversely, the figures for the early part of the century may be too low, although it is possible that the increase in smuggling at that time was partly offset by the tendency of exporters to overstate the value of their shipments after the removal of export duties in 1700 and 1721.[2] But the basic threefold division of the century is so pronounced that it is unlikely that however we measured the rate of change, and whatever deficiencies there may be in the statistics, the broad outlines of the picture would be seriously affected.

2. THE COURSE OF INDUSTRIAL CHANGE

What light does this evidence on overseas trade cast on the growth of the home economy and particularly its industrial sector? Does the other evidence we possess suggest that industrial growth followed broadly the same course as the development of foreign trade, or did the marked expansion of trade in the third quarter of the century simply reflect an increase in its relative importance in the national economy? Some answers to these questions can be deduced from the available indicators of industrial growth during the eighteenth century, some of which are set out in Table 15, and, in particular, from data on the development of the two main industry groups, the textile and the mining and metal industries.

The outstanding feature of the textile industries in the eighteenth century was, of course, the emergence and phenomenal expansion of the Lancashire cotton industry in the last quarter of the century. Estimates of the output of cotton goods are usually based on figures of raw cotton imports, though it should be remembered that until the seventies cotton cloth was a compound of linen warp and cotton weft, and imports of cotton covered only about half the raw material actually used in the industry. It is clear that the expansion of the new, factory industry in the last quarter of the century was of a quite different order

of the period has recently endorsed Davenant's view that even during the interlude of peace between the wars of 1689–97 and 1702–13, the volume of trade barely regained the level it had reached in 1686–8. See R. Davis, 'English Foreign Trade', *loc. cit.* p. 161. The decennial rates of growth in the periods marked off by the years 1697–1704, 1735–44, 1765–74 and 1795–1804 work out at 10, 20 and 26 per cent respectively.

[1] Between 1772–3 and 1797–8 our estimates of net imports c.i.f. record an increase in the volume of trade of 75 per cent, compared with 71 per cent if we measure the increase at 1796–8 prices.

[2] Cf. G. N. Clark, *op. cit.* pp. 15–16, 34–5.

Table 15. *Selected indicators of eighteenth-century industrial growth*

	Retained imports of raw cotton (m. lb.)	Raw and thrown silk Imports (000 lb.)	Raw and thrown silk Retained imports (000 lb.)	Flax (rough) imports (000 cwt.)	Linen yarn (raw) imports (m. lb.)	Scottish linen stamped for sale (m. yards)	Bar-iron imports (000 tons)	London coal imports (000 London chaldrons)	Cornish copper ore production (000 tons)	Cornish tin production (tons)	Tin retained for home use (tons)	Strong-beer production (000 barrels)	Wood imports (£000)	Glass production (000 cwt.)
1695–1704	1·14	525	—	34	2·1	—	16·4	327	—	1,323	232	3,446	114	—
1700–1709	1·15	499	—	34	2·1	—	16·0	339	—	1,426	308	3,673	114	—
1705–1714	1·00	482	—	34	2·1	—	16·3	355	—	1,476	174	3,387	112	—
1710–1719	1·35	557	—	42	2·8	—	17·3	389	—	1,453	194	3,483	115	—
1715–1724	1·68	629	—	44	3·1	—	19·0	433	—	1,396	326	3,744	135	—
1720–1729	1·55	675	—	48	2·7	—	19·7	468	—	1,482	333	3,669	146	—
1725–1734	1·44	685	—	66	2·7	3·87	21·5	475	6·6	1,632	345	3,588	143	—
1730–1739	1·72	645	—	80	2·7	4·53	25·5	475	7·7	1,667	278	3,606	138	—
1735–1744	1·79	563	—	74	2·8	4·81	24·2	484	7·4	1,691	290	3,512	136	—
1740–1749	2·06	552	—	79	3·1	5·68	22·5	480	6·3	1,744	251	3,536	140	—
1745–1754	2·83	607	—	98	3·6	7·50	26·6	492	9·1	2,159	474	3,679	153	60
1750–1759	2·81	670	—	113	4·2	9·04	29·3	508	13·8	2,658	937	3,777	168	78
1755–1764	2·57	777	—	119	4·9	10·82	33·0	527	16·7	2,669	1,023	3,818	176	94
1760–1769	3·53	906	—	127	5·2	12·42	39·7	582	19·5	2,728	913	3,775	203	116
1765–1774	4·03	946	—	129	6·5	12·58	44·9	634	25·2	2,851	990	3,744	239	131
1770–1779	4·80	950	—	131	8·4	12·84	44·5	653	28·8	2,751	1,089	3,957	248	130
1775–1784	7·36	1,683	—	125	9·1	14·68	43·0	666	29·7	2,657	808	4,220	249	121
1780–1789	15·51	1,132	—	132	9·0	17·49	44·1	709	33·3	2,958	918	4,329	275	131
1785–1794	24·45	1,177	1,093	—	—	19·38	—	771	37·1	3,327	945	4,690	—	155
1790–1799	28·64	1,181	1,094	242	8·7	20·89	49·9	825	46·7	3,245	822	5,278	489	157
1795–1804	42·92	1,128	1,041	317	8·8	21·42	43·0	875	52·9	2,881	861	5,407	558	167

Sources: Retained imports of raw cotton—1697/8–1780, A. P. Wadsworth and J. L. Mann, *The Cotton Trade and Industrial Lancashire, 1600–1780* (1931), pp. 520–1; 1781–1804, E. Baines, *History of the Cotton Manufacture* (1835), p. 347. Scottish linen stamped for sale, 1728–1804, A. J. Warden, *The Linen Trade, Ancient and Modern* (1864), p. 480. London coal imports—1694/5–1698/9, 1704/5–1708/9, J. U. Nef, *The Rise of the British Coal Industry* (1932), vol. II, p. 381; 1700–3 and 1710–1800, Ashton and Sykes, *The Coal Industry of the Eighteenth Century* (1929), pp. 249–51. Copper ore sold at public ticketings in Cornwall, 1726–71, W. Pryce, *Mineralogia Cornubiensis* (1778), p. xv; 1771–1804, Sir Chas. Lemon, 'Statistics of the Copper Mines of Cornwall', *Journal of the Statistical Society*, vol. I (1838), p. 70. Cornish tin production—1695/6–1804/5, J. Carne, *Journal of the Statistical Society*, vol. II (1839), *The Stannaries*, pp. 256–7; 1750–1804, J. Carne, *Journal of the Statistical Society*, vol. II (1839). Strong-beer production—1695/6–1804/5, Customs Library, Excise Revenue Accounts. Glass production (other than common bottles)—1746/7–1804/5, Customs Library, Excise Revenue Accounts. Retained imports of raw and thrown silk—1786–1804, Mrs Schumpeter and *S.P. (1806)*, vol. XIII. All other import figures (English, 1700–89; British, 1792–1804) are taken from Mrs Schumpeter. In 1789–90, English imports of the selected woods given by Mrs Schumpeter accounted for 84 per cent of British imports of selected woods; raw flax, 57 per cent; linen yarn, 89 per cent; bar iron, 90 per cent.

of magnitude from the growth of the old, domestic industry in the first seventy years. In the first four decades growth was slow, and raw cotton imports increased by only about one-third. In the late forties the tempo certainly quickened and in the next quarter of a century raw material imports more than doubled. But this was a pale anticipation of what was to come, for in the last twenty years they increased more than eightfold—from five or six million pounds about 1780 to over fifty million pounds in 1800.[1]

Here then is a pattern of growth which, in both its magnitude and timing, accords very well with the view that the industrial revolution became effective in the last twenty years of the century. For other branches of the textile industry, however, the picture is rather different. The only continuous statistics available on the output of the woollen industry in the eighteenth century are those for the production of broad and narrow cloths in the West Riding of Yorkshire. Unfortunately, this series does not cover the whole of the Yorkshire output, and for much of the period the figures relate to pieces of cloth which probably varied substantially in length. Moreover, we know that the output of the West Riding was growing in relative importance during the eighteenth century, owing to the decline of the older textile centres in East Anglia and the south-west, so that the series almost certainly gives a distorted impression of the growth of the industry as a whole. There are a number of contemporary guesses at the output of Britain's premier industry which were mostly based on estimates of the raw material consumed. An analysis of these has suggested that the industry was steadily expanding in the early part of the century, but that towards the end its rate of growth began to decline. From the end of the seventeenth century up to about 1741, the average rate of growth was apparently about 8 per cent per decade. Between 1741 and 1772 it seems to have risen to 13 or 14 per cent and then to have dropped back to as little as 6 per cent in the last quarter of the century.[2]

Since these estimates relate only to isolated years they are inconclusive in respect of the timing of the apparent expansion of the industry in the middle of the century; and in any case the evidence provided by such contemporary guesswork can only be tentatively used. But a similar impression is conveyed by the rather stronger evidence for the other two branches of the textile industry. Before 1700 the Scottish linen industry was insignificant and its rise to national prominence was one of the striking features of Scotland's economic history in the earlier part of the eighteenth century. In 1710 the total output of the whole country was estimated at only $1\frac{1}{2}$ million yards,[3] and even in 1728 the quantity stamped for sale was not much more

---

[1] See below, pp. 182–92, where the growth of the cotton industry is discussed at greater length.

[2] See Phyllis Deane, 'The Output of the British Woollen Industry in the Eighteenth Century', *J. Econ. Hist.*, vol. XVII (1957), pp. 207–23.

[3] A. J. Warden, *The Linen Trade, Ancient and Modern* (1864), p. 432.

than 2 million yards. But by the early forties production for the market had risen—somewhat unevenly—to about 4·7 million yards, and in 1763 it was over 12 million. After 1763 the rate of growth was substantially reduced, but the industry continued to expand and by 1800 the output was roughly double what it had been forty years earlier. If detailed production statistics of the English industry were available they, too, would probably produce a logistic curve, though the rate of growth of the English industry was certainly lower than that of its newer and smaller Scottish counterpart, and it is possible that in the last quarter of the century the English output actually fell. According to the contemporary estimates available, the annual production may have risen from 21 million yards about 1730 to 26 million in 1754.[1] By 1770 it seems likely that the output of the English industry was in the region of 33 million yards.[2] For 1783, on the other hand, there is a doubtful estimate quoted by Macpherson that the total output of the British linen industry was worth £1·75 m., and that it was declining.[3] These were a set of undocumented conjectures for which Macpherson himself expressly disclaimed responsibility. But the view that the English linen industry was declining is supported by other contemporary opinion. Oddy, writing in 1806, gave a good deal of space to the decline of the linen manufacture in Great Britain, which he attributed largely to 'the unprecedented rapid increase of the cotton manufacture; in which the capital, labour and attention of the manufacturers are employed, encouraged by the fashion of the times'.[4]

In the case of the silk industry, the problem of measurement is comparatively simple since all the raw material of the industry had to be imported,[5] and here there can be little doubt of the marked expansion of the industry in the middle decades of the century. It will be seen from Table 15 that imports of raw and thrown silk increased comparatively slowly in the first four decades; and annual figures show that in the early forties they fell lower than they had been at the beginning of the century; but in the next forty years they roughly doubled. At the end of the century, on the other hand, they were checked at the peak

---

[1] *A Letter from a Merchant who has left off trade, to a Member of Parliament* (1738), p. 21; Warden, *op. cit.*

[2] See below, pp. 201–3, where estimates of the linen industry at the end of the eighteenth century are further discussed.

[3] Macpherson, *Annals of Commerce*, vol. IV, p. 15.

[4] J. Jepson Oddy, *European Commerce* (1805), p. 583. It should be noted, however, that Horner, using Oddy's figures for imports of flax and yarn, arrived at the opposite conclusion to Oddy's. The explanation may lie in the fact that flax imports into Great Britain, and particularly into England, showed a tendency to increase in the last fifteen years of the century, and yarn imports to fall. This is probably a consequence of the adoption of flax-spinning machinery in England. But there is no doubt that the import statistics suggest that the period of fastest and most steady expansion in the English industry occurred between 1740 and 1770. Unfortunately, it is difficult to use these figures as the basis of output estimates, since part of the linen yarn imported went to the cotton industry, and some of the flax used was produced at home.

[5] Although it should be noted that the import figures available for most of the century make no allowance for re-exports. In the early seventies just under 13 per cent of the raw and thrown silk imported was re-exported.

they had reached in the early eighties, and it was not until the second decade of the nineteenth century that growth was resumed.

It would seem, then, that the phenomenal expansion of the cotton industry in the last quarter of the century was offset to some extent by a fall in the rate of growth of other branches of the textile industry from the peak which they had reached in the middle decades. In this con-

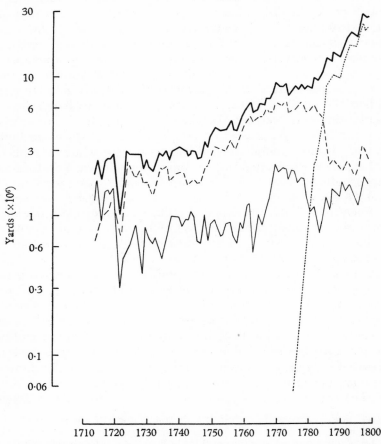

Fig. 3. Printed goods charged with duty, 1713–98: ———— total printed goods; ————
printed linens, cotton-linens and stuffs; ————foreign calicoes. . . . . British calicoes;
[*Source:* Customs Library, Excise Revenue Accounts.]

nection it is interesting to examine the statistics of the quantity of printed goods charged with duty during our period. Fig. 3 illustrates the growth of both the total output of printed goods and the major components of which the aggregate is composed. It is clear from the diagram that a crucial turning-point in this sector of the textile trades came in 1745 and that the revolution in the cotton industry in the 1770's represented the continuation—or restoration—of a rate of growth which had been initiated thirty years before. Of course, it is true that the output of printed linens and cotton linens in the middle of the century must have constituted a much smaller proportion of total textile production than did British-made calicoes at the end, and there is no doubt that the rise of the cotton industry in the last quarter of the century increased the rate of growth of textile output as a whole. But it may be doubted whether this rise was more significant than the earlier upsurge which resulted from less spectacular but more widespread changes which affected all branches of the textile industry in the middle of the century.

A similar conclusion is suggested by the data for the mining and metal industries. If we focus on the fortunes of the iron and steel producers, we must conclude that the rapid growth of Britain's capital goods industries dates from the 1780's. There are no reliable statistics of iron output in the early part of the century, but the traditional view is that about 1720 the production of pig-iron in England was not more than 25,000 tons, and that for the next twenty or thirty years it was stationary or declining.[1] More recently, however, it has been argued that the contemporary estimates of output on which this view was largely based may be misleading. Judging by the erection of new blast furnaces, there seems to have been no protracted period of inactivity, and it is possible that in the century before 1760 output may have increased by upwards of 10,000 tons.[2] Nevertheless, it remains true that the growth of the industry must have been comparatively slow before 1760, and even between 1757 and 1788 the rate of increase can hardly have reached as much as 40 per cent per decade.[3] Between 1788 and 1806, on the other hand, the decennial rate of growth was over 100 per cent.[4]

But again, the evidence for other industries in the group suggests that the acceleration of output in the last quarter-century may have been less of a break with past trends than the earlier upsurge. So far as we can judge, the beginning of the rapid expansion of coal production, which steadily accelerated until the end of the second quarter of the nineteenth century, may be dated from the late forties, and Professor Nef has suggested that between 1760 and the 1780's the output of coal may have risen from barely 5 million tons to over 10 million.[5] In the

---

[1] T. S. Ashton, *Iron and Steel in the Industrial Revolution* (1924), pp. 97–8, 235–8.

[2] M. W. Flinn, 'Revisions in Economic History: XVII. The Growth of the English Iron Industry, 1660–1760', *Econ. Hist. Rev.*, second series, vol. XI (1958), pp. 144–53. See also A. H. John, 'War and the English Economy, 1700–1763', *Econ. Hist. Rev.*, second series, vol. VII (1955), pp. 331–2, where it is suggested that there was some growth stimulated by war demand in the 1740's.

[3] In 1757 the output of bar iron was estimated at 18,000 tons and in 1788 at 38,000 tons.

[4] See below, pp. 221–3, where the output estimates for the end of the eighteenth and early nineteenth centuries are discussed further.

[5] J. U. Nef, *The Rise of the British Coal Industry* (1932), vol. I, pp. 19–20; vol. II, pp. 353–7. The expansion of the industry is certainly understated by the figures of London imports given in Table 15, since it is generally agreed that in the canal era the output of the inland coalfields grew much more rapidly than that of the coastal areas which supplied the London market. But whether in fact the effects of cheaper transport could have been as strongly felt in the third quarter of the century as Nef's figures imply, it is impossible to say. According

non-ferrous metal industries also, the major advance coincided with the application of Newcomen's engine in the Cornish mines in the 1740's. In the tin-mining and allied industries[1] in the eighteenth century progress was mostly concentrated in the sudden upsurge of production which is recorded at the end of that decade, while in the case of copper mining, the year 1748 marks the beginning of a great wave of expansion which lasted for nearly forty years. After 1770, the advance of production in Cornwall was slower, but for fifteen years the industry's rate of growth was maintained by a new source of supply opened in the Isle of Anglesey.[2] By the mid-eighties the output of metallic copper in Cornwall and Anglesey amounted to over 8,000 tons, probably eight or even ten times the Cornish production forty years earlier[3]. In the closing years of the century, the output of the Anglesey mines rapidly declined,[4] and although the production of ore in Cornwall was still increasing, the industry was facing diminishing returns.[5] It is probable, therefore, that from 1786 to the end of the century the total output of ore from the two main regions was more or less stationary, while the production of metallic copper seems to have dropped to about 7,000 tons.

The importance of these developments in the non-ferrous metal industries in the third quarter of the century should not be under-estimated, for in the 1780's the mining and smelting of copper was Britain's major metal industry. At current prices, the output of the Cornish and Anglesey mines in the mid-eighties was worth roughly

to the estimates of coal production contained in the *Report of the Royal Commission on Coal in the U.K.* in 1871 (vol. III, p. 32), total output did not reach 10 million tons until the end of the century. These estimates, however, were directly derived from the figures of coal shipments and made no allowance for the decline in the importance of sea-borne coal, at any rate before the 1780's.

[1] Until the middle of the eighteenth century, the main industrial use of tin was in the manufacture of pewter. In the 1690's, however, the manufacture of tin-plate, which had long been a German monopoly, was introduced into Britain, and from the 1740's the rapid growth of the industry provided a new domestic market for tin. The temporary decline in the quantities of tin retained for consumption at home at the end of the eighteenth century was probably due to the increasing replacement of pewter in common use by earthenware. Judging both by the export statistics and the establishment of new tin-plate works, the output of tin-plate continued to expand very rapidly at that time, and early in the nineteenth century it stimulated a renewed expansion of tin production. Cf. W. E. Minchinton, *The British Tinplate Industry* (Oxford, 1957); E. H. Brooke, *Chronology of the Tinplate Works of Great Britain* (Cardiff, 1944).

[2] Before 1770, copper-mining was of comparatively minor importance outside Cornwall, though Ecton mine in Staffordshire, which in 1781 produced 12 tons of fine copper a week, seems to have been reopened about 1739. Some copper must also have been mined in other parts of the country during this period, as smelting was apparently started in Lancashire about 1717, and there was a works at Middleton Tyas in Yorkshire about 1750. See J. Farey, *General View of the Agriculture and Minerals of Derbyshire*, vol. I (1815), p. 354; *Gentleman's Magazine*, vol. XXXIX, p. 59; G. P. Bevan, *British Manufacturing Industries*, vol. I (1876), p. 87.

[3] Sir Charles Lemon, 'Statistics of the Copper Mines of Cornwall', *Statistical Journal*, vol. I, p. 70; H. Hamilton, *The English Brass and Copper Industries to 1800* (1926), pp. 180, 209.

[4] *House of Commons Committee Reports*, vol. X, p. 671.

[5] Between 1785 and 1800 the copper content of the Cornish ores fell from 12 per cent to 9 per cent.

£600,000 per annum, or about double the gross value of the estimated output of pig-iron in 1788.[1] Not all of this was finally manufactured in Great Britain of course. But from the late forties until the late eighties the supply of copper to domestic industries probably grew at least as fast as the export trade.[2] In the second quarter of the century, the annual supply of copper to the home market, net of all copper exports, probably fluctuated between 400 and 850 tons. By the sixties, on the other hand, the quantities retained at home had reached over 2,000 tons, and by the eighties more than 5,000, before falling to under 3,000 at the close of the century.[3] It should be remembered that in the 1780's the spectacular rise of the Anglesey mines temporarily glutted the market: in October 1787, the Cornish Metal Company held an unsold stock of 6,654 tons of cake copper, and though this was reduced slightly in the next year or so, the company had over 5,000 tons on hand at the end of the decade.[4] Even so, it is clear that something like 4,000 tons of manufactured copper was disposed of annually in the home market in the 1780's, and it is not surprising that in the next decade, when copper production fell and exports continued to increase, complaints of shortages and high prices in the home market led up to the official inquiry of 1799.[5]

It is unlikely that the general impression which has emerged from this review of developments in the textile, mining and metal industries would be greatly modified by further research in other industries. Most of the available indicators confirm the view that the beginning of rapid industrial growth must be sought before the last quarter of the century. Admittedly there seems to have been no real increase in the output of strong beer before 1775; and although there is some evidence of earlier growth in the soap and leather industries, the movement was interrupted in the former industry in the fifties and in the latter in the sixties, so that it was not until the last quarter that growth became both relatively rapid and sustained. On the other hand, it is clear that the 1740's constitute a landmark in the history of several other branches of industry. Thus, the annual output of tallow candles fluctuated between 29 and 38 million lb. from 1711 to 1741, and then rose fairly steadily to well over 60 million lb. at the

[1] These estimates are based on price data from Tooke's *History of Prices*, vol. II, p. 406, and R. Wissett, *A Compendium of East Indian Affairs* (1802), vol. II (no pagination).

[2] It is difficult to give precise figures because the trade accounts do not distinguish between exports of sheet copper and finished goods. Both are classified as 'wrought'. See Table 16 below.

[3] In making these estimates we have assumed that until 1770 the Cornish mines were responsible for about 80 per cent of the total copper production and that the copper content of the Cornish ores during that period varied between 12 per cent and 16 per cent. The latter assumption is based on some estimates by Le Play, who appears to have had access to information from men in the industry which is not available today. Cf. F. Le Play, *Description des Procédés Métallurgiques* (Paris, 1848), p. 398.

[4] Hamilton, *op. cit.* pp. 175, 195–6.

[5] 'Report from the Committee, appointed to enquire into the state of the Copper Mines and Copper Trade of this Kingdom', *House of Commons Committee Reports*, vol. x (1799), pp. 651–728.

end of the century.[1] Similarly, according to Dr Coleman's estimates, paper production was virtually stationary in the early part of the century, but increased more than threefold between 1740 and 1800, a rate of growth almost as high as that achieved in the first half of the nineteenth century, after the introduction of the paper-making machine.[2] Indeed, here, as in the printed-goods trade, there is some reason to suppose that it was economic growth which called forth technological change, rather than vice versa. Finally, as a pointer to developments in the building industry—perhaps the most important omission from this analysis—it may be significant that timber imports rose steadily in the second half of the eighteenth century, while the output of glass (other than common bottles) charged with duty rose from a mere 1,400 tons in 1746–7, the first year for which figures are available, to over 7,000 tons in 1777, and continued to rise until the outbreak of war in the 1790's.

All this does not mean that there was no acceleration in the rate of growth in the eighties and nineties. But it does mean, as the trade statistics suggested, that the acceleration was at least a two-phase process, and that its origins must be sought in the remarkably pervasive if sometimes unobtrusive stimuli which seem to have influenced practically every sector of the industrial economy in the 1740's. Indeed, a comparison of the production data with the export statistics summarised in Table 16 would seem to suggest that, if the trade records err, it is in understating rather than overstating the magnitude of the break which occurred in the middle of the century. For if there was a time when foreign trade was growing faster than the output of the major export industries it was in the first half of the century, and, in particular, in the years between 1725 and 1745. It was then, when nearly all the production indicators record a period of comparative stagnation, that several branches of the export trade registered some of their greatest advances. It seems probable that almost the whole of the increase in the output of wrought iron was sent abroad during this period; and while the home consumption of copper and brass seems actually to have fallen from 1725 to 1745, exports were booming.[3] After 1745, on

[1] The excise series for soap, leather (hides and skins) and candles are discussed in more detail in the section on agriculture. See below, p. 71 *et seq.*

[2] D. C. Coleman, 'Industrial Growth and Industrial Revolutions', *loc. cit.*, and the same writer's *The British Paper Industry, 1495–1860* (Oxford, 1958), pp. 90, 345–6.

[3] It should be noted, however, that although exports of copper and brass had also grown rapidly before 1725, total output probably grew even faster. Between 1697–9 and the mid-twenties, exports more than doubled, but whereas in 1697 the production of copper in England, according to Houghton, was only 160 tons, in 1726 the output of ore in Cornwall alone had reached 5,000 tons—an amount which might be expected to yield at least 600 tons of metallic copper, and probably more. Until the eighteenth century England had imported substantial quantities of brass and copper manufactures, and in the second and third decades of the century most of the output of the infant domestic industries was absorbed by the home market in lieu of imports. It was only in the second quarter of the century, when the home market seems to have been temporarily saturated, that the contrast between the growth of the export trade and stagnation at home became so pronounced. Cf. Hamilton, *op. cit.*; J. Houghton, *Husbandry and Trade Improved*, vol. II (1727 ed.), p. 187.

the other hand, when output at home began to increase more rapidly, the rate of growth of exports tended to decline, and in the case of the copper and brass industries at least, the expansion of total output almost certainly began to outstrip the advance of the export trade. Much the same is true of the coal industry. Between 1701–10 and 1741–50, exports increased by more than 150 per cent while shipments of coal to London increased by less than 40 per cent. In the next forty years, on the other hand, exports increased by 60 per cent and London imports by 53 per cent, while total output, if Nef is right, more than doubled.

Table 16. *Selected eighteenth-century exports*

	Woollens (£000)	Cottons (£000)	Linens (000 yds.)	Silks (000 lb.)	Iron and Steel (tons)	Copper Un-wrought (£00)	Copper Wrought (tons)	Brass (tons)	Tin (tons)	Coal (£000)
England										
1697–1704	2,427	16	178	39	1,829	3	52	63	1,115	51
1700–9	2,809	13	196	40	1,619	12	43	65	1,198	53
1706–15	3,228	8	299	57	1,724	42	56	73	1,312	65
1710–9	3,222	8	379	59	2,158	36	89	89	1,316	80
1715–24	3,106	15	453	49	2,446	16	86	110	1,138	96
1720–9	3,116	16	586	47	2,866	89	88	149	1,148	105
1725–34	3,248	12	688	49	3,380	146	122	227	1,282	107
1730–9	3,581	15	864	50	4,125	260	156	324	1,373	119
1735–44	3,554	15	1,411	54	5,262	683	211	421	1,404	131
1740–9	3,453	11	2,211	54	6,676	620	245	551	1,495	134
1745–54	3,823	38	3,512	61	8,684	157	327	739	1,685	155
1750–9	4,339	86	5,145	92	9,326	39	416	795	1,721	163
1755–64	4,614	162	7,178	126	9,838	14	650	936	1,646	161
1760–9	4,448	227	8,288	107	13,376	—	977	1,275	1,815	n.a.
1765–74	4,356	236	9,142	77	16,770	—	1,186	1,580	1,861	339
						(tons)				
1770–9	3,991	247	8,184	66	14,603	127	1,273	1,480	1,843	335
1775–84	3,363	388	6,549	75	11,574	367	1,579	1,104	1,942	332
1780–9	3,518	756	7,522	91	14,035	578	2,022	1,103	2,104	404
Great Britain										
1792–9	5,425	2,896	15,164	115	27,150	88	4,260	3,122	2,281	510
1795–1804	6,323	5,371	14,992	98	30,717	37	4,450	3,323	1,975	487

Sources : Woollens (at 1709 rates)—1697–1708, see Appendix 1, below, pp. 322; 1709–17 and 1725–37, Sir Josiah Banks, *The Propriety of Allowing Qualified Exportation of Wool* (1782), p. 83; 1718–24 and 1738–53, Smith, *Memoirs of Wool*, vol. II (1757), pp. 210, 280; 1754–71, Bischoff, *Comprehensive History of the Woollen and Worsted Manufacture*, vol. II (1842), Appendix table VI; 1772–1804, Mrs Schumpeter. All other figures are based on Mrs Schumpeter. Those for linen have been converted into yards on the assumption that one piece=35 yards. All figures exclude Irish linens. Unwrought copper was entered at value in the early part of the century, and in the first few years it was usually valued at £100 per ton. The break in the coal series is due to a change in the measures and rates of valuation in 1765. For purposes of comparison, it may be noted that in 1789–90 English woollen exports accounted for 96 per cent of the total British exports of woollens, cottons 93 per cent, linens 77 per cent, silks 96 per cent, iron and steel 98 per cent, and coal 96 per cent. Scottish exports of non-ferrous metals were negligible.

Admittedly, the cotton industry appears to deviate somewhat from the general trend, for in the first half of the century exports were virtually stationary, and it was only in the 1750's that they started their meteoric ascent.[1] But in the linen trade the pattern is almost as clear

[1] For the explanation of the sudden expansion of cotton exports in the 1750's, see Wadsworth and Mann, *The Cotton Trade and Industrial Lancashire, 1600–1780* (1931), pp. 157 ff. According to the trade records, exports rose from £20,000 in 1750 to £167,000 in 1760 and no less than £399,000 in 1763. In the sixties, the gross output of the whole industry was estimated at about £600,000 per annum. (E. Baines, *History of the Cotton Manufacture* (1835), p. 361.) The relationship between the official values and current prices in the 1760's is uncertain, but even so it would appear that practically the whole of the increase in the

as in the metal and mining industries. In the early decades of the eighteenth century, linen exports practically doubled every ten years, and although output was also increasing, even the rapidly growing Scottish industry could not match the advance of the export trade. In the second half of the century, however, the rate of growth of linen exports rapidly declined and from 1760 onwards exports and home production seem to have moved in step.

In the nature of the case this argument cannot be conclusive, since we can only compare the production of individual commodities with the fortunes of the corresponding branches of the *export* trade, and not the total volume of production with the volume of exports *and* imports: in other words, we cannot make an adjustment for changes in the proportion of output exported which were due not to an increase or a decrease in the importance of foreign trade in the economy, but simply to a change in the terms of trade. Moreover, as we have already seen, the acceleration in the growth of net imports in the second half of the century was much more marked than in the case of exports.

It is possible to argue that the upturn in the forties did not mark the 'start' of industrial growth. Just as the data reveal a wave of expansion beginning in the forties and slackening in the seventies before the next upturn in the last two decades of the century, so there may have been an earlier wave which evaporated in the second quarter of the eighteenth century. Indeed, if we were to judge by the only national output series dating right back to the Middle Ages, namely the statistics of tin output, we should have to set the beginnings of the upward movement in the middle of the seventeenth century. For four centuries the tin industry had known secular fluctuations in production but no real growth, and in the reign of James I the output was the same as it had been in the reign of King John. In the second half of the seventeenth century, however, after a disastrous fall in production during the Civil War, the output doubled, and since that time each successive century has seen a further wave of expansion. But then, if we take the figures of coal shipments for a guide, we might be tempted to set the beginning of the upward movement in the sixteenth century.

The trouble, of course, is that until the eighteenth century we have no indicators of the growth of the economy as a whole as distinct from that of isolated sectors. In the first quarter of the eighteenth century most of the available indicators record an upward movement. But since continuous trade statistics are not available before 1697 and most of the excise series date from the second decade of the eighteenth century we cannot be certain that this does not merely represent a short-lived recovery 'boom' after the long wars with Louis XIV from 1689 to 1713. We have already noted that in the short interlude of

output of the industry in the early part of the century was swallowed up in this great expansion of the export trade. After 1763, the growth of exports temporarily slackened, and it was not until the last two decades of the century that the growth of the export trade again began to outstrip home consumption.

peace between 1698 and 1701 the volume of trade was probably no greater than it had been in the 1680's, and it will be seen from Fig. 2 that the overall percentage increase in the volume of imports and exports between 1700 and 1717 was no greater than it was in the next seventeen years. Again it will be noted that in the first quarter of the eighteenth century the rate of increase of coal shipments to London seems to have been even faster than it was after 1760. But if, as we are able to do in this case, we extend the series back into the seventeenth century, we find that this was largely due to a recovery in the second decade of the eighteenth century from a temporary recession during the wars. Actually, the average rate of increase between 1681–90 and 1721–30 was about the same (13 per cent per decade) as it was for coal shipments alone in the period after 1760.

Even so it is clear that the coal trade *was* expanding in the first quarter of the eighteenth century, and it must be admitted that there are other signs of movement in the economy at that time which contrast sharply with the stagnation of the second quarter. It was in the 1690's that the tin-plate manufacture was first introduced into England, and copper mining was revived after a lapse of over half a century. Moreover, we know that this was a period of technological innovation, even though some of the developments of the period—such as Newcomen's engine and Abraham Darby's discovery of a means of smelting iron with coal—had to wait another forty or fifty years before they were widely applied.

In sum, then, it is probable that most of the rather modest progress made in the first half of the eighteenth century took place in the first twenty to twenty-five years, and that the movement was then checked for about twenty years before the much stronger, many-sided wave of expansion which began in the 1740's and gathered increasing momentum in the ensuing decades. We still cannot determine the precise extent of the advance in the course of the century. With the reservations just noted, it seems fair to assume that the volume of imports and exports may provide us with a reasonably accurate index of the growth of those industries which entered largely into overseas trade. But although most industries played some part in foreign trade, they were obviously not all affected in the same degree. Moreover, it seems clear that industries which were mainly dependent on the home economy, both for their supplies of raw materials and for a market for their products, tended in general to expand much less rapidly than the major export industries. We have seen that the woollen industry probably increased its output by something like 150 per cent in the course of the century, and most of the newer export industries grew very much faster. But although some of the minor home industries doubled or even trebled their output in the same period, others, such as the leather and brewing industries, barely kept pace with the growth of population. The excise statistics provide a basis for measuring the growth of these industries with some degree of confidence; and if we combine this information with that provided by the trade series we should be able to form an impression of the overall industrial advance. But before we tackle this problem we must pause to consider in some detail the much more serious problems of measurement connected with the other main sector of the British economy.

3. THE ROLE OF AGRICULTURE

Even at the end of the eighteenth century well over a third of the occupied population earned their living in agriculture, and the industry was probably responsible for almost as large a percentage of the national income. Clearly, therefore, the evidence for this sector will largely determine our view of the growth of the economy as a whole, while the timing of agricultural change will necessarily affect our interpretation of the origins of industrial growth. Unfortunately there are virtually no agricultural statistics for the eighteenth century, or, indeed, for a long time after,[1] and we must largely rely on qualitative evidence, on the guesses of contemporaries and on the indications provided by evidence on the numerous and important industries ancillary to agriculture.

For corn there are no production or quasi-production series which might be regarded as reliable guides,[2] and we cannot place much faith in the pattern of change which might emerge from a comparison of the scattered estimates of contemporaries. On the other hand, prices, imports and exports are all known, and the per capita consumption of corn can have varied only within limits which were certainly much narrower than in the case of most other commodities. An attempt has indeed been made by a leading modern authority on eighteenth-century agricultural output to estimate the growth in wheat production during this period on the assumption that per capita consumption did not change.[3] The results of this inquiry suggested that in the course of the eighteenth century wheat output rose from 29 to 50 million bushels per annum, as a result of a rise in the average yield from 20 to 22 bushels per acre, and an increase in the acreage under crop of some 800,000 acres. These calculations are, however, of only limited value for our present purposes, for there is little doubt that the consumption of wheat bread became more widespread in the course of the eighteenth century, so that the output of wheat probably grew more rapidly than corn production as a whole. Fussell adopted a more conservative estimate than other writers of the increase in the *proportion* of the population who ate wheat bread,[4] but since he relied on Fin-

---

[1] Detailed agricultural statistics first became available in 1866.

[2] There are, of course, excise series for hops, malt, beer, starch and spirits, but the first two of these relate only to relatively small and unrepresentative parts of the total output, while the relationship between the rest and the variations in corn output over long periods is at best indirect.

[3] G. E. Fussell, 'Population and Wheat Production in the Eighteenth Century', *History Teachers' Miscellany*, vol. VII (1929), pp. 65–8, 84–8, 108–11, 120–7.

[4] He put the proportion as high as 80 per cent in 1700 and 90 per cent a century later.

laison's estimates of the total population which give a much lower figure for 1700 than any other authority, he concluded nevertheless that the number of wheat-eaters practically doubled in the course of the century. Moreover, the use of Finlaison's population figures makes his estimates a particularly unreliable guide to trends in production over short periods.[1] But, given a satisfactory estimate of the per capita consumption of all kinds of grain, it might be possible to generalise Fussell's method and arrive at a reasonably accurate impression of the probable changes in corn production as a whole.

A convenient starting-point for this inquiry is provided by the calculations made by a well-informed and judicious contemporary. Writing in 1766, Charles Smith made elaborate estimates of the average production and consumption of corn in England and Wales during the first sixty-five years of the eighteenth century.[2] He first estimated the amount of each kind of grain used in the making of bread. To do so, he divided the country into six regions on the basis of his own knowledge and that of travellers and acquaintances, and the transactions of the London corn market: London and the south-east, where nearly 90 per cent of the population ate wheat bread; the south-west, where about three-quarters were presumed to eat wheat and the remainder barley; the west, where nearly 70 per cent ate wheat and most of the rest barley or rye; two northern regions, where only about 30 per cent were wheat-eaters, a somewhat higher percentage ate oats, and the remainder used varying proportions of barley and rye; and finally, Wales, in which nearly all bread was made from barley or rye. On the basis of the hearth-tax returns, Smith reckoned that the population during the period 1700–65 had fluctuated around 6 million, a figure which agrees almost exactly with the results of the best modern scholarship in this field.[3] Of this total, 3,750,000 were supposed to eat wheat, a number which 'if any thing' he had 'set rather too low',[4] 739,000 barley, 888,000 rye and 623,000 oats. According to Smith, wheat-eaters consumed on the average one quarter of grain per annum, and the rest rather more.[5] He also made an allowance for the substantial quantities of grain used for other purposes, of which easily the most important were the production of malt, as measured by the excise figures, and horse fodder, which he estimated at eight times the London consumption, as indicated by the quantities of oats brought to London by water plus a notional addition for a small quantity of land supplies. On the basis of these calculations, Smith arrived at an estimated

---

[1] Finlaison's estimates were published in the 1831 *Census* and seem to have enjoyed a considerable vogue for some years afterwards. But the methods he employed are uncertain and his results have been superseded by the later work of Farr, Brownlee and Talbot Griffith which has been discussed in more detail elsewhere in this volume. The short-period trends of his series resemble those of the estimates given by Rickman in earlier *Census* volumes, which were based on the assumption of a constant baptism rate. Finlaison's figures would, however, imply that this rate *fell* during the eighteenth century.

[2] *Three Tracts on the Corn Trade and Corn Laws* (1766).

[3] Brownlee's figures suggest an average population of 6,082,000 for this period.

[4] *Op. cit.* p. 183.　　　　[5] 11 bushels of barley, 9 of rye, and 23 of oats.

annual consumption of just over 13½ million quarters, or almost exactly 18 bushels per head of the population.

Smith's figures can, of course, be criticised, and they certainly rely heavily on arbitrary guesswork.[1] In particular, it may be argued that his estimates of the amount of corn used in the making of bread were too high, and that the amount of wheat used was probably nearer 6 bushels per head than 8—although whether in this case it is better to rely on the actual consumption in modern industrial society or the opinion of a well-informed contemporary must remain a matter for individual judgment.[2] A more important question, however, is whether the total consumption per head—either at 18 bushels or at only 16— remained roughly constant during the eighteenth century. It is unlikely that the pattern of consumption was stable over such a long period, but the indications of change do not all point in the same general direction. There is little reason to suppose that there was any substantial change in per capita consumption of bread during the century. If there were, contemporaries do not seem to have been aware of it. Probably the diet of ordinary people became more varied as a result of rising incomes and the average consumption of bread may even have fallen slightly. In the latter part of the century, however, real wages apparently fell in many districts and it is probable that many who in earlier decades had started to eat meat, now had to eat more bread instead: certainly, as we shall see, there is little to suggest that the consumption of meat continued to rise at this time. On the other hand, since the price of wheat at the turn of the century was roughly treble what it had been in the 1730's and 1740's,[3] it seems unlikely that the *average* consumption per head could have been much higher than it was in the first half of the century.[4] As regards the other uses of grain, there is little doubt that the production of malt lagged behind the growth of population during the century, and indeed the excise figures suggest that it was virtually stationary. But again we know that horses were replacing oxen for draught purposes at this time, and it is quite possible that the decline in the relative importance of barley for malting was to some extent offset by an increase in the acreage under oats. It would be rash to assume that such changes neatly cancelled one another out. But it still seems plausible to assume that there was no very great change in the overall relationship between the consumption of cereals and the total population over the eighteenth century as a whole.

[1] As Fussell points out (*loc. cit.* p. 68), this objection was raised by Arthur Young, who, nevertheless, later made use of Smith's estimates for some calculations of his own.

[2] For the discussion of this question, see Fussell, *loc. cit.* pp. 66–7, and the authorities there cited, and the same writer's 'The Change in Farm Labourers' Diet during Two Centuries', *Economic History*, May 1927, pp. 268–74.

[3] There were some cases of actual starvation. T. S. Ashton, *The Eighteenth Century*, p. 235.

[4] If less corn was used in making wheat bread than other kinds, there would have been some decline in per capita consumption as a result of the increasing consumption of wheaten bread, although in a properly constructed index of corn production, weighted with the value of the different kinds of grain, this would be offset by the greater weight given to wheat.

If this assumption is accepted, and we multiply Brownlee's estimates of the population of England and Wales by 2·25, add net exports or deduct net imports,[1] and make an appropriate allowance for seed, we arrive at the results given in Table 17. Smith assumed that seed-corn was equal to 10 per cent of the gross produce. This proportion was probably a trifle low, but bearing in mind the possibility that his estimates of consumption may be too high, it seems likely that the figures for the gross output given in the table may not be far wide of the mark.

Table 17. *Estimates of corn output in England and Wales in the eighteenth century*

(000's and 000 quarters)

	Population (E. & W.)	Home consumption	+ Net exports − Net imports	Net output	Gross output
1700	5,826	13,109	184	13,293	14,770
1710	5,981	13,457	362	13,820	15,355
1720	6,001	13,502	491	13,993	15,547
1730	5,947	13,381	343	13,723	15,248
1740	5,926	13,334	522	13,855	15,395
1750	6,140	13,815	1,006	14,821	16,468
1760	6,569	14,780	485	15,265	16,961
1770	7,052	15,867	− 250	15,617	17,353
1780	7,531	16,945	− 238	16,706	18,563
1790	8,247	18,556	− 672	17,884	19,871
1800	9,024	20,305	− 1,313	18,991	21,102
1810	10,309	23,196	− 1,202	21,988	24,431
1820	12,088	27,198	− 2,112	25,086	27,873

Source: See text.

The figures suggest that output rose from 14·8 million quarters at the beginning of the century to 21·1 million in 1800—an increase of about 43 per cent. In the first half of the century, the country had a small but growing surplus of grain for export which in later years was converted into a deficit. But at no time during this period could the net exports or imports of grain have constituted more than a small fraction of the home consumption, and in view of the population figures it seems clear that, as the table suggests, most of the increase in total output must have been achieved after 1750. It is impossible to have much faith in the short-term movements implied in the estimates,

[1] There are numerous printed sources for these. Detailed annual figures of the imports and exports of wheat are given in D. G. Barnes, *A History of the English Corn Laws* (1930), pp. 299–300, and period averages of the trade in other grains in Lord Ernle, *English Farming, Past and Present* (1936 ed.), p. 500. The figures used here are based for the most part on the quinquennial averages given in 'S.C. on the Corn Trade', *S.P. 1812/13*, vol. III, pp. 483–4. Those given in the table are averages of the periods 1697–1705, 1706–15, 1715–24, 1725–34, etc. It should be noted that the figures for later years refer to Great Britain and not England and Wales, although the output estimates are intended to relate to the latter throughout.

though they probably indicate correctly the general directions, if not the precise magnitudes, of change. Roughly speaking, the 120 years covered by the table appear to fall into five fairly distinct trend periods: a period of slow growth during the first two decades, when both population and exports increased, followed by twenty years of stagnation, when the levels of population and exports changed comparatively little. Then came thirty years of definite, though somewhat irregular, progress, which was checked by the deficient harvests of the 1760's, followed by another thirty years of much more steady growth from 1770 to 1800, when output appears to have risen by about 7 per cent per decade; and finally, the period after 1800, when the rate of growth seems to have risen even further to about 15 per cent per decade. In considering the validity of these short-term movements, it may be reasonable to overlook the effect of possible long-term changes in the pattern of consumption on the *level* of demand, but not the effect of abrupt changes in prices on the actual quantity demanded. Since the demand for grain was probably inelastic, the margin of error involved may not be large, but it would be wise to recognise that the estimates given in the table may exaggerate the increase in production in the 1760's and again after 1790, for at both these periods the prices of grain were exceptionally high. For most of the century, however, there were no violent changes in the trend of prices which might vitiate the broad pattern of change outlined here.[1] In particular, it should be noted that in the seventies and eighties, prices were fairly stable, and in the late forties and early fifties they were still comparatively low after a gradual decline in the early part of the century, and there seems no obvious reason to doubt, therefore, that in both these periods there was a marked increase in the rate of growth, as the figures of population, exports and imports imply.

As a limited check on the plausibility of the output figures on which these hypotheses are based, we may perhaps consider their implications in terms of the acreages required to produce them. At the end of the century, the estimated output of 21 million quarters could have been obtained from about 6 million acres of arable land, assuming that this was divided in roughly equal proportions between wheat and rye, with a yield of $2\frac{1}{2}$–3 quarters per acre, and oats and barley, with a yield of 4–$4\frac{1}{2}$ quarters.[2] After allowing for seed, 3 million acres of wheat and rye plus imports would have provided a quarter per head for about 8 million people, a figure which seems consistent with what we know about the prevalence of wheat-eating at that time; and the assumption that the acreages under barley and oats were similar in extent agrees with contemporary and later accounts of the distribution of land under

[1] A possible exception should be noted in the case of the decade *c.* 1710–20, when prices fell nearly 25 per cent. For decade averages of wheat prices, see Table 23 below, p. 91.

[2] The yields are based on the estimates given in the 'Second Report from the S.C. on Waste Lands', *House of Commons Reports*, vol. IX, pp. 219–21, and on national averages calculated from the county reports on agriculture during the period 1800–16 which are tabulated in J. R. McCulloch, *A Statistical Account of the British Empire* (1837), p. 482.

the various crops.[1] Moreover, it seems probable that about three-fifths of the total arable land was under corn and beans,[2] so the figure of 6 million acres for cereals alone is consistent with the best contemporary estimates that the total arable acreage in England and Wales at this time was about 11 million acres.[3]

The position in 1700 is more obscure. There was a general consensus of opinion at the beginning of the eighteenth century that wheat yields were in the neighbourhood of 20 bushels per acre;[4] and although information for rye is much less plentiful, we shall not be far out if we assume that the average yield was about the same. In the case of barley and oats, the produce seems to have varied widely on different soils, but on the whole the sources suggest that both may have averaged about 30 bushels per acre.[5] Hence if the proportions given by Smith for the different crops in the early part of the century applied in 1700, the estimated output at that date would have required a sown acreage of about 4·8 million acres, of which perhaps 2·2 million would have been under wheat and rye, and the rest under barley and oats. Even if the estimated yields were a trifle optimistic, it seems clear that the suggested output could easily have been produced from the 10 million acres, including fallow, which, according to Gregory King, were devoted to cereals and legumes at the end of the seventeenth century.[6] King's estimates of the grain output are, however, much lower than ours: his figures for the net output of cereals only total 61 million bushels, and even with a more generous allowance for seed corn, which he reckoned at 20–25 per cent of the *net* produce, the gross output would still not come to more than 75 million bushels, or 9,375,000 quarters. If King's estimate of the arable acreage was about right, it would be hard to reconcile such a low figure for total output with the evidence of the contemporary agricultural writers: certainly the only figure which he gives explicitly—barley at only 15 bushels per acre[7]—seems much too low. Our figures, on the other hand,

[1] See, for example, J. Middleton, *View of the Agriculture of Middlesex* (1807); McCulloch, *op. cit.* p. 529; Braithwaite Poole, *Statistics of Commerce* (1852), p. 100; Caird, *English Agriculture* (1851), p. 521, and the official statistics from 1866. Poole estimated the sown acreage under grain crops at 7·8 million and the yield at 34 million quarters. Caird was more conservative and put the figures at 6·8 million and 29 million respectively.

[2] Middleton, *op. cit.* p. 640.

[3] The estimates are tabulated and discussed by G. E. Fussell, 'Population and Wheat Production', *op. cit.* p. 108. See also 'Select Committee on Emigration', *S.P. 1827*, vol. v, p. 361, for a similar estimate which is reprinted in Ernle, *op. cit.* p. 503. Middleton and Sir John Sinclair gave higher figures of 14–15 million acres, but both these writers tended to exaggerate.

[4] See Fussell, 'Population and Wheat Production', *op. cit.* p. 111.

[5] Robert Plot, *Natural History of Staffordshire* (1686), pp. 340–3; John Mortimer, *Whole Art of Husbandry* (1707), pp. 100–5; Giles Jacob, *The Country Gentleman's Vade Mecum* (1717), pp. 5–7; R. Bradley, *Complete Body of Husbandry* (1727), pp. 295–7. The yields given for barley are 30 bushels (Plot), 16–24 (Mortimer), 20–40 (Jacob), and 40, tithe paid (Bradley). Only Mortimer and Jacob give figures for oats which are similar to those for barley. According to Plot the yield of rye was rather higher than wheat; according to Mortimer it was lower.

[6] *Two Tracts by Gregory King*, edited by G. E. Barnett (Baltimore, 1936), p. 36.

[7] *Ibid.* p. 39.

would imply that an increase in the total output of grain in the eighteenth century was achieved by a modest rise in yields per acre of rather more than 10 per cent, and an increase in the sown acreage of perhaps 25 per cent. No great weight can, of course, be given to such estimates. But in the present state of the data they represent the best guess we can make.

What about the products of the grasslands? Here there are three types of evidence which we may usefully consider: contemporary estimates of the number of cattle and sheep and their average weight and yield in terms of wool and food; statistics of the number of cattle and sheep sold at Smithfield market, which are available annually from 1732 onwards; and finally, the indirect evidence provided by the output of industries which depended on agriculture for their supply of raw materials. These data do not enable us to measure the growth of the livestock section of the industry with any degree of precision; but together they may perhaps give us some indication of the direction and character of change.

Contemporary estimates of livestock suggest strongly that the output of wool and mutton increased considerably during the eighteenth century—much faster than the growth of corn production—while the supply of beef, and presumably also dairy produce, changed comparatively little. The figures for sheep and wool have been discussed elsewhere.[1] According to Gregory King, the numbers of sheep in England and Wales totalled about 11 million, and the best considered of later estimates suggest that the number may have risen to 16·6 million by 1741 and to 26 million at the beginning of the nineteenth century. In terms of wool produced this may have represented an increase from 40 million lb. in 1695 to 57 million in 1741 and to 94 million in 1805. The figures are, of course, conjectural, and it would not have been difficult to select others suggesting a different pattern of growth. We have already noted that King seems to have taken a rather pessimistic view of contemporary grain yields, and we shall see that there are also good grounds for suspecting that he may have underestimated the weight of cattle. Was his estimate of the number of sheep also too low? In the course of the eighteenth century, exports of woollen manufactures increased by about 150 per cent, which if anything was rather more than the estimated increase in the domestic output of wool. We might expect that in a century which saw the growth of a domestic linen industry and the meteoric rise of the cotton industry the proportion of the woollen output which was exported would tend to rise. On the other hand, we know that foreign markets were important to the British industry long before 1700, and even if the home consumption of woollen goods did no more than keep pace with

[1] See Phyllis Deane, 'The Output of the British Woollen Industry in the Eighteenth Century', *J. Econ. Hist.*, vol. XVII (1957), pp. 207–23; G. E. Fussell and Constance Goodman, 'Eighteenth Century Estimates of British Sheep and Wool Production', *Agric. Hist.*, vol. IV (1930), pp. 131–51.

the growth of population in the eighteenth century, it still seems likely that the domestic wool clip nearly doubled. The foreign-trade statistics support the impression given by the contemporary estimates that a substantial proportion of the overall advance was made before 1740: between 1699–1701 and 1738–42 the annual exports of woollens at the 1709 rates of valuation rose from £2½ m. to nearly £3½ m., an increase of almost 40 per cent; and at the same time, the annual imports of raw wool had fallen from about 7 million lb. to about 2 million, and contined to fall until the 1760's, before rising again to 8 million lb. at the beginning of the nineteenth century.

In contrast, contemporary estimates of the number of cattle suggest little variation in the course of the century, and certainly no increase. Gregory King put the numbers at the end of the seventeenth century at 4½ million, Arthur Young in 1779 at less than 3½ million, while in 1832 Mulhall reckoned the cattle population of the whole of the United Kingdom at only 5·2 million.[1] Such figures imply that if there was any significant increase in meat production in the course of the eighteenth century, it must have been due to an increase in the weight or quality of the cattle, or to a more rapid turnover of the total stock. According to Davenant, King estimated the weight of contemporary bullocks killed at Smithfield at 370 lb., whereas for the end of the eighteenth century Sir John Sinclair asserted that the average weight was 800 lb. Most of the evidence suggests that King's figure was too low,[2] and Sinclair's too high. The mass of contemporary estimates for different breeds which were assembled by Fussell indicate little change in the weight of the beasts in the half-century or so after 1770, and the isolated figures available at the beginning of the century are not very different from those quoted for the end. It seems probable that there was some increase in the size of cattle during the period, although the nature of the evidence makes it difficult to express this in quantitative terms.[3] In the case of beef bought for the Navy, the size of the beasts was fixed

[1] G. E. Fussell, 'The Size of English Cattle in the Eighteenth Century', *Agric. Hist.*, vol. III (1929), pp. 160–81. Other nineteenth-century estimates were higher, but not above King's. McCulloch, *A Statistical Account of the British Empire* (1837), p. 495, suggested there may have been just over 4 million in England and Wales, including horses, or 5·2 million in Great Britain. Poole, *Statistics of Commerce* (1852), p. 59, reckoned the British total at 4·2 million plus 1½ million horses.

[2] In defence of King, Fussell pointed out that it was unlikely that the largest cattle were sent to Smithfield at the end of the seventeenth century, and according to McCulloch, *Statistical Account*, p. 493, King's figure, unlike Sinclair's, was exclusive of offal—although McCulloch forgot this qualification on p. 587 when estimating the increase in meat consumption! In fact, however, King estimated the average yield of the 800,000 cattle including calves which he thought were slaughtered annually in England and Wales at 200 lb. per beast.

[3] Of the four references given by Fussell for the early part of the century, Defoe's examples were obviously exceptional, Bradley was stating an objective rather than a fact ('Fatting cattle should be . . . when fat' 600–640 lb.), while the details of cattle sales at Holkham in Norfolk relate to what had already become one of the most progressive estates in the country. (Cf. R. A. C. Parker, 'Coke of Norfolk and the Agrarian Revolution', *Econ. Hist. Rev.*, second series, vol. VIII (1955), pp. 156–66.) This leaves us with Giles Jacob, who reckoned that a large bullock weighed 500–600 lb., and a medium-sized beast 400–500 lb. These figures are still higher than King's but somewhat lower than those commonly quoted a century later, although it should be remembered that the breed is unspecified.

by contract, and whereas in 1683 a standard ox for salting was required to weigh 5–5½ cwt., by the end of the eighteenth century the weight stipulated had risen to 6–7 cwt.[1] an increase of roughly 24 per cent. Similarly, it may be noted that, according to a more plausible, if less frequently quoted estimate than that associated with Sir John Sinclair, the weight of both cattle and sheep sold at Smithfield increased by about a quarter between 1732 and 1795.[2] These figures are unlikely to understate the increase, since they relate to towns and take no account of the gradual disappearance of heavy plough oxen which would have tended to raise the average weight in country districts at the beginning of the period. On the other hand, this factor, coupled with the efforts of the cattle-breeders, presumably resulted in some improvement in the quality of the stock during the century, and in the reduction of bone and offal. Moreover, if the total stock remained constant there would have been an increase of about 25 per cent in the annual supply of beasts available for slaughter as a result of the earlier age of fattening. According to King, less than a fifth of the stock were slaughtered each year, whereas in the first half of the nineteenth century, the proportion commonly given was one-quarter.[3] Even so, on this evidence, it is difficult to believe that the supply of beef did more than keep pace with the growth of population in the eighteenth century; and it would follow that a significant increase in per capita consumption could only have come about as a result of a greatly increased consumption of mutton.

At first sight, this conclusion appears to conflict with the evidence provided by the Smithfield figures, which are summarised in Table 18. Sales of both cattle and sheep increased during the period covered by the figures; and in the eighteenth century there is certainly no evidence of an increase in the number of sheep as compared with cattle. There are some expected differences in the movement of the two series. In the forties and early fifties a severe cattle plague swept England which is said to have resulted in the loss of half a million cattle;[4] during these years a sharp decline in the sales of cattle at Smithfield was largely offset by an increase in the numbers of sheep. But then, after 1750, cattle sales recovered, while the numbers of sheep fell slightly, and from 1770 or thereabouts the two series march in step. From 1732–40 to the end of the century the sales of sheep increased by 42 per cent and of cattle by 43 per cent; and it is only in the opening decades of the nineteenth century that the numbers of sheep sold began to increase more rapidly than cattle.

To some extent this phenomenon may be due to the peculiarities of the London market. In the eighteenth century, sheep were reared

[1] Beveridge, *Prices and Wages in England from the Twelfth to the Nineteenth Century*, vol. 1 (1939), p. 548.

[2] 'S.C. on Waste Lands', *House of Commons Reports*, vol. IX (1795), p. 203.

[3] McCulloch, *Statistical Account*, p. 495; Poole, *Statistics of Commerce*, p. 59.

[4] C. F. Mullett, 'The Cattle Distemper in Mid-Eighteenth Century England', *Agric. Hist.*, vol. XX (1946), pp. 144–65.

mainly for their wool: they were not usually killed until they were three years old, and comparatively few lambs were slaughtered for their meat. According to King, 3,300,000, or just under 30 per cent of the total stock, were slaughtered annually; a century later the proportion was about the same, and may even have been smaller.[1] Now presumably the old wool sheep—like plough oxen—would have been consumed in the countryside and not sent to the London markets, and it is quite possible that the supply of saleable mutton did not increase much faster than beef. But if this interpretation is correct, it would, of course, imply that the shift from beef to mutton was even more striking in country districts than the overall national estimates suggest. Without specific information about the diet of the farm population it is not possible to confirm this hypothesis. It may be significant, however, that at Winchester College the consumption of mutton seems to have risen by about 20 per cent in the eighteenth century, although purchases of beef fell by more than half.[2]

What is clear from the Smithfield figures, is that the consumption of meat in general showed no significant increase during this period. In the second half of the eighteenth century, the combined sales of cattle and sheep increased by just under 48 per cent. During the same period, the population of the four counties in the London area increased by 63 per cent,[3] and it is probable that the numbers in the metropolitan area served by Smithfield grew even faster. Even allowing for some increase in the weight of the beasts sold, it appears that the total supply barely kept pace with the growth of population; and after 1800 it may well have lagged behind.[4]

However, there are good reasons for supposing that conditions in London may have been unrepresentative, and it would certainly be rash to assume that the Smithfield figures—which probably account for only about 10 per cent of the total consumption of England and Wales—give a good index of either the absolute or per capita increase in the meat supply during the period. More general, though

[1] According to Middleton (*Middlesex*, p. 644), about 36 per cent of the total stock were killed each year, of which about one-fifth were lambs, three-fifths three-year-olds and the rest breeding ewes of about five years of age. According to John Luccock (*Nature and Properties of Wool* (1809), p. 148), who must be regarded as the major contemporary authority on this subject, only 6·8 million sheep and lambs were slaughtered annually, or only 26 per cent of the estimated stock of 26·1 millions.

[2] Beveridge, *Prices and Wages in England*, vol. 1 (1939), p. 35. It is interesting to note that in the case of an institution like Greenwich Hospital, beef, veal and mutton were apparently in composite demand in the eighteenth century, since they were all recorded under the one heading 'flesh'. Perhaps for this reason there was no significant change in the relative prices of beef and mutton, which were usually the same, although in the case of the Westminster School and Abbey contracts, beef was cheaper than mutton at the beginning of the century, and dearer at the end.

[3] See below, p. 103. The counties referred to are Middlesex, Surrey, Kent and Essex.

[4] E. J. Hobsbawm, 'The British Standard of Living, 1790–1850', *Econ. Hist. Rev.*, second series, vol. x (1957), p. 58. Since this was written, however, it has been pointed out that the Smithfield data constitute an unreliable guide to changes in London meat consumption, owing to the growing importance of alternative sources of supply. See R. M. Hartwell, 'The Rising Standard of Living in England 1800–1850,' *Econ. Hist. Rev.*, second series, vol. XIII (1961), p. 410.

Table 18. *Indicators of eighteenth-century meat production*

	Smithfield cattle (000's)	Smithfield sheep (000's)	Combined meat index	Tallow candles (m. lb.)	Soap (m. lb.)	Hides and (skins (m. lb.)
1711–1720	—	—	—	(30·8)	(24·9)	—
1716–1725	—	—	—	33·3	26·0	—
1721–1730	—	—	—	34·3	26·3	(28·8)
1726–1735	—	—	—	34·3	26·5	28·5
1731–1740	(84)	(565)	100	35·8	27·1	29·4
1736–1745	82	542	97	33·7	26·3	28·7
1741–1750	79	570	97	32·6	26·4	27·5
1746–1755	72	633	96	35·8	28·4	28·8
1751–1760	78	616	99	37·5	28·9	29·9
1756–1765	84	609	103	40·3	29·0	31·4
1761–1770	82	614	102	42·0	29·9	31·8
1766–1775	86	607	104	42·1	30·6	31·9
1771–1780	95	649	114	45·3	32·6	32·9
1776–1785	99	686	119	48·4	35·1	33·7
1781–1790	98	687	119	49·4	36·8	35·0
1786–1795	104	711	125	53·6	41·0	36·9
1791–1800	114	756	135	58·8	46·4	38·8
1796–1805	120	799	142	64·1	50·9	39·6
1801–1810	128	886	154	69·0	—	43·0
1806–1815	133	939	161	72·0	—	47·7
1811–1820	131	952	161	76·8	—	47·3

Sources: The figures for Smithfield cattle and sheep are given in 'Report of the Select Committee on Waste Lands', *House of Commons Reports*, vol. IX (1795), pp. 202–3, for the period 1732–94, and in *Statistical Illustrations of the British Empire* (1825), p. 61, from 1782 onwards. We have used the former source up to 1794, although in the early nineties, but not before, the figures it gives are somewhat lower than those given in the later publication. The excise figures are from the Excise Revenue Accounts in the Customs Library.

indirect, evidence is provided by the excise series for tallow candles, soap, and hides and skins, which are also summarised in Table 18. The difficulty with such series is, of course, to know whether they reflect variations in the supply of raw materials provided by agriculture or in the demand of the industries using those materials. This is particularly true of the figures for tallow candles and soap. It appears that substantial, though declining, quantities of candles were made at home during this period, and the industry whose output the excise series may be presumed to represent was in any case largely localised in London.[1] Moreover, the series is vitiated by the fact that in the eighteenth century imports of tallow more than quadrupled: by 1796–8 the quantities retained for use in Britain had reached 37·5 million lb. and we have of course no means of knowing what proportion of this considerable amount was used in the manufacture of candles. Similar objections apply to the series for soap, which was made from butcher's fat, and it seems unlikely that either set of figures reflects at all accurately the long-term changes in the meat supply. On the other hand, as Professor Ashton has pointed out, the fluctuations in the quantity of tallow candles charged with duty agree closely with the Smithfield sheep series, in the period before 1770—although the trends are different—while the series for soap reflects the effects of the cattle

[1] T. S. Ashton, *The Eighteenth Century*, pp. 59–60.

disease in the 1750's.[1] It seems possible, therefore, that over comparatively short periods these figures may indicate changes in supply, and it is of some interest to note that both series suggest an upward movement at the beginning of the eighteenth century followed by the stagnation which is characteristic of all the indicators in the second quarter. Moreover, it should be noted that most of the increase in tallow imports took place in the last thirty years of the eighteenth century. Between 1699–1701 and 1772–4 the official value of tallow imports increased by only 54 per cent, which, if anything, was probably less than the increase in the output of candles during the same period. It may be reasonable to conclude, therefore, that on the whole this series supports the impression derived from the contemporary estimates that there was a substantial increase in the numbers of English sheep in the early part of the century; and, indeed, by extrapolation it appears that the increase in the output of tallow candles between 1695 and 1740 was almost exactly the same as the estimated increase in the number of sheep.[2]

The series for hides and skins is much more useful. A large proportion (nearly 90 per cent) of the total quantity of hides and skins which paid duty were charged by weight, and the series will, therefore, take some account of changes in the size of the beasts, though not of reductions in bone and offal.[3] It is clear that the leather industry must have absorbed the hides of virtually all the large cattle which were slaughtered in England and Wales each year,[4] and by the end of our period there were substantial imports of hides. The series is, however, subject to two limitations as an index of total meat production. In the first place, if we assume that a sheepskin produced about one pound of leather, it appears that only about half the annual supply of sheepskins found their way to the tanners and tawers, and not much more than a quarter were charged duty by weight. Since a bullock apparently produced about twenty-eight times as much leather as a sheep,[5] but only about ten times as much meat, the weight of sheep in the series given in the table is still further reduced. Secondly, detailed annual figures of hide imports are not available for most of our period, and since those which are refer to the number of hides and not their weight it is possible to make only a crude and partial allowance for the effect of increasing imports on the overall figures.

[1] *Ibid.*

[2] The significance of this is rather uncertain, since contemporary estimates of the sheep population, and certainly the one for 1741, often relied heavily on the Smithfield and excise data. Nevertheless the series provides some check on the comparability of different estimates over time. It should be noted that the excise series does not support the view, suggested by the contemporary estimates of the output of wool, that the rate of growth was significantly higher from 1740 to 1770 than in other periods of expansion.

[3] E. J. Hobsbawm, *op. cit.* pp. 65–6. The small proportion of the total which paid duty by the piece or *ad valorem* have been ignored here.

[4] At least 80 per cent of the totals given in the table refer to the skins of large cattle, and if about a million cattle were slaughtered annually, it seems unlikely that their hides would produce more than 28 million lb. of leather. Cf. Poole, *Statistics of Commerce* (1852), p. 215.

[5] *Ibid.*

Even so, the figures strengthen the impression derived from other sources that in the second half of the eighteenth century, and still more at the beginning of the nineteenth, the supply of beef failed to keep pace with the growth of population. It will be observed that with the exception of the years of the cattle plague the crude series given in the table follows a path remarkably similar to the estimated growth of corn production shown in Table 17. After remaining at about the same level for the first twenty years, output fell sharply in the 1740's, and then moved steadily upward, with only a temporary check in the 1760's. Between 1750 and the end of the century the overall increase indicated by the figures amounted to 37 per cent, and after that the rate of advance was apparently even faster. But on a rough estimate it appears that the leather content of imported hides retained for home consumption rose from 1·8 million lb. in 1772–4 to 4·3 million lb. in 1796–8, and by 1810–15 the figure was apparently approaching 20 million.[1] The import figures relate to Great Britain, whereas the output figures given in the table refer only to England and Wales and are, of course, incomplete. Nevertheless, it is difficult to avoid the conclusion that the increase in the home-produced supplies of beef, after 1770, if not before, was only about half that suggested by the figures for hides and skins, while in the opening years of the nineteenth century they may have suffered an absolute decline.[2] It is not surprising to find, therefore, that by the end of the eighteenth century, England was drawing heavily on Irish beef and dairy produce, and in 1796–8 retained imports of provisions, which included beef, bacon, pork, butter and cheese, were not much smaller by value than the corresponding figures for corn.[3]

If we now try to summarise the impressions derived from this survey, we may perhaps take the estimates of corn production given in Table 17 as an index of the progress of agricultural production as a whole, at any rate for the eighteenth century. The indicators discussed above suggest that, with the partial exception of the 1740's, when a series of bumper harvests and a 'prodigious increase'[4] of sheep coincided with the disastrous years of the cattle plague, the short-term movements in agricultural production all follow a similar course. In general, it appears that the production of wool and mutton ran ahead of corn production during the century, while beef and butter lagged behind, with the net result that the prices of cereals and animal products

[1] The figures for 1810–15 are based on a return in *S.P. 1830*, vol. xxv, p. 263, which relate to gross imports. The figure of 20 million lb. is based on the assumption that about 5 per cent of hides imported were re-exported.

[2] According to McCulloch (*Dictionary of Commerce* (1882 ed.), pp. 808–9), Scottish output of leather in the 1820's amounted to about 10 per cent of the English total. Assuming that the quantity of hides and skins constituted 90 per cent of the English total, we may tentatively estimate the total British output of leather from home-produced hides and skins at about 42 million lb. in the excise years ending 1797–9, and at about 40 million lb. in the closing years of the Napoleonic Wars.

[3] At 1796–8 prices, the figures were £2·1 m. and £2·6 m. respectively.

[4] Smith, *Memoirs of Wool* (1757), cited by W. Curtler, *A Short History of English Agriculture* (1909), p. 172.

moved in the same general direction throughout the century, and, if the contemporary estimates may be taken as a guide, the gross value of the output of the two branches of the industry was roughly equal at the beginning and the end of the century. During the French Wars, however, the balance was certainly disturbed, and a big increase in the output of grain was achieved only by bringing more land under the plough at the expense of the nation's meat supply.

Finally, although there can be no doubt that the increase in agricultural output was much greater after 1750 than before, the absolute figures give a misleading picture of the real achievements of the industry in the first half of the century. We have no statistics of the agricultural population before 1801, but, judging by the estimates of county populations discussed in the next chapter, it seems probable that the numbers in agriculture fell in the first half of the eighteenth century and increased thereafter. In the first fifty years the whole of the increase in population was concentrated in seven industrial counties, and the population of the six counties where, at the time of the 1811 census, agricultural influences were strongest, actually fell by about 9 per cent.[1] After 1750, on the other hand, the population of the industrial areas continued to grow more rapidly than the rest, but even the predominantly agricultural counties increased in numbers by over 25 per cent. If these figures are taken at their face value, and the figures of corn production are assumed to be roughly representative of agricultural output as a whole, it would appear that the output per head in agriculture increased by about 25 per cent in the eighteenth century, and that the whole of this advance was achieved before 1750.[2] Not much weight can be placed on such slender evidence, and in part no doubt the results may be explained by the fact that in the middle of the century harvests happened to be exceptionally good, while fifty years later they were exceptionally bad. On the other hand, the figures are consistent with the impression derived from much recent research in this field: they suggest that the enclosure movement of the latter part of the century was directed more towards increasing yields per acre and extending the area under cultivation than at economising the use of human labour; and that, in so far as the *relative* increase in the industrial population in the eighteenth century was made possible by a significant increase in agricultural output per head, its origins, at least, must be sought before the classical age of the great improvers.

4. TRENDS IN TOTAL AND PER CAPITA REAL OUTPUT

Much further research will be necessary before it is possible to measure at all confidently the course and magnitude of eighteenth-century

---

[1] The counties are Bedfordshire, Cambridgeshire, Hereford, Huntingdon, Lincolnshire and Rutland.

[2] Judging by the population estimates for 1781 given in the next chapter, it would appear that agricultural productivity may actually have fallen in the third quarter of the century and recovered thereafter.

economic growth. All we shall do here is to attempt to extract the overall implications of the statistical evidence discussed in earlier sections.

We argued above, first that the combined totals of net imports and domestic exports provide a crude index of the growth of those industries which entered largely into overseas trade, though they probably overstate the increase in industrial output as a whole, owing to the slower rates of growth of industries catering largely for the home market; and secondly, that our estimates of grain output should represent with reasonable accuracy the progress of the agricultural sector. There can be little doubt, on this evidence, that there were two major turning-points in the growth of the economy during the eighteenth century. If we are to make a more general quantitative assessment of the process of growth and relate it to changes in the size of the population, it is clearly necessary to make an attempt, however tentative, to combine the sectoral statistics into national aggregates. We have therefore constructed a series of index numbers which are designed to illustrate the probable trends in the growth of both total and per capita real output in the course of the century. This series is set out in Table 19.

The index numbers given in the table are decennial averages, roughly centring on the years specified.[1] Those relating to the 'export industries' and to agriculture are based simply on the totals of net imports plus domestic exports and on the series for grain output which were discussed above in sections 1 and 3. The index for industries producing largely for the home market, is a weighted average of the excise series for beer, leather (hides and skins), candles and soap.[2] The weights used in the construction of this index[3] were based on rough estimates of the value of output in the industries concerned *circa* 1700. These estimates, which were derived from the statistics of the physical quantities charged with duty and price data,[4] relate to gross output, but an arbitrary allowance was made for the fact that, so far as one can judge from the prices of raw materials used, the value added in brewing constituted a much smaller proportion of the gross output than in the other industries concerned.

So far we have not discussed the contribution made by Government and the service industries to British economic growth in the eighteenth century. But clearly some allowance had to be made for these sectors in preparing the index numbers of total output. In the absence of

---

[1] The index for the output of the 'home industries' relates to the excise years running from midsummer 1695 to midsummer 1705, etc., most of the others to the calendar years 1695–1704, etc. For most of the period the fiscal year roughly corresponded to the harvest year: but from the beginning of the nineteenth century the accounts were made up to 5th January.

[2] The output of British spirits was deliberately excluded from this index. It proved impossible to devise suitable weights for this series, and since its movement is quite different from the others, and the number of series available is in any case small, its inclusion could give a highly misleading picture of the overall trends.

[3] Beer, 35; leather, 57; candles, 5; soap, 3.

[4] Beveridge, *Prices and Wages in England*, vol. 1 (1939).

information on the development of service industries during the period, we assumed, quite arbitrarily, that rents and miscellaneous services increased at the same rate as population; and the index for them is therefore based on Brownlee's estimates of the population of England and Wales. An attempt was, however, made to arrive at a more considered estimate of the contribution made by the government sector. Detailed annual figures of net government expenditure are available for the whole of the eighteenth century,[1] and our index is based on the figures of total expenditure on civil government and defence adjusted for changes in the price level during the period.[2] Unfortunately, the official figures do not distinguish between the amounts paid to those in government employment and other forms of government expenditure. It seems unlikely that the proportion spent on wages and salaries changed substantially as between the beginning and end of the eighteenth century, but equally it seems probable that it did vary in periods of peace and war, owing to the relatively greater importance of expenditure on military supplies in war-time. For this reason the index may well exaggerate the increase in the contribution made by Government in war-time and its contraction in the intervals of peace.

The weights employed in combining these series to form an index of total output are given in brackets at the head of each column in the table, and require little further comment here. They are based partly on contemporary estimates of the national product which are discussed fully elsewhere,[3] and partly on our estimates of the output of the 'home industries' at the beginning of the century. Two points of explanation should be made here. Gregory King's estimates suggest that the value added in the woollen manufacture at the end of the eighteenth century amounted to about £3 m., or about one-third of the total net output of industry.[4] Since at that time the other textile and metal industries were of comparatively minor importance and the combined output of the brewing and leather industries cannot have been very much smaller than that of the woollen industry, it seems likely that in 1700 the 'home industries' must have been responsible for at least another third of the total industrial output. Secondly, it should be noted that as grain prices were unusually low in 1688, and King may in any case have underestimated the importance of agriculture, we have attributed 43 per cent of total output to the agricultural community—a figure somewhat closer to the share of 45 per cent implied by Young's estimates for 1770—in place of the 40 per cent which King's figures suggest.

[1] *S.P. 1867*, vol. xxxv.

[2] As price deflator we used a simple average of the Gilboy-Schumpeter index numbers of the prices of producer goods and consumer goods (exclusive of cereals). The series for producer goods ends in 1799, and for the years 1800–5 inclusive we used the Silberling index.

[3] See pp. 155–64.

[4] See Phyllis Deane, 'The Output of the Woollen Industry', *op. cit.* p. 209, and Table 35, p. 156, below.

Table 19. *Index numbers of eighteenth-century real output*

(1700 = 100)

	Export industries (18)	Home industries (12)	Total industry and commerce (30)	Agriculture (43)	Rent and services (20)	Government and defence (7)	Total real output (100)	Average real output
1700	100	100	100	100	100	100	100	100
1710	108	98	104	104	103	165	108	105
1720	125	108	118	105	103	91	108	105
1730	142	105	127	103	102	98	110	108
1740	148	105	131	104	102	148	115	113
1750	176	107	148	111	105	172	125	119
1760	222	114	179	115	113	310	147	130
1770	256	114	199	117	121	146	144	119
1780	246	123	197	126	129	400	167	129
1790	383	137	285	135	142	253	190	134
1800	544	152	387	143	157	607	251	160

Sources: See text.

It need hardly be emphasised that the data summarised here represent a set of hypotheses about the course of eighteenth-century economic growth, rather than a set of conclusions. Certainly we can attach little credence to the figures for individual decades. Apart from the possible errors in the index for the government sector to which we have referred,[1] it should be remembered that the index of agricultural output probably exaggerates the increase in production in the 1740's, since it makes no allowance for the effects of the cattle plague at that time. Again, the available indicators for the export industries give no indication of the decline in output in the seventies which is apparent in the foreign trade series, and it seems probable that our index seriously misrepresents the position in that decade. Fortunately, errors in the individual series may to some extent cancel each other in the aggregate, especially if, as seems likely, government orders in war-time helped to make good the temporary loss of export markets. Nevertheless, a wide margin of error remains. Nor can we be sure that the series accurately reflect long-term trends. Even if the evidence gives us some confidence in the indices for most sectors of the economy, the assumption underlying the

[1] The effect of the violent fluctuations in the index for the Government sector on the national aggregates can easily be illustrated. If this sector is omitted from the total and the weights of the industrial and agricultural sectors are correspondingly increased, the figures work out as follows:

	Total real output	Average real output		Total real output	Average real output
1700	100	100	1760	137	121
1710	104	101	1770	147	122
1720	109	106	1780	151	117
1730	111	109	1790	189	133
1740	113	111	1800	231	147
1750	123	117			

index for rents and services may well be false and so invalidate any deductions which we might make about the behaviour of the national aggregates. It is reassuring to observe that the major conclusion suggested by the series, that total output rather more than doubled in the course of the century, is consistent with the impression derived from the contemporary national income estimates. Moreover, our estimate that the output of industry and commerce roughly quadrupled agrees fairly well both with the implications of the national income estimates and with Hoffmann's index of industrial production, although, as we should expect from our earlier discussion, the figures given in Table 19 suggest a much higher rate of growth than Hoffmann's in the third quarter of the century.

In order to fix an upper limit to the rates of growth consistent with the data, we recalculated the indices of total and per capita real output, still on a 1700 base, but on the optimistic assumption that the whole industrial and commercial sector grew at the same rate as international trade. Next, we adjusted the component series given in Table 19 to an 1800 base, and reweighted the aggregates in terms of the prices prevailing at the end of the century. By then, the share of industry and commerce had risen to about 40 per cent of the total, while that of agriculture had fallen to roughly 33 per cent.[1] But agricultural prices were exceptionally high at the end of the century, as a result of war, population pressure and a number of bad harvests, and the estimates given in Table 19 imply that, in terms of 1700 prices, the share of agriculture had dwindled to less than 25 per cent of total output by 1800. The effect of adopting an 1800 base is to give a relatively large weight to the agricultural sector, and thus to arrive at a deliberately conservative estimate of the overall advance.

The results of these calculations are summarised in Fig. 4 and Table 20, in which twenty-year averages have been used to minimise the effect of errors in the index numbers for individual decades. There are significant differences between the rates of growth suggested by the three series, but in each case the pattern of change of both total and per capita output is broadly similar. All three series for total output clearly illustrate the three main phases in the process of eighteenth-century growth to which we have referred. In the early part of the century there are few signs of growth in the economy as a whole. As we might expect, the advance seems to have been most rapid in the first decade or two, but in the whole period ending *circa* 1745 the rate of growth of total output averaged less than 0·3 per cent per annum (2·6 per cent per decade). There can be little doubt that there was a marked acceleration in the rate of growth after 1745: for

---

[1] In the revised series, the 'home industries' are given a weight of 6 per cent of the total output as compared with 34 per cent for the export industries. The 1800 weights for the various components of the home industries index are: beer, 20; leather, 66; candles, 8; soap, 6. They are based largely on the information contained in Eden's estimates of British industrial output which are printed in Macpherson's *Annals of Commerce*, vol. IV (1805), p. 549.

twenty years it averaged about one per cent per annum, and although the pace slackened in the next two decades it seems to have maintained a level which was more than double that prevailing in the early part of the century. In the 1780's there was a further advance and the estimates suggest that in the closing years of the century the economy was expanding at the rate of 1·8 per cent per annum (or 19·1 per cent per decade).

Table 20. *Estimated annual percentage rates of growth of eighteenth-century real output*

	Total real output			Average real output		
	(i)	(ii)	(iii)	(i)	(ii)	(iii)
1695/1715–1725/1745	0·3	0·4	0·2	0·3	0·4	0·1
1725/1745–1745/1765	1·0	1·1	0·8	0·6	0·8	0·5
1745/1765–1765/1785	0·7	0·8	0·6	0·0	0·1	0·0
1765/1785–1785/1805	1·8	2·1	1·5	0·9	1·1	0·6

Sources: See text.

(i) 1700 base, *including* home industries; (ii) 1700 base, *excluding* home industries; (iii) 1800 base, *including* home industries.

The series for real output per head suggests a slightly different picture. It will be observed that the pattern of change suggested by the series for total output is in many respects remarkably similar to the course of population growth which has been discussed elsewhere in this volume; and though an allowance must certainly be made for the influence of the population figures on our estimates of total output, the correlation still seems too significant to be ignored. For most of the eighteenth century total output appears to have grown faster than population, but for the first eighty years the variations in the rates of growth are so similar that the alteration of trend in the second half of the century, which is such a marked feature of the growth of total output, is much less apparent in the series for output per head. Before 1745, when total output grew very slowly, the population also changed very little, with the result that average real output rose, slowly but fairly steadily at the rate of about 2½ per cent per decade. After 1745, on the other hand, the sharp increase in the rate of growth of total output soon appears to have been swallowed up by the population increase which began at the same time. It is true that for twenty years per capita output seems to have grown more than twice as fast as it had done before. But with the continued expansion of numbers and the somewhat slower growth of total output in the sixties and seventies, the advance was halted, and over the four decades ending in 1785 the average rate of increase was almost exactly the same as it had been in earlier decades. At the end of the century, however, there was a crucial change. After 1785, both total output and population were growing much faster than before, but the former now began to draw decisively ahead of the latter. For the first time, per capita output started to increase by nearly nine per cent per decade—or at more than three times the average rate for the rest of the period under review.

It is important to note that the pattern of growth implied by these estimates differs radically from that which we deduced from the most carefully considered contemporary estimates of the national income. Although, as we noted, the increase in real incomes over the century as a whole appears much the same from both sets of evidence, the national income estimates imply that a period of rising real incomes per head

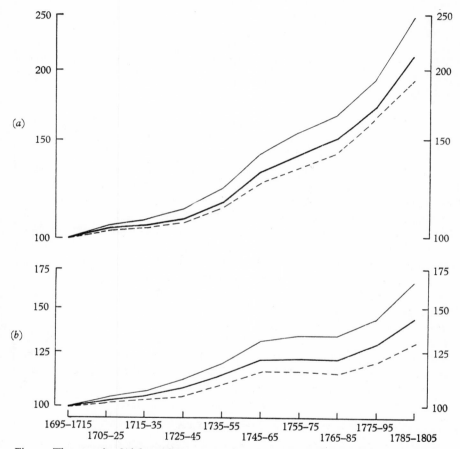

Fig. 4. The growth of eighteenth-century real output: (*a*) real output, (*b*) real output per head. ——— 1700 base, *excluding* home industries; ——— 1700 base, *including* home industries; – – – – 1800 base, *including* home industries.

in the early decades was followed by a phase of stagnation or even decline in the last thirty years.[1] The explanation of the discrepancy probably lies in the fact that the attempt to use contemporary estimates of the national income as a measure of long-term changes in the rate of growth necessarily rests on the assumption that these estimates are not only plausible guesses at the order of magnitude of the national product,

[1] See Phyllis Deane, 'The Implications of Early National Income Estimates', *op. cit.* p. 35; 'The Industrial Revolution and Economic Growth', *op. cit.* p. 167.

but that they can also be treated as directly comparable with one another over time. It is difficult to reconcile this assumption with the statistical evidence which has been discussed above. A comparison of the estimates of Gregory King and Arthur Young, for example, implies that in money terms the output of English agriculture roughly trebled between 1688 and 1770; and even allowing for a substantial rise in agricultural prices during that period, we are still left with an increase approaching 100 per cent. But in order to accept such a figure we should have to discount the evidence that the growth in meat output during the period was comparatively modest, and at the same time believe that in Arthur Young's day the average Englishman consumed far more bread than his great-grandfather at the end of the seventeenth century.

It is true that some calculations by Joseph Massie for 1759–60, which are more obviously comparable with Gregory King's, imply much less optimistic estimates of the various components of the national income than Arthur Young's a decade or so later.[1] On the other hand, as we have pointed out elsewhere, a study of Massie's estimates suggests that they are not internally consistent.[2] If, in the aggregate, therefore, they happen to yield a figure which is more consistent with other evidence, the result must be considered, to some extent at least, fortuitous. It seems difficult to escape the conclusion that while the best contemporary estimates may provide us with some indication of the structure of the national product at particular points in time, they do not yield trustworthy independent evidence of long-term changes in the national aggregates.[3] Whatever reservations we may have about the statistical materials assembled in this chapter, they provide a better basis for assessing the probable trends in eighteenth-century growth. They suggest that although the turning-point in the growth of the absolute levels of output came much earlier than has sometimes been assumed, the last two or three decades of the eighteenth century saw the beginning of the comparatively rapid rise in real incomes per head.

5. THE MECHANICS OF EIGHTEENTH-CENTURY GROWTH

What explanations can we offer for the pattern of growth we have traced? We shall not attempt here a detailed analysis of the factors responsible for the revolutionary changes in the British economy which began to take place in the latter part of the eighteenth century. Nor do we wish to over-simplify what was clearly a highly complex process.

---

[1] For a discussion of Massie's estimates, see Peter Mathias, 'The Social Structure in the Eighteenth Century: A Calculation by Joseph Massie', *Econ. Hist. Rev.*, second series, vol. x (1957), pp. 30–45. After an allowance for omissions, they suggest a total national income of £80–£90 m., as compared with the figures of £48 m. and £127 m. derived from the King and Young estimates respectively.

[2] Phyllis Deane, 'The Industrial Revolution and Economic Growth', *op. cit.* pp. 166–7.

[3] See below, pp. 155–64, where the structural implications of the contemporary national income estimates are explored.

But we shall comment on certain aspects of that process, and in particular on the part played by three of the major variables—population, harvests, and overseas trade.

There can, of course, be no doubt of the central importance of overseas trade in the expansion of the economy during this period. Apart from the intangible, but nonetheless vital, part which commercial contacts played in widening man's economic horizons, the possession of extensive overseas markets and the comparatively low costs of sea transport in the early stages of economic growth enabled Britain's export industries to enjoy economies of scale, and, at the same time, provided the home economy with supplies of the imported foodstuffs and raw materials on which it increasingly depended. We cannot verify our assumption that the growth of the industries producing exportable products kept pace with the expansion of international trade, which more than quintupled in volume during the century. But it is clear that the major export industries, and those domestic industries which supplied them with some of their raw materials, such as coal-mining and soap-making, enjoyed higher rates of growth than most other branches of economic activity.

This does not necessarily mean that the quickening tempo of economic expansion in the second half of the eighteenth century can be directly attributed to the accelerated growth of foreign trade during that period. Indeed, an examination of the evidence suggests that, if there was a causal relationship between the growth of foreign trade and the growth of national income, it was of a more complex character and operated in a different direction than has usually been supposed. We shall argue here that the expansion of the British export trade was limited by the purchasing power of Britain's customers, and that this in its turn was limited by what they could earn from exports to Britain.

There are two obvious ways in which a largely autonomous growth of foreign trade might be expected to stimulate expansion at home. If the demand for British exports increased, either as a result of expanding demand in existing markets, or the acquisition of new ones, the income of British exporters would tend to increase and ultimately to communicate itself to other sections of the community. Alternatively, if the world supply of goods which Britain imported increased, their prices would tend to fall, and in this way, too, British real incomes might rise. In either case, the terms of trade would tend to move in Britain's favour. In fact it looks as if the accelerated growth of foreign trade in the second half of the eighteenth century was associated with an *adverse* movement of the terms of trade. It is true that over the period from 1745 to 1800 as a whole, the gross barter terms of trade seem to have moved somewhat in Britain's favour, whereas between 1700 and 1745 they had gone strongly against her.[1] But in neither period was the movement continuous, and for most of the years when trade was expanding relatively rapidly—in the late forties and late

[1] See Table 85, pp. 319–21.

fifties, and again in the last twenty years of the century—the terms of trade were generally adverse, the only marked exception being the years immediately following the American War of Independence. Of course, the gross barter terms of trade constitute an unreliable guide to changes in relative prices, unless it is possible to assume that the balance of trade was constant. But such price data as we have do not permit a satisfactory index of the commodity terms of trade. The scraps of information now available are summarised in Table 21.

Table 21. *Eighteenth-century price relatives: imports and exports*

(Five-yearly averages centring on the year specified)

(1753 = 100)

	Imports				Exports					
	Sugar	Tea	Iron (bar)	Raw materials	Broad-cloth	Hats and stockings	Linens	Iron (anchors)	Non-ferrous metals	Coal
1700	120	—	—	163	—	—	—	—	—	—
1705	106	[347]	—	166	—	—	—	—	—	—
1710	125	329	86	176	92	—	—	107	67	145
1715	100	227	91	146	100	118	—	102	68	100
1720	68	157	104	138	101	115	—	109	77	112
1725	82	147	114	107	97	125	—	104	97	98
1730	66	170	96	110	95	118	82	101	108	94
1735	64	94	83	95	96	107	80	100	103	94
1740	84	115	82	120	91	99	86	101	99	103
1745	109	120	81	153	95	97	87	101	95	118
1750	95	117	86	147	95	100	95	100	95	107
1755	107	109	96	125	96	103	93	101	102	122
1760	[129]	153	103	154	108	113	89	109	91	131
1765	—	84	93	152	119	113	98	115	98	118
1770	—	71	98	129	132	107	102	115	99	107
1775	—	70	95	148	139	101	96	—	87	119
1780	[128]	76	107	206	138	93	99	—	85	138
1785	103	84	116	149	143	102	101	—	95	126
1790	145	84	115	137	165	102	85	—	96	132
1795	184	81	132	170	171	102	81	—	109	159
1799 (3 years)	181	87	167	218	174	102	91	—	118	171

Sources: IMPORTS.—Sugar: R. B. Sheridan, 'The Sugar Trade of the British West Indies from 1660 to 1756' (unpublished London University Ph.D. thesis, 1951), 1698–1758; T. Tooke, *A History of Prices*, vol. II (1838), p. 414, 1782–1800. Tea: average price of tea sold by the East India Company, exclusive of duty, based on R. Wissett, *A Compendium of East Indian Affairs* (1802), vol. II (no pagination), 1706–1800. Iron (bar): price on re-export from East India Company's Commercial Journals, 1708–1800. Raw materials: unweighted average of price relatives for hemp, pitch, tar, oil (train) and tallow, 1698–1800, from Beveridge, *Prices and Wages in England*, 1939, vol. I.

EXPORTS—Broadcloth: average value of East India Company's exports, 1708–1800, East India Company's Commercial Journals. Hats and stockings: unweighted average of price relatives, 1712–1800, from Beveridge, *op. cit.* Linens: average value of linens stamped for sale in Scotland, 1728–1800, A. J. Warden, *The Linen Trade, Ancient and Modern* (1864), p. 480. Iron (anchors): East India Company's Commercial Journals, 1708–1772. Non-ferrous metals: unweighted average of price relatives for lead, 1708–1800, from the East India Company's Commercial Journals; brass, 1732–1800, and manufactured copper, 1752–1800, from Wissett, *op. cit.*, vol. II. Coal: Beveridge, *op. cit.* p. 731, 1698–1800.

Some of the data are of doubtful value, and the series for broadcloth and linens—which are indicators of average values, not prices—are included here only as a first approximation. Nevertheless, the movements of the individual series are sufficiently clear and well synchronised to justify a few preliminary hypotheses about the probable trends of relative prices.

For most of the century, export prices were comparatively stable, and movements in the terms of trade were largely determined by fluctuations in the prices of imports. The latter tended to rise during war and to fall back to more normal levels when peace was concluded. During the War of the Spanish Succession, for example, import prices were high, but fell rapidly for about twenty years after the Treaty of Utrecht. In the mid-thirties they began to rise, and this movement, combined with a fall in the prices of major exports, such as woollens, non-ferrous metals and iron, which seems to have begun in the 1720's, produced an adverse movement in the terms of trade in the thirties and forties. When the War of the Austrian Succession ended in 1748, import prices fell again, and the terms of trade began to turn in Britain's favour. This movement was again reversed during the Seven Years War, but became more marked in the 1760's, when a fall in import prices[1] was accompanied by a significant rise in the prices of exports. During the American War of Independence, import prices again soared, only to plummet with the return of peace. Finally, in the late eighties and nineties, there was a marked increase in the prices of both imports and exports, but the former rose faster than the latter.

Thus, excluding the period of the American war and its aftermath, it appears that the years of most rapid expansion after 1745 were years in which the terms of trade were adverse, whereas in periods when the rate of growth of foreign trade sank to the low levels prevailing in the earlier part of the century, the terms of trade were moving in Britain's favour. In the light of this evidence, it is difficult to see the expansion of trade as a largely exogenous factor which quickened the pace of industrial growth. The dramatic recovery of foreign trade after the American War no doubt gave a temporary fillip to the home economy which helps to explain the general boom in the 1780's. More generally, however, it seems that the explanation of the higher average rate of growth in the second half of the century should be sought at home rather than abroad.[2]

---

[1] Detailed statistics of sugar prices are not available for the years 1759–81. It appears, however, that in 1760 the price of West Indian Muscovados in London was about 40s. per cwt. It dropped slightly in the sixties and early seventies, and by 1775 stood at 32s. During the American War, the price roughly doubled, and then fell back to just under 40s. by 1783–4. L. J. Ragatz, *The Fall of the Planter Class in the British Caribbean, 1763–1833* (New York, 1928), p. 167. See also, R. Pares, 'The London Sugar Market, 1740–1769', *Econ. Hist. Rev.*, second series, vol. IX (1956), pp. 254–70.

[2] It is interesting to note that Britain's territorial acquisitions during the Seven Years War do not seem to have had any immediate effect on the rate of growth of her overseas trade. It is true that from a commercial point of view this was easily the most satisfactory of eighteenth-century wars, and all branches of foreign trade were expanding during this

ne explanation may lie in the character of Britain's overseas kets during this period. An outstanding feature of British trade ... ing the eighteenth century was its increasing reliance on colonial markets. In 1700, over four-fifths of English exports went to Europe, and only a fifth to the rest of the world.[1] By the end of the century, on the other hand, this relationship was almost exactly reversed. Even in absolute terms, British goods made little headway in the protected markets of her European rivals. Some progress was made in the first half of the century, but in the last fifty years an extension of trade with Russia and the Baltic was more than offset by the decline in exports to North-West Europe and the Mediterranean. Hence the increase in British exports in the course of the century was almost entirely due to the expansion of trade with the new, colonial markets in Ireland, America, Africa and the Far East.

The most important of these markets from the standpoint of the British manufacturer were North America and the West Indies. Britain's trade with these areas formed a virtually closed system from which competitors were rigorously excluded, and in consequence she was able to increase her exports to America more than twentyfold in the course of the century. But for the same reason the colonists' demand for British goods was largely dependent on the value of the goods which they in turn could sell to her. This was particularly true of the West Indian Islands and the tobacco colonies on the American mainland. The highly specialised economies of the plantations, verging in some cases on monoculture, meant that the incomes of the colonists—and hence their demand for the imported goods on which they relied for their continued existence—were almost entirely derived from the sale of their export crops. And, under the Navigation Acts, the staple crops of these plantations could be sold only in other colonial markets or to the mother country.[2] Similar restrictions were not extended to the grain, furs and naval stores of the northern colonies until 1766, and Britain's direct imports from them were relatively small. But in

period. But a glance at the records is sufficient to show that the expansion was general, and cannot simply be attributed to trade with the conquered territories. Moreover, when the war was over, despite the gains in Canada, India and the West Indies, which were ratified by the Peace of Paris, the trade boom also came to an end.

[1] See Table 22.

[2] Insofar as the colonists could augment their incomes by borrowing, the direct dependence of their demand for imports on their export earnings would, of course, be modified. The development of the plantations depended heavily on British capital, and in the periods of low prices at the beginning of the century the planters were often in debt to their London factors. In the second half of the century, however, when prices rose, there was a marked increase in absentee ownership as the planters returned to England to live on the income from their estates. In this connection, it is interesting to note that whereas the gross barter terms of trade seem to have moved *against* Britain in the first half of the century as a whole, the series given in Table 21 suggest that the movement of relative prices was favourable to the mother country. After 1750, on the other hand, this disparity was certainly reduced and may have been reversed. As far as it goes, therefore, the evidence appears to be consistent with the view that the growth of exports in the early part of the century was partly the result of British overseas lending, and that the income from these investments later helped to finance the swelling volume of British imports.

Table 22. *Geographical distribution of eighteenth-century foreign trade*

(£000's)

	English imports				English re-exports				English exports			
	1700-1	1730-1	1750-1	1772-3	1700-1	1730-1	1750-1	1772-3	1700-1	1730-1	1750-1	1772-3
1. North-West Europe	1,387	1,424	1,120	1,086	1,333	1,800	1,790	3,009	1,941	1,475	2,458	1,461
2. The North	541	690	1,084	1,446	86	71	90	187	241	186	314	290
3. The South	1,650	1,715	1,445	1,769	233	234	248	459	1,478	2,321	3,562	2,132
4. British Islands	285	325	695	1,303	159	345	609	1,102	144	275	695	912
5. North America	372	655	877	1,442	106	208	384	522	256	351	971	2,460
6. West Indies	785	1,586	1,484	3,080	131	183	140	169	205	374	449	1,168
7. East India	775	943	1,101	2,203	11	32	68	69	114	116	585	824
8. Africa	24	43	43	80	64	128	99	285	81	105	89	492
9. The Fisheries	—	6	7	21	—	—	—	—	—	—	—	—
Grand total	5,819	7,386	7,855	12,432	2,136	3,002	3,428	5,800	4,461	5,203	9,125	9,739

	British imports				British re-exports				British exports			
	1772-3	1780-1	1789-90	1797-8	1772-3	1780-1	1789-90	1797-8	1772-3	1780-1	1789-90	1797-8
1. North-West Europe	1,220	2,172	1,841	2,426	3,865	1,280	2,664	8,056	1,539	2,298	2,640	2,063
2. The North	1,629	2,092	2,572	3,304	206	117	346	914	314	364	508	820
3. The South	1,793	748	2,573	1,273	464	123	282	180	2,143	755	2,229	975
4. British Islands	1,437	1,818	2,563	3,127	1,262	1,079	1,056	1,286	1,008	1,162	1,377	1,641
5. North America	1,977	219	1,351	1,666	605	419	468	364	2,649	1,359	3,295	5,900
6. West Indies	3,222	2,322	4,045	5,982	176	217	202	489	1,226	1,295	1,690	4,612
7. East India	2,203	1,749	3,256	5,785	69	35	77	75	824	821	2,096	1,640
8. Africa	80	29	87	62	285	90	282	437	492	165	517	650
9. The Fisheries	27	42	188	248	—	—	2	1	—	—	—	—
Grand total	13,595	11,189	18,476	23,903	6,930	3,359	5,380	11,802	10,196	8,218	14,350	18,298

Key: North-West Europe includes Flanders, France, Germany, Holland and Belle-Isle. The North includes Denmark and Norway, East Country, Poland, Prussia, Russia and Sweden. The South includes Gibraltar, Italy, Portugal and Madeira, Spain and the Canaries, Straits, Turkey and Venice. British Islands include Ireland, the Isle of Man and the Channel Islands. The Fisheries include Greenland, Iceland and the Northern and Southern Fisheries.

Sources: P.R.O. Customs 3 and 17. All figures exclude prize goods. The totals are those given in the ledgers and no allowance has been made for the revaluation of woollen exports from 1709. The figures do not, therefore, provide an accurate index of changes in the volume of trade between 1700-1 and 1730-1.

practice the northerners seem to have paid for a large part of their heavy imports of British manufactures by selling their own produce in the southern colonies and West Indian islands.[1] Thus, directly and indirectly, the fortunes of the most rapidly growing section of Britain's export trade were closely bound up with the fortunes of the southern planters. And since it was a cardinal objective of Britain's commercial policy to obtain her imports of primary products on the terms most favourable to the mother country, the chief limiting factor to the growth of her exports was the restricted purchasing power of her colonial customers. The only occasions in the eighteenth century when exports increased and the terms of trade were favourable the Spanish Succession and American Wars, during which the total volume of trade, and in particular imports, had fallen sharply. The prices of imports rose in war time, but this was probably mainly due to the increased costs of freight and insurance, and so was of little benefit to the producers. With the return of peace, Britain's customers were able to clear their accumulated stocks, and though the prices of imports fell in the mother country, the volume of imports and exports rose together. But these were recovery booms, and as soon as the immediate effects of the wars had passed, the normal relationship between the terms of trade and the volume of exports reasserted itself.

The association between the growth of exports and the terms of trade does not mean, however, that the *total* volume of trade always tended to grow faster when the movement of relative prices was unfavourable to the mother country. Until technical change began to exert a decisive influence on manufacturing costs,[2] the rate of expansion of the combined totals of imports and exports mainly depended on Britain's demand for imports, which seems to have been fairly elastic in the eighteenth century. In the first half of the century, both exports and imports tended to fluctuate with the price of imports, therefore, but in opposite directions. Hence it made little difference to the overall rate of commercial expansion which way the terms of trade happened to move. From 1715 to 1730, when the supply of imports outstripped the growth of home demand, Britain enjoyed the benefits of cheap colonial produce at the expense of her export trades. In the thirties and early forties, when the supply of imports dwindled, mainly, it appears, as a result of crop failures and restrictions on output in the West Indian islands,[3] exports increased; but until the outbreak of war in 1739 the overall rate of commercial growth was almost exactly the

[1] For the organisation of the American trade at this time, see, *inter alia*, E. R. Johnson and others, *History of the Domestic and Foreign Commerce of the United States*, 2 vols. (Washington, 1915); L. J. Ragatz, *op. cit.*; R. Pares, *War and Trade in the West Indies* (Oxford, 1936).

[2] When this happened (notably in the early decades of the nineteenth century) the expansion of British trade was again associated with an adverse movement in the terms of trade. This, however, reflects the familiar inverse relation between the productivity increment and the terms of trade.

[3] See R. Pares, *War and Trade in the West Indies, op. cit.* p. 474.

same as before. It was only after 1745, when the volume and prices of imported goods rose together, that the pace of commercial expansion began to quicken. It seems clear that at the end of the century this increased demand for imports was stimulated by Pitt's reform of the customs duties, and we know, for example, that tariff reductions resulted in a prodigious expansion of the Jamaica coffee plantations,[1] and in the rapid growth of legal imports of tea, in the last twenty years of the century. But for most of the century, the burden of import duties was rising, and if we want to understand the growing import demand, we must look for the factors which were promoting economic expansion at home.

As we have already observed, it is impossible not to be struck by the close connection between the pattern of growth at home and the course of population change,[2] and it is natural to inquire how far the two were causally related. Recent research has done much to emphasise the part played by population increase in easing the labour scarcity which seems to have been an outstanding feature of the British economy in the late seventeenth and early eighteenth centuries, and in providing the labour force on which the industrial system rested.[3] But at first sight the correlation seems too close to fit this explanation. For an increase in population might be expected to have a significant effect on the supply of labour only after an interval of sixteen or eighteen years[4]; even when all allowances have been made for the uncertainty of the statistics and the possible influence of child labour, it does not seem possible for the acceleration in the rate of economic growth in the 1740's and again in the 1780's to have been directly due to an increase in the size of the labour force, at any rate as a result of population increase. Nor is it obvious that an increase in population would have promoted an acceleration in the rate of economic growth through its effect on demand. For although an increase in the number of mouths to be fed and bodies to be clothed may enlarge wants, will it necessarily increase effective demand? Clearly, therefore, if we are to understand the significance of the population changes, we must consider some of the other factors in the situation.

A good deal of recent discussion has been devoted to the effects of variations in harvests on agricultural prices and the distribution of incomes. In an economy still so largely dominated by agriculture, it

[1] Cf. L. J. Ragatz, *op. cit.* p. 42.

[2] It should be noted that in this respect our findings agree remarkably well with the results of a regional study ,'The Vale of Trent, 1670–1800', by J. D. Chambers, which were published in 1957 as a supplement to the *Economic History Review*. In the discussion which follows, we have drawn heavily on Professor Chambers' valuable remarks on the economic implications of demographic change.

[3] See, for example, D. C. Coleman, 'Labour in the English Economy of the Seventeenth Century', *Econ. Hist. Rev.*, second series, vol. VIII (1956), pp. 280–95; J. D. Chambers, 'Enclosure and Labour Supply in the Industrial Revolution', *ibid.*, second series, vol. V (1953), pp. 319–43.

[4] Cf. T. R. Malthus, *Principles of Political Economy* (1836), pp. 254, 319–20; Karl Marx, *Capital*, vol. I (Everyman ed.), pp. 700–1.

is, of course, natural to ascribe a major role to changes in the fortunes of the farming community, and the debate on the consequences of high and low agricultural prices is probably as old as the English Corn Laws. Professor Ashton, following Adam Smith, has suggested that in the eighteenth century good harvests meant, not only an increased return to human effort in the agricultural sector, but also an increased demand for labour to gather the harvest, higher real wages, and hence an increase in the demand for the products of industry.[1] As an explanation of short-run fluctuations, this theory is plausible enough, although the evidence at our disposal makes it difficult to check. Certainly the influence of harvests can be detected in fluctuations in output in many of the industries for which production data are directly available, but since these were mainly industries which, in the short run at least, depended on agriculture for their supply of raw materials, it does not follow that this was entirely due to the income effects of good harvests.

Here, however, we are mainly concerned with long-term trends, and several students have argued that the effects of a series of good harvests may have been very different. For owing to the inelastic demand for foodstuffs—and especially cereals—good harvests meant, not only a rise in real wages, but a fall in agricultural incomes. In the short run this might not be important, since the losses in one year could be made good in the next. But the combination of a succession of good harvests with a stationary population may well have had such a depressing effect on the demand from the agricultural sector as to offset the stimulus which the industrial economy derived from high or rising real wages. It is true, of course, that over a period of years it may be difficult to distinguish improvements in agricultural productivity due to favourable climatic conditions from those due to technical change. The suggestion here, however, is simply that variations in the internal terms of trade between workshop and farm may have had a similar effect on the home demand for industrial goods as did changes in import and export prices on the fortunes of the export trade. And since it is probably fair to assume that the demand for cereals was less elastic than that for sugar and tobacco, it is possible that the economy as a whole may have lost more from sagging demand for industrial goods than it gained from abundant supplies of agricultural products. As Professor Habakkuk puts it: 'The low or stationary agricultural prices of the earlier decades of the century had a depressing effect on agricultural investment and indirectly on the demand for industrial goods. The rising prices over most of the second half of the century stimulated agricultural investment and led to increased demand for industrial goods; they led not so much to a shift of income between the industrial and agricultural sectors as to an increase in the income of both.[2]'

For the first six decades of the eighteenth century there is a good

[1] T. S. Ashton, *An Economic History of England: The Eighteenth Century, op. cit.* pp. 60–1.

[2] H. J. Habakkuk, 'Essays in Bibliography and Criticism: The Eighteenth Century', *Econ. Hist. Rev.*, second series, vol. VIII (1956), pp. 437–8.

Table 23. *Index numbers of the price of wheat in relation to the prices of producer and other consumer goods*

(1700/1 = 100)

	Wheat prices	Other prices	Index of relationship
1695–1705	122	105	116
1700–1710	105	98	107
1705–1715	121	99	122
1710–1720	109	97	112
1715–1725	92	92	100
1720–1730	99	93	106
1725–1735	94	90	104
1730–1740	84	86	98
1735–1745	86	88	98
1740–1750	84	91	92
1745–1755	90	88	102
1750–1760	101	91	111
1755–1765	106	96	110
1760–1770	117	96	122
1765–1775	141	97	145
1770–1780	136	102	134
1775–1785	132	108	122
1780–1790	142	1.10	129
1785–1795	148	113	131
1790–1800	196	128	153
1795–1805	250	[146]	170

Sources: Wheat prices—average of prices at London and Winchester from Beveridge, *op. cit.* pp. 81, 567 (B). Other prices—unweighted average of index numbers for producer goods (− 1800/1) and consumer goods (exclusive of cereals) from E. B. Schumpeter, 'English Prices and Public Finance', 1660–1822, *Review of Economics Statistics*, vol. xx (1938), pp. 21–37. All figures relate to harvest years beginning and ending at Michaelmas in the years specified.

deal of evidence in support of at least the first part of this hypothesis. It is difficult to measure changes in relative prices, but it appears from Table 23 that at the end of the seventeenth century, and for the first two decades of the eighteenth, the prices of cereals were, on the average, higher, both absolutely and in relation to those of producer goods and other consumer goods, than they were to be at any time in the next thirty or forty years. According to Mrs Gilboy's figures, money wages rose little, if at all, at this time, and real wages may even have fallen slightly[1]; and it is possible that the modest industrial expansion suggested by the scanty evidence for the period may have owed something at least to agricultural prosperity. It is true that prices were not consistently high throughout this period, and for most of the first decade of the century they were a good deal lower than in the years immediately before or after. It is significant, however, that in the second decade nearly all the statistical series indicate a definite advance in output which coincides, not only with the foreign-trade boom which marked the end of the long wars with Louis XIV, but with the period of generally high agricultural prices from 1708 to 1717. In the next

[1] See above, pp. 19–22.

twenty-five years, on the other hand, when the output of industrial goods seems to have been virtually stationary, agricultural prices were low and tended to fall even in relation to a generally sagging price-level.[1] During the early part of this period, the export trade was also in the doldrums, and it would seem that the production of goods for the home market was at any rate maintained. It should be noted, however, that the fall in agricultural prices was temporarily arrested in the late twenties, with the result that the average price level of the twenties was not much below that for the previous decade. In the thirties and early forties, on the other hand, when the export trade revived, there was no corresponding increase in the total volume of industrial output, and in some sectors, notably the mining and metal industries, the supply of goods to the home market seems to have dropped sharply. It is significant, therefore, that it was precisely in this period that agricultural prices reached their lowest point, and, while money and real wages were exceptionally high, that there are signs of a sharp depression amongst the farming community, marked by the accumulation of large arrears of rent and, in some cases, even the appearance of vacant holdings.[2] It was not till after 1743, when agricultural prices started their long climb and rent arrears began to disappear, that the home market for industrial goods revived, and, at the same time, the rising demand for imports helped to produce a further expansion of the export trade.

Whether it is also true, as the estimates given in Tables 19 and 20 imply, that the national income as a whole tended to grow more rapidly when agricultural prices were relatively high, it is difficult to say in the absence of reliable statistics of grain output. In so far as prices rose as a result of increasing demand for agricultural produce, this is, of course, likely to have been the case. But when prices rose simply as a result of bad harvests, there is no reason to assume that the increased demand for industrial goods more than offset the loss in agricultural output. There appears, however, to be a strong prima-facie case for the view that the growth of the home market for industrial goods was closely bound up with the fortunes of the agricultural community, in much the same way as the growth of the export trade depended on the prosperity of the primary producers overseas.

Two obvious explanations may be suggested. In the first place, it should be noted that until 1750 periods of comparatively high agricultural prices were not only periods of population expansion at home,

[1] It seems likely that the figures given in Table 23 understate the relative fall in agricultural prices for much of this period. This is because the index we have used for other prices includes the prices of animal products which moved in much the same way as the price of cereals, and because it is heavily weighted with imported products which were also falling in price for much of this period. The index may also rather understate the rise in the general price level in the 1760's (and hence somewhat exaggerate the rise in the relative price of cereals), since, as we have seen, import prices were low at that time, but the prices of most industrial products seem to have been rising.

[2] See G. E. Mingay, 'The Agricultural Depression, 1730–1750', *Econ. Hist. Rev.*, second series, vol. VIII (1956), pp. 323–38.

but of growing overseas demand for grain. Corn exports rose in the first quarter of the century, and again in the late forties; from the early twenties until the early forties they were virtually stationary. Exports of corn were encouraged by bounty during this period, but for the most part, the increase in the incomes of farmers, landlords and middlemen exporters associated with an increase in grain exports represented a net addition to incomes at home.

Second, and more important, however, the expectation that the redistribution of incomes arising from low corn prices should have stimulated industrial demand assumes that the marginal propensity of wage-earners and the non-agricultural sector as a whole to consume manufactured goods was in fact higher than that of farmers and land-lords. If England had been a society in which the market and taste for manufactured goods was highly developed, and in which, at the same time, the agricultural community tended to hoard its gains, such an assumption might be warranted. But it was not. For centuries English agriculture had had extensive ties of varying strength with the market, and by the eighteenth century it was largely organised on a capitalist basis: the typical farmer was not a peasant toiling for his own sub-sistence, but an employer of wage-labour holding his land at an economic rent from men who not infrequently ploughed their profits back into agriculture, or into transport, industry and trade. Much industrial output was produced by agricultural wage-earners or their families on a domestic basis. On the other hand, it is probably true that in England, as in any other largely pre-industrial economy, the economic horizons of the mass of the population tended to be narrow, and the range of consumer goods small. Hence the demand for manu-factured goods may have been relatively inelastic, and a rise in real wages may have led, not to an increase in their consumption, but to an increase in leisure—or, as contemporaries unanimously complained, to 'idleness'. Probably rising real wages did stimulate an increase in the consumption of some goods, and it is significant that the thirties and early forties witnessed the height of the gin mania. But evidently the demand for gin was not sufficient either to arrest the fall of agricul-tural prices or to provide the basis for rapid industrial growth.

When prices rose, on the other hand, agricultural incomes also rose and, at the same time, industrial artisans and the wage-earning popula-tion as a whole had to work harder to maintain their traditional standard of life. It is not surprising, therefore, that the rise in prices after 1743 seems to have been associated with a modest rise in total output per head. Moreover, it is important to note that the rise in the price of foodstuffs was brought about, not by a decline in agricultural output—indeed the evidence suggests that the yield of the soil in the decades after 1745 must have been substantially greater than it had been before—but mainly by an increase in the number of mouths to be fed. For a growing population and the increase in the size of families which it brought tended to transform the position of the labouring population. Not only did it give an immediate stimulus to wants, but it also meant that, as families grew up and population too continued to expand at an increasing rate, competition in the labour market began to replace the traditional scarcity.[1] From about the middle of the eighteenth century it is possible to discern a significant change in the attitude of contemporaries towards the labouring population. Complaints of the recalcitrance of labourers diminished and some writers began to argue that high, not low, wages provided the greater incentive to industry.[2] By 1776 Adam Smith could assert that the problem among piece-workers, at least, was not that they were idle, but that overwork tended to 'ruin their health and constitution in a few years'.[3]

In these circumstances, food would necessarily constitute the first claim on available incomes, and since the agricultural community was thus assured of an expanding market for its produce, the significance of harvest variations began to change. Provided that farmers and landlords continued to spend or invest their additional incomes, it might make little difference to industrial demand whether the prices of food were low or high. And if the addition to total output resulting from favourable harvests was no longer offset by losses in the industrial sector we might expect the national income as a whole to rise most rapidly when the prices of food were comparatively low. This, indeed, is what the data suggest. As we have seen, it appears that the period from the mid-forties until the early sixties was one of all-round expansion in both industry and agriculture. Despite the very heavy exports of grain in the ten years after 1745 and the unprecedented expansion of population in that and the ensuing decades, the rise in agricultural prices was at first comparatively modest, and their average level rose no higher than in the first two decades of the century.[4] Gradually, however, the growing population began to press against the available resources: exports of corn dwindled, and, with the poor harvests of the late sixties and early seventies, prices rose much more steeply, and Britain was for the first time compelled to import substantial quantities of grain. This brought a sharp increase in agricultural investment. Until the late fifties, the farming community evidently had little incentive to indulge in ambitious schemes of agricultural improvement.

---

[1] Cf. J. D. Chambers, 'The Vale of Trent', *op. cit.* pp. 4–5.

[2] A. W. Coats, 'Changing Attitudes to Labour in the Mid-Eighteenth Century', *Econ. Hist. Rev.*, second series, vol. XI (1958), pp. 35–51.

[3] *Wealth of Nations* (Everyman ed.), vol. I, p. 73.

[4] Probably the increase in agricultural incomes was greater than the rise in prices suggests, since output was also increasing and it seems unlikely that costs per unit of output were rising and they may well have been falling. Apart from the possibility, which most recent research suggests, that costs had fallen since the beginning of the century, as a result of the gradual improvement in agricultural methods, it is difficult to believe that there could have been an increase in the labour force in the decade after 1745 large enough to account for the very large increase in grain output which our estimates imply. It seems reasonable to assume, therefore, that the apparent increase was in part due to abundant harvests and possibly also to the sale abroad of stocks accumulated in previous years.

From 1730 to 1744, the number of enclosure bills presented in Parliament had averaged about forty per decade, and in the ten years ending in 1754 the total was only forty-nine. In the next ten years, however, the number jumped to 283, and in the following decade to 531.[1] There is no evidence that this wave of investment directly stimulated industrial demand, but it does not seem to have been accompanied by any contraction of the home market for industrial goods. High agricultural prices may have contributed to the trade recession of the early seventies, which appears to have been particularly severe in the linen trade,[2] but in the ten years ending in 1774, the volume of industrial goods consumed at home seems to have risen more than in previous decades. At the same time, however, the rise in the internal price-level no doubt contributed to the favourable swing in the external terms of trade during this period, and hence to the stagnation in the export trade; and since the output of agriculture and of the industries dependent on the land was almost stationary, it is not surprising that our estimates suggest a fall in the overall rate of expansion in both the major sectors of the economy, certainly in relation to the rapidly growing population, and possibly also in absolute terms.[3]

In the late seventies, the effects of enclosures began to make themselves felt. The price of corn was stabilised and, as other prices probably continued to rise as a result of the high cost of imports during the American War, its 'real' price dropped. After 1777, the wave of enclosures ebbed, and for a time, at least, arrears of rent testify to comparatively depressed conditions for the farming community.[4] But again there seems to have been a steady growth in the home market. Despite the virtual collapse of foreign trade in the war years, the available indicators suggest that the rate of growth of even those industries

---

[1] The annual numbers of enclosure bills from 1719–1835 are given in *S.P. 1836*, vol. VII, Part 2, p. 501. The decade totals are as follows:

1720–9	25	1760–9	385	1804	782
1725–34	37	1765–74	531	1800–9	847
1730–9	39	1770–9	660	1805–14	983
1735–44	41	1775–84	451	1810–9	853
1740–9	36	1780–9	246	1815–24	368
1745–54	49	1785–94	280	1820–9	220
1750–9	137	1790–9	469	1825–34	177
1755–64	283	1795			

In considering these figures, it should, of course, be remembered that they do not constitute an index of total agricultural investment, nor do they cover enclosures by agreement.

[2] Cf. D. Macpherson, *Annals of Commerce*, vol. III (1805), pp. 546–7.

[3] It has been suggested that the rise in agricultural prices at this time may have been due, not to population pressure, but to an increasing demand for food as a result of rising real incomes stemming from developments in other sectors of the economy. (A. J. Youngson, *Possibilities of Economic Progress* (1959), p. 123 n.) If this were so, it would mean, of course, that we may have seriously underestimated the increase in agricultural output. But if real incomes were rising, we should expect the demand for such commodities as beer and meat to be much more seriously affected than that for bread. In fact, however, the excise series support the view that the production of these commodities lagged behind the growth of population.

[4] G. E. Mingay, 'The Agricultural Depression', *op. cit.* p. 326.

which were normally most dependent on overseas markets was only slightly lower than in the previous decade. And when the return of peace brought with it a great revival of foreign trade, while prices of agricultural produce remained comparatively low, the economy experienced a new wave of expansion which was checked only by the combined effects of commercial difficulties, population pressure and bad harvests during the Napoleonic Wars.

Thus it appears that the importance which economic historians have recently ascribed to demographic factors—or, more precisely, the balance between population and other resources, and particularly land —in shaping the pattern of eighteenth-century economic growth is justified. In the early part of the century, Britain already had a relatively well-developed commercial agriculture, capable of supporting a larger industrial population than she in fact possessed. Moreover, she had acquired extensive overseas markets for the products of her industries, and colonial territories producing cash crops of foodstuffs and raw materials which complemented the products of the mother country. But since these territories were, in the strictest sense of the term, economic dependencies, largely cut off from outside influences, the expansion of the markets they provided was closely bound up with the development of the metropolitan economy. Although a large and probably growing proportion of Britain's industrial output was exported during this period, the growth of her overseas trade seems to have been held back by the slow pace of advance at home. Yet there appears to have been no serious shortage of capital at this time, and, as Professor Ashton has emphasised, interest rates were generally low.[1] Nor does slow technological advance appear to have been a limiting factor,[2] for the pace of *innovation* was even slower, at any rate in the metal industries; and some of the technical developments of the first two decades of the century, such as the Newcomen engine, the use of coal and coke in the smelting of iron, and the introduction of a successful means of producing tinplate, had to wait until the fifth and later decades before they were extensively applied. On the other hand, we know that labour was scarce in the early eighteenth century, and the stagnation of population aggravated this problem and contributed to the depression of both agricultural incomes and the demand for industrial goods.

It may be asked why the scarcity of labour did not stimulate labour-saving innovations, and why low agricultural prices did not encourage the migration of capital and labour from agriculture to industry. The answer to both questions may be that to some extent they did. Certainly landlords seem to have experienced difficulty in finding tenants,[3] and in the worst period of the agricultural depression there were some cases

---

[1] T. S. Ashton, *An Economic History of England: The Eighteenth Century, op. cit.* p. 29.

[2] The 'dip in the curve of scientific progress', which Prof. Bernal dates from as early as 1698, seems to have been even more striking than the slow tempo of technical advance. See J. D. Bernal, *Science in History* (1954), pp. 358 ff.

[3] G. E. Mingay, 'The Agricultural Depression', *op. cit.* pp. 328–30.

of vacant holdings. It has been argued that in the period from 1680 to 1740 big farmers and landlords were in the strongest position, and it is possible that the pressure of the land tax and the competition of larger and more efficient estates drove some of the lesser gentry and yeomen to abandon the land for other pursuits.[1] We shall see in the next chapter that the first half of the eighteenth century witnessed a significant movement of population from the rural areas to London and, less strongly, to some of the industrial counties. Moreover, this was not—as it seems to have been in later decades—simply a movement of the surplus population engendered by a high rate of natural increase, for as we have already noted, the population of several of the agricultural counties actually fell. On the other hand, the wage statistics suggest that the depression was not severe enough to reduce the demand for agricultural labour sufficiently to check the upward pressure on wage rates, while a succession of favourable seasons was not likely to generate a strong movement out of agriculture.

Similar considerations apply to the course of technological change. The limited technical innovations of the second quarter of the century were indeed largely aimed at economising labour, particularly in the textile industries. But labour scarcity is more likely to induce rapid technical progress in an expanding economy than in one where demand is limited and output virtually stationary. It was not until economic expansion was well under way, in the 1760's and seventies, when the pressures of a growing population were beginning to stimulate investment in measures designed to economise other resources, such as land (enclosures) and coal (canals), that the great labour-saving inventions of the eighteenth century laid the basis for the revolution in the textile industries and the introduction of the factory system.[2] Nor was it entirely by chance that these discoveries came when they did, for by the 1760's competitions were being held for the best inventions.[3] There is not much doubt that the widespread improvements and innovations in agriculture, transport[4] and industry helped to maintain if not to increase real incomes per head in the last quarter of the century. But it seems equally clear that the quest for technical improvement which gave rise to these revolutionary innovations was itself stimulated by the great upsurge of population which began a generation before.

[1] H. J. Habakkuk, 'English Landownership, 1680–1740', *Econ. Hist. Rev.*, vol. x (1940), pp. 2–17.

[2] Cf. T. S. Ashton, *The Industrial Revolution, 1760–1830* (1948), pp. 91–2.

[3] P. Mantoux, *The Industrial Revolution in the Eighteenth Century* (1928), p. 220; M. H. Dobb, *Studies in the Development of Capitalism* (1946), pp. 270–1.

[4] Little has been said here about the developments in transport, though it would be difficult to overestimate the importance of falling transport costs in promoting the growth of the home market. It should be noted, however, that the advances in this field also date from the period when economic expansion and population growth were beginning to make expenditure on the improvement of communications financially attractive: the first canals were begun in the late fifties, and the great age of the turnpikes was from 1745 to 1760.

CHAPTER III

INDUSTRIALISATION AND POPULATION CHANGE IN THE EIGHTEENTH AND EARLY NINETEENTH CENTURIES

SOMETHING has already been said about the broad trends in the growth of population during the two and a half centuries covered by these studies. But in view of the importance which we have attached to population growth in shaping the pattern of economic change traced in the last chapter, it may be worth attempting to probe somewhat deeper into the demographic revolution which marked the early stages of industrialisation. The connection between economic and demographic change at this time has long been a topic of interest to economic historians, but the nature of the causal relationships involved remains a matter for dispute. Opinion is divided between the classical theory, held by economic writers from Smith to Marx, that the growth of population was engendered by the demand for labour of an expanding industrial economy, and the contrary view that the Industrial Revolution was itself a response, in part at least, to the challenge afforded by a rising population. It is not surprising that this should be so, since, as we have seen, even the proximate causes of population growth during this period are still a matter for debate. This is partly because the attempt to measure changes in birth and death rates before the first Census of Population and before the civil registration of births and deaths is a hazardous undertaking whose results are open to question; but it is also true that the amount which can be deduced from the global statistics alone is strictly limited. We know that the increase in population was accompanied by fundamental changes in its distribution, and before we can hope to give a convincing explanation of the national upsurge we need to know much more about these regional variations in the pattern of growth—how far they can be attributed to internal migration and how far to differences in the rate of natural increase, and to what extent changes in birth and death rates also varied from place to place. It is not possible to answer such questions satisfactorily on the basis of the national records alone, and most of the relevant information which has so far been assembled relates to the nineteenth century rather than the eighteenth. But although, as Professor Habakkuk has remarked, a complete account will 'need a generation of collaborative work on parish registers and other local sources',[1] something can be gleaned from the available national statistics. In this chapter, therefore, we shall attempt to sketch some

---

[1] H. J. Habakkuk, 'English Population in the Eighteenth Century', *Econ. Hist. Rev.*, second series, vol. VI (1953), p. 130.

of the outlines of the picture and to venture a few preliminary hypotheses which, it is hoped, may before long be tested by detailed local research.

1. THE CHANGING DISTRIBUTION OF POPULATION

In an analysis of the process of population growth and its connection with industrialisation, it would clearly be desirable to distinguish between the growth of urban and rural areas. On the other hand, it is obvious that until the introduction of factory production on a large scale, industrialisation and urbanisation were not necessarily synonymous, and, in the eighteenth century at least, information for different counties may be as illuminating as the differences between town and country. It so happens that the early censuses—which constitute the starting-point of our inquiry—provide us with the data for each county in summary form, and the adoption of a different basis of analysis would not only be laborious, but would also raise the largely intractable problems of urban boundaries and populations.[1] For these reasons, the main unit considered here will be the geographical county.

Until 1801, there are no reliable statistics of the population of the different counties in England and Wales. The best estimates of the total population—those made by Farr, Brownlee and Talbot Griffith[2] —were obtained by estimating the natural increase of the population from the figures of baptisms and burials recorded in the parish registers, and then counting backwards from the enumerated population of 1801. This method assumes that eighteenth-century population figures were not seriously affected by migration, and though the assumption may be warranted for the country as a whole,[3] it certainly cannot be applied to smaller units. The early census volumes contain some estimates made by Rickman of the county population in 1700 and 1750, which were apparently derived from the figures of recorded births on the assumption that the baptism rates in each county remained constant throughout the eighteenth century. But since the baptism rate for the country as a whole rose considerably, his estimates of the county populations in 1700 are, on the average, too low; and since most of the increase in the baptism rate seems to have taken place before 1750, it is also likely that his figures seriously exaggerate the rate of population growth in the first half of the century.[4] Towards the end of his life,

---

[1] For a discussion of the boundary problem and its implications at the beginning of the following century, see Barbara Hammond, 'Urban Death-Rates in the early Nineteenth Century', *Economic History*, No. 3 (January 1928), pp. 419–28. There are, of course, no reliable statistics and few trustworthy estimates of urban populations before 1801.

[2] John Brownlee, 'The History of the Birth and Death Rates in England and Wales . . .', *Public Health*, vol. XXIX (1916), pp. 211–22, 228–38; G. Talbot Griffith, *Population Problems of the Age of Malthus* (Cambridge, 1926), chapter II.

[3] G. T. Griffith, *op. cit.* pp. 5–6.

[4] The changes in the national birth and death rates in the course of the eighteenth century are discussed in more detail below, pp. 122–35. The argument here, and in much of what follows, assumes that the estimates of the population of the country as a whole, which were made by Farr, Griffith and Brownlee, were approximately correct. The assumption may

however, Rickman made more elaborate estimates which were published after his death in the introduction to the 1841 census. These new calculations were based on figures supplied by the parish clergy of the number of births, deaths and marriages registered in each county in 1699–1701 and 1749–51, as well as some earlier periods which need not concern us here. Assuming in each case that the average number of entries in the parish registers at each date bore the same relationship to the total population as they did in 1800–1, Rickman made three sets of estimates of the population of each county, and then took a simple average of the three.

Now clearly, the assumption underlying the resulting averages is that errors in the individual series due to changes in baptism, burial and marriage rates in the course of the eighteenth century tended to cancel each other out.[1] Taking the century as a whole, there is some evidence that this was the case, and, indeed, Rickman's final figure for the population of England and Wales in 1700, 6,045,000, falls neatly between those given by Farr, on the one hand, and Brownlee and Talbot Griffith, on the other, which were mentioned above as the best available national estimates of the population in the eighteenth century. More important, Rickman's figures for individual counties agree surprisingly well with some independent estimates for the end of the seventeenth century which were made by Gonner on the basis of the hearth-tax returns furnished by Gregory King.[2] There are a number of exceptions, but apart from the figures for Middlesex and Devonshire —where, as we shall see, arithmetical errors may be involved—most of the significant discrepancies can be attributed to boundary differences. In the north, for example, there are wide variations in the figures for individual counties, but the regional totals are almost identical.

Unfortunately, however, we have at present no similar set of independent estimates of the county populations in the middle of the eighteenth century, and it is by no means certain that the assumption underlying Rickman's estimates holds good at the later date. True, the baptism rate rose and the burial rate fell in the eighteenth century, but whereas most of the increase in the former occurred before 1750, the decline in the latter only became significant after that date. It is not surprising, therefore, that Rickman's second set of estimates, which

be questioned, and it has been variously argued that Brownlee's estimates, for example, (which have been utilised throughout this volume) either overstated or understated the size of the population in 1701, according to the point of view of the authors concerned. In defence of Brownlee, it can be said that his figure agrees fairly well with a quite independent estimate referred to below which was made by Gregory King at the end of the seventeenth century on the basis of the hearth-tax returns. It may be that both King and Brownlee were wrong, but until more evidence is available it seems reasonable to assume that they were not far wide of the mark.

[1] Not, as has sometimes been implied, that all three rates remained constant. If the estimates really involved such an assumption they would be worthless.

[2] E. C. K. Gonner, 'The Population of England in the Eighteenth Century', *J. Roy. Statist. Soc.*, vol. LXXVI (1912–13), pp. 261–96. The hearth-tax returns given by King referred to 1690.

yield a figure for the total population in 1750 of 6,517,000, also appear to exaggerate the increase in the population as a whole in the first half of the century, though fortunately to a much smaller extent than the first. If we could accept the assumption made by Gonner, that errors in the aggregate figures are likely to be spread evenly over the country, this objection to the estimates might not be serious. But, in fact, it is most unlikely that changes in baptism and burial rates were the same in different parts of the country, and hence there is a possibility that Rickman's county figures may be quite seriously in error in individual cases.

These limitations should be borne in mind when considering the evidence summarised in Table 24 as the figures given for the county population in 1701 and 1751 are based on Rickman's averages. Two corrections have, however, been made. In the first place, Rickman's figures have been adjusted throughout so that the total populations in 1701 and 1751 agree with Brownlee's estimates for those years. This procedure will not affect the relative position of the individual counties at either date, and hence any incidental errors which may arise from local variations in the changes in baptism, burial and marriage rates will remain. But in general the adjusted series should represent more accurately than Rickman's the contrast in the rates of increase between the first and second halves of the eighteenth century. Secondly, Rickman's figures for Middlesex have been rejected and replaced by estimates of our own.[1] In view of the inadequacy of the data on which they are based, the figures cannot be conclusive. But two things may be said in favour of the revised estimates. The trend they suggest is more in keeping with the course of population growth suggested by Rickman's figures for the other three counties in the London area— Surrey, Kent and Essex; and the combined figures for all four counties in 1701 are within 2 per cent of the corresponding total derived from the hearth-tax returns. Unfortunately, it is not so easy to revise Rickman's estimates for Devonshire, which are also open to suspicion, and

---

[1] According to the estimates derived from the hearth-tax returns, the population of Middlesex at the end of the seventeenth century was less than half a million. Rickman, however, gives figures of 730,000 for 1700, and 553,000 for 1750. Unfortunately, the detailed evidence on which his estimates were based was not published, and until 1780 we now have figures of baptisms and burials only for isolated years at decade intervals, and annual marriage data only from 1754. But apart from the general implausibility of Rickman's estimates, to which Gonner drew attention, the information we do possess suggests very strongly that they were mistaken. The implied decline in the population between 1700 and 1750 is apparent in all three of the series on which his final averages were based. Yet the number of baptisms and burials recorded rose between the two dates. On recomputing the estimates from the available data, it appears that Rickman's figures for 1750 were probably correct, but that those for 1700 were in both cases too high. Secondly, his estimate from the marriage data of 253,000 for the population in 1750 is impossibly low. The corresponding figure for 1700 is nearly 580,000, and if we extrapolate backwards on the basis of the number of marriages recorded in the latter part of the century, it is clear that the population in 1750 must have been over 500,000. Accordingly, we have replaced Rickman's estimates from the baptisms and burials for 1700 and from the marriages for 1750 by our own, and have finally struck new averages. It is these averages which underlie the estimates for Middlesex given in Table 24.

the figures for this county should therefore be treated with the greatest reserve.[1]

To trace the connection between economic and demographic change, it would clearly be desirable to have estimates of county populations less widely separated in time. It is doubtful whether it is possible, in the present state of our knowledge, to obtain satisfactory figures for each decade, but as a first step we made estimates comparable to Rickman's for the year 1781. These estimates were also adjusted to bring the total for England and Wales into line with Brownlee's figure for 1781, and the results are shown in detail in column 3a of Table 24. As a check on the reliability of the figures, we then made a second series of estimates which are set out in column 3b. These were based on the marriage data alone, but to eliminate the effect of fluctuations in the marriage cycle, eleven-year averages of the number of marriages from 1776 to 1786 and from 1796 to 1806 were employed. In most cases the differences between the two series are comparatively small. In twenty-four of the forty-three counties the discrepancies are less than 5 per cent, and in only two, Bedfordshire and the East Riding of Yorkshire, do they exceed 10 per cent. Nevertheless, such differences are large enough to complicate any short-term analysis. In the case of Bedfordshire, to take an extreme example, it depends on which figure is preferred whether the apparent increase in population in the second half of the eighteenth century took place largely before or after 1781.

In general, it seems likely that the second set of estimates, from the marriage data alone, represents the closest approximation to the truth. In the last two decades of the century, the baptism and marriage rates for the country as a whole were almost stationary, while the burial rate showed a sharp decline. We should expect, therefore, the estimates obtained by Rickman's method to be too high, and in fact the unadjusted total for England and Wales came to 8,193,000 compared with Brownlee's figure of 7,531,000. The uncorrected total from the marriage data alone, 7,204,000, is much nearer the mark, and if an adequate allowance could be made for the armed forces[2] and for the fact that the returns for the years after 1800 were rather more complete

---

[1] In this case the error appears to lie in the estimates from the marriage data. On the basis of the number of marriages, Rickman estimated the population at 357,000 in 1700 and 370,000 in 1750. But since the enumerated population in 1801 was only 343,000, and the trend of marriages was strongly upward in the latter part of the eighteenth century, it is difficult to see how such extraordinarily high estimates were obtained. It would, of course, be possible to correct the estimate for 1750 by extrapolation, as in the case of Middlesex, and then to strike new averages; but in the absence of the necessary marriage data there is no means of checking the figure for 1700. It is conceivable that the figures for Devonshire given in Table 24 correctly indicate the trend of population in the first half of the century, but, as the estimates from the hearth-tax returns imply, they may well overstate its *level* by something like 30 per cent.

[2] Since soldiers and sailors abroad could presumably not be married in England, our estimates were based on the ratio between the number of marriages from 1776 to 1806 and the *de facto* population in 1801. In practice, however, the movement of troops in and out of the country probably means that the marriage rates obtained in this way were somewhat too high and the estimates of population for 1781 correspondingly low.

Table 24. *Estimated population of England and Wales, by counties, 1701–1831*

	1701	1751	1781 (a)	1781 (b)	1801	1831
A. Agricultural						
Bedfordshire	52,978	55,407	63,612	56,551	65,416	96,547
Berkshire	76,790	85,977	104,309	108,696	112,701	147,008
Buckinghamshire	75,291	81,723	100,137	97,733	110,873	148,161
Cambridgeshire	81,113	72,674	87,002	81,777	92,198	145,558
Essex	168,527	180,465	222,946	207,739	233,664	321,044
Herefordshire	74,210	70,426	84,752	88,428	92,038	112,450
Hertfordshire	72,602	76,457	96,679	91,577	100,691	144,938
Huntingdonshire	31,533	30,258	41,433	37,879	38,767	53,784
Lincolnshire	179,095	153,270	210,153	195,078	215,213	321,001
Norfolk	242,511	221,255	240,102	256,081	282,096	394,399
Oxfordshire	84,005	89,227	101,010	102,144	113,119	153,851
Rutland	15,404	11,742	15,444	15,708	16,878	19,601
Suffolk	161,245	159,577	195,373	188,981	217,147	299,618
Sussex	97,199	94,315	124,289	126,478	164,396	275,374
Wiltshire	150,307	157,206	180,927	184,614	191,015	242,831
Wales*	386,636	419,676	507,588	493,242	558,830	815,162
Sub-total	1,949,446	1,959,655	2,375,756	2,332,706	2,605,042	3,691,327
B. Mixed						
Cheshire	100,221	107,648	154,279	163,343	197,871	338,116
Cornwall	122,403	131,901	173,860	157,473	194,278	304,290
Cumberland	90,182	81,060	100,804	105,972	120,972	171,571
Derbyshire	113,998	100,734	132,345	134,197	166,285	239,812
Devonshire	331,119	306,524	291,158	291,959	353,948	499,986
Dorset	87,427	88,318	112,490	102,633	119,000	161,026
Hampshire	108,409	134,148	186,252	174,513	226,667	317,781
Leicestershire	79,123	91,649	101,613	109,573	134,233	199,197
Monmouthshire	26,467	29,524	37,451	37,104	47,037	99,223
Northamptonshire	112,130	111,834	135,514	133,920	135,962	181,334
Nottinghamshire	85,145	85,009	107,347	105,647	144,829	227,837
Shropshire	117,369	126,072	144,696	149,501	172,989	225,421
Somerset	214,096	222,526	240,880	252,834	282,487	408,702
Westmorland	40,134	35,951	39,631	38,579	42,945	55,654
Worcestershire	102,721	95,764	121,165	129,943	143,780	213,719
Yorkshire, E. Riding	72,042	73,626	107,351	85,769	139,706	206,528
Yorkshire, N. Riding	118,652	107,524	148,145	157,745	163,275	192,881
Sub-total	1,921,638	1,929,812	2,334,981	2,330,705	2,786,264	4,043,078
C. Industrial and commercial						
Durham	112,724	130,091	133,264	140,433	165,479	256,738
Gloucestershire	155,216	203,000	225,520	232,304	258,814	391,330
Kent	155,694	168,679	232,973	222,070	317,442	484,492
Lancashire	238,735	317,740	422,328	421,031	694,202	1,351,745
Middlesex	582,815	590,165	643,220	677,843	844,240	1,373,460
Northumberland	118,380	139,011	146,201	147,568	162,115	225,395
Staffordshire	124,151	140,562	188,977	190,492	246,786	415,085
Surrey	130,965	133,427	201,670	199,062	277,630	491,751
Warwickshire	97,387	124,760	171,816	177,701	214,835	340,359
Yorkshire, W. Riding	238,848	303,098	454,293	459,083	583,324	987,225
Sub-total	1,954,915	2,250,533	2,820,262	2,867,587	3,764,867	6,317,580
England and Wales	5,826,000	6,140,000	7,531,000	7,531,000	9,156,171	14,051,986

* The Welsh counties are not distinguished in Rickman's estimates.

Sources: See text. The estimates for 1801 and 1831 are based on census data. A number of minor corrections were made to the figures given in the early census volumes in the census of 1841, but these revisions also took into account boundary changes after 1801. We have therefore taken the uncorrected figures of the *de facto* population of each county and then adjusted them so that the totals agree with the revised figures for England and Wales including members of the armed forces.

than the earlier ones, it is probable that the figure would be almost exactly the same as Brownlee's. Moreover, as in 1750, it is unlikely that the upward bias in the estimate obtained by Rickman's method operated to the same extent in every county. For, although it is likely that the population was increasing everywhere at the end of the eighteenth century, the number of burials actually declined in some areas, while in others it rose as fast as the number of baptisms.

On the other hand, we cannot discount the possibility that in some areas there were significant changes in the marriage rate during this period which, in the aggregate, tended to cancel one another out. The estimates from the marriage data are also open to the objection that though they may be more accurate they are less directly comparable with the estimates used for earlier years. And finally, it should be noted that the figure for at least one county, the East Riding of Yorkshire, is almost certainly seriously in error. This is because the break in the marriage series for this county after 1800 is unusually large, and presumably, therefore, the returns for the eighteenth century were more defective than elsewhere. Hence it seems likely that the estimate given in column 3*b* is too low. Fortunately, if we group a number of counties together, such individual errors often cancel each other out, and for the purposes of regional analysis it makes little difference which set of estimates we adopt. But it is clear that the figures for individual counties must, to say the least, be used tentatively.

Since the estimates given in the table are for the most part similar to those used by Gonner, consideration of the broad changes they reveal need not detain us long. The outstanding feature, of course, is the rapid growth, absolute and relative, of the industrial and commercial counties. In 1701 each of the groups distinguished[1] accounted for about a third of the population of England and Wales, but by 1831 the share of the industrial and commercial group had risen to 45 per cent, while that of the agricultural counties had fallen to 26 per cent. This process did not take place evenly, and it was in the south London counties of Kent and Surrey and the newer industrial centres— Monmouth and Cheshire in the second group, and Lancashire, Staffordshire, Warwickshire and the West Riding of Yorkshire in the third— that growth was most spectacular. Each of these counties increased more than threefold in the course of the period, while the population of the mining counties of Northumberland and Durham on the northeastern seaboard barely doubled, and in the old textile centres in East Anglia and the south-west the rate of growth was, for the most part, even lower.[2]

[1] The classification adopted, necessarily somewhat static, is based on the occupational data given in the 1811 census. The first group consists of those counties where, in 1811, the majority of families drew the bulk of their income from agriculture, while the second, or mixed, group comprises those which were predominantly non-agricultural, but in which the proportion of families relying mainly on agriculture for their livelihood was above the national average of 36 per cent.

[2] A comprehensive classification of the new and old industrial counties is scarcely possible. But if we could classify English counties according to their industrial importance in 1700

Side by side with the rise of the new industrial centres went an increasing concentration of population and a shift in its centre of gravity from the south towards the north. According to Gonner, the density of population in 1700 (excluding the counties in the London area) ranged from 141 inhabitants per square mile in Worcestershire to 54 in Westmorland.[1] A century later the population of Westmorland was almost unchanged, but others had more than doubled their numbers, and Lancashire, which now headed the density list, had 353 to the square mile. At the beginning of the eighteenth century, the most thickly populated counties, apart from Lancashire, which was already beginning to develop rapidly, were those in midland and southern England, but later in the period we find more and more of the most populous counties located to the north-west of a line from the Severn to the Wash. Taking this area as a whole—which includes a number of sparsely populated rural areas, such as the Lakeland counties, the North Riding of Yorkshire, Lincolnshire, Hereford and parts of Wales, as well as the growing industrial centres—we find that its share in the total population rose from 43½ per cent in 1701 to 50 per cent in 1831, most of this advance apparently being achieved in the second half of the eighteenth century.

One other aspect of the changes in the structure of the population during this period may be noted here. Gonner remarks that the rise of the industrial counties was not accompanied by an absolute decline of the rural areas, and in general the statement is true. But in the first half of the eighteenth century, when the population of England and Wales increased by only about 5 per cent, the population of the industrial counties was already growing relatively fast. Three of the six listed above increased their numbers by more than 25 per cent, while some of the older industrial counties—such as Gloucestershire in the West Country textile area and Northumberland and Durham in the north-east—were still expanding. It is not surprising, therefore, to find that in sixteen other counties the population actually fell during this period, and in six of them—Cumberland, Westmorland, Derbyshire, Lincolnshire, Rutland and Cambridgeshire—the decline was apparently 10 per cent or more. It was only after 1750, when the pace of population growth markedly quickened, that these largely rural counties began to share in the general advance. In the next thirty years the agricultural counties increased in numbers almost as fast as the industrial and commercial group, though this improvement in their relative position was not maintained. Between 1781 and 1801 the industrial and commercial counties grew by 31–34 per cent, compared with 25–28

these old textile centres would certainly be much more prominent. In 1811 all the East Anglian counties come into the agricultural group, despite the proximity of Essex to London, while in the south-west only Gloucestershire qualifies as industrial and commercial, largely because it included Bristol, which, for much of the eighteenth century, ranked as the second city and port in the kingdom.

[1] These are Gonner's figures which are based on Rickman's unadjusted population estimates.

per cent in the previous thirty years, whereas in the agricultural counties the increase fell from 19–21 per cent in the period 1751–81 to only 10–12 per cent from 1781 to 1801.

2. MIGRATION AND NATURAL INCREASE

How far were these changes in the distribution of population brought about by migration and how far were they due to variations in the rate of natural increase?

If we can estimate the surplus of births over deaths in each county and compare the figures obtained with the estimated increase in population on the basis of the data given in Table 24, we should, in principle, get an answer to this question. There are, however, a number of practical obstacles to such a procedure. The Parish Register Abstracts of the early censuses provide us with detailed information about the number of baptisms and burials recorded in each parish in every year after 1780, but before that date we have the figures only for every tenth year. Hence estimation of the total number of baptisms and burials in the period before 1780 involves the assumption that the isolated figures available are in fact representative of each decade. Even if this assumption is warranted for the country as a whole—and it has recently been questioned[1]—it is obvious that it may involve quite serious errors in the case of particular areas. Secondly, the information for the eighteenth century given in the Parish Register Abstract of the 1801 census was found to contain a number of duplicate entries and omissions, and revised totals for England and Wales, but *not* for the individual counties, were published in 1811.[2] The figures for baptisms and burials were affected to approximately the same degree, so the revision did not make much difference to the natural increase implied by the 1801 figures, but again it is possible that there were more serious errors in some areas.

These difficulties are, however, minor compared with the wider problem of assessing the relationship between the figures of baptisms and burials recorded in the parish registers and the actual number of births and deaths. The question at issue here is not simply whether the ratios devised by Brownlee and Talbot Griffith for converting baptisms and burials into birth and deaths give approximately the right answer for the country as a whole, for unfortunately the coverage of the parish registers varied considerable from county to county. Some indication of the magnitude of the discrepancy after the introduction of civil registration is given by a table in the introduction to the Parish

[1] J. T. Krause, 'Changes in English Fertility and Mortality, 1781–1850', *Econ. Hist. Rev.*, second series, vol. XI (1958), p. 53n. Krause points out that the use of this assumption to measure Swedish population growth would exaggerate the natural increase between 1750 and 1780 by over 61 per cent.

[2] The revised figures are 6 or 7 per cent higher than those given in 1801 (excluding the supplementary figures given in that year), and the difference is roughly constant throughout the century.

Register Abstract of the 1841 census comparing the entries in the parish registers with the officially recorded number of births and deaths in the year 1839–40. An examination of this table shows that in Monmouth, for example, nearly a third of the deaths and over half the births recorded in the civil registers escaped entry in the parish returns, although at that time even the civil registers were probably incomplete, and in Shropshire, at the other end of the scale, the baptisms slightly exceeded the number of recorded births.

Fortunately it is unlikely that the problem was as serious in the eighteenth century. The virtual breakdown of the system in some areas in the early nineteenth century seems to have been due to the spread of nonconformity and the strain placed upon the ecclesiastical organisation by the growth and changing distribution of population. But this means, of course, that the information for 1839–40 cannot be used as a basis for correcting the data given in the parish registers for earlier years. In the West Riding of Yorkshire, for example, the birth–baptism and death–burial ratios for 1839–40 work out at $1 \cdot 78$ and $1 \cdot 23$ respectively; and if we were to use these ratios to correct the figures of baptisms and burials for the first half of the eighteenth century, we might be led to the conclusion that the early development of the Yorkshire woollen industry was accompanied by the exodus of nearly a quarter of a million people, or slightly more than the entire population of the area in 1701. In the circumstances, it might seem preferable to use the figures of baptisms and burials as they stand, rather than attempt to correct them by ratios which might give equally inaccurate and, for most of the period with which we are concerned, probably more misleading answers than the crude data from the parish registers. But since the registration of births was usually more deficient than that of deaths, the figures of baptisms minus burials tend to understate the natural increase of population. This means, of course, that if we compare the actual increase in population with the surplus of baptisms over burials, some counties which were in fact losing population by migration will appear to be gaining, and, in the aggregate, the gains of the 'immigrant' counties will greatly exceed the losses of the rest. In the period 1801–30, for example, the discrepancy amounts to nearly $1 \cdot 3$ million, even though the figures of baptisms and burials employed were taken from the summaries given in the 1831 census which included the parish clergy's estimates of supposed omissions. Accordingly, we decided to convert the figures of baptisms and burials[1] into births and deaths on the basis of national average conversion ratios derived from Brownlee's calculations, and it is these adjusted figures which form the basis of the estimates given in Table 25.[2]

[1] For the period 1801–30 the figures of baptisms and burials used included the parish clergy's estimates of omissions. Although these estimates were clearly grossly over-optimistic, their inclusion probably means that the variations in the coverage of the statistics are less serious than would otherwise be the case.

[2] Brownlee's own ratios naturally refer to the corrected figures of baptisms and burials given in the 1811 census for the eighteenth century and in the totals for each decade after

Table 25. Migration and natural increase, 1701–1831

	1701–1751			1751–1781			1781–1801			1801–1831			1839–40	
	Estimated increase of population	Estimated natural increase	Net gain (+) or loss (−) by migration	Estimated increase of population	Estimated natural increase	Net gain (+) or loss (−) by migration	Estimated increase of population	Estimated natural increase	Net gain (+) or loss (−) by migration	Estimated increase of population	Estimated natural increase	Net gain (+) or loss (−) by migration	Births Baptisms	Deaths Burials
A. Agricultural														
Bedfordshire	2,429	−3,735	6,164	1,144	8,953	−7,809	8,865	9,726	−861	31,131	36,563	−5,432	1·52	1·21
Berkshire	9,187	17,370	−8,183	22,719	31,176	−8,457	4,005	26,889	−22,884	34,307	59,632	−25,325	1·11	1·03
Buckinghamshire	6,432	2,340	4,092	16,010	19,163	−3,153	13,140	18,276	−5,136	37,288	55,280	−17,992	1·33	1·10
Cambridgeshire	−8,439	8,349	−16,788	9,103	8,291	812	10,421	12,865	−2,444	53,360	57,972	−4,612	1·25	1·13
Essex	11,938	−31,843	43,781	27,274	5,271	22,003	25,925	28,188	−2,263	87,380	111,413	−24,033	1·18	1·09
Herefordshire	−3,784	18,997	−22,781	18,002	23,049	−5,047	3,610	21,717	−18,107	20,412	42,266	−21,854	1·06	1·05
Hertfordshire	3,855	1,479	2,376	15,120	10,189	4,931	9,114	17,473	−8,359	44,247	56,517	−12,270	1·27	1·13
Huntingdonshire	−1,275	−5,496	4,221	7,621	911	6,710	888	4,415	−3,527	15,017	20,555	−5,538	1·47	1·17
Lincolnshire	−25,825	1,460	−27,285	41,808	38,350	3,458	20,135	46,552	−26,417	105,788	146,062	−40,274	1·12	1·05
Norfolk	−21,256	16,261	−37,517	34,826	59,849	−25,023	26,015	63,131	−37,116	112,303	177,661	−65,358	1·12	1·05
Oxfordshire	5,222	18,065	−12,843	12,917	27,603	−14,686	10,975	27,049	−16,074	40,732	64,004	−23,272	1·12	1·07
Rutland	−3,662	6,561	−10,223	3,966	3,703	263	1,170	3,804	−2,634	2,723	8,320	−5,597	1·15	1·01
Suffolk	−1,668	12,607	−14,275	29,404	41,803	−12,399	28,166	55,632	−27,466	82,471	136,161	−53,690	1·33	1·11
Sussex	−2,884	31,962	−34,846	32,163	41,211	−9,048	37,918	53,854	−15,936	110,978	132,448	−21,470	1·05	1·13
Wiltshire	6,899	30,035	−23,136	27,408	23,305	4,103	6,401	34,632	−28,231	51,816	95,728	−43,912	1·23	1·10
Wales	33,040	118,275	−85,235	73,566	144,050	−70,484	65,588	99,418	−33,830	256,332	264,747	−8,415	1·91	1·21
Sub-total	10,209	242,687	−232,478	373,051	486,877	−113,826	272,336	523,621	−251,285	1,086,285	1,465,329	−379,044	1·29	1·11
B. Mixed														
Cheshire	7,427	10,785	−3,358	55,695	42,287	13,408	34,528	35,336	−808	140,245	99,743	40,502	1·47	1·21
Cornwall	9,498	21,856	−12,358	25,572	58,069	−32,497	36,805	57,384	−20,579	110,012	147,475	−37,463	1·40	1·06
Cumberland	−9,122	33,504	−42,626	24,912	37,444	−12,532	15,000	24,500	−9,500	50,599	70,644	−20,045	1·13	1·06
Derbyshire	−13,264	42,315	−55,579	33,463	53,244	−19,781	32,088	43,003	−10,915	73,527	99,038	−25,511	1·40	1·06
Devonshire	−24,595	6,150	−30,745	−14,565	60,609	−75,174	61,989	71,921	−9,932	146,038	209,274	−63,236	1·18	1·04

Dorset	891	13,479	−12,588	14,315	24,263	−9,948	16,367	22,576	−6,209	42,026	66,991	−24,965	1·13 · 1·02
Hampshire	25,739	25,388	351	40,365	34,436	5,929	53,154	44,938	7,216	91,114	140,833	−49,719	1·13 · 1·12
Leicestershire	12,526	23,436	−10,910	17,924	28,052	−10,128	24,660	23,192	1,468	64,964	70,987	−6,023	1·52 · 1·16
Monmouthshire	3,057	7,749	−4,692	7,580	6,858	722	9,933	4,999	4,934	52,186	20,952	31,234	2·06 · 1·48
Northamptonshire	−296	13,699	−13,995	22,086	14,157	7,929	2,042	14,720	−12,678	45,372	61,871	−16,499	1·38 · 1·13
Nottinghamshire	−136	19,511	−19,647	20,638	27,076	−6,438	39,182	36,288	2,894	83,008	92,862	−9,854	1·48 · 1·17
Shropshire	8,703	23,836	−15,133	23,429	51,438	−28,009	23,488	45,823	−22,335	52,432	88,001	−35,569	0·98 · 1·04
Somerset	8,430	10,751	−2,321	30,308	60,465	−30,157	29,653	52,791	−23,138	126,215	148,540	−22,325	1·17 · 1·09
Westmorland	−4,183	10,172	−14,355	2,628	16,815	−14,187	4,366	10,060	−5,694	12,709	25,200	−12,491	1·03 · 1·03
Worcestershire	−6,957	19,127	−26,084	34,179	28,785	5,394	13,837	29,470	−15,633	69,939	84,417	−14,478	1·27 · 1·11
Yorkshire, E. Riding	1,584	5,252	−3,668	12,143	21,525	−9,382	53,937	25,074	28,863	66,822	83,847	−17,025	1·08 · 1·02
Yorkshire, N. Riding	−11,128	37,003	−48,131	50,221	50,451	−230	5,530	39,162	−33,632	29,606	86,661	−57,055	1·07 · 1·02
Sub-total	8,174	324,013	−315,839	400,893	615,974	−215,081	455,559	581,237	−125,678	1,256,814	1,597,336	−340,522	1·26 · 1·10

C. Industrial and commercial

Durham	17,367	24,139	−6,772	10,342	20,502	−10,160	25,046	12,353	12,693	91,259	90,434	825	1·20 · 1·06
Gloucestershire	47,784	29,275	18,509	29,304	45,345	−16,041	26,510	51,505	−24,995	132,516	153,966	−21,450	1·19 · 1·17
Kent	12,985	−7,742	20,727	53,391	25,063	28,328	95,372	55,935	39,437	167,050	182,063	−15,013	1·14 · 1·06
Lancashire	79,005	37,387	41,618	103,291	116,402	−13,111	273,171	146,852	126,319	657,543	474,009	183,534	1·65 · 1·61
Middlesex	7,350	−456,276	463,626	87,678	−177,451	265,129	166,397	−18,415	184,812	529,220	132,430	396,790	1·44 · 1·27
Northumberland	20,631	24,311	−3,680	8,557	20,942	−12,385	14,547	11,767	2,780	63,280	74,582	−11,302	1·46 · 1·01
Staffordshire	16,411	45,353	−28,942	49,930	71,042	−21,112	56,264	60,174	−3,880	168,299	165,841	2,458	1·31 · 1·05
Surrey	2,462	−71,671	74,133	65,635	−23,625	89,260	78,568	15,400	63,168	214,121	98,764	115,357	1·31 · 1·25
Warwickshire	27,373	15,486	11,887	52,941	23,968	28,973	37,134	51,920	−14,786	125,524	97,758	27,766	1·35 · 1·03
Yorkshire, W. Riding	64,250	109,726	−45,476	155,985	164,747	−8,762	124,241	130,539	−6,298	393,901	366,679	37,222	1·78 · 1·23
Sub-total	295,618	−250,012	545,630	617,054	286,935	330,119	897,280	518,030	379,250	2,552,713	1,836,526	716,187	1·46 · 1·27
England and Wales*	314,000	316,688	{+691,485 / −694,172}	1,391,000	1,389,786	{+487,352 / −486,140}	1,625,175	1,622,888	{+474,584 / −472,297}	4,895,815	4,899,191	{+835,688 / −839,667}	1·36 · 1·18

* The figures given in the first column do not add up to the totals for England and Wales, because of rounding. Similarly, the totals of column 2 do not coincide with the estimated increase in population as given in column 1, nor do the total gains and losses in column 3 exactly balance, because the multipliers used in converting baptisms and burials into births and deaths were correct only to three decimal places.

It will be apparent that these estimates are highly tentative. As an indication of the probable nature of the errors involved in those for the early nineteenth century we show the birth–baptism and death–burial ratios for each county in 1839–40. For the second half of the eighteenth century, all the estimates presented here—and in most subsequent calculations—have been based on the population figures for 1781 given in column 3*b* of Table 24, but the reader can, of course, gauge for himself the effect of using the alternative estimates in column 3*a*.[1] In general, it must be assumed that the estimates of migration for individual counties may be seriously in error, and the most we can hope is that they correctly indicate the direction of movement in most cases. However, in considering broad changes in the total volume of internal migration during the period, it is not essential to have precise figures for individual counties. If we recompute the estimates for the second half of the eighteenth century on the basis of the alternative population estimates for 1781, the resulting figures for the total volume of migration are within 5 per cent or less of those given in Table 25.[2] Secondly, although an examination of Table 25 suggests that in 1839–40 parish registration was in general more defective in immigrant counties than in those which had lost part of their natural increase, this seems to have affected the baptisms and burials to roughly the same extent. Indeed, if we estimate the number of births and deaths in the immigrant counties in 1839–40 from the parish register data, on the basis of the national birth–baptism and death–burial ratios in those years, we find that, if anything, we somewhat *over-estimate* their natural increase. If the same is true in earlier periods, it follows that the estimates of the total volume of migration given in Table 25 may be too low; but it seems reasonable to assume that they are more reliable than those for individual counties.

1801 without the additions made by the clergy to cover omissions. To allow for the difference in our data, the ratios actually used in this and subsequent calculations were obtained by dividing the figures of baptisms and burials employed here into Brownlee's estimates of the number of births and deaths. The resulting birth–baptism ratios for each of the four subperiods work out at 1·323, 1·323, 1·326 and 1·208 respectively, and for deaths–burials at 1·284, 1·276, 1·281 and 1·149. Incidentally, the lower ratios for 1801–30 should not be taken as an indication that the figures we have used for the early nineteenth century necessarily represent a larger proportion of the actual number of births and deaths than those for the eighteenth century. For in order to estimate the number of deaths Brownlee simply assumed that the death–burial ratio was constant throughout the period, and in consequence he concluded that there was only a small increase in the birth-baptism ratio in the early nineteenth century. But the assumption is questionable, and we have made use of Brownlee's calculations here, not because we accept his assumptions for the nineteenth century, but simply because they form the basis of the estimates of population in the eighteenth century which we have adopted as the best available.

[1] If these estimates are used, they suggest, for example, that Bedfordshire lost 748 by migration from 1751 to 1781, and 7,922 from 1781 to 1801, and that the East Riding gained 12,200 and 7,281 in the same periods. It will be noted that these figures imply that the East Riding gained by migration from 1751 to 1781, whereas, according to Table 25, it lost. In the same way, Worcestershire, and perhaps Rutland, may actually have been losing population at this time, while in the next two decades Hampshire may have been losing and Cheshire gaining.

[2] The actual figures (in thousands) work out at +512 and −511 for the period 1751–81, and +488 and −486 for 1781–1801.

Several features of the table call for comment. In the first place, it will be noted that the net volume of movement from county to county tended to increase throughout the period, though at a slower rate than we might expect. At the beginning of the nineteenth century, the net amount of migration in each decade was about double what it had been a hundred years earlier; but it is somewhat surprising that in the first half of the eighteenth century, when the total population was almost stationary, the amount of internal migration was not much smaller than in the succeeding period which saw the beginnings of both rapid industrialisation and population growth.

Secondly, it seems clear that for most, if not all, of the period under review, the bulk of the migrant population went to the four counties in the London area, Middlesex, Essex, Kent and Surrey. In the case of Middlesex alone, the number of burials recorded consistently exceeded the baptisms until the second decade of the nineteenth century, and taking the area as a whole, the same is true until the last decade of the eighteenth, so that, without the heavy influx from other districts, the population of the area must have declined. In this case we can probably give a more accurate idea of the size of the influx than is possible for other immigrant areas. It so happens that by multiplying the figures of baptisms and burials for Middlesex and Surrey in 1701–50 by the national conversion ratios, the excess of deaths over births is actually increased, despite the fact that the births–deaths *ratio* is, of course, higher than that for deaths–burials. This means that the disparity between the surplus of burials over baptisms and the estimated increase of the population of the area as a whole in the first half of the century is about 80,000 *less* than the estimated amount of immigration into the four counties as shown in Table 25. There is no reason to assume that the national conversion ratios are correct for the London area, where the parish registers, at any rate in the Metropolis itself, were probably more defective than in most other districts; but it is worth noting that even if the London records were as deficient in the early eighteenth century as they were a century later, it would still be true that the Surrey registers understate and the Middlesex only slightly exaggerate the excess of deaths over births. Unless, therefore, the underlying population estimates are very seriously at fault, it seems reasonable to conclude that the amount of immigration into the area during this period was somewhere between five and six hundred thousand. After 1750 the importance of the influx into the London area certainly declined, both in relation to the total volume of migration and, with the gradual disappearance of the excess of deaths over births, as a factor in the growth of the population of the area itself. Nevertheless, the drift towards 'the great wen' continued on a large scale; in absolute terms it was probably maintained and may even have increased.[1]

[1] Cf. M. C. Buer, *Health, Wealth and Population in the Early Days of the Industrial Revolution* (1926), pp. 32–4, for a similar estimate of the extent of immigration into London in the eighteenth and early nineteenth centuries.

Apart from this movement towards London, it is clear that a good deal of the migration which took place in the early part of the eighteenth century had little to do with the expansion of the newer industrial areas. In the first half of the century, for example, about 40 per cent of the migrants attracted to areas outside London apparently went, not to the Midlands and the North, but to Gloucestershire and Hampshire, Bedfordshire, Buckinghamshire and Hertfordshire, and even, it would seem, to the fenland county Huntingdon. In the case of Huntingdonshire, and perhaps also Bedfordshire, it may be possible to attribute the apparent gain to the uncertainty of the statistics, and it must be admitted that, a century later, the baptism registers of both were more than usually defective. But in general the results suggested by Table 25 are quite consistent with what we should expect in an age before the process of industrialisation had begun to dominate the pattern of demographic change, when population was relatively stable, and when the internal movements which took place would tend to reflect variations in the fortunes of particular areas. Thus it is not surprising to find that the home counties were apparently attracting population at the end of a period which had witnessed the steady expansion of the London food market,[1] nor to learn that a large part of the rapid growth of Gloucestershire in the early part of the century, to which we referred earlier, can be attributed to the losses of other counties in the south-western textile area. It is more difficult to explain the influx into Hampshire, which appears to have continued for most, if not all, of the eighteenth century, and then died away only to reappear before the middle of the nineteenth.[2] But in part it may be connected with the rapid growth of Portsmouth in the eighteenth century, which, though less than half of the size of the northern industrial towns in 1801, ranked with Bath as one of the largest towns in the South, outside the old centres of London, Bristol and Norwich. The fact that vagrancy constituted a serious problem in eighteenth-century Hampshire, has been attributed to the poverty of labourers in agriculture after 1750.[3] But if the statistics can be trusted, it looks as if the problem may have originated more in the real or imaginary attractions of Hampshire to the inhabitants of neighbouring counties than in the poverty of the indigenous population.

What is surprising is the comparatively minor role played by migration in the early development of the main industrial areas. It is true that the group of industrial and commercial counties listed in the table show a net gain from the rest of the country throughout the period under

[1] See F. J. Fisher, 'The Development of the London Food Market, 1540–1640', *Econ. Hist. Rev.*, vol. v (1935), pp. 46–64, for the effects of the growth of the London market on the earlier history of the home counties.

[2] For immigration into Hampshire in the 1840's, see the comparison of the inter-censal increase in population with the surplus of births over deaths given in the *Thirteenth Annual Report of the Registrar-General* (1854), pp. 194–5, 200–1. At that time it appears that Portsmouth was the main centre attracting immigrants, though some went to Southampton, Winchester and the Isle of Wight.

[3] *V.C.H. Hampshire*, vol. v, pp. 429–31.

review. But this was largely due to the influence of London, and if the metropolitan counties are omitted, the group as a whole seems actually to have *lost* by migration, at any rate until 1780. Nor can this be attributed to the decline in the fortunes of Gloucestershire after 1750, or to the comparative eclipse of Northumberland and Durham during the canal era. For if we focus attention on the six newer industrial counties[1] which were the pace-makers in population growth, exactly the same is true, and it is not until after 1800 that the statistics clearly reveal a general movement of population to these new industrial centres. We know that the South Wales–Monmouth area—represented here by Monmouth alone—was a relatively late starter in the industrial race, and this may partially explain why Monmouth apparently lost part of its natural increase in the first half of the eighteenth century. But what about the other districts? Of the four industrial counties which grew most rapidly in the eighteenth century, Lancashire and Warwickshire certainly attracted migrants on a large scale. From 1751 to 1781 the natural growth of Lancashire seems temporarily to have outstripped its actual increase in numbers, and the same appears to have happened in Warwickshire from 1781 to 1801. But for most of the period, both counties depended on fairly heavy immigration, and in the first half of the century, though not in the second, their growth must be attributed primarily to this factor. The growth of Staffordshire and the West Riding, on the other hand, seems to have owed little or nothing to migration, and unless we assume that the parish registers for these counties were more than usually complete, it seems clear that they were losing population throughout the eighteenth century. In the early nineteenth century, they do appear in the list of immigrant counties, and at the time of the 1851 census the net number of immigrants in Staffordshire amounted to over 39,000, or 6 per cent of the resident population, compared with 11 per cent in the neighbouring county of Warwickshire.[2] Even by this date, however, it is clear the immigration into the West Riding was of only marginal importance. The figures given in the 1851 census do not distinguish the three Yorkshire Ridings, and it has been assumed that the small net gain registered by the county as a whole concealed a larger movement of population from the East and North Ridings to the industrial West.[3] But returns furnished by the Registrar-General for the first complete decade of civil registration suggest that it was not the industrial West but the 'metropolitan' East Riding which then relied most heavily on immigration. In the 1840's the net gain by the West Riding was less than 7,500, or under 5 per cent of the increase in the population of the area, compared with nearly 15,000, or 45 per cent of the population increase of its smaller eastern neighbour, and over 185,000, or more than 50

[1] I.e., Lancashire, Staffordshire, Warwickshire and the West Riding in the industrial group and Cheshire and Monmouth in the mixed group.

[2] *1851 Census*, Part II, vol. I, p. clxxxii.

[3] A. Redford, *Labour Migration in England* (Manchester, 1926), p. 165 and Appendix, Map A.

per cent of the inter-censal growth in numbers of its great industrial rival in the west.[1]

It seems clear, then, that if the West Riding and Staffordshire increased in relative importance this must have been due, in the eighteenth century at least, to the greater fecundity of their population. Even in Lancashire and Warwickshire, however, natural increase was by no means a negligible factor. To facilitate a rough comparison between the different counties, we have estimated the average annual rate of natural increase in each county, on the assumption that the population grew at constant rates in each of the four sub-periods during the 130 years under review.[2] The results of these calculations, together with rates of migration for each county calculated in the same way, are shown in Table 26. The figures are very crude, of course, and the rates given will be subject to some extent to the influence of migration, for wherever there were significant movements of population, these will clearly have affected the number of births and deaths recorded, and there is no means of estimating the net reproduction rates of the indigenous populations. Nevertheless, it is interesting to observe that, for most of the eighteenth century, both Lancashire and Warwickshire seem to have enjoyed rates of natural increase significantly above the national average.

More important, however, is the fact that both these counties appear to fall within a wider area of relatively high natural increase. This is particularly clear in the case of Lancashire, for seven of the ten counties with the highest rates of natural increase in the eighteenth century as a whole constituted the belt of counties—Cumberland, Westmorland, the North and West Ridings of Yorkshire, Derbyshire, Staffordshire and Shropshire—which all but enclose the Lancashire–Cheshire textile area. To illustrate this point more clearly, the counties given in the table have been grouped on a regional basis, and these regions are also marked on the accompanying map. It will be noted that in both the periods before 1780 the rate of natural increase of this north-western group of counties as a whole was considerably above that prevailing elsewhere, and only in the last twenty years of the century was the gap substantially reduced. Now if the concentration of such high rates of natural increase in a particular area related to a comparatively short period of time there might be some simple demographic explanation of the phenomenon, such as a temporarily favourable age structure. But the persistence of such a situation for the best part of a century calls for a more general explanation. Its significance becomes apparent when we consider the migration rates, for it will be noted that five of the seven counties listed above—i.e. excluding Staffordshire and the West Riding—were precisely those which, together with Rutland, Herefordshire and possibly Sussex, lost the biggest proportion of their

---

[1] *Thirteenth Annual Report of the Registrar-General*, pp. 196–7.

[2] The method used in making these estimates is described in more detail in the discussion of birth and death rates. See below, pp. 122–135.

Table 26.

Average annual rates of migration and natural increase, 1701–1830

(per thousand)

	Rates of natural increase				Rates of migration			
	1701–50	1751–80	1781–1800	1801–30	1701–50	1751–80	1781–1800	1801–30
North-West								
Cheshire	2·1	10·6	9·8	12·7	− 0·6	3·3	− 0·2	5·2
Cumberland	7·8	13·4	10·8	16·3	− 10·0	− 4·5	− 4·2	− 4·6
Derbyshire	7·9	15·2	14·4	16·4	− 10·4	− 5·7	− 3·6	− 4·2
Lancashire	2·7	10·6	13·4	16·0	3·0	− 1·2	11·6	6·2
Shropshire	3·9	12·5	14·2	14·8	− 2·5	− 6·8	− 6·9	− 6·0
Staffordshire	6·9	14·4	13·8	17·1	− 4·4	− 4·3	− 0·9	0·3
Westmorland	5·4	15·0	12·4	17·1	− 7·6	− 12·7	− 7·0	− 8·5
Yorks., N. Riding	6·5	12·8	12·2	16·3	− 8·5	− 0·1	− 10·5	− 10·7
Yorks., W. Riding	8·1	14·6	12·6	15·9	− 3·4	− 0·8	− 0·6	1·6
Total North-West	5·6	12·9	12·8	15·8	− 3·4	− 2·2	0·8	1·2
North								
Durham	4·0	5·1	4·0	14·5	− 1·1	− 2·5	4·2	0·1
Herefordshire	5·3	9·7	12·0	13·8	− 6·3	− 2·1	− 10·0	− 7·1
Leicestershire	5·5	9·3	9·5	14·4	− 2·6	− 3·4	0·6	− 1·2
Lincolnshire	0·2	7·4	11·4	18·4	− 3·3	0·7	− 6·4	− 5·1
Monmouthshire	5·5	6·9	6·0	10·0	− 3·4	0·7	5·9	14·9
Northumberland	3·8	4·9	3·8	12·9	− 0·6	− 2·9	0·9	− 2·0
Nottinghamshire	4·6	9·5	14·6	16·9	− 4·6	− 2·3	1·2	− 1·8
Rutland	9·7	9·1	11·7	15·2	− 15·2	0·6	− 8·1	− 10·2
Warwickshire	2·8	5·3	13·3	11·9	2·2	6·5	− 3·8	3·4
Worcestershire	3·9	8·6	10·8	15·9	− 5·3	1·6	− 5·7	− 2·7
Yorks., E. Riding	1·4	9·0	11·3	16·3	− 1·0	− 3·9	13·1	− 3·3
Wales	5·9	10·5	9·5	13·0	− 4·2	− 5·2	− 3·2	− 0·4
Total, North	4·1	8·2	9·8	14·3	− 3·0	− 1·8	− 1·5	− 1·0
London area								
Essex	− 3·7	0·9	6·4	13·5	5·0	3·8	− 0·5	− 2·9
Kent	− 1·0	4·3	10·5	15·4	2·6	4·9	7·4	− 1·3
Middlesex	− 15·6	− 9·3	− 1·2	4·1	15·8	14·0	12·2	12·2
Surrey	− 10·8	− 4·8	3·3	8·8	11·2	18·1	13·4	10·3
Total London	− 10·8	− 4·8	2·7	8·2	11·4	11·4	9·6	7·4
South								
Bedfordshire	− 1·4	5·3	8·0	15·2	2·3	− 4·7	− 0·7	− 2·3
Berkshire	4·3	10·7	12·1	15·4	− 2·0	− 2·9	− 10·3	− 6·5
Buckinghamshire	0·6	7·1	8·8	14·3	1·0	− 1·2	− 2·5	− 4·7
Cambridgeshire	2·2	3·6	7·4	16·5	− 4·4	0·4	− 1·4	− 1·3
Cornwall	3·4	13·4	16·4	20·0	− 1·9	− 7·5	− 5·9	− 5·1
Devonshire	0·4	6·8	11·2	16·5	− 1·9	− 8·4	− 1·5	− 5·0
Dorset	3·1	8·5	10·2	16·1	− 2·9	− 3·5	− 2·8	− 6·0
Gloucestershire	3·3	7·0	10·5	16·0	2·1	− 2·5	− 5·1	− 2·2
Hampshire	4·2	7·5	11·3	17·4	0·1	1·3	1·8	− 6·1
Hertfordshire	0·4	4·1	9·1	15·5	0·6	2·0	− 4·4	3·4
Huntingdonshire	− 3·6	0·9	5·8	14·9	2·7	6·6	− 4·6	− 4·0
Norfolk	1·4	8·4	11·7	17·7	− 3·2	− 3·5	− 6·9	− 6·5
Northamptonshire	2·4	3·9	5·5	13·1	− 2·5	2·2	− 4·7	− 3·5
Oxfordshire	4·2	9·6	12·6	16·1	− 3·0	− 5·1	− 7·5	− 5·9
Somerset	1·0	8·5	9·9	14·5	− 0·2	− 4·2	− 4·3	− 2·2
Suffolk	1·6	8·0	13·7	17·7	− 1·8	− 2·4	− 6·8	− 7·0
Sussex	6·7	12·5	18·6	20·5	− 7·3	− 2·8	− 5·5	− 3·3
Wiltshire	3·9	4·6	9·2	14·8	− 3·0	0·8	− 7·5	− 6·8
Total, South	2·2	7·6	11·2	16·5	− 1·6	− 2·8	− 4·5	− 4·7
England and Wales	1·1	6·8	9·8	14·3	± 2·3	± 2·4	± 2·8	± 2·4

population by migration in the eighteenth century. An obvious inference is that the rise of Lancashire stimulated the growth of population in the surrounding areas, and that part of the population increase was then siphoned off into Lancashire itself. If so, it would seem that,

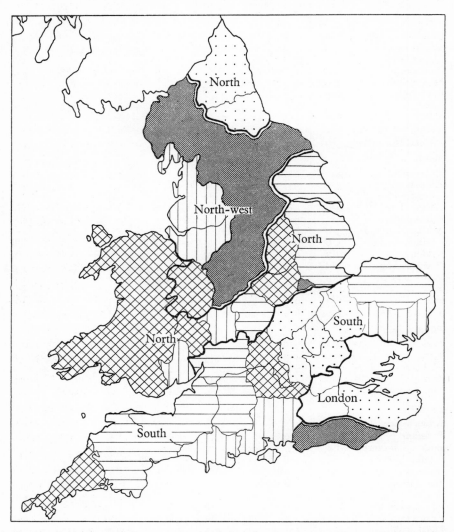

Fig. 5. Average annual rates of natural increase, 1701–1800. Rates per thousand: 9·5×, 7·5–9·4, 6–7·4, 4·5–5·9, 0–4·4, negative.

in the early part of our period at least, the supply generated was in excess of the demand, for until 1750 the surplus of baptisms over burials in this 'catchment area' as a whole—even without an adjustment for the defects of parish registration—was larger than the estimated increase of population. This does not mean, of course, that all the emigration from individual counties in the area can be attributed to the overflow of the surplus population produced by a high rate of natural increase: on the contrary, as we have seen, in the first half of the eighteenth century the population of no less than four of the counties in this region, Cumberland, Westmorland, the North Riding and Derbyshire, suffered an absolute decline. Nevertheless, the rate of natural increase achieved was already such that, despite these individual losses, and despite the loss by migration apparently suffered by the area as a whole, the population of the region increased both absolutely and in relation to that of the rest of the country.

In the second half of the eighteenth century, the pace of population growth quickened everywhere, but it was during this period that the biggest relative growth of the North-West took place. Nevertheless, the excess of births over deaths still accounted for most of the estimated increase in population, and for thirty years (as can be seen from Table 27) the area continued to show a small loss by migration. After 1780 the growth of the North-West appeared to outstrip its powers of natural increase, and for the first time the figures suggest a small net gain from other areas. But by this time, as we have already noted, local variations in the rates of natural increase, which had been so pronounced earlier in the century, were beginning to disappear. For the nineteenth century, the differences recorded for about three-quarters of the counties shown in Table 26 must be regarded as well within the margin of error of the statistics, and in the North-West as a whole the rate of natural increase seems, if anything to have been slightly below that in the South. This is what we might expect to happen with the growth and spread of industry if, as the eighteenth-century figures suggest, the process of industrialisation was itself a potent factor in the growth of population. Yet even at this stage, most of the migration which helped to swell the numbers in the growing industrial centres seems to have depended on the relatively high rates of natural increase of comparatively nearby areas, and the statistics suggest little in the way of a drift of population from the predominantly rural South to the industrial North. Throughout the eighteenth century, not only the north-western catchment area, but the whole of the wider region north and west of the line from the Severn to the Wash—which includes all the major industrial centres of the nineteenth century—had been losing a substantial part of its natural increase by migration; and although this flow from north to south seems to have been checked by the early nineteenth century, the balance of movement in the opposite direction remained negligible. In short, the conclusion drawn by Professor Cairncross that 'the North of England triumphed over the South, mainly by superior fertility (and not as we used to be taught by attracting migrants)', appears to be at least as true of the early phases of industrialisation as in the period after 1840 to which his evidence relates.[1]

[1] A. K. Cairncross, *Home and Foreign Investment, 1870–1913* (Cambridge, 1953), p. 79.

Table 27. *Migration and natural increase by regions**

(ooo's)

	North-West	North	North and North-West	London	South	London and South
% population, 1701	20·3	23·2	43·5	17·8	38·7	56·5
Population increase, 1701–51	138	75	213	35	66	101
Estimated natural increase, 1701–51	350	284	634	−568	250	−318
Net migration, 1701–51	−212	−209	−421	602	−184	418
% population, 1751	21·5	23·2	44·7	17·5	37·8	55·3
Population increase, 1751–81	500	302	801	234	356	590
Estimated natural increase, 1751–81	604	387	991	−171	570	399
Net migration, 1751–81	−104	−85	−190	405	−214	191
% population, 1781	24·2	22·9	47·1	17·4	35·6	52·9
Population increase, 1781–1801	569	309	877	366	381	748
Estimated natural increase, 1781–1801	535	367	902	81	640	721
Net migration, 1781–1801	33	−58	−25	285	−258	27
% population, 1801	26·1	22·2	48·3	18·3	33·4	51·7
Population increase, 1801–31	1,589	1,002	2,591	998	1,307	2,305
Estimated natural increase, 1801–31	1,476	1,077	2,553	525	1,821	2,346
Net migration, 1801–31	113	−75	38	473	−515	−41
% population, 1831	28·3	21·6	49·9	19·0	31·1	50·1

* If the alternative estimates of population for 1781 are used, there are minor differences in the figures of migration obtained, but the direction of movement is in each case the same.

It may be objected that the statistics for the earlier period are much less reliable; it is true that the conclusions drawn from the material at our disposal must be regarded as tentative. Nevertheless, an examination of the possibilities of error in this particular case is somewhat reassuring. For although the argument is based on the application of national conversion ratios to the regional totals of baptisms and burials, it is virtually certain that in the early nineteenth century the parish registers were, on the whole, more defective in the North than in the South. In 1839–40 the surplus of baptisms over burials was 39 per cent of the natural increase recorded by the civil registers in the North-West and only 32 per cent in other parts of the North, compared with 50 per cent for the counties in the London area and 66 per cent for the rest of the South. Clearly, therefore, the figures given in Table 27 for the early nineteenth century are more likely to over-estimate than under-estimate the movement of population from south to north, and it is quite probable that even at that time the movement was actually in the other direction. Further back, of course, the position is more obscure. It so happens that in 1839–40 the coverage of the parish baptism registers in many of the more rural counties of the North was relatively good; and if, as seems likely, the breakdown of the registration system in some of the industrial counties was a comparatively recent phenomenon, it is possible that for a large part of the eighteenth century registration in the North was on the average no worse than in the South. But unless we are prepared to go further and assume that it was in fact better in the North than the South, the conclusions we have suggested will not be seriously affected.

One obvious question remains. If it is true that the growth of the North was in general due, not to migration, but to its relatively high rate of natural increase, and if, as we have suggested, this high rate of natural increase can be attributed to the influence of industrialisation on the rate of population growth, why is it that within the North there should have been such marked disparities between the experience of different industrial counties? Why does the growth of the West Riding and Staffordshire seem to have been almost exclusively due to their exceptionally high rates of natural increase, whereas Lancashire and Warwickshire, which grew more rapidly than their neighbours, had lower rates of natural increase and relied more heavily on the immigration of the surplus population from surrounding areas? We should, of course, expect both the supply of, and the demand for, migrant labour to be greatest in the most rapidly expanding centre in a particular region, and it is not surprising that Lancashire and Warwickshire should have attracted more immigrants than their neighbours. But this would hardly explain the virtual absence of net immigration into Staffordshire and the West Riding, or the relatively low rates of natural increase in Lancashire and Warwickshire. We must, therefore, look elsewhere for the main explanation, and it seems likely that it may rest in the differences in the industrial structure and distribution of population in the counties concerned.

In both Lancashire and the West Riding industrial development in the eighteenth century meant to a large extent the growth of domestic industries in rural areas; but in Lancashire, with the growth of the port of Liverpool and the early development of an industrial and commercial centre in the Manchester area, a significant proportion of the population was already living in towns. By 1801, Lancashire was by far the most densely populated county in England outside the London area, and most of its inhabitants, then as now, were packed into a comparatively small area south of the River Ribble. It is difficult to give statistics of urbanisation as such, owing to the uncertainty of urban boundaries, but judging by the figures given in one analysis[1] it appears that about 40 per cent of the population of Lancashire lived in nine towns with more than ten thousand inhabitants each, and nearly 25 per cent in Liverpool and Manchester alone. In the West Riding, on the other hand, the concentration of population was much less pronounced. At the beginning of the eighteenth century the county was relatively thinly populated, and although by the end it had risen to third place in the density list with 212 to the square mile, there were

[1] R. Price Williams, 'On the Increase of Population in England and Wales', *J. Statist. Soc.*, vol. XLIII (1880), pp. 462–96.

only five towns of moderate size which together embraced only just over 20 per cent of the population. Despite the growth of Leeds and Sheffield, the West Riding was still for the most part a county of industrialised villages.[1]

A similar contrast is apparent in the development of Staffordshire and Warwickshire. The density of population in the two midland counties was remarkably similar through the eighteenth century, and in 1801 both of them had about the same number of people to the square mile as the West Riding. But the internal distribution of the population was very different. Staffordshire was, of course, rich in the minerals on which the midland industries were based and it was already a relatively populous industrial area at the end of the seventeenth century. But even with the most elastic definition of urban boundaries[2] it had no town remotely comparable to Birmingham, which, lying in the north-western corner of the neighbouring county, between the mineral ores of the 'Black Country' proper and the older industrial area in the Coventry district, rapidly became the industrial centre of the region. On the other hand, the growing urban concentration in north Warwickshire had no counterpart in the southern part of that county, which remains predominantly rural even today, whereas in Staffordshire the growth of the small industrial towns and colliery villages in the south was balanced by the rise of the potteries further north. In other words, the inhabitants of Staffordshire—like those of the West Riding—seem to have been fairly evenly dispersed, and the division between town and country, industry and agriculture, was still indistinct. In 1801, no more than a quarter of the population—and probably much less—lived in towns with more than 10,000 inhabitants, while in Warwickshire 42 per cent of the population lived in Birmingham and Coventry and over a third in Birmingham alone.

Now we should, of course, expect there to be more migration in districts where the growth of population was uneven and involved the rapid development of towns. This would be the case even if the rate of natural increase in urban areas was the same or, up to a point, higher than in rural districts; but in reality the rate of natural increase in eighteenth-century towns was usually low, and sometimes, as in the case of London, negative. The growing industrial towns of the North did not regularly have the huge excess of burials over baptisms which was characteristic of the metropolis; but neither did they enjoy as favourable a balance of life over death as the rural districts which surrounded them. In Birmingham and Manchester, for example, so far as we can judge from the isolated data available, the baptisms

[1] According to another analysis, only 31 per cent of the population of the West Riding lived in towns with over 4,000 inhabitants in 1801, compared with 45 per cent in Lancashire and Cheshire combined. See T. A. Welton, 'On the Distribution of Population in England and Wales, and its Progress . . . from 1801 to 1891', *J. Roy. Statist. Soc.*, vol. LXIII (1900), pp. 527–89.

[2] In 1801, the *parish* of Wolverhampton (the unit taken by Price Williams) had a population of over 30,000, but the town itself was less than half that size.

exceeded the burials in only five decades of the eighteenth century, and in Liverpool in six, compared with eight or nine in the case of the counties to which they belonged. Thus it seems clear that if industrial expansion tended to stimulate population growth urban conditions did not. Hence when, as in Staffordshire and the West Riding, industry was widely diffused, it seems to have resulted in a rapid growth of population and little or no immigration from outside. But when, as in Lancashire and Warwickshire, industrial development meant that a large proportion began to live in towns, we find that the county as a whole had a relatively small surplus of baptisms over burials, and it was compelled to draw heavily on the natural increase of its neighbours.

In conclusion, however, it should be noted that part of the different experience of these counties may simply be an accident of geography. For if the extent of migration was associated with the growth of towns, much may depend—in an analysis based on a county classification— not merely on the percentage of the population living in urban areas, but on the size and location of individual towns. Such evidence as we possess suggests that migrants usually travelled comparatively short distances, and in the case of Birmingham, for example, the majority of the immigrants at the beginning of the eighteenth century apparently came from Staffordshire and Warwickshire, and most of the remainder from Worcestershire and Shropshire. Moreover, even within the three counties immediately adjacent to Birmingham, most of the immigrants apparently came from the parts nearest the town rather than further away.[1] If the growth of the town had no influence on the population increase in its immediate neighbourhood, this would make little difference, since presumably those who moved into the town would tend to be replaced by others from further afield, and in this way the town would become the centre of a series of converging waves of immigration whose ramifications might extend over a very wide area. Something like this seems to have happened in the case of London; but in the case of Lancashire and its surroundings, it seems more likely that the growth of the northern industrial centres tended to stimulate population in the districts from which immigrants were drawn and thus reduced the need for replacements from outside the immediate urban catchment areas. If this was so, then clearly a county in which the bulk of the urban population was concentrated in one centrally situated town or, alternatively, spread over a number of smaller and scattered urban centres, would be likely, other things being equal, to attract less immigrants from outside and to have a higher rate of natural increase than one which happened to have a large urban concentration near the county boundary. But when, as in Warwickshire, the large urban concentration was close to the boundary with a county of the former type, the contrast between them would be sharpened. If more people had lived in Warwick and Leamington instead of Birmingham, or if the

---

[1] W. H. B. Court, *The Rise of the Midland Industries, 1600–1838* (1938), pp. 48–50.

urban population of Staffordshire had been concentrated in the neighbourhood of West Bromwich or Walsall, the position of the two counties might have been reversed, even though the actual proportion of towndwellers in each case remained the same. Nor can the 'accidents' of urban location be ignored in considering the demographic history of the West Riding, since Leeds is situated in the heart of that county and probably attracted very few immigrants from outside. Sheffield, it is true, is close to its southern boundary, but it must be remembered that the statistics we have given are designed to illustrate the *net* movement of population across county boundaries, not its absolute volume. The West Riding's gains on account of Sheffield may have been more than offset by its losses to the nearby Manchester area and to the East Riding, which in 1801 had a relatively larger urban population,[1] and at times relied much more heavily on immigration, than its industrial neighbour.

These explanations of the differences in the pattern of demographic evolution in the major industrial counties are largely speculative, and it is not at present possible to check the assumptions on which they are based. But perhaps enough has been said to indicate that a closer analysis of the complex relationship between urbanisation, industrialisation and population growth should throw a clearer light, not only on the changing distribution of population, but on the determinants of its overall increase during this critical period.

3. CHANGES IN BIRTH AND DEATH RATES

The primary conclusion drawn from the preceding discussion was that the increase in the share of the industrial areas of the country in the rising population of England during the early stages of industrialisation must be attributed to the relatively high rates of natural increase obtaining in the North-West during that period. It seems unlikely that this broad conclusion would be altered by the removal of the serious defects in the underlying statistics. It is more difficult to suggest a confident hypothesis concerning the mechanism by which this high rate of increase was achieved. Quite apart from the difficulties of estimating the number of births and deaths from the parish register data, it can be argued that the assumptions underlying the basic population estimates for the eighteenth century render any figures of local birth and death rates obtained from them virtually worthless. This is so of figures derived from Rickman's first set of estimates— which assumed a constant baptism rate—and to some extent the objection applies to deductions from the estimates given in Table 24.[2]

---

[1] Thirty-four per cent of the total population according to Price Williams.

[2] Talbot Griffith (*op. cit.* p. 10) thought that the adoption of Rickman's first set of estimates would only invalidate estimates of the birth rate and that they were therefore preferable to the second. But this is nonsense. Clearly, 'death-rates' calculated on the basis of these figures would simply reflect changes in the ratio of deaths to births, and would coincide with the actual death rates only if the assumption on which the population estimates were based was valid. But, as Griffith himself shows, that assumption was false.

On the other hand, the figures calculated for 1701 are largely supported by estimates, for roughly the same date, based on the hearth-tax returns, which do not involve any assumptions about the behaviour of baptism and burial rates. For 1781 also we have two sets of estimates, and though they are not independent, their underlying assumptions differ, and it is possible to feel some measure of confidence that the totals for the main regions and for many of the individual counties are reasonably reliable. As for the 1751 estimates, it is probably safe to assume that the increase in population in the first half of the eighteenth century was generally very small, and the margin of error involved in the absolute figures can hardly be large, even if they may sometimes give a misleading impression of the rate or even direction of change. If the estimates we have do represent the level of population at different periods more or less correctly, they can be used to indicate the major changes in birth and death rates, despite the methodological objections to them. But it remains true that calculations based on this material will at best be crude, and we have at present no means of measuring the short-term fluctuations in birth and death rates. Hence, we shall be mainly concerned in this section with the movement of the absolute numbers of births and deaths over time, and we shall attempt to relate these movements to population changes only in the most general terms. Fig. 6 illustrates in graphic form the fluctuations in the estimated numbers of births and deaths from decade to decade and the probable trends in population in each of the major regions considered in the previous section, while Tables 28 and 29 give estimates of the long-term changes in the average birth and death rates in each region and county during the 130 years under review. In Table 28 separate figures are given for each of the four sub-periods, but in view of the uncertainty of the mid-century population estimates for individual counties, no attempt has been made in Table 29 to distinguish the rates for 1751–81 and 1781–1801.

Instead, two alternative estimates are given of the average rates prevailing in the second half of the century as a whole, the first based on the population estimates for 1781 given in column 3a of Table 24 and the second on the estimates in column 3b of the same table.[1] For these calculations, we have simply divided the average annual number of births and deaths in each of the four sub-periods by the average annual population in thousands, on the assumption that the population grew at constant rates in each sub-period.[2] It is, of course, unlikely that population grew at constant rates during these periods. Moreover, it could be argued that even on this assumption it would have been preferable to calculate separate rates for each year, or at least decade, and then to average the rates obtained. It is reassuring to note,

---

[1] These are weighted averages of rates separately calculated for each of the periods 1751–80 and 1781–1800.

[2] I.e.,
$$\frac{P^1 - P^0}{\log_e P^1 - \log_e P^0}$$

however, that when we calculate the birth and death rates for England and Wales as a whole by these methods the results are almost exactly the same as the corresponding averages of Brownlee's rates for each decade.

Before we consider the implications of this material, it may be useful to summarise the present state of the debate about changes in the national birth and death rates during the period. Until 1780 or 1790, the differences in trend between the various estimates of these rates are not significant and the direction of the changes indicated by the figures, as distinct from their interpretation, has not been seriously questioned. At the beginning of the eighteenth century, the birth rate was about 32 per thousand, according to Brownlee and Farr, or a few points lower if Griffith's coefficient is preferred. About the second decade of the century, the birth rate began to increase, and by the 1740's it had apparently risen by five or even six points. Thereafter the increase was much more gradual, but the general movement was slightly upward until about 1790, when the rate is variously estimated at between 35 and 40 per thousand. In the early part of the century the rise in the birth rate was more than offset by an increase in mortality, which rose steadily from 26–30 per thousand at the beginning of the century to 33–37 per thousand in the 1730's. In the twenties and thirties the total number of deaths probably outnumbered the births; but in the forties the death rate started to decline, and by the sixties it had fallen almost to the level of the first decade, only to rise again slightly in the 1770's.

The increase in population in the generation or so before 1780 must, therefore, be attributed partly to a relatively high birth rate, and partly to a decline in the death rate from the peak reached in the 1720's and 1730's. But both these phenomena may be regarded as the normal demographic reaction to a period of high mortality[1]; and clearly much depends on what happened in the half-century after 1790. It is here, however, that we enter disputed territory. Brownlee's figures suggest that, if anything, the birth rate declined slightly during this period, and according to Griffith it fell by about three points. If they are right, it follows that the acceleration in the rate of population growth after 1780 was entirely due to a further and dramatic fall in the death rate, which, according to Brownlee, dropped from 28·6 in the 1780's to 21·1 in the second decade of the nineteenth century. But Griffith and Brownlee both assumed that the ratio of deaths to burials did not alter during this period, and Griffith also assumed a constant birth–baptism ratio. These assumptions and the conclusions based upon them have recently been seriously challenged by J. T. Krause, who argues that the apparently low level of mortality in the 1810's is in fact evidence, not of a decline in the death rate, but of the breakdown in parish registration.[2] He points out that it is unlikely that mortality was lower at the end of the Napoleonic Wars—as Griffith's and Brownlee's figures imply—

[1] See H. J. Habakkuk, 'English Population in the Eighteenth Century', *loc. cit.* pp. 120–2.
[2] J. T. Krause, 'Changes in English Fertility and Mortality, 1781–1850', *Econ. Hist. Rev.*, second series, vol. XI (1958), pp. 52–70.

than in most subsequent decades of the nineteenth century, especially since the evidence of the 1821 census shows that the age structure at that time was not conducive to a low death rate. Nor, he suggests, have any convincing reasons been advanced for expecting a fall in the death rate in the generation after 1780; apart from the doubt which has recently been cast on the medical evidence, the consensus of opinion at present tends to the view that the standard of life of those closest to the margin of subsistence probably fell between 1790 and 1820, and improved thereafter.

At the end of his article, Krause suggests that the death rate may actually have *risen* during this period. In order to sustain this view he first estimates the number of births in the second decade of the nineteenth century and then deducts the inter-censal increase in population to obtain the number of deaths in the same period. His estimate of the number of births, however, involves the assumptions that the recording of the 0–9 age group in the 1821 census was defective and that the survival ratio of this group was slightly lower in 1811–20 than in the 1840's. Both assumptions are plausible, but it must be admitted that the latter to some extent begs the question at issue. Moreover, his calculations imply that while the birth–baptism ratio was high from 1811 to 1820, the death–burial ratio was even higher. It is not altogether clear why this should have been so. We know that after 1838 the registration of births was much more defective than that of burials, and Krause apparently accepts the usual view that a similar discrepancy existed in the latter part of the eighteenth century. Most of the factors which may have been responsible for a deterioration of registration in the intervening period would have applied to the baptisms as well as the burials, and it is doubtful whether the omissions from the registers of the deaths of members of the armed forces would by itself have been sufficient to reverse the normal relationship.[1] The point is not that Krause's chief conclusion—that the birth rate was the *major* variable behind the upsurge of English population during the Industrial Revolution—is false; it may well be correct. But at present the evidence does not seem so overwhelming that we are justified in completely reversing the picture suggested by the crude statistics, defective as these undoubtedly are. What is certainly true, however, is that the possibilities of error involved in the use of these statistics in the early nineteenth

[1] It is usually suggested that the registration of deaths by the parish clergy was more complete than that of births because the disposal of a corpse, unlike infant baptism, is a physical necessity as well as a religious duty. It is true that the private burial grounds associated with the rise of nonconformity provided an alternative to the Anglican churchyard for sections of the population to whom the rites of the Established Church had little or no appeal; and for this reason the gap between the birth–baptism and death–burial ratios may have narrowed at the beginning of the nineteenth century. But why should it have disappeared? Krause has since explained that although most Anglicans were presumably baptised in the established church, many were in fact buried in nonconformist burial grounds during this period. This certainly strengthens his case, but as Professor Glass has pointed out in the same volume, there are still good reasons for doubting his conclusion that there was no decline in mortality at this time. See *Population in History,* ed. D. V. Glass and D. E. C. Eversley (1965), pp. 7, 16–17, 392.

century are even more serious than the data for the first years of civil registration would suggest. For it is the crux of Krause's argument that parish registration deteriorated sharply before 1820 and improved again thereafter; and if he is right the statistics will not only give a biased impression of the trend but will also distort the fluctuations from decade to decade.

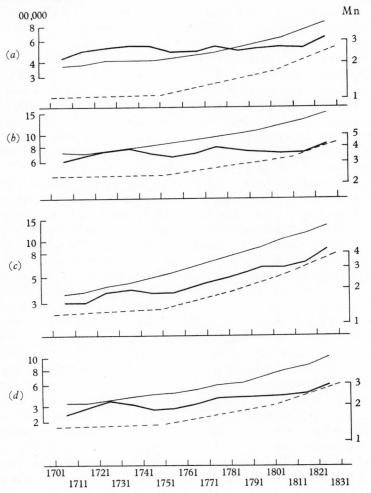

Fig. 6. Births, deaths and populations by regions, 1701–1831: ———— births ($\times 10^5$); ———— deaths ($\times 10^5$); – – – – population ($\times 10^6$). (*a*) London area, (*b*) the South, (*c*) the North-West, (*d*) the North.

It is not to be supposed that the regional figures which we propose to discuss here, and which are, in effect, based on the crude statistics, will elucidate these problems. But they may discourage the tendency, which seems to be inherent in most discussion of the subject, to seek a single explanation of population change. For it is evident that in the eighteenth century the relative importance of birth and death rates

Table 28. *Average regional birth and death rates, 1701–1830**

(per thousand)

	Birth rates				Death rates			
	1701–50	1751–80	1781–1800	1801–30	1701–50	1751–80	1781–1800	1801–30
North-West	33·6	39·6	39·8	38·5	28·0	26·7	27·0	22·7
North	32·6	35·1	35·1	35·4	28·5	26·8	25·3	21·0
North and North-West	33·1	37·3	37·6	37·1	28·2	26·7	26·2	22·0
London Area	38·0	38·5	37·9	35·2	48·8	43·3	35·1	27·0
South	32·8	36·6	37·1	37·2	30·6	29·0	26·0	20·6
London and the South	34·5	37·2	37·4	36·4	36·4	33·6	29·1	23·0
England and Wales	33·8	37·2	37·5	36·8	32·8	30·4	27·7	22·5
Brownlee's averages	33·9	37·1	37·5	36·9	32·7	30·5	27·8	22·5

* If the alternative population estimates for 1781 are used, the birth and death rates obtained for both 1751–81 and 1781–1800 are slightly higher in the case of London and the North-West and slightly lower for the other two regions. The differences are largest in the North-West, but the overall trends are not affected and in no case does the discrepancy amount to more than 0·4 per thousand.

varied considerably in different localities, and it is possible that the same may have been true for the early nineteenth century.

Let us examine first the statistics for the London area. As we should expect, in the first half of the eighteenth century, when the gin mania was at its height, the death rate in the metropolitan counties was abnormally high. Over the whole period it averaged 49 per thousand, and even if the death–burial ratio is too high, it seems likely that in London itself, where the effects of gin-drinking were most acutely felt, the annual mortality was 50 per thousand or more. In common with other districts the trend of deaths was upward until the 1730's, and in this case very heavy mortality seems to have persisted in the 1740's. After 1750, however, there was a marked fall in the number of deaths, and although there was a temporary increase in the seventies, the number of recorded burials did not regain and finally surpass the level of the 1730's and 1740's until the opening decades of the nineteenth century, when the population had roughly doubled. It may well be that the estimates given in Table 28 exaggerate the dramatic fall in the death rate during this period, and particularly after 1800, but there can be no doubt that there was a significant decline in mortality in this area in the second half of the eighteenth century. Moreover, although the possibility of a temporary rise in mortality during the Napoleonic Wars cannot be discounted, it is probable that, in the first thirty years of the nineteenth century, it was, on the average, lower than in the latter part of the eighteenth. Even on the assumption that the death–burial ratio averaged 1·5 from 1801 to 1830—as against 1·21 for this region in 1839–40—the death rate was still lower than in the last twenty years of the eighteenth century, and considerably below the average of the third quarter.[1] By the first years of civil registration, the death rate in the rural districts round London ranged from 17·9 in Surrey—the lowest in the country—to 20·2 in Essex, and even in the metropolis itself it was only about 25·3, or about half the average rate a century before.[2]

In contrast, it is difficult to find evidence of a significant rise in the birth rate in the London area during the eighteenth and early nineteenth centuries, and certainly none that was sustained over a long period. At the beginning of the eighteenth century the birth rate was already high, and well above the national average, although it was still considerably below the mortality rate, and indeed the rate of natural *decrease* in London at this time was roughly double the rate of *increase* anywhere else in the country. In the first three decades the number of births tended to increase, but in the thirties and forties the advance was checked, and in Middlesex there was an absolute decline. In the third quarter of the century, the estimated birth rate was slightly above the average for the first fifty years, but the increase in the recorded number of baptisms was already tending to lag behind the probable growth of population; and even if in fact the birth rate temporarily rose at the beginning of the nineteenth century to 40 per thousand or more, it is difficult to escape the conclusion that the major long-term factor in the increase in population in London after 1750 was the decline in mortality from the disastrous levels prevailing in the first half of the eighteenth century.[3]

The main outlines of the developments in the London area are already familiar, for they have been more closely examined than events elsewhere and have certainly coloured the commonly accepted view of the importance of a falling death-rate during this period.[4] When we turn to the North-West, on the other hand, the picture looks very different. Unless registration was already more defective in this region

---

[1] Rickman estimated that a third of the deaths in London itself were not recorded in the parish registers, and although he was undoubtedly over-optimistic in thinking that most of the omissions were included in the returns as printed, some of them certainly were. And even if Rickman underestimated the deficiency of the registers in the metropolis itself, it is difficult to believe that the death–burial ratio for the whole region could have averaged more than 1·5 throughout the first thirty years of the nineteenth century. Incidentally, it should be noted that recent research suggests that Brownlee probably overestimated the death–burial ratio for the country as a whole in the eighteenth century, just as he probably underestimated it for the beginning of the nineteenth. It is unlikely, however, that the death–burial ratio adopted here is too high for the London area in the latter part of the eighteenth century, since London was the one district which already had a significant number of private burial grounds before 1800. See J. T. Krause, *op. cit.* pp. 55–7.

[2] *Eighth Annual Report of the Registrar-General* (1847–8), p. liv. The rates refer to the years 1838–45.

[3] According to the Registrar-General's returns for 1839–45, the birth rate had dropped back to 25·3 in Middlesex and 31·1 in the metropolis, which was certainly considerably below the level a century before. It is generally agreed, however, that by that time the birth rate for the country as a whole had started to fall.

[4] See, *inter alia*, M. D. George, 'Some Causes of the Increase of Population in the Eighteenth Century as Illustrated by London', *Economic Journal*, vol. XXII (1922), pp. 325–52; J. R. Brownlee, 'The Health of London in the Eighteenth Century', *Proc. Roy. Soc. Med.*, vol. XVIII (1925), Part II, Epidemiology Section, pp. 73–85.

than elsewhere, it seems that at the beginning of our period both birth and death rates in the North-West—and particularly the latter—were below the national average and the difference between the two, even in the first half of the eighteenth century, already indicates a relatively high rate of natural increase. From 1710 to 1750 the curve of births rose much more steeply, both absolutely and in relation to the probable increase in population, than elsewhere; and although the number of deaths also increased in the twenties and thirties, the balance of births over deaths, in sharp contrast to other parts of the county, was not only positive in those years, but was actually larger in absolute terms than in the first two decades of the century. When the wave of mortality ebbed in the forties the high birth rate was maintained, and in the 1750's the North-West entered a period of sustained natural growth: the region apparently experienced neither the rise in mortality in the seventies nor the quickening of population growth in the 1780's which seem to have occurred in other districts, and for half a century the births and deaths mounted at almost constant, and remarkably similar, rates.

This population 'take-off' (which, incidentally, lends added support to the assessment of developments in the 1740's given in the last chapter) must be regarded as one of the outstanding features of the demographic history of the area. To some extent it can be attributed to the decline and stabilisation of the death rate after the high mortality of the twenties and thirties. But the major factor was the rise in the birth rate, for whereas the latter averaged 39·7 per thousand, or more, in the second half of the century, compared with 33·6 from 1701 to 1750, the death rate had fallen by little more than one point, and probably tended to rise again towards the end of the period. Nor was this pattern peculiar to one or two parts of the region, although there were, of course, internal variations. In some counties, notably the West Riding and Cheshire, the rise in the birth rate was comparatively modest—perhaps because the birth and death rates were both relatively high at the beginning of the century—and in these counties the fall in the death rate after 1740 seems to have played a greater part in the growth of population than in other parts of the region. But in general the picture suggested by the figures for the area as a whole appears to reflect surprisingly closely the developments in the individual counties of which it is composed.

In the first two decades of the nineteenth century, there was a second acceleration in the tempo of population growth in the North-West which, if the statistics can be trusted, was entirely due to a fall in the death-rate. It is possible, indeed probable, that for the area as a whole this impression is spurious, for we know that in 1839–40 at least a third of the births and nearly a quarter of the deaths in this region escaped registration by the Anglican clergy. In some of the rural parts of the region, where registration was comparatively good, there may well have been a fall in the death rate at this time, but in the industrial areas, and particularly the West Riding and Lancashire, it seems more likely that the true explanation should be sought in a further increase in the birth rate. But even if the evidence of the statistics is accepted at its face value this would not alter the conclusion that the primary reason for the enormous increase in population which accompanied the industrialisation of the North-West was the sharp rise in the birth rate in the early part of the eighteenth century.

The other two regions fall somewhere between the extremes offered by London and the North-West, and in both of them population growth appears to have been due to the combination of a rise in the birth rate and a falling death rate, certainly before 1780 and possibly thereafter. There can be little doubt of the importance of the birth rate, which rose in both regions in the first half of the eighteenth century, though less markedly than in the North-West. Moreover, the figures suggest that the numbers born in the South continued to increase more rapidly than the total population in the second half of the eighteenth century, while in the North there seems to have been a further rise in the birth rate after 1780, with the result that, even on the basis of our defective statistics, it appears that the birth rate was, on the average, slightly higher in both these regions in the first three decades of the nineteenth century than it had been at the end of the eighteenth.[1] The death rate is a little more difficult to assess. It would probably be wrong to accept the conclusion suggested by the burial figures that the decline in mortality was more spectacular after 1780 than before; but, as in London, the impression is strong that the death rate was in general somewhat lower after 1800 than before. Krause points out that the growth of nonconformity was by no means insignificant even in the South, and comparatively high death–burial ratios are certainly to be found in some of the southern counties in the early years of civil registration.[2] But the *average* death–burial ratios in 1839–40, in both the rural South and the northern counties outside the north-western catchment area—despite the inclusion in the 'North' of Wales and Monmouth—work out at $1 \cdot 1$ and it is unlikely that by using Brownlee's coefficient of $1 \cdot 2$ we can have underestimated the average death rates in these regions during the first three decades of the century. Yet, if allowance is made for the fact that the parish register returns given in the 1801 census were incomplete, it appears that these death rates were slightly below the corresponding *burial* rates in the previous period.

Within two such large and heterogeneous regions significant differences in the causes of demographic change might be expected. It is dangerous to lean too heavily on the shaky materials at our disposal, but a few remarks may perhaps be appropriate. In the South, the local variations seem to have been comparatively small. In nearly all the counties in the group the death rate tended to fall fairly steadily after

[1] The figures probably understate the rise much more in the North than the South, for in 1839–40 the birth–baptism ratio averages about $1 \cdot 4$ in the northern counties, compared with $1 \cdot 2$ in the South.

[2] J. T. Krause, *op. cit.* pp. 55–6.

Table 29. *Average county birth rate and death rates, 1701–1830*

(per thousand)

	Birth rates				Death rates			
	1701–50	1751–1800		1801–30	1701–50	1751–1800		1801–30
		(a)	(b)			(a)	(b)	
North-West								
Cheshire	35·8	38·7	37·6	35·8	33·8	28·2	27·4	23·1
Cumberland	29·1	35·8	34·9	38·1	21·3	23·1	22·5	21·8
Derbyshire	33·4	40·6	40·3	37·3	25·5	25·7	25·5	20·9
Lancashire	29·1	40·9	41·0	40·6	26·4	29·3	29·3	24·5
Shropshire	33·1	38·6	38·0	36·2	29·2	25·2	24·8	21·3
Staffordshire	37·2	43·4	43·3	40·3	30·3	29·2	29·1	23·2
Westmorland	31·7	39·4	40·0	38·2	26·3	25·6	25·9	21·1
Yorks., N. Riding	32·3	37·0	35·9	36·3	25·7	24·0	23·2	20·0
Yorks., W. Riding	38·3	40·5	40·3	38·0	30·2	26·7	26·6	22·1
North								
Durham	33·0	36·3	35·4	37·1	29·0	31·5	30·7	22·6
Herefordshire	28·0	31·7	31·0	33·1	22·7	20·9	20·4	19·1
Leicestershire	32·4	37·9	36·6	35·9	26·9	28·1	27·1	21·5
Lincolnshire	39·0	38·7	40·2	40·2	38·8	30·0	31·2	21·8
Monmouthshire	32·5	28·2	28·3	28·4	27·0	21·7	21·8	18·5
Northumberland	26·8	27·1	27·0	33·5	23·0	22·7	22·6	20·5
Nottinghamshire	31·2	39·9	40·2	39·2	27·5	28·5	28·7	22·3
Rutland	38·1	39·4	39·0	35·8	28·3	29·1	28·9	20·6
Warwickshire	34·8	40·2	39·6	34·8	32·0	31·6	31·1	22·9
Worcestershire	34·2	39·2	37·9	38·7	30·3	29·4	28·4	22·7
Yorks., E. Riding	40·8	36·7	41·1	40·3	39·3	27·9	31·2	24·0
Wales	30·1	31·3	31·8	31·6	24·2	21·3	21·7	18·6
London Area								
Essex	31·9	34·4	35·7	36·5	35·5	31·4	32·6	23·0
Kent	42·4	44·5	45·5	41·7	43·3	37·8	38·8	26·3
Middlesex	37·0	37·1	36·1	33·2	52·6	43·3	42·2	29·1
Surrey	45·2	40·2	40·4	33·6	56·0	41·8	42·0	24·9
South								
Bedfordshire	32·4	34·9	37·0	36·6	33·8	28·8	30·6	21·4
Berkshire	36·4	39·4	38·6	37·0	32·1	27·9	27·3	21·6
Buckinghamshire	35·8	37·6	38·1	37·0	35·2	29·9	30·3	22·7
Cambridgeshire	35·6	37·9	39·0	40·5	33·4	32·9	33·9	24·0
Cornwall	34·3	38·5	40·5	38·2	30·8	24·7	25·9	18·2
Devonshire	26·1	35·8	35·7	37·5	25·7	27·3	27·3	21·0
Dorset	33·0	33·4	34·9	35·4	29·9	24·6	25·8	19·4
Gloucestershire	34·5	35·9	35·3	35·3	31·2	27·4	27·0	19·3
Hampshire	36·9	37·1	38·3	39·1	32·7	28·3	29·3	21·7
Hertfordshire	34·1	35·2	36·2	37·0	33·7	29·3	30·1	21·5
Huntingdonshire	38·9	36·6	38·3	37·7	42·5	33·9	35·5	22·7
Norfolk	34·6	40·9	39·6	38·8	33·2	30·9	29·9	21·1
Northamptonshire	33·2	33·3	33·5	35·0	30·7	28·8	29·0	21·9
Oxfordshire	34·2	38·0	37·8	37·0	30·0	27·1	27·0	20·9
Somerset	29·3	34·3	33·5	34·9	28·4	25·0	24·4	20·4
Suffolk	34·1	37·7	38·4	37·6	32·5	27·6	28·0	19·9
Sussex	39·1	44·6	44·2	40·5	32·4	29·5	29·2	20·0
Wiltshire	30·1	31·0	30·7	34·4	26·2	24·6	24·3	19·6

Source: See text.

1740, with a momentary break in the 1770's[1]; and in all but Hunting-donshire, the estimated birth rate was higher in the second half of the eighteenth century than it had been in the first. True, the continuing rise in the birth rate after the death rate had started to fall was apparently confined to the south-western textile area and to some of the East Midlands counties which were comparatively close to the growing industrial centres in the North. But it may be significant that several of the other counties in the region had relatively high birth–baptism ratios in 1839–40, and there are, in fact, only five in which there is no obvious reason to suspect a further rise in the birth rate in the latter part of the eighteenth century. Moreover, two of these, Sussex and Berkshire, were insulated by their geographical position from the stimulus of industrial growth,[2] and two more, Norfolk and Gloucestershire, were by southern standards urbanised counties in which industry was relatively, if not absolutely, in decline.[3]

Further north, in the rather mixed belt of counties adjoining the north-western catchment area, the picture is more complicated. The general quickening of population growth in the second half of the eighteenth century had singularly little effect on the industrial counties on the north-eastern seaboard of England, and in both Northumberland and Durham changes in birth and death rates in the course of the century were comparatively small. After 1780 the population of these counties seems to have been swollen by immigrants, but it was not until the early nineteenth century that the figures suggest a marked rise in the rate of natural increase, which appears to have been due both to an increase in the birth rate and, possibly, a decline in mortality.[4] It is, therefore, in the industrial counties of the Midlands and their immediate neighbours that we must look for the clearest evidence of a rising birth rate in the eighteenth century. For in these counties, as we might perhaps expect, the pattern of demographic change bears a close family

---

[1] The apparent exception in the case of Devonshire, where the estimated death rate was higher in the second half of the century than the first, is almost certainly due to an error in the population estimates for 1701 and 1751. See above, p. 102. The same factor would, of course, also account for the disproportionately large increase in the birth rate in this county in the eighteenth century.

[2] It will be noted that in the case of Sussex, although the birth rate seems to have been lower after 1800 than before, it was still unusually high. It is possible that this was in part due to the relatively efficient registration of births in this county by the parish clergy. But Krause has shown by an analysis of the census data that in 1821 the fertility ratio was also exceptionally high in Sussex, a fact which he attributed to the operation of the poor-law. (*Op. cit.* p. 68.)

[3] The fifth was Oxfordshire. In 1801, about a quarter of the population of Gloucestershire lived in Bristol, while Norwich, King's Lynn and Yarmouth (each with over 10,000 inhabitants) together accounted for nearly 23 per cent of the population of Norfolk.

[4] It will be noted that the increase in the birth rate is more apparent in the figures for Northumberland despite the high birth–baptism ratio for that county in 1839–40. This is probably in part because the parish clergy in that county seem to have made a much more realistic estimate of the number of unentered baptisms than was the case elsewhere, and in 1801–10, for example, they put the figure at about 21 per cent of the registered total. But since, of course, the figures we have used here take no account of omissions before 1801, this may mean that we have somewhat post-dated the rise in the birth rate, even though registration was probably more defective after 1801 than before.

resemblance to that in the North-West. Apart from Monmouthshire, where registration was notoriously defective, all the counties in the area experienced a significant rise in fertility, and in Nottinghamshire the increase seems to have been greater than in any county in the North-West, except Lancashire. The death rate, on the other hand, changed little during this period, and in Nottinghamshire and Leicestershire it was, on the average, higher in the second half of the eighteenth century than it had been in the first. After 1780, or thereabouts, the picture is more obscure. In most of the counties in the area, there may have been some decline in mortality, for the registration of burials was in general comparatively good. But it is equally likely that the birth rate continued to rise. Possibly in Worcestershire, certainly in Herefordshire, and even to some extent in Monmouthshire, a small increase is indicated by the estimates given here, and in Nottinghamshire and Leicestershire there was only a small decline, although in 1839–40 both these counties had birth–baptism ratios well above the national average. Somewhat surprisingly, Warwickshire appears to be an exception to the general trend. In 1839–40 the birth–baptism ratio here was only 1·35, yet our estimate of the average birth rate for the first three decades of the nineteenth century is about five points lower than for the second half of the eighteenth. It is by no means certain that these figures should be accepted at their face value: the statistics suggest that there was a sharp fall in the birth rate in the first decade of the nineteenth century and that it was then stabilised at the lower level, but it may well be that there was simply a substantial, if temporary, deterioration in registration, particularly in Birmingham. At least it seems possible, however, that in Warwickshire, and perhaps also in the neighbouring county of Staffordshire—which is here included in the north-western region— the birth rate was a less potent factor in the growth of population at this time than it was both in the other midland counties and in the textile and mining districts further north.

To sum up, it seems probable in the light of recent research that the decline in mortality played a smaller part in the expansion of population during the Industrial Revolution than has sometimes been supposed, and that the dramatic fall in the death rate came after the population upsurge had passed its peak. As we emphasised at the outset of this chapter, much local research will be needed before any firm conclusions can be advanced about the forces at work, and the present very superficial survey can in no sense be regarded as a substitute for such studies. There can be no doubt that the tentative suggestions we have made about the demographic fortunes of individual counties will require revision in the light of further work. But the evidence at our disposal suggests that in general the fall in mortality which did occur in the late eighteenth and early nineteenth centuries was most marked in London and the rural areas, while the expansion of population in those districts which felt the direct influence of industrial growth was much more clearly due to an increased birth rate.

In the nature of the case, the materials considered here do not cast much light on the underlying causes of this changing pattern of fertility and mortality. It seems clear that the rise in the birth rate was closely connected with the process of industrialisation, although it remains an open question whether this increase took place primarily as a result of earlier marriage, greater fertility, or even an increase in illegitimacy. The position in regard to the death rate, however, is more obscure. Recent work has tended to suggest that the high mortality in the 1720's and 1730's may be connected with climatic conditions and epidemics, and in so far as the general level of mortality was lower after the sharp fall in the 1740's, this may have been partially due to the comparative absence of epidemics during that period.[1] Certainly there is little reason to suppose that the large number of burials in the second quarter of the century can be attributed to a shortage of food, for, as we have seen, this was a period of relatively low food prices and high real wages. In London, such indications as we have of a rise in the standard of living of the labouring classes relate to the early part of the century, and there seems to be no economic change after 1740 which would account for the apparently dramatic fall in mortality at that time. It seems more likely that the explanation must lie in the improvement in the Londoner's health and sanitary conditions which followed the gin age, and if this was connected with economic conditions at all, it must have been due, not to rising material standards, but to the effect on the prices of grain of a growing population elsewhere. It is, of course, possible that in rural districts some part was played by the gradual disappearance of local famines and greater resistance to infection connected with the more *regular* supply of food to the rural population, which we might expect to follow from improvements in transport and a progressive rise in agricultural incomes.[2] But it seems probable that the decline in mortality in eighteenth-century England was in the main due to factors largely independent of the process of economic growth.

This does not mean, however, that the growth of population was itself an independent variable. In conditions of demographic equilibrium birth and death rates tend to fluctuate directly, and not inversely; so the question remains why the fall in the death rate was not accompanied by a decline in fertility.[3] Of course, we should expect it to take some time for social habits to become adjusted to changed conditions and the fall in the death rate would not at once be offset by a corresponding decline in fertility. However, it remains a question why, outside London, the birth rate not only failed to decline, but in most cases continued to rise, for seventy or eighty years after the death

[1] Cf. J. D. Chambers, 'The Vale of Trent', *op. cit.*; T. S. Ashton, *An Economic History of England: The Eighteenth Century*, pp. 3–4.

[2] In this connection, it is worth noting that although the general level of agricultural prices rose steeply in the second half of the eighteenth century, *fluctuations* became much less pronounced.

[3] See S. H. Coontz, *Population Theories and the Economic Interpretation* (1957), pp. 170–1.

rate had started to fall. It is surely significant also that the rate of natural increase of different regions of England in the eighteenth century should have been so closely connected with the pace of economic advance in these regions.

On the other hand, it would be wrong to suggest that the increase in population was simply a function of economic growth, and exercised no independent influence on the course of economic change. As we saw in the last chapter, it can be argued that in the conditions of eighteenth-century England population growth was itself a powerful agent of economic expansion. Furthermore, it seems clear that the rise in the birth rate which was mainly responsible for the increase of population in the northern cradle of British industrialism took most of its effect in the first half of the eighteenth century; that is to say, in the period immediately *before* the marked quickening in the tempo of economic and demographic change which occurred after 1745. Thus the evidence appears to be consistent with the view that the growth of population was both a consequence and, in its turn, a cause of economic change. We have seen that the late seventeenth and early eighteenth century was a period of modest economic expansion in which there was a tendency for wages to increase, and which was certainly notable for vigorous complaints of labour scarcity; and it was in the second decade of the eighteenth century that the birth rate apparently started to rise. But in the next decade both economic expansion and population growth seem to have been checked by a sharp rise in the death rate which, if we are right, had comparatively little to do with economic conditions in England. It was only in the 1740's, when the wave of mortality ebbed, that the effects of the rise in the birth rate made themselves felt in a new and unprecedented wave of population growth and economic expansion. This in its turn was followed by a further modest rise in the birth rate and a continuing fall in the death rate in areas comparatively remote from the major centres of economic growth, which laid the basis of a further advance in the 1780's. And when the full story comes to be told, it may well appear that at each stage in the process, the growth of population, itself produced by economic changes in the generation before, was one of the factors which drove the British economy upwards on the path of sustained growth.

CHAPTER IV

CHANGES IN THE INDUSTRIAL DISTRIBU-TION OF THE LABOUR FORCE AND EMPLOY-MENT INCOMES IN THE NINETEENTH AND TWENTIETH CENTURIES

AN industrial revolution characteristically entails extensive changes in the industrial distribution of the labour force. The long-term trends involved in this process are of three main kinds. First of all there is a fall in the proportion of the labour force engaged in agriculture, and an associated rise in the proportions engaged in manufacturing and extractive industries. Secondly there is an increase in the specialisation of labour, which at certain stages in the process means an increase in the proportions engaged in the service industries and at all times involves a widening of the range of occupations employing labour on a full-time basis. Thirdly there is an increase in the proportion of the total population regularly and fully committed to gainful economic activity.

These broad tendencies are generally arrested, or at any rate greatly reduced, when industrialisation is complete. In Britain there has been relatively little change in the proportion of the labour force in agriculture since the beginning of the twentieth century. Labour has continued to develop new specialisations, but some of the simpler and more repetitive operations are beginning to be taken over by machines. Economic opportunities continue to expand, but as real incomes and social standards improve, the proportion of the voluntarily unoccupied —students, housewives, and retired persons—also grows.

In the course of the nineteenth and early twentieth centuries, however, the changes in the distribution of the labour force were among the most significant aspects of the story of British economic growth. It is difficult to measure them satisfactorily because they were so radical and extensive as to escape all yardsticks. Indeed there is a limit to which we can usefully attempt to push back in time our estimates in this sphere; a limit which is defined less by the scarcity of data than by the inapplicability of our concepts. It is possible that we have gone beyond these limits and that our estimates for the distribution of the labour force before, say, 1841, or 1831, are so beset by the conceptual difficulties of allocating individuals to specific industries or occupations that the results have no clear meaning.

Certainly it does not seem possible to say anything precise about the distribution of the labour force in the pre-industrial era when the major manufactures were domestic industries subordinate to agriculture, and when many of the labourers, even in capitalistic industries like building or metal-working, moved from industrial to agricultural occupations at times of harvest or planting, and when domestic servants were often as occupied with their master's trade or industry as with his household. Peter Stubs, the eighteenth-century industrialist whose career in the second half of the century has been described by Professor Ashton, was innkeeper, maltster, brewer and filemaker, at one and the same time.[1] When a writer in the early eighteenth century calculated that nearly 965,000 people were engaged in the British woollen industry he may not have exaggerated as wildly as is commonly supposed.[2] If every woman who occasionally spun, every child that helped its parents by carding, and every man who occasionally worked a loom were included in the total, they would together constitute a substantial proportion of the population. As late as 1841 the census returns for Ireland (then still at a pre-industrial stage) recorded something quite close to a proportion of one in eight for persons engaged in the textile industries.[3] The point is not that the figures are inaccurate (they may be that too), but that they do not attempt to measure what we want to know.

The consequence is that when we try, for example, to convert Gregory King's elaborate estimate of the distribution of the population *circa* 1688 to something approaching an estimate of the distribution of the labour force, we find a proportion for those primarily engaged in agriculture which varies from about 60 per cent to about 80 per cent (according to the assumptions we make about the way his estimate for servants fits into his pattern of families, and according to the assumptions we make about the distribution of labourers and servants) and for trade and industry of between 11 and 30 per cent. If we can make no allowance for domestic industry, and we cannot distribute 'labouring people and outservants', between agricultural and non-agricultural occupations, we cannot get any closer to the truth than this.

In what follows, therefore, we have confined our attention to the nineteenth and twentieth centuries: and even these calculations are exceedingly crude and inaccurate for the early years of the nineteenth century.

I. THE EVIDENCE OF THE CENSUS RETURNS

The industrial distribution of the labour force has been deduced from the Census of Population returns, and these—especially for the first half of the century—are highly unsatisfactory.[4] The first census

---

[1] T. S. Ashton, *An Eighteenth Century Industrialist* (1939).

[2] See *A Short Essay upon Trade in General but more enlarged on that branch relating to the woollen manufactures of Great Britain and Ireland, etc., etc.*, by a Lover of his Country. The estimates in this pamphlet have been examined by Deane, 'The Output of the British Woollen Industry in the Eighteenth Century', *J. Econ. Hist.*, June 1957, pp. 210–12.

[3] 665,239 persons were attributed to the textile industries in Ireland at the 1841 census out of a total population of 8·175 million. More than half a million of these were women over fifteen—presumably part-time domestic spinners.

[4] Apart altogether from the fact that they are based on an occupational rather than an industrial classification of individuals.

attempt to collect occupational data in any detail was made in 1831. Before then all that was attempted was a rough classification of persons (1801) and of families (in 1811 and 1821) by two main classes of industry: (1) agriculture, and (2) trade and manufactures, with a third, residual, group to take all those who could not obviously be allocated to one of the two main branches of economic activity. The results of the 1801 attempt to obtain returns of the numbers of persons dependent for their livelihood on these two main activities are generally regarded as worthless. Rickman in the report of the 1821 census, for example, makes the following comment: 'The Question of 1801 relating to the occupations of persons was found in practice to produce no valuable result. In some instances a Householder seemed to understand that the Females of his Family, his Children and Servants ought to be classed with himself, but generally these appear to have been referred to the third class as being neither Agricultural nor Commercial.'[1]

Rickman was more optimistic about the results of the 1811 and 1821 censuses, but the 'other' group was still something of a rag-bag. The 1821 report states that it 'appears to consist chiefly of superannuated labourers and widows resident in small tenements: this may serve to show that scarcely any information can be drawn from the numbers which appear in the Third or Negative Class'.[2] Since we may assume, moreover, that domestic servants, and other earners who were not heads of families, have been classed with the economic activity of the head of the household, the results of the 1811 and 1821 censuses are also unsatisfactory for our purposes.

The occupational returns of the 1831 census are more informative in this respect but they relate to adult males (i.e. males of the age of twenty and over) and female domestic servants: and the breakdown is detailed only for those engaged in what was called 'retail trade or handicrafts'. For the remainder a few broad groups have been distinguished: (1) agriculture (distinguishing employing occupiers, non-employing occupiers, and paid labour), (2) manufacture, (3) capitalists, bankers, professional and other educated men, (4) labourers in non-agricultural occupations, and (5) other adult males not in domestic service. In addition, for this as for the earlier censuses, men in the Army and Navy and merchant seamen, whether at home or abroad, are enumerated separately from the rest of the population.[3]

It is inevitable that such broad distinctions should be imprecise at the margins, and this lack of precision was accentuated in 1831 by the fact that the economy was undergoing a radical transformation of its structure. The distinction between 'handicrafts' and 'manufactures' is particularly difficult to define at this distance in time, although it is possible that it was clear enough to contemporaries. Examination of

[1] *S.P. 1822*, vol. xv.
[2] *Ibid.*
[3] There is a problem here, since we are concerned at the moment with Great Britain only, of eliminating the Irish share in the Army, Navy, etc., group.

the list of occupations detailed in the 'retail trade and handicraft' category, for example, shows that it includes, besides building, road transport and some categories of wholesale trade, a number of occupations which were treated as manufacturing activities in the later censuses.[1] There are even some occupations belonging to industries which were largely attributed to manufacture in the 1831 census itself —e.g. metal industries and textile industries.[2] We know, moreover, that the handicraft group was intended to include 'masters, shopmen, journeymen and apprentices or any capacity requiring skill in the business' and that the unskilled workers in these industries were specifically allocated to the group of non-agricultural labourers. Probably the deciding factor which determined the enumeration of an individual with the retail trade and handicraft group of industries rather than the manufacturing groups was, besides his skill, the fact that he was a self-employed person dealing directly with the purchaser of final products rather than a factory employee or an out-worker. Probably also, the self-employed artisan class was relatively more important at this stage and earlier than it was at the later stage of industrialisation.

The 1841 census was the first to attempt a record of all income-earners, men, women and children, but a comparison of its results with the corresponding data for 1851, 1861 and 1871 suggests that it was an incomplete record—the proportion omitted varying with the industry concerned and being particularly high in those industries which employed a large number of women and children. It is not surprising that this should have been so since the family often operated as a unit for employment as well as self-employment purposes. It was a common practice for manufacturers to contract for whole families through the head of the family, and in a community with a relatively large number of small family businesses the distinction between occupied and unoccupied members of family must have been difficult to establish consistently.

Since all the censuses from 1831 onwards distinguished adult male workers (i.e. those aged twenty and over) it is possible to arrive at estimates of total labour force in 1831 and 1841 by extrapolating backwards on the assumption that in each industry the percentage of adult males to all other employees was relatively constant from one decade to another. Broadly speaking, this seems a reasonable assumption, but it could obviously give misleading results for industries which were undergoing rapid structural change. And it obscures what seems to have been an important characteristic of the process of industrialisation, namely, the tendency for economic opportunities for child and female

[1] Wood and furniture, shipbuilding, printing, fur and leather, dressmaking, shipbuilding, watches, toys and musical instruments, food and drink, and paper.

[2] The list includes blacksmiths, iron founders, weavers, dyers, etc. But although all the adult male blacksmiths may well be there, it is clear that only a very small proportion of, say, the weavers or the dyers are included.

employment to increase. It seems likely that the proportion of women and children in full-time gainful employment increased during the first half of the nineteenth century, and although this was partly a consequence of shifts in the importance of different industries, it is still probable that if we extrapolate backwards from 1851 (even for a relatively detailed industrial breakdown) we may overstate the size of the effective labour force in 1841 and still more in 1831. However, in spite of this qualification it was felt that the results of the 1851 census were sufficiently representative of the age and sex composition of each industry's labour force in the middle half of the century to permit the deduction of reasonably reliable, if rough, estimates for 1841 and 1831 from the census returns for these three years.

For the second half of the nineteenth century the census results were reasonably complete although the system of classification adopted in the returns was not sufficiently unambiguous to permit a satisfactory analysis either by occupation or by industry. There were always shifts in definition and treatment from one census to another and these have continued to complicate the results up to the mid-twentieth century. Often these ambiguities and shifts were unexplained and only detailed research would uncover them. Charles Booth, who made a systematic analysis of the occupational returns with the object of producing comparable results for the period 1841–81, has dealt with some of the major discrepancies for these years and we have therefore accepted his detailed tables as our starting-point in estimating industrial distribution up to 1881.[1] For the years 1881–1911 there is an analysis in the General Report of the 1911 census which offers a comparable series of figures and we were able to make these broadly comparable to the series extracted from the Booth analysis for 1841–81 by shifting various groups of dealers to the trade and commerce group of industries.[2] After 1911 there is a fresh break in the series, and although the 1921, 1931 and 1951 industry analyses can be regarded as comparable with each other for most purposes, they are only very broadly comparable with those for earlier years.[3]

[1] Charles Booth, 'Occupations of the People of the United Kingdom 1801–81', *Journal of the Statistical Society*, vol. XLIX (June 1886). Discussing the problem of comparability, and referring in particular to the results for 1851, 1861, and 1871, for example, he writes that ' . . . though the broad plan of classification remains much the same as in 1851, huge transpositions of numbers have been made from one class to another: the domestic class in one census includes the larger part of the population and in the next is reduced by more than half: 350,000 persons in England alone (consisting of the wives and other relatives of farmers, etc.) are taken from the agricultural class of one census and placed in the unoccupied class of another: the partially occupied wives are in no two successive censuses classed alike. . . .'

[2] *S.P. 1917–18*, vol. XXXV. The practice was to include dealers in commodities under the same broad heading as manufacturers of these commodities. These were separately listed in the *General Report* of the 1911 census, but for the earlier years, although most large groups of dealers were separately distinguished, the process of re-classification involved some degree of estimate.

[3] There were differences, moreover, in the groups classified by occupation or industry as the school-leaving age crept up. The 1811–1911 census analysis referred to the occupied population over the age of ten, the 1921 census to those over twelve, the 1931 census to over fourteen, and the 1951 census to those over fifteen.

2. THE CHANGING DISTRIBUTION OF THE LABOUR FORCE

1801–1951

Table 30 summarises the results of an attempt to produce comparable estimates of industrial distribution for each census year. It is subject to wide margins of error. The figures for the first three or four benchmark years are of course exceedingly tentative, being based on extrapolation of trends and proportions deduced from the 1841–61 returns. These are mainly order-of-magnitude estimates. For the years 1841 onwards the basic data are fuller, but conclusions based on comparisons between one decade and the next should be drawn with caution in view of the differences in classifications involved. This reservation is particularly important in connection with the 'trade and commerce' and 'domestic service' groups of industries for which problems of definition have been consistently difficult. The census returns were never precisely comparable with each other, however, and the extent of their comparability diminishes as we go back in this. Not until the period after the First World War do satisfactory industry analyses become available, and the estimates in Table 30 are thus largely based on adjusted occupational data.

Although the exact percentages will not stand close analysis on a decade by decade basis, certain broad trends in the distribution of the British labour force stand out unequivocally from this table. The decline in the proportion engaged in the agriculture–forestry–fishing group of industries, from probably over a third of the total labour force at the beginning of the nineteenth century to 5 per cent in the middle of the twentieth, seems to have proceeded without appreciable interruption, and at a fairly steady pace with the exception of two periods (in the 1840's and again in the first decade of the twentieth century) when there was a notable slackening in the rate of change. The proportion engaged in public service fell in the first half of the nineteenth century from the inflated levels characteristic of a major war, changed little for most of the rest of the century, but began to rise in the twentieth century, so that by 1951 the public, professional and miscellaneous services group of industries accounted for about 22 per cent of the total British labour force. By contrast the domestic-service group of industries, after showing some tendency to increase for most of the nineteenth century, began to decline at the turn of the twentieth century, and dropped to negligible importance in the total by 1951.

The distinction between the manufacturing group of industries and the trade and commerce group cannot be established unambiguously at any point in the nineteenth century and no significant conclusions can be drawn from changes of one or two per cent in their respective shares between one decade and the next. It would appear, however, that it was in the first thirty years of the nineteenth century that the main shift of labour took place towards the mining, manufacturing and building group of industries. After that it was the turn of the trade and transport group of industries, which increased their share from perhaps 12½ per cent of the occupied population *circa* 1831, i.e. immediately before the railway age, to about 22½ per cent *circa* 1891.

Table 30. *Estimated percentage distribution of the British labour force, 1801–1951*

(as percentages of the total occupied population)

	Agriculture, forestry, fishing	Manufacture, mining, industry	Trade and transport	Domestic and personal	Public, professional and all other
1801	35·9	29·7	11·2	11·5	11·8
1811	33·0	30·2	11·6	11·8	13·3
1821	28·4	38·4	12·1	12·7	8·5
1831	24·6	40·8	12·4	12·6	9·5
1841	22·2	40·5	14·2	14·5	8·5
1851	21·7	42·9	15·8	13·0	6·7
1861	18·7	43·6	16·6	14·3	6·9
1871	15·1	43·1	19·6	15·3	6·8
1881	12·6	43·5	21·3	15·4	7·3
1891	10·5	43·9	22·6	15·8	7·1
1901	8·7	46·3	21·4	14·1	9·6
1911	8·3	46·4	21·5	13·9	9·9
1921	7·1	47·6	20·3	6·9	18·1
1931	6·0	45·3	22·7	7·7	18·3
1951	5·0	49·1	21·8	2·2	21·9

Sources: Rough estimates of the total labour force 1801–21 were made after calculating proportions of men, women, boys and girls of different age groups, extrapolating from the 1851 census. The industry split was estimated partly extrapolating and partly by compiling data for specific industries: the results are little more than guesses. The 1831 figures were similarly calculated, but in addition we had an incomplete set of occupation returns for 1831. The 1841–81 estimates were based on Booth's analysis published in the 1886 *Journal of the Statistical Society*, scaling up the 1841 figures by analogy with the proportions engaged in each industry by sex and age groups returned at the 1851 census. The 1891–1911 estimates owe a good deal to our analysis made for the 1911 census, *S.P. 1917–18*, vol. xxxv, for occupied persons of ten years and over: for 1911 the dealers included with other industries were detailed separately in the *General Report* of the Census for 1891 and 1901 it was necessary to extract them from the detailed returns and some degree of estimate was involved in allocating them to the trade and commerce group. We tried throughout to include members of the armed forces and merchant navy at home and abroad, but unemployed persons and before 1881 retired persons are generally included. The 1921, 1931 and 1951 figures are from the census industry analyses: for 1921 they refer to occupied persons of twelve years and over, for 1931 to those fourteen and over, and for 1951 to those fifteen years and above.

This seems to be as far as we can go in drawing conclusions from such broad percentages. To analyse the shifts in the labour force in greater detail it is necessary to examine the estimates of actual numbers for a larger selection of industries and this can only usefully be attempted for years in which the census returns include a reasonably complete occupational classification. Table 31 shows the underlying estimates in somewhat greater detail and in terms of numbers occupied rather than in percentages. The estimates are particularly crude for the year before 1841 and are given here for comparative purposes only. It should be noted, moreover, that up to and including 1871, persons described as 'retired' from any stated occupation were classified by that occupation, but that in 1881 (and subsequently) such retired persons (with the exception of officers in the Army and Navy, the clergy and medical practitioners) were included with the unoccupied sector of the population. Hence there was a fall in the percentage described as occupied from about 47 per cent at the 1861 and 1871 censuses to about 45 per cent at the 1881 census.

It appears that, in terms of numbers occupied, British agriculture reached its peak in the middle of the nineteenth century. In 1851, with a working population of more than 2 millions, it was still the most important British industry. But by 1871 there were more persons in domestic service than in agriculture, and more in commerce and finance (excluding transport) than in either. By 1881 there were probably fewer people in agriculture than there had been in 1801 though the population of Great Britain had increased some two and a half times.

Table 31. *Estimated industrial distribution of the British labour force, 1801–1951*

(millions of persons)

	Agriculture, forestry, fishing	Mining and quarrying	Manufactures	Building	Trade	Transport	Public service and professional	Domestic and personal	Total occupied population
1801	1·7		1·4		0·5		0·3	0·6	4·8
1811	1·8		1·7		0·6		0·4	0·7	5·5
1821	1·8		2·4		0·8		0·3	0·8	6·2
1831	1·8		3·0		0·9		0·3	0·9	7·2
1841	1·9	0·2	2·7	0·4	0·9	0·3	0·3	1·2	8·4
1851	2·1	0·4	3·2	0·5	1·0	0·5	0·5	1·3	9·7
1861	2·0	0·5	3·6	0·6	1·2	0·6	0·6	1·5	10·8
1871	1·8	0·6	3·9	0·8	1·6	0·7	0·7	1·8	12·0
1881	1·7	0·6	4·2	0·9	1·9	0·9	0·8	2·0	13·1
1891	1·6	0·8	4·8	0·9	2·3	1·1	1·0	2·3	14·7
1901	1·5	0·9	5·5	1·3	2·3	1·3	1·3	2·3	16·7
1911	1·6	1·2	6·2	1·2	2·5	1·5	1·5	2·6	18·6
1921	1·4	1·5	6·9	0·8	2·6	1·4	2·1	1·3*	19·3
1931	1·3	1·2	7·2	1·1	3·3	1·4	2·3	1·6*	21·1
1951	1·1	0·9	8·8	1·4	3·2	1·7	3·3	0·5*	22·6

Sources: Even with this degree of rounding these figures must be used cautiously for the attempt to derive an industry classification from occupational returns, which were all that were available before 1921, is subject to considerable margins of error. This would affect particularly the trade and commerce group of industries, and the domestic and personal group where the differences produced by different classifications or methods of estimate may constitute a high proportion of the labour force attributed. Note that these figures include unemployed persons, retired persons before 1881 and armed forces and merchant navy serving abroad before 1921.

* Private domestic service only.

One feature of the fall in the agricultural labour force which does not emerge from the overall figures in Table 31 deserves particular notice, however, This is the fact that the loss of labour was almost entirely a loss of hired labourers, not a decline in the number of farmers. Apart from a fall of about 8½ per cent in the 1870's, and a rise of about 13 per cent between 1911 and 1921, the number of British farmers has shown remarkably little tendency to vary.[1] Farmers (excluding relatives) thus accounted for about 15 per cent of the occupied population in agriculture in 1851, about 20 per cent in 1911 and about 27 per cent in 1951.

Unfortunately we do not have a status classification for other industries until the twentieth century, but it may be presumed that during the period of rapid industrialisation the tendency was for the proportion of employers and self-employed to fall rather than to rise. This presumption might be confirmed by a detailed scrutiny of census occupational returns—but it is borne out for certain industries by the increase in the proportion of factory workers or of workers employed by public services and utilities.

The manufacturing group of industries expanded their labour force most rapidly in the period immediately following the Napoleonic Wars. In the first decade of the nineteenth century they probably absorbed less than a quarter of the occupied population of Great Britain. By 1841 (perhaps already by 1831) they had expanded their share to about a third, and from then until the First World War they grew, in numbers at any rate, more or less in step with the total British labour force. They still claimed only a third of the labour force in 1911, but in 1921 their share had reached 36 per cent, and in 1951, 39 per cent.

Thus in the first three decades or so of the nineteenth century agriculture and manufacturing industry changed places in relative importance as measured by the number of jobs provided. The process of change in the composition of the labour force slowed briefly in the second quarter of the century. Between 1831 and 1841 the numbers (though not the proportion) occupied in agriculture expanded and manufacture merely maintained its share. Then the industries whose growth had been stimulated by industrialisation—mining, transport and trade—began to gather momentum and to absorb an appreciable body of workers. The numbers in mining and quarrying and in transport more than doubled between 1841 and 1871 and again between 1871 and 1911. There was almost a doubling of the numbers in the trade and commerce group between 1861 and 1891. Between 1841 and 1891, when the share of agriculture in the labour force halved, the proportion in mining grew from 3 per cent to 5 per cent, in transport from 4 per cent to 7 per cent, and in trade from about 10 per cent to about $15\frac{1}{2}$ per cent.[2]

It may be presumed, therefore, that the shift of labour to more productive occupations has continued throughout the 150 years under review in Table 31, though not always at the same pace. It is notable,

[1] See J. R. Bellerby, 'The Distribution of Manpower in Agriculture and Industry, 1851–1951', *The Farm Economist*, vol. IX, No. 1 (1958), p. 2, where the fact that 'there was no secular trend whatever in the size of the farmer class in Great Britain' between 1851 and 1951 is commented upon. The census figures for earlier years are inadequate, of course, but if we put any reliance on the 1831 returns we should deduce that there were then between 350,000 and 400,000 farmers in Great Britain, which suggests a sharp fall between then and 1851 when there were about 303,000.

[2] However, the trade figures should be used with caution since these are highly vulnerable to differences in classification between census and census.

however, that the domestic-service group (defined broadly in all estimates derived from occupational returns) maintained and at times increased its share for much of the period before the First World War. Even on a more restricted definition (indoor domestics), between 10 and 12 per cent of the labour force was employed in domestic service for most of this period. The fact that such a high proportion of the working population remained in this relatively unproductive occupation set certain limits to the rate at which average overall productivity could expand before the Second World War.

In sum, we can distinguish three main periods in which the pattern of change in the distribution of the labour force took characteristically different shapes. The first seems to have been a period in which the main emphasis of change lay in the shifts between agriculture and manufacture. According to our estimates this occurred particularly rapidly between *circa* 1811 and 1831 but was probably an important characteristic of the whole half-century before 1831.

The second period, lasting from *circa* 1831 to the First World War was characterised by a continuing fall in the share of agriculture and no noticeable trend in the share of manufacture. The rapidly expanding sectors were mining and transport, but even at the end of the period these together absorbed only about 15 per cent of total labour force compared with about 7 per cent at the beginning, a gain which represented only about half of the percentage lost by agriculture. In effect, much of the slack created by the falling share of agriculture was absorbed by relatively slowly expanding industries, and the changes in the distribution of the labour force over this period of roughly three-quarters of a century were not striking.

By contrast there has been a considerable change in the twentieth-century pattern. Both world wars created considerable dislocation in the economy, and this makes it difficult to put a long-term interpretation on the post-1913 figures. But there does seem to have been a new and accelerated kind of change in process in the second quarter of the twentieth century. Certainly the 1951 pattern differs appreciably from the 1911 pattern, and the direction of change was already evident in the interwar period. Agriculture continued to decline, but the numbers in mining and domestic service have contracted so much more rapidly that these two industries, which in 1911 accounted for more than 20 per cent of the British labour force, absorbed only 6 per cent in 1951. Manufacturing industry which had grown in step with working population for nearly a century suddenly began to grow faster and expanded its share from about a third of the total in 1911 to about 36 per cent in 1921, and 39 per cent in 1951. Equally notable has been the rise in the numbers occupied in the industries supplying public and professional services which began to expand their share appreciably at the very end of the nineteenth century, and have grown from 8 per cent to 11 per cent in the period 1911–31 and again to nearly 15 per cent in 1951.

Table 32. *Distribution of the labour force in manufacturing industry*
1891–1951

(as percentages of the totals in the manufacturing group)

	1891	1911	1921	1951
Bricks, pottery, glass	3·2	3·0	2·7	3·8
Chemicals	1·7	2·6	3·1	5·1
Metals, machinery, vehicles	24·3	29·0	36·9	45·5
Textiles	28·2	22·6	18·8	11·5
Clothing	24·8	20·1	12·5	8·0
Food, drink, tobacco	4·1	5·6	9·0	8·7
Wood	4·7	4·8	4·4	3·5
Paper	4·9	6·4	5·8	5·9
Other manufacturing	4·1	5·9	6·9	8·0

Sources: as for Tables 30 and 31.

Notes: Changes in classification are likely to affect the food, drink, and tobacco considerably, and the other manufacturing groups to a lesser extent. In particular it is doubtful whether the expansion in the share of the food, drink and tobacco industries between 1911 and 1921 was quite as great as indicated above. For the remainder of the industries listed here these classification problems were of minor importance and can safely be ignored.

Both years for which the interwar data are available are somewhat unsatisfactory as bench-marks in this comparison; 1921 because it was a post-war year and 1931 because it was a depression year. We have selected 1921 as being less distorted on the whole than 1931. The differences are not great.

The change in the composition of the labour force in the second quarter of the twentieth century is equally striking when the manufacturing group is considered in greater detail. For the increase in its overall share was accompanied by fairly substantial shifts of labour within the group. Outstanding among these was an inflow of labour into the metals, machinery and vehicles group, and an outflow from the textiles and clothing industries. The change of emphasis had begun to develop in the second half of the nineteenth century, but it was not until the First World War that the numbers in the textile and clothing group began to decline absolutely as well as relatively. Between 1921 and 1951 the metals, machinery and vehicles group expanded its labour force at roughly twice the rate of the national total. By 1951 it accounted for 45 per cent of the total British labour force, and the textiles and clothing group for less than 20 per cent compared with 31 per cent in 1921 and over 50 per cent in 1891. Table 32 illustrates these changes in the structure of the manufacturing industry of Great Britain since the end of the nineteenth century. Its other interesting feature is the steady increase in the labour force of the chemicals industry.

In conclusion, some reference should perhaps be made to the history of the Irish labour force. The above analysis has been conducted entirely in terms of the occupied population of Great Britain because the divergent history and varying weight of Ireland in the United Kingdom total enormously complicates the problem of interpretation. Before the famine, in 1841, the Irish working population was apparently about 47 per cent of that of Great Britain: by 1851 it had fallen to less than a third, by 1911 to about 17½ per cent (i.e. less than 10 per cent of the then United Kingdom total). After the First World War when the Irish Republic had left the United Kingdom the remaining Irish population accounted for less than 3 per cent of the British labour force.

The chief Irish industry was, of course, agriculture. In 1841, according to Booth's analysis of the Irish census returns, more than half of the occupied population was engaged in the agricultural group of industries, and of about 27 per cent engaged in manufacturing the vast majority (over 90 per cent) were in the textiles and dress industries.[1] The exodus which followed the famine was largely an exodus from agriculture. As in Britain, it was a flight of agricultural labourers, and the number of farmers, though fluctuating, showed no definable secular trend over the next century. Between 1851 and 1861, however, the number of contract workers on Irish farms halved and the number of farmers rose by 9 per cent.[2] By 1911 there were more farmers in Ireland than agricultural labourers (including farmers' relatives). Ireland with about 43 per cent of its occupied population in the agricultural group of industries was less industrialised than Britain a century before.

Table 33 gives the figures for the United Kingdom as a whole for 1851, 1881 and 1911. After 1921 the Irish component of the United Kingdom total is fairly small.

Table 33. *Distribution of the occupied population of the United Kingdom*[1]

(in millions of persons)

	1851	1881	1911
Agriculture, forestry, fishing	3·6	2·6	2·3
Mining and quarrying	0·4	0·7	1·2
Manufacturing	3·9	4·5	6·1
Building and construction	0·6	1·0	1·2
Trade and commerce[3]	1·2	2·2	3·1
Transport	0·4	0·8	1·7
Domestic service[4]	1·5	2·4	2·2
Public and professional service[5]	0·5	0·8	1·5
All other	0·6	0·7	0·8
Totals occupied[2]	12·7	15·7	20·2

Sources and notes: [1] Figures for 1851 and 1881 from Booth's analysis, *Journal of the Statistical Society* (1886). Figures for 1911 from the *General Report* of the 1911 census, *S.P. 1917–18,* vol. xxxv.

[2] Including retired and unemployed persons for 1851. Excluding retired but including unemployed 1881 and 1911.

[3] Including dealers classified under the manufacturing trades in the census returns.

[4] Including outdoor and extra domestic service.

[5] Not including army and navy serving abroad.

[1] Domestic spinners (female) accounted for a large proportion of these.

[2] For a careful analysis of the manpower structure of the agricultural population 1851–1951, see F. D. W. Taylor, 'United Kingdom Numbers in Agriculture', *The Farm Economist,* vol. VIII, No. 4 (1955).

3. THE INDUSTRIAL DISTRIBUTION OF INCOMES FROM
EMPLOYMENT 1801–1951

Problems of estimation

There exists a good deal of information on money wages in Great
Britain during the nineteenth and early twentieth centuries and it
seemed worth making the attempt to use the wage data and the occupational analyses discussed in the previous section to arrive at estimates
of incomes from employment. There were two major problems of
estimation involved in this calculation. The first arose out of the
inadequacies of the wage data, and the second from the fact that the
pre-1911 census returns do not provide a status classification distinguishing employed persons from employers and self-employed.

The first industrial wage census was made in 1886, another inquiry
was made in 1892, and there was another and more satisfactory inquiry
for 1906.[1] From the 1880's onwards there are sufficient data to give a
reasonable basis for estimates of year-to-year changes in total wages
for the principal industries and indeed for the economy as a whole.[2]
Before 1880 the data are numerous, but they are so scattered and incomplete that any attempt to deduce total wage bills from them is
complicated by considerable uncertainty as to the quality of the
material. If the data for the early decades of the nineteenth century
are not grossly unrepresentative (and there is no reason to suppose that
they are) we may hope that the estimates of average earnings which
we have based on them reflect the relative and absolute orders of
magnitude involved. But the possibility that inadequate records
reflect abnormal rather than normal conditions should be borne in
mind; and even on the most favourable assumptions as to the repre-
sentativeness of the available data considered as a whole it is impossible
to claim much precision for the resulting estimates.

The wage data embedded in government reports and numerous contemporary surveys or *ad hoc* inquiries were extensively worked over by
Bowley and Wood, whose wage studies have been referred to above in
the section on the course of money wages.[3] Their researches were not
exhaustive or final, and for particular occupations, or industries, or
years, more reliable or conclusive estimates could be made by exploit-
ing other sources of wage data and re-interpreting the raw material
used by them. The Bowley-Wood collection of data was so extensive,

[1] 'Returns of Rates of Wages', *S.P. 1889*, vol. LXX; *1890*, vol. LXVIII; *1890–1*, vol. LXXVIII;
1892, LXVIII; for the 1886 census 'Report on the Wages of the Manual Labour Class', *S.P.
1893–4*, vol. LXXXVIII, pt. II. 'Earnings and Hours Enquiry', *S.P. 1909*, vol. LXXX; *1910*,
vol. LXXXIV; *1911*, vol. LXXXVIII; *1912–13*, vol. CVIII; for the 1906 census.
[2] Cf. A. L. Bowley, *Wages and Income since 1860* (Cambridge, 1937), p. xiii. 'The basic
point for this book is chosen as 1880 by which date the figures are sufficient for fairly precise
statements'.
[3] For detailed reference to the Bowley-Wood data see the section cited, pp. 18–28, above.
Most of their results were published in the *Journal of the Royal Statistical Society* for 1898, 1899,
1900, 1901, 1902, 1905, 1906, 1909, and 1910; and in the *Economic Journal* for 1898, 1899,
and 1904; and in Bowley's *Wages and Income since 1860*.

however, and their experience in the problems of handling this kind of material such, that it seemed reasonable to regard their results as acceptable indicators of orders of magnitude and long-term trends. Bowley did not publish the industrial details of his wage-bill estimates (which are annual from 1860 to 1936), so that it is impossible to compare them with other data for specific industries or to explore their structural implications. However, for agriculture, shipbuilding, engineering, building, cotton, wool, and printing, Bowley and Wood published indices or averages back to the first decade of the nineteenth century or the last quarter of the eighteenth. In addition they gave indices for mining, iron, and merchant shipping back to 1840 and some more general indices back to 1790. Other sources were used to supplement their data for occupations which they did not investigate, e.g. domestic service, government and the armed forces, teaching and other professions.[1]

Before we could apply this miscellany of wage data to our estimates of industrial distribution, however, it was necessary to estimate the number of employed persons in each main industry group. It was not possible to do this satisfactorily throughout the period. The year 1901 is the earliest for which the census returns were sufficiently detailed to permit a satisfactory estimate of status distribution,[2] and for 1801 and 1811 there were Colquhoun's rough estimates of the labourers (as distinct from the 'persons employing capital') in each industry.[3] But for the intervening years there was little information except where the detail of census returns happened to indicate status.[4] Before 1881 the census returns do not even distinguish retired persons, and for no year is it possible to calculate the numbers of the unemployed. The most difficult task, however, was to arrive at estimates of the numbers of self-employed. Our estimates suggested that about 19 per cent of the occupied population fell into this category at the beginning of the century, that the proportion rose to a little over 20 per cent in the couple of decades after the Napoleonic Wars and then began to fall

[1] For domestic service the main sources of information were J. J. Hecht, *The Domestic Servant Class in Eighteenth Century England* (1956); W. I. Leyton, 'Changes in the Wages of Domestic Servants during Fifty Years', *J. Roy. Statist. Soc.*, vol. LXXI (1908); and there were numerous other sources which gave data for particular periods, e.g. G. R. Porter, *Progress of the Nation* (1847), and C. S. Peel, 'Homes and Habits', in G. M. Young's *Early Victorian England*. For incomes earned by government employees and armed forces, the main sources were the financial accounts summarised in *S.P. 1868–9*, vol. xxxv, the relevant Army and Navy estimates, and various *ad hoc* reports and returns giving salaries, etc., earned in the public service.

[2] The 1901 returns were combined and analysed by Bowley for a committee of the British Association and published in the *Journal of the Royal Statistical Society* for December 1910. For convenience we used this analysis as our starting-point for the 1901 estimates.

[3] P. Colquhoun, *Treatise on Indigence* (1806) and *Treatise on the Wealth, Power and Resources of the British Empire* (1815).

[4] Farmers are usually distinguished from their labourers, for example, and shopkeepers were often separately entered. But for the earlier years it was necessary to estimate the proportion of relatives in the 'farmers and relatives' group, and the estimates become less reliable as we go back in time both because the census returns were less informative and because it became more difficult to extrapolate the 1901 status proportions.

sharply in the late 1830's and the 1840's, reaching something of the order of 11 or 12 per cent at the end of the century. The basis for estimate was exceedingly slight and the implications are spelt out here to facilitate checking our results rather than because they are thought to have much intrinsic value.

The wage-bill estimates are thus crude and unfortunately we can say little about the probable directions of bias. Because it was impossible to allow for the incidence of unemployment, there is a probability that the overall and industry totals are too high for some years—particularly towards the beginning of the century when the evidence suggests that irregular work and short time characterised most forms of wage-earning activity. A parliamentary return for 1803 gave the total number of adult paupers in receipt of regular outdoor relief in England and Wales as 336,199 and the numbers relieved in workhouses as 83,468. A further 305,889 beggars and vagrants received occasional relief. We have estimated that there were about 3·9 million employed persons in Great Britain at that time, so that we might deduce from these figures that something like one in ten of the population was in regular receipt of poor-relief. In view of the current practice of supplementing wages out of poor-relief it is impossible to say what this means in terms of unemployment but it may well have been considerable. It is also likely that we were more likely to overstate the total in a trough year (e.g. 1801 and 1811) when we were unable to assess the volume of cyclical unemployment and to understate in a peak year (e.g. 1831) when overtime was being worked. In sum it is probable that our estimates for the early decades (particularly 1801 and 1811) overstated total wages and salaries—though not, unfortunately, that the overstatement was of the same order of magnitude from year to year or from industry to industry. By the end of the century, however, they tend to fall below overall estimates based directly on Bowley's wage bills.[1]

In making the wage estimates for 1801–81 we used Bowley's and Wood's last available estimates of average wages and their trends to calculate average earnings in each census year for agriculture, mining, the textiles and dress industries, metals and engineering and other manufacturing, and to provide bases for estimates for certain broad industry groups for which we had little or no wage data covering the period as a whole (e.g. trade and transport).[2] For central government

[1] Our estimates are for wages and salaries earned in Great Britain and Bowley's for wages only earned in the United Kingdom. Adding an estimate for wages and salaries earned in Ireland to our estimates and of salaries to Bowley's estimates we can obtain two series that should be comparable. The results of this comparison give almost the same figure for 1881 and differences of 5 and 6 per cent for 1891 and 1901 respectively. For 1861 our figure is about 2 per cent below Bowley's estimate (adjusted for salaries) for 1860–4 and our 1871 estimate about 9 per cent below the corresponding Bowley total for 1870–4. These are obviously very crude checks. All that they suggest is that we reach results of roughly the same order of magnitude as did Bowley and that our estimates tend to be lower than his.

[2] In the decade and a half before the First World War Bowley and Wood published a large number of articles presenting and revising the results of their researches into wages. We chose the latest revisions we could find. See footnote 5 on p. 22.

we derived our estimates directly from the government accounts and included superannuation and incomes paid to British armed forces at home and abroad. For domestic service a variety of sources was used to provide estimates of average earnings in cash and in kind.[1] For professional occupations we collected information from a miscellany of sources (government committee reports, departmental estimates, ecclesiastical returns, etc.) and, at best, succeeded in reaching very rough estimates of levels of earnings. We made no attempt to distinguish salaries from wages.

The 1901 estimates are more satisfactory because it was possible to use the various wage inquiries undertaken by the Labour Department of the Board of Trade as well as the estimates made by Bowley for various salaried occupations.[2] For the years after the First World War reliable estimates have already been published. We accepted the Chapman and Knight estimates for the period 1920–38,[3] and the official estimates published in the United Kingdom National Income White Papers and Blue Books for later years. The post-First World War estimates are all for the United Kingdom (i.e. Great Britain and Northern Ireland), but, since the Irish share of incomes from employment was under 2 per cent of the total,[4] they can be regarded as broadly comparable to our nineteenth-century estimates for Great Britain.

The results of these calculations are shown in Table 34. It is hardly necessary to emphasise further the tentative nature of the pre-First World War figures. Undoubtedly more reliable results could be secured by more careful and time-consuming methods of estimation. These can be used with reasonable confidence however to give a broad picture of the long-term change in the distribution of British incomes from employment. They cannot be presumed to offer satisfactory estimates of the incomes earned in any particular industry for a given year.

The general pattern reflected in Table 34 has already been commented upon in the previous section. The fall in the share of the agricultural group of industries throughout the period and of the domestic service group in the twentieth century are outstanding features of this pattern. So also is the rapid rise of the mining, manufacturing and building group during the period of industrialisation, and again in the twentieth century. The change in the structure of the agricultural industry, as its labourers drifted away from it, is brought out by the steep decline in the share of agricultural employment incomes over the past century.

One aspect seems to stand out more sharply here than in earlier

---

[1] See footnote 1 on p. 149 for references.

[2] See footnotes 1 and 3 on p. 148 for references.

[3] Agatha L. Chapman and Rose Knight, *Wages and Salaries in the United Kingdom, 1920–1938* (1953).

[4] The Irish share in the U.K. total of wages and salaries probably reached its peak of about 15 per cent in the 1830's and had dropped to about 7½ per cent by 1881. In the period immediately preceding the First World War it was probably about 5 per cent.

British Economic Growth

Table 34. *The industrial distribution of British wages and salaries,*[1] *1801–58*

(in £m. and as a percentage of total wages and salaries)

	Agriculture, forestry, fishing	Mining, manufacturing, building[2]	Trade and transport	Domestic service	Public,[3] professional, and all other	Totals
Great Britain						
	(£m.)	(£m.)	(£m.)	(£m.)	(£m.)	(£m.)
1801	26·0	23·0	10·5	12·8	31·8	104·1
1811	36·4	28·8	16·4	15·7	42·8	140·2
1821	29·3	37·5	17·7	16·6	31·5	132·6
1831	28·4	48·8	20·3	19·2	31·7	148·4
1841	33·8	68·6	27·4	26·9	34·6	191·4
1851	39·7	92·1	37·3	27·4	50·1	246·6
1861	45·3	125·9	50·5	35·0	58·7	315·4
1871	44·4	166·1	84·7	45·5	67·7	408·4
1881	43·9	195·1	116·7	51·7	88·4	495·3
1891	41·8	241·1	153·2	70·6	107·1	613·9
1901	40·6	317·8	178·1	78·5	148·3	763·3
1911	45·8	369·1	205·4	87·0	176·1	883·6
United Kingdom						
1921[4]	117·4	1,285·9	666·1	184·4	533·4	2,787·2
1931[4]	74·6	969·6	638·2	148·5	468·4	2,299·3
1938[4]	72·4	1,299·7	747·4	175·9	594·9	2,890·3
1951[5]	278·0	3,971·0	1,933·0	95·0	2,182·0	8,459·0
1958[5]	348·0	6,505·0	3,083·0	92·0	3,385·0	13,413·0
Great Britain						
	(%)	(%)	(%)	(%)	(%)	(%)
1801	25·0	22·1	10·1	12·3	30·6	100·0
1811	26·0	20·5	11·7	11·2	30·6	100·0
1821	22·1	28·3	13·3	12·5	23·8	100·0
1831	19·1	32·9	13·7	12·9	21·4	100·0
1841	17·7	35·9	14·3	14·1	18·1	100·0
1851	16·1	37·3	15·1	11·1	20·3	100·0
1861	14·4	39·9	16·0	11·1	18·6	100·0
1871	10·9	40·7	20·8	11·2	16·6	100·0
1881	8·9	39·4	23·5	10·5	17·9	100·0
1891	6·8	39·3	24·9	11·5	17·5	100·0
1901	5·3	41·6	23·3	10·3	19·4	100·0
1911	5·2	41·8	23·3	9·9	19·9	100·0
United Kingdom						
1921	4·2	46·1	23·9	6·6	19·1	100·0
1931	3·2	42·1	27·8	6·5	20·4	100·0
1938	2·5	45·0	25·9	6·1	20·6	100·0
1951	3·3	46·9	22·9	1·1	25·8	100·0
1958[5]	2·6	48·5	23·0	0·7	25·2	100·0

Sources and Notes: N.B. The United Kingdom includes Great Britain and Northern Ireland, Southern Ireland is excluded throughout.

[1] Excluding directors' fees and employers' insurance contributions. These latter are, of course, only appreciable after the First World War.

[2] Including gas, electricity, water.

[3] Including superannuation payments by government.

[4] Agatha Chapman and Rose Knight, *Wages and Salaries in the United Kingdom, 1920–1938* (1953).

[5] C.S.O., *National Income and Expenditure, 1959* (H.M.S.O., 1959).

tables, however. This is the considerable burden of largely unproductive income carried by the economy during the Napoleonic Wars period. Column 5 is a composite heading, but it consists largely of incomes paid out by public authorities.[1] In the Napoleonic Wars more than a fifth of the national wage and salary bill was met by government. This does not equal the much more crushing weight of administrative and defence incomes carried by the economy in more recent wars, but it was nevertheless a heavy burden for a relatively backward economy.[2]

Finally, it may be noted that the main twentieth-century trends which we traced to 1951 have continued into the 1950's. Domestic service and agricultural employment incomes have continued to decline in relative importance and the share of the mining, manufacturing and building group has continued to rise.

[1] Our totals for the nineteenth century are inflated by government superannuation and pension payments, which may be strictly definable as transfers rather than incomes. In so far, however, as these are the pensions of public servants, they are as much 'incomes from employment' as the employers' contributions which we include for later years.

[2] There are no official estimates of the incomes paid by public authorities during the Second World War. But in 1945, when the pay and allowances of the armed forces alone amounted to over 22 per cent of total incomes from employment, the total share of public authorities was probably not far from 31 per cent of the national wage and salary bill.

CHAPTER V

THE CHANGING STRUCTURE OF NATIONAL PRODUCT

BRITAIN'S transformation from the relatively unspecialised, pre-industrial type of economy of the early eighteenth century to the industrialised economy of the late nineteenth and early twentieth centuries was associated with a marked change in the rate of economic growth. This much is obvious from a general view of the economic history of the past two and a half centuries. What is not obvious is the order in which these changes took place. Did rapid economic growth precede, accompany or follow the major changes in industrial structure? What can we infer about the causal connections between the process of industrialisation and the rate of growth in average real incomes? To answer these questions it is necessary to assess the timing and magnitude of the structural changes involved.

In this chapter an attempt will be made to trace the main changes in the structure of national product by estimating its industrial distribution at a series of bench-mark dates covering the whole of the period under consideration in this book. Unfortunately the bench-mark dates were determined by the data available and are not close enough to indicate specific turning-points. Nor were the basic data sufficiently full to permit definitive estimates of net output for each major industry or industrial group. These data problems impose progressively more serious qualifications on our conclusions as we go back in time. We shall therefore consider the estimates in a series of time-periods related to the character of the data and we shall discuss problems of estimation in each period before attempting to draw any conclusions from the results.

The problems which arise from the scarcity of data will be explicit in the following discussion. There is, however, a second group of problems which may not always be self-evident though they introduce equally important qualifications into attempts to measure the changing structure of national product through the process of industrialisation. These are the problems involved in trying to arrive at objective, long-term measurements of structural change for an economy which is also changing in structure and content.

Reference has already been made to the difficulty of defining manufacturing industry at the beginning of the nineteenth century when the distinction between the small-scale manufacturer and the shopkeeper was not only blurred but shifting.[1] For earlier periods it may be just as difficult to distinguish between agriculture and mining when the land-owner was commonly engaged in both industries. Or again, where the

---

[1] See above, pp. 138–9.

unit of production is the family the domestic servant is often indistinguishable from the agricultural labourer or the tradesman's assistant. Examples of these problems of definition could be multiplied, though in practice they are often overlooked because the basic data are insufficient to show them up. Students of comparative economic growth in the modern world will recognise them as manifestations of familiar problems involved in the attempt to apply the concepts of relatively specialised economies to those which are imperfectly specialised.[1] In spite of the obstacles in the way of measuring structural change through time the attempt to express the evidence in quantitative terms is an important prerequisite to any assessment of the relative significance of different factors in the process. It is important to remember, however, that there is a large subjective element in the quantitative approach.

I. STRUCTURE OF NATIONAL PRODUCT IN THE EIGHTEENTH CENTURY

Evidence on the overall size and structure of national product in the eighteenth century is so incomplete that it raises more questions than it answers.[2] All that we have for the period which preceded the industrial revolution are the contemporary estimates for England and Wales made by Gregory King for *circa* 1688 and by Arthur Young for *circa* 1770. Although both sets of estimates are interesting in that they reflect well-informed contemporary views of economic structure, it is putting a severe strain on their independent validity to extract from them measures of the order of magnitude of structural change between 1688 and 1770.

For what the comparison is worth, however, it is made in Table 35, where we have rearranged and interpreted the details of the King and Young estimates in order to place them in juxtaposition. That this arrangement and interpretation involved some highly arbitrary judgments will be evident from the notes to the table.

The conclusions suggested by this comparison are somewhat restricted in view of the definitional problems and exceedingly tentative in view of the data problems. Taking them at their face value, however, the first and perhaps most surprising implication is that agriculture's contribution to total national product actually increased in the period under review. There is a general agreement that there were important changes in agricultural techniques during the eighteenth century considered as a whole. The fact that the population grew by probably about 57 per cent between 1701 and 1801 and was still growing faster each decade,[3] while imports of food were negligible, has always

---

[1] Cf., for example, P. T. Bauer and B. S. Yamey, 'Economic Progress and Occupational Distribution', *Economic Journal*, December 1951; and A. G. B. Fisher, 'A Note on Tertiary Production', *Economic Journal*, December 1952.

[2] The evidence is discussed at length in Deane, 'The Implications of Early National Income Estimates, etc.', *op. cit.*

[3] Using Brownlee's estimates. Various estimates of eighteenth-century population growth are possible but none of them justify the loose statement that population *doubled* in the course of the century. Cf. Ernle, *English Farming, Past and Present* (1936), p. 266.

Table 35. *The structure of national product before the industrial revolution*

(Rounded figures for England and Wales: based on Gregory King and Arthur Young)

	Circa 1688		Circa 1770	
	£m.	As % national income	£m.	As % national income
1. Agriculture	19·3	40	58·2	45
2. Manufacture, mining, building	9·9	21	30·3	24
3. Commerce	5·6	12	17·0	13
4. Professions and domestic service	7·4	15	14·9	11
5. Government and defence	3·3	7	5·7	4
6. Rent of housing	2·5	5	4·0	3
7. Total national income	48·0	100	130·1	100

Sources: The 1688 figures are based on estimates in 'Natural and Political Observations and Conclusions upon the State and Condition of England', reprinted in George E. Barnett, *Two Tracts by Gregory King* (Baltimore, 1936). The 1770 figures are mostly based on estimates by A. Young in *Political Arithmetic* (London, 1779), Part II, where he sums up and averages the estimates in his *A Six Months' Tour through the North of England*, vol. IV (London, 1770), and in *The Farmers' Tour through the East of England*, vol. IV (London, 1771): but we have occasionally preferred the estimates in the *Tours* for some details. See Deane, 'The Implications of Early National Income Estimates, etc.', *op. cit.*, for a discussion of these estimates.

Notes: 1. Agriculture. For King's estimates see George Barnett, *op. cit.*, pp. 36–7: we have excluded £1 m. for hay consumed by cattle but no other raw materials or purchased service. If we approach it by another route, i.e. by summing the incomes of those who may be presumed to have gained most of their livelihood from agriculture, we get a total of over £25 m. But in view of the unspecialised character of these occupational classifications (freeholders, for example, would include house-owners and miners, and cottagers would include domestic spinners and weavers) this is obviously too high. Young's estimates of agricultural output are amongst the most detailed and well considered of his estimates: it is well possible that they are overestimates since they are based on the results and costs of the farmers whom Young himself visited and who were probably above average in output and efficiency.

2. Manufactures, mining, etc. This is a residual in the 1688 estimates; for the derivation of the national income total see Deane, 'The Implications of Early National Income Estimates', *op. cit.*: it probably overstates the share of the manufacturing group of industries rather more in 1688 than in 1770. We have accepted Young's earlier (*Northern Tour*) estimate for the woollen manufacture since it fitted in better with other contemporary evidence: Young includes inland fishing with mining and timber industries and we have put it with this group.

3. Commerce. For 1688 includes King's estimates of incomes of merchants and traders by sea, plus shopkeepers and tradesmen plus a proportion of his estimates for seamen and labourers. For 1770 includes Young's estimates—for artisans and shopkeepers, foreign commerce and shipping and other commercial.

4. Professions and domestic service. Includes our estimate of domestic service which seems to cover a broader group of activities in 1688 than in 1770: probably some of the incomes which we have attributed to domestic service in 1688 found their way into domestic manufacture or commerce in 1770.

5. Government and defence. For 1688 includes persons in offices, naval and military officers, common soldiers and 50 per cent of common seamen—excluding poor-relief incomes for soldiers and seamen. For 1770 includes Young's broad estimates of incomes paid out of public revenue after excluding national debt interest.

weighed heavily in support of the view that there was a substantial expansion in agricultural output during the course of the eighteenth century.[1] The problem is to establish when it occurred and how it compared with developments in other sectors of the economy. For if there was really an increase in the contribution of agriculture to national income in the period immediately preceding the industrial revolution this opens up an interesting field of speculation concerning the preconditions of British economic growth.

We have described elsewhere in this book our own efforts to quantify the evidence on agricultural output in the eighteenth century. They led us to the conclusion that real output in agriculture increased by about 17 per cent between *circa* 1700 and *circa* 1770 compared with about 44 per cent for total real output and about 21 per cent for population.[2] It is not possible to reconcile this result with an increase in the share of agriculture in the national income without postulating an increase in relative agricultural prices on a scale which is not borne out by the available price data. We should hesitate to place great weight on any of these tentative calculations, but their implication that the share of agriculture fell rather than rose over this period seems to us strong enough to throw doubt not only on the Young estimates, which have always been suspect in this sector,[3] but also on the King estimates. We would conclude that the Young estimates certainly overstated the share of agriculture, that the King estimates may have understated it, and that it probably accounted for between 40 and 45 per cent of national income for most of the first three-quarters of the eighteenth century.

The second hypothesis that emerges from the comparison in Table 35 is that there had been only a small increase in the proportion of national product due to manufacturing industry, including mining and building. We have no reason to reject this hypothesis as thus broadly stated, but the conclusion of the previous paragraph implies a warning against accepting the underlying figures too literally.[4] What the comparison does not reveal, though this is readily suggested by a comparison of the details of Young's and King's estimates, is the greater diversification of manufactures and the greater degree of specialisation in 1770. *Circa*

---

[1] Cf. the statement by R. N. Salaman in *The History and Social Influence of the Potato* (Cambridge, 1949), that 'for at least fifty years prior to 1770 the workers of this country were free from anxiety as to their immediate needs in food and shelter to an extent unknown to later generations'.

[2] See above, pp. 62–75.

[3] There seems little doubt that Young had a tendency to overestimate agricultural output (see Deane, 'The Implications of Early National Income Estimates', *op. cit.* p. 24), but the effect of this bias on the structural implications of his estimates may be reduced by a general tendency to overstate in areas of ignorance.

[4] If Young overestimated the share of agriculture he may have underestimated the share of industry. More probably, however, it was the share of the trade and transport group of industries which were relatively understated in his estimates. Similarly, if King understated agriculture he may have overstated industry: but here again we should be more inclined to doubt the estimate for share of professional and personal services implied in his calculations than the share of manufacture, mining and building.

1688, for example, King's estimates imply that the woollen manufacture accounted for more than 30 per cent of this rather miscellaneous group of industries, and no other industry approached it in importance. Young's estimates attribute only about 23 per cent of the value of the manufacturing group to the woollen and worsted industries and assess the metal manufactures at roughly the same level of importance.[1]

The third hypothesis suggested by the comparison in Table 35 is that the burden of government declined in the course of this period. It was to rise sharply during the Napoleonic Wars. But in 1770 costs of administration were apparently relatively low, and in the light of the financial history of this period it is not difficult to accept the implication that government was more efficient *circa* 1770 than *circa* 1688.

In sum, and making all allowances for defective data, it does not appear that there was much change in the broad structure of English output over the period of eighty years following the Glorious Revolution. The manufacturing group of industries probably increased their share (from rather more than a fifth including mining and building to something less than a quarter) and broadened their base. The contribution of agriculture does not seem to have altered significantly. The burden of government and defence probably diminished. It is possible that the rate of change was more rapid at the end of the period than at the beginning. We have estimated, for example, that the overall rate of growth in total national output rose from under half of one per cent per annum in the first four decades of the eighteenth century to nearly 1 per cent in the period 1740–70.[2]

2. THE STRUCTURE OF INDUSTRY AT THE BEGINNING OF THE NINETEENTH CENTURY

For the first decade of the nineteenth century the information available on national product and its composition is fuller and more satisfactory than that available for any previous decade. This is so, first because there were several reasonably careful estimates from well-informed sources; second because the results of the new income-tax assessments provided a check on some of these estimates and a source of new data; and third because the first population census provided reliable data on an important dimension of the economy—the number of its people.

The principal estimates available for the years around the turn of the century are those by Pitt, who calculated British 'taxable' income in connection with the introduction of the income tax in 1799, by Beeke and Bell, who attempted independently of each other's (but not of Pitt's) estimates to calculate total national income of Great Britain on a similar basis, and by Colquhoun, who took the 1801 population returns as his starting-point and tried to produce an up-to-date version

---

[1] Even using the higher of Young's two estimates of woollen-manufacturing output.
[2] See above, p. 80.

of Gregory King's 1688 table of incomes for England and Wales.[1] These estimates have been discussed in detail elsewhere.[2] Here it may be noted that if we adjust them by excluding national debt interest and poor-relief incomes and adding an estimate for domestic service, they all imply a national income for Great Britain of between £200 m. and £250 m.

Colquhoun also made a later and much more elaborate national-income calculation for 1812.[3] In many ways, this is a more carefully considered and informative calculation than his earlier estimate, but it is for the United Kingdom as a whole and the Irish component is both highly dubious and difficult to disentangle.[4] An attempt to extract it, largely on the basis of his estimates for the national capital (which are detailed by countries), suggested a national-income total for Great Britain of £330 m. in 1812.[5] This is a credible total, but examination of the details does not inspire confidence in its composition.

The contemporary estimates are an important part of the evidence for the period. It is true that they were largely guesswork and that they were made at a time when attempts to quantify the known features of the economy were too rarely based on or checked by specific statistical data. But they were produced by relatively objective observers who were well acquainted with current sources of economic and statistical information and who took the trouble to seek advice from the contemporary experts in particular fields of economic activity. In some cases they published revised figures which took account of the advice and criticism evoked by an earlier publication.

Since these estimates were made, however, the stock of quantitative information about the British economy has increased, and although most of the new data refer to later time-periods they do throw some light on probable dimensions at the beginning of the century. We were able, for example, to reach rough estimates of total incomes from employment in each census year, largely by applying the results of the Bowley and Wood compilations of wage data to extrapolations of mid-century census-of-occupation results.[6] These estimates, together with the results of the income-tax assessments which were available for the period 1800–14, provided the basis for independent estimates of the

---

[1] H. Beeke, *Observations on the Produce of the Income Tax and its Proportion to the Whole Income of Great Britain* (1800); Benjamin Bell, *Essays on Agriculture* (Edinburgh, 1802); and P. Colquhoun, *Treatise on Indigence* (1806).

[2] Phyllis Deane, 'Contemporary Estimates of National Income in the First Half of the Nineteenth Century', *Econ. Hist. Rev.*, vol. VIII, No. 3 (April 1956).

[3] P. Colquhoun, *Treatise on the Wealth, Power and Resources of the British Empire*, 2nd ed. (1815).

[4] The Irish component is particularly dubious for two reasons—first, because neither Colquhoun nor the contemporaries whose advice he sought were well equipped to assess incomes and output in Ireland, and secondly, because there were no population figures for Ireland. Later estimates suggest that Colquhoun's figures for Irish population should be increased by roughly a quarter.

[5] See Deane, *Econ. Hist. Rev.*, vol. VIII, *op. cit.* p. 342, for a discussion of this attempt.

[6] See above, pp. 148–53, for a description of these estimates.

national income of Great Britain at the beginning of the nineteenth century.

The income and property tax was chargeable on all incomes above £60 until 1806 when the exemption limit was dropped to £50 to cover those who had stated their incomes fractionally below £60.[1] The tax covered a substantial proportion of the incomes earned in Great Britain at this period, and if the assessments were reasonably reliable they reflected an important proportion of the national income. A discussion of the income-tax assessments and of their usefulness as a basis for national-income estimation is given in Appendix II. There it is estimated that the national income of Great Britain amounted *circa* 1801 to about £232 m. and *circa* 1811 to about £301 m. The earlier figure is quite close to the estimate which we derived from a study of the Pitt, Beeke and Bell calculations for *circa* 1800, and the 1811 figure is nearly 9 per cent below the estimate which we derived from Colquhoun's figures for *circa* 1812.[2]

A distribution of these totals by industries can be made only on highly arbitrary assumptions. The employment estimates were based on calculations for each of the main industry groups and are thus readily divisible. Some of the tax assessment data are also easy to distribute. For example, much of Schedule A and the whole of Schedule B incomes can be allocated to agriculture, and most of Schedule E is attributable to government services. It is the Schedule D incomes which are most intractable, partly because they are the most unreliable group of assessments,[3] and partly because they represent a medley of profit incomes from a wide variety of sources—from trade, transport, manufacture and the professions. Accordingly the estimated division in Table 36 between incomes earned in trade and manufacture is particularly crude. We believe that it is more likely to overstate the trade and transport component than the manufacturing, mining and building group, but the distinction between the two is very uncertain.

The most interesting implication of the estimates in Table 36 is that agriculture increased its share in national income during the war period. Most of this increase can be attributed to the incidence of war inflation which drove up agricultural rents and prices faster than other elements in the price system. It is probable that there was also an increase in the volume of agricultural output during the war period. The demand for food resulted in an extension of the cultivated area, and increased wages probably forced farmers to use agricultural labour

---

[1] It is interesting to note that this seems to have made a negligible difference to the total of incomes assessed under Schedule D which was most subject to evasion. See Table 87 in Appendix II.

[2] Deane, 'Contemporary Estimates of National Income in the First Half of the Nineteenth Century', *op. cit.* It need hardly be said that these discrepancies between our independent estimates and those derived from contemporary calculations are within the margin of error of both.

[3] We made rough evasion-allowances of one-third to one-half of Schedule D incomes and it is not at all certain that these were adequate to cover all understatement for this group.

Table 36. *The structure of British national product at the beginning of the nineteenth century*

(Estimates based on tax assessment and wage data)

	1801 £m.	1801 As % total national income	1811 £m.	1811 As % total national income
1. Agriculture	75·5	32·5	107·5	35·7
2. Trade and transport	40·5	17·5	50·1	16·6
3. Manufactures, mining and building	54·7	23·6	62·5	20·8
4. Housing	12·2	5·3	17·2	5·7
5. Government and defence	22·8	9·8	32·4	10·8
6. Domestic, professional and all other	26·2	11·3	31·4	10·4
7. Total national income	232·0	100	301·1	100

Sources and Notes: 1. Agriculture. Includes gross assessments to Schedule A (lands), Schedule B and our estimates of incomes from employment in agriculture.

2. Trade and transport, and 3, Manufactures, mining and building. The distinction between these two items was reached by adding to our wage and salary estimates for each group, estimates of the share of each in (*a*) Schedule D assessments, (*b*) Schedule D evasion and (*c*) unassessed own account incomes (after allowing for profits from professions). All Schedule A profit incomes were attributed to the manufacturing group and for the rest it was assumed that assessed incomes were largely attributable to the maufacturing group and evasion and unassessed incomes to the trade group. These arbitrary assumptions gave only the flimsiest basis for the distinction and the division should accordingly be treated with more than usual reserve.

4. Housing. For 1801 estimated from Eden's estimates of rent distribution. For 1811 housing assessments under Schedule A plus a small allowance for unassessed housing.

5. Government and defence. Based on an analysis of government accounts for an estimate of incomes from employment in government and the armed forces.

6. Domestic, professional and all other. From our estimates of incomes from employment in domestic and professional occupations plus an allowance for profits, etc., incomes equivalent to about 50 per cent of estimated wage and salary incomes earned in professional occupations.

more effectively. The rate of enclosure at nearly 53,000 acres per annum was higher in the period 1802–15 than for any other period in British history.[1] It has been estimated that the English acreage under potatoes increased by at least 60 per cent in the period 1795–1814.[2]

The trade and manufacturing groups of industries seem to have expanded less than population. The tentative nature of the estimates for these items and the flimsy basis of the split between them has already been stressed. The only other data which might throw light on these results are the overseas trade returns and the Hoffmann index of industrial production. If we compare the triennium 1800–2 with 1810–12, for example, we find that the gross value of overseas trade (imports, domestic exports and re-exports) at current prices changed little over the decade; if anything it fell slightly.[3] But this is what one

[1] Gilbert Slater, *The English Peasantry and the Enclosure of Common Fields* (1907), estimated that 739,743 acres of common pasture and waste were enclosed in the period 1802–15 compared with 752,150 acres in the four decades 1761–1801. Appendix A, p. 267.

[2] R. N. Salaman, *History and Social Influence of the Potato* (1949), p. 613.

[3] Using Imlah's estimates of current values of imports and re-exports, *op. cit.* p. 37.

would expect in wartime. In so far as there was an increase in the value of trade it must have been due to an expansion in internal trade. Hoffmann's index, measured over the same period, points to a rise of about 26 per cent in the volume of British industrial production.[1] That there was some fall in the prices of British industrial goods seems certain. The problem is to measure it. A comparison of the declared and official values of British domestic exports suggests a price fall of 16 per cent over this period: on the other hand a comparison of Imlah's price relatives for domestic exports suggests a fall of only 5 per cent. But the official values were largely based on 1696 prices: and in any case the basket of goods entering into the export trade in the first decade of the nineteenth century cannot be taken as representative of the total output of the British manufacturing and mining group of industries.

The other items in Table 36 show movements which are small but plausible. An increase in the share of housing and of government and defence and a fall in the share of domestic and professional services are familiar characteristics of war conditions.

If we now take a longer view and compare the proportions in Table 36 with those in Table 35 we find that they suggest a substantial fall in the share of agriculture and a rise in the share of the trading and manufacturing group of industries taken together. The results of the first quarter of a century of relatively rapid industrialisation are apparently reflected in a fall in the share of agriculture from between about 40 and 45 per cent of national product to between 32 and 36 per cent. The share of the trading and manufacturing group increased from between 33 and 37 per cent to between 37 and 41 per cent. For a combination of reasons—statistical and conceptual—it is difficult to say much about the manufacturing group as distinct from the trading group. But if the implication that the mining, manufacturing and building group failed to increase its share in the national product between *circa* 1770 and the first decade of the nineteenth century seems surprising, it should be remembered that there had been a marked fall in relative prices and that in real terms the share of this group had certainly increased. It should also be remembered that in the first decade of the nineteenth century the economy was distorted by a major war which inflated agricultural prices, restricted overseas markets and drew a large proportion of the able-bodied population into government service.

For some industries, however, the changes which occurred between 1770 and 1801, and even between 1801 and 1811, were quite spectacular. These were the truly revolutionary developments of the period, the features which distinguished it from the pre-industrial era and which gave the process of economic growth the impetus that kept it rolling without serious check for more than one and a half centuries.

[1] W. G. Hoffmann, *British Industry 1700–1950*, translated by W. O. Henderson and W. H. Chaloner (1955). Table 54, using his index of industrial production including building.

The cotton industry was the outstanding example. If it is easy to overestimate its contribution to the national standard of living in the early stages of the industrial revolution, it is important not to underrate its own pace of change and its strategic significance in the broader process. The story of the growth of the cotton industry is told elsewhere in this book.[1] Here it may be recalled that in the half-century preceding 1811 it grew from a position of negligible importance to that of the major British industry. *Circa* 1770 it contributed only about half a million pounds a year to the British national income. By 1801–3, with a net value added of about £11 m., it accounted for nearly 5 per cent of total national income and was second only to the woollen industry. By 1811–13 it had outstripped wool and contributed about $7\frac{1}{2}$ per cent of national income. Retained imports of raw cotton, which are a conservative indicator of the volume of output for the industry in this period, had increased by a factor of 19 in the space of about fifty years.

At the same time it may be noted that the other textile industries which were cotton's less progressive competitors did not cease to grow, though they declined in relative importance from about 8 per cent of national income in 1770 to about 7 per cent in 1801 and about 6 per cent in 1811. In effect, by 1811 more than a half of the output of the manufacturing group of industries was attributable to textiles, compared with about 40 per cent at the turn of the century and about 36 per cent in 1770.[2] Thus most of the growth in the output of British industry between 1801 and 1811 seems to have been attributable to textiles and in this the cotton industry was the leading branch.

It is not difficult to think of reasons why textiles should have set the pace in the process of industrialisation. They served a mass market at home and abroad. The raw materials and the finished products were light and transportable. They were the principal beneficiaries of an unusually fruitful crop of labour-saving inventions that developed towards the end of the eighteenth century. In so far as they demanded skill it was traditional skills that were required. In time they tended to require less rather than more skill and to provide an outlet for large quantities of unskilled labour, particularly the child labour which was so abundant in the period of falling infant mortality and rising birth rates. Their capital equipment could be built up gradually by small discrete outlays of capital, and indeed during this period the worker himself could often be made to provide the loom or the jenny, and the working space, and to hire the auxiliary labour required. In sum, the textile industries were peculiarly well adapted to development by a low-income community and seem to have suffered less from the

---

[1] See below, pp.182–92.

[2] It should be borne in mind that the 1770 figures refer to England and Wales and those for 1801 and 1811 to Great Britain. For most purposes of structural comparison, the difference is probably of negligible importance since Scotland's share in the population of Great Britain was only about $14\frac{1}{2}$ per cent and her share in British national product was even smaller. Inclusion of Ireland with a population of about half the size of Great Britain would make a considerable difference, however.

discouraging effects of foreign trade restrictions and high taxation than any other industry.

Before the wars ended, assessed incomes (including national debt interest) had risen by a further £15 m. and national income by perhaps about £13 m. Then the war boom broke and peace ushered in a period of dislocation and distress from which it is difficult to extract a clear picture of the course of structural change.

3. THE PERIOD OF INDUSTRIALISATION

Whatever may have been the effect of the war on the process of industrialisation there is no doubt that the post-war years saw a relatively rapid expansion.[1] Unfortunately the period from the end of the war to the beginnings of the railway age in the late 1830's is one for which the national-income data are especially deficient. There are no income-tax assessments for the period 1816–41. The 1821 population census provided very little information on occupations and the 1831 occupational analysis was sketchy and was in any case limited to adult males and domestics of all types. There are various contemporary estimates for this period, but apart from Lowe's calculations for the early 1820's there are no contemporary assessments on which we could place any reliance.[2]

Under the circumstances we were obliged to depend on Lowe[3] for an estimate of total national income in 1821 and to calculate its industrial distribution largely with the aid of our estimates of incomes from employment.[4] For 1831 we reached a set of highly tentative figures for the main components, on the basis partly of the incomes from employment estimates, partly on certain *ad hoc* data available for this period (e.g. inhabited-house duty returns), and partly on extrapolations from the income-tax assessments which began in 1842–3.

From the 1840's onwards the wage-bill estimates were based on relatively complete[5] occupation returns and we again had income-tax assessments on which to base estimates of the non-wage items. These data are far from satisfactory as a basis for national-income estimation.

---

[1] Cf. W. G. Hoffmann, *British Industry 1700–1950*, translated by W. O. Henderson and W. H. Chaloner (1955), p. 32. 'The period 1793–1817 may be regarded as a break in a period of particularly rapid industrialisation.' The evidence for 'particularly rapid industrialisation' is thin: estimates of the eighteenth century trend depend largely on raw-cotton imports, output of West Riding woollens and London coal imports; but for most of the nineteenth century the Hoffman index rests on a broader base and its implications are accordingly of greater interest.

[2] Pablo Pebrer's estimate for 1831 in *Taxation, Expenditure, Power, Statistics and Debt of the whole British Empire* (1833) is for the United Kingdom as a whole: but in any case a close scrutiny of its details suggests that it is too carelessly put together to be acceptable even as a starting-point. See Deane, *Econ. Hist. Rev.*, vol. VIII, *op. cit.*, for a discussion of this and some of the other estimates produced during this period.

[3] Joseph Lowe, *The Present State of England* (1822).

[4] See above, pp. 148–53.

[5] The 1841 occupation returns were obviously deficient but it was possible to adjust them (industry by industry and in relation to sex and age) to arrive at a reasonably complete account.

Indeed it is not until the 1880's that there is enough information to justify the construction of annual estimates with reasonable confidence that they can be expected to reflect the year-to-year variations.[1] But as indicators of the principal orders of magnitudes involved at bench-mark dates the figures based on wage-bill estimates and income-tax assessments do have some independent validity.

The tax returns are not analysed in sufficient detail to indicate the industrial distribution of assessed incomes although it is possible to distinguish most agricultural incomes and there are some public com-panies which are industrially classified (railways, canals, ironworks, gasworks, mines and quarries, for example). Hence our estimates of the industrial distribution of national output for the period 1841–81 were based on:

(1) our wage-bill estimates which were constructed on an industry basis;

(2) our estimates of the numbers and earnings of the self-employed;

(3) the industrial distinctions which could be deduced from the returns of assessed incomes;

(4) some arbitrary assumptions as to the probable distribution of those Schedule D and unassessed self-employment incomes for which no detail was available: these assumptions in their turn were heavily dependent on our employment income estimates; and

(5) the estimates of United Kingdom agricultural net incomes for the period 1867 onwards made by the Oxford Agricultural Economics Research Institute.[2]

The result is that we have some confidence in our estimates of agricul-tural incomes and a highly tentative view of our estimates of the split between the manufacturing, mining and building group of industries on the one hand, and the trade and transport group on the other. If the data problems discussed in the last few paragraphs are added to the conceptual problems referred to at the beginning of this chapter the significance of the split appears even more doubtful. Clearly it is only within very broad statistical and definitional limits that the resulting figures are acceptable.

Table 37 presents the results of these estimates distinguishing the principal industry groups. They build up to a set of what we have called 'national income' aggregates for Great Britain: in this connec-tion, however, it is important to note two things about these aggregates. First, that the data on such items as capital consumption and stock appreciation are not sufficient to permit a precise estimation of net national income. Generally, however, it may be assumed that the

---

[1] This is possible, moreover, only after the 'unscrambling' operations which Prest per-formed on the income-tax assessments. *Economic Journal* LVIII (1948), *op. cit.*

[2] We are indebted to Mr J. R. Bellerby for making the annual estimates available to us. The deductions for Ireland were our estimates, however, and are inevitably crude.

Table 37.

The industrial distribution of the national income of Great Britain, 1801–1901

(in £m. at current prices, and as percentages of total national income in each year)

	Agriculture, forestry, fishing (£m.)	Manufacture, mining, building (£m.)	Trade and transport (£m.)	Domestic and personal (£m.)	Housing (£m.)	Income from abroad (£m.)	Government, professional and all other (£m.)	Total national product (£m.)
1801	75·5	54·3	40·5	12·8	12·2	—	36·8	232·0
1811	107·5	62·5	50·1	15·7	17·2	—	48·1	301·1
1821	76·0	93·0	46·4	16·6	17·9	3·0	38·1	291·0
1831	79·5	117·1	59·0	19·2	22·0	3·9	39·3	340·0
1841	99·9	155·5	83·3	26·9	37·0	6·2	43·6	452·3
1851	106·5	179·5	97·8	27·4	42·6	10·4	59·0	523·3
1861	118·8	243·6	130·7	35·0	50·3	19·9	69·7	668·0
1871	130·4	348·9	201·6	45·5	69·4	39·5	81·3	916·6
1881	109·1	395·9	241·9	51·7	89·1	59·5	103·9	1051·2
1891	110·9	495·2	289·6	70·6	104·0	94·3	123·8	1288·2
1901	104·6	660·7	383·0	78·5	134·2	106·5	175·5	1642·9
	(%)	(%)	(%)	(%)	(%)	(%)	(%)	(%)
1801	32·5	23·4	17·4	5·5	5·3	—	15·8	100·0
1811	35·7	20·8	16·6	5·2	5·7	—	16·0	100·0
1821	26·1	31·9	15·9	5·7	6·2	1·0	13·1	100·0
1831	23·4	34·4	17·3	5·7	6·5	1·1	11·6	100·0
1841	22·1	34·4	18·4	6·0	8·2	1·4	9·6	100·0
1851	20·3	34·3	18·7	5·2	8·1	2·0	11·3	100·0
1861	17·8	36·5	19·6	5·2	7·5	3·0	10·4	100·0
1871	14·2	38·1	22·0	5·0	7·6	4·3	8·9	100·0
1881	10·4	37·6	23·0	4·9	8·5	5·8	9·9	100·0
1891	8·6	38·4	22·5	5·5	8·1	7·3	9·6	100·0
1901	6·4	40·2	23·3	4·8	8·2	6·5	10·7	100·0

N.B. Figures have been rounded and therefore do not add exactly to totals.

Sources and notes: (1) For 1801 and 1811 estimates see notes to Table 89, below.

(2) The 1821 estimates include Lowe's total, his estimate for agriculture, our estimates for government, professional and other services and for housing, and our split of the residual between manufactures and building and transport and trade.

(3) Our estimates for 1831 throughout. Based on our wage-bill and housing estimates plus extrapolation of 1841 figures by analogy employment incomes for agriculture and manufacturing and foreign trade for the trade and transport group.

(4) 1841–1881 estimates based on our estimates for wage bill (see Table 34) and housing, income-tax assessments 1842–3 onwards, Bellerby's estimates of U.K. agriculture incomes 1867 onwards, and Imlah's estimates of net interest and dividends from abroad.

(5) Agriculture, forestry, fishing. Based on Bellerby's estimates for 1867 onwards extrapolated and reduced to a Great Britain basis by means of our estimates of agricultural wages bill and the income-tax assessments.

(6) Manufacture, mining, building. Where income-tax assessments are available this includes a proportion of Schedule D (trades and professions), the proportion estimated on the basis of the distribution of employment incomes between the manufacturing, etc., group and the trade and transport group; it also includes profits from quarries, gasworks, iron-works, etc., and a proportion of incomes from self-employment. The allowance for evasion of Schedule D (trades and professions) was estimated at 50 per cent of assessed incomes for 1841, 1851 and 1861, at one-third for 1871, at 25 per cent for 1881 and 1891, and at 10 per cent for 1901.

(7) Trade and transport. Includes a proportion of Schedule D (trades and professions), allowing for evasion, as described in note (6), and a proportion of self-employment incomes plus profits from canals and railways in the United Kingdom.

(8) Incomes from self-employment. This is a very crude figure based on our estimates of the numbers of self-employed (excluding farmers) and on the assumption that the average earnings for this group was equivalent to the average non-agricultural wage plus 50 per cent.

(9) Housing. There are three sources of information on residential housing: (a) the population censuses which give numbers of inhabited houses, (b) the inhabited house duty returns available for 1821 to 1833 and 1851–2 onwards which give rent distribution tables for rents of over £5 for 1821–24, over £10 for 1825 to 1833, over £20 for 1851–2 to 1873–4, and for all houses (charged and uncharged) for 1874–5 onwards, (c) the income-tax returns of houses and messuages charged to Schedule A, which, however, do not distinguish between houses and other buildings. These different sources have different definitions of what constitutes a 'house' (sometimes the same source contains variable definitions as between one year and another) so that the final estimates are by no means as reliable as the abundance of data

might lead one to expect. For 1901 we derived the estimate from the figures given in Prest and Adams, *Consumers' Expenditure in the United Kingdom 1900–1919.*

(10) Government and defence. These estimates made for our wage-bill aggregates and based on government expenditure accounts could be refined by a more intensive study of the estimates and accounts for this period. At present they contain a good deal of estimation by fixed proportions based on the detailed extraction of the wage and salary component of mixed items for only one or two years of the series.

(11) Professional incomes. Besides the estimates made for our wage-bill aggregates this includes a token allowance of 5 per cent of Schedule D (trades and professions) after allowing for evasion.

(12) Domestic service. Includes other personal service as well as indoor domestics.

(13) Incomes from abroad. Derived from Imlah's estimates of net interest and dividends from abroad. A. H. Imlah, *Economic Elements in the Pax Britannica, op. cit.* No attempt has been made to extract the Irish share from this total on the assumption that British incomes from Irish sources not elsewhere included were at least as large as the Irish share in total U.K. incomes from abroad.

(14) Total national income. These totals are by addition of separate estimates for the main items except in the case of the 1821 figure when we used Lowe's estimates plus net income from abroad to provide the aggregate. For 1801, 1811, 1831 and 1841 (though not, of course, for 1821) our estimates are independent of the contemporary estimates and it is therefore interesting to compare them.

	Our estimate	Estimates derived from contemporaries	
	£m.	£m.	
1801	232	228	(After Beeke and Bell, *c.* 1800)
1811	301	330	(After Colquhoun, 1812)
1831	340	424	(After Pebrer, 1831)
1841	452	445	(After Spackman, 1841)

See Deane, *Economic History Review*, vol. VIII (1956), for a discussion of the contemporary calculations and of the estimates which can be derived from them. It will be seen that the discrepancies are well within the margin of error of the estimates except perhaps for 1811–12, when there is a difference of the order of 10 per cent, and 1831, when it is nearly 25 per cent. The direction of these differences accords with expectations: that is to say, it is more likely on the whole that Colquhoun overestimated the total and it is fairly certain that Pebrer over-estimated, perhaps considerably. However, our basis for the 1831 estimates was very weak and it may well be that it is itself an underestimate.

incomes are gross incomes, inclusive of both capital consumption and incomes from abroad, and that the national-income aggregates relate to gross national income or gross national product.

Secondly, it must be emphasised that where the Great Britain and the United Kingdom estimates used in this book overlap, neither series of aggregates is sufficiently precise to permit the extraction of the Irish totals as residuals. The Irish residuals seem to be about the right order of magnitude in terms of the United Kingdom estimates: that is to say, they fall between 15 and 20 per cent of the United Kingdom total before the famine and its aftermath, and between 5 and 9 per cent after.[1] Obviously, however, this represents a wide range for the Irish total and we can draw no useful conclusions for Ireland from these estimates.

In view of the limitations on the estimates in Table 37 it is necessary to restrict ourselves to those conclusions which do not depend heavily on the results for any one year and which will stand up to fairly wide margins of error in the basic figures. This means in effect that we should not put too much weight on the shifts suggested for a single decade, and that we should not try to read too much into the fluctuations in the share of somewhat heterogeneous groups of industry.

The features which then emerge significantly from Table 37 are as follows:

1. The revolutionary decline in the share of agriculture, which fell from probably more than a third of the national product in the first decade of the nineteenth century to about 6 per cent in the first decade of the twentieth. This fall was interrupted only by the war years at the beginning of the nineteenth century, when—as is usual in wartime—there was a marked increase in agricultural prices and some increase in output.

2. The somewhat uneven rise in the share of the mining, manufacturing and building group of industries over the century, from perhaps less than a quarter to about 40 per cent of the total. This rise was interrupted in the first decade, in the second quarter and possibly also in the 1880's. It was steepest in the period immediately following the Napoleonic Wars.

3. The increase in the share of the trade and transport group of industries starting in the 1820's and continuing, virtually without interruption (except possibly in the 1880's), throughout the period.

4. The growth in the share of incomes from abroad from under 1 per cent at the beginning of the century to more than 7 per cent at the end.[2]

---

[1] For 1851, when Bellerby's estimate suggests a total of about £613 m. for the United Kingdom, our estimate for Great Britain is about £523 m. If both are right the Irish share was about 14½ per cent for a corresponding population share of 24 per cent. This may be rather high, but even an adjustment to 10 per cent is within the margin of error of either the United Kingdom or the Great Britain estimate.

[2] We have no estimates for the first two decades, but it can be assumed that during the war years, when Britain was subsidising her European allies on a substantial scale, the flow was outwards rather than inwards.

By the turn of the century net incomes from abroad accounted for roughly the same proportion of national product as the agricultural group of industries.

For the other sources of income distinguished in Table 37 the main trends of interest seem to be: (a) the moderate rise in the share of housing, which was largely accomplished in the first half of the century when the rate of population growth was greatest, (b) the narrow range of fluctuation in the share of the domestic-service group which seems to have accounted for between 5 and 6 per cent of British national income for most of the nineteenth century, and (c) the decrease in the share of the government, professional and all other groups of services in the first half of the century: this was largely due to the reduction in the burden of government from the inflated totals of the war years, when incomes earned in government and defence probably accounted for more than 10 per cent of national product, to the peaceful, free-trading, Victorian levels of between 3 and 5 per cent.

Evidently the revolutionary changes in the structure of national product which took place during the nineteenth century were not smooth and continuous in their operation. The estimates will not support detailed, decade-by-decade comparisons, but they justify long-term analyses. If we consider the shape of change over a series of twenty- or thirty-year periods certain conclusions emerge quite convincingly. The first is that the period of greatest structural change fell within the first three to four decades of the century, particularly in the two decades immediately following the Napoleonic Wars. To some extent the post-war spurt was intensified by the effect of the war in distorting and retarding the pattern of growth: but probably this would have been a period of relatively rapid change even without a war to complicate the process. There was a substantial fall in the share of agriculture (amounting to perhaps 13 to 14 per cent in the period 1811–41) and an equally substantial gain in the share of the mining, manufacturing and building group of industries. If we exclude government and defence, and housing, both of which strongly reflected the wartime distortion, there seems to have been little change during the first three or four decades in the relative importance of the other groups distinguished in Table 37. Indeed, during the 1830's and 1840's the rate of structural change was apparently quite low for all groups.

The rate of change accelerated again in the 1850's and more rapidly in the 1860's and 1870's. Between 1851 and 1881 the agricultural group lost nearly 10 per cent of its share in national product and the trade and transport group together with net incomes from abroad absorbed a further 8 per cent. During the last two decades of the century the pace of change slackened appreciably. The agricultural industry had fallen to a relatively low level of importance so that its continued decline made a very much smaller impact on the national framework. Only coal-mining among the major industries continued to expand its share of national product at an appreciable rate.

These conclusions are based on current-price estimates; and to compare relative rates of growth in different sectors of the economy it is necessary to allow for some widely divergent price movements. Again there are serious data problems involved. The price indices for the period leave much to be desired and the resulting real-product estimates are even less precise than the current-value figures. Nevertheless, imprecise though they are, they have some significance and their implications warrant further consideration.

Table 38. *Nineteenth-century rates of growth in the real product of Great Britain*

(Compound percentage rates per annum for decade averages measured over thirty-year periods)

Decades	Total national product	Agriculture, forestry, fishing	Manufactures, mining, building	Trade and transport
1801/11–1831/41	2·9	1·2	4·7	3·0
1811/21–1841/51	2·9	1·5	3·7	2·5
1821/31–1851/61	2·3	1·8	2·3	2·8
1831/41–1861/71	2·2	1·3	3·0	2·8
1841/51–1871/81	2·5	0·7	2·7	3·2
1851/61–1881/91	3·2	0·5	3·5	3·7
1861/71–1891/1901	3·3	0·7	3·5	3·6

Sources: Estimates in Table 37 deflated by Rousseaux price indices averaged over periods of nine years. To deflate the gross-product totals for the agricultural group of industries we used his index for agricultural products; for the manufactures, mining and building group his index for industrial products; and for trade and transport and all other industries his composite index. The totals, for British national product, represent a sum of the industry totals thus deflated. The decade average was estimated as an average of the bench-mark years in each case—thus the estimate for 1801/11 was an average of the estimate for 1801 and 1811. See Paul Rousseaux, *Les Mouvements de Fond de l'Economie Anglaise 1800–1913* (Louvain, 1938), pp. 266–7. The base of the index is an average of the years 1865 and 1885.

Comparative rates of growth in total real product are shown in Table 38. We have used the Rousseaux price index to deflate our estimates of product at current prices and have measured the growth rates in terms of decade averages over successive thirty-year periods. Thus we have attempted to estimate the rate of growth between the first and fourth decades, the second and fifth decades, and so on. Measured in this way, the thirty-year growth rates vary from 2·2 per cent to 3·3 per cent. For the period as a whole, i.e. for the span between the first and tenth decades of the century, the compound rate of growth works out at 2·8 per cent per annum.

The striking feature of these estimates is the deceleration they imply for the middle of the century. For most of the first half of the century the rate of growth seems to have been in the region of 2·9 per cent. But there was a mid-century span in which—if we compare 1831/41 with 1861/71—the rate drops to 2·2 per cent. It must be borne in mind of course that our decade averages are averages of two bench-mark years in each case, and that if the cyclical abnormalities were in the same direction for two consecutive bench-mark years this would tend to distort some of the calculated rates of growth. A convenient characterisation of the cyclical circumstances of industrial years can be obtained from Thorp's *Business Annals* for England, and for our bench-mark years these are as follows[1]:

1801	Depression: revival
1811	Deep depression
1821	Slow revival
1831	Recession: depression
1841	Depression
1851	Prosperity
1861	Uneven prosperity
1871	Prosperity
1881	Mild prosperity
1891	Industrial recession
1901	Mild depression

If these characteristics exerted an appreciable influence on our bench-mark estimates (which are often based as largely on data for adjacent years as for the year in question) then we might expect the calculated growth rates to contain an *upward* bias for 1821/31–1851/61 and 1831/41–1861/71 and a *downward* bias for 1861/71–1891/1901. This would not alter our conclusions either about the mid-century deceleration or about the later acceleration.

In effect, therefore, we would conclude that after an early spurt (which may have been exaggerated by recovery from a wartime retardation) the economy seems to have gone through a period of rather slower growth. This was the period when most of the British railways were built and there was unprecedentedly heavy investment in mines, blast-furnaces, steam-driven machinery and ships. Presumably this expansion in capacity bore fruit in the second half of the century when the rate of growth rose to levels which represent an all-time peak for comparable periods of time.

The relative rates of growth are also interesting. The early spurt was primarily due to a high rate of growth in the mining, manufacturing and building group of industries, but in the second half of the century the pace seems to have been set by the trade and transport group. As was to be expected, the agricultural group expanded relatively slowly throughout the period, but during the first six decades this sector was by no means a passive contributor to the overall momentum of British economic growth. Not until the second half of the nineteenth century did the long-term rate of growth of British agriculture begin to decline, and not until the last three or four decades did it fall appreciably below 1 per cent per annum.

One of the factors which helped to inflate the overall rate of growth at the beginning of the century was, of course, the high rate of population growth. Between 1801 and 1831 the population of Great Britain

[1] W. L. Thorp, *Business Annals* (New York, N.B.E.R., 1926), pp. 162–73.

grew at an average rate of about 1·5 per cent per annum: this was probably the peak period for British population growth. Between 1811 and 1841 the rate was 1·4 per cent; between 1821 and 1851, 1·3 per cent; and from then until the end of the century the rate settled at about 1·2 per cent per annum. However, it is probable that the decline would have continued had it not been checked in the three or four decades following the famine by the influx from Ireland, whose population declined by more than 3½ million between 1846 and 1890.

By confronting the real-product estimates described in this chapter with the estimates of the industrial distribution of the occupied population which formed the subject of chapter IV, some impression can be obtained of the relative rates of productivity growth implied by these data. It will be evident, however, from what has already been said, that the results of such a calculation are inevitably rough, particularly for the individual sectors. Neither the census occupational analyses nor the income-tax returns give a firm basis for distinguishing between industries; and the combination of the two sets of estimates to give relative rates of 'productivity' growth is a hazardous procedure. However, there is no reason to suppose that the data distort the overall rates for the economy or that they fail to reflect the main trends for the broad sectors distinguished here.

Table 39. *Nineteenth-century rates of growth in the average real product of Great Britain*

(Compound percentage rates per head of the occupied population in each sector)

Decades	Total national product	Agriculture, forestry, fishing	Manufactures, mining, building	Trade and transport
1801/11–1831/41	1·5	1·1	2·2	1·1
1811/21–1841/51	1·4	1·2	1·8	1·1
1821/31–1851/61	0·9	1·3	0·6	0·5
1831/41–1861/71	0·9	1·1	0·7	0·4
1841/51–1871/81	1·4	1·1	1·5	1·0
1851/61–1881/1891	2·0	1·4	2·4	1·6
1861/71–1891/1901	2·2	1·5	2·3	1·9

Sources: For real-product estimates see notes to Table 38 in this chapter. For occupied population see notes to Table 30 in chapter IV.

The estimates of growth in average real product per head which are given in Table 39 reinforce the impression of a post-war spurt (though this is not so impressive when allowance is made for population increase), a mid-century slackening in the pace of growth and a later acceleration to unprecedented levels. They suggest, moreover, that it was a decline in the rate of growth of productivity in the manufacturing, mining and building group of industries that contributed most effectively to the deceleration in the rate. For the trade and transport group still accounted for a relatively minor fraction of total national output and the average rate of growth for the agricultural group seems actually to have exceeded the national average during the period 1821/31–1861/71—the period which covers the 'Golden Age of Agriculture'. The later acceleration was supported by an increase in the rate of growth per head for each of the sectors distinguished in Table 39: but it is significant, in the light of later developments, that for the manufacturing group the average rate had ceased to grow at the end of the century when for both the trade and transport group and the agricultural group the trend was still upwards.

4. INDUSTRIAL STRUCTURE IN THE TWENTIETH CENTURY

There were no censuses of production either for industry or agriculture in nineteenth-century Britain and estimates of the structure of national product are both broad and rough. For the twentieth century it is possible to make more detailed and reliable estimates—at any rate for the commodity-producing trades and for the public utilities—though not unfortunately at annual intervals.

The first census of industrial production was taken in 1907, when there was also a census of agricultural production. It was preceded by an inquiry into the earnings of manual labourers (1906). The second (1912) census of industrial production was incomplete, largely because work on the returns was interrupted by the war and never finished, but also because it exempted firms employing less than five workers.[1] The next full census was taken in 1924, and this was followed by the censuses of 1930 and 1935. The Second World War again interrupted the series, and the next industrial census was delayed until 1948.

Largely on the basis of the production census results and the tax assessments for the relevant periods we have made estimates of the structure of national product for three bench-mark years in the first half of the nineteenth century—1907, 1924 and 1935. For the interwar period we also relied heavily on the exhaustive wage and salary estimates made by Chapman and Knight.[2] The results of our estimates are summarised in Tables 40 and 41. They are more satisfactory than the estimates given above for the nineteenth century but they could certainly be improved by a more thorough exploration of the data for individual industries not covered by the production censuses. It is doubtful, however, whether the published data would permit much refinement of the highly tentative estimates reached for the commercial industries (distribution and finance), which are the most vulnerable of our figures.[3]

The Irish component of the United Kingdom total has been much

---

[1] The main results of the 1912 census were published in the reports on the 1924 census wherever they were sufficiently complete to justify inclusion for comparative purposes.

[2] Agatha Chapman and Rose Knight, *Wages and Salaries in the United Kingdom 1920–1938* (Cambridge, 1953).

[3] A more detailed analysis of the original tax assessments than is available in Inland Revenue reports would help to improve these estimates but there is still a dearth of information on unassessed profit incomes in this group.

less important in the twentieth century than in the nineteenth century. This is partly because the Irish population has been declining in numbers and partly because of the secession of Southern Ireland after the First World War. Until 1923 when the Irish Free State became independent, the Irish contribution to the United Kingdom total was not, however, negligible. In the 1900's it accounted for between 9 and 10 per cent of the total population and for between 20 and 25 per cent of the net output of agriculture, for example. After 1923 the Irish part of the United Kingdom contained less than 3 per cent of its population and contributed only about 2 per cent of its total national product.[1] At this stage the inclusion of Ireland makes little difference to the structural pattern, at any rate in terms of the broad industrial categories considered here. To facilitate comparison with our nineteenth-century estimates we have therefore excluded Ireland from the 1907 and 1924 estimates in Table 40. For the more recent years it has not been considered necessary to exclude Ireland.

The estimates for each industry in Table 40 are again expressed as percentages of gross national income or product. The basic United Kingdom totals are derived from Prest's national-income series plus Jeffery's and Walters' addition for incomes of charities, etc., plus an estimate of capital consumption made by extrapolating the C.S.O. estimate for 1938 on the basis of the Jefferys and Walters series for depreciation.[2]

Consideration of the data summarised in Table 40 and their comparison with the corresponding nineteenth-century estimates (see Table 37) suggests the following broad conclusions on structure.

1. The rapid decline in the contribution of agriculture to the national product was still in progress at the turn of the century. In the period of roughly a quarter of a century preceding 1907 the share of the agricultural group of industries had roughly halved. By then it had the same weight in the economy as the mining and quarrying group and was less important than either the textiles and clothing group or the metals and engineering group. The decline continued during the first quarter of the twentieth century, but much less rapidly, though it probably accelerated a little after the First World War. By 1924 it had gone almost as far as it could go.

2. But if agriculture was still in rapid relative decline at the end of the nineteenth century and the beginning of the twentieth, the mining–manufacturing–building group, taken as a whole, showed no marked increase. Within the group there was some structural change as the leading industries in the British industrial revolution grew more slowly and new industries were introduced. Textiles alone, which accounted for about 10 per cent of national income in 1881, contributed only

---

[1] In 1948 Northern Ireland's population was about 2·7 per cent of the United Kingdom total and its gross domestic product about 2 per cent.

[2] Jefferys' and Walters' estimates of depreciation are 74 per cent of the C.S.O. estimate for 1938 and less than 60 per cent for the average of the seven years 1946–52. *Income and Wealth Series*, vol. v (1956), and C.S.O., *National Income and Expenditure 1958*.

Table 40. *The industrial distribution of the national income of Great Britain in the first quarter of the twentieth century*

	1907		1924	
	Value of output at current prices (£m.)	As percentage of national income gross of depreciation (%)	Value of output at current prices (£m.)	As percentage of national income gross of depreciation (%)
1. Agriculture, forestry, fishing	120·1	6·0	168·5	4·1
2. Mines and quarries	119·4	6·0	227·5	5·6
3. Engineering and metal manufactures	164·3	8·2	332·6	8·1
4. Textiles and clothing	159·5	8·0	312·3	7·6
5. Food, drink and tobacco	85·5	4·3	277·0	6·7
6. Paper and printing	32·6	1·6	95·5	2·3
7. Chemicals	21·0	1·1	77·4	1·9
8. Wood industries	20·6	1·0	37·6	0·9
9. Miscellaneous manufactures	29·4	1·5	96·8	2·4
10. Gas. electricity, water	31·0	1·6	71·9	1·7
11. Building and contracting	74·4	3·7	127·3	3·1
12. Rents of dwellings	148·4	7·4	265·2	6·4
13. Commerce	358·4	18·0	735·5	17·8
14. Transport	188·9	9·5	498·5	12·1
15. Government and defence	59·6	3·0	187·0	4·5
16. Professions, charities and miscellaneous	202·5	10·1	395·6	9·6
17. Domestic service	75·8	3·8	141·4	3·4
18. Income from abroad	143·8	7·2	220·0	5·3
19. Errors and omissions	39·7	—	−146·5	—
20. National income gross of depreciation	1,995·5	100·0	4,121·1	100·0

Sources and notes: 1. Agriculture, forestry and fishing. The 1907 census of production covered the agricultural and fishing industries. We used the revised figure for Great Britain published by the Ministry of Agriculture and Fisheries, *The Agricultural Output and the Food Supplies of Great Britain* (1929). For 1924 we used the agricultural estimates given by Bellerby in *The Farm Economist*, 1953, and added for fishing on the basis of the Chapman and Knight wage and salary estimates.

2–11. *Mines and quarries, manufacturing, gas, etc., building and contracting.* These are the industries covered by the censuses of production. We included public buildings and road construction in building and contracting. Some estimate was involved in distinguishing the Irish component for certain industries where disclosure regulations prevented a full county analysis in the census reports.

12. Rents on dwellings. For 1907 we based our estimates on Prest's figures of expenditure on housing rents. For 1924 we extrapolated Prest's 1919 figures on the basis of unhabited housed duty data. A. R. Prest and A. A. Adams, *Consumers' Expenditure in the United Kingdom 1900–1919* (Cambridge, 1954).

13–14. Commerce and transport. These estimates were calculated from a variety of sources, principally on the income-tax assessments for profit incomes and on estimates of total wages and salaries. For 1907 we used Bowley's estimates of shop assistants' earnings (*Wages and Income since 1860*, op. cit. p. 76), the earnings inquiry data for railway wages (*S.P. 1912–13*, vol. cviii), the British Association report on 'The Amount and Distribution of Income (other than wages)', *J. Roy. Statist. Soc.*, December 1910, and the Inland Revenue reports. For 1924 we used Chapman and Knight, op. cit., and the Inland Revenue reports. Income from abroad and financial services are included with 'Commerce'.

15. Government and defence. For 1907 we calculated the wages and salaries paid by

government from the *Appropriation Accounts*. For 1924 we used Chapman's estimates, *op. cit.*

16. Professions, charities, etc. For 1907 we used the estimates in the British Association report, *op. cit.*, and Jefferys' estimates of the incomes of charities. For 1924 there were Chapman's estimates of wages and salaries and (residually) the Inland Revenue reports.

17. Domestic service. For 1907 we made an estimate based on the occupation census numbers and average earnings based for males on the 1893–4 inquiry into the wages of the manual labour classes (*S.P. 1893–4*, vol. LXXXIII) and for females on Miss Collett's report on domestic servants (*S.P. 1899*, vol. XCII). In both cases an allowance was included for the value of board and lodging. The resulting estimate is about 17 per cent higher than Prest's estimate for expenditure on domestics in 1907. For 1924 we accepted Chapman's estimates.

18. Income from abroad. Net investment income as calculated by Imlah (*op. cit.*) for 1907 and Board of Trade (*op. cit.*) for 1924. These figures relate to the United Kingdom. If the Irish figures were calculated and the flow between Great Britain and Ireland accounted for it is likely that these estimates would be slightly higher than shown.

19. Errors and omissions. This represents the difference between the sum of items 1–17 and item 19. It need hardly be said that this figure bears no relation to the overall margin of error in the estimates.

20. National income. Based on Prest (*Economic Journal*, 1948, *op. cit.*), Jefferys and Walters (*Income and Wealth Series V, op. cit.*) for the incomes of charities, etc., and the C.S.O. estimates for 1938 (*National Income and Expenditure, 1957* (H.M.S.O., 1957)) which we accepted as the most reliable of all these estimates and to which we adjusted the earlier estimates to match. The totals include an allowance for capital consumption made by extrapolating the C.S.O. estimate for 1938 on the basis of Jefferys' and Walters' depreciation estimates.

about $4\frac{1}{2}$ per cent of the 1907 total.[1] After 1907 the expansion of some of the newer, lighter, more miscellaneous industries induced a recovery in the importance of the manufacturing group. The share of the textile and clothing industries continued to decline and the other great staples (mining and quarrying and iron and steel manufactures) also lost in relative importance. But there were notable increases in the share of the food, drink and tobacco, paper and printing, chemical and miscellaneous other industries between 1907 and 1924.

3. In spite of the highly tentative nature of our estimates for the trade and transport group of industries, there is no doubt of their growth in relative importance, a growth which seems to have been almost uninterrupted since the 1830's. For most of the period of industrialisation it was the transport sector—particularly railways—which contributed most strongly to the increase in the weight of this group: and if British railways ceased to increase their net output as rapidly in the fourth quarter of the nineteenth century as they had in the third there were the profits and interest receipts from colonial and foreign railways and the British canals to be taken into account. The growth in incomes from abroad was indeed one of the most striking features of the three or four decades which preceded the outbreak of the First World War. Between 1886–7 and 1914–15 assessed incomes from abroad (so far as these could be distinguished by the Board of Inland Revenue) roughly trebled in value.[2] In 1907 total net investment incomes from abroad were estimated to be worth about £120 m., which is of the same order

[1] See pp. 211–14.
[2] *Fifty-ninth Report of the Commissioners of H.M. Inland Revenue, for the year 1915–16* (H.M.S.O., 1916). During the same period total national income roughly doubled.

of magnitude as the estimated net output of the agricultural or of the mining and quarrying group of industries.[1] Shipping incomes were estimated to account for a further £85 m.,[2] which compares with £117 m. for the total working receipts of the railways of Great Britain.

4. The other conclusions suggested by these estimates are less striking. It is, however, of interest to note the slow decline in the share of dwelling rents and of domestic service, dating from before the beginning of the twentieth century in both cases. On the changes in the contribution of the government and defence group (which tend to vary from one year to another in response to non-economic and temporary factors such as war) it is relevant to say that part of the twentieth-century increase represents a transfer from private professional services and is associated with the government's increasing assumption of educational and medical responsibilities.

Table 41 carries the estimates of industrial structure up to 1955. This time the estimates are for the United Kingdom as a whole, but the divergencies from the Great Britain proportions are inconsiderable as can be seen from a comparison of the 1924 results in Table 41 with those in Table 40. Again the totals are for gross national product. The 1935 estimates are based, like the 1924 estimates, largely on the Census of Production, the Chapman and Knight wage and salary estimates and the income-tax returns. The 1949 and 1955 estimates are from the 1957 Blue Book, the breakdown for manufacturing being partly estimated.

Two world wars and a great depression produced certain temporary distortions in the economic structure of the United Kingdom during the first half of the twentieth century. These are particularly evident in the figures for 1935 and 1949. The abnormally low share of most commodity-producing industries in 1935, for example, reflects the depression from which British agriculture and industry were only just beginning to recover. The abnormally high share of agriculture which characterised the later war years was still in evidence in 1949. But even for 1955 the low level of dwelling rents, for example (and to some extent the high level of building activity), is attributable to restriction which accompanied the war and which (at least as far as rent restrictions were concerned) were still almost in full force. These abnormalities make it difficult to extract a clear picture of the long-term trends in the twentieth century.

If we focus attention mainly on 1924 and 1955, both years in which the economic aftermath of war had largely (but by no means entirely) subsided, we find that the following broad conclusions indicated by the results in Table 41.

1. The most significant structural change in this thirty-year period seems to have been a substantial increase in the share of the manufacturing group of industries together with gas, electricity and water, and

---

[1] Board of Trade estimate published in *Board of Trade Journal*, vol. cx (1923).
[2] *Ibid.*

building and construction. For this group the increase was from 34½ per cent of gross national product in 1924 to 44½ per cent in 1955. The mining and quarrying industries tended to decline in relative importance for most of the present century, but even if we include these, the mining–manufacturing–building group of industries as a whole accounted for 48 per cent of the gross national product in 1955 (compared with 40 per cent in 1924, 38 per cent in 1935, and 45 per cent in 1949). For the average of the ten years 1949–58 it was nearly 47 per cent. Taken at its face value, therefore, the comparison between 1924 and 1955 suggests a higher rate of industrialisation than at any time since the first three or four decades of the nineteenth century.

Table 41. *Distribution of the gross national product of the United Kingdom, 1924–55*

	(1) 1924		(2) 1935		(3) 1949		(4) 1955	
	£m.	%	£m.	%	£m.	%	£m.	%
1. Agriculture, forestry, fishing	176	4·2	175	3·9	691	6·2	787	4·7
2. Mines and quarries	228	5·4	139	3·1	407	3·7	580	3·4
3. Engineering and vehicles	199	4·7	269	6·0	1226	11·0	2259	13·4
4. Metal manufactures	137	3·3	154	3·4	560	5·1	912	5·4
5. Textiles	219	5·2	160	3·5	471	4·2	562	3·3
6. Clothing	105	2·5	97	2·1	198	1·8	245	1·5
7. Food, drink and tobacco	280	6·7	232	5·1	391	3·5	617	3·7
8. Paper and printing	97	2·3	118	2·6	251	2·3	448	2·7
9. Chemicals	78	1·9	93	2·1	245	2·2	487	2·9
10. All other manufactures	135	3·2	160	3·5	401	3·6	619	3·7
11. Gas, electricity, water	73	1·7	111	2·5	226	2·0	400	2·4
12. Building and construction	129	3·1	187	4·1	612	5·5	972	5·7
13. Rents of dwellings	268	6·4	292	6·5	297	2·7	534	3·2
14. Commerce	744	17·8	884	19·6	1820	16·5	2659	15·7
15. Transport and communications	501	12·0	483	10·7	915	8·2	1392	8·2
16. Government and defence	192	4·6	210	4·7	1012	9·1	1562	9·3
17. Domestic service	144	3·4	154	3·4	103	0·9	96	0·6
18. Income from abroad	220	5·2	185	4·1	160	1·4	177	1·0
19. All other including errors and omissions	267	6·4	413	9·1	1143	10·1	1584	9·3
20. Total gross national income inclusive of capital consumption and income from abroad	4192	100·0	4516	100·0	11129	100·0	16892	100·0

Sources and notes: 1. For 1924 estimates see notes to Table 40. The 1935 estimates were reached for the most part in the same way. It was necessary, however, to adjust the 1935 Census of Production results (which were complete only for firms of more than ten employees). The addition for small firms was made by applying to numbers employed in these firms the average net output of the smallest group of firms covered in each industry, i.e. the firms employing eleven to twenty-four persons.

2. The 1949 and 1955 estimates are largely drawn from the 1958 Blue Book on *National Income and Expenditure* (Table 16 on pp. 11–12). We used the industry breakdown given in Tables 17 and 29 of the Blue Book for wages, salaries and company trading profits, which together accounted for over 93 per cent of incomes earned in manufacturing, as a basis for distinguishing items 3–10.

2. This twentieth-century industrialisation differs, however, from the industrial revolution of the early nineteenth century in that it has been balanced not by a decline in agriculture (which seems to have reached

the permanently low level of 4 to 5 per cent of peacetime national product) but by a fall in the relative importance of the commercial and transport group of industries, including, among these, incomes from abroad. In 1924 investment incomes from abroad were estimated at more than 5 per cent of gross national product. In 1955 they had fallen to about 1 per cent. The decline in shipping incomes was also considerable and was more than sufficient to outweigh the growth of the motor-transport industry.

3. Two other major structural shifts of long-term significance have taken place since the outbreak of the Second World War. One is the decline of domestic service to an economic activity of negligible value in the British economy; the other is the doubling in the relative weight of government's contribution to the gross national product. The decline in the importance of domestic service was already evident at the beginning of the century; it was jolted to a new low level by the Second World War, since when the total incomes of domestic servants have continued to decline in absolute as well as in relative terms although the gross national product has more than doubled. The growth of the government sector reflects the remarkable extension of the responsibilities of public authorities in the United Kingdom. More than a third of the product of government in 1955 was attributable to incomes from employment in public health and education. About 26 per cent was spent on the incomes of the armed forces, but in 1924 this proportion had been about 36 per cent. It seems clear that costs of administration *per se* have also increased. In 1955 incomes earned in public administration exclusive of armed forces, public health or educational service accounted for 3·6 per cent of gross national product; whereas in 1924 incomes earned in government service, excluding the armed forces but including state health and educational services, was only 2·9 per cent.

4. In conclusion it may be noted that the structural changes of the past thirty to forty years have shown marked tendencies towards a decline in the importance of industries with a relatively low product per worker, and a growth in those with a relatively high average product. The obvious examples are the decline in domestic service and mining, and the growth of highly capitalised industries (such as gas, electricity and water) or of the salaried and professional services (government, health and education). Within the manufacturing group itself similar changes have been taking place. The expanding groups have been chemical, metal manufactures, electrical engineering and vehicle-building trades; and the declining groups have been textiles, clothing, and food, drink and tobacco, all of which are industries with a characteristically low average product per worker.

5. TWO AND A HALF CENTURIES OF INDUSTRIAL CHANGE

Finally, if we try to take a broad view of the changing shape of the British economy over this whole period and think of it mainly in terms of three components—the agricultural group, the manufacturing group, and the trade and transport group of industries—we can distinguish four main phases in the process of industrialisation.

The first was the pre-industrial phase. Agriculture was by far the most important industry. Until the last two or three decades of the eighteenth century it seems to have lost very little ground. During this period the manufacturing and commercial sectors of the economy gradually expanded their share, without, however, being clearly distinguishable from each other.

In the second phase, which began in the second half of the eighteenth century, and was somewhat retarded by the Napoleonic Wars, the manufacturing industry expanded its share strongly and developed characteristics which distinguished it sharply from either the commercial sector or from pre-industrial manufacture. Meanwhile agriculture was losing ground in relative, though not absolute terms, and by 1831 it accounted for less than a quarter of the gross national product of Great Britain compared with rather more than a third at the turn of the century.

The third phase began with the building of the railways; slowly at first, for relatively little structural change is discernible for the 1830's and 1840's, when productivity seems to have been growing more slowly in industry and commerce than in agriculture. It was in the third quarter of the century that the trade and transport industries began to expand strongly, and to a lesser extent the mining and building industries. The volume of international trade reached its peak rate of growth of over $4\frac{1}{2}$ per cent per annum in the period 1841–71. The product of agriculture began to decline in absolute terms and agriculture's share in the national total accordingly declined sharply, though agricultural productivity, measured in terms of real output per person occupied, continued to grow at a fairly steady pace until the last quarter. By 1881 it accounted for not much more than 10 per cent of the national total, and by 1901 for about 6 per cent. The third phase—characterised by expansion in the trade and transport group and rapid decline in the importance of agriculture—seems to have lasted until the First World War. By 1924 our rough estimates suggest that the trade and transport group accounted for nearly 30 per cent of national product compared with about 23 per cent in 1881 and 18 per cent in 1841.[1] Incomes from abroad had reached their peak near the turn of the century at about 7 per cent of gross national product.

The final phase is not easy to define, because war and depression have obscured long-term trends. What does emerge from a comparison of the 1920's and 1950's suggests a new phase of industrialisation possibly comparable in extent to the process which characterised the early decades of the nineteenth century. By this time the agricultural group of industries was too small significantly to affect the shape of the

---

[1] These percentages should be regarded as tentative, but the rise they suggest is not in doubt.

British economy, and the growth in the share of manufacturing industry has been compensated by a relative decline in the share of the trade and transport group. According to our estimates the contribution of commerce and transport to gross national product has fallen from an average of possibly more than a third (including net incomes from abroad) in the interwar period to about a quarter in the 1950's. The next stage may well be characterised by relative expansion in the other service industries, excluding domestic service (which has virtually disappeared) but dominated by the services which are generally included in the government sector in this country.

CHAPTER VI

THE GROWTH OF THE NINETEENTH-CENTURY STAPLES

THE description of the changing structure of national product given in the previous chapter is sketchy. It does no more than outline a framework and suggest how it has developed through time. To take the next step and to explain the process of change or to locate the crucial turning-points we require a finer industrial classification and a less widely spaced set of bench-mark years. This entails a major programme of research involving special studies of industries for which the essential quantitative data are scattered through a variety of contemporary sources or buried in hitherto unexplored private records. Nor is it simply a question of digging out the figures. The task of converting the output and price data of a particular industry into estimates of its contribution to national income is complex even when the data have been objectively recorded with this kind of purpose in view. When they must be extracted from records kept for administrative or fiscal or private accounting purposes or deduced from input or cost data or similar partial indicators, the conversion requires specialised knowledge of the technical and economic circumstances of each industry concerned.

Although the readily available data do not permit a complete chronologically continuous analysis of each major industry's contribution to the national product, it is possible to be more specific than we have been so far about the role of some of the key industries in the process of industrialisation. In this chapter we shall consider the contribution of four industrial groups which played a major part in the industrial revolution and which, partly for that reason, are relatively well documented. These are textiles, mining, iron and steel and transport—the industries which became the staples of the industrialised economy. We shall focus attention on the nineteenth century since this was the period which covers most of the British industrial revolution and for which there are no census-of-production data: and we shall be concerned primarily with the growth of output. If our discussion of the bases and procedure of the estimates seems to be lengthier than is required to support the somewhat limited conclusions we have drawn from them, it is because they could certainly be improved upon and those who want to adapt or improve may find this amount of detail a useful starting-point.

I. THE TEXTILE INDUSTRIES

(a) Cotton

Cotton was the leading industry in the British industrial revolution and the rapidity of its early growth may have owed something to the fact that it was essentially a new industry. During approximately the first three-quarters of the eighteenth century it was a minor trade, little more than a subsidiary occupation for a few thousand agriculturalists. Its finished product was a compound of linen warp and cotton weft, and its expansion was restricted on the demand side by the limited market for these coarse cottons, and on the supply side by the relatively low productivity of spinners dependent on the hand-wheel. The selling value of its product was estimated by contemporaries at a mere £600,000 in the 1760's.[1]

The new inventions which became effective in the 1770's and 1780's transformed the industry without, in the first instance, robbing it of its domestic character.[2] Arkwright's water-frame (patented in 1769) produced cotton yarn of unprecedented strength and permitted the use of cotton for warp as well as weft.[3] When Hargreaves' spinning-jenny was patented a year later it contained sixteen spindles and multiplied by something like the same proportion the output of the individual spinner. Crompton's mule (patented in 1779), combined the principles of the jenny and the rollers and produced a smoother and finer yarn. Thus within a few years the principal limitations on the side of supply were removed and the product of the industry was greatly improved.

The effects of the water-frame and the jenny are perceptible in the rise of raw-cotton imports in the 1770's, but it was in the 1780's and 1790's that these began to multiply. Between 1780 and 1800 there was an increase of about eightfold, and since the yarn spun grew finer on the average, as well as stronger, the raw-material inputs understate the increase in output. By 1812, according to Ellison, 'one spinner could produce as much in a given time as 200 could have produced before the invention of Hargreaves' jenny'. These revolutionary developments changed the character of the industry. Spinning began to be concentrated in factories. Weavers would now rely on an uninterrupted supply of yarn and could afford to engage full time in manufacture. Their numbers increased rapidly. They began to crowd into the towns. Improvements in other processes helped to accelerate the rate of growth. There were improvements in bleaching and dyeing; carding, scutching and roving machines were introduced; steam power made it possible to locate factories where no water power was available: the introduction of Whitney's ginning machine in the United States in the

---

[1] This is Postlethwayte's estimate later elaborated by Baines, who related it to 1760–6. See Edward Baines, *History of the Cotton Manufacture in Great Britain* (1835), p. 361. Net output, according to Baines, would not have been more than about £300,000.

[2] See, for example, A. P. Wadsworth and Julia Mann, *The Cotton Trade and Industrial Lancashire* (Manchester, 1931), p. 506: 'One cannot avoid the conclusion that the new machinery spread quickly in England because the whole community was interested in it.'

[3] This, of course, was not the first of the textile inventions. Kay's flying shuttle (patented in 1733 and probably in general use by the 1760's) had raised productivity among weavers and thereby put pressure on the spinners. The slowness with which it spread and provoked an effective response from the spinning side is in interesting contrast to the developments which took place in the 1770's and 1780's.

last decade of the century provided another major impetus by greatly reducing the price of the raw material.

The spectacular progress of the cotton industry captured the imagination of contemporaries and a number of estimates of the value of its output were made at the end of the eighteenth century and beginning of the nineteenth. Most of them were based on the figures of retained imports of cotton wool. Since this was by far the principal raw material of the industry it is an indicator of some importance. However, it does not reflect changes in quality. It is also unsatisfactory for the early stages of the industry's development when an important proportion of cotton wool was used for candlewicks rather than for manufactured cottons.[1] Nor, since imports tended to fluctuate sharply from year to year, is it a satisfactory reflection of total output in any particular year.

A summary of the contemporary estimates or of estimates derived from contemporary sources for the half-century or so during which the cotton industry was created is given in Table 42. They are shown for groups of years rather than for particular years since the year-to-year changes in imports (from which most of the estimates are eventually derived) are considerable. It is unlikely that the industry as a whole fluctuated to this extent from year to year, though while it was largely domestic in character, supply tended to be elastic and highly variable in the short run.

The transformation of the cotton industry took less than three decades In the early 1770's value added by manufacturing to the cost of cotton raw material was less than half of one per cent of English national income. By 1802 it was probably between 4 and 5 per cent of the national income of Great Britain, and by 1812 between 7 and 8 per cent.[2] By then it had outstripped the woollen industry. Colquhoun gives £23 m. for value added in the cotton industry of the United Kingdom in 1812 and £18 m. for the woollen industry. Both are probably exaggerations but reflect the contemporary view of the relative contribution of the two industries to the national income. Rather more than a decade earlier Eden had estimated the product of the cotton industry of Great Britain as £10 m. and the woollen at £19 m.: the former may have been underestimated and the latter overestimated, but the superiority of the woollen industry does not seem to have been in any doubt. Our estimates suggest that in terms of value added the cotton industry had drawn ahead by the beginning of the century, but that, in terms of the value of final product, the two industries were still roughly level in the middle of the first decade. By 1815–17, which is

[1] An estimate quoted in Macpherson, *Annals of Commerce*, vol. IV (1805), p. 133, and originating in a contemporary pamphlet entitled *An Important Crisis in the Calico and Muslin Manufacture in Great Britain*, gives the amount used for candlewicks in 1787 as 1·5 million lb. out of a total import of 22·6 million lb. In the same source it was estimated that some 2 million lb. of the cotton-wool imports of this year were mixed with silk or linen goods.

[2] Net output was, of course a smaller percentage of national income, and if we relate it to the national income of the United Kingdom (instead of Great Britain or England and Wales) we get a still smaller percentage.

Table 42. *Estimates of cotton-industry output, 1760–1816*

	Retained imports[1]		Gross value cottons	Value added[2]	Exports at current prices[3]
	(m. lb.)	(£m.)	(£m.)	(£m.)	(£m.)
1760	3·4	0·2	0·6[4]	0·4	0·3
1772–74	4·2	0·2	0·9[5]	0·6	0·3
1781–83	8·7	1·0	4·0[6]	2·0	n.a.
1784–86	16·1	1·6	5·4[5]	3·8	0·9
1787–89	24·7	2·3	7·0[5]	4·7	1·6
1795–97	26·5	2·6	10·0[7]	7·4	3·7
1798–1800	41·8	5·7	11·1[8]	5·4	5·1
1801–03	54·3	4·0	15·0[9]	11·0	9·3
1805–07	63·1	4·5	18·9[10]	14·4	12·5
1811–13	65·0	5·3	28·3[11]	23·0	17·4
1815–17	99·7	8·3	30·0[12]	21·7	17·4

Sources and Notes: (1) Annual figures of retained imports, obtained from the Custom House Accounts, are published by A. P. Wadsworth and Julia L. Mann, *The Cotton Trade and Industrial Lancashire, 1600–1780* (Manchester, 1931). The same source summarises the price data available for the eighteenth century. For the nineteenth century, customs returns and value figures for raw cotton are published in parliamentary returns and other contemporary sources.

(2) I.e. value added to the cotton wool. It includes other raw materials such as coal and it includes purchased services.

(3) These are estimates based on published figures of official values except for 1815–17 when they are the declared values as given in the customs returns. When Irving made his estimate of exports at current prices for the years 1796–8 they were about a third above official values. By 1814 (year ended 5 January 1815) the declared values were about 13½ per cent above official values: thereafter they fell below. Official values have been converted to an estimate of current values by adding one-third for years up to and including 1798–1800 and by interpolating on the assumption that the proportion fell steadily from 1798 to 1814.

(4) Baines' estimate based on Postlethwayte. There is an earlier estimate giving £200,000 for the value of the industry *circa* 1760, but retained imports of cotton wool in 1760 were only a quarter of what they were in 1766, so that a discrepancy of this order of magnitude is not surprising if estimates were based on import data.

(5) *Observations on the Advantages which this Country draws from a Free and Unfettered Importation of the Raw Material of Cotton Wool* (London, 1789).

(6) *An Important Crisis in the Calico and Muslin Manufacture in Great Britain.* Quoted in Macpherson, *Annals of Commerce*, vol. IV (1805), p. 132. The estimates by this author differ slightly from estimates for the same years made by the author of *Observations on the Advantages, etc.* (see previous note). But they are small discrepancies in relation to the margins of error of both sets of estimates. Macpherson (vol. IV, p. 15) quotes an 'estimate of the annual produce and condition of the principal manufactures of Great Britain . . . published about this time' (1783) in which cotton is given a value of £960,000 (gross). Macpherson was surprised that no mention was made of the fact that it was 'increasing with astonishing rapidity'. However, if the estimate is taken as referring to a date five or six years earlier, it is not inconsistent with the other contemporary estimates quoted in this table.

(7) Macpherson, *Annals of Commerce*, vol IV (1805), pp. 528–9, quotes estimates of the values for muslins and calicoes only in 1796; for Scotland he gives £3·109 m. and for England and Wales £6·553 m. By this time muslins and calicoes were the most important sections of the industry but the estimates quoted are probably rather high.

(8) Eden's estimates made for the Globe Insurance Company and quoted by Macpherson *op. cit.*, vol. IV, p. 549, give £10 m. for cotton of which £6 m. for home consumption and £4 m. for exports. The figure for exports is almost certainly an understatement—even on the average of 1796–8 they exceed £4 m. This estimate is therefore found by adding our figure for current value of exports to Eden's value of £6 m. for home consumption.

(9) From a pamphlet, *Observations on the Cotton Trade of Great Britain*, quoted pp. 429–33 of Lauderdale, *An Inquiry into the Nature and Origin of Public Wealth and into the Means and Causes of its Increase* (1804).

(10) By extrapolating backwards on the basis of retained imports Ellison's estimates for 1815–17.

(11) P. Colquhoun, *Treatise on the Wealth, Power and Resources of the British Empire* (1815), p. 91, for an estimate of value added, to which we have added an estimate of the current value of imports.

(12) Thomas Ellison, *The Cotton Trade of Great Britain* (London, 1886), p. 56. Ellison's estimate of the cotton wool consumed in the industry on an average of these three years was 92·6 million lb. He gives estimates of stocks of cotton wool in Great Britain from 1811 onwards.

the period to which Ellison's first estimates relate, the total wage bill of the industry was probably between £8 m. and £9 m.[1] According to Sinclair, the Scottish share in the industry's total produce had reached over £6·2 m. in 1812, which was about 22 per cent of the total for Great Britain.[2] The Irish share was probably negligible at this stage.

From the second decade of the nineteenth century until the First World War the cotton industry continued to be the major British textile industry and it continued to grow. Over the century as a whole its rate of growth, measured by its input of raw material,[3] was about 3½ per cent per annum but at a falling rate in the second half. For the first fifty years the rate was over 5 per cent per annum. In the quarter of a century following the end of the Napoleonic Wars it reached about 6½ per cent per annum.

There are numerous estimates of the value of gross output of the cotton industry during the nineteenth century. The best seem to be those compiled by Ellison and brought up to date by him at various periods.[4] Table 43 lists these estimates for the years for which they are available and interpolates estimates also based on import and export data. The resulting series is probably a fair reflection of the changing volume of gross output at current prices. It should be noted, however, first that the estimates are designed to cover the bleaching, dyeing and finishing industries associated with the cotton industry, and secondly, that the 'value added' estimates, derived by subtracting the estimated cost of cotton consumed, contain the value of raw materials other than cotton. Estimates made by Ellison suggest that other raw materials and purchased services amounted to about 37 per cent of this gross-value-added concept in 1859–61 and about 40 per cent in 1880–2.[5] This may be high. It is not possible to make satisfactory estimates of net output, but it can probably be assumed that it is somewhere in the region of two-thirds to three-quarters of the value-added series in Table 43, the proportion falling in later years.

Ellison's estimates for wages and salaries seem generally to be rather high, especially for the earlier period, since they are formed by multiply-

---

[1] G. H. Wood, 'Statistics of Wages in the Nineteenth Century—The Cotton Industry', *J. Roy. Statist. Soc.*, June 1910, gives estimates of numbers employed and average weekly wages. Assuming forty-nine weeks in a year, his estimates for 1815–17 give annual wage bills of £10·2 m., £8·6 m. and £8·0 m. respectively. For 1814 it exceeded £12½ m., but this seems to have been its peak value for the first half of the century.

[2] Sir John Sinclair, *General Report of the Agricultural State and Political Circumstances of Scotland*, vol. III (1814), p. 317. According to an alternative estimate the total sales of the Scottish section amounted to nearly £7 m.

[3] Consumption of raw material per unit of product varied from time to time because the character of the product varied. Finer counts of yarn, for example, required less cotton but were generally a superior product in terms of value per yard. On the whole the use of input data tends to understate the rate of growth in real output of cotton in the nineteenth century, both because of a refinement of the product and because of economies in the manufacturing process which reduced the waste of raw material.

[4] See especially Thomas Ellison, *Cotton Trade of Great Britain* (1886), and 'Report on the Relation of Wages in certain Industries to the Cost of Production, *S.P. 1890–1*, vol. LXVIII.

[5] Ellison, *op. cit.* p. 123.

ing weekly wage rates by 52. On the other hand, Wood's estimates relate only to operatives in weaving and spinning factories and hand-loom weavers. They omit domestic spinners, handloom weavers' assistants, and operatives in bleaching, dyeing and printing establishments. Wood estimated rates of wages and numbers employed in each year for the workers in which he was interested, but not their total wage bill. The wage and salary figures in Table 43 are based largely on Wood's estimates together with an addition for categories omitted by him, based on Ellison's estimates. In all cases it was assumed that forty-nine weeks were worked in a year, so that the series is insensitive to the effects of booms and recessions on temporary unemployment and on the amount of short time or overtime, though it is designed to reflect the more permanent changes in labour force from year to year.

Using raw-cotton imports as an index of the volume of output we may say that (leaving aside the period of transformation at the end of the eighteenth century) the cotton industry's peak period of growth was the quarter of a century following the Napoleonic Wars. In the first quarter of the nineteenth century it increased by a factor of about 3. Between *circa* 1816 and *circa* 1840 the multiplier was $4\frac{1}{2}$. It began

Table 43. *Development of the cotton manufacture of the United Kingdom, 1819–1917*

Annual averages for 3-yr. periods	(1) Imports of raw cotton (m. lb.)	(2) Value final product (£m.)	(3) Value added to raw material (£m.)	(4) Wages and salaries (£m.)	(5) Exports as percentage value of final product
1819–21	141	29·4	23·2	10·2	52·8
1824–26	169	33·1	26·7	11·5	51·1
1829–31	249	32·1	25·3	10·7	56·4
1834–36	331	44·6	31·2	10·9	50·4
1839–41	452	46·7	34·3	10·9	49·8
1844–46	560	46·7	34·7	10·6	55·4
1849–51	621	45·7	30·2	11·4	60·8
1854–56	802	56·9	37·4	14·0	61·4
1859–61	1,050	77·0	47·7	18·0	63·8
1864–66	771	97·3	43·1	17·6	64·0
1869–71	1,155	104·9	58·0	21·6	67·1
1874–76	1,274	101·6	66·0	26·7	70·1
1879–81	1,386	94·5	62·7	25·8	74·0
1883–85	1,401	100·5	64·7	27·2	68·5
1889–91	1,684	101·2	63·8	30·9	71·4
1894–96	1,558	84·7	55·4	32·7	78·6
1899–1901	1,510	89·2	57·2	33·8	78·8

Sources: Estimates in columns 2 and 3 are Ellison's for the following years (references in brackets are to page numbers in his *Cotton Trade of Great Britain*): 1815–17 (p. 56); 1819–21, 1829–31, 1844–6 (p. 60); 1859–61 (p. 123); 1874–6, 1879–81, 1883–5 (pp. 308–9). The estimates for other years are ours, using Ellison's figures as a starting-point. Import and export data from the trade returns. Wages and salaries estimated from Wood's series of numbers employed and average weekly wage, assuming forty-nine weeks worked in the year and adjusting for categories not included by Wood. But see M. Blaug, 'The Productivity of Labour in the Lancashire Cotton Industry during the Nineteenth Century'. *Econ. Hist. Rev.*, Vol. XIII (1961), for a different set of estimates of final product and a critique of Ellison's estimates.

to slacken pace in the late forties but was still growing strongly until the cotton famine created by the American Civil War. The rate of increase in the twenty-five years preceding 1860 was roughly the same as in the first quarter of the century, that is to say raw-cotton imports roughly trebled. In the last quarter of the nineteenth century the total increase was barely 20 per cent, though imports continued to grow erratically, until the beginning of the First World War.[1]

The overseas market absorbed an important proportion of the cotton industry's output from the very beginning. It was at its minimum in the period of maximum growth following the Napoleonic Wars. During most of the first three or four decades of the century (with the possible exception of the first decade and the late 1820's) the home market seemed to be growing faster than the overseas market. Thereafter the converse was true and by the end of the century the declared value of exports amounted to about 79 per cent of estimated final product compared with the previous peak of 66 per cent (1805–7, see Table 42) and about 50 per cent in the 1830's.

Estimates of the net output of the cotton industry are thus highly tentative. This is enough, however, to suggest the relative size of its contribution to national income. Net output can be assumed to lie somewhere between value added to raw material and total wages and salaries. If we take it to be about two-thirds of value added,[2] we may say that cotton accounted for between 2 and 3 per cent of the United Kingdom national income *circa* 1801, about 4 per cent (possibly rising to $4\frac{1}{2}$ per cent in some years) from the early 1820's to the mid-1840's, and a generally falling percentage thereafter. By 1907 it was very little more than 2 per cent again. In terms of the national income of Great Britain it weighed more heavily in the total, of course, though the difference was only appreciable for the first half of the century, during most of which the cotton industry accounted for over 5 per cent of the national income of Great Britain.

It is impossible to say how much of the gap between gross values added and total wages and salaries, as estimated for Table 43, is due to other raw materials and purchased services and how much to profits, rents and interest. The relative proportion must have changed through time. Other raw materials, for example, would have accounted for a larger proportion of costs when the final raw material became more fully processed (as undoubtedly happened during the course of the century) or when fashion dictated a higher proportion of other textiles in the mixture fabrics based on cotton.

But, however generously we allow for factors of technical change or

[1] Output, however, was increasing faster than input; cf. the report by William Whittam, *England's Cotton Industry* (U.S. Dept. of Commerce and Labour, Bureau of Manufactures, 1907), p. 10: 'England uses between 30 and 35 lb. of cotton per spindle per year and the annual consumption per spindle has shown a slow but steady decline for several years, indicating that the products of her mills are gradually assuming a finer and lighter character. Continental Europe and Great Britain combined use 70 lb. per spindle per annum.'

[2] It was about 63 per cent at the time of the 1907 census but probably higher at the beginning of the nineteenth century.

fashion in determining the size of the gap, there seems little doubt that its increase in the 1830's and 1840's reflects a marked increase in the share of profit in net output. It is significant, moreover, that this coincided with the period of maximum growth in the cotton industry. According to the estimates in Table 43, wages and salaries fell from about 44 per cent of gross value added *circa* 1821 to 35 per cent *circa* 1835 and to less than a third in the 1840's. The wage fraction apparently recovered in the third quarter of the century, when it varied between 37 per cent and 41 per cent of gross value added. At the end of the century it seems to have risen to about 59 per cent.[1]

Various factors can be held to account for the decline and subsequent rise of the wage fraction. The decline in the second quarter of the century can be largely explained as a consequence of the adoption of power-using machinery which took place in the twenties, thirties and forties. Estimates by Ellison and others suggest that the labour cost per unit of output practically halved in spinning and more than halved in weaving during this period.[2] The later improvements in productivity were much less marked, and indeed there is some evidence of a rise in the labour cost of the weaving at the end of the century.

The reasons for the later recovery and still later sharp increase in the wage fraction are less obvious. In view of the great and still growing importance of female labour in cotton the upward trend in women's wages was probably a major factor.[3] The displacement of child labour by adults and the reductions in hours worked may also have been significant, however.[4] Table 44 illustrates the considerable change which took place in the personnel of the industry during the last three-quarters of the century. In 1835 more than 13 per cent of the workers in the cotton industry were children: probably another 25 to 30 per cent at least were young persons of thirteen to eighteen years of age.[5]

[1] The estimates of wages and salaries in Table 43, derived from Ellison, are almost certainly rather generous, even when it is remembered that they include salaried personnel and also operatives in processing industries (bleaching, dyeing, etc.). The absolute amounts involved in these estimates should therefore be regarded with caution.

[2] F. Merttens, 'The Hours and the Cost of Labour in the Cotton Industry at Home and Abroad', *Transactions of the Manchester Statistical Society*, 1893–4, p. 128, quotes and extends some of Ellison's estimates of labour cost per lb. of final product thus:

	1829–31	1844–46	1859–61	1880–82	1891–93
	d.	*d.*	*d.*	*d.*	*d.*
Spinning	4·2	2·3	2·1	1·9	1·6
Weaving	9·0	3·5	2·9	2·3	2·6

[3] G. H. Wood in 'Factory Legislation considered with Reference to the Wages, etc. of Operatives protected thereby', *J. Roy. Statist. Soc.*, vol. LXV (June 1902), concluded (p. 308) that 'During the era of factory legislation, that is since the "Ten Hours" Act (1847) and its extension, in a more or less modified form to other industries than textiles, women's wages have risen by about 66 per cent while the average increase for the United Kingdom is about 45 per cent. The increase, too, has been progressive, while the United Kingdom numbers underrate stationariness or a fall during the eighties.'

[4] Possibly part of the decline in the wage fraction in the thirties was due to an increase in the proportion of child or young persons' labour relatively to the proportion of adult males. But we have no employment statistics for the industry before the first Factory Inspectors' reports in the 1830's.

[5] In 1839 only 58 per cent of the industry's employees were over the age of eighteen.

Table 44. *Age and sex distribution of cotton operatives, 1835–1907*

(as percentages of total employed in cotton factories)

	Children under 14 (%)	Women and girls (%)	Young men 14–18 (%)	Adult males over 18 (%)
1835	13·1	48·1	12·4	26·4
1850	4·5	55·6	11·2	28·8
1862	8·8	55·7	9·1	26·4
1868	10·3	55·1	·8·5	26·1
1874	13·9	53·7	8·3	24·1
1878	12·8	54·9	7·2	25·1
1885	9·9	56·0	8·0	26·1
1890	9·1	55·9	8·2	26·8
1895	5·8	58·8	7·8	27·6
1901	4·0	60·8	7·1	28·1
1904	3·4	60·6	7·1	28·9
1907	3·2	60·6	7·9	28·3

Source : Compiled from factory inspectors' returns by G. H. Wood, 'The Statistics of Wages in the Nineteenth Century: The Cotton Industry', *J. Roy. Statist. Soc.*, vol. LXXIII (June 1910), p. 607.

By 1907 the proportion of employees under eighteen in the cotton factories was only 26 per cent, including about 3 per cent under fourteen who were employed half time. At the same time there were considerable reductions in working hours: and since these were more drastic for children than for adults they reinforced the trend towards a more adult labour force. In effect, from 1850 onwards child labour was generally half-time labour, and after 1874 textile factories were prohibited from employing children under ten. For women and young persons in textile factories the legal limit on the number of hours worked per week was fixed at 69 in 1844, 60 in 1850, 56½ in 1874 and 55½ in 1901.[1] Since they constituted about two-thirds of the labour force their normal day tended to determine the maximum for adult males, whose hours of work were legally unlimited.

Some of these improvements in working conditions may have resulted in increased labour productivity, and in so far as they saved labour there would have been no tendency for the wage fraction to rise. However, it is likely that this compensating factor was less effective for the later improvements than for the earlier ones. In the earlier period there were important improvements in labour productivity as a consequence of the new machinery.

An impression of the progress of new investment in cotton machinery can be obtained from the estimates in Table 45. After 1835, when factory inspectors' reports became available, they are reasonably reliable. For earlier periods than those covered by Table 45 the data are scanty but they suggest a fairly rapid development of the spinning branches of the industry at the end of the eighteenth century and the

[1] It was not until 1850, when a legal limit was put on the normal working day, that these maxima became effectively enforceable.

beginning of the nineteenth. It has been estimated that there were about 1·7 million spindles in existence in the early 1780's and between 4 and 5 million by 1812: at this latter date there were probably about 2,400 power-looms operating and perhaps 200,000 handlooms.

In the fifteen years or so spanning the 1830's and early 1840's the number of spindles practically doubled and the number of power-looms quadrupled. It was the handloom weaver who bore most of the burden of the industry's transformation to power. While the cotton capitalists' profits expanded at an unprecedented rate the number of handlooms fell to a quarter of the number operating in the 1820's. By the 1850's the handloom weaver contributed a negligible proportion of the industry's output of woven goods. Dr Blaug's estimates of fixed capital at constant prices suggest that the cotton industry expanded its equipment at a rate averaging over 3 per cent per annum over the period 1834–60, rising to about 4½ per cent in the 1860's and falling below 2 per cent in the following decade and a half, i.e. between 1871 and 1886.[1]

Table 45. *Capital equipment of the cotton industry, 1819–1903*

	Spindles (millions)	Looms (thousands)	
		Hand	Power
1819–21	7·0	240	14
1829–31	10·0	240	55
1844–46	19·5	60	225
1850	21·0	40	250
1861	30·4	3	400
1870	38·2	—	441
1878	44·2	—	515
1885	44·3	—	561
1890	44·5	—	616
1903	47·9	—	683
1914	59·3	—	805

Sources: Clapham, *Economic History of Modern Britain*, vol. 1 (1939), pp. 143–4; Wood, *J. Roy. Statist. Soc.*, 1910, *op. cit.* p. 594. Ellison, *The Cotton Trade of Great Britain* (1886), pp. 68–9, 325; and for the later years, Board of Trade, *Thirteenth Abstract of Labour Statistics* (1907–8).

In sum, therefore, cotton became the most important British manufacturing industry during the first decade of the nineteenth century. By 1811 it employed about 100,000 factory operatives in spinning-mills and perhaps another quarter of a million handloom weavers and their auxiliaries. This was when the total British occupied population was about 5½ million persons. As an object lesson in the advantages of industrialisation its influence was no doubt considerable. But its impact on the national economy was still small in absolute terms. Its contribution to the British national income was only between 4 and 5 per cent: it offered employment opportunities on a smaller scale than the armed forces. Moreover, at this stage the industry's development was still one-sided. Cotton-spinning and cotton-ginning techniques had been

[1] M. Blaug, 'The Productivity of Capital in the Lancashire Cotton Industry during the Nineteenth Century', *Econ. Hist. Rev.*, Vol. XIII, 1961.

mechanised, with important consequences for cost of production of yarn, but the weaving branch was still essentially a domestic industry operating with much the same techniques as it had used for most of the eighteenth century.

It was after the Napoleonic Wars that the industry's rate of growth accelerated to maximum effect. In the 1820's, 1830's and 1840's, when its net output accounted for rather more than 5 per cent of the British total, its input of raw cotton was growing at a rate of more than 5 per cent per annum. This was the period of the most complete industrial revolution in the cotton industry. Steam power transformed the process of production, halved labour costs and brought spinners and weavers alike into the factory system.

In the period of mechanisation of the cotton industry the capitalist manufacturer found himself in a peculiarly favourable position. He could shift the main burden of adjustment to technical change to the domestic producers, who owned the handlooms which were being rendered obsolete. He could readily contract or expand the working time of a large unorganised labour force mainly composed of women and children or young persons, for it was not until the 1850's that maximum-hours legislation became effective. Nor was there much competition for this unskilled semi-dependent labour force until the industrial revolution gathered momentum in other industries and provided additional openings for women and children in industry. At the same time the cotton manufacturer was producing a commodity with a mass market and no near substitutes until technical change spread to other textile industries and other countries.

These were temporary advantages, however, and the latter part of the nineteenth century was a period of decelerating growth for the cotton industry. The prices paid for labour and for raw cotton were rising. The direct cost of innovation was growing. Labour productivity grew more slowly. The market for the final product could be expanded only by greater dependence on overseas markets. The industry continued to grow until the First World War, and by the beginning of the twentieth century it accounted for rather more than 2 per cent of national income and employed more than half a million full-time workers (more than three-quarters of them adult). At the time of the 1907 census of production cotton was still a major British industry, but its net output amounted to less than half of that of coal-mining, was second to the engineering trades, and was less than 10 per cent greater than either the building and contracting or the brewing and malting trades.

(b) Wool

The woollen and worsted industries were the staple manufactures in pre-industrial Britain and at the beginning of the nineteenth century their joint contribution to the national income appears to have been of the same order of magnitude as that of the cotton industry. There were numerous contemporary estimates of the output of wool and of the industry's progress throughout the eighteenth and nineteenth centuries.[1] During the nineteenth century these estimates were generally arrived at by summing the principal cost items. Figures of the industry's consumption of wool were calculated on the basis of estimates of the number of sheep and their average fleece and records of international trade in raw wool. Estimates of the numbers employed (broad guesses in the early part of the century) were applied to estimates of average earnings to give a wage bill for the industry. Other costs (including other raw materials such as soap and purchased services) and profits, rents and depreciation were generally added by means of more or less arbitrarily determined percentages. Since it was not until 1867 that a census of livestock gave an empirical basis for estimating the number of sheep in the United Kingdom, and since employment data were not collected for the industry until the 1841 population census, the estimates produced in the first two-thirds of the century were based largely on guesswork and could not be expected to indicate more than the orders of magnitude involved.

For most of the second half of the century annual estimates of the industry's consumption of wool and of the domestic wool clip were made by the Board of Trade on the basis of the import and export records and of various estimates compiled by merchants.[2] Another series of estimates was made by the Committee on Industry and Trade which reported in 1928, and these, which are based upon tables compiled by the Bradford Chamber of Commerce,[3] give annual averages for consecutive quinquennial periods between 1779 and 1927. When the two series overlap (1855–1908) they are not always identical, but the discrepancies are negligible and we therefore have reasonably reliable annual estimates for the second half of the century and rough estimates of quinquennial averages for most of the first half. The quantity data for the nineteenth century are summarised in column 1 of Table 47.

It is of some interest to compare the later estimates of the domestic clip with contemporary estimates. After 1867 when annual livestock censuses made it possible to base calculations on fairly reliable though by no means accurate data the careful contemporary estimates are close to the results in Table 47, as indeed we might expect. Archibald Hamilton's estimate of a domestic clip of 160 million lb. for the period 1867–70, for example, compares favourably with the Board of Trade

---

[1] For a discussion of the eighteenth-century contemporary estimates and their implications see Deane, The Output of the British Woollen Industry in the Eighteenth Century, *op. cit.*

[2] 'Statistical Tables and Charts Relating to British and Foreign Trade and Industry, 1854–1908', Cmd. 4954, *S.P. 1909*, vol. CII, pp. 16–2. Estimates for the domestic wool clip were taken by the Board of Trade from Messrs. Schwartz and Co.'s trade circular and those of the consumption of shoddy, mohair, etc., were made by the Bradford Chamber of Commerce.

[3] Frederic Hooper, *Statistics relating to the City of Bradford and the Woollen and Worsted Trades of the United Kingdom* (1898 et seq.). These series were returned regularly by the Bradford Chamber of Commerce up to 1940. They are quoted in the 'Report of the Committee on Industry and Trade', *Survey of Textile Industries* (1928), p. 275.

figures of 159 millions for 1865–9 and 160 millions for 1870–4.[1] An
estimate by the Board of Agriculture for 1905–6 was constructed on the
basis of questionnaires sent out in each of these two years to wool-
buyers and wool-growers.[2] It suggested a total output of about 121
million lb. for Great Britain, which, with an estimate for Ireland of
12 million provided by the Irish Board of Agriculture, gives a total only
slightly in excess of the Board of Trade estimates for 1905 and 1906.[3]
By this time, however, the domestic clip accounted for less than 18 per
cent, by weight, of the woollen raw material of the industry. It is for
the earlier decades that errors in the estimates of British wool assume
considerable significance.

The estimates which were made during the first two-thirds of the
century are probably less reliable than the figures of domestic clip
given in Table 47 because the earlier investigators were working in
ignorance of the results yielded by later statistical surveys. There is a
time limit, however, to all backward extrapolations, and when we get
back to the beginning of the century it is arguable that these later
estimates are no more reliable than the best of the contemporary
estimates. Some account should therefore be taken of the latter.

Table 46 gives estimates derived from the most convincing contemporary sources. These figures are all higher than the later estimates
made by the Board of Trade or the Bradford Chamber of Commerce
in spite of the fact that they represent conservative views by contemporary standards. Luccock's results were considerably lower than those
of his contemporaries and recent predecessors. Yet they suggest an
input (including imports) of over 120 million lb. *circa* 1800. The 1828
figures, which are based on the estimates generally attributed to
Hubbard (and are 14 per cent higher than the Board of Trade estimates
for 1825–9), are in fact an understatement of Hubbard's position. He
based these results on the assumption that the number of sheep in
England and Wales had not changed but that the weight of fleece had
increased substantially, largely as a result of a shift in favour of long-
woolled sheep. Many later investigators took this assumption to mean
that Hubbard thought the stock of sheep had stayed constant,[4] but in
his oral evidence to the House of Lords Committee he said that he had
'not the slightest doubt' that there were then a greater number of sheep
in England than in 1805. And in a footnote to the table in which he
applied his own estimates of fleece weights to Luccock's estimates of
sheep, county by county, he wrote: 'In this table no notice is taken of
the improved state of Agriculture: but from information obtained as to
the number of sheep kept one-fifth may be added to the weight of the

[1] Archibald Hamilton ,'Wool Supply', *Journal of the Statistical Society of London*, vol. xxxiii
(December 1870).

[2] Board of Agriculture and Fisheries, *Production of Wool in Great Britain in 1905 and 1906*
(H.M.S.O., 1907).

[3] *S.P.*, *1909* vol. cii, *op. cit.* The Board of Trade quinquennial average for 1905–8 was
131·2 million lb.

[4] E.g. J. McCulloch, *op. cit.*, vol. 1 (1839), p. 496.

Table 46. *Estimates of sheep and wool output in the first half of the nineteenth century: derived from contemporary sources*

	1800		1828	1841	
	Sheep (m.)	Wool (m. lb.)	Wool (m. lb.)	Sheep (m.)	Wool (m. lb.)
England	26·1	94·4	108·9 ⎫	24·0	103·4
Wales	0·6	2·2	2·2 ⎬		
Scotland	2·9	10·3	11·9	3·4	15·0
Ireland	2·0	7·2	8·3	2·1	9·1
United Kingdom	31·6	114·1	131·3	29·6	127·5

Sources: The estimates for England in 1800 are Luccock's (Sir John Luccock, *The Nature and Properties of Wool* (London, 1805)); those for England in 1828 and for Wales in 1800 and 1828 are Hubbard's (Minutes of Evidence taken before the Committee of the Lords on the State of the British Wool Trade', *S.P. 1828*, vol. VIII, pp. 232–3. For Scotland in 1800 and 1828 we used Sir John Sinclair's estimate of the numbers of sheep, based on data collected by survey at the end of the eighteenth century (Sir John Sinclair, Appendix to the *General Report of the Agricultural State and Political Circumstances of Scotland*, vol. II (Edinburgh, 1814), p. 135): this we applied to Luccock's and Hubbard's estimates of average fleece for 1800 and 1828 respectively. For Ireland in 1800 and 1828 we used McCulloch's 1839 estimate of 2 million sheep with Luccock's and Hubbard's fleece averages (J. McCulloch, *Statistical Account of the British Empire*, vol. I (1839 ed.), p. 496): 1841 the results of official census of livestock were available. The 1841 estimates of sheep for England and Wales are McCulloch's (*op. cit.*, vol. II (1846 ed.)) and the 1841 fleece average was estimated to fall between Hubbard's estimate for 1828 and Hamilton's for 1868.

table of 1800 and would give the increase 148,587 packs instead of 69,933'.[1] In other words, he contemplated an addition of about 18·877 million lb. for the extra sheep, which would bring his 1828 estimate to about 150 million lb.

It is probable that Hubbard's estimate was too high even in its most conservative form. Later investigators produced much lower estimates of the number of sheep, and although the possibility of a substantial increase and then a decline in their number cannot be ruled out altogether, it seems unlikely on the whole.[2] Luccock's estimates, while consciously conservative, may still have been coloured by the climate of exaggeration which had prevailed throughout the eighteenth century in writings on the woollen industry. McCulloch's estimate of 127·5 millions in 1841, however, is not very much higher than the Board of Trade estimate of 125 millions for the period 1840–4.

In sum, the contemporary estimates of woollen inputs made during the first three decades of the nineteenth century imply a lower rate of growth for the first half-century than the estimates summarised in

[1] *S.P. 1828*, vol. VIII, *op cit.*

[2] G. R. Porter (*Progress of the Nation* (1847 ed.), p. 175) read Hubbard carefully enough to observe that he believed in an increase in the number of sheep by one-fifth since 1800— and accepted this view; but he read Luccock less carefully and applied the increase to Luccock's estimate of sheep shorn only (excluding slaughtered sheep) and attributed this incomplete total to England and Wales. Thus he reached a figure of 25·3 million sheep for England and Wales, which is actually less than Luccock's estimate for England but which looks quite plausible in the light of later estimates and presumably in the light of the views prevailing in his own time. Cf. McCulloch's estimate given in Table 46.

Table 47. More specifically, if we accepted Hubbard's estimate for *circa* 1828 we should find no increase in inputs between the late 1820's and the late 1830's and an increase of under 35 per cent for the second quarter of the century. Accepting Luccock's estimate for *circa* 1800 we should find an increase of less than 50 per cent in the first four decades of the century instead of over 70 per cent as suggested by the Board of Trade estimates. We have concluded that the contemporary estimates were based on an exaggerated view of the size of the domestic wool clip and have accordingly accepted the later Board of Trade figures. But these are also highly conjectural and the possibility that the figures in Table 47 overstate the industry's rate of growth during the first half of the nineteenth century should certainly be borne in mind.

Table 47. *The growth of the United Kingdom woollen industry, 1805–1908*

Annual averages	(1) Quantity of wool consumed (m. lb.)	(2) Value woollen raw materials (£m.)	(3) Percentage woollen raw materials imported	(4) Estimated value final product (£m.)	(5) Estimated net value added (£m.)	(6) Value exports woollen manufactures as percentage final product
Circa 1805	105·0	8·5	31	22·3	12·8	35
1820–24	140·0	8·2	32	26·0	16·6	23
1825–29	153·3	8·9	37	27·0	16·8	19
1830–34	171·1	10·3	46	28·8	17·0	19
1835–39	177·9	12·9	37	31·1	16·7	20
1840–44	188·0	9·9	41	32·7	20·8	19
1845–49	209·5	10·6	43	34·5	21·4	20
1850–54	241·0	13·1	49	36·4	20·3	25
1855–59	262·6	14·7	49	38·4	20·2	26
1860–64	312·2	20·1	49	47·6	22·1	30
1865–69	374·3	24·5	49	56·7	24·9	37
1870–74	453·5	24·5	51	59·6	25·9	43
1875–79	477·5	24·9	55	54·0	18·0	33
1880–84	496·5	20·3	65	56·6	23·3	33
1885–89	539·4	18·6	74	60·4	26·9	32
1890–94	622·2	19·6	74	59·7	23·3	29
1895–99	686·4	21·0	80	61·5	21·8	27
1900–04	655·6	19·6	84	63·4	23·2	25
1905–08	744·2	26·7	82	70·3	21·1	29

Sources: (1) Balfour Committee on Industry and Trade, *Survey of Textile Industries* (1928), p. 275. (2) and (3) For prices of domestic clip (1812–73), Bradford Chamber of Commerce series of prices, quoted Cathcart, *Journal of the Agricultural Society of England*, vol. XI (London, 1875); for 1874–1908, average declared export price. For prices imports, Tooke, *op. cit.*, vol. II, to 1837; Hamilton, *J. Statist. Soc.*, vol. XXXIII (1870), for period to 1854; after 1854, trade values. (4) and (5) See text, net value is calculated residually. (6) Official returns of exports by Irving, Porter's tables and the *Statistical Abstracts*.

If we regard these estimates of wool intake as an indication of the progress in total output we may deduce that it grew only a little faster than population in the first three or four decades of the century. It began to gather momentum in the late 1840's and 1850's, but its peak period of growth took place after the middle of the century, particularly in the 1860's and early 1870's. In the quarter of a century between 1845–9 and 1870–4 inputs of raw wool more than doubled. At this period it was probably growing a little faster than the cotton industry. By this time, however, 50 per cent of the value of the wool consumed in the industry was imported, and from then on the domestic clip was actually declining.[1] Before the First World War the import proportion of woollen raw materials was over 80 per cent. The domestic clip was then back at its early nineteenth-century level after having increased by nearly 60 per cent in the first three-quarters of the century.

The second column of Table 47 contains our estimates of the value of woollen raw materials. They were complicated by the fact that wool is a commodity with a wide range of qualities and types, each having a distinctive price level and a distinctive price trend. We were therefore obliged to seek appropriate price quotations in a variety of sources. For the domestic clip we used Luccock's valuations for the beginning of the nineteenth century, a series prepared by the Bradford Chamber of Commerce for the period 1812–73, and the average declared export price for the period 1874–1908.[2] For shoddy we used Jubb's average for years before 1854 and the average import price thereafter.[3] For imports we found estimates from various contemporary sources up to 1839 and derived an average from Hamilton's import price series up to 1854.[4] After 1854 imports were valued at their imputed or declared values as recorded in the trade statistics.

In the eighteenth century it had been common for writers on the wool industry to calculate the value of final output as a multiple of their estimates of the value of the wool used. While the price of wool was relatively steady and methods of production fairly static this was probably as good a rule-of-thumb as any, though prices and processes changed over long periods and hence the multiplier required revision from time to time. By the nineteenth century, however, when the pace of change was considerable, the results of such a calculation were much more doubtful, although it was still used as a method of estimating final product.[5] Early in the century it was usual to assume that the value of

[1] Recovered wool was rising and this source more than compensated for the fall in the domestic clip in terms of volumes. There was a great difference in quality, however.

[2] Luccock, *op. cit.* The Bradford Chamber of Commerce series was quoted by Earl Cathcart in 'Wool in Relation to Science with Practice', *Journal of the Agricultural Society of England*, vol. xi (1875).

[3] Samuel Jubb, *The History of the Shoddy Trade* (London, 1860).

[4] Tooke, *History of Prices 1793–1837*, vol. ii, gives prices of Spanish wool from 1782–1837, but after the first decade of the nineteenth century Spanish wool was largely replaced by German wool, and that in its turn by Australian wool.

[5] Informed contemporaries were of course well aware of the dangers of such a calculation. Cf. the evidence of Benjamin Gott, merchant manufacturer of Leeds, to the House of Lords Committee in 1828, quoted in James Bischoff, *A Comprehensive History of the Woollen and Worsted Manufactures*, etc.), vol. ii (1842), p. 194: 'Whatever be the cost of wool, 50 per cent upon that would be the price of the article when in a complete state of manufacture for sale. The expense of manufacturing does not always, however, depend upon the value of the raw material . . . if from any circumstance that same quality of wool was double the price it is now the manufacturing expense would remain the same.'

short clothing wool would be doubled by the process of manufacture and that the worsted industry (using long wool) multiplied by at least 4 the value of its raw material.[1] McCulloch in the first (1837) and second (1839) editions of his *Statistical Account of the British Empire* accepted a multiplier of 3 for the industry as a whole, based on Stevenson,[2] but revised the latter's cost structure. But in his 1847 and 1854 editions he abandoned altogether the multiplier method of estimate and built up a final-product total which was only about twice the value of the wool.[3] James, referring to the worsted industry at mid-century and calculating its value *circa* 1856, wrote: 'It will quickly be observed that whilst in former years the value of the manufactured goods was three and four times that of the raw material it is now only about doubled. This arises partly from the present excessive price of wool; but of late years the cost of manufacture has been much lessened from the use of combing machines and the great improvements in the processes of spinning and weaving, etc.'[4] By 1907 when the first Census of Production returns became available the value of final product was only one and a half times the value of all raw materials (including chemicals and fuel, for example). However, the value of *woollen* raw materials (including alpaca, mohair and shoddy) was still only about 45 per cent of final product. By then the total gross value of the industry's output exceeded £70 m.

In the second half of the century detailed estimates of the value of total output were made by Baines and James (covering the woollen and worsted branches of the industry respectively) and by Sir Jacob Behrens, President of the Bradford Chamber of Commerce.[5] A combination of Baines' and James' estimates suggests a value of final product of about £38·4 m. *circa* 1856–7 and Behrens estimated that it was £60·4 m. by 1884. An earlier estimate by Behrens for 1866 gave the value of the worsted industry as £33·6 m. compared with James' estimate of £18 m. for 1857.[6] These are sketchy bases for an estimate

---

[1] John James, *History of the Worsted Manufacture in England* (1857), p. 371, writing of the worsted industry *circa* 1810, comments: 'Neither does it seem inaccurate to quadruple the value of the wool in order to ascertain the whole cost of the piece. Although wages had risen, and what is more to the purpose, much finer descriptions of goods had begun to be made, yet probably the cost of production had, on the whole, lowered since the latter part of last century, because of the application of spinning machinery and of the flying shuttle increasing so greatly the power of production.'
[2] In the section on England in the *Edinburgh Encyclopedia*, edited by D. Brewster, vol. VIII Part 2 (1830).
[3] J. R. McCulloch, *Statistical Account of the British Empire*, 1st ed. (1837), vol. II, p. 48; 2nd ed. (1839), vol. I, pp. 626 *et seq.*; 3rd ed. (1847), vol. I, pp. 650 *et seq.*; 4th ed. (1854), vol. I, pp. 658 *et seq.*
[4] James, *op. cit.* p. 543.
[5] Edward Baines, 'The Woollen Manufacture of England with Special Reference to the Leeds Clothing District'. Paper read before the British Association for the Advancement of Science in 1858 and reprinted in Thomas Baines, *Yorkshire Past and Present*, vol. I (1877), James, *op. cit.*, also quoted in Baines, *op. cit.* Evidence of Sir Jacob Behrens (February 1886) to the Royal Commission on the Depression in Trade and Industry, *S.P. 1886*, vol. XXI, p. 478.
[6] Quoted in Thomas Baines, *op. cit.*, vol. I, p. 694.

of the long-term trends in output, but values of exports are available from official sources, and the estimates of these well-informed contemporaries can be interpreted and extrapolated on the reasonably plausible assumption that the home market was a function of total population, consumption per head increasing during the earlier part of the century by analogy with the increase suggested by Baines' and James' estimates for 1856–7 and the Census of Production results for 1907.

These are the broad assumptions which underlie the estimates given in the fourth column of Table 47. Except in the sixties when Behrens' estimates permit a more adequate assessment of an important spurt in the output of the worsted industry—for the home market as well as for the export market—the estimates are insensitive to fluctuations in demand on the home market. However, it seems reasonable to assume that the fluctuations were not very great and comparison of our estimates with the most convincing of the contemporary estimates confirms the view that they are of the right order of magnitude although the margin of error probably varies between 10 per cent and 20 per cent.

To convert these estimates of gross output to net output, and hence to arrive at approximations to the industry's net contribution to national income, it was necessary to calculate the value of the raw materials consumed. The most important of these were the woollen raw materials whose values have been estimated in column 2 of Table 47. For other raw materials there is some information in the contemporary estimates by McCulloch, Youatt, Baines and James and in the 1907 Census of Production.[1] For the early years of the century we extrapolated contemporary estimates of other raw materials (dyes, soaps and chemicals being then the most important of these) by analogy with the amount of wool consumed in the industry. From the middle of the century onwards other textiles and coal began to be important inputs and the estimates were interpolated on the assumption that their value increased steadily through the century. In fact, of course, the increase was certainly irregular as new processes were introduced and new tastes developed. However, even by 1907 woollen raw materials were still the most important item of cost in the industry and for these our estimates were based on fairly reliable quantity series. The estimates of net value added which were reached residually after deducting raw materials from total output should of course be treated with very great reserve. They contain margins of error probably exceeding 20 per cent.

Although the woollen industry was outstripped by the cotton industry in the first decade of the nineteenth century its net output still accounted for between 4 and 5 per cent of British national income in the 1820's. Thereafter its relative importance declined. By mid-century it contributed not much less than $3\frac{1}{2}$ per cent of British national income, and

---

[1] These sources have already been referred to above. Youatt's estimates are quoted in James' Appendix.

by the beginning of the twentieth century its contribution probably did not reach 1½ per cent.

With the exception of the worsted section (which was technically closer to cotton and followed more closely in its wake) the industry was slow in adapting the new textile innovations to its requirements. The rate of mechanisation (and less directly the pace of new investment) can be roughly gauged by the factory inspectors' returns of machinery installed in textile factories. When the first returns were compiled (1835) only 5,127 power-looms were reported in woollen and worsted factories.[1] The corresponding figure for cotton factories was 109,626. By 1839 only 36 per cent of the spinning-engines in woollen factories were driven by steam power.[2] For cotton (and also for worsted) the proportion was 71 per cent. By 1850 the number of power-looms in woollen and worsted factories had increased to over 42,000 (more than three-quarters weaving worsteds) and the horsepower capacity of woollen and worsted machinery had roughly doubled by comparison with 1835.

In effect, in terms of the horsepower capacity of machinery installed, the rate of mechanisation (and probably of new investment) in the woollen industry as a whole reached its peak in the 1850's and 1860's. In the eleven years 1839–50 horsepower increased by 21 per cent: between 1850 and 1861 by 92 per cent: between 1856 and 1867 by 138 per cent, and in the decade 1861–71 by 79 per cent.[3] Most of the advance before 1850 took place in the worsted section of the industry. In the 1850's worsted factories were still developing power more rapidly than woollen factories, but in the 1860's woollen factories were growing rather faster than worsted factories—largely because of a marked increase in the number of power-looms in the woollen branch.

Table 48. *Spindles and looms in the woollen industry, 1850–1904*

	Spindles (millions)			Power-looms		
	Wool and shoddy	Worsted	Total	Wool and shoddy	Worsted	Total
1850	1·595	0·876	2·471	9,439	32,617	42,056
1861	2·183	1·289	3·472	21,770	43,048	64,818
1870	2·703	1·821	4·524	48,218	64,654	112,272
1878	3·684	2·097	5·781	57,738	87,393	145,131
1885	3·360	2·227	5·587	59,710	79,931	139,641
1890	3·448	2·403	5·851	62,880	67,391	130,271
1904	2·901	2·938	5·839	51,789	52,725	104,514

Sources: S.P. 1850, vol. XLII; S.P. 1862, vol. LV; and for 1870–1904, Board of Trade 13th Abstract of Labour Statistics (Cmd. 5041, 1910).

[1] Porter, *op. cit.* p. 204.
[2] Porter, *op. cit.* p. 173.
[3] *S.P. 1850*, vol. XLII; *S.P. 1857* (Sess. 1), vol. XIV; *S.P. 1862*, vol. LV; *S.P. 1867–8*, vol. LXIV, and *S.P. 1871*, vol. LXII. In 1850 nearly a third of the power was water-power: in 1839 it was about 37 per cent: by 1871 water-power accounted for only 11 per cent of the horsepower of machinery in woollen and worsted factories.

After the 1870's the rate of new investment seems to have slowed down very markedly. Although the figures in Table 48 give no indication of the improvements in existing machinery or of the replacement of obsolete machines, it does seem reasonable to deduce from them that new investment in the woollen industry proceeded at a much slower pace in the last two decades of the century than it had at any period since the early 1830's.

It is impossible to calculate the wage bills corresponding to the net output estimates in Table 47—at any rate for the first three-quarters of the century—because the employment data are inadequate. There are reasonably reliable, though discontinuous, statistics of the numbers employed in the factories, but although the worsted trade was largely a factory industry by the 1850's this could not be said of the woollen industry proper until the 1870's, and even at this late stage the number of handloom weavers was not negligible.[1]

According to the census returns about 299,000 persons were engaged in occupations concerned with the woollen and worsted manufactures of the United Kingdom in 1851. In the previous year the factory inspectors had reported 154,180 persons in woollen and worsted factories. At least half of these engaged in the woollen manufacture were working either in their own homes or in workshops not using power and hence not liable to inspection under the Factory Acts. Eighty-five per cent of the 45,000 attributed to the woollen and worsted industry in the Irish census returns, for example, were women spinners and it is impossible to say how many of them were fully employed.[2]

By the last two decades of the century, however, the factory inspectors' returns probably provide a reasonably good approximation to total employment in the industry and these suggest that the numbers employed fluctuated between about 250,000 and about 300,000 according to the state of trade. But from 1890 onwards there was a marked tendency for the numbers to decline. The wage bill in the fourth quarter of the century and the first decade of the twentieth was probably between £9½ m. and £10½ m. except in years of particularly severe depression. In 1907 it accounted for about 50 per cent of net value added. Half a century before, the wage fraction had probably been less than a third.

(c) Linen and jute

At the beginning of the nineteenth century the linen industry was predominantly Irish though it was a manufacture of some importance

---

[1] In 1871 there were 37,052 handlooms operating in the U.K. (mostly weaving wool) compared with 50,830 power-looms in wool and shoddy and 64,659 in worsted weaving. The number of power-loom weavers was only 70,880, whereas each handloom required a single operator.

[2] In the previous census returns (1841) Ireland accounted for nearly a third of the totals attributed to the woollen and worsted industries, and of these, 95 per cent were women spinners. Clearly these returns require a great deal of further analysis before they can be treated as employment aggregates.

in all three countries of the British Isles. Ireland's predominance was then a relatively recent phenomenon, associated with the sudden rise of the English and Scottish cotton industry in the last two decades of the eighteenth century. The cotton industry had never gained much of a foothold in Ireland even in its domestic stage and when it was almost a subsidiary of linen. When it began to adopt mass-production techniques requiring capital, a docile labour force and good communications, Ireland—poor, wild and inaccessible—could not compete with the cotton manufacturers of Lancashire and the West of Scotland. The Irish linen industry, on the other hand, being relatively free from competition for its labour and capital, was able to expand when its English and Scots counterparts were giving way to cotton.

The industry received a good deal of attention from eighteenth-century governments and pamphleteers—particularly in Ireland and Scotland where it was a relatively major manufacture—and there are a variety of contemporary estimates and statistical series describing its progress through the eighteenth century. There are figures of Irish exports from near the beginning of the century and also of Scottish linens stamped for sale, but there is little reliable information on the output of the English linen industry or on Irish output retained for home consumption or on Scottish subsistence output. On these matters we are obliged to depend on contemporary estimates.

From these data we may deduce that for at least the first half of the eighteenth century the English linen industry was more important than either the Irish or the Scottish manufacture in the United Kingdom total, but that the latter were growing faster. By *circa* 1770 Irish output seems to have reached roughly the same level as English output. For 1770–71 an estimate of Irish output was made by Robert Stephenson, an overseer employed by the Linen Board, on the basis of information collected during his 1770 tour.[1] If we accept Stephenson's figures we get an estimate for Ireland (including domestic consumption) of about 38 million yards valued at £2·525 m.[2] Scottish output stamped for sale was about £0·634 m. in 1770, and the combined output of the two countries (including a small allowance for Scottish subsistence output) was thus probably in the region of 51 million yards valued at about £3·2 m. Estimating English consumption of yarn[3] and applying a conversion factor we get an estimate of 33 million yards for the English output.[4] This is probably generous, and perhaps the £2·5 m. which it

[1] Robert Stephenson, *Observations on the Present State of the Linen Trade of Ireland* (1784), p. 86.

[2] C. Gill, *The Rise of the Irish Linen Industry* (1925), refers to an 1802 estimate of 6 yards per head consumed in Ireland and compares it with Stephenson's estimate of 5 yards per head, with the conclusion that the latter must be understated.

[3] Stephenson, *op. cit.*, estimated the value of exports of Irish yarn to England, and Somerville (quoted by Alex J. Warden, *The Linen Trade Ancient and Modern* (1867 ed., p. 370) estimated English output of flax. On these bases it would seem that English yarn output must have been about two-thirds of imported Irish yarn and that total English consumption of yarn must have been over 118,000 cwt.

[4] John Horner, *The Linen Trade of Europe during the Spinning-Wheel Period* (1920), p. 225, suggests a conversion factor of 3,550 cwt. to a million yards for the English industry.

represents was the peak value of the English linen industry before the cotton industry became an important competitor.

In effect, therefore, we have calculated that the gross output of the linen industry of the United Kingdom had reached a value of about £5·7 m. *circa* 1770 and that the Irish and English branches each accounted for about 44 per cent of the total. Of this rather more than a half, or between £3 m. and £3½ m. represented a net contribution to national income. In England alone this cannot have amounted to more than about 1½ per cent of national income, if indeed it was as much.

Estimates for the beginning of the nineteenth century suggest that the English linen industry was declining.[1] This marks the beginning of a new phase in the English linen industry, a phase characterised by the adoption of flax-spinning machinery and by increased production of yarn which was then exported to Ireland and Scotland where weaving costs were much lower than in England. By about 1806 the combined value of the Scottish and Irish output (taking a five-year average centred on 1806 and assuming an average of about 5 yards per head for Irish home consumption) was in the region of 88 million yards valued at about £5½ m. If we accept Warden's estimate of £3 m. for British output,[2] we find a total gross output for the United Kingdom of about £7·6 m. representing about 118 million yards.

For the first quarter of the nineteenth century there is more information available, though there is still a problem of assessing the volume of total home consumption, particularly English domestic consumption. Figures of Irish exports to Great Britain and of Scottish linen stamped for sale—most of which totals were consumed within the United Kingdom—partially fill the gap. In addition there are some figures of sales in Irish markets and some estimates by Gill, based on these figures, of Irish home consumption, for the second and third decades.[3] It was possible on these materials to build up a series consisting of estimates of Irish home consumption, Irish exports, British exports and Scottish linens stamped for sale and to calculate volume of output in the first quarter of the century by extrapolating from an estimate of 118 million square yards for 1804–8.

The only other basis for an estimate of total output of the industry over this period is Ellison's estimates of the raw material consumed by the linen industry in 1798–1800 and 1829–31.[4] Making allowance for a probable decline in English and Scottish output at the turn of the century the conclusion suggested by Ellison's figures is that the 1829–31 output was in the region of 209 million yards, which agrees reasonably well with our estimate of about 180 million yards for 1821–5. An attempt to break down the United Kingdom totals as between countries

---

[1] This is supported by contemporary opinion. See above, chapter II, p. 53.

[2] Warden, *op. cit.* p. 661. Eden estimated the value of the product of the linen industry *circa* 1800 at only £2 m. (quoted in Macpherson, *Annals of Commerce*, vol. IV (1805), p. 549).

[3] Gill, *The Rise of the Irish Linen Industry* (1925), p. 277.

[4] T. Ellison, *History of the Cotton Trade* (1886), p. 120. His estimates were 108·607 million lb. for 1798–1800, and 193·778 million lb. for 1829–31.

suggests that English output had fallen to less than a quarter of the total by the beginning of the nineteenth century and risen again to over a third at the end of the first quarter. The English industry after declining in response to competition from cotton seems to have recovered its momentum with the introduction of spinning machinery at the beginning of the nineteenth century and to have grown rather faster than the Irish industry in the first three decades.

For the middle of the century some more acceptable but still imprecise estimates are given by Ellison.[1] These were built up from estimates of raw material used, wages and salaries paid, and other costs of production, and they suggest a final value of product of about £15·1 m. in 1856, £15·6 m. in 1859–61, £17·7 m. in 1863, from £20 to £25 m. in the cotton famine of 1864–7, and back to under £18 m. by 1880–2. At the time of 1907 census, total value of output calculated in a manner so far as possible comparable to our previous estimates, was only about £12·3 m.[2] Using Ellison's estimates as a basis and calculating raw material inputs from imports of flax and Irish acreages under the crop it was possible to make rough estimates of the volume and value of the linen industry's output for selected years in the nineteenth century.[3]

Table 49. *The output of the United Kingdom linen industry,*
1770–1907

Circa	Index of raw material imports (1803 = 100)	Estimated gross value product (£m.)	Estimated net output at 60% gross output (£m.)
1770	74	5·7	3·4
1803	100	7·2	4·3
1812	110	9·2	5·5
1823	159	12·5	7·5
1830	196	14·0	8·4
1845	191	14·0	8·4
1856	243	15·1	9·1
1860	218	15·6	9·4
1863	240	17·0	10·2
1866	323	23·0	13·8
1875	260	18·0	10·8
1881	270	17·0	10·2
1891	204	13·5	8·1
1907	197	12·3	7·2

Source: See text.

[1] Ellison, *op. cit.* p. 124.

[2] Value of linen piece goods in the United Kingdom + value linen yarn exported (1907) + value made-up output of weaving firms + bleaching + thread and similar articles.

[3] For most years there were estimates of Irish output made by the Flax Supply Association and these are used by Ellison, *op. cit.* p. 120; by Warden, *op. cit.* p. 411, and Supplement to the 1867 ed., p. 13; and by R. Lloyd Patterson in his article on 'The British Flax and Linen Industry', in Sir Wm. Ashley's *British Industries* (1903). See also Dundee Trade Report Association, *Statistics of the Linen Trade* (Dundee, 1855).

For an industry whose fortunes fluctuated as much as the linen industry's the use of bench-mark dates as a basis for assessment of its rate of growth is hazardous. But in broad and relative terms there seems to be little doubt about the picture which emerges from Table 49. It would appear that the linen industry never recovered the importance it had in the British economy before the industrial revolution transformed the cotton industry. *Circa* 1770 it accounted for roughly 30 per cent of the United Kingdom output of textiles and perhaps $1\frac{1}{2}$ per cent of its national income. In the last few years of the eighteenth century there may have been some absolute decline in the linen industry to set off against the very rapid rise in the cotton manufacture. By the beginning of the nineteenth century its share in the net output of all textiles had fallen below 20 per cent though its contribution to national income was still probably nearly $1\frac{1}{2}$ per cent. The introduction of spinning machinery into the English industry induced a period of relatively rapid growth. English factory labour provided yarn for the cheap domestic labour of Ireland and Scotland. But although this was a time in which the rate of growth was probably more rapid than at any other period it did not compare with the pace of the advance in cotton. Thereafter in the second and third quarters of the century (if we exclude its sudden expansion when the cotton famine crippled its most serious rival) the industry grew only very slowly and the last few decades were again a period of decline.

The English section of the industry began to decline in mid-century. Numbers employed fell from 27,421 in 1851, to 18,680 in 1871 and 4,956 in 1901.[1] In Scotland it was not until the 1870's that the decline began and by this time the jute industry was beginning to absorb much of the capital and labour that had hitherto been confined to linen proper. Ireland's linen industry, though it failed to maintain the peak output of the cotton famine period, was nevertheless fairly prosperous in the seventies and eighties. Assisted by the adoption of the power-loom and by the retirement of English competition, it grew steadily until the end of the century. By 1907 the Irish branch accounted for about 61 per cent of the final value of product, the Scottish branch for nearly 29 per cent and the English branch for under 10 per cent. In terms of numbers employed the English share had fallen to under 5 per cent by 1901 and the Irish share was nearly 70 per cent.[2] English output in current-value terms was less than half what it had been at the end of the Napoleonic Wars.

The fraction of the industry's output produced for foreign markets was variable, but the long-term trend was upwards. At the beginning of the nineteenth century the proportion of gross product exported seems to have been under 20 per cent. By the twentieth century it was

---

[1] Board of Trade, *Memoranda and Statistical Tables and Charts on British and Foreign Trade and Industrial Conditions* (H.M.S.O., 1903, Cmd. 1761), p. 362.

[2] Board of Trade, *Second Series of Memoranda and Statistical Tables, etc.* (H.M.S.O., 1904. Cmd. 2337), p. 456.

commonly 50 per cent. In linen as in the other textile industries the expansion which followed the Napoleonic Wars seems to have been largely absorbed by the home market, whereas the decline that set in towards the end of the century was partly mitigated (or at any rate postponed) by an expansion of sales to foreign countries.

Finally, it may be noted that the weaving section of the linen industry remained a largely domestic manufacture until well into the second half of the nineteenth century. In 1850 there were only 3,748 power-looms, and in Ireland—where most of the linen piece goods made in the United Kingdom were finally woven—the number was only 88. Even in 1868, after the extraordinary stimulus of the cotton famine, there were not many more than 31,000 power-looms operating in the industry and, of these, Ireland and Scotland had nearly 13,000 each. In England the industry had already begun to decline and in Scotland it was to decline in the last two decades. But in Ireland investment continued to grow steadily until by 1910 there were 935,000 spindles (82 per cent of the United Kingdom total compared with 41 per cent in 1850) and 36,000 power-looms (63 per cent of the United Kingdom total).

For Scotland the decline in the linen industry was more than offset by the growth of the jute industry. Small quantities of jute were imported in the late eighteenth century and the early nineteenth century for making doormats and similar articles. But it was not until the 1830's that experiments were made in manufacturing bagging and sacking articles from jute[1] and not until the 1860's that the industry emerged as a manufacture of any importance. From the first it was largely concentrated in Dundee and its vicinity. Information on the value of output in the industry is scanty. There are figures of jute imports and exports, and there is, of course, the Census of Production return for 1907, from which we can deduce that the value of the industry's product was then about £6·8 m. If we extrapolate back from this point to *circa* 1870 on the basis of imports of raw material and allow for the change in prices since 1870, we may conclude that the current value of output of the industry in 1870 was about £3 m. Volume of output increased by two and a half times the 1870 level before the end of the century. Jute output was probably worth between £5 and £6 m. by the 1880's. The volume of output in 1907 does not seem to have been much different from the 1890 volume but prices were temporarily higher.

Table 50 summarises these estimates. Again the results are exceedingly crude and do no more than indicate the rough orders of magnitude involved. Hemp products (cord, rope, etc.) accounted for a gross output of about £1½ m. in 1907 and probably for less than £1 m. in 1870.

---

[1] Cf. Warden, *op. cit.* p. 72: '. . . manufacturers unanimously disapproved of it.' By the mid-1860's, again according to Warden, p. 79, 'The various descriptions of Jute goods now manufactured are legion—sackings, baggings, hessians, hop pocketing, osnaburgs, ducks, carpeting, etc.'

Table 50. *Estimated output of the jute industry, 1870–1907*

	Volume	£m.
1870	100	3·1
1880	173	5·0
1890	264	6·5
1907	263	6·8

Source: See text.

(d) Silk

Quantitative information on the progress of the silk industry is seriously incomplete. The fact that its raw material had to be imported means that we have a more or less continuous indicator of its level of input and hence, indirectly, of its level of output. But there are no indicators of the value of this output apart from a very few contemporary estimates whose reliability we were unable to assess.

It was never a major British industry, though, like linen, it was of some significance in the pre-industrial stage. Estimates of input and output which were given to the 1765 Committee of the House of Commons by a manufacturer suggest that the imports of raw and thrown silk imported during the five years 1767–71 would have yielded plain silk goods to a gross value of about £1·8 m.[1] For this period Arthur Young estimated that the net value added by the silk and cotton industries was in the region of £1·5 m. and that the net value of the cotton industry's output was probably about £0·5 m. We are probably using figures of roughly the right order of magnitude if we put the total final value of British silks (including dyeing and printing), at a little over £2 m. and net value added at roughly £1 m. *circa* 1770.

Macpherson quotes a doubtful set of estimates for 1783 which suggests that the total product of the silk industry was worth nearly £3½ m. and that it was increasing.[2] Imports of raw material in 1780–4 were running at an annual rate which was 50 per cent above the level for the period 1767–71 and were more than twice as great in 1783 and 1784, so that the estimate conforms with the scanty evidence we have. The data suggest that the industry's output rose to a peak which may have yielded a gross output worth as much as £3½ m. at current values of the early 1780's. This level was not maintained however. The volume of input in 1786–90 was below the 1780–4 level and was about the same level in the period 1796–1800. Thus in the last two decades of the century when the cotton industry was making spectacular progress the silk industry seems to have stagnated and declined.

Prices, however, were rising. At this time the current value of silk manufactures exported was in the region of £600,000—roughly twice their 'official' values.[3] If the value of the industry's gross product was

[1] *House of Commons Journal*, vol. xxx (1765).
[2] In *Annals of Commerce, op. cit.*, vol. iv, p. 15.
[3] Irving's estimate for 1796–8 gives Great Britain's exports at £610,552 including about £25,000 to Ireland. The official value of exports at this time was about £308,700.

about £3 m. at the end of the century, exports accounted for about 20 per cent, which is rather larger than their share earlier in the century but could be explained by the fact that French competition was more effectively checked by war than by trade protection measures. Judging by a comparison of the declared and official values, prices of British silk manufactures continued to rise till towards the end of the first decade of the nineteenth century and after that they started to fall quite sharply. It was in this first decade also that inputs of raw material began to rise markedly.

Colquhoun estimated that the total value of the gross output of the silk industry *circa* 1812 was in the region of £3 m. of which he attributed £1 m. to the value of the raw material.[1] Of this, all that can be said is that it does not conflict with the other evidence that we have. It seems, however, to have represented a somewhat larger volume of output than the turn-of-the-century estimates of £3 m. which we also found plausible. The declared value of exports averaged about £523,000 over the period 1808–12, or probably a little more than one-fifth of total output.

The second decade of the nineteenth century saw a definite expansion in the industry stimulated by technological improvements, particularly in the throwing sections. The third saw a more rapid growth which was apparently a direct and immediate result of the removal of trade restrictions on imports. Imports of raw, waste and thrown silk more than doubled between 1801–5 and 1819–23; and the proportion of raw silk, which had been little more than half of the total in the mid-eighteenth century and about 70 per cent in the boom of the early 1780's rose to between 85 per cent and 90 per cent at the end of the second decade of the nineteenth century. This was a consequence of the substantial growth in the English throwing industry and meant that a relatively high proportion of the final cost of manufacture was now incurred within Great Britain. Prices continued to fall in consequence. The declared value of pure silk manufactures, which had been about three and a half times the official values at the beginning of the century, were less than twice as high in 1823. By 1827 after the removal of the large duties on imported silks, raw and thrown, declared values of pure silk manufactures were only about a third higher than the official values. Average annual imports nearly doubled in the decade between 1819–23 and 1829–33. They were to treble again in the three decades between 1829–33 and 1859–63.

This growth was achieved behind a high wall of protection. The industry had never been in a position to face French competition in a free market. The effectiveness of the French challenge was due to three main reasons—cheap labour costs in France, the cheaper raw material (some of which was actually produced in France and none of which had so far to travel as the English raw material) and the superior fashion quality of the French goods. A silk mercer giving evidence

[1] P. Colquhoun, *Treatise on the Wealth, Power and Resources of the British Empire*, p. 92.

before the 1765 committee of the House of Commons said, for example, that 'the Trade in England is greatly confined for want of taste, there being no comparison between the taste of France and England'.[1] Similar evidence was given before the 1821 and 1831 committees. When, in 1864, the Cobden treaty removed the protective duty of 15 per cent on foreign silk manufactures further growth of the silk industry was finally checked. By 1875 imports of silk manufactures, which had been under £2 m. in 1854, were over £7·3 m., and by 1880 they exceeded £13·3 m. After rising to a gross output peak of perhaps more than £17 m. in the early 1860's the British silk industry wilted in the face of foreign competition to probably not more than about £13 m. *circa* 1875 and to under £5½ m. in 1907.

Estimates of the value of output of the silk industry in the nineteenth century are few and seldom reliable. From the evidence of manufacturers and merchants to two select committees on the industry which reported in the first half-century we can get some idea of the orders of magnitude involved. Applying the values, costs, wastage proportions, etc., stated by manufacturers before the 1821 Commission, to the imports for the period 1818–20, for example, we get £6·5 m. for the final value of output, of which raw materials account for £3·4 m. and wages and salaries for £2·3 m.[2] Porter writing in 1831 estimated that each pound of silk raw material would be manufactured into a finished product worth about £2·37, which for about 4·2 million lb. suggests a final product worth about £9 m.[3] Again, *circa* 1839, he calculated that the annual value of silk manufactures consumed in the United Kingdom 'is considerably above £12 millions'.[4] The declared value of exports indeed rose from just over half a million pounds per annum in the period 1818–20 to about £842,000 in the period 1834–6, which was a rise of over 65 per cent. The export figures of 1835 and 1836 were peak figures which were not reached again until the 1850's, but even so it would not be surprising to find that home consumption had increased by at least as much, and a figure of £11 m. or £12 m. for the total gross value of the industry's output at the end of the 1830's does not seem impossibly high.

McCulloch, however, produced a more conservative set of estimates for *circa* 1836 and it is sufficiently thoughtful to deserve serious consideration.[5] They suggest a total gross output of about £10½ m. *circa*

---

[1] *House of Commons Journal*, vol. xxx (1765), p. 210.

[2] *S.P. 1821*, vol. vii, 'Second Report by the Lord Committee . . . to Inquire into the Means of Extending and Securing the Foreign Trade of the Country'. However, in the evidence before the Committee it was stated by a manufacturer (p. 4) 'that the value upon Raw Silk is increased nearly fourfold in the course of manufacture and that the whole value of our silk manufacturers cannot be stated at less than £10 millions annually, which, with the exception of a very trifling proportion to the whole, is used for home consumption'. It is fairly certain that this was a considerable overestimate.

[3] G. R. Porter, 'Treatise on the Silk Manufacture', in *The Cabinet Cyclopedia*, by Dionysius Lardner (1831), p. 88.

[4] G. R. Porter, *Progress of the Nation* (1847 ed.), p. 582.

[5] J. McCulloch, *Account of the British Empire*, vol. i (1839), pp. 682–90.

1836, of which £4·0 m. was attributed to raw materials and purchased services and £3·7 m. to wages and salaries. This of course is only an 'order of magnitude' estimate and it is appreciably lower than Porter's figure of over £12 m. for roughly the same period. It must however be remembered that the silk industry was a luxury industry which was subject to severe fluctuations from year to year. Imports of raw materials, for example, ranged from under 3 million lb. in 1829 to over 6 million lb. in 1836. The declared value of exports, which were about £268,000 in 1829, had risen to £972,000 in 1835 and fallen back again to £503,700 in 1837. Gross value of output may well have exceeded an annual amount of £12 m. for some years in this fourth decade of the nineteenth century but it seems unlikely on the whole that the average sustained value was much in excess of £10½ m.

McCulloch repeated his 1836 estimate in the 1847 edition of his *Account of the British Empire*, with the comment that 'circumstances have changed but little in the interval'. This is plausible. The volume of raw material used had increased about 16 per cent between 1834–8 and 1844–8, but prices were still falling and it is possible that the average value of output in the mid-forties was still under £11 m.

For the rest of the nineteenth century there are no reputable estimates of the value of the industry's output and we have no reliable bench-mark until 1907 when, according to the Census of Production returns, the gross output of the silk industry amounted to rather less than £5½ m. We can, however, make some rough estimates for the intervening period on the basis of input and employment data and these are summarised in Table 51.

Table 51. *The nineteenth-century silk industry*

Circa	Volume (1801–5 = 100)	Value final product (£m.)	Contribution to national income (£m.)	Numbers employed (000)
1770	87	2	1	—
1800	100	3	2	—
1812	110	3	2	—
1819	186	6½	3	—
1836	449	10½	6½	80
1847	521	11	6½	100
1860	1068	17	9	150
1875	723	13	7	72
1890	873	9	5	58
1907	826	5½	2	40

Source: See text.

The silk industry did not lend itself readily to mechanisation, and at the peak of its growth, in the early 1860's, only about a third of the numbers engaged in the industry were employed in factories. Within the silk factories (they reached a total of 771 in 1861) there were, even by 1867, as many as seven persons employed for every unit of steam horsepower available. Cotton factories had a higher steam horsepower ratio than this as early as 1835. Power-looms began to be introduced extensively into the industry in the 1850's and 1860's, but even by 1867 there were only 14,625 of them. This was less than half the number in the linen industry (another slow starter in the process of mechanisation) and only an eighth of those in the woollen and worsted industries.

(e) The textiles and clothing industries

The textiles and dress industries, considered as a group, reached the peak of their importance in the British labour market in the middle of the nineteenth century. At the time of the 1851 census about two and three-quarter million people (10 per cent of the total population and 21·4 per cent of the occupied population) were working in this group of manufactures.[1] Between 10 and 11 per cent of them were under the age of fifteen. The proportion of children at work was already decreasing under the influence of factory legislation and educational progress but the children constituted a convenient reservoir of labour for the industry until the twentieth century. When textiles were booming, the proportion of children in the factories rose. When textiles were in depression, they were the first to be cast off.

After mid-century the proportion of the working population engaged in the textile and clothing industries began to decline. So, less rapidly, did their absolute numbers. By 1871 the numbers had fallen to about 2·6 million and their proportion of the occupied population to 17·7 per cent. The only other groups of industries to employ a labour force of comparable size were the agriculture and fisheries group, which accounted for 19·5 per cent in 1871, and the domestic-service group, where the proportion was 15·2 per cent.

Among the manufacturing industries, of course, the textiles and clothing groups were still typical of British industry. Of over 130,000 factories and workshops which came under the control of the Factory and Workshop Acts in 1871 more than 61,000 were in the textile and clothing group.[2] They accounted for about 52 per cent of the steam-power capacity of British factories and 63 per cent of their water-power capacity. The only other manufacturing group of comparable importance at this stage was the metal manufacturing group with more than 18,000 establishments, 634,000 employees, and over a third of the steam-power capacity of all factories and workshops.

The industries discussed in the preceding four sections do not, of course, cover the whole of the textile group but they do represent most of it. In 1871 they accounted for over 70 per cent of all the employees in the textiles and clothing factories and workshops and their progress

[1] These figures are from Booth's analysis of the census returns and they therefore exclude dealers. Charles Booth, *op. cit., J. Roy. Statist. Soc.*, vol. XLIX (June 1886).

[2] Factories, broadly speaking, were establishments using power. Workshops were all places of work where children, young persons, or women were employed. So factories and workshops together covered most manufacturing establishments in the United Kingdom which were of more than a minimum size.

provides a good indicator of the role of the group as a whole. Table 52 summarises our estimates of net output for these industries at various years in the period 1770–1870, based on the data brought together in the earlier sections of this chapter.

Table 52. *Net output of the principal textile industries of the United Kingdom,*
1770–1870

(in millions of pounds at current values)

Circa	Cotton (£m.)	Woollen and worsted (£m.)	Linen (£m.)	Silk (£m.)	Totals (£m.)	As percentage national income
1770	0·6	7·0	3·4	1·0	12·0	9
1805	10·5	12·8	7·6	2·0	32·9	10
1821	17·5	16·6	12·5	3·0	49·6	14
1836	21·8	16·7	8·4	6·5	53·4	11
1845	24·3	21·1	8·4	6·5	60·3	11
1850	21·1	20·3	8·7	7·0	57·1	10
1855	26·2	20·2	9·0	8·0	63·4	10
1860	33·0	21·2	9·4	9·0	72·6	10
1865	30·1	25·0	13·5	9·0	77·6	9
1870	38·8	25·4	12·3	8·0	84·5	9

Source: Rough estimates based on the 'value added' and 'net output' calculations made in the preceding sections, pp. 182–211 above. Since these are based to some extent on input data, there may be some double counting in the total in respect of mixed materials.

The evidence suggests that the principal textile industries (excluding the clothing group) accounted for as much as 14 per cent of the United Kingdom national income in the early 1820's. The minor textiles (lace and hosiery, for example) were then of small significance in relation to the total and their inclusion would probably not alter the percentage when expressed in these round terms. By the 1850's and 1860's, however, the industry was expanding its range of products considerably and the minor products (including the mixtures) were by no means negligible. In 1871, for example, we have calculated that the gross value of jute products alone reached 15 per cent of the corresponding total for the linen industry.[1]

We also attempted in our studies of the individual industries, to measure their progress in terms of volume indices, largely on the basis of input data. By weighting these volume indices with the proportions suggested by our net value of output estimates it is possible to construct a rough index of the growth in net product for the textile industry as a whole. This is given in Table 53.

This series puts into perspective the spectacular growth of the cotton industry in the last three decades of the eighteenth century, a growth which amazed contemporaries and has injected a strong upward bias into many later interpretations of the overall rate of progress associated with the early stages of the industrial revolution. Between *circa* 1770 and *circa* 1800 retained imports of cotton wool increased by a factor of

[1] See above, p. 206.

Table 53. *Index of the growth in real net output for textiles, 1770–1870*

Averages of five years centring on	1800 = 100
1770	76
1780	84
1790	89
1800	100
1805	112
1810	118
1815	127
1820	199
1822	212
1827	288
1832	360
1837	463
1842	612
1847	632
1852	803
1857	1050
1862	863
1867	1056
1872	1481

Sources: Volume indices for individual industries estimated from input and output data discussed in relevant sections of this chapter. Weights based on the net output estimates in Table 52.

more than 14. But its relative importance at this period was such that for the textile industry as a whole real net output apparently grew by only about a third. This was not very much greater than the increase in population over the same period.

It is true that the cotton-wool imports on which we have based our volume index of the growth of the cotton industry does not allow for quality changes, and that the coarse cottons which were its typical product in the 1770's were greatly inferior to the fine calicoes of the early 1800's. However, even on the assumption that quality improved as rapidly as inputs and that the real rate of progress in cotton should be doubled, we still find that the textile industry as a whole grew only about half as fast in the last three decades of the eighteenth century as in the first two decades of the nineteenth, and only a quarter as fast as in the 1820's and 1830's.

We would conclude from this attempt to measure the growth of real net product in the textile industry that its peak rate of growth was achieved in the two decades following the Napoleonic Wars when real output, as measured in Table 53, increased some three and a half times. Then, when the share of textiles in the national income may have been between 11 and 14 per cent, the impact of their very rapid progress on the overall rate of economic growth of the United Kingdom must have been especially significant.

Progress continued to be rapid into the forties and fifties, when real output doubled again. There was a setback as a consequence of the cotton famine and a sharp recovery in the late 1860's. The industry never recovered the impetus it had had in the three or four decades before the middle of the century, but it continued to grow overall. In the three and a half decades between *circa* 1872 and *circa* 1907 there was an increase in real product which amounted to about 80 per cent if we include jute, and might prove to have been somewhat higher if we were to include other minor textiles. This was a higher rate of growth than we found for the corresponding three decades or so at the end of the eighteenth century.

Most of the late-nineteenth-century growth was attributable to the continued expansion of the cotton industry. The silk industry and the English and Scottish linen industries were of negligible importance by the beginning of the twentieth century and the wool industry accounted for not much more than a quarter of textile output. By then, however, it is doubtful whether all the textile industries together contributed as much as 5 per cent of the national income of the United Kingdom.

2. THE MINING INDUSTRY

The mining industry has a long history in Britain and played an important part in the early stages of the industrial revolution, but it was not until the second quarter of the nineteenth century that it began to make an appreciable direct contribution to the national income. At this stage, that is in mid-century, iron, copper, lead and tin all figured prominently in the total product of the industry. The pithead value of the metal ores mined was then between 30 and 40 per cent of the value of the coal; and the other, so-called 'earthy minerals' (clay, building stone, slates, etc.) must have been not far short of the value of the metal ores.[1] When valued after smelting, the aggregate output of the metals mined in the United Kingdom was nearly as great as that of coal. After mid-century, however, coal output continued to grow in volume and value and most other metals (except iron) declined. By 1900 the pithead value of coal mined in the United Kingdom was roughly six times the values of metals smelted from British ores and more than twenty times the value of the ores mined.

There were no reliable mineral statistics until the 1850's when Robert Hunt began to compile them in connection with the Geological Survey. Earlier estimates tended to be largely conjectural, although there are figures for Cornish copper and tin which throw some light on the volume and value of these metals and of course there is a good deal of information of varying degrees of quality on the iron industry.[2] For the most part, however, the quantitative information available on other minerals than coal, records output or value not at the mine or the quarry, but after some further process of production (e.g. smelting of metals). In this section, therefore, we shall be primarily concerned with tracing the quantitative history of the coal industry though we shall try to set it in the broader perspective of the mining industry as a whole wherever data are available.

[1] *Mineral Statistics of the United Kingdom for 1858.*   [2] See above, p. 55.

For coal there are numerous contemporary estimates from the end of the eighteenth century onwards, but it is difficult to assess their reliability or to select between them when they vary.[1] Clapham started from the estimates given in the 1871 Coal Commission report and linked them to the official 1855–7 figures by sketching a curve on the assumption that the progression was 'fairly smooth throughout the forty years after Waterloo'.[2] In broad terms this curve suggests a plausible picture of the industry's growth during the first half-century. It may be doubted, however, whether the progression was as smooth as Clapham chose to assume. The coal series that do exist (imports into London, exports to foreign countries and to Ireland, total coastal shipments, etc.) suggest a more jerky progress, and the iron industry, which was the most important industrial consumer, also grew somewhat fitfully in the four or five decades after the wars.

It is possible by searching the parliamentary returns for the first half of the century to compile series for total coal imports into London, and total coal exports to foreign countries and to Ireland. It is also possible to calculate roughly the consumption of coal in the iron industry by applying an appropriate coefficient per ton of pig-iron (ranging from 7 *circa* 1800 to 6 *circa* 1855). In 1855 these 'measurable' components of total coal output were estimated to amount to nearly 50 per cent of total output. Half a century earlier when coal was largely produced for the domestic consumer it is unlikely that they accounted for as much as 30 per cent of total output. We are left with a remainder (i.e. British consumption outside of London or the areas supplied by London and excluding the iron industry) for which we have no series on which to base a direct estimate. The assumption that this remainder grew at the same rate as London consumption, permits extrapolation back from the official 1855 figures to reach the series of output estimates given in Table 54.

It may be that this assumption is more plausible for the earlier part of the period concerned than it is for the latter part when industries accessible to the coalfields (e.g. the textile industries of Lancashire and Yorkshire) may have been adapting to steam-power techniques more rapidly than the London manufacturers. Whether the areas outside London and its hinterland were increasing their consumption faster than the London area is, however, open to doubt. In the cotton industry, which was generally ahead of other industries in adopting new techniques, steam-power did not predominate in spinning until the 1830's and in weaving until the 1840's.[3] The direct demand of the

---

[1] A discussion of these early estimates is given in vol. III of the report of the 1871 Coal Commission, *S.P. 1871*, vol. XVIII; Clapham also discusses them briefly. J. H. Clapham, *An Economic History of Modern Britain*, vol. I, pp. 430–31.

[2] Clapham, *op. cit.* p. 431.

[3] There are various estimates of the growth in number of power-looms in cotton. See, for example, G. H. Wood, *J. Roy. Statist. Soc.*, June 1910, *op. cit.*, and Samuel Andrew, 'Fifty Years of the Cotton Trade', Paper read to the Economic Section of the British Association at Manchester, 1887. See also Clapham, *op. cit.* pp. 143 *et seq.*

new steam transport industries (as opposed to the indirect demand through construction of iron ships and railway equipment) probably accounted for a minor proportion of home consumption until the 1850's. In sum, if we exclude the iron industry, which was the most important single factor in the rising demand for coal in the first half of the century, the increasing home consumption was probably largely due to the growing fuel requirements of the broad mass of domestic consumers and small manufacturers: and as far as these groups are concerned there is no reason to suppose that the London area with its large population and variety of small industries provides a distorted picture of the trend for the rest of the country.

If the areas outside London were taking up coal at a faster rate than the London area by the 1830's and 1840's, we may have underestimated the industry's rate of growth in the last fifteen to twenty years of the period 1800–55 and overestimated the absolute levels of output in the first three or four decades of the century. It seems doubtful, however, whether an acceptable estimate for *circa* 1800 would fall below the commonly quoted estimate of about 10 million tons[1] or that 1841 output was as low as Samuel Salt's estimate of about 28½ million tons.[2]

Table 54. *Nineteenth-century coal output*

	Total U.K. output (millions of tons)	Value at pithead (£m.)	Proportion of output exported (%)
1800	11·0	2·8	2·0
1816	15·9	5·2	2·5
1820	17·4	5·7	1·4
1825	21·9	6·9	1·4
1830	22·4	6·9	2·2
1835	27·7	7·6	2·7
1840	33·7	8·8	4·8
1845	45·9	9·2	5·5
1850	49·4	10·3	6·8
1855	61·5	16·1	8·1
1860	80·0	20·0	9·2
1865	98·2	24·5	9·3
1870	110·4	27·6	13·4
1875	131·9	46·2	13·5
1880	146·8	62·4	16·3
1885	159·4	41·1	19·3
1890	181·6	75·0	21·3
1895	189·7	57·2	22·6
1900	225·2	121·7	25·9
1905	236·1	82·0	20·1
1913	287·4	146·0	32·8

Sources: After 1850 all figures from the *Statistical Abstracts of the U.K.* Before 1850, see text. Output estimates 1800–50 on the basis of exports to foreign parts and Ireland, London imports, and estimated consumption by iron industry. Values 1800–45 at half price of best Newcastle coals at port of shipment. Exports 1820 onwards from Porter's tables in *S.P., 1833*, vol. XLI, and *Statistical Abstracts*; 1800 estimated from Newcastle and Sunderland exports, Porter, *op. cit.* p. 280. For 1816 exports see *S.P. 1818*, vol. XIV.

[1] *S.P. 1871*, vol. XVIII.   [2] Samuel Salt, *Statistics and Calculations* (1845), p. 46.

The output estimates thus arrived at for the first half of the nineteenth century do not differ greatly from the figures cautiously suggested by Clapham.[1] They do, however, imply a rather more variable rate of growth than he envisaged. In particular the rate of growth seems to have slackened markedly in the late 1820's and the late 1840's, in the latter case after an abnormal spurt of progress in the early 1840's. In terms of the total amounts of coal raised, the industry seems to have grown fastest between 1830 and 1865 when total output increased some four a half times. In the next quarter of a century output barely doubled. The 1913 level of output was never exceeded. For most of the interwar period coal output was between 220 and 250 million tons. Since the Second World War it has generally been between 200 and 225 million tons.

The value figures for the years before 1850, for which no pithead price data are available, are merely token estimates. The prices that have been recorded are f.o.b. values for exports and prices of best Newcastle coals at place of shipment and on arrival in London. All are above pithead price and there is a wide range between. In 1835, for example, when the average f.o.b. price was 6·59s. per ton,[2] the price of first-quality coals at Newcastle and Sunderland was 11s. and at the London Coal Exchange best Newcastle coals were fetching 20s. 3d.[3] In the late 1850's the average f.o.b. price for goods shipped to foreign buyers averaged nearly 80 per cent above the pithead price. Hence in evaluating output estimates for the period 1800–45 at approximately half the price of Newcastle coals we cannot hope to do more than obtain a very rough indication of the probable trend in the gross output of the industry.

If the price structure of the industry is taken into consideration it is surprising that output expanded as much as it did in the first three decades of the century. Most branches of the iron industry, of course, enjoyed the benefits of being situated near the place of production. But the majority of other consumers had to bear heavy costs of transport by sea and a system of central and local government duties which together exceeded the original pithead price. On the assumption that the average British consumer outside the iron industry paid as much as the Greenwich Hospital contract price per ton of coal the final retail sales value in the immediate post-war years must have exceeded £25 m. for an output worth between £5 m. and £7 m. at the pithead. Retail

---

[1] Clapham, *op. cit.* p. 431. 'If an output of some 15,000,000 tons for Great Britain be accepted as a starting-point, some such progression as the following may be suggested as not unlikely: 1826, 21,000,000 tons; 1836, 30,000,000 tons; 1846, 44,000,000 tons; 1856, 65,000,000 tons.

[2] *Board of Trade Report on Wholesale and Retail Prices* (1903), p. 13.

[3] Porter, *op. cit.* p. 280. In the war years, when retail prices were inflated by high transport costs and heavy duties, the differential between the Newcastle and London price was very much larger than this. For example, in 1814, when the Newcastle price was 13s. the London Coal Exchange was 44s. 8d. and at the Royal Hospital, Greenwich, the contract price had risen to 48s. 9d. per ton. Consumers in less accessible or well-organised markets than London must often have faced higher prices than this.

prices began to fall in the late 1820's, partly as a consequence of increasing competition in the industry, and even more rapidly in the 1830's, after the coal duties were lifted. By 1834 the Greenwich Hospital contract price, which had been over £2 until Waterloo and over 30s. until 1828, had dropped to 14s. 11d. per ton. In 1835 it was 16s. 8d. and the final sales value of coal output was probably not more than treble the pithead value.

The output figures in Table 54 are valued gross of the costs of materials and purchased services and they therefore correspond to the Census of Production definition of gross output. These costs constitute a relatively small proportion of pithead price in coal-mining—probably between 10 per cent and 15 per cent of gross value for the period covered in Table 54, though after the First World War when the industry became more mechanised the proportion rose.[1] It would therefore appear that coal-mining accounted for under 1 per cent of British national income at the beginning of the nineteenth century, rather less than 2 per cent for most of the second quarter, rising, however, to about 6 per cent at the end of the century.

The coal industry's changing rate of growth can be partly explained in terms of the changes in the character of its market which have been considerable during the past one and a half centuries. At the beginning of the nineteenth century the principal market was the household market or the small domestic manufacturers which were practically indistinguishable from it. Apart from the iron industry, which probably absorbed between 10 and 15 per cent of coal output even at the very beginning of the century, the principal industrial consumers must have been brickmakers, brewers, distillers, bakers, potteries, and copper and tin smelters. The steam engine was still restricted by Watt's patent until 1800, and by the high costs of transporting coal until much later.[2] Exports to places outside the British Isles took only about 2 per cent of total output and we have estimated that the household market absorbed between half and two-thirds of all coal consumed in Great Britain and Ireland.

Forty years later the metal processing industries (largely iron) and the mines were probably taking about 28 per cent of total coal output. Exports had risen to nearly 5 per cent. Steam navigation by road and rail were in their infancy and the urban gas industry was spreading to cities outside London—together they may have taken as much as 3 per cent of the 1840 coal output. Steam was the chief source of power in

---

[1] Materials and purchased services amounted to 12½ per cent of gross output at the time of the 1907 Census of Production. However, in 1950 the mining and quarrying group's purchases from other industries amounted to about 23 per cent of final output (excluding goods and services supplied by the transport and distributive group but including imports). See 1955 *Blue Book on National Income and Expenditure* (H.M.S.O., 1956), Table 17.

[2] See John Lord, *Capital and Steam-power 1750–1800*, p. 176. 'The number of engines in Great Britain and Ireland in the year 1800 was 321 representing a total horsepower of 5,210'. This, however, relates to only Boulton and Watt engines, which may not have accounted for more than a third of the engines then operating. See A. E. Musson and E. Robinson, 'The Early Growth of Steam-power', *Econ. Hist. Rev.*, 2nd Series vol. XI, 1959.

the textile industries, though in the weaving branch the handloom weavers had only just begun to decline in numbers.[1] But it is doubtful whether all manufacturing industry outside the metal industries accounted for as much as a third of all coal produced in the United Kingdom, and private households probably took nearly as much as, if not more, than the general manufacturing group. Our estimates of the distribution of coal output in 1840 are shown in Table 55.[2]

This was the period of fastest advance in coal-mining. In the fifteen years between 1830 and 1845 coal output is estimated to have doubled at least. Exports multiplied by a factor of five, iron industry demands apparently more than doubled, and imports into London—stimulated by a fall in prices of about a third compared with less than 7 per cent registered by most general price indices[3]—increased by about 80 per cent.

The detailed estimates of coal consumption in different industries compiled for the 1871 Coal Commission reflect the fact that by 1869 coal was primarily a producers' good. In consequence coal-mining

Table 55. *Estimated distribution of coal in the United Kingdom*

(as percentages of U.K. coal tonnage raised)

	(1) 1840 (%)	(2) 1869 (%)	(3) 1887 (%)	(4) 1913 (%)	(5) 1929 (%)	(6) 1955 (%)
Iron industry	25	30	16½	11	10	12
Mines	3	6½	6½	6½	5	4
Steam navigation	1½	5	12½	6	6	6
Gas and electricity	1½	6	6	8	11	32
General manufacturing	32½	26	26	22½	22½	28½
Domestic	31½	17	17½	13½	15½	16½
Exports	5	9	15	32½	30	6

Sources: N.B. There are rounding errors which prevent some of these columns from adding to 100 but the 1955 column exceeds 100 because it includes imports amounting to about 5 per cent of U.K. output.

(1) Our estimates based on the detailed industry estimates made for 1869 on behalf of the 1871 Coal Commission. McCulloch estimated that *circa* 1846 over 50 per cent of coal output went to domestic consumption and 'smaller manufacturers'.

(2) Estimates made for the 1871 Coal Commission. *S.P. 1871*, vol. XVIII.

(3) Estimates from Richard Price-Williams, 'The Coal Question', *J. Roy. Statist. Soc.*, vol. LII (March 1889), p. 38.

(4) From estimates by J. H. Jones, 'The Present Position of the British Coal Trade', *J. Roy. Statist. Soc.*, vol. XCIII (1930), p. 33; also from estimates given in the *Ministry of Fuel and Power Statistical Digest 1956* (H.M.S.O., 1957), Tables 66 and 78.

(5) and (6) *Ministry of Fuel and Power Statistical Digest, op. cit.*

[1] According to the Factory Inspector's reports there were over 3,000 steam engines at work in textile mills in 1839, generating a horsepower of over 74,000 compared with 28,000 horsepower generated by water.

[2] They are based on extrapolation of the very detailed estimates for 1869 made for the 1871 Coal Commission and almost certainly over-estimate the share of industry.

[3] Comparing prices of best coals at the ship-side in London, 1829–31 and 1844–46 respectively (three-year averages in each case), with the various wholesale commodity indices available for this period.

was to become the most vulnerable of all British industries to foreign competition and trade recession. It was vulnerable both directly because it was sending an important proportion of its output overseas, and indirectly because a fall in the output of any power-using industry tended to involve a corresponding fall in the demand for coal. It was also vulnerable to technical innovation in other industries since many of the cost-reducing innovations which were adopted by hard-pressed British producers involved economy in the use of fuel.

The effect of this instability on the side of demand, combined with the inelasticity of supply and diminishing returns which were long-standing problems of the industry, can be seen in the fluctuating value of its product after about 1870. Coal prices varied so widely from one year to another that in a quarter of a century net output could range from about 5 per cent of national income in 1881 to about 3 per cent in 1886 and again to over 6 per cent in 1900 and about 4 per cent in 1905, although tonnage raised grew almost without interruption throughout this period and never fell by as much as 10 per cent (or grew by as much as 15 per cent) as between one year and another.

By the beginning of the twentieth century the mining industry employed nearly a million persons, compared with about 300,000 in 1851 and about 200,000 in 1841. Coal was then the only British mineral of importance. In 1907 the output of all mines and quarries covered by the Census of Production (excluding manufactured fuels) accounted for nearly $5\frac{1}{2}$ per cent of the national income of the United Kingdom, and of this more than 90 per cent was attributable to coal. Nearly half the pig-iron produced in the United Kingdom was made from foreign ores. Half a century earlier (in 1858) the mining and quarrying fraction of the national income may have amounted to as much as $3\frac{1}{2}$ per cent of the national income, but of this the coal-mining proportion was only 60 per cent, iron ore accounted for between 9 and 10 per cent, tin, copper and lead mines for about $12\frac{1}{2}$ per cent, and the other minerals (including stone, clay, etc.) for perhaps $18\frac{1}{2}$ per cent.

Coal has remained the major source of British mining incomes during the first half of the twentieth century and the problems which emerged during the last quarter of the nineteenth century largely persist. By 1913 nearly a third of the coal output of the United Kingdom went to foreign markets, but world output of coal was then eight times as large as it had been half a century before, whereas British output had merely trebled. After the First World War the competition in foreign markets and from other fuels developed rapidly. New economies were effected in the use of coal. World depression intensified the home-market recession which began late in 1929. Exports never recovered their pre-war levels and in recent years the net export of coal has been a negligible proportion of total output. By 1956 the proportion of national income earned in mining and quarrying was down to about 4 per cent, but it had been even lower (at about 3 per cent) in the interwar depression years.

3. THE IRON INDUSTRY

The iron industry was one of the leaders in the British industrial revolution which, like the cotton industry, was suddenly transformed in the last two decades of the eighteenth century. Cort's discovery (patented in the 1780's) made it possible to produce iron with coal for all purposes except steel-making, and Watt's steam engine (first installed for blasting in 1776) made generally available the strong blast necessary to the coke smelting process. From then on the industry rapidly escaped from dependence on foreign bar-iron and diminishing supplies of domestic timber and was able to use the relatively abundant British resources of iron ore and coal. The transition from charcoal to coke iron was almost complete by the end of the century.

Statistical evidence bearing on rates of growth in the iron industry at this period is imprecise, but the broad trends are clear enough. According to Schubert the number of coke furnaces in blast rose from seventeen in 1760 to fifty-three in 1788 and eighty-one in 1790.[1] By 1805 there were 177 furnaces in blast, most of them coke furnaces.[2] Total output of pig-iron seems to have rather more than doubled between *circa* 1760 and 1788, but in the next seventeen or eighteen years it roughly quadrupled.[3]

By the beginning of the nineteenth century, therefore, output of pig-iron seems to have been in the region of 250,000 tons.[4] The transition from charcoal to coal was more or less complete and imports of foreign bar-iron were falling rapidly. In the quinquennium 1801–5 retained imports of bar-iron averaged 31,000 tons per annum: in the following quinquennium the average fell below 19,000: in the decade 1787–96 the average had been over 45,000 tons.[5] The success of the new British iron is reflected in the growth of exports. In the quinquennium 1796–1800 these averaged roughly 45,000 tons of pig-iron (or pig-iron

---

[1] H. R. Schubert, *History of the British Iron and Steel Industry* (1957), p. 333. Apparently fourteen coke furnaces were erected in the 1760's and early 1770's.

[2] *Ibid.* p. 335. Scrivenor's figure (quoted by Ashton) is of 173 furnaces *circa* 1806, of which only 11 were charcoal furnaces. See H. Scrivenor, *History of the Iron Trade* (1854), p. 99. T. S. Ashton, *Iron and Steel in the Industrial Revolution* (1924), p. 98, footnote.

[3] The commonly quoted estimate for 1720 is 17,350 tons of pig-iron; and although recent researches suggest that there may have been some growth from then on, even the most generous interpretation of the evidence does not imply an estimate of more than 30,000 tons for *circa* 1760. See M. W. Flinn, 'The Growth of the English Iron Industry 1660–1760', *Econ. Hist. Rev.*, August 1958, for a recent survey of the evidence. For the 1788 and 1805 estimates see Schubert, *op. cit.* p. 335.

[4] This is the figure commonly accepted in the debate on the iron excise in the spring of 1806. See *Hansard Parliamentary Debates*, vol. VII (1806), 9 May. It seems to have been based on a return which has been variously reproduced by different authorities and generally attributed to 1806. See Scrivenor, *op. cit.* p. 99; Ashton *op. cit.* p. 98 (quoting Scrivenor); and R. Meade, *The Coal and Iron Industries of the United Kingdom* (1882), p. 834. Schubert is the only writer who has given an original source for his figure of 250,507 tons: he attributes it to the Boulton and Watt Collection (returns of 1805) in the Birmingham Reference Library.

[5] See the returns by Irving, *S.P. 1806*, vol. XII, and *S.P. 1814–15*, vol. X, and an Irving return of 1 March 1799 quoted by Macpherson, *op. cit.*, vol. III, p. 469.

equivalent), in the quinquennium 1801–5 over 52,000 tons and in the next three years over 67,000 tons.[1] Even the Navy began to drop its resistance to British coke iron in the middle of the first decade.[2]

The output figures are rough and different sources give varying figures for each region: but the totals given by the different sources are generally of the same order of magnitude, and since they are based on returns made by the ironmasters they are probably roughly reliable. When we try to convert them to value terms in order to measure them against national-income aggregates the difficulties are more serious. Essentially it is a problem of finding appropriate prices. The basic product, pig-iron, passes through a wide variety of finished forms (from fire-grates to cutlery) and of mixtures with other materials (such as tinplate or machinery). What we wanted as a starting-point was an approximation to the wholesale value of all commodities in which iron or steel was the principal component.

Our best source of information on prices of the products of the iron and steel trades at the beginning of the nineteenth century was Irving's figures of the 'real' or 'current' values of British iron and steel exports.[3] We used Irving's total 'real' values for exports, valued government consumption at the price paid by the Navy for its purchases of British iron,[4] and home consumption at average export prices for cast-iron, nails and wrought iron. This gave a rough figure for gross value of final product.

It was crude for several reasons. First of all because Irving's 'real' or 'current' values were clearly not current prices: at best they were an approximation to the average prevailing price for each main group considered.[5] Secondly because we were obliged to adopt arbitrary assumptions as to the proportions of the output cast and wrought

---

[1] *S.P. 1806*, vol. XII; *S.P. 1814–15*, vol. X. The export figures for 1809, 1810 and 1811 were destroyed by fire. Wrought iron has been converted to a pig-iron equivalent on the assumption that 1 ton of bar or wrought iron contained 33 cwt. of pig.

[2] *S.P. 1806*, vol. XII, for return of British and foreign iron tonnage consumed by the Navy (all yards except Deptford).

[3] Irving's 'real' values are set out in detail in *S.P. 1804*, vol. VIII. He applied them (at a constant level) to iron exports for the period 1796–1805 to get a set of real values for iron and steel exports distinguishing pig, bar, nails, wrought iron and hardware, ordnance and tinplate.

[4] *S.P. 1806*, vol. XII, *op. cit.*, for Navy purchases. Vansittart, in speeches on the Iron Duty Bill, estimated that government consumption of iron was 15,000–20,000 tons. We have taken it to be 20,000 tons. *Hansard Parliamentary Debates*, vol. VII (1806).

[5] The behaviour of current iron prices at this period is somewhat obscure. Tooke's pig-iron series, which is the only one we have going back before 1800, is astonishingly constant. Gayer, Rostow and Schwartz, *Growth and Fluctuation of the British Economy 1790–1850*, vol. II (1953), p. 845, attribute the constancy to 'the prevalence of price fixing in the industry. . . . From 1804–1816 the monopoly control of the pig-iron price appears to have been completely successful, for the price was absolutely constant during this period.' But control did not necessarily imply price fixity through time. Ashton, *Iron and Steel in the Industrial Revolution* (1924), p. 181, summarising the evidence in the minutes of meetings of the principal iron-masters of Yorkshire and Derbyshire, 1799–1928, writes: 'In the case of pig iron control appears to have been most completely exercised, and quarter by quarter the changes in demand were reflected in the value of each grade: between 1808 and 1824 for example the price of No. 1 pig was altered no fewer than 17 times and varied between £7 and £9 a ton.'

respectively.[1] Thirdly because the export values probably included merchants' profits and some of the shipping costs. On the other hand, we did not attempt to apply the prices of the more highly processed commodities, such as cutlery, which were relatively more important in the export trade than in the home trade.

The figure of £16·2 m. thus arrived at is more likely to overestimate than to underestimate the final gross value of products of the British iron and steel trades *circa* 1805.[2] It should be borne in mind, however, that it includes besides the output of mines, blast-furnaces and iron-works, the whole, or a large part, of the output of a wide range of manufacturers, from village smiths to Sheffield cutlers and makers of steam engines. Our estimates for the textile industries suggested a gross product of about £22 m. for woollen manufactures and about £18 m. for cottons *circa* 1805.[3] It is not surprising to find that iron and steel trades figured third on the list of British manufacturing trades, with a total gross product not far short of the cotton industry's.

Deducting estimates of the value of coal used in the manufacture and of the value of imported bar-iron[4] gives a figure of about £14·7 m. for the industry's net contribution to the national income. This includes the output of the iron mines and is larger than the value of the iron manufacture proper. On the assumption that the national income of Great Britain was in the region of £250 m. *circa* 1805 the iron industry, thus widely interpreted, contributed nearly 6 per cent of it. In these terms, that is in relation to the national income, it was of the same order of importance as the cotton industry and somewhat less important than the woollen industry if we include the value of British wool in the latter's net product.

There are no other plausible output estimates for the iron industry until 1818. From then until 1854, when the series compiled by the Inspectors of Mines and the Geological Survey begin, there are scattered contemporary estimates of pig-iron tonnage which cannot be depended upon to give more than orders of magnitude for total output. Partly because the industry was highly vulnerable to periods of boom and slump these early estimates for particular years must be used cautiously, even when they are reasonably well documented.[5] In Table 56 they are grouped, wherever possible, to give estimates which can be related to periods of about five years rather than to particular

---

[1] We assumed that 50 per cent of the iron consumed at home was cast and the remainder wrought and that 30 cwt. of pig-iron gave 20 cwt. bar or wrought iron. These proportions are based on contemporary estimates. See, especially, David Mushet, *Papers on Iron and Steel* (1840).

[2] The only contemporary estimate which we have for this period is Eden's figure of £6 m. for the final value of hardware and cutlery products only *circa* 1803.

[3] See above, pp. 196 and 185.

[4] Coal consumption was estimated at a little over 7 tons of coal per ton bar iron imported.

[5] Most of the contemporary estimates are reprinted in the following publications: Porter, *Progress of the Nation, op. cit.*; Richard Meade, *The Coal and Iron Industries of the United Kingdom* (1882); Isaac Lowthian Bell, *The Iron Trade of the United Kingdom* (1886); also in *S.P.*, vol. XXI (1886); *Annual Statistical Report of the Iron, Steel and Allied Trades Federation* (1916).

years. The later estimates, also given in quinquennial averages in Table 56, become less useful as indicators of the industry's volume of output as steel became a more important proportion of the final product, i.e. in the 1880's and later.

If its progress is assessed in terms of its output of pig-iron the British iron industry seems to have reached its peak rates of growth at, or a little before, mid-century. In the two decades between 1830–4 and 1850–4 annual pig-iron output quadrupled, giving a rate of growth comparable to that achieved in the two decades preceding 1805 when the transition from charcoal to coke iron was in progress. Rapid growth—involving at least a trebling of output every two decades—was maintained from the early 1820's until the early 1860's, though the iron industry's progress was always rather erratic. Moderate growth (at least a doubling of output every two decades) was maintained throughout the first three-quarters of the century. Thereafter growth became even more erratic and slowed rapidly. In the two decades ending 1900–4 pig-iron output increased by only 3 per cent: steel output, however, almost trebled. If account is taken of the improved quality of product that this involved (e.g. by weighting the steel and non-steel components at the prices of 1900–4) it would appear that there was an increase in real output of about 23 per cent between 1880–4 and 1900–4.[1]

An attempt to assess the weight of the iron industry in the national economy by putting a value on its product again raises the problem of finding appropriate prices. The problems of calculating the inputs and value of inputs of raw materials and of eliminating double counting are even more intractable. We were obliged to be content with a very rough measure of gross product, based on a selection of what seemed to be the most appropriate export prices; and a mere indicator of net output, arrived at by deducting the estimated value of coal consumed and imported ore from the gross product estimates.

The gross-product estimates are summarised in Table 56. They are intended to cover all products of the iron and steel industry (including the mining section) except the engineering, shipbuilding and vehicle trades. In fact they overstate the total, so defined, by double-counting some commodities which are the final product of one branch of the industry and the raw material of another. They may also, because they are based on export prices, overstate the fluctuations in values between periods of depression and periods of boom.

They are compared, in Table 56, with figures of exports of the principal iron and steel products distinguished in the trade statistics. This comparison suggests that during the first half of the nineteenth century the industry's growth was associated with a substantial growth of the home market for iron and steel goods, but that there was a sudden shift in the early 1850's to very much greater dependence on the export trade. In the last quarter of the century the growth of production for

[1] At the prices of 1880–4 the increase was over 50 per cent.

Table 56. *Growth of the iron and steel industry, 1805–1907*

Annual averages for	(1) Production of pig-iron (000 tons)	(2) Estimated value of gross product (£m.)	(3) Exports as percentage of gross product
Circa 1805	250	16·21	23·6[7]
Circa 1818	325	9·15	29·6[7]
1820–24	428[4]	11·01	21·4
1825–29	658[5]	17·89	16·5
1830–34	689[4]	13·78	22·7
1835–39	1,150[5]	22·72	21·5
1840–44	1,278[5]	19·06	28·5
1845–49	2,000[6]	34·44	24·1
1850–54	2,757[5]	35·72	38·7
1855–59	3,526	47·06	39·5
1860–64	4,152	54·37	40·5
1865–69	4,904	65·02	42·1
1870–74	6,378	113·51	40·5
1875–79	6,381	102·44	32·8
1880–84	8,366	122·36	37·2
1885–89	7,661	103·47	40·1
1890–94	7,285	112·20	38·5
1895–99	8,638	122·29	36·2
1900–04	8,639	123·85	42·0
1905–07	9,944	142·54	50·0

Sources: (1) From various sources (see footnote on p. 223). For the period before 1854 we used estimates relating to 1805, 1818, 1820, 1823, 1825, 1827, 1828, 1830, 1833, 1835, 1836, 1839, 1840, 1842, 1843, 1844, 1847, 1850, 1852.
   (2) Estimated by applying triennial average export values to output statistics and using results to extrapolate 1907 census figure.
   (3) Exports defined to include iron and steel, hardware and cutlery, tin-plate, machinery (after 1824), implements and tools (1839 onwards), telegraphic wire (1825 onwards). Quinquennial averages except where otherwise stated.
   (4) Two years only.
   (5) Three years only.
   (6) 1847 only.
   (7) Triennial averages centring on date specified.

the home market seems to have been negligible, although imports of iron and steel products increased nearly sixfold in quantity and more than threefold in value between 1870–4 and 1900–4.

It is not possible with the data presently available to make a satisfactory series of estimates of the industry's net contribution to the national income. However, we can arrive at a rough indicator of this net contribution by deducting from our gross-product series annual estimates of the value of coal and imported ore consumed by the industry each year.[1] The resulting totals are expressed in Table 57 as percentages of the national income at decennial intervals. They can be assumed to be in excess of the industry's true net contribution to national income.[2]

[1] Coal is certainly the industry's major raw material, but since economies in its use were occasionally of special importance it is not a good indicator of other raw-material inputs.

[2] The iron industry is here defined to include iron-ore mining and manufacturing of goods largely composed of iron, except vehicles.

Table 57. *Share of the iron industry in the national product of Great Britain, 1805–1907*

Circa	Gross output (less coal and imported ore) as percentage gross national product
1805	5·9
1818	3·4
1821	3·6
1831	3·6
1841	3·8
1851	6·2
1861	7·6
1871	11·6
1881	10·3
1891	7·5
1901	5·8
1907	6·4

Sources: Coal consumption estimated as a function of pig-iron output and valued at an estimated pithead price. Iron-ore products from the trade returns. These were deducted annually from our gross-product estimates, summarised by quinquennia and applied to national-income totals calculated in chapter v.

In the first decade of the nineteenth century when prices of iron and steel products were inflated by war conditions, and not yet reduced by falling costs due to the new techniques, average values were at record levels. They dropped rapidly in the post-war period, and the value of output—as grossly defined for the purposes of Table 57—fell from nearly 6 per cent of British national income *circa* 1805 to about 3½ per cent in the next three decades. The proportion began to rise markedly in the 1840's, which represented the height of the railway age in Britain, and in these relative terms the iron industry continued to grow in importance until the early 1870's. In absolute terms the 'nineteenth-century zenith' of output and exports was reached in 1882 when the relative rate of growth of the industry had already begun to slacken pace.[1]

The manufacturing section of the industry was then second only to cotton among British factory industries. In 1871 blast furnaces, iron-mills and foundries absorbed about 25 per cent of the steam power generated in factories and workshops in Great Britain and about 40 per cent of their adult male labour force.[2] During the quinquennium 1870–4 profits from ironworks accounted for over 17 per cent of the gross assessments under Schedule D: in 1875–9 the proportion was 14 per cent. Even in absolute terms assessed profits from ironworks never

---

[1] 'American railway building in 1879 and then world railway building swept the British iron and steel export breathlessly up to its nineteenth-century zenith in 1882.' D. L. Burn, *The Economic History of Steel Making, 1867–1939* (Cambridge, 1940), p. 73. 1882 was also the nineteenth-century peak for pig-iron output.

[2] *S.P. 1871*, vol. LXII. If we include establishments making ships, machinery, nails, bolts and screws, tiles, saws and tools, cutlery and locks, the proportion of steam power generated rises to 31 per cent and the proportion of adult male employees in factories and workshops to 78 per cent.

again reached the levels they attained in 1874 and 1875.[1] The earnings of labour were also relatively high in the early 1870's. The wages of puddlers in the Midlands, for example, rose from 8s. 6d. per ton in 1869 to 13s. 3d. in 1873, and were back to 7s. 6d. by 1878. The percentage unemployed in the ironfounders' trade union fell to the record low level of 1·4 per cent in 1872: there were only five other years during the whole of the period 1851–1903 when it dropped below 3 per cent.[2]

The mining branch of the industry also reached its peak in the early 1870's. In 1873 the value of ore produced from British mines exceeded £7½ m., a level which it never reached again until the post-First World War inflation. By the beginning of the twentieth century the product of British iron-ore was worth only half what it had been towards the end of the third quarter of the nineteenth.

In sum, the evidence suggests the following trends for the British iron industry. After its sudden rise to prominence at the end of the eighteenth and very beginning of the nineteenth century, the industry grew slowly, if at all, in the later Napoleonic War and immediate post-war years, expanded more or less in step with the rest of the economy in the 1820's and 1830's, when it accounted for rather less than 3½ per cent of national income, and grew rapidly in the 1840's, and more rapidly in the 1860's to reach its high relative importance of the 1870's. At that stage we have tentatively estimated that direct incomes earned in all branches of the iron industry amounted to something like 10 per cent of the national income of Great Britain. By the turn of the century the share seems to have roughly halved.

In the international context the decline in the relative importance of the British iron industry was, of course, more marked. British pig-iron, which had accounted for more than half of the world supply in 1870, had fallen to only 20 per cent by 1901: and for British steel the fall over the same period was from 43 per cent to 16 per cent.[3] The industry was losing ground to foreign competitors even in the home market. Imports of iron and steel manufactures were by the early 1900's running at levels of between a quarter and a third of British exports of iron and steel goods, instead of the 5 to 10 per cent levels which had prevailed in the early 1870's.

The evidence on capital formation is a good deal less accessible than the output data. Some impression of the pace of capital formation can be gained by examining the figures available on numbers of furnaces in existence. For blast furnaces the figures are given in Table 58.[4] The number in existence appears to have been growing at the rate of fifteen or sixteen per annum on the late 1820's and by as many as twenty-seven per annum in the 1850's. They reached their maximum in 1875, by which time 959 had been built, but numbers actually in

---

[1] The assessments were based on the profits of the preceding year.

[2] Board of Trade, *Second Series of Memoranda, Statistical Tables and Charts on British and Foreign Trade and Industrial Conditions* (Cmd. 2337, 1904), p. 87.

[3] British Iron and Steel Federation Yearbook, *Statistics of the Iron and Steel Industries* (1936).

[4] It would, of course, be naïve to regard these as an investment series for they take no account of the considerable changes in capacity of the typical blast furnace over this period.

Table 58. *Numbers of blast furnaces, 1806–1910*

	Totals built	of which in blast
1806	216	161
1823	266	250
1830	372	300
1839	538	396
1847	623	433
1852	655	497
1855	763	589
1860	872	582
1865	919	657
1870	923	664
1875	959	629
1880	924	567
1884	908	575
1890	n.a.	349
1895	n.a.	344
1900	n.a.	403
1905	n.a.	345
1910	n.a.	336

Source: British Iron and Steel Federation Yearbook, *Statistics of the Iron and Steel Industries* (1939).

blast did not rise above 683 (in 1873) and by the first decade of the twentieth century (taking an average of those in blast in each year 1901–10) they were only half the 1873 peak. The expansion which took place in the second and third quarters were associated with the development of new fields of coal or of ore (in Scotland in the 1830's, in the Cleveland ore-field in the 1850's and in the Cumberland-Lancashire field in the 1860's). In the last quarter of the century, however, the industry showed markedly less tendency to move into new areas, in response to changes in the availability of raw material, and what redistribution did occur developed more slowly than in the past.[1]

Investment in puddling furnaces also increased sharply in the third quarter of the century. Between 1860 and 1870 the number of puddling furnaces had increased from 3,452 to 6,699, and in spite of the indications that many of them were to be rendered obsolete by the substitution of steel for malleable iron they numbered 7,575 by 1875. Many of these enterprises were short-lived, however, and by 1884 there were only 4,577 in existence, 'and of these many were idle'.[2] Investment in steel equipment there certainly was in the fourth quarter, but it seems to have been slow not only by comparison with the past record of the

[1] See Howard G. Roepke, 'Movements of the British Iron and Steel Industry, 1720–1951', *Illinois Studies in the Social Sciences*, vol. XXXVI (Urbane, 1956).

[2] See Lowthian Bell's evidence to the Committee on the Depression in Industry and Trade. *S.P. 1886*, vol. XXI. Cf. also T. H. Burnham and G. O. Hoskins: 'The period under review saw the wrought iron industry reach its zenith but already doomed by the advent of the large-scale steel making process. The struggle was not, however, given up without fighting to the bitter end and money was spent liberally to put the industry on an economic basis. Between 1875 and 1885 £4,660,000 capital was invested in puddling furnaces, but it was nearly all lost.' *Iron and Steel in Britain 1870–1930*, p. 162.

British industry but even more by comparison with foreign countries. In the eighties and nineties, according to Burn, 'the rate of modernising was as certainly less in Great Britain than in the States or the continent, as the volume of innovation was less, if modernising be measured by the proportion of output handled by modern methods'.[1] And at the beginning of the twentieth century there was stagnation not only of production and foreign trade but also of structure. Works important in 1904 had been already important in 1880 and for the most part had grown little since.[2]

In short the evidence suggests a marked expansion in new investment in the iron industry in the second, and even more in the third quarter of the century, followed by at best a maintenance of existing capacity if not a tendency to reduce investments in the fourth quarter.

4. THE TRANSPORT INDUSTRY

The growth of transport in the United Kingdom had its direct impact on the national income in two main ways.[3] First, because investment in new means of transport stimulated the building, contracting, iron and engineering industries; and secondly, because the creation of new transport capacity led to an increase in the output of transport services. The construction phase was a dominant feature of British economic growth and fluctuations in the second quarter of the nineteenth century; the direct expansion of transport services assumed some importance in the second half. Partly because the data on construction are on the whole more accessible than the data on net output, but also because the various construction booms came at a time when their absolute weight in the national economy made them especially significant, we shall be concerned largely in this section with the pace of expenditure on new investment in transport rather than with the increase in the output of transport services.

(a) The railway industry

For the first quarter of the nineteenth century iron railway construction was limited to small-scale localised railroads operated by horse power or by stationary engines. Those that went beyond the bounds of a private estate and were more than adjuncts to a mine or ironworks required an Act of Parliament, so that there is some record of their length and of their costs of construction. Francis lists twenty-nine of these small local railways built in the first twenty-five years of the century.[4] Only the Stockton and Darlington Railway, opened in 1825,

---

[1] D. L. Burn, *op. cit.* p. 185.   [2] *Ibid.* p. 219.

[3] The indirect consequences of the growth of transport—the reduction in costs and prices for other sectors of the economy—are not considered here; but they made an important contribution to the British rate of economic growth towards the end of the nineteenth century.

[4] J. Francis, *A History of the English Railway: its Social Relations and Revelations, 1820–45*, vol. 1 (1845), pp. 57–64. G. Porter, *Progress of the Nation* (1847 ed.), pp. 329–32, has a similar list. These lists show mileages opened at 1845 or thereabouts, and hence, for the lines in operation by 1825, they include some extensions made after 1825.

exceeded twenty-five miles in length, though important extensions to existing lines were projected and in some cases carried through eventually.

By the end of 1825 there were between 300 and 400 miles of iron railroad in the United Kingdom, representing a total capital investment of probably less than £1½ m.[1] The opening of the Stockton–Darlington line, the first to be designed for steam traction and for passenger traffic, was the beginning of the railway era, although it took time still for the new form of transport to develop. Horse-drawn coaches were used for passenger traffic on the Stockton–Darlington line for some years, and even in 1840 there were several public lines dependent entirely on horse traction or on stationary engines.

Railway companies were an important constituent of the promotion 'mania' of 1825. According to Francis, 'A capital of £21,942,500 was demanded for railways in 1824–5 on which £219,425 was actually paid: what became of the money it would be difficult now to say though there cannot be a doubt that to the great mania of 1825 England is indebted for her railway system'.[2] The collapse of the boom brought a more subdued atmosphere to the railway capital market but in the next five years (1826–30) 287 miles and a capital of over £4 m. were sanctioned by Parliament and 71 miles were opened to traffic. Expenditure on railroad construction was not far short of £1½ m. in this quinquennium and the capital invested in the railways by the end of 1830, including private railroads, was probably between £2½ and £3 m. By the end of 1840 the value of capital invested in railways, including land, parliamentary expenses and ancillary businesses, was near £48 m[3] of which perhaps 8 per cent represented the value of rolling stock.[4]

Table 59 indicates the phasing of this stage in the railway construction boom. Figures of mileages sanctioned and opened and of capital authorised derive originally from Bills or Acts of Parliament relative to railways. There are numerous published contemporary analyses of these, some of which differ slightly from the figures in Table 59 because of differences in the method of attributing the Bills or Acts of a particular session to the year in which they were introduced or passed. Dr Mitchell's estimates of capital expenditures give a picture of the distribution of railway investment through time.

The impact on the U.K. economy of expenditure on railway construction began to be significantly large in the second half of the thirties and rose to a crescendo a decade later. By the triennium

---

[1] Estimated from contemporary lists. [2] Francis, *op. cit.*, vol. 1, p. 135.
[3] Estimated from data given by F. Whishaw, *The Railways of Great Britain and Ireland* (London, 1840); J. S. Jeans, *The Jubilee Memorial of the Railway System* (London, 1875); W. L. Steel, *The History of the London and Northwestern Railway* (London, 1914); C. J. Allen, *The Great Eastern Railway* (London, 1955); and from material in *S.P. 1839*, vol. x, and *S.P. 1846*, vol. xiv.
[4] B. R. Mitchell has compiled from company accounts annual estimates of gross capital formation by U.K. railway companies distinguishing expenditures on permanent way, rolling stock, ancillary business and land. See his 'The coming of the Railway and United Kingdom Economic Growth,' *Journal of Economic History*, September 1964.

Table 59. *United Kingdom railway investment, 1800–46*

Years (inclusive	(1) Mileage sanctioned	(2) Mileage opened to traffic	(3) Capital authorised (£m.)	(4) Expenditure on railway capital formation	
				(a) Totals (£m.)	(b) Per annum (£m.)
1800–20	—	190	—⎫	1·5	—
1821–25	62	27	—⎭		
1826–30	287	71	4·0	1·0	0·2
1831–37	2,120	443	51·4	11·5	1·6
1838–40	104	957	11·0	27·4	9·1
1841–43	160	546	12·6	14·9	5·0
1844–46	8,043	1,084	207·0	50·2	16·7

Sources: (1) H. G. Lewin, *Early British Railways* (London, 1825) for figures to 1844.
(2) H. G. Lewin, *op. cit.*, for figures to 1844. *S.R. 1847–8*, vol. XXVI (Report of Commissioner of Railways 1847–8), for 1845–6.
(3) G. Porter, *Progress of the Nation* (1847 ed.), p. 332, for figures to 1845. *S.P. 1857–8*, vol. LI, for 1846. These figures are not additive.
(4) Estimated from contemporary lists up to 1830. Later figures from B. R. Mitchell, *op. cit.* They exclude land and parliamentary expenses.

1838–40 expenditure on construction and railway stock was running at a rate of over £9 m. per annum. By 1844–6 (after a recession to half the 1838–40 level in 1841–3) it had risen to an annual rate of over £16½ m., which was roughly 3 per cent of the national income and over 28 per cent of the declared value of U.K. produce exported. The higher rate of expenditure in 1844–6, as compared with 1838–40, was inflated by the construction of Scottish and Irish railways which developed a few years later than the English network. In Scotland, the 1844–6 expenditure was almost twice as high as the 1838–40 expenditure, and in Ireland, where it was negligible in the earlier triennium, the 1844–6 rate of expenditure had expanded by a factor of about thirty.

Capital raised by the railway companies in the triennium 1844–6 was £58·8 m. of which £37·8 m. (representing between 6 and 7 per cent of the national income) was raised in 1846.[1] By this time (year ending June 1846) total traffic receipts were running at over £7½ m. per annum.[2]

The great railway construction peak, however, was in 1847, when more than a quarter of a million men were employed in constructing 6,455 miles of railways. A further 47,218 persons were engaged in operating them, so that a total of over 300,000 persons were directly

[1] *S.P. 1847–8*, vol. XXVI.
[2] *Ibid.* Total traffic receipts for the year ended 30 June 1843 were £4·5 m.: for 1843–44 they were £5·1 m. for 1844–5, £6·2 m., and for 1845–6, £7·6 m. These are less than the true totals since not all the companies made returns. For *circa* 1840, figures given by Whishaw, *op. cit.*, suggest that the annual rate of revenue from traffic receipts was rather more than £2·1 m.

employed in the railway boom. This was at a time when the total gainfully occupied population (males and females) was in the region of 12 million persons. In 1847 alone *total* railway expenditure exceeded £52 m., which was not far short of the declared value of U.K. domestic exports and approached a tenth of the total national income. In the three years 1847–9 an average of nearly 1,000 miles of new railway line were opened annually.

By the end of 1850, 6,621 miles of railway line were open to traffic. In that year for the first time there were rather more persons employed in operating railways than in constructing them and in the following year total traffic receipts exceeded the total increase in paid-up capital for the first time. It was in the late 1850's that operating profits began to be of the same order of magnitude as the annual

Table 60. *The growth of the railway industry, 1845–60*

	Construction activity			Operating activity		
	(1)	(2)	(3)	(4)	(5)	(6)
	Mileage under construction (mid-year)	Numbers employed (mid-year) (000)	Annual gross capital formation (£m.)	Mileage open (mid-year)	Numbers employed (mid-year) (000)	Traffic receipts (£m.)
1845	—	—	13·0	—	—	6·2
1846	—	—	30·2	—	—	7·6
1847	6,455	257	43·9	3,505	47	8·5
1848	2,958	188	33·1	4,252	53	9·9
1849	1,504	104	24·9	5,447	56	11·8
1850	864	59	13·1	6,308	60	13·2
1851	734	43	9·9	6,698	64	15·0
1852	738	36	9·7	7,076	68	15·7
1853	682	38	10·2	7,512	80	18·0
1854	889	45	12·7	7,803	90	20·2
1855	880	39	11·3	8,116	98	21·5
1856	963	36	9·0	8,506	102	23·2
1857	1,004	44	9·6	8,942	110	24·2
1858	1,014	38	9·3	9,324	109	24·0
1859	993	40	9·9	8,796	116	25·7
1860	1,051	54	11·0	10,201	127	27·8

Sources: (1), (2), (4) and (5)—*S.P. 1847–8,* vol. XXVI; *S.P. 1857–8,* vol. LI, and later returns in the same series of returns to Parliament. (3) from Mitchell, *op. cit.* p. 335.

(6)—*Statistical Abstracts* for figures 1847 onwards; *S.P. 1847–8,* vol. XXVI, for 1845–6. Figures in column (3) are of the total gross capital formation of the railway companies.

increase in capital invested in the railways. This decade of the fifties saw the end of the railway construction boom and the growth in the importance of the railways as an industry in their own right. Table 60 illustrates the period of transition.

Construction activity on the railways never again played as large a role in the U.K. economy as it had done in the late 1840's, although there were later bursts of activity due to special circumstances. There was a notable burst, for example, in the 1860's when the mileage of lines opened annually to traffic again exceeded an average of 500 and the peak capital expenditure reached £28 millions in 1865. Another upsurge of expenditure took place in the mid-1970's when the iron rail was in process of conversion to the steel rail. After 1870 no important new long line was constructed, but the work of adding branches and link lines went on, though at a decelerating rate, and in the 1880's involved such major construction projects as the Severn Tunnel and the Forth Bridge. In the last decade or so of the century there was increasing expenditure on widening the capacity of the system, on replacing the broad gauge sections of the Great Western with the standard narrow gauge that would link it effectively with the rest of the railway system, on extending the four-track mileage and on improving locomotives and coaches.

Operational activity on the railways climbed throughout the century whether measured in terms of traffic receipts, working expenses or operating profits. Table 61 illustrates the development of the railway

Table 61. *Development of the railway industry in the second half of the nineteenth century*

(in annual averages for each decade)

	Gross capital formation (£m.)	Lines opened (miles)	Traffic receipts (£m.)	Operating profit (£m.)	Estimated net output (£m.)
1845–54	20·1	587	12·6	(6·5)	8·9
1850–59	10·5	397	20·1	(10·5)	14·3
1855–64	13·4	474	26·9	14·1	19·2
1860–69	18·1	514	34·6	17·6	24·4
1865–74	18·2	366	44·9	21·8	31·0
1870–79	18·7	255	55·4	25·3	37·3
1875–84	19·5	242	62·9	28·6	42·3
1880–89	16·5	225	67·4	30·9	45·5
1885–94	15·7	204	73·5	32·1	48·7
1890–99	19·0	176	83·2	33·8	53·4

Sources: Statistical Abstracts for figures 1854 onwards. *S.P. 1857–8*, vol. LI, for previous years. Working expenses are available from 1854 onwards, so they were estimated as a proportion of traffic receipts for the earlier years and the operating profit is therefore given here in brackets. Gross capital formation from B. R. Mitchell, *op. cit.*

industry in the second half of the nineteenth century. The last column of this table is a crude attempt to measure the growth in net output of the industry, on the assumption that it was roughly equivalent to 40 per cent of working expenses plus total operating profit throughout the half-century.

(b) Shipping

The tonnage statistics of registered shipping go back to the end of the eighteenth century, and since the industry was of considerable strategic importance there is a good deal of price and value information available in the parliamentary reports of the nineteenth century. An attempt to convert these data into series indicative of the levels and trends of activity attributable to the shipping industry is shown in Table 62.

The first column of this table represents an attempt to measure the annual value of new British ships built during each decade of the nineteenth century. It was obtained by applying an estimated average value per ton of new ships to the published figures of sail and steam tonnage built and registered in the United Kingdom. The growth in relative importance of steam and iron ships meant an expansion of the foreign market for British built ships and the series in column 2 takes

Table 62. *The growth of the United Kingdom shipping industry*

(annual averages in millions of pounds)

	(1) Value tonnage built and registered in United Kingdom	(2) Value tonnage built in United Kingdom	(3) Net shipping earnings from the rest of the world
1795–1804	2·0	2·1	n.a.
1800–09	2·2	2·3	n.a.
1805–14	2·5	2·6	n.a.
1810–19	2·7	2·9	n.a.
1815–24	1·9	2·0	9·7
1820–29	1·7	1·8	9·3
1825–34	1·9	2·0	9·9
1830–39	2·1	2·2	11·2
1835–47	2·5	2·6	12·9
1840–49	2·5	2·7	14·6
1845–54	3·2	3·5	16·5
1850–59	4·7	5·2	20·6
1855–64	6·8	7·9	28·6
1860–69	8·8	9·9	37·5
1865–74	11·6	14·6	46·6
1870–79	13·0	16·3	51·1
1875–84	14·9	17·9	56·6
1880–89	13·8	17·1	58·7
1885–94	11·6	14·5	57·3
1890–99	12·4	16·0	59·1
1895–1904	14·0	18·7	64·1
1900–08	16·7	22·6	75·7

Sources: (1) Figures of tonnages built and registered in the United Kingdom, *S.P. 1806*, vol. XII; *S.P. 1814–15*, vol. VIII; *S.P. 1852*, vol. XLIX, and *S.P. 1909*, vol. CII. Estimates of construction costs 1830–1938 based on estimates by K. Maywald in 'The Construction Costs and the Value of the Merchant Fleet', *Scottish Journal of Political Economy*, vol. III (February 1956), p. 50: we related Maywald's figures of total cost per ton to the new steamer tonnages and of hull cost per ton to the sailing-ship tonnages, after converting to net tonnage equivalents on the assumption that net registered tonnage was two-thirds of gross registered tonnage per steamer and 95 per cent for sailing-ships.

(2) For the basic tonnage figures 1858–1908 see *S.P. 1909*, vol. CII: the estimates for earlier years are extrapolated in relation to the tonnages built and registered in the U.K. and on the assumption that exports of sailing-ships were of negligible importance. Values estimated as for column 1.

(3) Decade averages calculated from the annual series of net shipping earnings in Albert H. Imlah, *Economic Elements in the Pax Britannica*, pp. 70–5. Includes freight charges on imports and exports (net of expenses incurred abroad) but does not include coasting trade: based on British registered tonnage figures of sail and steam adjusted in accordance with total British entries in each category and an index of freight rates.

some account of this by measuring the total value of ships built in the United Kingdom whether registered there or not. Since tonnage built for foreigners was not distinguished until the 1850's this involved estimating the proportionate annual tonnages sold to foreigners for the first half of the century. The third column summarises Professor Imlah's estimates of net shipping earnings, i.e. 'the credits due to the United Kingdom after allowing for the expenditure of British shipping abroad'.[1] It may be regarded as an indicator (though not an estimate) of the direct contribution of the shipping industry to the national income.

Measuring these estimates against the corresponding national-income figures illustrates the relative importance of the industry at different periods of the nineteenth century. At the beginning of the century the annual value of investment in new shipping was probably not much more than one-half of 1 per cent of the national income of the United Kingdom. The net value of the shipbuilding industry's output was probably less than this even if we allow for ship repair services. In relative terms shipbuilding does not seem to have advanced appreciably until the second half of the century. It may have declined somewhat in the period after the Napoleonic Wars. The value of ships constructed began to rise markedly in the late 1840's when iron ships began to be built in increasing numbers; by the 1860's the annual value of tonnage built and registered in the United Kingdom exceeded 1 per cent of the national income. This was still the age of sailing-ships, however. Not until the 1870's did new steamship tonnages begin to overtake new sailing-ship tonnages. The shipbuilding industry appears to have reached the peak of its relative importance in the decade 1875–84 when the estimated value of new ships built in the United Kingdom exceeded 1·6 per cent of the national income. In this decade less than 30 per cent of the new tonnage was under sail. But by then nearly 17 per cent of the total value of new construction was for foreign owners, a proportion which had risen to over a quarter in the first decade of the twentieth century.

In sum, therefore, the rate of investment in and construction of new ships began to accelerate in the 1840's. Between the decades 1845–54 and 1855–64 the value of new construction more than doubled. It was still growing faster than national income in the 1860's and 1870's, but it slumped sharply—in absolute as well as in relative terms—in the late 1880's. It was expanding again at the turn of the twentieth century but not as rapidly as before, and it did not again reach the levels of relative importance that it had achieved in the 1870's.

The series for net shipping earnings also shows its maximum rate of expansion in the 1850's and 1860's but it reached and passed its peak less abruptly. The expansion began in the 1830's and the setback of the late 1880's represented only a small fall in absolute values. Net shipping earnings are not equivalent to net output of shipping services

[1] Albert H. Imlah, *op. cit.*

since they exclude the coasting trade and include stores and services purchased from British sources. Nevertheless, it seems reasonable to deduce from this series that shipping services made their major contribution to the national income in the decade 1875–84. In that decade net shipping earnings, which averaged between 4 and 5 per cent of the United Kingdom national income for most of the fifty years beginning 1860, exceeded 5 per cent.

Investment in ships involved investment in docks and harbours which it would take much detailed research to evaluate fully. Some indication of its chronological distribution, however, is provided by data made accessible by other investigators. London Docks were largely rebuilt in the first quarter of the century. The sums authorised for expenditure on them in the period 1799–1815 amounted in all to £5·4 m.[1] It has been estimated that total new capital expenditure on British docks and harbours exceeded £8 m. in the first two decades of the nineteenth century. The dock area of Liverpool was more than doubled between 1825 and 1846, and in Hull (the third British port) the area was almost trebled between 1863 and 1885.[2] According to a parliamentary return published in 1876, a total of over £9½ m. was spent by government on the harbours of the United Kingdom in the first three-quarters of the nineteenth century.[3] Of this about half was spent between 1850 and 1870 and nearly a quarter between 1812 and 1832. In the peak decade of the 1850's public expenditure on U.K. harbours averaged over £300,000 per annum.

(c) Other transport

The main impetus towards investment in roads and canals came in the early decades of the industrial revolution. In the case of roads it seems likely that a slowly developing improvement preceded the beginnings of rapid economic growth by several decades. The pace of new investment in roads during the eighteenth century can be gauged, for example, from the statistics of the Road Acts which were involved in the establishment of Turnpike Trusts and which generally signified increased expenditure on road maintenance. In the first half of the eighteenth century these Acts were being passed at the rate of about eight a year. Between 1750 and 1770 there were more than forty a year, in the next two decades slightly less, between 1791 and 1810 the average was over fifty, and between 1810 and 1830 over sixty a year.

An analysis of the Acts by regions affected, and a comparison with the corresponding regional areas, indicates that in the first half of the eighteenth century the new Trusts were relatively concentrated in the home counties (Middlesex, Kent, Surrey, Sussex, Hampshire, Berk-

---

[1] Walter Stern, 'The First London Dock Boom and the Growth of the West India Docks', *Economica* (1953).

[2] See Phyllis Deane, 'Capital Formation in Britain before the Railway Age', *Economic Development and Cultural Change* (1961). See also (Clapham *op. cit.*, vol. II, p. 522).

[3] *S.P. 1876*, vol. LXV.

shire, Oxfordshire, Bedfordshire, Hertfordshire); indeed, the south-eastern counties had more than their share of this kind of activity throughout the period 1700–1830.[1] Between 1750 and 1790 the midland counties (including Derbyshire, Staffordshire, Warwickshire, Nottinghamshire, Northamptonshire, Shropshire and Leicestershire) were responsible for 23 per cent of the Road Acts and less than 7 per cent of the area of England. It was not until the process of industrialisation was in full swing, between 1790 and 1830, that the Road Acts began to affect Yorkshire, Lancashire and Cheshire to an extent that was out of proportion to their joint area. By the 1830's the railway age had begun and expenditure on roads attracted a diminishing proportion of the national resources until the advent of motor transport in the twentieth century.

Evidence on actual amounts spent on the roads is inadequate and scattered. It has been estimated that over £2 m. was spent on road repairs by Turnpike Trusts alone in 1809.[2] In addition there was the national expenditure on highways (£1·3 m. in England and Wales in 1812 and £1·454 m. in 1814) and the county rate expenditure on highways and bridges. An attempt to extract from the parliamentary returns and other sources[3] details of all kinds of expenditure on the roads and bridges of the United Kingdom suggests that by 1813 it may have been in the region of £3½ m., and in 1821 over £3·0 m. In the 1830's and 1840's expenditure on roads was generally in the region of £3½ m. and rose very slowly thereafter, so that by the beginning of the twentieth century (1908–9) it was still only about £5·2 m. In effect, therefore, it was during the first quarter of the nineteenth century when expenditure on roads and bridges probably averaged between £3 m. and £3½ m. per annum that they absorbed an important proportion of U.K. resources, perhaps over 1 per cent of the national income.

The construction of the British canal system also took place largely between 1760 and 1830. The first modern canals were the Sankey Brook, from the St. Helens' coalfield to the Mersey, opened in 1757, and the Duke of Bridgewater's from the Worsley mines to Manchester opened in 1761.[4] There was a small burst of canal-building activity in the 1760's and early 1770's followed by a lull and then a spectacular burst of activity in the 1790's. There was another minor boom in the

[1] An analysis of Road and Canal Acts by time and region is given in W. T. Jackman, *op. cit.*, vol. I, p. 743. Probably they provide a better indication of the location of capital and enterprise available for investment in roads than of the volume of industrial traffic using them.

[2] Charles Singer, E. J. Holmyard, A. R. Hall and Trevor I. Williams, *op. cit.*, vol. IV, p. 530, in an article by R. J. Forbes. This, however, seems rather high, even allowing for the wartime wage inflation.

[3] See, especially, *S.P. 1818*, Vol. XVI; *S.P. 1834*, Vol. XIV; *S.P. 1836*, Vol. XIX; *S.P. 1833*, Vol. XV; *S.P. 1840*, Vol. XXVII; *S.P. 1852–3*, Vol. XCVII; and for Ireland, *S.P. 1931*, Vol. XVII; *S.P. 1831–2*, Vol. XVII; *S.P. 1860*, Vol. XXXVIII. Also *Life of Thomas Telford*, edited by John Rickman (1838), for Highland roads and bridges.

[4] Singer, Holmyard, Hall and Williams, vol. IV, *op. cit.* p. 563, in an article by Charles Hadfield. 'In 1750 there were over 1,000 miles of navigable river in Great Britain, and in 1850 about 4,250 miles of inland navigation in addition to a considerable mileage in Ireland.'

late 1830's and 1840's as existing canals were extended and new ones built to link up with the new railway system.

The canals were extensively documented in the contemporary literature, both in parliamentary and other sources. Numerous calculations of their global cost exist—based on such data as average cost per mile or capital authorised—neither of which bases provides a satisfactory starting-point for overall estimates covering an extended period of time. Costs of construction, for example, varied widely as between one decade or district and another and between one canal and another; while capital authorised for particular canals might bear little relation either to total capital called upon to total spent on construction. We have estimated, tentatively, that between *circa* 1755 and *circa* 1835 about £20 m. was spent on the construction and improvement of British inland navigation, of which perhaps £2½–3 m. before 1790, between £5 and £6 m. in the 1790's under the influence of the canal mania, and the remaining £11 m. or so in the period 1801–35.[1]

(d) All transport

The development of substantial new transport facilities, which absorbed at times a considerable proportion of the nation's resources, was a distinctive feature of the growing economy of the nineteenth century. To assess the overall impact of these developments we attempted to aggregate the estimates for different sectors. In the present state of our knowledge the attempt must be subject to serious reservations. There is no way of directly estimating expenditure on road and canal vehicles (coaches, wagons, barges, etc.) and our information on construction is clearly incomplete. Aggregation of the estimates referred to in the preceding sections is thus likely to understate gross transport expenditure.[2] Nor, since the data at our disposal was more plentiful for some periods than others, is the understatement likely to be consistent as between one decade and another.

For what they are worth, however, estimates based on the incomplete data examined so far suggest the following broad conclusions:

1. The provision of new or improved transport facilities absorbed under 2 per cent of gross national expenditure in Great Britain at the end of the eighteenth century and beginning of the nineteenth. In

---

[1] See Deane, 'Capital Investment in Great Britain before the Railway Age', *op. cit.*, for the bases of these estimates. It should be noted that much higher estimates have been made. Rennie, for example, in a calculation quoted by Urquhart A. Forbes and W. H. R. Ashford in *Our Waterways* (1908), pp. 135–6, estimated that by 1839 a total of £30·7 m. had been spent in Britain on improving inland navigation and constructing canals. Possibly this was the source of Samuel Salt's frequently quoted figure of £31 m.: see *Statistics and Calculations* (1845), p. 87, though the latter relates it to the period 1760–1824. At any rate, we came to the conclusion, after examining published data for individual canals, that these estimates were too high.

[2] We were trying to obtain as close an approximation as possible to gross capital formation in transport but it was not possible to distinguish capital from maintenance expenditure for roads.

earlier decades the proportion must have been a good deal less. At this stage expenditure on communications was concentrated largely on roads, ships, canals and docks—in that order of importance.

2. Expenditure on railways became the most important component in the total during the 1830's, and at the peak of their construction boom (1847–8) they involved an aggregate outlay which approached 10 per cent of United Kingdom national income. By the 1840's the expansion of transport facilities probably accounted for more than half of gross domestic fixed capital formation.

3. The peak for all transport seems to have been reached in the 1870's which saw the mass conversion of railways to steel and of ships to steam. For that decade our rough total for capital expenditure on transport approached 4 per cent of the national income of Great Britain. The sailing-ship tonnage did not fall below the steamer tonnage until 1882 and new ships accounted for about half of our estimated total transport expenditure in the 1880's.

4. By the 1890's the massive expenditures on transport were being reduced. At the turn of the century it is unlikely that the total amounted to much more than 2 per cent of British national income.

The impact of the nineteenth century developments in communications on the growing British economy is only partially reflected, however, in measures of the flow of expenditures on new transport facilities. The industry took a steadily increasing proportion of national income— how much larger we cannot say, but it is relevant that the trade and transport group of industries were estimated to have expanded their share of British national product from about 17 per cent at the beginning of the century to about 23 per cent at the end: the bulk of the sharp increase from about $19\frac{1}{2}$ per cent *circa* 1861 to 22 per cent *circa* 1871 seems to have been due to the transport group. The industry contributed to the growth of national output not only by virtue of its own productivity increases but also by reducing the costs of other industries. Between 1820 and 1866 the cost of carriage of bulky goods halved for hauls served by railway.[1] Between the quinquennia centring on 1871 and 1911 respectively, for example, the Isserlis index shows a fall of over 40 per cent in tramp-shipping freights.[2]

In effect it was the multiplicity of its linkages with the rest of the economy that gave the transport industry its key role in British economic growth. It might indeed be said to have played not one but a series of parts in the process. In the early stages of the industrial revolution the developments in transport were crucial in unifying the economy and in lifting the barriers to urbanisation. The replacement of the pack-horse by the wagon, the barge and the regular coaching service, and the reduction of journey time on the main highways by 1830 to between a third and a fifth of what it had been in 1750, transformed the national

---

[1] *S.P. 1867*, vol. xxxviii, Pt. I, gives comparative data for Bristol–London and Birmingham–London at selected dates.

[2] L. Isserlis, 'Tramp Shipping Cargoes and Freights', *J. Roy. Statist. Soc.*, 1938, p. 122.

pattern of economic opportunity without appreciably increasing the industry's share in the national income or its claim on the national capital. With the development of the railway and the iron steamship in the middle decades of the nineteenth century the industry entered upon another role. Its massive expenditures demanded new levels of capital formation and directly stimulated the growth of large-scale heavy industries—themselves highly capital-intensive. When the railway system had been largely built and the shipping fleet largely converted from sail to steam the industry played yet another part and its influence was again reflected more in the growth of national output than of national capital. It is difficult to overestimate the contribution of the transport industry in promoting the great specialisation of the nineteenth century and in reducing costs of production and consumer prices within the United Kingdom.

By the beginning of the twentieth century the transport and communications group of industries were estimated to account for about 10 per cent of the national product of Great Britain.[1] By the 1920's with the new developments in road transport its share had grown to about 12 per cent. Probably it was then at the peak of its direct importance in the national economy. But even in the recent post-war period, when its share has dropped below 8 per cent, it still exerts powerful direct and indirect pressures on the shape of economic development. The growth of the motor industry, for example, has been a significant feature of the changing pattern of British industry and British exports in the mid-twentieth century.

[1] See above, Tables 37 and 41, for estimates of the distribution of national product in the twentieth century.

CHAPTER VII

LONG-TERM TRENDS IN THE FACTOR COMPOSITION OF NATIONAL INCOME

So far our analysis of the process of economic growth has been focused largely on the industry composition of British national product. In this chapter we propose to examine the material from another vantage point and to consider its factor composition. It is well known that there are insuperable difficulties in the way of measuring factor shares so that they approximate at all closely to the 'pure' factor incomes of economic theory. Although modern national-income calculations generally distinguish income from employment, there remains, for example, a question of imputing to labour its share of the earnings of self-employed persons. To take another example, rents do not measure the return on the factor of production land, but rather the earnings derived from the ownership of land and buildings.[1] In a relatively urbanised community subject to a high degree of rent restriction it is doubtful whether we can derive any useful measure of the share of land *per se*. In the end it seems best to focus on incomes from employment as being the least ambiguous of the factor shares. This section is thus primarily concerned with the long-term trend in incomes from employment as currently defined in the National Income Blue Books, i.e. inclusive of salaries, directors' fees and employers' insurance contributions. We shall try to arrive at estimates of the share of this income category in the national income over as long a period as the data will permit.

It should be emphasised that what we are trying to measure is a somewhat wider category of incomes than most previous investigators have considered with reference to U.K. conditions. Bowley's estimates of the national wage bill were estimates of wages exclusive of salaries but inclusive of shop assistants' incomes,[2] and this is the series which Prest reproduced as a main component of his national-income estimates.[3] Phelps Brown and Hart were also interested in wages in their narrow sense, and they excluded shop assistants' wages.[4] The wage fraction whose stability Keynes regarded as 'a bit of a miracle'[5] and which

---

[1] Cf. *National Income Statistics, Sources and Methods* (H.M.S.O., 1956), p. 332: 'Rent might better be regarded as a form of trading profit—the surplus on operating account derived from the business of hiring real estate—than as the earnings of a specific and distinguishable factor of production.'

[2] A. L. Bowley, *Wages and Income since 1860* (Cambridge, 1937).

[3] A. R. Prest, 'National Income of the United Kingdom, 1870–1946', *Economic Journal*, March 1948.

[4] E. H. Phelps Brown and P. E. Hart, 'The Share of Wages in National Income', *Economic Journal*, June 1952.

[5] J. M. Keynes, 'Relative Movements in Real Wages and Output', *Economic Journal*, 1939.

Kalecki discussed in his theory of income distribution[1] was a still narrower concept; it was calculated in terms of the employee incomes which are most responsive to cyclical changes in output and hence might be expected, *a priori*, to fluctuate with it in the short period.

The object of the distinction between wages and salaries is not always clear. Theorists may be concerned either with the reward of labour in its purest form (i.e. excluding the property and entrepreneurial components which may be assumed to inflate salaries), or with the variable, as opposed to the fixed, labour costs of the economy. The statisticians base their distinction on a variety of criteria which seem on the face of them to have very little to do with either of these theoretical considerations—on the manual or non-manual character of the activity, for example, on the period or size of the payment, on degree of participation in the production process, on the collective or individual character of the wage-bargain, and so on.

When salaries were a relatively unimportant fraction of the total and when most employees were manual and unskilled workers, the distinction may have been both meaningful and easy to draw. This may have been so for the United Kingdom for most of the period 1860–1914. Nowadays, however, wages (as defined according to the present conventions of the Central Statistical Office) account for only about 60 per cent of total incomes from employment; the amount of capital and special ability involved in the wage-earning activities of skilled operatives in mechanised industry is greater than that involved in numerous clerical occupations which now fall into the salaried group; and the importance of the occupations which can only be classified arbitrarily (policemen, firemen, shop assistants, works foremen, etc.) has become quite large.[2] It is thus difficult to see what useful purpose—theoretical or practical—the distinction serves, and we have preferred to focus on employment incomes taken as a whole rather than an arbitrarily defined section of them.

Basically what is required for our immediate purpose are estimates of total net national income at factor cost and of the totals of wages and salaries paid in each year. The data are such that it is necessary to consider the problem in terms of three time-periods: (1) the period

---

[1] M. Kalecki, *Theory of Economic Dynamics* (1954). Cf. p. 39: 'The application of the theory of income distribution to the analysis of long-run changes in the relative share of wages and salaries in income would be difficult because of the growing importance of salaries in the sum of overheads and profits as a result of increasing concentration of business.' In effect Kalecki focused attention on the share of wages in the private sector (excluding government employees).

[2] The Central Statistical Office makes its distinction largely on the basis of the definitions adopted for the Census of Production, i.e. operatives are treated as wage-earners and administrative, technical and clerical staff are treated as salary-earners. Shop assistants, policemen and firemen are treated as wage-earners, and works foremen as salary-earners. See *National Income Statistics Sources and Methods, op. cit.* pp. 72–3. Some of the 'doubtful' categories are defined otherwise by other U.K. government departments and represent a recent change of mind for the C.S.O. itself. See H. R. Kahn, 'The Distinction between Wages and Salaries', *Scottish Journal of Political Economy*, June 1956, for a discussion of the different definitions, past and current, in U.K. government departments.

since the First World War when the wage and salary estimates and the national-income estimates are reliable enough to make year-to-year shifts in the proportion interesting, (2) the period from *circa* 1870 to the beginning of the First World War when the employment-income estimates and the national-income estimates are based on a sufficiently satisfactory foundation of evidence to suggest convincing broad trends but are not sufficiently precise to support detailed analysis of year to year variations; and (3) the period before about the middle of the nineteenth century when all estimates of national income and its major components are extremely tentative and all conclusions drawn from them are suspect unless strongly supported by other kinds of data.

I. INCOMES FROM EMPLOYMENT SINCE THE FIRST WORLD WAR

Official estimates of national income are available for the period 1938–1959, and Prest's and Stone's estimates for the period 1920–1937 were adjusted by Jefferys and Walters to include some minor items excluded from the earlier series. Some adjustments had to be made to the C.S.O. estimates to produce comparable figures for the war years but they were not important in relation to the totals. For wages and salaries (including directors' fees and employers' national insurance contributions) in the interwar years we relied on the Chapman and Knight estimates, and for 1938–56 on the C.S.O. estimates.[1]

The results of all these calculations are shown annually in Table 63. In this period of thirty-six years the share of employees in the national income increased from near 60 per cent of the national income in 1920 to about 73½ per cent in 1958. Most of the increase took place in the war years when the proportion jumped from about 62 per cent in 1939 to about 72 per cent in 1945.

Most of the increase, moreover, was due to increases in the non-wage components of employment income. Salaries, as can be seen from Table 64, have tended to increase their share of total national income throughout the period. This is partly a consequence of shifts from the own-account and employer groups but much more largely a result of changes in the structure and organisation of industry—an expansion of the numbers engaged in administrative and professional occupations. Employers' insurance contributions have also expanded greatly since the First World War and forces' pay has been a relatively larger component of employment incomes since the Second World War than it was in the interwar period. In effect the non-wage components rose from 20 per cent of national income in the 1920's to 29 per cent in the 1950's whereas for the wage fraction proper the rise was from about 39 per cent to about 43 per cent—the whole of which increase was attributable to the Second World War.

---

[1] For sources in detail see notes to Table 63.

Table 63. *National income and incomes from employment, United Kingdom,*
1920–59

(in £m.)

	(1) Net national income at factor cost	(2) Incomes from employment	(3) Incomes from employment as percentage of national income
1920	5,787	3,469	59·9
1921	4,572	2,857	62·5
1922	3,962	2,426	61·2
1923	3,951	2,332	59·0
1924	4,029	2,391	59·3
1925	4,091	2,434	59·5
1926	4,030	2,353	58·4
1927	4,268	2,517	59·0
1928	4,277	2,511	58·7
1929	4,301	2,558	59·5
1930	4,076	2,497	61·3
1931	3,779	2,393	63·3
1932	3,681	2,367	64·3
1933	3,846	2,411	62·7
1934	4,004	2,515	62·8
1935	4,238	2,604	61·4
1936	4,525	2,751	60·8
1937	4,759	2,909	61·1
1938	4,816	3,022	62·8
1939	5,191	3,212	61·9
1940	7,171	4,839	67·5
1941	7,142	4,498	63·0
1942	7,887	5,017	63·6
1943	8,403	5,415	64·4
1944	8,439	5,809	68·8
1945	8,357	6,034	72·2
1946	8,087	5,732	70·9
1947	8,587	6,199	72·2
1948	9,556	6,766	70·8
1949	10,208	7,220	70·7
1950	10,710	7,600	71·0
1951	11,720	8,459	72·4
1952	12,727	9,097	71·5
1953	13,607	9,608	70·6
1954	14,580	10,253	71·0
1955	15,416	11,205	72·7
1956	16,698	12,218	73·2
1957	17,635	12,913	73·2
1958	18,341	13,397	73·1
1959	18,931	13,933	73·6

Sources: The Blue Book on *National Income and Expenditure 1960* (H.M.S.O., 1960) gives data for 1938 and 1948–58 inclusive. The Blue Book for 1957 gives 1946–7 figures and the 1959 Blue Book the latest 1958 estimates. For the war years we used the White Papers, *National Income and Expenditure of the United Kingdom 1938–46* (Cmd. 7099, H.M.S.O., 1947) and *National Income and Expenditure of the United Kingdom, 1947* (Cmd. 7371, H.M.S.O., 1948), adjusting the estimates in the White Papers to conform to the revised definitions in the latest Blue Book.

For the inter-war years we used Prest's national-income estimates (*Economic Journal* (*1948*), *op. cit.*) adjusted to conform with the C.S.O. 1938 estimate and to include employers' insurance contributions and incomes of non-profit-making institutions and incomes of non-residents. The two last were derived from James B. Jeffery and Dorothy Walters, 'National Income and Expenditure of the United Kingdom', in *Income and Wealth Series V* (Bowes and Bowes, 1955).

For wages and salaries and employers' insurance contributions for the interwar years we used the estimates in Agatha L. Chapman, assisted by Rose Knight, *Wages and Salaries in the United Kingdom 1920–1938* (Cambridge University Press, 1953).

Table 64. *The components of United Kingdom employment incomes,*
1920–58

(as percentages of total national income by decades)

	Wages (%)	Salaries (%)	Forces' pay (%)	Employers' statutory insurance contributions (%)	Total employment incomes (%)
1920–29	39·4	17·6	1·9	0·8	59·7
1925–34	38·8	19·4	1·6	0·9	60·7
1930–39	39·0	20·2	1·7	1·1	62·0
1946–55	43·1	21·6	2·9	4·0	71·6
1950–58	43·2	22·4	2·4	4·4	72·4

Sources: Chapman and Knight, *op. cit.*, and Blue Book as for Table 63. The official estimates do not provide comparable figures for the period 1940–5 because the C.S.O. treated shop assistants as salary-earners in estimates published before 1953.

2. INCOMES FROM EMPLOYMENT BEFORE THE FIRST WORLD WAR

There are no satisfactory national-income or wages and salaries estimates for the years of the First World War. The period 1915–19 is accordingly a gap in the statistics. Before 1915, however, estimates based on Bowley's and Wood's wage studies and Stamp's income series can be carried back to 1860 with a degree of confidence which diminishes markedly as we go back before 1880.

For the period 1870–1914 Prest calculated national income on the basis of Bowley's estimates of wages and intermediate incomes and of his own estimates of assessed incomes.[1] Later Jefferys and Walters adjusted Prest's national-income estimates upwards to cover employers' insurance contributions, incomes of co-operative societies, hospitals and other non-profit-making bodies, to exclude incomes of non-residents and to allow for an assumed understatement of agricultural incomes.[2] We accepted Jefferys' and Walters' estimates for employers' insurance contributions and incomes of non-profit-making bodies and non-residents but rejected their addition for agricultural incomes.[3] We carried the Prest estimates for profits and evasion back to 1860 on the basis of Stamp's true comparable series of taxable income,[4] and we also

[1] See A. L. Bowley, 'Tests of National Progress', *Economic Journal*, 1904, for 1860–80 wage estimates, and *idem*, *Wages and Income since 1860, op. cit.*, for their continuation to 1914. A. R. Prest, *op. cit., Economic Journal*, 1948.

[2] Jefferys and Walters, *op. cit.* pp. 23–5.

[3] The justification for the Jefferys' and Walters' adjustment in respect of farm incomes is contained in an early estimate of agricultural incomes made by Bowley on the basis of the Census of Production taken in the first decade of the twentieth century. (A. L. Bowley, *Division of the Product of Industry* (Oxford University Press, 1919), p. 15.) This suggested that the tax records understated farm incomes by some £26 m. *circa* 1911. Recent estimates made by the Agricultural Economic Research Institute at Oxford indicate that Bowley's census estimates were faulty and do not justify the upward adjustment. I am indebted to Mr J. R. Bellerby of the Agricultural Economics Research Institute for this information.

[4] J. C. Stamp, *British Incomes and Property* (London, 1916), pp. 318–19.

carried back Bowley's estimate of intermediate incomes from 1880 to 1860 on the assumption that there was a slow linear increase in these incomes. Essentially, therefore, our national-income series is the series calculated by Prest, extrapolated to 1860 and adjusted to allow for: (1) a small increase in intermediate incomes 1870–80, (2) the exclusion of incomes of non-residents, (3) the inclusion of incomes of non-profit-making bodies 1870–1914 and employers' insurance contributions 1909–14. The second and third of these adjustments were made by Jefferys and Walters. None of the adjustments affect the Prest national-income estimates by more than about 1 per cent.

To calculate the wage and salary totals it was necessary to estimate the salaries below £150 included in intermediate income and the assessed salaries included in the profits and evasion categories.[1] We accepted Bowley's estimate of unassessed salaries for 1911[2] and extra-polated them back by analogy with the wage bill. Stamp's series of 'true comparable incomes over £150' assessed to Schedule E provided the basis of our estimate of assessed salaries.[3] These estimates of assessed and unassessed salaries were then added to the Bowley wage-bill estimates to give annual estimates of wages and salaries back to 1860. We extrapolated to 1860 on the basis of our own estimates of wages and salaries in 1851 and 1861.

The results of these estimates are summarised in Table 65, which compares the employment incomes proportion with the shares of two other major components of national income—rents and the profits and property incomes remaining after employment incomes and rents have been deducted.

What light these results shed on the problem of whether the factor of production labour has enlarged its share of national income depends on how narrowly we define its reward. Those who regard wages (as distinct from salaries or employers' insurance contributions) as a proper measure of the share of labour will find confirmation in these tables for the view that, except in so far as it was forced up by the full-employ-ment conditions of the Second World War and its immediate after-math, the share of labour has been relatively constant over the long period. In the half-century before the First World War this relative constancy was a characteristic of total employment incomes. There were year-to-year fluctuations: but between 1860 and 1914 the share of wages and salaries never fell as low as 46 per cent or rose above 51 per cent. Much of the upward jump in the course of the Second World

---

[1] Prest did not consider Schedule E incomes separately, but by adjusting his estimates of incomes earned under Schedule A, B, C and D to Stamp's 'true comparable series' of *all* taxable incomes he did in effect cover them within his profits and evasion totals. Phelps Brown and Hart (*op. cit.*, *Economic Journal*, 1952) took salaries as equivalent to intermediate incomes as calculated by Prest (by linear extrapolation of Bowley's estimate for 1911) plus shop assistants which Prest included in his wages total. But not more than a quarter of Bowley's 1911 estimate of intermediate incomes was attributable to salaries and no account is taken of them of assessed salaries.

[2] Bowley, *Wages and Income since 1860*, p. 96.

[3] Stamp, *op. cit.* pp. 272–3.

Table 65. *The distribution of United Kingdom national income, 1860–1959*

(in average decade percentages of total national income)

	Wages and salaries (%)	Rents (%)	Profits, interest and mixed incomes (%)
1860–69	48·5	13·7	38·9
1865–74	47·6	13·0	39·4
1870–79	48·7	13·1	38·2
1875–84	48·8	13·9	37·3
1880–89	48·2	14·0	37·9
1885–94	49·2	13·0	37·8
1890–99	49·8	12·0	38·2
1895–1904	49·6	11·6	38·8
1900–09	48·4	11·4	40·2
1905–14	47·2	10·8	42·0
1920–29	59·7	6·6	33·7
1925–34	60·7	8·1	31·2
1930–39	62·0	8·7	29·2
1935–44	64·0	6·7	29·3
1940–49	68·8	4·9	26·3
1946–55	71·6	4·2	24·2
1950–59	72·4	4·9	22·7

Sources: Wages and salaries based on Bowley's wage-bill estimates and our estimates of salaries as described in text. Rents are Phelps Brown's and Hart's estimates based on Schedule A (*op. cit.*, *Economic Journal*, 1952), C.S.O. estimates (excluding depreciation) for later years and our extrapolation for missing years. Profits, etc., incomes as a residual after calculating national income by method described in text on basis of Prest estimates. For 1920–59 estimates see notes to Tables 63 and 64 above.

War was due to the increase in non-wage incomes; for wages alone the increase was from about 39 per cent to about 43 per cent.

For employment incomes as a whole the trend since 1914 has been so unmistakeably upwards as to suggest to those who see little significance in the distinction between wages and salaries a strong presumption in favour of an increase in the share of labour. Probably the quality of labour has been improved by social investment in education and training. Certainly there has been some increase in the numbers employed and a corresponding decrease in the numbers dependent on profits and mixed incomes. Employees represented about 87 per cent of the gainfully occupied population in 1911, 90 per cent in 1921, and 93 per cent in 1951. Between 1911 and 1921 the rise in this proportion was largely due to a fall in the proportion of own-account workers, and between 1921 and 1951 to a fall in the proportion of employers though the self-employed group continued to fall in relative importance. These changes are illustrated in Table 66. But neither the institutional changes which turned employers into employees, nor the process of capital accumulation implied in the improved quality of labour, nor a combination of the two, seems sufficient to account for an increase in the employee share from about 47 per cent in the decade before the First World War to about 72 per cent in the decades following the Second World War.

Table 66. *Distribution of the occupied population by industrial status, 1911–51*

(as percentage of the total occupied population of Great Britain, including unemployed but excluding retired persons)

	Employers	Own account	Employees[2]
1911[1]	4·6	8·2	87·2
1921	3·8	6·3	89·9
1931	n.a.[3]	6·1	n.a.[3]
1951	2·2	5·0	92·8

Sources: Censuses of England and Wales and Scotland. *Notes* [1] The 1911 census does not distinguish status for all industries but it is possible to estimate employed and own-account workers for the few occupations in which they are not distinguished. [2] 1911 returns refer to population aged ten and over, 1921 to twelve and over, 1931 to fourteen and over, and 1951 to fifteen and over. In 1911 there were about 500,000 occupied persons aged ten to fifteen. [3] The 1931 census distinguished between managerial, own-account and operatives so that it is not possible to distinguish employers from employed persons. But between 1931 and 1951 the managerial group fell slightly—from 5·7 per cent to 5·4 per cent. Unless the employed managers increased appreciably faster than the employed population in general there was only a small fall in the proportion of employers between 1931 and 1951.

It is unfortunately not possible to split the other components of national income into more interesting categories. It seems fairly clear, however, that rents have declined considerably in relative importance since about the middle of last century. This is not surprising for an economy which was rapidly shifting resources from agricultural to industrial uses. The trend since the First World War is not so clear. It is difficult to allow adequately for the effect of wartime restrictions in building (or in building repairs) in temporarily reducing rents in both post-war periods, or for the effects of the exclusion of Southern Ireland in depressing land rents in the first post-war period.[1] But in any case, by the 1920's rents were a relatively inconsiderable component in the national income. It was the miscellaneous group of entrepreneurial and property incomes which lost ground to labour.

That the strains and stresses of war should drastically shift the pattern of factor shares is not surprising. It is more surprising, in view of the previous record of stability, that the shifts should be not only sustained but continuing.

3. EMPLOYMENT INCOMES BEFORE 1860

If employment incomes displayed a marked stability in the second half of the nineteenth century and showed a marked rising tendency in the first half of the twentieth, what can we say of their earlier history?

[1] Bowley estimated that about 4 per cent of the home-produced income of the U.K. in 1911 was attributable to Southern Ireland, which then accounted for under 7 per cent of the population of Great Britain and Ireland. See *Wages and Income since 1860*, p. 83. By 1930 the Irish Republic accounted for about 6·6 per cent of the population of Great Britain and Ireland. Hence even on relatively extreme consumptions concerning the importance of rents and wages and salaries in Southern Ireland in the decade 1905–14 it is doubtful whether its exclusion would raise the wage and salary percentage to 48, or drop the rent percentage below 9·5.

The attempt to carry these calculations back before the 1860's leads into hazardous paths. We can estimate the occupational distribution of the employed population on the basis of the occupation censuses for 1851 and 1841: and, as has been demonstrated in chapter IV, there are enough wage and salary data to permit rough estimates of average earnings in the chief occupations at these times. These give the basis for rough bench-mark estimates of the total wage and salary bill. We can also carry back the profits data to *circa* 1841 on the basis of Stamp's true comparable series of taxable incomes and we can extrapolate intermediate incomes on reasonably plausible assumptions.

There are two reasons why this process yields an inconclusive result. The first is that rough bench-mark estimates will not do for the purpose of indicating trends. The year-to-year variations in the share of employment incomes could be quite large: and if the estimates for a particular year are subject to an additional area of uncertainty because they involve wide margins of errors they can tell us nothing at all about the direction of change.

The other reason is that as soon as we carry any of our economic measures for the United Kingdom back through the middle of the nineteenth century we are faced with the Irish problem. In 1841 Ireland accounted for nearly 31 per cent of the population of the United Kingdom and in 1861 for less than 20 per cent. In the intervening two decades the Irish economic experience diverged catastrophically from that of the rest of the United Kingdom.

In effect, therefore, for periods between 1801 and 1851 the Irish component of the United Kingdom is so large and its structure so different that it is difficult to read any meaning into the composite total. It does not seem possible to visualise any set of economic aggregates which would measure overall growth for the United Kingdom on a comparable yardstick throughout the nineteenth century. If we want to compare the end of the century with the beginning or even with its middle we must first distinguish the Irish component.[1]

For figures of national income and its structure in the first half of the nineteenth century we are largely at the mercy of the contemporary estimates. The numerous difficulties in the way of deriving estimates of employment incomes by applying the wage and salary data available in contemporary records and government reports to the occupational returns of the decennial censuses have already been discussed in chapter IV. One of these is the problem of extracting the number of self-employed persons. Except in a few occupational categories (e.g. farmers, shopkeepers, lawyers and doctors) we have no means of

---

[1] Oddly enough this is easier to do for the first half of the century than for the second. In the earlier period the basic statistics often did not include Ireland at all. There was no population census even before 1821. And Ireland did not come into the scope of income-tax assessment before 1853–4. So contemporary national-income investigators either excluded Ireland from their calculations altogether or included it by extrapolating on the basis of Great Britain's experience. We may not be able to measure the national income of Ireland with much confidence but we can plausibly exclude it from such calculations.

estimating the proportions employed as opposed to the employers or the self-employed. Before 1881 retired or unoccupied persons are attributed indiscriminately to the occupation claimed by them. We may extrapolate from the more complete returns at the end of the century to provide estimates of the employed population in, say, 1871 or 1861, but if we carry this process back much further we find ourselves feeding into the statistics the characteristics which we want to deduce from them. It seems highly probable on *a priori* principles that the proportion of self-employed persons in manufacturing, for example, diminished and the proportion of employed persons grew considerably between 1801 when Britain was essentially a pre-industrial economy and, say, 1871, when it was to all intents and purposes an industrial economy. But this is precisely the kind of hypothesis which we want to be able to check and quantify with our measures of long-term growth. If we assume the answer into our estimates of numbers employed we cannot say that the resulting wage-bill estimate tells us much about the proportion of national product attributable to income from employment.

A similar problem is raised by our ignorance of the overall quantitative significance of unemployment in the early phases of the industrial revolution. Bowley and Wood took account of seasonal differences in employment in assessing wage rates for different industries, and by the second half of the century there were trade-union records which gave some indication of the relative year-to-year incidence of unemployment in important industries. But in the early part of the century the probability is that unemployment took the form of short time rather than complete idleness, that it was widespread throughout the economy and that it was highly variable from year to year. Certainly it is difficult to conceive of any way of allowing for it quantitatively, although poor-relief records might give some idea of its fluctuations.

To accept the contemporary estimates as being more satisfactory reflections of broad proportions than any new estimates which we could build up for ourselves from the records still available, is not to attribute to them the quality of independent and reliable statistical evidence. Since the statistics on which they were originally based are generally less complete than those available to national-income investigators for the period 1870–1914 we should expect them to be less reliable. What they may suggest, however, are some hypotheses concerning the broader long-term trends in the wage fraction. They may indicate, for example, whether the shift from property and entrepreneurial incomes to labour incomes which emerges from the statistics of the past eighty or so years was less pronounced than the shifts which characterised the period of the industrial revolution proper or preceded it.

An analysis and combination of the most plausible elements from each group of estimates which were published at the beginning of the nineteenth century suggested a total national income for Great Britain *circa* 1801 of £228 m., of which £100 m. was attributable to labour incomes.[1] The implication was therefore that at the beginning of the nineteenth century labour incomes accounted for about 43·9 per cent of national income. If this were so, it would seem that although labour incomes had increased their share of national income in the course of the industrial revolution, this increase was smaller than that which occurred in either the First World War or in the Second World War. The *circa* 1801 estimates also suggest that rents of land and houses accounted for about 19½ per cent of the national income of Great Britain, so that other property incomes and other entrepreneurial profits must have accounted for about 36½ per cent or not very much less than they were after the First World War.

Our own estimates of wages and salaries of Great Britain, when compared with the corresponding estimates of gross national product at decade intervals during the nineteenth century, suggest a proportion of 44·9 per cent *circa* 1801 and 46·5 per cent *circa* 1811 falling to about 42·3 per cent *circa* 1841, and fluctuating between 43·6 per cent and 47·6 per cent during the remaining bench-mark years for the century.[2] In view of the difficulty of distinguishing self-employed from employees for the purposes of these calculations, and also the possible variations of the bench-mark years from adjacent years, no great weight can be put either on the absolute proportions suggested or on the decade-to-decade changes. However, it is perhaps significant that for the first four decades our estimates fluctuated between 42·3 per cent and 46·5 per cent, and for the next six decades between 44·5 per cent and 47·6 per cent. Perhaps the most significant feature of these estimates is the minor character of the shifts they imply.

If we now try to push these calculations back to the earliest of the contemporary national-income estimates, i.e. to 1688, we find that in England and Wales rents of land and housing were estimated to account for about 27 per cent of national income.[3] But the distinction between mixed incomes and labour incomes is here so obscure that it is difficult to make any estimate of incomes from employment that can be regarded as even broadly comparable with modern concepts. If we assume that all the nobility (including gentlemen) were self-employed or property-owners; and that the incomes of persons in offices, clergymen, 'artizans and handycrafts', military and naval officers, common soldiers and seamen, labouring people and outservants, cottagers and paupers (excluding poor-relief incomes) and domestics were all classified as

---

[1] There was a fairly close agreement between the contemporary estimates for this period although there were considerable differences in methods and assumptions. The agreement, however, is evidence not so much of the reliability of the estimates but of their validity as a reflection of the views held by well-informed contemporaries, for it may be assumed that they were acquainted with each others' estimates. See Deane, 'The Implications of Early National Income Estimates, etc.', *op. cit.*, and *idem*, 'Contemporary Estimates of National Income, etc.', *op. cit.*, for detailed discussions of these estimates.

[2] See above, Tables 34 and 37.

[3] *Two Tracts by Gregory King, op. cit.* p. 30, gives rent of lands = £10 m., of housing about £2 m. and of all other hereditaments about £1 m.

labour incomes we can say that about 39 per cent of the national income seems to have fallen within this category and that non-rent property incomes and entrepreneurial profits accounted for 34 per cent.[1]

The fact is, however, that very few of King's categories could be classified unambiguously as 'incomes from employment' rather than as 'mixed incomes'. Artisans and craftsmen and persons in science and the arts must include numerous own-account workers as well as employed persons. Cottagers may have held their cottages like the modern agricultural labourer as a part condition of employment. The clergy may be regarded as land-owners rather than as employers. In a world where even government offices and military or naval commissions were openly bought and sold the employee was clearly not the typical earner. If we exclude all the categories which might embrace a high proportion of mixed incomes we are left with the labouring people and outservants, the domestics, the common soldiers and sailors, and possibly the clergymen: and their combined share in the national income according to King was only about 25 per cent.

We might conclude therefore that at the end of the seventeenth century the share of incomes from employment was between 25 per cent and 39 per cent of national income—possibly nearer the lower figure than the higher: and also that by the beginning of the nineteenth century it may have been in the region of 45 or 46 per cent.

This implies that there was a substantial shift towards pure wage incomes in the eighteenth century, i.e. before the industrial revolution gathered momentum on a broad front and before the period of rapid economic growth. The hypothesis that there was a radical change is borne out moreover by a comparison of King's estimates of 'the national income and the state of society' in 1688 and Colquhoun's 'general view of society' since 1801. About a fifth (by value) of the incomes detailed in Colquhoun's list fell in categories which were not distinguished by King presumably because they were not sufficiently important to justify separate mention at the end of the seventeenth century.[2] The most important of them were various kinds of capitalists —i.e. 'persons employing capital' in production—but they also include a large class of salaried employees—'clerks and shopmen'. Clearly the distinction between the profit-earner and the wage-earner, between master and employee, was more important and readily recognisable in Colquhoun's day than it had been a century earlier.

But even the incomes in Colquhoun's list which are apparently comparable to King's categories contain some significant differences of emphasis or breakdown. In King's day, for example, a gentleman was

[1] For Table 1, above, we adopted a somewhat different classification—included persons in science and the arts as 'employees' and excluded cottagers and paupers—and reached a proportion of about 37 per cent. See above p. 2, and Deane, 'The Implications of Early National Income Estimates, etc.', *op. cit.* p. 10.

[2] Colquhoun himself draws attention to the change in the structure of society by detailing separately 'Persons not included in the Gregory King's estimate'. See his *Treatise on Indigence, op. cit.* p. 23.

a near-exclusive rank in society, analogous to the temporal or spiritual lords or to the baronets or the knights. When Colquhoun wrote, it was not social rank which determined the gentleman but the unearned character of his income, and he indicated this by the description 'Gentlemen and ladies living on income'. It is worth noting further that Colquhoun thought it useful to distinguish labouring people in husbandry from those in 'mines, canals, etc.' and that he specified labourers and merchants in the group which included artisans and craftsmen but did not distinguish them. By then also the incomes earned by officers in the public service or in the army or navy were predominantly salary-type incomes despite the continuation of the practice of selling commissions.

In sum, therefore, the specialisation of factors of production, giving rise to conceptually distinct categories of income, which was barely discernible in England at the end of the seventeenth century, was already a marked feature of the pattern of income distribution by the beginning of the nineteenth. Exactly when and in what circumstances the change occurred, however, it is impossible to say. We are dealing with a period of more than a century for which it is generally agreed that there were considerable changes in the economic framework of society. It would be interesting to know how gradual the process was and how much of it occurred before or after the marked quickening of industrial activity which took place in the last quarter of the eighteenth century.

The indications are that a significant proportion of the change had taken place before then. By 1775 Adam Smith was stating with conviction, but also with the emphasis of a discoverer, that 'The whole produce of the land and labour of every country, or what comes to the same thing, the whole price of that annual produce, naturally divides itself, it has already been observed, into three parts; the rent of land, the wages of labour and the profits of stock; and constitutes a revenue to three different orders of people: to these who live by rent, to those who live by wages, and to those who live by profit. These are the great original and constituent orders of every civilised society, from whose revenue that of every other order is ultimately derived.'[1]

But even earlier than this, in 1766, David Hume asserted, in a letter to Turgot, 'that, besides the Proprietors of Land and the labouring Poor, there is in every civilised Community a very large and a very opulent Body who employ their Stocks in Commerce and who enjoy a great Revenue from their giving Labour to the poorer sort. I am persuaded that in France and England the Revenue of this kind is much greater than that which arises from Land: For besides Merchants, properly speaking, I comprehend in this Class all Shop-keepers and

[1] Adam Smith, *The Wealth of Nations*, Cannan edition, vol. 1, p. 248. See an article by Ronald L. Meek, 'Adam Smith and the Classical Concept of Profit', in the *Scottish Journal of Political Economy*, June 1954, for a discussion of the extent to which Adam Smith was a pioneer in recognising the importance of this basic distinction between rent, wages and profits.

Master-Tradesmen of every species.'[1] And earlier still, in 1760, Joseph Massie drew up a table of families distinguished by income and social group which differed from the King table, on which it was obviously modelled in that it distinguished 'master manufacturers' from 'manufacturers and Labourers' where King saw only 'artizans and handycrafts'.[2]

It would seem reasonable to conclude from these contemporary analyses that an appreciable part of the shift towards specialisation of factor incomes had occurred before the last quarter of the eighteenth century. The capitalist 'manufacturer' or 'tradesman' was by midcentury a character of some importance in the eyes of contemporaries. At the end of the seventeenth century such a well-informed observer as Gregory King had not thought it worth distinguishing him from the ordinary artisan.

These are qualitative conclusions and it is doubtful whether the attempt to push quantitative comparisons of factor shares across the period of the industrial revolution into the pre-industrial era is conceptually feasible. The problem is that the analytical concepts which may be appropriate in a specialised economy do not find readily recognisable counterparts in the unspecialised economy. Nor do we have to go back to the seventeenth century to encounter this kind of difficulty. Any pre-industrial phase throws up numerous examples. In measuring employment incomes at the beginning of the nineteenth century, for example, we chose to include the earnings of the handloom weaver. The fact that the cottage weaver or spinner owned his own equipment and may even have hired his own assistants, did not seem to us to turn him into an entrepreneur or a self-employed person. His relationship to the capitalist who provided his raw material and collected and marketed the final product seemed to be essentially an employee-master relationship. But there is obviously an arbitrary element in this kind of decision and the significance of the arbitrary factors in the classification increases as we go back in time.

The point is not that the arbitrary factors disappear altogether for the modern period but that they are comparatively unimportant on the whole. At the present day self-employment incomes account for between 9 and 10 per cent of net national incomes.[3] If we excluded directors' fees from employment incomes it would involve adjustments

---

[1] Quoted by Meek, *Scottish Journal of Political Economy*, June 1954, *op. cit.* p. 149.

[2] Joseph Massie, *A Computation of The Money that hath been exorbitantly Raised upon the People of Great Britain by the sugar planters in one year from January 1759 to January 1760, etc.* A broadsheet published in 1760. See Peter Mathias, 'The Social Structure in the Eighteenth Century: a Calculation by Joseph Massie', *Econ. Hist. Rev.*, vol. x, No. 1 (August 1957), for a detailed analysis of Massie's table and a comparison with King's and Colquhoun's tables.

[3] For 1956 the proportion was 9·1 per cent. This is for *net* incomes from self-employment as a percentage of net national income. See the 1957 *Blue Book on National Income and Expenditure, op. cit.*, Tables 1 and 59, for estimates of gross incomes and stock appreciation; and the Cohen Council Report, p. 59, for estimates of capital consumption. *First Report of the Council on Prices, Productivity and Incomes* (H.M.S.O., 1958).

of only about 2 per cent,[1] and although rents are not a homogeneous group of incomes they are a recognisably distinct category of earnings, and in any case they are small in relation to the total national income. In effect, for the recent period, the conceptual problems involved in distinguishing employment incomes from other kinds of earnings are not great enough to dilute our conclusions concerning the striking increase in the wage fraction.

4. CONCLUSIONS

Briefly, therefore, if it is possible to accept the national-income and wage-bill estimates we have been considering as reasonably reliable measures of what they purport to measure, our conclusions might be summed up as follows. The share of employees in the national income grew significantly in the period before industrialisation gathered momentum on a sufficiently broad front to induce sustained economic growth. The proportion seems to have changed comparatively little in the nineteenth century and early twentieth century in spite of a structural transformation of the British economy. In the period of most rapid economic growth therefore the employee share has apparently been fairly stable. But there has been a very marked increase since 1914, an increase which was apparently associated directly with the impact of two world wars but has been more or less continuous in the period before and after the Second World War.

The relative stability of the employee share in the nineteenth century is, on the face of it, surprising. As between one industry and another there are considerable differences in the contribution of labour to the factor cost of production. In 1956, for example, incomes from employment constituted less than 41 per cent of the net output of the agriculture, forestry, fishing group of industries, and about 86 per cent in the case of the mining and quarrying group. For government, of course, most of value added is attributable to labour. If there were much change in the structure of British industry in the nineteenth century we might expect the employee fraction to have altered appreciably—unless there were compensating factors involved in the process.

It has been pointed out, however, that, other things being equal, some degree of compensation is to be expected. Changes in the relative importance of the component industries should not in general be expected to make much difference to the variability of the national employee fraction unless there is some intercorrelation between the industry employee fractions.[2] Thus, if the industry employee fractions

---

[1] Chapman and Knight, *op. cit.* p. 22. They reached their interwar maximum of about $2\frac{1}{2}$ per cent of employment incomes in the later twenties.

[2] See Robert M. Solow, 'A Skeptical Note on the Constancy of Relative Shares', *American Economic Review*, vol. XLVIII (1958). Statistical analysis of U.S. data for selected years in the period 1929–53 shows that the observed variance in the overall wage fraction through time was not significantly different from what it would have been if the industries concerned had maintained fixed shares in the national total. 'If anything the aggregate share fluctuated a bit *more* than the hypothesis of independence would indicate.'

vary independently the explanation for a stable employee fraction must be sought in the stability of the component industry employee fractions. If the national employee fraction shows a rising trend the explanation may be either that there are some general forces tending to push up the corresponding fraction in most industries or that there is some tendency for industries with a high wage fraction to gain in relative importance.

One explanation for a rising employee share during the transition from a pre-industrial to an industrialised economy is the tendency for employment incomes to gain at the expense of mixed incomes as the number of self-employed persons falls and the number of employees grows. It is precisely because the statistics do not distinguish between employee and employed that we have been unable to make satisfactory estimates of the employee share during the early nineteenth century. Our estimate that there was a substantial fall in the wage fraction between the end of the seventeenth century and the end of the eighteenth is blurred by the same problem.

Indeed it may be said that, in comparing the relatively stagnant pre-industrial economy depicted by Gregory King at the end of the seventeenth century with the growing economy described by Colquhoun in the early nineteenth century, the significant difference is not the change in the relative shares of capital and labour—however these are measured. It is the shift from the subsistence sector to the exchange economy. In 1688 the cottagers, paupers and vagrants together accounted for 24 per cent of total population and received between 5 and 6 per cent of total income in King's 'scheme of the income and expence of the several families of England'.[1] By 1801 when Colquhoun drew up a comparable table the paupers and the vagrants were still there (the poor—in some form—are always there) but the cottagers, swallowed up no doubt by the eighteenth century enclosure movement, were no longer worth mentioning. We may conclude that, except in Ireland and in the highlands and islands of Scotland (where a small crofter group has lasted into the twentieth century), the subsistence producer had virtually disappeared from the British economy when the industrial revolution began.

A sufficient explanation of the long-term constancy of the employee fraction between the 1860's and the decade before the First World War must await detailed statistical analysis of the trends in the component industry wage fractions. But since we have no prior reason to suppose that there was a tendency either for changes in industrial structure to be biased towards industries carrying a high employee fraction or for the shifts in the relative importance of labour and capital (or their

---

[1] The subsistence sector was already, of course, far less important than it is currently in some of the modern underdeveloped economies in which an industrial revolution is said to be in progress. Cf. The Federation of Rhodesia and Nyasaland, where, according to the official estimates for the quinquennium 1954–8, it accounted for over 60 per cent of the population, and about 18 per cent of national income.

relative bargaining power) to be large enough to produce appreciable variations in the pattern of income distribution, the observed constancy is not as miraculous as has sometimes been supposed.

What does seem surprising is the remarkable rise in the share of employment incomes during the twentieth century. Again it must be emphasised that an adequate explanation must await detailed statistical analysis of the component industry trends. At a broader level of analysis, however, we may suggest that there were two major factors in the rise of the national employee fraction over the last half century.

First and most important was the effect of two world wars, each of which produced a sharp increase in the share of wages in the national income, presumably as a consequence of the labour scarcity involved in total war. The fact that the increase in the wage fraction was maintained after the First World War is perhaps more surprising than the fact that it was maintained after the Second World War when the wartime labour scarcity was prolonged in a period of abnormally full employment.

Secondly, it is evident that there has been a marked increase in the power and influence of trade unions since the First World War and even more since the Second World War. It seems reasonable to attribute part at least of labour's increasing share in the national income to political and institutional developments which have improved its bargaining power.

It may also be argued that there has been some shift of labour from industries with a low employee fraction (such as agriculture) and into industries with a high employee fraction (such as government and manufacturing). However, Table 67, which illustrates the changing composition of the wage and salary bill, shows that the shifts were by no means all in one direction. Whether on balance the twentieth-century structural changes have contained an important degree of bias towards industries with a high labour content is dubious.

Table 67. *Industrial composition of United Kingdom wages and salaries, 1901–56*

(as percentages of total incomes from employment)

	1911	1921	1938	1956
Agriculture, forestry, fishing	5·2	4·2	2·5	2·6
Mining and quarrying	7·0	7·0	4·7	4·6
Manufacture	28·0	31·6	32·0	38·7
Building and contracting	6·0	6·1	6·4	6·9
Gas, electricity, water	0·9	1·5	2·0	1·9
Transport and communication	}23·2{	11·0	9·9	9·0
Trade and commerce		13·0	16·0	13·1
Government and defence	8·2	9·1	8·8	8·9
Miscellaneous other	21·5	16·6	17·8	14·4

Sources: Chapman and Knight, *op. cit.*, for 1921 and 1938; 1957 Blue Book, *op. cit.*, for 1956. Our estimate for 1911 which is for Great Britain only.

Finally, it is clear that there has been a continuing increase in the proportion of employees—both because the shift from self-employed to employed has continued and because there has been a tendency for enterprise to be organised on a company basis so that entrepreneurs and own-account workers are transformed into salaried employees. It should be noted, however, that there is no evidence to show that the trend towards an increase in the proportion of employees has appreciably accelerated during the last fifty years (it rose from 87 per cent in 1911 to 93 per cent in 1951) by comparison, for example, with the half-century before the First World War when the wage fraction was so lacking in secular trend.

CHAPTER VIII

LONG-TERM TRENDS IN
CAPITAL FORMATION

WHERE the basic statistics are few it is generally easier to compile estimates of the ways in which national income is earned or produced than of its disposition. It is rarely that the statistician of an under-developed country, for example, is able to make an independent cal-culation of the expenditure side of the national-income account. To do so would involve expensive *ad hoc* collections of data that are not normally necessary for routine administrative purposes. Students of historical trends are faced with the same kind of problem. Aggregate statistics of consumers' expenditure or of capital formation are rarely needed for ordinary administration. Those who require them face the labour of building up their own aggregates from a mass of incomplete and small data and barely relevant indicators. Naturally enough this is a task which becomes more formidable as we go back in time both because the raw material must be quarried from less and less accessible sources and because the prospects of obtaining reasonably reliable results are less and less encouraging.

In this chapter we shall be largely concerned with one aspect of the disposition of national resources—the long-term trend in capital accumulation. The conceptual problems involved in defining and measuring capital in a way that lends itself to long-term analysis are, of course, formidable. The task of amassing enough empirical evidence to justify estimates of the changing level and structure of capital forma-tion in the United Kingdom over a long period of time has never been systematically attempted. All that we shall try to do in this chapter is to consider, somewhat sketchily, a few of the rough measures which have been constructed by previous investigators, in the hope of deducing from them a broad view of the changing dimensions of the process of capital accumulation in the United Kingdom. We shall look at them from two points of view—first in relation to the changing rate of capital formation, and secondly in terms of the changing composition of the stock of capital.

I. CHANGES IN THE RATE OF CAPITAL FORMATION

We can take as our starting-point Gregory King's estimates for the seventeenth century. He calculated the value of the stock of capital at various points in the seventeenth century and for 1688 suggested an investment of £2·4 m., representing about 5 per cent of national income.[1] This figure related to what he described as the 'actual stock'

---

[1] See Table 1 above.

of capital, that is to say, it included plate, jewellery, coin, furniture and clothing and excluded buildings. If we adjust his estimate of capital stock to exclude household goods and include buildings, i.e. to approximate to what might be called the 'productive and reproducible national capital', we find that his figures suggest a rate of investment of about 6 per cent of national income in 1688 in relation to a capital stock of about £112 m.[1]

However, 1688 was a prosperous year and King clearly did not regard these results as indicative of a long-term average. For the following decade his estimates suggest a fall in the nation's capital and examination of his estimates of capital stock over the century as a whole suggest a long-term average of not more than 3 per cent.

All this is, of course, highly conjectural. At best it permits us to say that an intelligent contemporary guess suggests an annual rate of capital formation at the end of the seventeenth century of between 3 per cent and 6 per cent of national income. It tended to be highly vulnerable to short-term disturbances and in particular to the incidence of war. The limiting factors to an increase in the rate of capital formation seem to have operated more from the side of investment than from the side of saving. When profitable opportunities for investment existed there seems to have been no lack of funds—as may be judged from the rapidity with which the losses incurred in the Plague and the Fire of London were made good and by the ease with which the foreign trading companies and the Bank of England were able to raise very considerable sums in the early 1690's.[2]

There are no usable estimates of the overall level of capital formation available for the eighteenth century, nor indeed for the first half of the nineteenth century. The earliest years to which modern investigators have extended their researches are the 1850's, and for this period their estimates suggest an average rate of net capital accumulation exceeding 10 per cent of national income. By then the process of industrialisation was well advanced and the nation seems to have been accumulating capital at twice its pre-industrial rate. When, we may ask, did the upward shift take place?

Generally it has been assumed that this doubling of the rate of capital formation took place fairly rapidly.[3] Professor Rostow has visualised its compression into a space of two decades (1783–1802) in postulating 'as a necessary but not sufficient condition for the take-off that the proportion of net investment to national income (or net national

[1] The reproducible stock includes producers' equipment and inventories, £33 m.; livestock, £25 m. and buildings, £54 m. King calculated the value of the nation's capital stock for 1600, 1630, 1660 and 1688 (*op. cit.* p. 61) on the assumption that it was increasing at an average annual rate of between 1 and 1½ per cent per annum.

[2] See Deane, 'Capital Formation in Britain before the Railway Age', *op. cit.*, for a discussion of the evidence on these points.

[3] Cf. W. Arthur Lewis. *The Theory of Economic Growth* (1955), p. 208: 'All countries which are now relatively developed have at some time in the past gone through a period of rapid acceleration in the course of which their rate of annual net investment has moved from 5 per cent or less to 12 per cent or more. This is what we mean by an Industrial Revolution.'

product) rises from, say, 5% to over 10%'.[1] There are three reasons for doubting that the change was so compressed, however. The first is that there is some evidence for an increasing rate of capital formation before the last two decades of the eighteenth century. The second is that the developments which occurred in the last two decades, though impressive, were not massive enough to produce an impact of the magnitude required by the Rostow hypothesis. The third is that the railway age of the 1830's and 1840's had an impact on the economy which was totally unprecedented in its magnitude, and if we are looking for a stage of development in which the rate of capital formation may have shifted sharply upwards, this is the period which is more likely than any other to qualify.

The evidence on the levels of capital formation for the eighteenth century is far from conclusive. Indeed, for the first four or five decades it is difficult to find anything to justify the view that the level had risen, apart from a steady increase in the rate of urbanisation and an expansion in overseas trade in the 1740's. In the middle of the century, however, there is unmistakeable evidence of a rising rate of capital accumulation in roads, canals, buildings and agricultural enclosures. The pace of urbanisation accelerated. The first wave of investment in canals began in the 1750's and lasted until the late 1770's. Whereas it is difficult to say whether the earlier Road Acts reflected new capital formation or merely a more effective system of keeping old routes in repair, there is some justification for regarding the work of the first road engineers as providing net additions to the nation's capital.[2] If parliamentary enclosures can be taken as evidence of increased investment in the reproducible capital of agriculture (fences, buildings, equipment, livestock, etc.), the fact that the acreage statutorily enclosed in the period 1761–92 was seven times that of the preceding three decades is significant enough.

In sum, then, it seems certain that from about the middle of the eighteenth century the nation's stock of reproducible capital began to grow appreciably. So too did population and total incomes. To establish a rising trend in the level of capital accumulation relative to national income we must show that the increase in the capital stock outstripped that of population and income. This we cannot do with present evidence. At best we can record an impression that the rate of capital formation advanced and steadied, perhaps reaching a long-term average of 5 or 6 per cent before the American War depressed the economy.

While it seems reasonable to assume that most of the upward shift in the rate of capital accumulation took place in less than seven decades —i.e. between the early 1780's when the steam engine, the new textile machinery and Cort's puddling process were being introduced, and the late 1840's when the railway construction boom was at its height—it is

[1] W. W. Rostow, *The Stages of Economic Growth* (1960), p. 37.
[2] Metcalfe, the first road engineer, was active between 1765 and 1792.

difficult to believe that it was largely accomplished in the space of about twenty years at the end of the eighteenth century. For this implies that an average annual rate of capital formation of under £10 m. per annum in the early 1780's had been raised to over £20 m. per annum by the early years of the nineteenth century.[1]

The relevant quantitative date for the period are few and uncertain but they are not of the right order of magnitude to support the hypothesis. The leading sectors in the industrial transformation were the cotton and iron industries. The most important form of new non-industrial capital formation undertaken in this period was the construction of canals and docks. It might reasonably be supposed that the large increases in capital accumulation would appear in these sectors.

For the cotton industry a contemporary estimate put the capital in buildings and machinery at nearly £9¼ m. *circa* 1802:[2] an earlier estimate had valued the capital invested in the industry during 1783–7 at nearly £1 m., which represented a doubling of the stock existing in 1783; taken together these estimates suggest that roughly £8 m. were invested in the cotton industry during the last two decades. In the iron industry 216 blast-furnaces were said to be in existence by 1806, which, at a generous allowance of £50,000 apiece, would represent a total capital of about £11 m. a large part of which had been invested in the previous two decades—probably about £6½ m. in the previous decade and a half. The number of steam-engines in existence at the end of the century probably did not exceed 1,000, representing a total capital of less than half a million pounds.[3] An analysis of the evidence available on capital authorised and spent on canal, dock and harbour projects suggests that these may have accounted for a new capital formation of up to £1¼ m. annually in the last decade of the eighteenth and the first decade of the nineteenth century.

On the most generous assumptions concerning the planning of these investments it is difficult to see how the new capital construction in cotton, iron and transport could have stepped up the annual rate of capital formation by more than about 1½ per cent of national income by the turn of the century. Nor does there seem any reason to suppose that investment in other sectors was growing more rapidly than national income during this period.

It is doubtful, further, whether the rate of capital accumulation could have been appreciably accelerated in the first two decades of the nineteenth century when the economy was taking the strain of a major

---

[1] *Circa* 1802 the national income of Great Britain was probably about £230 m. In 1783, if we postulate a 20 per cent increase in the price level and no increase in average real incomes per head, the total may have been in the region of £160 m.: if we assume a greater price rise or some increase in real incomes the 1783 total would be less than £160 m.

[2] Lauderdale, *An Inquiry into the Nature and Origins of Public Wealth and into the Means and Causes of its Increase* (1804), p. 430, quoting a Glasgow writer's *Observations on the Cotton Trade of Great Britain*. These writers were inclined to exaggerate the importance of the cotton industry.

[3] See A. E. Musson and E. Robinson, 'The Early Growth of Steam Power', *Econ. Hist. Rev.*, April 1959, and John Lord, *Capital and Steampower, 1750–1800* (1923).

war and its depressed aftermath. We are therefore inclined to suppose that most of the upward shift in the national level of capital formation must have taken place in the period after 1815 and, in view of the dislocation which was involved in the re-establishment of the economy on a peacetime basis, probably after 1820. The statistical evidence on the growth of the major nineteenth-century industries which was considered in chapter VI tends to confirm this hypothesis and to suggest a further narrowing of the crucial period to between the 1830's and the 1860's.

For the cotton industry the transformation to power took place in the 1830's and 1840's. By this time cotton was a major industry, contributing 5 per cent or more of the British national income and it went on to expand its capital equipment at an annual rate which is estimated to have exceeded 4 per cent by the 1860's.[1] For the woollen industry the peak in mechanisation developed a decade or two later, i.e. in the 1850's and early 1860's. For the coal industry we found no investment data relating to the first half of the century, but if the most rapid expansion of capital coincided with the most rapid increase in output it probably came in the 1830's and early 1840's. For the iron industry the number of blast furnaces was growing most rapidly in the 1850's. The great boom in railway construction took place in the 1830's and 1840's, reaching its peak in the latter decade. For the transport industry as a whole we have estimated that the annual cost of new capital formation averaged about £11 m. in the 1830's and nearly £15½ m. in the 1840's, compared with between £5 m. and £6½ m. for most of the period 1790–1829.

Our tentative conclusions on rates of capital formation for the period up to about the middle of the nineteenth century can thus be summarised as follows:

1. It is impossible to say whether capital accumulation grew faster than the national income in Britain in the immediately pre-industrial period, i.e. between, say, 1688 when King's calculations suggest a long-term rate of capital formation of under 5 per cent of national income, and 1783 which marks the beginning of Professor Rostow's 'take-off' period.

2. There seems no doubt that there was an increase in the relative level of capital formation in the last two decades of the eighteenth century, but it is unlikely that it amounted to an increase of more than about 1½ per cent of the national income. Thus, if the rate of capital formation amounted to between 5 and 6 per cent of national income by the early 1780's, it may have reached about 7 per cent by the beginning of the nineteenth century.

3. Whether this level was maintained during the period of major war and its aftermath is doubtful. Certainly there is no reason to suppose that it was increased.

4. There does indeed seem to have been a period during which the

[1] M. Blaug, *op. cit.*

rate of investment increased rather suddenly, perhaps by as much as 2 per cent of national income in the 1830's and 1840's, probably by more than 3 per cent over the period 1830–60.

For the period before the First World War a number of annual total capital formation estimates are available.[1] They are all very rough and exceedingly tentative. With the exception of the Douglas series they are all direct descendants of the estimates made by Professor Cairncross in 1935 and amended for publication in 1953.[2] The Cairncross series have stood the test of time because they embody the results of much original and careful research and because to improve substantially upon them would involve a considerably larger project of research than the original. Most later estimates depend heavily upon them. It is appropriate therefore to recall the author's own warnings on the limitations of his material and the reasons for his hesitation in publishing it.[3]

In this chapter we shall be using Charles Feinstein's estimates for domestic fixed asset formation up to 1914 partly because they cover a longer time-period than any other, but also because they appear to be the most satisfactory. They also depend on Cairncross to a considerable extent. For the interwar period, 1920–37, we used Feinstein's and Maywald's estimates of gross capital formation in fixed assets,[4] and for the subsequent period, the official C.S.O. estimates published in the National Income Blue Book.

Stocks present a problem. What we need is an estimate of the value of the physical increase in stocks and work in progress. Over the past decade (1950–1959) this has averaged, according to the official estimates, about 1 per cent of national income, but there have been such wide annual variations that the average is meaningless. There was no basis at all for estimates of stock variations before 1914. Jefferys and Walters, following a precedent set by Phelps Brown, calculated stock changes on the assumption that they represented 40 per cent of the first difference between national-income estimates in successive

[1] See, for example, P. H. Douglas, 'An Estimate of the Growth of Capital in the United Kingdom, 1865–1909'. *Journal of Economic and Business History*, August 1930; J. H. Lenfant, 'Great Britain's Capital Formation, 1865–1914', *Economica*, vol. XVIII (May 1951); E. H. Phelps Brown and S. J. Handfield Jones, 'The Climacteric of the 1890's: A study in the Expanding Economy', *Oxford Economic Papers*, vol. IV (October 1952); James B. Jefferys and Dorothy Walters, 'National Income and Expenditure of the United Kingdom', *Income and Wealth Series* V, Bowes and Bowes (1955); C. H. Feinstein, 'Income and Investment in the United Kingdom, 1856–1914', *Economic Journal* (June 1961).

[2] A. K. Cairncross, *Home and Foreign Investment, 1870–1913* (Cambridge, 1953).

[3] *Op. cit.*, Preface, pp. xiv–xv: 'It would, no doubt, have been possible for me to have published the dissertation without amendment immediately after its completion. But I had too lively a sense of its deficiencies to have any wish to do so. . . . How often, nevertheless, have I since come on some series of mine dressed in unfamiliar uniform and marching and counter-marching in an impossible campaign! It has been this sight that has convinced me of the need to publish. . . . The statistical material may be worth using, but only if its limitations are exposed to all who wish to do so.'

[4] An early version of these estimates appeared in an article by Dr. K. Maywald, *London and Cambridge Economic Service*, June 1960. Dr. Feinstein's final revisions are in *Domestic Capital Formation in the Uniea Kingdom 1920–38*, Cambridge, 1965, and are summarised in B. R. Mitchell, *Abstract of British Historical Statistics*, Cambridge University Press, 1962, pp. 373–8.

years. Whatever might be thought of this method as giving an indication of magnitude, or of probable direction of change from one year to another, it is clearly irrelevant to an analysis of long-period trends. Since the First World War the problem of estimation has been further complicated by the effects of inflation or depression on the money values of existing stocks. Even for the relatively recent periods the resulting estimates are unreliable.[1] In view of these problems of estimation and on the assumption that changes in stocks and work in progress were unlikely to affect substantially long-period trends in the level of capital formation, we ignored this component. It must be borne in mind, then, that our estimates probably understate the annual rates of domestic investment, and if the assumption that there was no appreciable trend in the level of stocks is not justified they may distort the long-period trend in capital formation.

The problem of calculating capital consumption is a similar amalgam of empirical and conceptual difficulties. The existing data are scanty, and even were they abundant it would still be difficult to convert them into the kind of measure we want. Here, however, we are dealing with an item which cannot be ignored. Over the decade 1950–9 capital consumption is estimated to have accounted for 9 per cent of gross national product and 49 per cent of gross investment. Using Feinstein's estimates of domestic investment, depreciation and national income, and Imlah's estimates of foreign investment, we can calculate that over the decade 1860–9 the corresponding proportions were about $2\frac{1}{2}$ per cent of gross national income and about 21 per cent of gross investment (excluding stocks). Maywald's estimates for 1929–38 suggest a depreciation proportion of about 70 per cent of the gross capital formation total. These are weighty proportions, whatever margins of error are attributed to them.

With the aid of existing estimates, supplemented where necessary by some crude interpolations or extrapolations of our own, we were able to compile series of the other main components of national expenditure for a period of about a century. They are summarised in Table 68. Because the available estimates did not permit the construction of satisfactory series for capital consumption over this period we have confined attention to the gross aggregates. It should be remembered, however, that the maintenance of the existing stock of capital has constituted an increasing proportion of total capital accumulation. Perhaps its share has risen from about a fifth to about a half in the course of the past century; possibly it rose well above a half in the depressed interwar period when incentives for new investment were weak. Certainly there is no doubt of its relative importance in the twentieth century pattern of economic change.

[1] See Central Statistical Office, *National Income Statistics, Sources and Methods*, p. 309, where reference is made to 'two special features of the estimation of stock changes: the first is the absence of complete data, which is more marked in this field than in any other part of the system of national accounts . . .; the second is the problem, both conceptual and practical, of the appropriate valuation of stock changes.'

In effect then, Table 68 illustrates in very broad terms the way in which the pattern of disposal of gross national product has changed over the past century. The underlying estimates lack precision and detail and it has not always been possible to ensure complete comparability, but they may be good enough to indicate the major trends without distortion.

Table 68. *The disposition of resources in the United Kingdom, 1860–1959*

(annual averages in £m.)

	(1) Consumers' expenditure	(2) Public authorities' expenditure	(3) Gross capital formation in fixed assets	(4) Net foreign investment	(5) Expenditure generating gross national product (excluding stocks, etc.)
1860–69	815	50	69	29	963
1865–74	963	53	85	56	1,156
1870–79	1,082	60	105	51	1,297
1875–84	1,133	68	105	42	1,349
1880–89	1,162	77	85	68	1,392
1885–94	1,235	86	85	72	1,478
1890–99	1,363	104	113	52	1,632
1895–1904	1,547	148	161	41	1,898
1900–09	1,727	168	168	85	2,148
1905–14	1,877	169	141	161	2,347
1920–29	4,088	455	445	124	5,112
1925–34	3,913	427	403	28	4,771
1930–39	4,066	583	484	−50	5,084
1935–44	4,669	2,646	391	−398	7,308
1940–49	6,359	3,504	676	−487	10,052
1945–54	9,180	2,588	1,659	−58	13,369
1950–59	12,513	3,160	2,738	150	18,561

Sources: For details see Appendix Table 91. Briefly, most figures for the period 1938–59 were derived from the National Income White Papers and Blue Books; consumers' expenditure series 1900–45 are D. Rowe's estimates; public authorities' expenditures 1870–1938 are from Jefferys and Walters; domestic capital formation estimates are from Feinstein and Maywald; net foreign investments are from Imlah (1860–1913) and *Board of Trade Journal* for the inter-war period. The fifth column is a sum of the preceding columns.

We may deduce from the existing estimates that total net capital formation had passed the 10 per cent level by the 1850's and rose to what may well have been its nineteenth-century peak of about 12 per cent of gross national product at market prices in the period 1865–79,[1] The level fell back to about 10 per cent in the 1890's and rose again at the turn of the century: it may have exceeded the nineteenth-century peak in the decade before the First World War. The striking feature of the pre-1914 pattern, however, is its narrow range. Expressed as a proportion of gross national product at market prices average gross capital

[1] Cf. Cairncross, *op. cit.* p. 198: 'If one accepts the figures it would seem that the savings reached a major peak in 1872–4 and that this peak was not subsequently surpassed, although 1913 came close to it.'

formation, excluding stocks, varied between about 10 per cent and 13 per cent over the whole half-century ending in the First World War.

A somewhat more erratic picture emerges for the second half of the nineteenth century if we consider the estimates for domestic capital investment alone. There is the same rise to a peak (of about 8 per cent) in the 1870's, a fall, perhaps to under 6 per cent, in the decade 1885–94, and a rise again at the turn of the century. But it is significant that in the early twentieth century the tendency seemed to be for the level of home investment to fall rather than to rise. The peak in total capital accumulation which seems to have occurred in the decade before the First World War was largely due to an abnormally high rate of foreign investment. Investment at home seems to have been lower, relatively, than it had been at any time in the previous half-century with the exception of the depressed decade 1885–94.

The evidence indicates, in effect, that, at any rate from *circa* 1875, the tendency was for the average levels of foreign and domestic investment to move in opposite directions. The decade 1885–94, for example, which shows a trough in the domestic investment series provided a peak in the foreign investment series, and the reverse was true of the decade 1895–1904. The rate of foreign investment was rising from 1875–84 to 1885–94, and again from 1895–1904 to 1905–14. The reverse was true of domestic investment. Whether this implies that 'long run foreign investment was largely at the expense of home investment or vice versa', as Cairncross has argued,[1] is another matter. It is perhaps sufficient to assume that the volume of savings becoming available for investment was determined by the investment opportunities which presented themselves and that opportunities for foreign investment tended to be more attractive when domestic investment was in the doldrums. If as has been suggested elsewhere[2], one of the reasons for the slackening in the pace of British economic growth at the end of the nineteenth century and the beginning of the twentieth was the growth of foreign competition, it is not surprising that home and foreign investment opportunities tended to appear in inverse relation to each other.

Certainly the virtual disappearance of opportunities for foreign investment in the 1930's and after does not seem to have released any funds for domestic investment. The level of domestic investment prevailing in the interwar period stayed at a low and relatively constant level. Its recovery in the period after the Second World War was below the nineteenth-century peak levels, though probably a little above the average for the half-century preceding 1910. If the rate of capital accumulation in the United Kingdom is to be raised to the previous peak levels of between 14 and 15 per cent without a recrudescence of investment abroad it involves a much higher rate of domestic investment than has ever been sustained in this country.

In this connection it is worth noting that there is one important respect in which the United Kingdom pattern of national expenditure

[1] *Ibid.* p. 187. See also Brinley Thomas, *Migration and Economic Growth*, 1954.
[2] See above, p. 33.

has differed markedly in the post-Second World War period from the earlier pattern. In the decade 1950–59 the current expenditure of public authorities amounted to 21 per cent of net national income. True the tendency for public authority activity to absorb an increasing proportion of national resources can be traced back to the last quarter of the nineteenth century, though it was obscured by temporary, war-conditioned, leaps in government expenditure. It took from the 1860's to the 1930's to increase from about 6 per cent to about 12 per cent. Except possibly at the peak of the Napoleonic Wars and briefly during the Boer War the current expenditure of public authorities absorbed a lower proportion of national income than net capital formation throughout the nineteenth and early twentieth centuries. By the inter-war years, however, the current peacetime expenditure of public authorities was averaging between 10 and 12 per cent of national income with national capital formation of about 3 to 6 per cent. During the 1950's when current expenditure of public authorities was more than a fifth of national income the investment of public authorities accounted for about a quarter of total national investment.[1] The recent recovery in the level of capital accumulation in the United Kingdom to something approaching nineteenth-century levels, clearly owes something to the increase in public authority investment.

So far we have considered these capital formation estimates in current prices, without exploring their implications as additions to the economy's total stock of capital The conceptual and practical problems of converting capital formation data to a constant price basis are too formidable to be solved by the kind of rule-of-thumb methods we have been using in this chapter, and must await the results of a more careful piece of research. Meanwhile, however, a tentative assessment of the labour content of capital formation and—in this sense—of the corresponding changes in the volume of the annual addition to the capital stock can be obtained by deflating the estimates in Table 68 by an index of money wages. For this purpose we used Wood's index for the period 1850–1914, Bowley's for the period 1880–1936, and the Ministry of Labour index of money wages for the recent period. The results, crude though they are, suggest some interesting conclusions concerning the rate at which additions were made to the national stock of capital, and the relative magnitude of these additions as between one period and another. In the 1850's and 1860's the rate of capital accumulation, measured in terms of its labour input, seems to have been rising rapidly: it was more than half as much again in the 1870's by comparison with the decade 1855–64. It fluctuated at this sort of level until the turn of the century, and then began to rise again. Between 1890–9 and 1905–14 the increase in the annual rate of addition to capital rose slightly more than in the earlier period of rapid advance. So by the decade preceding the First World War the annual net addition to the stock

---

[1] If we include the capital formation of public corporations it brings the share of government-inspired investment up to 31 per cent of the national total.

Table 69. *Gross capital formation deflated by an index of money wages*

(annual averages in £m.: wages index based on 1914)

1855–64	137
1860–69	162
1865–74	205
1870–79	213
1875–84	199
1880–89	207
1885–94	237
1890–99	196
1895–1904	227
1900–09	274
1905–14	317
1925–34	256
1930–38	253
1950–59	558

Sources: Capital formation totals as in Table 68. Money wage index from Bowley, *Wages and Income since 1960*, extrapolated by Wood's index of money wages for dates before 1880 and Ministry of Labour index for recent period.

of capital seems to have been proceeding at about two and a half times its volume half a century before. The labour force had meanwhile increased by about 70 per cent. It is, however, significant that in the 1905–14 decade more than half of total gross capital formation took the form of additions to foreign assets which were to be heavily depleted during the First World War.

The interwar period saw a strikingly small flow of resources to capital formation. The deflated value for gross domestic capital formation was only 80 per cent of the pre-war level and foreign investment fell to a negative quantity in the 1930's. After the Second World War the flow recovered its momentum and in the decade 1949–58 annual total net investment was running at about 76 per cent of the average for the period 1905–14: but this time most of the increased flow was towards home investment. By then average domestic investment was about 50 per cent above the pre-First World War peak. The total occupied population had increased by somewhat less than this. We may conclude therefore that the annual net addition to domestic fixed capital is currently absorbing a higher proportion of labour resources than ever before.

2. CHANGES IN THE STRUCTURE OF THE NATIONAL CAPITAL

Considered estimates of the stock of capital in the United Kingdom are both few and unsatisfactory. Even for relatively recent periods the margins of error involved in the available estimates are discouragingly wide. Redfern used the perpetual inventory method to derive estimates of gross and net fixed capital at replacement cost for the years 1938, 1947 and 1952 but he was primarily interested in arriving at estimates of capital consumption and his figures for capital stock are no more than approximate.[1] More recently Barna's direct estimates of fixed assets in manufacturing industry only (based on a sample of fire insurance valuations) gave results which were 50 per cent above the Redfern figures for this category.[2] The fact that the raw material for such estimates becomes more scanty as we go back in time suggests additional reasons for regarding with caution calculations for earlier periods, of which the most careful are those made by Maywald for the interwar period.[3]

The estimates by Redfern, Barna and Maywald, uncertain though they are, do have the virtue of attempting to evaluate directly the physical stock of capital. For earlier periods the only estimates which are at present available are largely the result of capitalising current incomes. The capitalisation coefficients—in so far as they are not mere accounting conventions—measure stock-market expectations rather than values of real assets. There is little that such calculations as these can be expected to tell us about the long-term trends in the value of real capital or its changing rates of growth. Still less can they be used to measure changes in capital-output ratios, though they may show directions of change. What they should be able to do, however, is to indicate the changing structure of the national capital, though even here the analysis must be in very broad terms, for there is little breakdown of the estimates of industrial and commercial capital.

Gregory King's estimates for 1688 are particularly condensed. Out of an estimated total national capital of about £310 m. (excluding coin and household goods) about 64 per cent was attributed to land, about 17½ per cent to housing and about 8 per cent to livestock. The main interest of his calculation lies not in the actual figures, which must be entirely conjectural, but in their relative magnitudes. Land and buildings together accounted for more than 80 per cent of the productive national capital. The enormous importance attached to land, which is presumed to account for nearly two-thirds of the national capital, is significant. So too is the small share (not much more than 10 per cent) which he attributes to a broad category including 'Shipping and other Carriages, Engines and Instruments in Trade, Arts and employments in Naval and Military Stores (including defence works), Foreign and Domestic Wares, Commodities or Provisions'.

By the end of the eighteenth century, if we may judge by Beeke's estimates, land had fallen to 55 per cent of the total and buildings to about 14 per cent, while industrial and commercial capital outside

---

[1] P. Redfern, 'Net Investment in Fixed Assets in the United Kingdom, 1938–53', *J. Roy. Statist. Soc.*, 1955.

[2] T. Barna, 'The Replacement Cost of Fixed Assets in British Manufacturing Industry in 1955', *J. Roy. Statist. Soc.*, 1957.

[3] K. Maywald, 'Capital Formation in the United Kingdom', *London and Cambridge Bulletin* 34, in *The Times Review of Industry*, June 1960. It may be noted that Maywald's estimate of the gross capital stock at current prices at the end of 1938 was £23,553 m. Redfern's estimate was £15,818 m.

agriculture accounted for about 21 per cent. Investment in trade and industry was then a significant channel of new capital formation.

Table 70. *The structure of the national capital of Great Britain, 1798–1927*

(as percentages of the total national capital)

Circa	1798	1812	1832	1885	1912	1927
1. Land	55·0[3]	54·2[3]	54·1[3]	18·1[4]	6·9[4]	4·0
2. Buildings	13·8	14·9	14·1	22·1	25·9	22·1
3. Farm	8·7	9·3	9·2	5·2	2·5	2·3
4. Overseas securities	—[2]	—[2]	4·7[6]	8·2	12·0	7·6
5. Domestic railways				10·5	9·3	4·6
6. Industrial commercial and financial capital	20·8	19·8	16·2	30·2	33·7	47·2
7. Public property[5]	1·7	1·8	1·7	5·7	9·7	12·3
8. Total national capital[1]	100·0	100·0	100·0	100·0	100·0	100·0

Sources: Figures for 1798 from H. Beeke, *Observations on the Produce of the Income Tax, etc.* (London, 1800); figures for 1812 from P. Colquhoun, *Treatise on the Wealth, Power and Resources of the British Empire* (London, 1815); figures for 1832 from Pablo Pebrer, *Taxation, Expenditure, Power, Statistics and Debt of the Whole British Empire* (London, 1833). Lowe also made an estimate of the national capital but it was incomplete and based on a hasty interpretation of Colquhoun's estimate. The 1885 estimates are from R. Giffen, *Growth of Capital* (London, 1889); and the 1912 and 1927 estimates are from H. Campion, *Public and Private Property in Great Britain* (London, 1939).

Notes: 1 Excluding national debt and movable property (furniture, plate, etc.).
2 No estimate available: probably negligible.
3 Excludes standing timber which is included in the industrial capital.
4 Campion uses a markedly lower number of years purchase for 1911–13 than Giffen had done for 1885 and part of this difference is thus due to the method of estimate. Applying Campion's multiplier to Giffen's figures for 1885 would give about 15 per cent instead of about 18 per cent for land in 1885.
5 Excluding roads and military property.
6 Using Imlah's estimate of the accumulating balance of credit abroad. This is probably rather high.

The pattern of structural change suggested by the contemporary estimates for the nineteenth century is exhibited in Table 70. They imply that there was little secular trend discernible in the first third of the century, though in view of the uncertainty of the data it would be unwise to put much weight on this conclusion. The implied long-term trend is more dependable, at any rate in broad terms. Its main characteristics can be distinguished as follows:

1. The fall in the relative importance of land and of farmers' capital, which together declined from an estimated 63½ per cent of total national capital in the first quarter of the nineteenth century to about 6½ per cent at the end of the first quarter of the twentieth century.

2. The corresponding growth in the importance of industrial and commercial capital from about 20 or 21 per cent of the national total at the beginning of the nineteenth century to over 40 per cent in the fourth quarter, and to over 50 per cent *circa* 1927.

3. Within the category of industrial and commercial capital, the rapid growth and later decline of overseas investments.

4. The growth in the importance of buildings from about 14 or 15 per cent of the national capital at the beginning of the nineteenth century to between 22 and 26 per cent in the late nineteenth and early twentieth centuries.

5. The growth in the importance of public property from under 2 per cent in the early decades of the nineteenth century to over 12 per cent in the 1920's.

We are on hazardous ground when we try to take a narrower view of these estimates, particularly those for the early years. It may be doubted, for instance, whether the estimates available for the first half of the century are truly comparable (apart altogether from the margins of error involved) with those for the second half. The main difficulty lies in the different character of investment in land at the two periods.

In an economy as developed as Britain was in the second half of the nineteenth century it is a convenient and fairly realistic assumption that the value of land represents the aggregate of claims to a virtually static stock of assets. In considering the growth of physical capital, therefore, we may be justified in excluding land altogether in order to focus more sharply on the reproducible elements in the national balance sheet. In early nineteenth-century Britain, on the other hand, much of the investment in land must have represented extensions or improvements of the cultivated area. How much, we do not know, although it has been calculated that in less than a quarter of a century (1793–1815) about a million acres of common pasture and waste were statutorily enclosed.[1] The Enclosure Acts do not, of course, establish either the fact or the timing of additions to the area under cultivation, but they give some support to the hypothesis that investment in land constituted an important element in new capital formation during the first two or three decades of the nineteenth century.

We can say little on the basis of these estimates about the character of the non-agricultural investment in the early years of the century. An important component of the early estimates of national capital consisted of stocks of goods and work-in-progress. About $8\frac{1}{2}$ per cent of Colquhoun's and Pebrer's totals for the national capital is accounted for by this component. Beeke has a corresponding estimate of about £200,000 or about $13\frac{1}{2}$ per cent for capital in the home trade and in foreign trade: but part of this represents shipping (1·2 per cent in both Colquhoun's and Pebrer's totals) and part may be attributable to engines and machinery. For 'steam engines and other expensive

[1] Gilbert Slater, *The English Peasantry and the Enclosure of Common Fields* (1907), p. 267, gives a statistical summary of the Acts of Enclosure relating to common pasture and waste only, as follows:

	Acts	Acres enclosed
1727–1760	56	74,518
1761–1792	339	478,259
1793–1801	182	273,891
1802–1815	564	739,743
1816–1845	244	199,300

machinery' Colquhoun has an estimate of £60 m.[1] and Pebrer states that 'in 1803 the sum invested in steam engines and other expensive machinery was estimated at £40 millions; since when it has more than doubled'.[2] If these contemporary guesses are of the right order of magnitude they suggest that capital in machinery may have accounted for between 2 and 2½ per cent of the national capital at the very beginning of the century, about 3½ per cent *circa* 1812 and about 4 per cent *circa* 1832. But in real terms the weight of this component may have grown between 1812 and 1832 more than the current-price estimates would suggest, for this was a period in which the price of capital equipment fell considerably.

One conclusion which emerges from the data shown in Table 70 is that the radical change in both the level and structure of capital formation took place after 1830. We have no further estimates of national capital until 1865 for which Giffen made his first estimates for the United Kingdom. By this time a remarkable change had taken place in the pattern of investment and in the structure of the national capital.

Analysis of Giffen's estimates for 1865, 1875 and 1885 indicates that important changes in the national capital were still in progress in the two decades before 1885. Land was declining rapidly in relative importance; it accounted for about 33 per cent of the national capital in 1865, 26 per cent in 1875, and 19 per cent in 1885. Although farmers' capital seems to have been increasing in relative and absolute value up to 1865 and in absolute value up to 1875 it had begun to fall absolutely as well as relatively by 1885. Investment in buildings had grown and was still growing in relative importance, but it was the industrial and commercial channels which were apparently attracting the bulk of new investment at this period.

Unfortunately it is not possible to analyse the shift towards industrial and commercial investment in detail. This is because the income-tax data on which Giffen's estimates are based do not provide an adequate breakdown for the Schedule D assessments. There is evidence for a very few sectors. Railways seem to have reached the peak of their importance in the 1880's; by 1885 they accounted for about 12½ per cent of the national capital. Ironworks seem to have attracted an accelerated flow of new capital in the decade 1865–75 and then to have declined in absolute value in the following decade. Capital in gasworks grew strongly in the decade 1865–75 and still more strongly in the decade 1875–85. Investment abroad began to swell strongly in the 1870's. Between 1865 and 1885 the value of U.K. foreign investments (excluding direct investments other than railways) can be estimated, on the basis of Giffen's figures, to have increased some three and a half times.

---

[1] Colquhoun, *op. cit.* p. 56. Joseph Lowe, in his *Present State of England* (1823), pp. 82–3, states wrongly that Colquhoun made no allowance for manufacturing machinery and suggests for *circa* 1822 a total of £130 m. representing 'money in hand, advances to correspondents abroad, manufacturing machinery, tools and implements of mechanics'.

[2] Pebrer, *op. cit.* p. 345.

Table 71. *The national capital, 1865–1933. Estimated by the income method*

(in thousand millions of pounds at current prices)

	United Kingdom			Great Britain			
	1865	1875	1885	1885	1911–13	1926–28	1932–34
1. Buildings	1·0	1·4	1·9	1·9	2·9	4·1	4·6
2. Farm capital	0·6	0·7	0·5	0·4	0·3	0·4	0·4
3. Overseas investments	0·4	1·0	1·3	1·3	3·0	3·7	3·7
4. Railways and canals	0·4	0·7	1·0	1·0	1·1	0·9	0·8
5. Capital in industry, commerce and finance	1·0	1·6	2·1	1·9	3·8	8·7	7·8
6. Public property	0·3	0·4	0·5	0·5	0·8	1·7	2·1
7. Total reproducible capital	3·7	5·8	7·4	6·9	10·9	19·5	19·3
8. Net national income	0·8	1·1	1·1	1·0	2·0	4·2	3·8
9. Capital–output ratio	4·6	5·4	6·6	6·7	5·5	4·6	5·0

Sources: Capital estimates for 1865, 1875 and 1885 based on Giffen, *Growth of Capital*; for 1911–13, 1926–8 and 1932–4, based on Campion, *Public and Private Property in Great Britain*. Figures for net national incomes based ultimately on Feinstein and Prest, with adjustments to exclude Ireland where necessary. Overseas investments 1865–85 include (*a*) public funds less home funds, (*b*) dominion and foreign securities, (*c*) railway outside U.K. and (*d*) foreign investments not assessed for tax. Overseas investment 1912, 1927 and 1938 based on Imlah (adjusted), and Kindersley (adjusted by Bank of England estimates).

On the face of it the growth of capital appears to have been slower in the decade 1875–85 than in the previous decade. This conforms with the evidence of the estimates in Table 68 which suggest a capital formation proportion of 12 per cent in 1865–74 and 11 per cent in 1875–84. Giffen commented at length on the implication of his estimates. 'There is reason to believe that in the last decade the rate of increase on capital has been steadily declining. . . . Capital has to be invested for a smaller and smaller amount.'[1] However, he concluded that in real terms, i.e. after correcting for the fall in prices, the difference was negligible.[2]

Table 71 summarises estimates of reproducible capital made by Giffen and Campion. It also confronts them with the relevant national-income estimates. In so doing it raises a number of problems of principle and of interpretation.

To deduce capital–output ratios from capital aggregates derived by capitalising current incomes is, of course, a highly questionable procedure. It can be said that the income-based estimates of capital do not appear to give results that differ greatly from direct estimates where these exist. Using Maywald's direct estimate as a basis for the 1933 net national capital figure, for example, we find a ratio of about 4·3 instead of about 4·9 which the income method gives for 1933–4.[3] But

---

[1] Giffen, *op. cit.* p. 48. [2] *Ibid.* p. 56.

[3] Phelps Brown and Weber made a rough direct estimate for the United Kingdom in 1912–13 of £8,429 m. excluding foreign assets. If the latter amount to about £2½ m. this gives a total national capital for 1912–13 of about £10·9 m. for the United Kingdom as a

the direct estimates are themselves so uncertain and so few that this is not a particularly encouraging observation.

Even apart from this crucial difficulty of principle, however, the data are too crude and discontinuous to be conclusive. Had we an annual series of direct estimates for the period 1865–85, for example, it might lead us to a quite different view of the trend or the stability of the ratio. Secondly, it must be borne in mind that all these estimates are at current prices and that except for periods where the prices of capital and consumer goods moved in sympathy with each other the trends suggested by estimates at constant prices would not be the same as those suggested in Table 71. Thirdly, it should be noted that the importance of foreign assets and foreign incomes in the century before the Second World War was such that capital–output ratios calculated on the basis of domestic capital and income would again be quite different. Annual estimates made at 1912–13 prices by Phelps Brown and Weber, for example, indicate that the ratio of domestic capital stock to annual home-earned income flow 'declined from about 3·7 in the seventies to 3·3 in the nineties and rose again to 3·9 in 1912. In the interwar years it moved from about 4·0 to 3·6.'[1]

The intriguing feature of the capital–output ratios lies in their apparent rise during the nineteenth century and their subsequent fall. If we take into account the early nineteenth-century capital estimates which form the basis of Table 70 they suggest a capital–output ratio of about 3 or even less, so that the implied rise is substantial. Unless there was a considerable shift in the relative prices of capital and con-sumer goods (which would eliminate much of the rise were the estimates converted to constant prices), or unless there were contributory changes in the structure of the national capital, a rise of this order of magnitude is not, on the face of it, consistent with capital formation estimates of perhaps 6 or 7 per cent of national product at the turn of the century, rising to perhaps 14 per cent in the 1870's, while the rate of growth of national product rose from under 2 to over 3 per cent. Similarly, given a steady or slightly increasing rate of capital formation between *circa* 1885 and 1912 together with a slackening, even declining, rate of growth in national income, it is difficult to see why the capital–output ratio should have fallen.

It is true that there were structural changes which would have con-tributed positively to a rise and later fall in the capital–output ratio. Over the period covered by Table 71 the most striking shift has been the increase in the relative importance of overseas investment—which accounted for less than 10 per cent of reproducible capital in 1865 and about 18 per cent in 1885 and 25 per cent in 1912, and declined again to about 19 per cent in the interwar years. Another sector with a high

whole; which suggests a very moderate degree of over estimate in the 1911–13 figure of Table 71. See, 'Accumulation, Productivity and Distribution in the British Economy 1870–1938', *Economic Journal*, 1953.

[1] *Ibid.* p. 266.

capital–output ratio was railway and canal transport which increased its share of the reproducible capital total from about 11½ per cent to about 13½ per cent between 1865 and 1885 and had dropped back to about 4½ per cent in 1927. These were substantial changes, though they would not explain a rise (and later decline) in the net capital–output ratio of the order of 50 per cent.[1] In sum, the capital–output ratios supplied by the estimates in Table 71 do not appear plausible and this may be partly attributable to the fact that the capital estimates do not reflect the cumulated results of past investments: it may also be attributed in part to the failure of bench-mark estimates to indicate trends.

For earlier periods the data are even less complete and their implications correspondingly more obscure. It may be asked, for example, how the accelerated rates of growth which are estimated to have occurred for the British economy in the late eighteenth and early nineteenth centuries were obtainable with such a modest increase in the level of capital formation. We have estimated that the overall long-term rate of growth rose from under ½ per cent per annum in the first part of the eighteenth century to 1½ per cent at the end and to nearly 3 per cent in the first three or four decades of the nineteenth century. If these changes were not the consequence of a greatly increased rate of capital accumulation, to what were they due?

The basic difficulty is that of defining capital formation so that it bears some relation to productivity, and so that it can provide a meaningful picture of the transition from a pre-industrial to an industrial economy. When the British rate of growth first began to accelerate markedly, the most important type of capital asset in Britain was still land. The enclosure movement which had been gathering momentum in the second half of the eighteenth century reached its peak with the first decade or so of the nineteenth. Large sums were spent on enclosure —on legal fees, on buying out occupants, and on fencing land. The effect of this kind of investment on productivity would depend on what was done with it. The owner who turned it into parkland and hunting preserves was unlikely to raise the national income; indeed, he may have reduced it by depriving the subsistence cottager of his plot of land, and his rights of pasture on the common. On the other hand, if he used it to plant corn for sale, to breed cattle or sheep, or to introduce new systems of crop rotation, he would raise the productivity of the land. What was done with the enclosed land would depend on the general economic situation. In the earlier part of the period—in the third quarter of the eighteenth century, for example—enclosed land often was used for conspicuous consumption or as a way of hoarding the profits of merchants (the earnings of the returned nabobs, for example)

---

[1] Probably we are trying to explain too much here. Short-term factors may account for much of the difference between single-year estimates over the decade 1929–38; for example, annual calculations of the net capital–output ratio based on Maywald, *op. cit.*, and Kindersley, *Economic Journal*, 1939, for overseas assets, varied from 3·9 to 4·6 with an average for the decade of about 4·2.

or for farming experiments of limited value. When the growth of population and war conditions made food scarce the enclosed land was turned to good account—but a generation or more may have elapsed between the initial expenditure on enclosure and its productive use. Similarly with expenditure on roads and canals. It might take several decades and a change in the general economic situation before their productive potential bore fruit. In other words, it was nearly a century of developing investment in enclosures, canals and roads which produced the acceleration of economic growth in Britain in the late eighteenth and early nineteenth centuries; and it was population growth and war that brought them into full productive effect.

Nor is it necessary to assume that capital formation in industry kept pace with the growth of incomes. In its early stages the leading industry in the British industrial revolution was the cotton industry, and much of this was organised on an outwork system. The weaver was characteristically a handloom weaver operating a wooden loom in his own home, employing his own family as auxiliary labour: much even of the spinning was done in the workers' own homes. Until the spinning inventions of the end of the eighteenth century increased the rate of spinning so vastly, most looms were inadequately utilised and a weaver was typically a farmer who gave only part of his time to his loom. Specialisation involved the elimination of this kind of excess capacity. In such circumstances the amount of new fixed capital required was quite small in relation to the output it would generate. By working factory labour long hours and on shift systems throughout the night, capital and buildings could be, and were, used relatively more intensively in the first quarter of the nineteenth century than ever before. At the same time developments in the banking and communication system meant that the need for capital to hold stocks of raw materials was diminished. It was not until the railway age and the steel age that men began to build vast capital installations which inflated the rate of growth of capital out of all proportion to the current growth of income, so that they might reap a corresponding return at a later date.

In effect, it is of the essence of a pre-industrial economy that additions to capital are not always fully productive and it is one of the features of the process of industrialisation that it makes some forms of existing capital more productive than at the time of their creation. Finally it should be remembered that not all innovations which increase income require commensurate increases in the rate of capital formation. A new system of crop-rotation, a larger measure of know-how in the use of manure, for example, might raise yields without any additional capital. The limiting factor to development may be the human factor, restrained by ignorance, uncertainty and inertia from making the most productive use of resources.

CHAPTER IX

BRITISH ECONOMIC GROWTH IN RETRO-SPECT : A SUMMARY OF CONCLUSIONS

THIS book represents a first attempt to establish the main dimensions of British economic growth over a period of over two and a half centuries. Its results are tentative and fragmentary because the accessible data proved inadequate for a definitive and comprehensive account. There is need for much detailed research at the industrial or regional level before we can confidently describe the quantitative characteristics of British industrialisation. Nor, indeed, have we exhausted the relatively accessible resources. To explore and test the implications of our estimates requires more sophisticated techniques of analysis and a wider body of information than we have brought to bear upon them: it demands a closer study of individual sectors and par-ticular time-periods.

We made these estimates, however, in the belief that there were some insights to be gained by taking the very long view of British economic growth and by trying to express secular change in consistent quantita-tive terms, rough though the measurements necessarily were. The purpose of this chapter is therefore to look back over the whole period and to summarise what seem to be the most interesting general features of our results.

I. LONG-TERM TRENDS IN NATIONAL INCOME

The beginnings of rapid or sustained economic growth are evidently to be sought in the eighteenth century. True, it is possible to find a tendency towards industrialisation beginning in the sixteenth and seventeenth centuries, if not earlier: and there is still room for argument concerning the degree of industrialisation and the rate of growth which had been achieved by the beginning of the nineteenth century. But most economic historians would agree that an unprecedented accelera-tion in the rate of economic expansion associated with the beginnings of modern industry took place in Britain in the second half of the eighteenth century, and that this initiated a process of economic growth which, in absolute terms and at differing rates, has been maintained until the present day. Clearly, the character of the initial acceleration and its pre-conditions are of particular interest, not only to those who are seeking an explanation for the first industrial revolution, but also to those who are concerned with policies which may launch modern pre-industrial economies into a path of sustained growth.

Our first attempt to plot the course of national income in the eighteenth century was made in terms of the contemporary national estimates.[1] These were few in number and of doubtful value. Between Gregory King's estimates for England and Wales made at the end of the seventeenth century, and the crop of estimates which arose out of the first attempts to impose an income tax in Great Britain at the end of the eighteenth century, we found only two national-income calculations that merit serious consideration. The first of these is Joseph Massie's calculation of the incomes of the various social groups in England and Wales, made in 1759 as part of a polemic on the sugar trade.[2] The other is Arthur Young's estimate published a decade later in his *Political Arithmetic*. Because Young's estimates were extremely detailed and specific we analysed them with some care.[3] The conclusion that emerged was that Young tended to exaggerate, and that probably he overestimated agricultural incomes more than other components of his national-income total. The Young estimates after adjusting for apparent omissions suggested a total income of about £130 m. for England and Wales *circa* 1770, in relation to a population of some 7 millions. The Massie estimates (also adjusted for omissions) suggested a total of between £80 and £90 m. *circa* 1759 in relation to a population of about 6½ millions and possibly a slightly lower level of prices.[4] The disparity between the aggregates implied by these two sets of estimates is a fair measure of their failure to inform on the precise level of money incomes in the period immediately before industrialisation began to gather a modern momentum. The average may have been between £12 and £19 per head according to these figures.

Nor was this the only problem of interpretation which arose out of the attempt to apply the contemporary national-income estimates. In order to use them as a basis for measuring the rate of growth of real income in the second half of the century we had to form some view of the change in the value of money in a period of structural change and war inflation. For this purpose the available price indices were clearly inadequate, and although we might have improved on them as measures of short-term fluctuations in the general price level, by widening their scope,[5] it did not seem likely that we could arrive at a more acceptable estimate of the long-term changes in the value of money.

Accordingly we turned to other sources of data and tried to deduce

---

[1] Deane, 'The Implications of the Early National Income Estimates, etc.', *op. cit.*

[2] Massie's estimates are presented and discussed by Peter Mathias, 'The Social Structure in the Eighteenth Century: A Calculation by Joseph Massie', *Econ. Hist. Rev.*, second series, vol. x (August 1957).

[3] Deane, 'The Implications etc.', *op. cit.* pp. 20–25. See also above, pp. 155–8, where the Young estimates are used in estimating the structure of national product *circa* 1770.

[4] Mathias, *op. cit.*, did not use Massie's figures as a basis for a national income estimate but he summed them to a total of about £61 m. excluding domestic servants which none of the eighteenth-century investigators considered as contributing to the national aggregate.

[5] It is a question whether a general price level measured in this way has any significance at all in an economy where regional variations in the content of total incomes were so great as was obviously the case in eighteenth-century Britain.

from the qualitative and quantitative evidence available for individual industries and branches of economic activity the chronology of the process by which the British economy entered into a state of sustained economic growth. This chronology is discussed in detail in chapter II of this volume. Here we shall confine ourselves to stating, somewhat baldly, what we found to be the overall quantitative implications of the data.

Briefly, what we did to arrive at the overall estimates was to calculate volume indices for five groups of economic activity: (*a*) agriculture and ancillary activities, (*b*) industries entering largely into the export trade, (*c*) industries producing largely for home consumption, (*d*) government and defence and (*e*) rents and miscellaneous services. We calculated the volume of agricultural output at decade intervals by estimating corn production and meat output: we assumed that the growth of commerce and industries entering largely into international trade could be related to the volume of domestic exports and net imports: we calculated a volume index for the home market industries by combining certain of the excise series: we derived an index for the government sector by adjusting government expenditure for price changes: and we assumed that the service industries expanded with population. We weighted these according to the pre-industrial structure of output in which agriculture and ancillary activities accounted for 43 per cent of the total, industry and trade for 30 per cent, government and defence for 7 per cent, and miscellaneous services for 20 per cent.

Different systems of weighting are discussed above in chapter II; with any plausible set of weights the pattern seems to be the same. There is little evidence of growth in the first four decades of the century, but beginning in the 1740's there was a marked upward trend in absolute totals though little improvement in the rate of growth in incomes per head until the last two or three decades. A considerably sharper upward trend appears in the 1780's and 1790's.[1] To recapitulate the results summarised in Table 20, real national output is estimated to have grown at about 0·3 per cent per annum over the period before 1745, 0·9 per cent over 1745–85, and 1·8 per cent over the last two decades of the century. The corresponding rates of growth in output per head were 0·3, 0·3 and 0·9 per cent.

These crude growth rates are based on 1700 weights and by comparison with the similar calculations based on 1800 weights they have an upward bias. The reason is that prices of agricultural commodities, whose output expanded slightly less than population according to our estimates, rose much more rapidly than prices of domestic exports, whose expansion in real terms was three times greater than that of population. The disparity between the two sets of prices became particularly marked in the last two or three decades of the eighteenth century, and if we measure the overall rate of progress in our index

[1] This of course is the period to which Professor Rostow attributes the British 'take-off' (*Economic Journal*, *op. cit.* p. 31).

during the period 1785–1805 we get a rate of 1·5 using 1800 weights compared with 1·8 with 1700 weights. The contrast between the rates of stagnation, early growth and acceleration, characteristic of the three periods distinguished above, is as striking when measured in terms of 1800 prices, however, as in terms of 1700 prices.

The acceleration in the rate of growth found for the last two decades of the century is in accordance with what now seems to be the generally accepted view among economic historians.[1] We have tried to put a quantitative interpretation on that view. It must be remembered, however, that it rests heavily on the domestic exports series. In effect it has been assumed that over a fifth of national output rose in sympathy with the soaring volume of domestic exports. If international trade was indeed an 'engine of growth' of such significance, then we may fairly conclude that it was in the last two decades of the eighteenth century that national output began to grow faster than population.

These estimates relate to England and Wales only. If we were able to extend them to include Scotland and Ireland it may be supposed that the eighteenth-century rates of growth would seem lower. Certainly it would be difficult to find evidence for an acceleration of this order in Ireland, which by the end of the eighteenth century is estimated to have accounted for about a third of the population of the United Kingdom. On the other hand, it may be noted that estimates of Irish population in the eighteenth century (for what they are worth) imply a more rapid rate of population growth than in England and Wales.[2]

For the nineteenth and twentieth centuries we were able to make national-income estimates of our own or to make use of those provided by other investigators in order to provide bases for estimates of long-term economic growth. Prest's estimates of national income 1870–1913[3] and Jefferys' and Walters' estimates[4] of incomes not included by Prest (largely incomes of non-profit-making institutions) formed the main basis of our estimates of U.K. national income for the period 1870–1913 and these were extrapolated back to 1855 on the basis of Feinstein's estimates.[5] However, for the first six or seven decades of the nineteenth century the divergent experience of Ireland and the relative weight of the latter in the United Kingdom total, made it essential to exclude it in order to arrive at meaningful estimates of the levels and changes in British incomes. We therefore calculated the national product of Great Britain at decade intervals (for census years) throughout the nineteenth century. The results are shown in Table 72.

Converting these estimates to real terms presented a problem because of the lack of satisfactory price data. The only index covering the whole

---

[1] Cf. Asa Briggs, *The Age of Improvement* (1959), p. 18.

[2] See above, Table 2, p. 6.

[3] A. R. Prest, *op. cit.*

[4] James Jefferys and Dorothy Walters, *op. cit.*

[5] C. H. Feinstein estimates 'Income and Investment in the United Kingdom, 1856–1914', *Economic Journal*, vol. LXXI, (June 1961).

Table 72. *The national product of Great Britain in the nineteenth century*

(in £m.)

	National product at current prices	National product at constant prices	
		Total	Per head
1801	232	138	12·9
1811	301	168	13·2
1821	291	218	15·3
1831	340	312	19·1
1841	452	394	21·3
1851	523	494	23·7
1861	668	565	24·4
1871	917	782	29·9
1881	1,051	1,079	36·2
1891	1,288	1,608	48·5
1901	1,643	1,948	52·5

Sources: See text and notes to Table 37 above.

of the nineteenth century was the Rousseaux index of wholesale commodity prices based on an average of the years 1865 and 1885.[1] As an index of changes in the value of money it is exceedingly dubious but we have accepted it for broad comparisons over fairly long periods of time. These estimates suggest that the real national income of Great Britain increased by a factor of about 14 in the course of the nineteenth century, and that real national income per head roughly quadrupled. In both absolute and per capita terms the growth from decade to decade seems to have been positive and continuous for the whole period.

Unfortunately the data are too crude to measure changes in real incomes over shorter periods of time because there are serious deficiencies both in the money national-income estimates and in the price deflator. The use of the Rousseaux wholesale commodity index as a measure of the short-term relation between real and money incomes introduces an unknown margin of error into the real-income estimates throughout the period. The money national-income estimates are least satisfactory for the first half of the century. On the most optimistic view of the data on which they are based, however, each of the national-income estimates represents a bench-mark calculation which is more or less closely related to the experience of a particular year or short group of years and is thus subject to cyclical bias. Short-term deviations from the trends in the rate of growth or value of money become relatively less important when seen in larger perspective. We have therefore summarised the growth implications of the data in Table 72 by measuring them in terms of decade averages and relating them to periods of at least thirty years. The resulting estimates are set out in Table 73.

Before leaving the decadal figures, however, it is worth noting that

[1] Paul Rousseaux, *Les Mouvements de Fond de l'Economie Anglaise 1800–1913* (Louvain, 1938), pp. 262–7.

they imply abnormally low rates of growth in the first and sixth decades of the century and again in the last decade. It is easy to explain the relative stagnation in the first decade in terms of war conditions. It is not so easy to account for the apparent low rate of growth between *circa* 1851 and *circa* 1861. The difference is great enough to require explanation, even when allowance has been made for defective data. Perhaps the readiest explanation is the Irish famine, which reduced the population of Ireland by 30 per cent between 1845 and 1861 and flooded Britain with unskilled labour. But this is clearly not enough and closer study is required to resolve the problem posed by these estimates. The downturn of the 1890's has already been recognised and extensively discussed in terms of a 'climacteric' following the 'massive application of steam and steel' which is held to have carried the economy to its peak nineteenth-century rate of growth.[1]

Table 73. *Nineteenth-century rates of growth in British real product*

(compound rates per cent per annum)

	Total growth of national product	Growth of national product per head occupied population	Growth of national product per head total population
1801/11–1831/41	2·9	1·5	1·5
1811/21–1841/51	2·9	1·4	1·5
1821/31–1851/61	2·3	0·9	1·1
1831/41–1861/71	2·2	0·9	1·0
1841/51–1871/81	2·5	1·4	1·3
1851/61–1881/91	3·2	2·0	1·9
1861/71–1891–1901	3·3	2·2	1·7

Sources: As for Table 72.

The broader measurements in Table 73 suggest a long-term rate of growth beginning at rather less than 3 per cent per annum, slackening to between 2 and 2½ per cent in the middle decades of the century, and exceeding 3 per cent at the end. The slower mid-century rate of growth is even more marked in the per head figures which suggest a lower rate of growth in productivity at this stage. In sum, therefore, the process of acceleration in the United Kingdom rate of growth to its climax in the last quarter of the century seems to have been disturbed by three main factors—the retarding effect of the Napoleonic Wars, the sudden spurt in industrial growth which followed this retardation, and the Irish famine.

[1] E. H. Phelps Brown and S. J. Handfield-Jones, 'The Climacteric of the 1890's: A Study in the Expanding Economy', *Oxford Economic Papers*, 1952. This interpretation has been discussed by Coppock, who regards the apparent downturn of the 1890's as being too heavily dependent on the price indices used to deflate money incomes. By taking his cue from the somewhat earlier decline in industrial productivity he chooses to place the crucial watershed in the 1870's, attributing the subsequent downturn largely to the associated decline in British exports. D. J. Coppock, 'The Climacteric of the 1890's: A Critical Note', *Manchester School of Economic and Social Studies*, 1956.

Table 74 carries the story into the twentieth century in which the United Kingdom rate of growth, disturbed as it was by two world wars, appears to have been highly erratic. During both wars there was an absolute decline in real incomes per head and attempts to establish significant long-term trends for the twentieth century are thus not very conclusive. The results are further obscured by the inclusion of Southern Ireland up to 1920 and its exclusion thereafter. The sharp decline of the Irish population in the second half of the nineteenth century gives an upward bias to the rates of growth in real income per head during the early part of the period covered by Table 74.[1] The fact that the

Table 74. *United Kingdom rates of growth, 1855–1959*

Annual averages	National income at factor cost and current price (£m.)	National income per head at 1913 prices (£)
1855/64	685	21·2
1860/69	713	23·1
1865/74	936	26·1
1870/79	1,057	29·0
1875/84	1,106	31·0
1880/89	1,171	34·3
1885/94	1,291	38·5
1890/99	1,463	43·2
1895/04	1,649	46·0
1900/09	1,850	47·0
1905/13	2,087	48·6
1920/29	4,327	47·7
1925/34	4,035	49·9
1930/39	4,291	54·4
1935/44	6,212	63·9
1940/49	8,332	64·5
1945/54	10,807	62·5
1950/59	15,037	70·0

(Average percentage increase per head per decade (measures over twenty-year periods))

	(%)
1855/64–1875/84	23
1860/69–1880/89	24
1865/74–1885/94	24
1870/79–1890/99	25
1875/84–1895/04	24
1880/89–1900/09	19
1885/04–1905/14	13
1900/09–1920/29	1
1905/14–1925/34	1
1920/29–1940/49	18
1925/34–1945/54	13
1930/39–1950/59	14

(Annual rates of growth per head (decade averages measured over thirty-year periods))

1855/64–1885/94	2·0
1860/69–1890/99	2·1
1865/74–1895/04	1·9
1870/79–1900/09	1·6
1875/84–1905/14	1·5
1890/99–1920/29	0·3
1895/04–1925/34	0·3
1900/09–1930/39	0·5
1905/14–1935/44	0·9
1920/29–1950/59	1·3

Sources: As for Table 90, Appendix III, below.

[1] It should be noted that the annual rates of growth given in this table are not comparable with those in Table 73 for two reasons: (a) because the Irish component gives a spurious

two wars caused radical alterations in both the structure and level of prices should also be borne in mind for this throws doubt on real-income estimates which are arrived at by means of an overall price deflator.

In spite of the deficiencies of the data, however, and the erratic path of U.K. growth in the twentieth century it seems clear that long-term rates of growth have been substantially lower than those prevailing at the end of the nineteenth century. It is difficult to assess the contribution of war to this result because there has been no period of more than twenty years in the present century which has not been affected by war or its aftermath.

Looking back now over the whole period of two and a half centuries covered by this inquiry, it can be said that while we hesitate to put weight on the precise short-period changes suggested by our data, the shape of the long-period trends (sustained over periods of at least three decades) emerges fairly convincingly. The beginnings of sustained economic growth can be traced to the middle of the eighteenth century when the overall rate of growth seems to have risen to near 1 per cent per annum from probably not more than about 0·3 per cent per annum. At this stage, however, the expansion of the economy was apparently swamped by the growth of population which also dates from slightly before mid-century. There is little evidence of an appreciable acceleration in the long-term rate of growth of real incomes per head until the last two decades of the eighteenth century, when the average rate of growth seems to have approached one per cent per annum. The acceleration which then took place was significant, though perhaps not as spectacular or as sudden as has sometimes been suggested, because it marked the beginning of a more or less continuous upward trend. The rate of growth continued to accelerate into the nineteenth century, slackened in mid-century, recovered to record heights and then slackened again at the beginning of the twentieth century. Its pace has fluctuated and it has been thrown into temporary reverse by total war, but except over the period affected by the two world wars the long-term rate of growth has been positive (at an annual average rate generally in excess of 1 per cent) ever since the end of the eighteenth century.

2. THE ROLE OF POPULATION IN ECONOMIC GROWTH

Special interest attaches to the role of population in the early stages of economic growth, for the rapid expansion of national output which characterised the industrial revolution was accompanied by an equally revolutionary upsurge in the numbers of the people, and by a shift in the centre of gravity of the population from the south and east of the

upward lift to the United Kingdom figures, and (*b*) because the rates for Great Britain have been damped by comparing averages of bench-mark estimates rather than decade averages of annual figures.

country towards the north and west. This coincidence raises a number of vital questions. To what extent were the population changes a cause, and to what extent a consequence of the economic changes? Did population grow because output was expanding or did output expand in response to population growth? Was the internal distribution of the population determined by the changes in the location of industry or did the distribution of population set the stage for industrial expansion?

Most historians would agree that the population changes were both a cause and an effect of the concomitant economic changes. They differ, however, in their analysis of the mechanism of interaction, of the timing of cause and effect, and hence on the relative importance of the causal factors. It has commonly been assumed that the rapid increase in the population at the end of the eighteenth century was initiated by a fall in the death rate and that this in its turn was due to medical progress.[1] In this interpretation population growth was determined by exogenous factors. More recently Professor Habakkuk has suggested that the effect of the birth rate has been underestimated,[2] and medical historians, while accepting the primacy of the death rate, have argued that the medical advances of the eighteenth century were not such as would have affected the death rate.[3] More recently still it has been claimed that the evidence for a decline in the death rate at the end of the eighteenth century is itself unconvincing, and that the major factor must have been the birth rate.[4]

It is not possible to solve these problems of interpretation without making a substantial addition to the inadequate demographic data on which they are based. What is required is a large-scale study of the local records, particularly of the parish registers. An analysis of the county data given in the early censuses, however, suggests that part of the conflict of interpretation is due to the fact that there were considerable regional variations in the pattern of population growth.

The population of the counties which received the major impact of the industrial revolution (Lancashire, West Riding, Warwickshire, and Staffordshire) was already growing quite markedly in the first half of the eighteenth century, when the population of England and Wales increased by about 5 per cent, while in the predominantly agricultural

---

[1] Cf. T. H. Marshall, 'The Population of England and Wales from the Industrial Revolution to the World War', *Econ. Hist. Rev.*, vol. v (1935), reprinted in E. M. Carus-Wilson, *Essays in Economic History*, p. 333: 'It is generally agreed that the outstanding fact in the first period was a rapidly falling death rate. The cause of the fall is to be found mainly in the progress of medicine of which there is ample evidence.'

[2] H. J. Habakkuk, 'English Population in the Eighteenth Century', *Econ. Hist. Rev.*, second series, vol. vi (1953), p. 133, where it is argued that 'the acceleration of population growth was primarily the result of specifically economic changes, and in particular, of an increase in the demand for labour' which 'operated more via the birth-rate than the death-rate'.

[3] T. McKeown and R. G. Brown, 'Medical Evidence Related to English Population Changes in the Eighteenth Century', *Population Studies*, vol. ix (1955).

[4] J. T. Krause, 'Changes in English Fertility and Mortality, 1781–1850', *Econ. Hist. R.* Second series, vol. xi (1958).

counties population was stationary or falling. Some of the increase was due to internal migration, but the evidence suggests that internal migration in the eighteenth century was attributable more to the attraction of urban areas than to industrial expansion *per se*. For most of the period of 130 years ending in 1831, the lure of London and the home counties seems to have accounted for the bulk of internal migration, and the indications that Lancashire and Warwickshire owed some of their increase to migration, whereas Staffordshire and West Riding did not, can be plausibly explained by the existence of Liverpool, Manchester and Birmingham. If we take the north-west region as a whole, and compare it with the south-eastern counties taken together, our estimates suggest that although the north-western share in total population increased from 43·5 per cent to 48·3 per cent in the course of the eighteenth century, there was a substantial balance of net migration away from this area rather than towards it.

The data on which these estimates are based are defective, but when allowance is made for this there remains a high probability that the relative growth of the numbers in the industrial counties in the eighteenth century was due entirely to relatively high rates of natural increase in them and their immediate neighbours. In trying to measure relative birth and death rates on the basis of defective baptism and burial figures, we are on still more hazardous ground, but again the regional variations in the pattern constitute the most striking and convincing feature of the results.

London was clearly a special case. The fall in its death rate (from an estimated 48·8 in the first half of the eighteenth century to 27·4 in the first part of the nineteenth) was spectacular. On the other hand, we could find no evidence of a sustained increase in the London area birth rate up to 1831. It may even have declined from a level which was well above the national average in the first half of the eighteenth century.

In the north-west region, by contrast, it would seem that the first half of the century was characterised by a marked rise in the birth rate, and by a death rate which rose in the 1720's and 1730's and began to decline only in the 1740's. In the second half of the eighteenth century, the high birth rate which had been achieved in this area by 1750 was maintained and the death rate was stabilised at a level slightly below the average of the earlier period. If we focus attention on the counties which took the major impact of the industrial revolution, and their immediate neighbours, there seems little doubt that the rise in the birth rate was the primary factor in the population upsurge, and that most of it preceded the era of rapid industrial growth. It is questionable whether the rise in the birth rate in the first half of the eighteenth century was due to non-economic factors, or to rising agricultural productivity, or to a preceding and more generalised economic expansion that was reflected in labour shortage and rising real wages at the end of the seventeenth and very beginning of the eighteenth centuries.

We know, however, that the growth in the relative importance of the north-west had started well before 1750, and it seems reasonable to suppose that the demographic peculiarities of the region were to a large extent dependent on its changing economic fortunes. On the other hand, it is equally likely that population growth served, in its turn, to influence the course of economic change and that there was some connection between the beginnings of the population upsurge which began in the 1740's when declining mortality reinforced a rising birth rate, and the beginnings of the general economic expansion which also became apparent at that time.

The overall effect of these various movements in regional birth and death rates on the national level of population can be seen in Table 75. The eighteenth century seems to have opened with a tendency to population growth, but this turned to stagnation or decline as death rates rose in most parts of the country. The marked expansion of the North-West in the 1740's was countered by a continuing high level of mortality in London, which was still in the grip of the gin mania, to give a very moderate increase at the national level. When, in the second half of the century, the London death rate began its dramatic decline the population of the northern and western counties had already 'taken off' into steady and sustained growth. The slight

Table 75. *Rates of growth of population, 1701–1931*

(percentage increase per decade)

	England and Wales[1]	Great Britain[2]	United Kingdom
1701–11	+ 2·7	..	..
1711–21	+ 0·3	..	..
1721–31	− 0·9	..	..
1731–41	− 0·3	..	..
1741–51	+ 3·6	..	..
1751–61	+ 7·0	..	..
1761–71	+ 7·3	..	..
1771–81	+ 6·8	..	..
1781–91	+ 9·5	+ 9·0	..
1791–1801	+11·0	+10·2	..
1801–11	..	+13·7	+13·8
1811–21	..	+16·9	+16·0
1821–31	..	+15·2	+14·9
1831–41	..	+13·4	+10·8
1841–51	..	+12·5	+ 2·4
1851–61	..	+11·1	+ 5·8
1861–71	..	+12·7	+ 8·9
1871–81	..	+13·9	+10·7
1881–91	..	+11·2	+ 8·2
1891–1901	..	+12·0	+ 9·9
1901–11	..	+10·3	+ 9·1
1911–21	..	+ 4·6	+ 4·2
1921–31	..	+ 4·7	− 2·3[3]

Sources: 1 Based on Brownlee's estimates.
2 Registrar-General's estimates (estimated mid-year population).
3 1921 figures with Irish Republic, 1931 without.
.. Estimates not available.

deceleration in the 1770's could be attributed to a rise in mortality which the north-western counties seem to have avoided. It was not until the last two decades of the century that the London area's death rate fell low enough to permit a positive rate of natural increase so that it contributed directly to the new population upsurge which began in the 1780's.

By the beginning of the nineteenth century, the regional variations in birth and death rates were no longer so significant. The London area's death rate though still high was only 20 per cent above the national average (compared with nearly 50 per cent above in the first half of the eighteenth century). The rate of natural increase in the south-eastern portion of the country was over 89 per cent of that in the northern and western group of counties compared with 51 per cent in the second half of the eighteenth century, and − 21 per cent in the first half (when the rate of natural increase was negative in the South-East and positive in the North-West).

The upsurge that began in the 1780's continued to a peak in the second and third decades of the nineteenth century, when the rate of growth was in the region of 15 or 16 per cent per decade, and although this peak was not maintained, the decade rate of increase for Great Britain remained over 10 per cent until the second decade of the twentieth century, when it dropped to, and stayed at, under 5 per cent. As we saw in the previous section, there was a similar sharp drop in the rate of growth of average real incomes in the early twentieth century: but this preceded by about a decade the drop in the rate of population growth.

For most of the nineteenth century the changes in the rate of natural increase are of less significance in relation to economic growth than the changes in the rates of migration. These have been analysed elsewhere.[1] Briefly, however, it may be said that as the growth of factory production concentrated industry in the urban areas the movement to the towns was greatly accentuated. The nineteenth century was a period of rapid urbanisation which was closely associated with the pattern of industrial growth. Between 1841 and 1901 the English towns attracted nearly 3 million migrants and the colliery districts over half a million.[2] By contrast, the rural areas lost more than 4 million by migration. The net outflow from England and Wales as a whole during the second half of the nineteenth was in the region of a million: before 1851 the net balance of migration was probably inwards rather than outwards though most of this inflow was from Ireland or Scotland.

The relation of these migrations to economic growth has been explored by Professor Brinley Thomas, who found 'clear evidence of an inverse relation between the fluctuations of internal migration and home investment on the one hand and those of emigration (and capital

---

[1] A. K. Cairncross, *Home and Foreign Investment, 1870–1913* (Cambridge, 1953), pp. 65–83, and Brinley Thomas, *Migration and Economic Growth* (Cambridge, 1954).

[2] Cairncross, *op. cit.* p. 70.

exports) on the other'.[1] Here it may be sufficient to note that the first decade of the twentieth century, when the rate of growth of real incomes per head seems to have been significantly below nineteenth-century levels, was also the decade when for the first time the English towns showed a net outflow of population. During this decade, moreover, the net emigration from England and Wales seems to have been over half a million, which was half as much as the net outflow for the whole of the five previous decades.

3. CHANGES IN INDUSTRIAL STRUCTURE

The process of industrialisation involves radical changes in the industrial distribution of the labour force and the structure of national product, and it may be presumed that these shifts were associated with changes in the rate of growth in real incomes. Accordingly we attempted to measure these shifts in the pattern of industry with the object of relating them to long-term growth rates.

For the eighteenth century information was scanty. There were no labour force data and the contemporary national-income calculations were inconclusive. Our analysis of Gregory King's calculations, for example, suggested that agriculture accounted for about 40 per cent of national product *circa* 1688: the corresponding proportion suggested by Arthur Young's estimate was 45 per cent *circa* 1770. It is possible that the share of agriculture increased in this period, but when it is remembered (*a*) that our comparison of King's figures with other contemporary estimates left the impression that he may have underestimated agricultural incomes, (*b*) that Young almost certainly overestimated the share of agriculture, and (*c*) that both sets of estimates were subject to wide margins of error, it will be appreciated that conclusions based on this sort of information are, to say the least, uncertain. All that we can safely assume is that in pre-industrial England and Wales agriculture probably accounted for between 40 and 45 per cent of national product, manufacture mining and building for between 20 and 25 per cent, and distribution and transport for between 10 and 15 per cent. This leaves an indeterminate remainder (professions, domestic service, government and defence, rents of housing) which may have accounted for anything between 15 and 30 per cent of the total. What changes occurred between 1688 and 1770 it is not possible to say, but there is evidence that there was a positive increase, if only a small one, in the share of industry.

If our estimates of the rates of growth in eighteenth century real output are of the right order of magnitude, it was after 1780 that the rate turned strongly upwards in per head as well as in absolute terms. Since this advance appears to have been due to improved productivity in industry and trade, rather than in agriculture (which according to our calculations barely kept pace with rising

---

[1] Thomas, *op. cit.* p. 126.

population), we should expect the share of agriculture to have fallen during the last two or three decades of the century, and the share of industry and trade to have risen. This indeed is what seems to have happened if we compare the industrial structure suggested by our own national-income estimates for the early part of the nineteenth century with the pre-industrial structure implied by the Young and King estimates. By the first decade of the nineteenth century, the share of agriculture seems to have fallen to between 32 and 36 per cent (compared with 40 to 45 per cent before the beginnings of rapid growth) and the share of industry and trade to have risen to between 37 and 41 per cent (compared with 33 to 37 per cent in the earlier period).[1] These estimates relate to Great Britain and the earlier figures to England and Wales but it is unlikely that allowance for Scotland would make much difference to the conclusions.

Table 76 summarises the results of our estimates of the structure of national product of Great Britain. It will be seen that the share of agriculture in national product continued to decline throughout the nineteenth and early twentieth centuries, except in the first decade of the nineteenth century, when the statistical evidence suggests an increase. The statistics are far from conclusive, but the evidence for a retardation in industrial expansion and an acceleration in the volume and value of food output during the Napoleonic Wars is strong enough to make the result plausible.

Table 76. *The structure of the British national product*

(as percentages of total national income)

	Agriculture, forestry, fishing (%)	Manufactures, mining, building (%)	Trade, transport, and income from abroad (%)	Government, domestic, and other services (%)	Housing (%)
1801	32·5	23·4	17·4	21·3	5·3
1811	35·7	20·8	16·6	21·7	5·7
1821	26·1	31·9	16·9	19·3	6·2
1831	23·4	34·4	18·4	18·1	6·5
1841	22·1	34·4	19·8	17·8	8·2
1851	20·3	34·3	20·7	18·4	8·1
1861	17·8	36·5	22·6	17·9	7·5
1871	14·2	38·1	26·3	13·9	7·6
1881	10·4	37·6	28·8	14·8	8·5
1891	8·6	38·4	29·8	15·1	8·1
1901	6·1	40·2	29·8	15·5	8·2
1924	4·2	40·0	35·0	14·4	6·4
1935	3·9	38·0	34·4	17·2	6·5
1955	4·7	48·1	24·9	19·2	3·2

Sources: See notes to Tables 37 and 40 above. Figures for 1924–55 include Northern Ireland.

[1] See above, p. 162. The share of agriculture seems to have risen between 1801 and 1811 and the share of industry and trade to have fallen. This is a plausible enough result for a period in which industrial advance seems to have been retarded and agricultural output and prices to have been inflated by war conditions.

Taking the long view of the progress of agriculture, however, it is clear that the decline in its share tended to accelerate up to the beginning of the twentieth century, by which time it had fallen almost as low as it was going to fall. During the first three-quarters of the eighteenth century its share in national income may have declined slightly, but almost certainly by less than 10 per cent. During the half-century ending in the first decade of the nineteenth century, the decline probably did not exceed 20 per cent: during the half-century ending *circa* 1861 it fell by about 50 per cent and during the next half-century by about two-thirds. The last four decades of the nineteenth century constituted the period during which the major shift of resources from agriculture took place.

As far as industry was concerned the timing of the major shifts in relative importance was somewhat different. There had been a tendency for the manufacturing group to expand, albeit slowly, for most of the eighteenth century. The big change, however, took place in a fairly short period immediately after the Napoleonic Wars when the share of the mining, manufacturing and building group rose from under a quarter to over a third of national product. Thereafter the trend was generally upwards, but it fluctuated, and our estimates suggest that, as between *circa* 1831 and *circa* 1935, there was a difference of only 4 per cent in the percentage of national income accruing to this group of industries. Then, however, there was another shift towards manufacturing, and in 1955 this group claimed 10 per cent more of the national income.

The commercial and transport group of industries apparently expanded their share in national income in the last quarter of the eighteenth century, and remained at about 17 per cent of national income (apart from a wartime decline) until the 1830's. They grew most rapidly in relative importance in the fifties and sixties when their share (including incomes from abroad) expanded from under one-fifth to over one-quarter. They continued to increase their share in the last quarter of the nineteenth century (when incomes from abroad expanded) and again in the interwar period, by which time they accounted for over a third of national income, but their share had fallen back to about a quarter by 1955.

These are broad aggregates, of course, and obscure some of the more significant shifts in the components of national income. The evidence is sufficient to distinguish, for example, three service components whose shares have changed considerably over this period of the Industrial Revolution and its aftermath:

1. The housing percentages are shown in Table 76. They indicate a rise in the early part of the nineteenth century, fluctuation within a fairly narrow range ($7\frac{1}{2}$ to $8\frac{1}{2}$ per cent) for most of the remainder of the nineteenth century, and a fall during the twentieth century which was further precipitated during the rent restrictions of the Second World War and its aftermath.

2. The rise in the importance of the contribution of incomes earned on foreign property has been discussed in chapter v. These grew from a negligible fraction of the nation's total income in the beginning of the nineteenth century, to over 7 per cent at the end, and then dropped again, as two world wars decimated Britain's foreign assets, to a mere 1 per cent in the 1950's.

3. The virtual disappearance, in the twentieth century, of the kind of activity involved in the provision of domestic and personal services (which accounted for a steady 5 to 6 per cent of national product during most of the nineteenth century) has also been noted elsewhere.

In chapter vi we attempted to probe the aggregate of the mining, manufacturing and building industries, and to distinguish the industries which are generally believed to have played a key role in the industrialisation of the United Kingdom. These were textiles, iron and steel, coal, and steam transport. The quantities on which attention was focused were net value added, volume of output and levels of capital formation. The data were insufficient to permit precise or continuous estimates of these quantities: but in most cases it was possible to obtain some measure of the changing weight of net output, the rate of growth of real output at different periods, and the timing of investment activity.

Economic historians have attributed great weight to the textile industry as a leader in the process of industrialisation, and particularly to the British cotton industry. Certainly the cotton industry set an example of rapid growth which made a deep impression on contemporary imagination. Between the 1760's when the industry produced its coarse cotton-linen mixtures for a limited market and *circa* 1802 when the world market was spending almost as much on British calico as on British woollens, its share in the national income increased more than tenfold and its input of raw cotton by a factor of 14 or 15. It is impossible to assess the impact of this spectacular achievement in creating a climate of opinion favourable to industrial innovation. It is possible, however, to form some impression of the direct impact of the cotton industry on the national rate of growth by viewing it in the perspective of the textile industry as a whole and of the total national income.

We have estimated that *circa* 1805 the net value of the output of the cotton industry was nearly 5 per cent of the national income of Great Britain, and about 3½ per cent of that of the United Kingdom as a whole. At this time the value added to national income by all the textiles was estimated at about 11 per cent of the United Kingdom total. Cotton manufacturing, though already more important than either linen or silk, was thus still making a smaller contribution to net output than the woollen manufacture when the nineteenth century began. It seems to have outstripped the woollen industry in terms of net value of the manufacture sometime during the first decade.[1] But

---

[1] The term woollen industry is here used to cover the whole of the woollen and worsted industries.

in view of the fact that the basic cotton raw material was imported, and two-thirds or more of that used by the woollen industry was domestically produced, it is possible that the woollen industry continued to make a somewhat larger direct impact on British incomes than the cotton industry until towards the end of the second decade. It was not until the second half of the nineteenth century that the woollen industry made an appreciably smaller contribution to national output than the cotton industry, and not until the last quarter, when the linen and silk industries became of negligible importance, that cotton dominated the textile industry. By 1907 when the first census of production was taken for the United Kingdom the net output of the cotton trade was put at about £45 m. and all textile trades at about £94 m.[1] At the beginning of the twentieth century, therefore, cotton manufacturing accounted for between 2 and 2½ per cent of the United Kingdom national income.

It is thus possible to overstress the weight of cotton in the British economy at the end of the eighteenth and beginning of the nineteenth centuries. It may be worth noting that during the whole of the Napoleonic War period, the total value added to raw-cotton imports in the process of cotton manufacture was probably appreciably less than either the incomes earned by the employees of government (including the armed forces) or the interest on the national debt.

To say that the direct contribution of cotton to the national-income aggregates should not be overrated, however, is not to deny the strategic importance of the industry throughout most of the nineteenth century. Its rapid rate of growth (between 6 and 7 per cent per annum as measured by the input of raw cotton) in the quarter century following the Napoleonic Wars, and its relatively slow growth (under 0·7 per cent per annum) in the last quarter of the century, were trends of absolute as well as of symbolic significance in the overall progress of British real incomes.

Important also were its effects on the distribution of incomes between different factors of production. On the one hand it widened the range of economic activity for the most unskilled sectors of a growing labour force, and drove the traditional representatives of domestic industry, the handloom weavers, to accept the discipline of large-scale industry or the workhouse. In 1835, 13 per cent of the operatives in cotton factories were children under the age of fourteen, 48 per cent were women and 12 per cent youths or girls (aged eighteen or less). These were groups which would have found it difficult to obtain regular employment outside domestic service in the pre-industrial era.[2] The elimination of the handloom weaver took place in the twenties,

---

[1] *Final Report of the First Census of Production of the United Kingdom, 1907* (Cmd. 6320, 1912), p. 285. Including fibre rope, bleaching, finishing, etc., and cutting trades. If we exclude these subsidiary trades the textiles total comes to about £82 m. and the cotton industry accounted for about 55 per cent.

[2] They were still very vulnerable to temporary unemployment during trade depressions in the factory era.

thirties and forties. Between 1821 and 1831 their weekly wages fell by more than a quarter without appreciably affecting their numbers. Between 1831 and 1841 their average weekly wages held firm or even grew a little and the numbers halved.

On the other hand there is evidence of a shift in the distribution of cotton incomes from labour to capital. In the quarter of a century following 1820 the estimated net output of the industry grew by about 40 per cent in current-value terms, and its wage bill by only about 5 per cent. It is not surprising to find that the number of spindles almost trebled, and the number of power looms multiplied by a factor of 16 in this period. Investment in mills and in fixed equipment in the cotton industry was almost certainly a higher proportion of total national capital formation than might be suggested by the industry's share in national income.

In international trade, the cotton industry played a role which was out of all proportion to its share in total national output. At the end of the Napoleonic Wars, i.e. *circa* 1815, it accounted for about 40 per cent of the declared value of domestic exports.[1] The corresponding proportion for the woollen industry was only 17 per cent and was falling steadily. By *circa* 1820 the cotton industry's share had risen to 44 per cent of domestic exports, and during most of the period 1824–40 it varied between 47 per cent and 50 per cent, falling back to 44 per cent again *circa* 1845. During the quarter century ending in 1845 the volume of cotton manufactures exported increased some five times and their average price fell by about two-thirds.[2] At the same time imports of raw cotton were a substantial proportion of the total value of imports. They reached their peak of relative importance in the quinquennium centring on 1836 when they averaged 20 per cent of total net imports.

In effect, it was the textile trades which set the pace of United Kingdom exports in the period immediately following the Napoleonic Wars. As between the decades 1815–24 and 1825–34 the increase in the volume of all domestic exports was 40 per cent, but exclusive of cotton and woollens it was only 23 per cent. Textiles held their lead through the 1830's. By the 1840's other exports were growing as fast as cotton and woollen manufactures, and by the 1850's they were growing faster.[3]

By the 1840's, however, a new pacemaker emerged in the United Kingdom economy—railway construction. It began to exert a significant direct influence on the level of economic activity in the late 1830's, when expenditure on permanent way and rolling stock was estimated to approach an annual average of £10 m. After a brief recession in the early 1840's, railway construction grew again to about

[1] The export data in this paragraph are three-year averages centring on the year specified.

[2] Calculated from Professor Imlah's volume and value estimates. See Albert Imlah, *Economic Elements in the Pax Britannica* (1958), pp. 208–9.

[3] *Ibid.* for volume relatives of all domestic exports and domestic exports excluding cotton and woollen manufactures.

£12 m. per annum (equivalent to about 2 per cent of the national income) in the mid-1840's and then reached its climax in 1847 when there were more than 300,000 men directly employed in constructing and operating railways, and when the industry's total expenditure may have amounted to a larger sum than the value of total domestic exports from the United Kingdom. In the triennium 1847–9 nearly 1,000 miles of new railway were annually opened to traffic, compared with an annual average of about 270 miles in the previous decade, and about 400 in the following decade.

The construction boom was temporary, of course, but the output of transport services continued to expand. By mid-1850 there were more men employed in operating the railways than in building new track. In the following year railway traffic receipts for the first time exceeded new capital invested. In the 1860's the industry's average net output was almost twice the level of the 1850's and it continued to grow faster (though less and less faster) than total national income until the late 1880's.

The output of shipping services also expanded vigorously in the 1850's and 1860's according to Professor Imlah's estimates.[1] By the 1870's net shipping earnings and net railway output together accounted for between 8 and 9 per cent of total national income, and construction expenditure on all forms of transport probably absorbed between 11 and 12 per cent of gross national capital formation. By this time, however, the transport industry was expanding at a more modest rate and was no longer racing ahead of other sectors in the economy.

It is impossible to assess adequately the impact on the British economy of innovations in transport, for their indirect effects must have been at least as important as their direct effects. The accelerated growth of the iron and steel and coal industries in the late 1840's and the 1850's, for example, can clearly be related to the construction of new transport facilities and the consequent expansion of capacity. The repercussions in other industries may have been less conspicuous at the height of the transport boom, but it may be presumed that the strong expansion of railway and shipping output in the 1850's and 1860's reflects a correspondingly strong expansion in the industrialised economy. By the 1860's, if we may judge by the Hoffmann index of industrial production, the volume of industrial production was running at a level which was six times greater than in the first decade of the century; and although it had passed its peak rate of growth, it was still growing at the rate of about 3 per cent per annum. Table 77, which is based on the Hoffmann index of industrial production (excluding building) for the nineteenth century and the Lomax index for the twentieth century, illustrates the general pattern of industrial growth in the nineteenth and twentieth centuries.

A quite marked slackening of the rate of industrial growth appears from these data to have set in during the decade covering the late

[1] *Op. cit.* pp. 70–5.

1870's and early 1880's. An equally marked relative deceleration showed up also at this period in our estimates of net output of transport and appears even more marked in Professor Imlah's estimates of net income from abroad (interest, dividends, profits, commissions, etc.). In effect, it is evident in most of the sectors which benefited directly from the process of industrialisation, all of which seem to have passed their peak rates of growth within the period 1825–70. Real national income in the aggregate, however, appears to have gone on increasing its rate of growth for roughly another decade, that is until the late 1880's or early 1890's.[1]

Table 77. *The rate of growth of United Kingdom industrial production*

(percentage increase per decade)

	%		%
1800/09–1810/19	22·9	1865/74–1875/84	23·2
1805/14–1815/24	29·5	1870/79–1880/89	20·8
1810/19–1820/29	38·6	1875/84–1885/94	16·4
1815/24–1825/34	45·2	1880/89–1890/99	17·4
1820/29–1830/39	47·2	1885/94–1895/1904	20·7
1825/34–1835/44	43·0	1890/99–1900/09	17·9
1830/39–1840/49	37·4	1895/04–1905/14	18·0
1835/44–1845/54	38·7	1900/09–1910/19	12·2
1840/49–1850/59	39·3	1905/14–1915/24	4·0
1845/54–1855/64	33·2	1910/19–1920/29	14·1
1850/59–1860/69	27·8	1915/24–1925/34	23·8
1855/64–1865/74	34·6	1920/29–1930/38	25·8
1860/69–1870/79	33·2		

Sources: W. Hoffmann, *British Industry 1700–1950*, for an index of industrial production of the U.K. (excluding building) from 1800 to 1909. K. S. Lomax, 'Production and Productivity Movements in the United Kingdom since 1900', *J. Roy. Statist. Soc.* (1959), for an index of industrial production 1900–38. The two indices were linked on the base 1900–9. It should be noted that the Hoffmann index included Southern Ireland throughout and the Lomax index excluded it throughout.

This lag may be partly due to structural changes. The fact that a significantly larger proportion of the national income was being produced by sectors with a relatively rapid rate of growth (manufacturing, mining and transport, for example) and a significantly smaller proportion in industries which tended to grow relatively slowly if at all (agriculture, forestry, fishing, domestic service, for example) might account for an expanding rate of overall growth even though the former group had passed their peak. Professor Ashworth has shown, however, that in terms of the broad sectors distinguished in Tables 31 and 37, the redistribution of the labour force was not an important factor in raising the level of national income over the last quarter of the century. His calculations suggest that intersectoral redistribution would account for only 9·6 per cent of the increase in national income between 1871 and 1901. A finer disaggregation of industries might yield a different

[1] Cf. E. H. Phelps Brown and Handfield Jones, 'The Climacteric of the 1890's: A Study in the Expanding Economy', *Oxford Economic Papers*, October 1952; and D. J. Coppock, 'The Climacteric of the 1890's: A Critical Note', *Manchester School of Economic and Social Studies*, January 1956.

result, but there is no obvious reason to suppose that it would significantly increase the weight attributable to structural change in raising overall productivity at this period.[1]

We have not been able to calculate an industrial breakdown for the United Kingdom as a whole, but our estimates for Great Britain in Table 76, above, suggest that the share of the agricultural group fell very sharply in the last quarter of the nineteenth century. Table 78, which gives estimates of the share in total United Kingdom national income of net factor incomes earned in agriculture, confirms this impression and suggests, moreover, that it was in the 1880's that the decline was most rapid. Between the decade centring on 1875 and the decade centring on 1900 the share of agriculture more than halved. By the beginning of the twentieth century the agricultural industry was of minor significance and changes in its share could have very little influence thereafter on the United Kingdom rate of growth.

Table 78. *The share of agriculture in United Kingdom
national income, 1867–1934*

(Net factor incomes in agriculture as percentage total net national income, in decade averages)

	%		
1867–74 (8 years)	15·7	1890–99	7·6
1870–79	14·0	1895–1904	6·8
1875–84	11·9	1900–09	6·6
1880–89	10·0	1925–34	3·9
1885–94	8·7		

Sources: Estimates of net factor incomes in agriculture kindly provided by Mr J. R. Bellerby of the Oxford University Agricultural Economics Research Institute. Estimates of national incomes in Appendix III, Table 90.

During the twentieth century the share of agriculture continued to fall (though it recovered twice to over 6 per cent under the special and temporary stimulus of war), but until after the Second World War the most striking characteristic of the structural pattern was its relative stability. This impression persists even when a finer industrial breakdown is taken into consideration, as the data in Table 79 illustrate.

In effect, in spite of a world war and a major cyclical depression the British industrial structure seems to have changed little in the period of nearly three decades between 1907 and 1935. The mining industry had contracted its share to nearly half of what it had been at the beginning of the century. Some manufacturing industries continued the process of relative decline which had been even faster at the end of the nineteenth century—textiles and clothing, for example. Some were increasing their share—chemicals almost doubled their weight, for example. But, measured against the national framework, none of these represented substantial shifts of emphasis.

[1] W. Ashworth, 'Changes in Industrial Structure', *Yorkshire Bulletin of Economic and Social Research*, Vol. 17, May 1965, p. 69.

Table 79. *Twentieth-century industrial structure in the United Kingdom*

(as percentages of total national income)

	Great Britain only	Great Britain and Northern Ireland		
	1907 (%)	1924 (%)	1935 (%)	1955 (%)
1. Agriculture, forestry, fishing	6·0	4·2	3·9	4·6
2. Mines and quarries	6·0	5·4	3·1	3·4
3. Engineering and metal manufactures	8·2	8·0	9·4	19·5
4. Textiles and clothing	8·0	7·7	5·6	5·2
5. Food, drink and tobacco	4·3	6·7	5·1	4·1
6. Paper and printing	1·6	2·3	2·6	2·7
7. Chemicals	1·1	1·9	2·1	3·0
8. Miscellaneous manufactures	2·5	3·2	3·5	4·4
9. Gas, electricity and water	1·6	1·7	2·5	2·4
10. Building and contracting	3·7	3·1	4·1	5·7
11. Commerce	18·0	17·8	19·6	16·5
12. Transport	9·5	12·0	10·7	8·3
13. Government and defence	3·0	4·6	4·7	9·4
14. Domestic service	3·8	3·4	3·4	0·6
15. Rents of dwellings	7·4	6·4	6·5	3·2
16. All other, including errors and omissions	15·3	11·6	13·2	7·1

Sources: See notes to Tables 40 and 41 above. As will be seen there, the differences between the percentages for Great Britain in 1924 and those given above for Great Britain including Northern Ireland (which is the present United Kingdom) are negligible.

In the next two decades, however, the picture changed radically. The engineering and metal manufacturing group of industries more than doubled its share. Government's weight in the economy almost doubled as public service became a major British industry. Domestic service, which had contributed almost as much as agriculture to the national income of the 1930's, had practically disappeared by 1955. The manufacturing industries increased their share of national output from under 31 per cent in 1935 to over 41 per cent in 1955. These were the changes which were associated with a 3 per cent per annum increase in the index of industrial production between 1935 and 1955, as compared with a 1·7 per cent rate of increase between 1907 and 1935.[1]

4. LONG-TERM CHANGES IN FACTOR SHARES

The attempt to analyse national income by factor shares is complicated by the existence of mixed-income components for which the returns to labour and capital cannot be distinguished. In the United Kingdom of the 1950's these mixed incomes accounted for between 9 and 10 per cent of gross national product and can conveniently be ignored in any inquiries focused on short-term shifts in the relative shares of capital, labour or land. In most pre-industrial societies, on the other hand, the

[1] The Lomax index, *op. cit.* p. 192, shows 81·6 for 1907, 130·3 for 1935, and 234·5 for 1955. (1924 = 100.)

incomes earned by peasants, fishermen, traders and other self-employed persons constitute a substantial proportion of total national income. Indeed, the fall in this proportion would be, if we could measure it, a revealing indicator of the pace and level of industrialisation through time. Unfortunately the data do not permit quantification for the period when this would be of greatest interest; that is in the eighteenth and early nineteenth centuries. All that we can do for this period is to make a rough assessment of the probable directions of change.

If we take Gregory King's statistical picture of England and Wales at the end of the seventeenth century as our starting-point, we find that rents of land and housing were estimated to account for about 27 per cent of national income. Rent was a concept that was clear enough to seventeenth-century political arithmeticians to make their estimates acceptable in principle for our present purposes.[1] It is impossible, however, to distinguish at all clearly profits on capital, incomes from employment and incomes from self-employment. At best it can be said that on a most conservative interpretation employment incomes may have accounted for as little as 25 per cent of the national income of England and Wales at the end of the seventeenth century. On an extremely generous view they may have accounted for as much as 39 per cent. We do not have enough information to analyse the factor distribution of the incomes in the remaining 34 to 48 per cent, but it is safe to assume that a high proportion of them fell into the mixed-income group.

We cannot trace chronologically the transition to a more specialised economy, but it is evident that by the time Colquhoun imitated King's table of incomes at the beginning of the nineteenth century the distinction between the capitalist manufacturer or merchant, and the proletarian labourer was sufficiently important to be specified in many cases. Public offices and commissions in the forces were still liable to be sold but, in general, public servants could more reasonably be regarded as employees than as self-employed persons which they had often resembled a hundred years ago. The area of doubt is still considerable but probably less than 45 per cent of British national income was attributable to income from employment in 1801.

In chapter VI, above, we made estimates of incomes from employment at census years in the nineteenth century. But for most of the period there was no way of distinguishing employed from self-employed persons in the lower income groups, and these estimates are therefore not very useful for our present purposes. It is not until the second half of the century that we can find enough information in the census occupational returns and in Bowley's and Wood's wage and salary estimates to permit direct estimates of incomes from employment exclusive of the incomes of self-employed persons. The results of these estimates are summarised in Table 80.

[1] In this respect, of course, seventeenth-century England was a more highly specialised economy than many modern pre-industrial economies.

Table 80. *Estimates of the distribution of income by factor shares*

(as percentages of total national income)

	Employment incomes (%)	Rents (%)	Profits, interest and mixed incomes (%)
Circa 1688 (England and Wales)	25–39	27	34–48
Circa 1801 (Great Britain)	44	20	37
United Kingdom (annual averages)			
1860–69	49	14	38
1870–79	49	13	38
1880–89	48	14	38
1890–99	50	12	38
1900–09	48	11	40
1920–29	60	7	34
1930–39	62	9	29
1948–57	72	4	24

Sources: Figures for 1688 and 1801 based on contemporary estimates. For 1860 onwards see Table 65, above.

Two features of these results stand out above the crudeness of the data on which they are based. The first is the fall in the share of rents from possibly more than a quarter of national income in pre-industrial England and Wales to under 5 per cent in the present-day United Kingdom. The second is the relative constancy of the share of employment incomes in the half-century preceding the First World War, followed by the sharp increases which were associated with both world wars.

The fall in the share of land rents was a reflection of two main trends —the fall in the share of agriculture in the national income and the falling share of rents in the net factor incomes earned in agriculture. The decline in the relative importance of the agricultural industry was described in the previous section of this chapter. Between the 1860's and the early 1900's the industry fell to about two-fifths of its former significance. At the same time net rents, which had accounted for about 24 per cent of the net output of agriculture in the 1870's and about 25 per cent in the 1880's, had fallen to about 19 per cent in the first decade or so of the twentieth century, and to under 11 per cent by the 1930's.[1] Rents of dwellings seem to have reached a maximum of relative significance in the 1880's when they accounted for nearly 9 per cent of national income, and then to have declined to about 6½ per cent in the interwar period, and to about 3 per cent since the Second World War. In recent years institutional factors (war and rent restrictions, for example) have combined to depress house rents to artificially low levels.

It is more difficult to explain the trends in the share of employment

---

[1] These figures of the factor share of agricultural incomes are based on estimates kindly made available by Mr J. R. Bellerby of the Oxford Agricultural Economics Research Institute.

incomes. On the face of it, the fact that the wage fraction varies considerably as between one industry and another, for example, makes its overall constancy in a period of structural change somewhat surprising. It turns out, however, that the structural changes which occurred in the five or six decades before 1914 were not such as to produce marked shifts in the average wage fraction for all industries taken together.[1] All that can be deduced from its relative constancy is the absence of strong forces tending to depress or inflate the share of labour in the sum of British economic activity during this period. Conversely, of course, the leap in the employment incomes fraction from 48 per cent to 62 per cent as between the first and third decades of the nineteenth century, when the United Kingdom economy maintained a relatively stable structure, must be attributed to factors tending to inflate the share of labour in general.

The twentieth-century trends in the employment incomes percentage can be plausibly attributed to two main groups of factors. The first of these is the effects of full employment under the stress of total war which can be held to account for the sharp increases associated with the two world wars. The continuance of full employment and the bargaining strength it has given to organised labour in the period 1946–57 may also have contributed to the continuing increase in the share of employees since the Second World War.

The second group of factors which has tended to inflate or maintain the share of employees has been the institutional changes which have made for an increase in the proportion of relatively rigid labour costs (salaries and employers' insurance contributions, for example) as opposed to the more variable pure wage costs in the economy. These institutional changes may explain the maintenance of the share of employees in the interwar period, in spite of chronic unemployment. For although the employed sector as a whole absorbed an extra $2\frac{1}{2}$ per cent of national income as between 1920–29 and 1930–38, the gain to the sum total of directors' fees, salaries and employers' contributions more than outweighed this, and represented about $3\frac{1}{2}$ per cent of national income.[2]

To some extent the institutional factors inflating the share of the employed sector reflect changes in the status distribution of the occupied population. Between 1911 and 1921 the proportion of employers and self-employed persons fell from about 12·8 per cent of the occupied population of Great Britain to about 10·1 per cent. Between 1921 and 1951 there was a further fall to about 7·2 per cent.

---

[1] This can be checked by applying a fixed set of wage fractions to the industrial structure percentages in Table 75 above. Robert M. Solow has made this point in relation to more recent U.S. data and more detailed statistics in 'A Skeptical Note on the Constancy of Relative Shares', *American Economic Review*, September 1958, where the conclusion is reached (p. 622) that 'Short and long-run changes in the importance of various sectors are important economic facts. But they are not what accounts for the variance or lack of variance of over-all shares.'

[2] See above, Table 64.

In effect, therefore, the percentage of employed persons in the population increased from about 87 per cent to about 93 per cent over a period when their share in total national income increased from about 47 per cent to about 72 per cent.

Within the employed group itself it may be presumed that other and more significant status changes were taking place—shifts from wage to salary status, for example, or from unskilled to semiskilled occupations. The available data do not permit measurement of these changes. Indeed it is doubtful whether the conceptual distinctions (e.g. as between salaried staff and operatives, or between skilled and semi-skilled workers) are clear enough to justify attempts to specify these categories at all precisely. It does seem reasonable to conclude, however, that the marked increase in the share of the employed sector in the past four to five decades has been partly due to increase in the efficiency of the labour force, and this in its turn can be largely ascribed to increased investment in basic education and training.[1]

5. CHANGES IN THE RATE OF CAPITAL FORMATION

A systematic study of the long-term processes of capital formation in the United Kingdom required more resources than were available for this inquiry. We therefore confined ourselves in chapter VIII, above, to a brief review of the readily available evidence on its qualitative characteristics. In further distilling the conclusions suggested by this review, it should be borne in mind that the data used were sketchy in the extreme and the implications drawn must be regarded as particularly tentative. Much more detailed study of the data available for individual industries is required before the results can be regarded as conclusive.

Whether the proportion of British national income invested increased during the eighteenth century it is impossible to say on the evidence available to us. Gregory King's estimates suggest that net private saving *circa* 1688 was in the region of £2½ m., or rather less than 5 per cent of national income. Of this he calculated that about 70 per cent was invested at home, and the rest found its way into foreign lending. These are plausible enough estimates for pre-industrial England and Wales, but there is no check on them and no conclusive way of establishing their long-term significance. 1688 was a prosperous year, for example, and it is reasonable to suppose that the investment proportion was relatively high. An examination of King's estimates of the stock of capital at earlier dates in the seventeenth century—which are even more conjectural than the 1688 figures—suggest that the long-term

---

[1] Our estimates suggest, for example, that between *circa* 1881 and 1911, when the share of the employed sector showed no secular trend, the share of salaries increased very little —from about 10 per cent to about 13 per cent: and most of this may be eliminated if we exclude a fall in the employers' share due to incorporation of private firms. By the 1920's, however, salaries had increased their share to over 18 per cent and by the 1930's to 21 per cent.

average net capital formation might have been nearer 3 per cent of national income than 5 per cent. For the eighteenth century we found evidence of a slow acceleration of industrial growth beginning in the 1740's and reaching a crescendo in the last two or three decades. There is no doubt that in absolute terms the volume of capital formation increased. Certainly there was an increasing volume of investment in agricultural enclosures, in roads and bridges, in canals (amounting to a 'mania' in the early 1790's), in public and private buildings, and in mills and spinning-machinery. But national income also grew, and whether capital formation grew even as fast as absolute national income is an open question. The growth in output per head may have been attributable to a more productive use of savings rather than to a greater relative volume.

At the beginning of the nineteenth century, judging by Beeke's estimates, the national capital was still largely composed of agricultural capital. The value of land accounted for more than half of it. Even if we exclude land (and confine our attention to 'reproducible assets'), less than half of the total consisted of industrial, commercial and financial capital (including stock in trade, machinery, canals, and foreign assets): building and public property accounted for about a third and farmers' capital for nearly a fifth. As late as the early 1830's a contemporary estimate of the national capital suggests that its overall structure had changed little.[1] Industrialists may have been ploughing back profits at a greater rate than at the end of the eighteenth century, and farmers may have been putting more savings into fertilisers, improved breeding stock and farm machinery, than into enclosure of commons and waste. But the broad structure of the national product looked much the same to Pebrer as it had to Beeke three to four decades previously.

The evidence, such as it is, suggests that there had been some increase in the rate of additions to capital stock in this period. Our estimates of money national income implied an increase of about 50 per cent between *circa* 1800 and *circa* 1832. Estimates of national reproducible capital derived from Beeke and Pebrer suggest a corresponding increase of about 70 per cent. The reproducible capital–income ratio seems to have risen from 2·9 to 3·2. The evidence for these quantitative comparisons is flimsy in the extreme. But when it is borne in mind that Pebrer was more prone to overestimate than Beeke, the interesting thing about the former's estimates is that they suggest so modest an increase in the relative level of capital formation. Again it may be plausibly argued that a more effective use of savings might have had a more powerful influence on the rate of economic growth at this period than a higher propensity to save.

There are no estimates either of the overall value of the national capital or of the annual level of capital formation for the crucial period of the railway age. Study of the evidence for individual industries,

[1] Table 70, above, for details and references.

however, indicates that the level of capital accumulation expanded markedly between the 1830's and the 1860's. Tentatively we would conclude that most of the upward shift in the level of national investment which was associated with the industrial revolution in Great Britain took place during this period of three or four decades. By the late 1860's and during the 1870's it may have been running at an average level which was higher than at any comparable period before or since.

In the 1830's, 1840's and 1850's the cotton industry was being converted to power: in the 1850's and 1860's it was the turn of the woollen industries. The great railway boom took place in the late 1840's, but for transport in general our estimates suggest that the sustained rate of capital formation expanded suddenly from an average of about 2 per cent of national income for most of the period 1790–1829, to nearly 3 per cent in the 1830's, and between 3 and 4 per cent in the 1840's. The construction boom and the expansion of transport facilities both generated a wave of sympathetic investment in other industries. New blast-furnaces were being built at the rate of 27 per annum in the 1850's and the growth of the iron industry brought with it massive developments in iron- and coal-fields.

Yet the period 1831–61 is the one for which our national-income calculations suggested a lower overall rate of growth in real terms than at any other period of comparable length in the nineteenth century. The overall picture is, however, complicated by the Irish disaster, and in per head terms the mid-century slackening of the rate of growth is not as marked as it is for total national income. The subsequent acceleration reached the peak rates for the United Kingdom of about 3 per cent per annum in total real income and a little over 2 per cent in average real incomes in the period 1865–95.[1]

By the 1860's, judging from Giffen's estimates of the national capital, considerable changes had taken place in the characteristic pattern of British capital formation. Land still represented nearly a third of the value of total national capital, but it was declining rapidly in relative importance and by 1885 accounted for less than a fifth of the total. Farm capital was also relatively less important by the 1860's, and by the fourth quarter of the century it was falling in absolute value.

For the industrialised economy of the second half of the nineteenth century it is convenient to exclude land from the national capital calculations and to focus attention on reproducible capital. The changing pattern in the total, excluding land, is illustrated in Table 81, below.

Briefly, then, the existing data suggest that capital was growing markedly faster than output in the second and third quarters of the nineteenth century and more slowly than output in the following half-century. Between *circa* 1832 and 1885, when we found a trebling of the national income (at current prices), reproducible national capital

See Table 74, above.

seems to have expanded some fivefold. In the next half-century the value of national income quadrupled and that of national capital expanded only two and a half times.

Table 81. *Changes in the reproducible national capital of Great Britain,*
1832–1933

(as percentages of total national capital exclusive of land)

	1832 (%)	1865 (%)	1885 (%)	1913 (%)	1927 (%)	1933 (%)
Buildings	31	28	26	25	21	24
Farm capital	20	16	7	2	2	2
Overseas assets		10	18	25	19	19
Railways	45	12	14	9	4	4
Industrial, commercial and financial capital		27	29	32	45	41
Public property	4	8	7	7	9	11
Capital–output ratios	3·2	4·6	6·7	5·5	4·6	5·0

Sources: See above, Tables 70 and 71, for detailed references to the original estimates by Pebrer, Giffen and Campion.

The estimates on which these percentages and ratios are based are subject to major qualifications, apart altogether from the margins of error in the basic statistics. Being estimates for bench-mark years they tell us nothing about the turning-points. The evidence on capital flows suggests that the rate of growth in capital began to fall behind the rate of growth in output in the late 1870's: but more systematic study of the data on capital formation might suggest a later or an earlier turning-point. Nor do these estimates, being at current prices, throw any light on *real* rates of growth in the national capital. It is a reasonable presumption that there were significant changes in the relative prices of capital and consumption goods which, if measurable, might lead to substantially different conclusions concerning relative rates of growth of income and capital and the associated changes in the capital–output ratio. Finally it is important to recall here that the contemporary estimates were largely derived by capitalising current incomes and they reflect changes in the climate of expectations more effectively than changes in the physical stock of capital. But when all allowance is made for the inadequacies of the statistics, the evidence seems to point strongly to the conclusion that the proportion of national income devoted to capital formation and the capital–output ratio tended to grow for most of the period 1830–85 and to fall for most of the period 1885–1927.

The structural implications of the estimates in Table 81, broad though these are, are also interesting. In general the evidence suggests that the changes in structure between the early 1830's and 1860's were radical. Railways, steamships, power-driven machinery and blast-furnaces, which were apparently less important than traders' stocks in the 1830's, may have accounted for most of the industrial and commercial capital by the 1860's. By the 1880's railways alone were worth roughly twice the value of farm capital and the flow of capital overseas accounted for more savings than the whole of British agriculture. During the next half-century, when the national capital expanded relatively slowly the domestic railway system accounted for less and less of total capital, though investment in foreign railways still continued to attract British funds at the end of the nineteenth century and beginning of the twentieth. Total overseas assets seem to have accounted for near a quarter of the national capital immediately before the outbreak of the First World War. Thereafter opportunities for foreign investment declined sharply and after the Second World War (in 1948) it is doubtful whether overseas assets accounted for more than about 8 per cent of the net national capital.[1]

For the period since the middle of the nineteenth century there exist various estimates of the annual rate of capital formation. Those presently available are extremely rough, but they may perhaps be relied upon to indicate the main features of the long-period trends. Unfortunately they are deficient in two main respects: (*a*) because they include no acceptable long-term series for investment in stocks and work in progress, and (*b*) because the estimates for capital consumption are not comparable throughout the period. Over the decade 1950–9 the value of the annual increase in the physical volume of stocks and work in progress amounted to 6 per cent of gross fixed capital formation. Even the most recent estimates are exceedingly tentative, but we have no reason to suppose that there was any secular trend in the volume of stocks and work in progress, so it may be sufficient to assume that an addition of 5 or 6 per cent to the gross fixed capital series would give a reasonable approximation to total domestic investment in each decade.

The lack of acceptable capital consumption estimates is more serious. For one thing the difference between net and gross capital formation is quite large—in 1950–9 the C.S.O. estimates showed capital consumption equivalent to about 54 per cent of gross fixed capital formation. For another thing the gap may be presumed to have widened through time. The Feinstein estimates, for example, show a depreciation in the 1860's amounting to about 30 per cent of gross fixed capital formation. In any case it can probably be assumed that net domestic capital formation in the interwar period was only about half of the gross percentage shown in Table 82.

Taking these estimates as indicators of trend, however, it may be deduced that total gross investment rose to a peak in the late sixties and early seventies, declined in the last quarter of the nineteenth century, and exceeded its earlier peak in the decade immediately

[1] P. Redfern, 'Net Investment in Fixed Assets in the United Kingdom, 1938–53', *J. Roy. Statist. Soc.*, vol. 118 (1955), p. 158, estimates gross fixed capital 1947 as £21,173 m.; stocks, etc., can be calculated from the C.S.O. Blue Book to be £4,870 m.; and the Bank of England estimate of the nominal value of U.K. overseas securities was £2,274 m.

Table 82. *Trends in United Kingdom capital formation, 1860–1959*

(as percentages expenditure generating gross national product in decade averages)

	Gross domestic fixed capital formation (%)	Net foreign investment (%)
1860–69	7·2	3·0
1865–74	7·3	4·8
1870–79	8·1	3·9
1875–84	7·8	3·1
1880–89	6·1	4·9
1885–94	5·7	4·9
1890–99	6·9	3·2
1895–04	8·5	2·1
1900–09	7·8	3·9
1905–14	6·0	6·9
1920–29	8·7	2·4
1925–34	8·4	0·6
1930–39	9·5	−1·0
1950–59	14·8	0·8

Sources: As for Appendix III, Table 91.

preceding the First World War. The pre-war recovery was largely due to an increase in the flow of capital abroad which then reached an all-time peak (in decade averages) of over 7½ per cent of net national income.[1] In the interwar period gross domestic investment recovered but net home investment had fallen to negligible proportions. If we accept Dr Maywald's estimates of net domestic capital formation they suggest a level for the interwar decades which was lower in relation to national income than at any time since the first quarter of the nineteenth century—possibly even since the last quarter of the eighteenth. In the 1950's, on the other hand, net home investment has revived to a level which may not be far short of its mid-nineteenth-century peak.

From these highly tentative estimates and comparisons the following broad hypotheses concerning the role of capital in British economic growth suggest themselves. In the early stages of the industrial revolution the level of capital formation—measured as a percentage of national income—rose only slowly. At this period, covering the last quarter of the eighteenth century and the first quarter of the nineteenth, savings were being used more productively and a large proportion of the new developments were taking place in industries with a relatively low ratio of capital to income. Meanwhile, total real incomes had begun to grow rapidly at the end of the century, advanced more slowly in the period of the French wars and accelerated sharply in the aftermath. It was after this sudden leap in average incomes, that the massive changes in the size and character of British capital resources occurred. During a period of thirty or forty years beginning in the

[1] The percentages in Table 82 are expressed in terms of gross national product rather than net national income.

1830's the basic capital of the economy was transformed. The textile and iron industries expanded enormously and turned over to power-driven machinery. A vast railway network was built and a fleet of steamships launched. While the money value of national income roughly trebled, that of national capital seems to have been multiplied by a factor of five.

Many of the investment projects made in mid-century were of the basic kind which takes time to develop its full potential. During the next four or five decades—that is in the period beginning in the 1860's—they came to fruition and the long-term rate of growth reached its maximum.[1] The capital–output ratio probably continued to rise until the late 1870's or the 1880's. Real national income passed its peak rate of growth in the late 1880's or early 1890's. The level of net home investment sank to perhaps 5 per cent of national income in the decade preceding the First World War, and the capital–output ratio was falling. For most of the interwar period net home investment remained at depression levels, and foreign investment, which had provided a convenient alternative in earlier home depressions, had fallen to less than 1 per cent of national income.

The period which has elapsed since the end of the Second World War is too subject to war influences and too short in any case to justify any conclusions concerning a new long-term trend in capital formation. But it seems to have provided a break in the chronic stagnation of home investment which characterised most of the first half of the twentieth century.

6. LONG-TERM TRENDS IN THE VOLUME OF INTERNATIONAL TRADE

Throughout the past two and a half centuries international trade has been a strategic factor in British economic growth. Overseas markets gave an outlet to industries which would have operated less efficiently within the confines of domestic demand: imported raw materials provided bases for innovation and specialisation: foreign investment offered profitable employment to capital which found home prospects unattractive. It is only within the past century, however, that international trade has come to play a dominating role by virtue of its sheer weight in total economic activity.

Some idea of the changing weight of foreign trade can be obtained by comparing its value with the value of national income. At the end of the seventeenth century domestic exports of England and Wales were between 5 and 6 per cent of national income and imports between 9 and 10 per cent.[2] By the end of the eighteenth century these proportions had more than doubled—to about 13 per cent and 21 per cent

---

[1] See above, Table 74.

[2] At this period, and indeed for the whole of the eighteenth century, British imports were inflated by an important re-export trade.

respectively—but in the period of rapid industrial growth which followed the end of the Napoleonic Wars the home market seems to have responded more readily than the overseas trade and United Kingdom domestic exports averaged 10 per cent or less of national income for most of the first half of the nineteenth century. Imports began to expand in the late 1840's with the abandonment of the protectionist system, and exports followed. The change was rapid. In the early 1870's, when exports reached their peak in relative terms, they were equivalent in average value to about 22½ per cent of national income and imports reached their peak of nearly 36 per cent in the quinquennium 1880–4. Thereafter domestic exports have generally averaged between 16 and 20 per cent of national income, though they fell considerably below this level in the world depression of the 1930's and in the war and immediate post-war years. In the early 1950's domestic exports averaged about 20 per cent of national income and imports about 27 per cent.

Another aspect of this question of the quantitative relationship between economic growth and international trade can be explored by comparing relative rates of growth in their respective volumes. For the eighteenth century the official returns of imports and exports provide convenient volume indices because they were largely recorded at constant prices.[1] A study of the total volume of imports and exports (excluding re-exports) suggests that there were two significant turning-points in the history of the eighteenth century—the first in the 1740's and the second in the 1780's. This corresponds to the trends suggested by our study of the output and population series. After a sharp depression during the War of the Spanish Succession (1702–13) and a rapid post-war recovery, trade grew only slowly. Between 1700 and 1745[2] the volume of imports and exports increased by only 0·7 per cent per annum, and even up to the peak reached in the years immediately before the War of the Austrian Succession (1739–48) the average rate of growth was under 1 per cent. This, however, represented a distinctly faster rate of advance than that of total output which we have estimated

---

[1] I.e. at prices prevailing at the end of the seventeenth or at the beginning of the eighteenth century. Occasional changes in rates of valuation were made in the first decade or so of the century and a few commodities were entered 'at value' for a longer period, but for most forms of merchandise the rates became stereotyped very early in the eighteenth century. We carried out a check on the effectiveness of the official values as volume indicators by applying 1796–8 prices to quantities for selected years: we found that these gave much the same results for exports, and for imports and re-exports also until the last two decades of the century when the great expansion of certain colonial imports introduces serious divergencies between the alternative series. See Appendix I.

[2] The measurements are between averages of three years centring on the year specified. It would, of course, have been possible to obtain a higher rate of growth for the early part of the century if we had chosen any other group of years rather than the 'boom' years 1699–1701 as our base period. But this would have given a misleading impression of the progress actually achieved, since trade was exceptionally depressed during the wars of 1689–97 and 1702–13. Cf. Ralph Davis, 'English Foreign Trade 1660–1700', *Econ. Hist. Rev.*, second series, vol. VII (1954), p. 161, who estimates that the volume of trade in 1699–1701 was probably at about the same level as in 1686–8.

was growing at only about 0·3 per cent per annum in the first four decades of the century.

From 1745 to 1771, the rate of growth in international trade rose to 2·3 per cent, reaching 3 per cent in the years 1745–60 and averaging 1·5 per cent over the whole of the period 1737 to 1771. Between *circa* 1740 and 1770 we have estimated that national output was rising at the rate of about 0·9 per cent per annum. Finally, in the great upsurge of trade in the last twenty years of the century its rate of growth was no less than 4·9 per cent per annum, and even over the period 1771–99 it averaged 2·6 per cent when our calculations suggest that total output was growing at about 1½ per cent per annum.

Table 83. *Growth in volume of international trade and national income in the nineteenth century*

(compound rates per cent per annum)

	Volume exports	Volume exports and imports	Real national income
1801–31	2·9	2·6	2·7
1811–41	4·0	4·0	3·1
1821–51	4·7	4·4	2·8
1831–61	4·5	4·5	2·0
1841–70	4·9	4·6	2·3
1851–80	3·8	4·1	2·6
1861–90	3·1	3·5	3·5
1871–1901	2·3	2·9	3·1
1881–1911	2·7	2·5	2·4

Sources: For national-income estimates see Table 72 above. Trade figures based on Imlah's volume relatives, *op. cit.* pp. 94–8. Except where national-income figures are for bench-mark years all measurements are taken as between decade averages centring on years specified. The national-income estimates are for Great Britain, the trade figures for the United Kingdom.

The nineteenth-century trends are illustrated in Table 83, which is based on Professor Imlah's volume indices for United Kingdom trade and our own real national-income estimates. It shows an even stronger tendency for the total volume of trade to run ahead of the volume of total output, except in the first thirty years or so when the home market was probably expanding somewhat faster than overseas markets and at the very end when a new trend appeared. The timing of these changes is suggestive. The volume of international trade had achieved its peak rate of growth at a period when the expansion of national income was beginning to show some signs of slowing down: the former had passed its peak when the latter began to accelerate again. At this stage, however, the sheer weight of foreign trade in the sum total of British economic activity gave it a dominant role.[1] It is not too much to say that the foreign-trade sector was setting the pace for British economic

[1] In the quinquennium 1880–4 total imports reached their peak value of about 36 per cent of national income: for the rest of the period before the First World War the quinquennial averages lie between 29 and 32 per cent. They were still at this sort of level in the 1920's, but had fallen to about 20 per cent in the 1930's.

growth. It is thus not surprising that when the volume of British international trade ceased to grow, and even declined, in the interwar period the pace of growth in real incomes fell to less than half of its peak nineteenth-century rates.

Since the Second World War, however, there has been a marked change of direction, though it is still too soon to recognise a new long-term trend. In the decade which ended in 1957 United Kingdom exports of goods and services valued at 1948 prices expanded by over 60 per cent compared with about 40 per cent for all imports and 28 per cent for gross domestic product.

In sum, therefore, there was evidently a close relationship between the changing rate of Britain's economic growth and the volume of her international trade. Even in the eighteenth century when the absolute weight in the pre-industrial economy of her transactions with the rest of the world was less than half of what it has generally been in the industrialised economy of the past hundred years, it is probable that about a third of British industrial output was exported. The profits earned by the merchants carrying trade between the Americas, the Far East and Europe were a source of finance for investors in British agriculture and industry. The existence of exploitable international markets at the end of the eighteenth and beginning of the nineteenth centuries was probably crucial in initiating the process of industrialisation and the growth in real incomes which was associated with it. Similarly, at the very end of the nineteenth century, and more particularly during the first few decades of the twentieth century, the sharp decline in the long-term rate of growth can be associated with the prolonged stagnation or decline in British exports and the heavy reductions in British foreign assets.

7. TWENTIETH-CENTURY TRENDS

It would be satisfactory if we could conclude this survey of the salient long-term trends in British economic growth by indicating the features which seem to have most relevance for the future. If we could distinguish and evaluate those underlying trends which have shown some degree of persistence in the first half of the twentieth century, and which might reasonably be expected to continue into its second half, useful information might be provided for policy-makers and forecasters. It is extraordinarily difficult to do any such thing, however.

Two world wars and a major depression have chopped twentieth-century economic history into a series of short periods which have only the fact of their abnormality in common. The second decade and the fifth were distorted by total war. The third and the sixth were largely dominated by the wars to which they were an aftermath. The fourth was partly conditioned by a depression of unprecedented severity, and partly by the rearmament boom that preceded the Second World War. In twenty years' time it may be possible to deduce the long-term trends which have characterised these disturbed decades. At present any conclusions that are reached on this problem must be highly subjective.

It may be supposed, of course, that the British economy will continue to expand, for the long-term rate of growth in real incomes per head has been positive for at least the last one and a half centuries. Whether it will grow at the accelerated rate which has characterised the years since the Second World War or at the slower rate of the preceding period is a question of some interest, however. For the long-term rate of growth in real income per head over the twenty-year period 1938–58 has been about 2·4 per cent per annum. It was half that rate for the previous thirty years.

The attempt to distinguish in the statistical record of the 1950's the movements which could be regarded as a continuation of early twentieth-century trends is not rewarding. The only major trends which have continued virtually without interruption through the last half-century or more are (1) the growth in the importance of the economic activities falling within the sphere of government, (2) the increase in the share of national income accruing to employees, and (3) the decline in the importance of domestic service. Of these the last has gone so far that it can no longer be regarded as an important factor, and the second, except in so far as it is a consequence of the first, may be more an irreversible consequence of two major wars than a basic long-term trend.

It may reasonably be presumed that the public-authority sector will continue to expand as the industrialised society becomes more affluent, and certainly that it will not decline. This will have consequences for other sectors. It has already been noted, for example, that capital formation attributable to government and its agencies has in recent years accounted for near 30 per cent of all British capital formation, and hence for a good deal of the recent rise in the level of net domestic investment. Moreover, since government policy is consciously directed towards maintaining or increasing the rate of economic growth, its impact on the climate of expectations may be responsible for some of the increase (by comparison with the interwar period) in the level of private company investment, which accounted for about 47 per cent of total national investment in the decade 1949–58.

The implication of these tendencies for the future long-term rate of growth depends *inter alia* on the productivity of the capital accumulation which has been undertaken since the Second World War, and on the extent to which government is successful in maintaining a favourable climate of expectations for private investment. It may be that government current expenditures on health, education and research raise national productivity more than government expenditure on capital formation. Or it may be that the taxation required to support the growth of the public sector, and the rigidities introduced into the economy by the expansion of public corporations, tend to inhibit rather than to encourage an increase in productivity. These, however, are not problems which the statistical aggregates considered in this book can be expected to illuminate. The long-term significance of the fact that the British economy is currently growing appreciably faster than in the earlier part of this century (though not as fast as at some periods in the nineteenth century) is a question of great interest, but it remains a question.

APPENDIX I

STATISTICS OF EIGHTEENTH-CENTURY TRADE

(*a*) NOTE ON THE REVALUATION OF EIGHTEENTH-CENTURY
FOREIGN TRADE AT CONSTANT 1796–8 PRICES

In his estimates of the average values in current prices of British
foreign trade in the years 1796–8, Irving gives details of the value of
the imports and re-exports, and in most cases the average price, of
commodities and groups of commodities which altogether accounted
for over 98 per cent of the total value of imports and nearly 95 per cent
of total re-exports. The import prices were apparently intended to
include insurance and freight, and an examination of the estimates
suggests that Irving simply added an allowance of 15 per cent for
merchants' profit in order to obtain the price on re-export. A comparison of the prices given by Irving with those available in Tooke's
History of Prices shows that Irving's estimates were both careful and
accurate.

In order to estimate the value of re-exports at 1796–8 prices in the
years selected from 1772 onwards we multiplied the total quantities of
each commodity re-exported by the appropriate price in 1796–8. In
the case of groups of commodities, such as 'other linens', ships' hulls
and materials, wood, etc., where no price is available, we first calculated
the ratio of the value at current prices in 1796–8 to the official value of
the goods in the same years, and then multiplied the official values of
the quantities re-exported in earlier years by the same ratios. A similar
procedure was also adopted in the case of the small group of residual
items re-exported which were not detailed either by Irving or in the
official trade accounts.

The import calculations were complicated by the fact that all
Irving's estimates apparently include prize goods, but the surviving
trade records for the latter part of the century do not give details of
prize goods broken down by commodities. Where the prices of individual commodities are given by Irving we could adopt the same
procedure as in the case of re-exports. But in the case of groups of
commodities, where no price is given, there is no means of ascertaining
either the 'real' value in 1796–8 of imports exclusive, or the official
value of imports inclusive, of prize. It was therefore necessary to
obtain an appropriate conversion factor to cover all such groups of
commodities, and all prize goods, as well as the group of 'all other
articles' not detailed by Irving. This means that our estimates of
the values of imports at 1796–8 prices may be somewhat less accurate
than those for re-exports, although it should be noted that the 127

commodities for which price data are available[1] account for over 75 per cent of total imports in 1796–8, and a similar proportion in earlier years.

Irving's account of exports, which he estimated 'agreeably to the Prices Current, or to the Declared Value by the Merchants Exporters', is much less detailed than his accounts of imports and re-exports. No price data are given and only twenty-five commodities and groups of commodities are covered. In the case of twelve of the items on Irving's list it was possible to estimate the average price in 1796–8 from the data given; but for the others our estimates for earlier years have been based on the use of conversion factors of the type described above. Altogether, the items given in the list accounted for 73 per cent of the total value of exports in 1796–8, but since the composition of the major commodity groups varied from year to year and the prices of their components had probably changed in different degrees in the course of the century, the estimates we have made must be regarded as appreciably less reliable than those for the other two branches of foreign trade.

Before 1772 the official trade records give no account of the total quantities of imports and exports broken down by commodities, and for the early part of the century our estimates of the values of trade at 1796–8 prices have been based on the tables compiled by Mrs Schumpeter[2]. These relate only to imports and domestic exports, and for this reason we were unable to carry our estimates for re-exports back beyond 1772. Mrs Schumpeter's tables provided us with the relevant information for twenty-five commodities or groups of commodities in the case of imports and twenty in the case of exports. As a result of the changing structure of trade, the share of the imported items rose from less than half of total imports in 1702–3 to over 70 per cent in 1772–3, while the share of the exported items in total exports fell from nearly 85 per cent to just over 70 per cent in the course of the same period. For some of these items and for all other goods it was necessary, as before, to make use of appropriate conversion factors based on the data for the base-years 1796–8. Since Mrs Schumpeter's figures relate to English trade only, whereas the data for 1796–8 include Scottish trade, which was officially valued at different rates from the English, this method may be open to criticism. Our tests indicated that the overall margin of error involved for all commodities was in the neighbourhood of 1 per cent or less, and could therefore be safely ignored. But in the

[1] This total includes tea, for which the average price is not given by Irving. In this case, however, we were able to calculate the average price of tea sold by the East India Company in 1796–8 from the information given in *S.P. 1845*, vol. xlvi, p. 191, and hence to estimate the import price on the assumption that the company made a profit of 15 per cent on the transaction. In making this estimate of the average import price, an allowance was made for the fact that the quality of tea for home consumption and re-export differed. This was done by calculating the import price of both tea for home consumption and for re-export and then taking a suitably weighted average of the two.

[2] See Elizabeth Boody Schumpeter, *English Overseas Trade Statistics, 1697–1808* (1960). Through the courtesy of Professor Ashton, who edited this volume, we were able to see and to use Mrs Schumpeter's figures before they appeared in print.

case of exports of fish and glass, where the errors were more substantial, revised conversion ratios were obtained by first revaluing all exports in these groups in 1796–8 at the English official rates of valuation. Throughout the calculations it was also necessary to make appropriate adjustments to allow both for occasional changes in the rates of official valuation in the course of the period, and for the fact that in the case of exports the valuations employed by Mrs Schumpeter sometimes differ from those employed by the officials who compiled the official trade records.[1]

Since the relative prices of various commodities changed a good deal in the course of the century, it may throw some light on the interpretation of the results of our calculations if we give the ratios of the 'real' to the official values in 1796–8 of some of the more important imports and exports. These are set out in the table below. The differences between the ratios for imports and re-exports are, of course, mainly due to the fact that the real values of imports include insurance and freight, whereas the official values do not.

Table 84. *Ratios of the real to the official value of selected imports, re-exports and exports, 1796–8*

	Imports	Re-Exports		Exports
Brandy	2·53	1·39	Bark, tanners'	8·64
Calicoes, Indian	—	0·77	Beer	2·79
Coffee	0·83	0·46	Brass	1·96
Flax	1·01	1·08	Candles, tallow	2·11
Hemp	2·06	1·61	Coal	0·77
Iron, bar	2·05	1·76	Copper, wrought	1·34
Linens, Irish	1·97	1·55	,, unwrought	1·46
Oil, train	1·17	1·91	Cottons	1·40
Rum	2·90	0·98	Fish	1·01†
Silk, Bengal raw	1·69	1·09	Glass and earthenware	3·33†
,, thrown	0·83	0·77	Haberdashery	10·22
Sugar, brown	2·19	1·37	Iron and steel	1·82
Tallow	2·29	1·78	Lead	1·67
Tar	1·27	1·01	Leather	3·27
Tea	(1·31)*	1·39	Linens	1·36
Tobacco	3·50	2·02	Silks	2·05
Wheat	1·90	1·74	Tin	1·78
Wine, port	1·62	1·37	Woollens	1·45‡
Wood	—	8·36		
Wool, cotton	—	2·53		
,, Spanish	2·90	1·98		
Yarn, linen	2·37	—		
Totals, all goods	1·78	0·95		1·69

* Estimated as described in the text.

† The revised ratios if fish and glass and earthenware are officially valued at the rates in use in the English ledgers work out at 0·71 and 3·47 respectively.

‡ This figure is based on the official valuation of woollens at the rates in use from 1709 onwards. If the rates in use from 1703–8 are employed, the ratio is 0·83.

[1] This is because Mrs Schumpeter valued all exports throughout at the rates prevailing in 1703–8, and ignored changes before and after those dates.

(*b*) NOTES ON THE ESTIMATES OF THE OFFICIAL VALUES OF
IMPORTS, C.I.F.

Imports were officially valued in the eighteenth century on the basis
of the estimated cost of the goods in the country of origin, whereas
re-exports were valued at rates which were based on the price of the
goods on re-export from this country, i.e. at rates which included, in
addition to the original cost, the insurance and freight charges for
bringing the goods to this country, plus the merchants' profit and, in
some cases, duty. In order to estimate the cost of imports inclusive of
insurance and freight we therefore revalued them at the official rates
for re-exports in time (i.e. after the import duties had been drawn back),
less an appropriate deduction for merchants' profit. For this purpose
we assumed that the average profit of 15 per cent, which Irving allowed
in 1796–8, was also applicable at the beginning of the century, and
accordingly multiplied the re-export rates by a factor of 0·87.

It was not, of course, possible to revalue each commodity individually
for every year of the century, for detailed accounts of total imports
broken down by commodities do not exist before 1772. Accordingly,
we made use of Mrs Schumpeter's tables of imports, which relate to
English trade from 1700 to 1791, and British thereafter. These enabled
us to revalue about forty-five individual commodities, comprising from
50 to 60 per cent of the total value of English imports at first cost, for
the whole of the period 1700–91. With the help of the detailed accounts
preserved in the Public Record Office for the latter part of the century,
we then revalued the imports of a further eighty-five commodities for
the years 1772–4. The total value of all the commodities individually
estimated in this way exceeded the official value at first cost by 43 per
cent, and by assuming that a similar difference would apply to the
remaining imports—about 5 per cent of the total—we were able to
obtain an estimate of the value of all English imports c.i.f. for these
three years. From this total we deducted the value of the forty-five
commodities given in Mrs Schumpeter's list and divided the remainder
by the corresponding figure for the official value at first cost. This gave
us a conversion factor, similar to those used in the estimates of the value
of trade at 1796–8 prices, for all the commodities not specified by Mrs
Schumpeter. By applying this ratio to the official value of these commodities in the other years we were able to obtain estimates of the value
of all English imports c.i.f. for the whole period. In doing so it was
necessary to make an allowance for occasional changes in the official
rates of valuation in some of the earlier years, and this was done by
assuming that, on the average, the rates for those commodities not
specified by Mrs Schumpeter changed in the same way as those which
are. Before 1700 Mrs Schumpeter gives no details of the commodities
imported. In order to obtain rough estimates for the years 1697–9 we
therefore divided our estimates for 1700–1 by the official value of imports in those years, and applied this ratio to the official value of
imports for the earlier years.

For the figures of British imports from 1772 onwards, we first made estimates for the years 1772–4 in the same detail as for English imports. Next we subtracted the English total from the British to obtain an estimate for Scotland, which we divided by the official value of Scottish imports in the same years. This factor was then applied to the official value of Scottish imports in each subsequent year down to 1791. After 1791, when Mrs Schumpeter's figures refer to British imports, we used the years 1796–8 as a base-period and proceeded in the same way as for English imports. An estimate for British imports on a 1796–8 base was also made for the year 1791, and as this turned out to be just over 1 per cent lower than the corresponding estimate on a 1772–4 base, all the estimates for the years before and after the link year were slightly adjusted to eliminate the discrepancy. Finally, as a check on the reliability of the estimates, we treated the years 1780, 1781, 1789 and 1790 in the same elaborate detail as the base-periods 1772–4 and 1796–8. The results were in each case slightly lower than the original estimates, but in none of them did the difference amount to as much as 2 per cent.

Table 85. *Official values of eighteenth-century foreign trade*

| | Imports | | | | | Gross barter |
	First cost (£000)	C.i.f. (computed) (£000)	Re-Exports (£000)	Exports (£000)		terms of trade (1700 = 100)
England						
1697	3,344	(4,534)	1,096	2,257	(2,295)	
1698	4,608	(6,248)	1,608	4,220	(3,582)	103
1699	5,621	(7,622)	1,570	4,281	(3,655)	102
1700	5,840	7,902	2,081	4,303	(3,731)	100
1701	5,796	7,878	2,192	4,619	(4,049)	105
1702	4,088	5,572	1,144	3,592	(3,130)	117
1703	4,450	6,014	1,622	4,464	(3,888)	115
1704	5,329	7,261	1,804	4,294	(3,723)	119
1705						129
1706	4,064	5,350	1,447	4,743	(4,142)	157
1707	4,267	5,863	1,602	4,791	(4,173)	154
1708	4,699	6,028	1,495	5,069	(4,404)	147
1709	4,511	6,268	1,507		4,406	159
1710	4,011	5,396	1,566		4,729	158
1711	4,686	6,130	1,875		4,088	168
1712						140
1713	5,811	7,539	2,402		4,490	148
1714	5,929	7,765	2,440		5,564	145
1715	5,641	7,409	1,908		5,015	145
1716	5,800	7,699	2,243		4,807	140
1717	6,347	8,359	2,613		5,384	126
1718	6,669	8,557	1,980		4,381	129
1719	5,367	7,000	2,321		4,514	121
1720	6,090	8,162	2,300		4,611	133
1721	5,908	7,900	2,689		4,512	133
1722	6,378	8,537	2,972		5,293	133
1723	6,506	8,707	2,671		4,725	122
1724	7,394	9,890	2,494		5,107	118

Table 85 *(cont.)*

	Imports				Gross barter terms of trade (1700 = 100)
	First cost (£000)	C.i.f. (computed) (£000)	Re-Exports (£000)	Exports (£000)	
1725	7,095	9,518	2,814	5,667	119
1726	6,678	8,987	2,692	5,001	120
1727	6,799	9,196	2,670	4,605	116
1728	7,569	10,226	3,797	4,910	112
1729	7,541	10,230	3,299	4,940	112
1730	7,780	10,768	3,223	5,326	110
1731	6,992	9,659	2,782	5,081	119
1732	7,088	9,592	3,196	5,675	120
1733	8,017	11,064	3,015	5,823	123
1734	7,096	9,481	2,897	5,403	118
1735	8,160	11,114	3,402	5,927	129
1736	7,308	10,076	3,585	6,118	140
1737	7,074	9,794	3,414	6,668	154
1738	7,439	10,095	3,214	6,982	142
1739	7,829	10,766	3,272	5,572	133
1740	6,704	9,148	3,086	5,111	124
1741	7,936	10,657	3,575	5,995	140
1742	6,867	9,280	3,480	6,095	150
1743	7,802	10,966	4,442	6,868	164
1744	6,363	8,708	3,780	5,411	159
1745	7,847	9,314	3,333	5,739	178
1746	6,206	8,505	3,566	7,201	175
1747	7,117	9,357	3,031	6,744	175
1748	8,136	11,238	3,824	7,317	170
1749	7,918	10,814	3,598	9,081	179
1750	7,772	10,832	3,225	9,474	190
1751	7,943	10,874	3,644	8,775	183
1752	7,889	10,820	3,469	8,226	173
1753	8,625	11,818	3,511	8,732	166
1754	8,093	11,165	3,470	8,318	153
1755	8,773	12,188	3,150	7,915	154
1756	7,962	11,240	3,089	8,632	137
1757	9,253	14,670	3,755	8,584	149
1758	8,415	11,647	3,855	8,763	155
1759	8,923	12,348	3,869	10,079	168
1760	9,833	14,656	3,714	10,981	171
1761	9,544	13,297	4,069	10,804	171
1762	8,870	12,128	4,351	9,400	166
1763	11,199	15,731	5,146	9,522	166
1764	10,391	14,541	4,725	11,536	153
1765	10,981	15,315	4,451	10,122	149
1766	11,513	16,110	4,193	9,890	129
1767	12,074	16,738	4,375	9,492	126
1768	11,879	16,487	5,425	9,695	123
1769	11,909	16,269	4,454	8,984	123
1770	12,217	17,163	4,764	9,503	126
1771	12,822	17,996	5,905	11,219	127
1772	13,305	19,022	5,656	10,503	129
1773	11,560	17,087	5,944	8,976	125
1774	(13,098)	17,746	5,868	10,049	

Table 85 *(cont.)*

	Imports				Gross barter
	First cost (£000)	C.i.f. (computed) (£000)	Re-Exports (£000)	Exports (£000)	terms of trade (1700 = 100)
Great Britain					
1772	14,515	20,460	6,746	10,974	
1773	12,676	18,412	7,114	9,418	125
1774	14,300	19,174	6,732	10,557	121
1775	14,817	20,130	6,253	10,072	119
1776	12,449	17,231	5,051	9,705	113
1777	12,644	17,134	4,191	9,300	113
1778	10,976	15,300	4,046	8,208	112
1779	11,435	15,672	5,890	7,648	116
1780	11,715	15,770	4,785	8,814	106
1781	12,724	17,358	3,710	7,622	111
1782	(10,342)	(13,972)	(3,900)	9,110	112
1783	13,122	17,417	4,327	10,710	117
1784	15,273	20,762	3,827	11,274	105
1785	16,279	22,407	5,143	10,975	100
1786	15,786	21,744	4,476	11,830	97
1787	17,804	24,319	4,816	12,054	97
1788	18,027	24,774	4,748	12,725	100
1789	17,821	24,372	5,561	13,780	105
1790	19,131	26,015	5,199	14,921	114
1791	19,670	26,629	5,922	16,810	123
1792	19,659	26,454	6,568	18,337	122
1793	19,257	26,467	6,498	13,892	121
1794	22,289	31,068	10,024	16,725	114
1795	22,737	32,002	10,785	16,527	127
1796	23,187	31,173	11,417	19,102	137
1797	21,014	29,053	12,014	16,903	134
1798	27,858	39,925	13,919	19,673	134
1799	26,837	37,384	11,907	24,084	137
1800	30,571	42,347	18,848	24,304	141

Notes:

1. The sources of all figures prior to 1772 are P.R.O. Customs 3, and thereafter P.R.O. Customs 17. The accounts for the year 1782 are defective, and give no details of prize goods. The figures given in brackets for that year have, therefore, been based in part on the returns published in Macpherson, *Annals of Commerce,* vol. IV.

2. The figures for Great Britain relate to merchandise trade with all parts of the world, including Ireland, the Isle of Man and the Channel Islands. Those for England relate to trade with all parts of the world except Scotland. Particulars of sea-borne trade with Scotland before the Act of Union in 1707 are given in the sources, but have been excluded here for the sake of comparability.

3. The totals of imports and re-exports include prize goods throughout.

4. The figures for 1697 and 1698 refer to the years ending at Michaelmas. From 1699 to 1752 inclusive the accounts were made up to 25 December each year. After the change of calendar, they were probably made up to 5 January in the years following those specified, although the clerks who kept the old ledgers (P.R.O. Customs 3) continued to give the years as ending at Christmas throughout. There are some differences between the figures given in P.R.O. Customs 3 and 17 for the years 1772–80 (when the old series comes to an end), but these differences cannot be attributed to a discrepancy in the years.

5. Before 1706 the abstracts given in the ledgers do not distinguish exports of coin and bullion from exports and re-exports of merchandise. Return of bullion exports are given

Table 85 (*cont.*)

in *J.H.C.*, vol. xviii, p. 674, and P.R.O. C.O. 390/5.4, from 1699 onwards, and exports of gold and silver for 1697–9 in *House of Lords Papers*, new series, vol. iv, p. 436, but these are incomplete. In preparing the above table, therefore, the returns have been checked against the ledger entries, and so far as possible, all bullion exports have been excluded.

6. A wholesale revision of the official rates of valuation for woollen exports was introduced with effect from 1709. Before that date each type of woollen goods was valued at the same rate, but thereafter the valuation used depended on the country of destination. In order to make the figures of the volume of exports more nearly comparable over time, we have therefore deducted the official value of woollen exports from total exports for each year before 1709 and substituted estimates of the value of woollens at the 1709 rates of valuation. The latter were obtained by dividing the total value of woollen exports in 1709–12 at the revised rates, which are given in P.R.O. C.O. 390/5.18, by the corresponding totals given by Mrs Schumpeter for woollens at the 1703–8 rates of valuation; and then applying this factor to Mrs Schumpeter's figures for earlier years. The adjusted figures for total exports calculated on this basis are given above in brackets. Judging by the various series for woollens given below, it appears that a somewhat similar adjustment was made to the figures for woollen exports given in [Sir Josiah Banks] *The Propriety of Allowing Qualified Exportation of Wool* (1782), p. 83. It will be noted that our figures for the official values of woollen exports differ somewhat from Mrs Schumpeter's. This is because there were minor changes in the rates of valuation before 1703, whereas Mrs Schumpeter values woollens throughout at the 1703–8 rates; and because Mrs Schumpeter's figures apparently include trade with Scotland until 1707, and our figures exclude it.

Table 86. *Woollen exports, 1697–1708*

(£000)

	Mrs Schumpeter's figures	Official values	Valuation at 1709 rates	Banks' figures
1697	1,871	1,506	1,543	1,481
1698	3,168	3,254	2,617	2,455
1699	2,908	3,025	2,399	2,446
1700	2,989	3,043	2,472	2,542
1701	3,238	3,251	2,681	2,697
1702	2,617	2,629	2,167	2,193
1703	3,359	3,358	2,781	2,760
1704	3,327	3,324	2,754	2,740
1705	Records Missing			2,508
1706	3,503	3,498	2,898	2,903
1707	3,595	3,594	2,977	2,912
1708	3,875	3,875	3,210	3,257

7. The figure for imports at first cost in 1774 has been amended to allow for an error in the valuation of imports of spruce linen yarn. According to P.R.O. Customs 3/74, imports from Germany in that year amounted to 1,222,072 lb., but they were valued at 4s. 6d. per lb., instead of the usual rate of 4d. to 6d. (i.e. 5d.). The resulting value figure of £274,966 4s. was carried forward uncorrected to P.R.O. Customs 17/3, and in addition the quantity was entered as 1,122,072 lb. The uncorrected figure for total English imports at first cost in that year is £13,347,638.

8. Figures for Scottish trade from 1755 onwards are available in P.R.O. Customs 14, but they are not reproduced here, as the methods of classifying exports and re-exports differed slightly from those in use in the English ledgers. Although these differences persisted after 1772, the figures given in Customs 17 were based on a uniform classification for the whole of Great Britain.

9. The index of the gross barter terms of trade is given in the form of a three-yearly moving average (centring on the years specified) to eliminate random fluctuations due to the comparatively slow pace of ocean shipping in the eighteenth century.

NOTE ON INCOMES ASSESSED TO TAX IN THE NAPOLEONIC WARS

The income tax which was introduced by Pitt as an emergency measure in 1799[1] was temporarily abolished during the Peace of Amiens, re-imposed in 1803 under the name of the 'property' tax[2] and lasted until the end of the fiscal year 1815–16. It was so unpopular that all the records relating to it were ordered by Parliament to be destroyed. In fact the destruction was incomplete. Various returns had already been published in *Parliamentary Papers* and duplicates of the parish assessment and Receivers-General county returns, which had been deposited with the King's Remembrancer in accordance with ancient custom, had escaped destruction. These documents were not discovered until the 1930's when they were explored by Arthur Hope-Jones and formed the subject of his monograph, *Income Tax in the Napoleonic Wars*.[3] It would appear that all the records relating to incomes assessed (rather than to tax charged) did perish in the 1802 mashtub or the 1816 bonfire.[4] It was of course, the income details that the opponents of the tax wanted most to have destroyed, and except in so far as summary income returns happened to have been published in parliamentary papers before 1816 they seem to have been successful.

Hence most of the historians who have made use of the income-tax data to illustrate changes in general economic conditions have based their analyses on the tax assessment data rather than on the scattered income returns. Since the rate of tax and the scale of allowances varied considerably over the period the figures of tax yield or gross assessments are an unsatisfactory reflection of changes in income. Moreover, in spite of the apparent abundance of assessment figures it is extra-ordinarily difficult to construct an authoritatively consistent series of either gross or net assessments for the whole of the period. The returns from which the various published extracts have been compiled gave

[1] It was preceded by an unsuccessful attempt to tax incomes in 1798: this tax, which was charged on persons liable to assessed incomes, yielded less than £2 m.

[2] The property tax was, in spite of its name, intended as a tax on incomes over £60 per annum. It represented an attempt to collect tax at the source of income, and since most incomes over £60 were property incomes the tax was assessed on properties rather than on persons. Cf. the contemporary statement on the tax, given later in evidence to the Select Committee on Income and Property Tax and there attributed to the Board of Taxes: 'The present measure then must be considered as a tax on the first produce, gradually subsiding itself into a tax upon the income of the ultimate proprietor.' *S.P. 1852*, vol. IX.

[3] Arthur Hope-Jones, *Income Tax in the Napoleonic Wars* (Cambridge, 1939).

[4] Clapham states in his preface to Hope-Jones' volume that the sacks contained 'the complete or all but complete evidence about an episode of first importance in both political and economic history'. But Hope-Jones makes no mention of any evidence relating to incomes, and in so far as he uses the quantitative data himself his analysis is entirely in terms of either gross assessment or tax yield figures.

assessment data at varying levels of grossness for different years; and without exhaustive details of the deductions involved in each case it is impossible to be certain that the figures are comparable. The frequently quoted table in the 1870 Inland Revenue report added further confusion by introducing a number of copying errors.[1] An earlier Inland Revenue version of the summary table of assessments under each Schedule was published in 1852 in the Appendix to the Second Report of the Select Committee on Income and Property Tax.[2] This seems to have been free from gross copying errors. But users of this source can find ample scope for confusion by comparing it with the similar table printed in the text of the minutes of evidence of the report.[3] The Appendix table purports to relate to 'gross' assessments and the table in the text to 'net' assessments but there are a number of inexplicable identities and discrepancies.[4]

It may be possible by a diligent compilation and comparison of all the many scattered returns relating to gross and net assessments, deductions, and net yields to arrive at a comparable series of tax charged under each schedule and for each year. For our purposes, however, it would clearly be more interesting to be able to consider the returns of incomes assessed rather than of tax liabilities or payments.

The most elaborate set of returns relating to gross incomes assessed was published in 1813.[5] This gave for 1803–4, 1805–6, 1806–7, 1808–9 and 1810–11 an enormous amount of data, in many cases detailed by counties of England and Wales (though not by Scottish counties), on: (a) annual values of properties assessed and of various kinds of allowances, deductions and abatements under each Schedule, (b) gross assessments and net yields, and (c) income distribution tables for Schedule D incomes for 1806–7, 1808–9 and 1810–11. A similar detailed return for 1812–13 was published in 1815.[6] A more complete record of the 1803–4 assessments was published in 1806[7] and from this it is clear that certain centrally assessed incomes (mainly under Schedules C and E) were excluded from the county returns published in 1813.[8] For the earlier (1799–1801) version of the tax an income distribution analysis was published in 1802.[9] This covered all assessed incomes, unlike later income distribution tables which related to

---

[1] *S.P. 1870*, vol. xx. Gayer, Rostow and Schwartz (*op. cit.*, vol. i, p. 139 and footnote) noticed the discrepancy in the 1814 assessments and attributed it to an error of addition. Apparently, however, it was due to an error in the Schedule D figure. There are further copying errors in 1803 (Schedule A) and 1804 (total) items of this table, and the 1805 total contains an additional duty not included in the sector sub-totals.

[2] *S.P. 1852*, vol. ix, 2nd Report, p. 404.   [3] *Ibid.*, 2nd Report, p. 294.

[4] For example, the 'net' assessments for 1804 in the text table are higher than the 'gross' assessments in the Appendix table (though not for all schedules). The 1805, 1814 and 1815 assessments are identical except for a negligible difference under Schedule E.

[5] *S.P. 1812–13*, vol. xii.   [6] *S.P. 1814–15*, vol. x.

[7] *S.P. 1806*, vol. xii.

[8] Especially national-debt interest paid through the Bank and incomes from public offices.

[9] *S.P. 1801–2*, vol. iv.

Schedule D incomes only. There were also various other contemporary returns dealing with particular types of income (e.g. foreigners' incomes from national-debt interest which were exempt from the tax) and assessments for particular schedules. Finally there exist some much later parliamentary returns on this subject which are presumably copies of original returns published during the period of the tax's operation.

Table 87 summarises the gross incomes assessed to tax which we extracted or estimated from these sources.

Table 87. *Gross incomes assessed to tax, 1800–14*

(in £m.)

Year ended 5 April	A	B	C	D	E	All schedules
1800–01			No schedules distinguished			80·217
1803–04	38·691	24·280	11·918	34·854	5·609	115·352
1805–06	41·773	26·992	(13·900)	34·673	(7·000)	124·338
1806–07	44·835	28·453	(22·360)	34·570	(6·255)	136·473
1808–09	47·986	31·376	(24·028)	33·499	(8·628)	145·517
1810–11	51·886	33·376	(24·777)	34·402	(9·768)	154·209
1812–13	57·129	36·865	(26·508)	34·384	(10·623)	165·509
1813–14	56·702	36·337	(28·589)	36·080	11·381	169·089
1814–15	60·138	38·396	30·049	37·059	14·824	180·466

N.B. Figures in brackets are our estimates from assessment data. All other figures for particular schedules are from published returns.

Notes on Sources:

Schedules A, B and D: *S.P. 1806*, vol. xii, for 1803; *S.P. 1812–13*, vol. xii, for 1805, 1806, 1808, 1810; *S.P. 1814–15*, vol. x, for 1812; *S.P. 1823*, vol. xiv, for 1813 and for 1814 Schedule D, and *S.P. 1852*, vol. xxviii, for 1814 except Schedule D.

Schedule C: *S.P. 1806*, vol. xii, for 1803; and *S.P. 1852*, vol. xxviii, for 1814. The intervening figures interpolated by analogy with figures of the produce of the tax on this Schedule in *S.P. 1812–13*, vol. xii, and *S.P. 1823*, vol. xiv.

Schedule E: *S.P. 1806*, vol. xii, for 1803; *S.P. 1823*, vol. xiv, for 1813; and *S.P. 1852*, vol. xxviii, for 1814. Intervening figures interpolated on the basis of figures of the produce of the duty.

All Schedule totals: By addition except for 1800 which was given in *S.P. 1801–2*, vol. iv.

No information is available for 1815. According to a note in *S.P. 1830–31*, vol. xiv, 'the assessments under Schedules A, B, D and E for the year 1814–15 were continued for 1815 ending on 5th April 1816'.

The difference between the 1801 and 1803 totals is due largely to the more effective coverage of the 1803 Act with its collection-at-the-source procedure. Both taxes were intended to apply to all incomes over £60 per annum, but the later version brought a much larger group of people within range of the tax and the gross incomes in Table 87 actually include some incomes in the £60 and under income group who were exempted from tax.[1] If we add a similar proportion for

---

[1] The incomes exempted from tax because they were below the exemption limit amounted to £5·745 m. for England and Wales in 1803, and 291,490 persons were involved. *S.P., 1812–13*, vol. xii.

Scotland the incomes below £60 in the Great Britain total appear to have amounted to rather more than £6 m.

Unfortunately there are no records showing the number of persons covered by the 1803 returns, only the number of assessments under each schedule. An official estimate published in 1806 put the number of persons charged in England and Wales in 1803 at 1,059,314 compared with 303,772 assessed for income duty in 1800–1.[1] This seems an implausibly large number in relation to an estimated occupied population of under 4½ million, though of course the exemption limit was not very high at £60. Certainly these two sets of assessments are irreconcilable for it is inconceivable that about 320,000 persons (including Scotland) earned about £80 m. in 1800 and over a million earned £115 m. in 1803–4: for in both cases the exemption limit was £60.

It is not very helpful to say that the actual number of persons to whom the figure of gross incomes assessed relates probably lies between these two wide limits. But without making some fairly arbitrary assumptions it is not possible to be more specific. It is evident, on the one hand, that the 1800–1 returns provide a closer approximation to average incomes per person in the over £60 a year range because assessments were related to persons rather than to income: and on the other hand, that the 1803–4 returns come closer to the aggregate total of incomes earned within this range because the process of assessment by source of income permitted less evasion.

If we assume that all self-employed persons in agriculture were assessed and use our own estimate of about £400,000 for this group; that persons assessed to Schedule D in 1803–4 earned an average of £250 per annum (which was the average for all persons assessed in 1800)[2]; and that there was no double counting in the Schedule E (employment) assessments, we may deduce that the figure of £115·35 millions for gross incomes assessed in 1803–4 related to not more than about 600,000 persons. This would give an average of a little under £200 per annum, which is compatible with the 1800–1 returns on the assumption that the 1803–4 method of assessment brought a number of smaller incomes into account, some of which were not in the last analysis chargeable because they fell below £60 per annum. All this, however, is highly speculative.[1] What is reasonably certain is that the assessments under Schedule D were more likely to be understated than the assessments under Schedules A, B, C or E. In part this was due to the fact that Schedule D incomes were returnable net and the deductions for expenses were not in practice subject to the agreement of tax officials; whereas all other incomes had to be returned gross and the deductions had to be specifically claimed. In part also it is due to the

---

[1] *S.P. 1806*, vol. XII. The total numbers 'brought into charge' under each schedule add up to a total of 1,246,116.

[2] It should be noted, moreover, that the figure of 1,059,314 quoted above is an official estimate of the numbers *charged* to the property tax in the year 1803 in England and Wales. This, after allowing about 7 per cent for Scotland, suggests a gross income of only about £100 per annum per head of the taxed population.

fact that the new collection-at-the-source procedure made it particularly difficult for farmers, land-holders, dividend-receivers and salaried persons to evade assessment or to understate their incomes.

The conclusion that Schedule D assessments were undervalued is strongly supported by examination of the figures in Table 87. Between 1803 and 1812 when incomes assessed under Schedules A, B, C and E rose by an average of over 60 per cent Schedule D incomes did not rise at all. This is very difficult to credit. It is true that most of the industrial indices show a relative stagnation in this period and that the value of overseas trade rose little if at all[1]; but the population increased by about 14 per cent and there is no evidence of absolute decline in industrial output. The trend was still upwards, though not at the rate of the previous two decades. The yield of hawkers' and pedlars' licences (at a constant rate of tax) more than doubled between 1803 and 1812. The annual number of licences granted to retailers of tea and coffee, tobacco, sweets, wines and spirits rose by about 15 per cent between 1803 and 1812, which suggests that they were keeping in step with the population increase. Traders may not have been maintaining their share in the national income *vis-à-vis* the agricultural producers but there is no reason to suppose that their absolute incomes failed to grow at least in proportion to the increase in prices and population. In sum, it would appear not only that trading and manufacturing profits were difficult to assess at the point of first assessment but also that it was more difficult to adjust assessments upwards when profits increased.

It is interesting to note that the profits assessed under Schedule A (i.e. the profits which could be attached more or less directly to ownership of landed property such as mines, quarries and ironworks) were more responsive than the Schedule D profits. Between 1806 and 1812, for example, they increased by over 20 per cent, which was below the increase for land rents in general but was none the less considerable. Table 88 gives details of the Schedule A assessments for the years for which these are available.

Table 88. *Schedule A assessments, 1806–14*

(in £m.)

	1806	1808	1810	1812	1814
Lands	29·834	31·709	34·130	37·666	39·406
Tithes, manors, fines	2·046	2·194	2·418	2·652	3·022
Houses	11·914	13·042	14·179	15·534	16·259
Profits	1·041	1·041	1·159	1·277	1·451
Total Schedule A	44·835	47·986	51·886	57·129	60·138

Source: As corresponding Schedule A figures in Table 88 except for the 1814 details which were in *S.P. 1870*, vol. xx.

[1] The declared volume of British exports over the three years 1810–12 was almost exactly the same as for the triennium 1801–3 and the computed value of imports had increased by about 10 per cent. (Imlah, *op. cit.* p. 37.)

The property tax income assessments covered the bulk of the non-wage income earned in Great Britain and, in combination with our estimates of incomes from employment, should provide some sort of basis for estimating total national income. The two main difficulties involved in such an estimate are, first, the problem of assessing the degree of understatement in the assessed incomes, and second, the problem of calculating the incomes of unassessed self-employed persons (i.e. those earning under £60 per annum).

To construct estimates of national income for 1801 and 1811 respectively we took as our starting-point our own estimates of employment incomes for 1801 and 1911 and the tax assessment data for 1800–1 and 1803–4 on the one hand and 1810–11 and 1812–13 on the other. We allowed for evasion and for the unassessed self-employed population on the following assumptions: (1) That most of the evasion took place under Schedule D. (2) That evasion amounted to one-third of Schedule D incomes at the beginning of the decade and 50 per cent *circa* 1811 and that the evasion under Schedule A and B was balanced by the deductions for expenses under these heads. (3) That the average income of the unassessed self-employed averaged about £50 per annum.

On these assumptions we arrived at the following estimates of national income.

Table 89. *Estimated national income of Great Britain, 1801 and 1811*

(in £m.)

	1801	1811
1. Incomes from employment	104·1	140·2
2. Assessed profits, rents and other incomes from self-employment	96·9	123·8
3. Unassessed profit, etc., incomes	18·8	19·9
4. Housing	12·2	17·2
Total national income	232·0	301·1

Notes to items:

1. For incomes from employment see pp. 148–158 above. The probability is that these are overestimated because we have been unable to allow for short time and unemployment. However, in a period of relatively full employment this may not have been an important factor.

2. Includes gross Schedule A, B and D incomes excluding exempted incomes under £60 and including allowance for evasion equivalent to one-third per cent of Schedule D incomes for 1801 and 50 per cent for 1811. Schedule C incomes have been excluded since they are largely national-debt interest and Schedule E incomes because they are included in our estimates of employment incomes.

3. The estimates for numbers of unassessed self-employed persons are very rough, being arrived at residually after deducting numbers estimated to have been assessed to tax from our estimates of numbers of self-employed (see above, p. 149). It is very probable that we have underestimated the proportion of self-employed persons in the population and that this figure should be higher and the incomes from employment figure correspondingly lower.

4. Housing 1801 estimated from Eden (quoted Colquhoun, *Treatise on Indigence*, p. 59), who found an average rent of about £6·765 p.a. We have applied this to number of inhabited houses 1801 in England and Wales and an average which includes the highest rented group in London to the number for Scotland. Housing 1811 found by adding 16 per cent to assessed housing.

UNITED KINGDOM NATIONAL INCOME TABLES

(a) Annual Estimates

Annual estimates of national income for the United Kingdom are available back to 1855 and we have depended heavily on the work of other investigators for this period. The estimates for individual years must be regarded as subject to considerable margins of error, and since we have been concerned with long-term trends rather than year-to-year changes it seemed appropriate to discuss the data entirely in terms of decade averages. Those who prefer to examine the trends in the light of a different framework of periods will, however, require annual figures.

Much of the raw material of the British economic-growth inquiry is being published separately, with full annual detail, in an *Abstract of Historical Statistics* which is a companion volume to this book. We shall not reproduce series which are available either in the *Abstract* or in their original place of publication. In this Appendix we give some of the series which we have treated as basic but which have not appeared elsewhere in this form. The reader is warned against depending heavily on the results for particular years.

Table 90. *The growth of national income, 1855–1959*

	Net national income at factor cost and in current prices (£m.)	National income per head in current prices (£)	National income per head at 1913–14 prices (£)
1855	627	22·54	19·77
1856	656	23·42	20·54
1857	636	22·56	19·28
1858	624	21·98	20·74
1859	647	22·63	20·95
1860	684	23·77	21·03
1861	717	24·74	22·09
1862	731	25·00	22·12
1863	748	25·38	22·07
1864	784	26·42	22·97
1865	811	27·10	23·98
1866	834	27·66	24·27
1867	828	27·23	23·89
1868	824	26·85	23·76
1869	855	27·60	24·86
1870	923	29·53	26·84
1871	982	31·12	27·54
1872	1,037	32·53	27·11
1873	1,131	35·15	28·81
1874	1,132	34·83	30·29
1875	1,085	33·04	29·77

Table 90 (*cont.*)

	Net national income at factor cost and in current prices £m.	National income per head in current prices £	National income per head at 1913–14 prices £
1876	1,089	32·80	29·82
1877	1,096	32·64	29·67
1878	1,075	31·67	30·45
1879	1,024	29·85	29·56
1880	1,079	31·16	29·68
1881	1,118	32·00	31·38
1882	1,161	32·98	32·33
1883	1,190	33·57	33·24
1884	1,142	31·97	33·65
1885	1,124	31·21	34·29
1886	1,140	31·39	35·27
1887	1,169	31·94	35·89
1888	1,251	33·92	37·69
1889	1,339	36·01	39·15
1890	1,405	37·48	41·19
1891	1,392	36·82	40·03
1892	1,367	35·85	40·28
1893	1,336	34·71	39·00
1894	1,383	35·59	42·37
1895	1,449	36·94	44·51
1896	1,477	37·30	44·94
1897	1,528	38·21	46·04
1898	1,610	39·87	46·91
1899	1,683	41·28	46·90
1900	1,768	42·96	45·70
1901	1,735	41·77	46·93
1902	1,750	41·77	46·94
1903	1,736	41·09	45·66
1904	1,754	41·16	45·74
1905	1,832	42·62	46·84
1906	1,952	45·02	47·89
1907	2,050	46·87	48·32
1908	1,940	43·97	47·79
1909	1,987	43·63	47·79
1910	2,078	46·26	48·19
1911	2,154	47·55	49·02
1912	2,288	48·14	47·66
1913	2,395	52·47	51·95
1914	2,294	49·77	50·27
1920	5,787	123·60	47·72
1921	4,572	103·74	43·59
1922	3,962	89·29	43·99
1923	3,951	88·60	43·38
1924	4,029	89·70	47·21
1925	4,091	90·79	47·79
1926	4,030	89·10	46·89
1927	4,268	94·03	51·11
1928	4,277	93·84	51·00
1929	4,301	94·17	51·46
1930	4,076	88·87	49·93
1931	3,779	82·02	48·53
1932	3,681	79·44	47·86

Table 90 *(cont.)*

	Net national income at factor cost and in current prices (£m.)	National income per head in current prices (£)	National income per head at 1913–14 prices (£)
1933	3,846	82·67	51·03
1934	4,004	85·80	52·96
1935	4,238	90·42	55·82
1936	4,525	96·11	58·60
1937	4,759	100·64	59·55
1938	4,816	101·40	58·95
1939	5,182	108·50	60·95
1940	7,141	148·07	73·30
1941	7,085	146·94	66·19
1942	7,806	161·28	68·34
1943	8,306	170·24	69·49
1944	8,257	168·46	67·38
1945	8,285	168·46	66·06
1946	8,087	164·31	58·06
1947	8,587	173·23	57·36
1948	9,556	190·87	58·55
1949	10,208	202·69	60·69
1950	10,710	211·59	61·33
1951	11,720	231·82	62·32
1952	12,727	250·92	63·52
1953	13,607	268·85	66·88
1954	14,580	287·10	70·20
1955	15,416	302·46	71·67
1956	16,698	326·08	73·94
1957	17,635	342·72	75·66
1958	18,341	354·90	76·16
1959	18,931	364·16	77·98

Sources:

1. National income totals. Central Statistical Office Blue Book on *National Income and Expenditure, 1960*, for 1949–59; and 1957 and 1959 editions for 1938 and 1946–8. *National Income White Paper, 1938–46*, Cmd. 7099, for 1939–45. A. R. Prest, 'National Income of the United Kingdom 1870–1946', *Economic Journal*, 1948, for basic national-income estimates 1870–1937. These were adjusted by the addition of employers' national insurance contributions and income of non-profit-making organisations from James Jefferys and Dorothy Walters, 'National Income and Expenditure of the United Kingdom 1870–1952', *Income and Wealth Series V*, p. 24, and Agatha Chapman and Rose Knight, *Wages and Salaries in the United Kingdom 1920–1938*. Adjusted totals were extrapolated to 1855 on the basis of Charles Feinstein's estimates of national income, *Economic Journal*, 1961, p. 384.

2. Population figures used to convert to per head terms were Registrar-General's latest estimates.

3. Price index to deflate to 1913 prices was derived from London and Cambridge Economic Service retail price index *Bulletin*, *Times Review of Industry*, June 1960, and the retail price index in A. L. Bowley, *Wages and Income since 1860* (1937), pp. 121–2.

Table 91. *The disposition of gross national product at market prices,*
1860–1959

(as percentages of the total)

	Consumers' expenditure (%)	Public authorities' expenditure (%)	Gross domestic fixed capital (%)	Net foreign investment (%)	Expenditure generating gross national product at market prices (£m.)
1860	85·2	6·3	5·6	2·9	822
1861	86·1	6·1	6·1	1·7	848
1862	85·6	5·7	7·3	1·4	876
1863	84·3	4·9	7·8	2·9	931
1864	84·3	4·7	8·6	2·4	977
1865	83·5	4·5	8·6	3·4	1,010
1866	83·7	4·4	8·8	3·1	1,054
1867	84·1	5·0	6·8	4·1	1,028
1868	85·2	5·3	5·6	3·6	1,025
1869	84·8	5·1	5·7	4·5	1,056
1870	84·5	4·9	6·7	3·9	1,129
1871	82·4	4·6	7·1	5·8	1,218
1872	80·7	4·3	7·5	7·4	1,319
1873	82·6	4·1	7·2	6·0	1,357
1874	82·2	4·2	8·4	5·2	1,366
1875	82·9	4·5	8·8	3·8	1,348
1876	84·3	4·6	9·4	1·7	1,336
1877	85·0	4·7	9·4	1·0	1,333
1878	85·4	4·9	8·5	1·3	1,312
1879	84·3	5·5	7·3	2·9	1,254
1880	85·1	5·2	7·1	2·7	1,347
1881	83·1	5·2	6·8	4·9	1,354
1882	83·4	5·3	7·1	4·3	1,388
1883	84·0	5·4	7·1	3·5	1,416
1884	82·9	5·4	6·5	5·1	1,401
1885	83·4	6·1	6·0	4·5	1,365
1886	83·1	6·0	5·1	5·8	1,355
1887	83·3	5·7	4·7	6·3	1,395
1888	83·1	5·4	5·1	6·3	1,428
1889	83·4	5·4	5·6	5·5	1,471
1890	82·2	5·6	5·8	6·5	1,525
1891	83·9	5·7	6·0	4·4	1,567
1892	83·9	5·9	6·5	3·8	1,566
1893	84·5	6·1	5·9	3·4	1,551
1894	84·9	6·3	6·3	2·5	1,552
1895	85·0	6·6	5·9	2·5	1,572
1896	83·7	6·5	6·4	3·5	1,651
1897	83·1	6·7	7·7	2·5	1,696
1898	83·1	6·8	8·9	1·3	1,763
1899	81·4	7·2	9·2	2·2	1,874
1900	79·7	9·1	9·4	1·9	2,040
1901	79·4	9·9	9·1	1·6	2,092
1902	79·8	9·3	9·4	1·6	2,094
1903	80·8	7·9	9·2	2·2	2,091
1904	81·4	7·4	8·8	2·5	2,102
1905	80·9	7·2	8·1	3·8	2,137
1906	80·3	6·9	7·5	5·4	2,192
1907	79·8	6·7	6·6	6·8	2,260
1908	80·8	6·9	5·4	6·9	2,232
1909	81·3	7·3	5·4	6·1	2,241

Table 91 (cont.)

(as percentages of the total)

	Consumers' expenditure (%)	Public authorities' expenditure (%)	Gross domestic fixed capital (%)	Net foreign investment (%)	Expenditure generating gross national product at market prices (£m.)
1910	80·2	7·4	5·3	7·2	2,328
1911	79·7	7·2	5·0	8·2	2,417
1912	79·8	7·2	5·2	7·9	2,501
1913	78·3	7·2	6·0	8·5	2,628
1914	79·1	7·9	6·0	7·1	2,536
1920	77·2	9·9	9·1	3·8	6,548
1921	78·3	9·4	9·1	3·2	5,601
1922	79·0	9·2	8·7	3·1	4,940
1923	80·2	8·6	8·0	3·2	4,720
1924	81·4	8·5	8·3	1·8	4,726
1925	81·3	8·5	9·1	1·1	4,857
1926	82·6	8·9	8·4	0·2	4,733
1927	80·4	8·6	8·7	2·3	4,934
1928	80·0	8·4	8·9	2·7	5,024
1929	80·6	8·6	8·8	2·0	5,040
1930	81·5	9·0	8·9	0·6	4,915
1931	84·2	9·6	8·5	−2·2	4,590
1932	84·4	9·5	7·3	−1·1	4,435
1933	83·5	9·3	7·2	—	4,492
1934	82·4	9·2	8·6	−0·1	4,689
1935	80·8	9·5	9·1	0·6	4,949
1936	80·1	10·3	9·9	−0·3	5,175
1937	79·2	11·3	10·6	−1·0	5,500
1938	76·5	13·3	11·5	−1·2	5,826
1939	71·4	20·5	12·1	−4·0	6,273
1940	63·5	43·9	3·6	−11·0	7,328
1941	56·8	50·7	2·1	−9·5	8,582
1942	54·6	50·3	2·2	−7·1	9,391
1943	52·0	52·9	2·0	−6·8	9,940
1944	53·8	51·8	1·0	−6·5	10,111
1945	78·0	44·4	6·2	−8·7	10,114
1946	71·0	22·7	9·2	−3·0	10,077
1947	75·8	16·7	11·5	−4·0	10,438
1948	71·7	14·8	12·2	1·2	11,880
1949	70·1	15·6	12·7	1·5	12,659
1950	68·8	15·2	12·7	3·2	13,620
1951	71·7	17·3	13·6	−2·7	14,098
1952	66·9	18·2	13·4	1·4	15,910
1953	66·7	18·1	14·1	1·1	16,907
1954	67·0	17·5	14·4	1·1	17,987
1955	68·4	17·0	15·1	−0·5	18,890
1956	66·6	17·1	15·4	0·9	20,455
1957	66·4	16·7	15·8	1·1	21,562
1958	66·4	16·4	15·6	1·5	22,685
1959	66·9	16·8	15·6	0·6	23,491

Sources:

1. Consumers' expenditure. For 1947–59 figures see C.S.O. Blue Books on *National Income and Expenditure*, 1960, 1959 and 1957 editions. For 1900–46 estimates by D. A. Rowe, see *Abstract of Historical Statistics*. For 1870–1899 see Jefferys and Walters, *op. cit.* pp. 8–9. Earlier years by extrapolation on basis retained imports and national-income estimates.

Table 91 *(cont.)*

2. Public authorities' expenditure, recent years, see C.S.O. Blue Books and White Papers. For 1870–1937 see Jefferys and Walters, *op. cit.* pp. 8–9. Earlier years extrapolated on basis public expenditure accounts.

3. Gross domestic fixed capital. Estimates for period 1860–1914 by Charles Feinstein, *Economic Journal*, June, 1961; for 1920–37 by K. Maywald, as revised by Charles Feinstein for *Domestic Capital Formation in the United Kingdom, 1930–1938* to be published; for recent years see National Income Blue Books and White Papers.

4. Net Foreign Investment, 1860–1913 figures from A. H. Imlah, *Economic Elements in the Pax Britannica*, pp. 70–75; 1914–37 from *Board of Trade Journal* estimates published annually in February from 1923; 1938–59 figures from National Income Blue Books and White Papers.

5. Expenditure generating gross national product. By addition other four columns of this table. Makes no allowances for additions to stocks or for changes in money value of stocks.

(*b*) *Reconciliation of National Income or Product Estimates*

In the course of this study we made three largely independent estimates of nineteenth-century national income. The choice of method in each case was determined partly by the viewpoint we wanted to illuminate in a particular context and partly by the nature of the available data. (1) To map out the broad changes in industrial structure we built up estimates of the gross national product of Great Britain for each census year 1801–1901. These are in Table 37. (2) To trace the time-path of total national income we followed Prest in using income tax and wage data as a basis for a series of annual estimates of the net national income of the United Kingdom from 1855 onwards. These are in Table 90. (3) To illustrate the pattern of change in the way the nation laid out its resources as between consumption, investment and public expenditure, we summed expenditure estimates to produce an annual series of expenditure generating gross national product of the United Kingdom from 1860. These are in Table 91.

In principle these three approaches constitute the basic components of a complete set of national accounts. In practice there were significant gaps in our knowledge which meant that we could not articulate them without doing a great deal more research. The estimates of gross national product for Great Britain could be brought into line with the estimates of net national income for the United Kingdom only after deriving satisfactory estimates for the national product of Ireland on the one hand, and for capital consumption on the other. The third approach which was at market prices could be conceptually matched with the other two by deducting indirect taxes and adding subsidies: but especially for years before 1900 its major component—consumers' expenditure—was so crudely estimated that its totals were too unreliable to set against the other two estimates with any confidence.

It may however be helpful to indicate the extent and the direction of the differences between the three sets of estimates by attempting a rough reconciliation. That is the purpose of Table 92. Column 1 of this table is formed by adding to the totals in Table 37 a crude estimate of the national product of Ireland based on an assumed average income per head. Column 2 adds to the estimates in Table 91 Feinstein's admittedly rough estimates of depreciation. Column 3 deducts indirect taxes and adds subsidies to the relevant figures in Table 91. The figures in brackets are rough extrapolations which are very much less reliable than the other figures in Table 92. It is our view that the differences between columns (1) and (2) are well within the margins of error of both sets of estimates, but that in assessing the differences between column (3) and either of the other two columns more weight should be given to the wider margin of error involved in the third approach.

Table 92.   *Three Approaches to an Estimate of United Kingdom G.N.P.*

(In millions of pounds at current prices)

	(1)	(2)	(3)
1841	526	(560)	(516)
1851	589	(592)	(631)
1861	755	734	(859)
1871	1,030	1,009	1,145
1881	1,170	1,146	1,272
1891	1,410	1,431	1,474
1901	1,777	1,784	1,960

Source: See text and notes to Tables 37, 90 and 91.

336

LITERATURE

This does not set out to be a comprehensive bibliography of British economic growth. Nor indeed is it an exhaustive list of works consulted or used in the course of the inquiry of which this book is the outcome. It is a brief alphabetical list of the books, pamphlets and articles specifically referred to in this book and is designed to save readers who want a past reference from having to toil through the footnote jungle in search of it. There are no references to papers in the *Sessional Papers* series and place of publication is given only for non-British publications. A more exhaustive, classified bibliography of statistical sources and commentaries is contained in the *Abstract of Historical Statistics* which is being published as a companion to this volume.

Allen, C. J., *The Great Eastern Railway*, 1955.
Andrew, Samuel, *Fifty Years of the Cotton Trade*. Paper read to the Economic Section of the British Association at Manchester, 1887.
Anon. *Observations on the Advantages which This Country Draws from a Free and Unfettered Importation of the Raw Material and Cotton Wool*, 1789.
Anon. *An Important Crisis in the Calico and Muslin Manufacture in Great Britain*, 1788.
Ashley, Sir William, *British Industries*, 1903.
Ashton, T. S., *Iron and Steel in the Industrial Revolution*, 1924.
Ashton, T. S., *An Eighteenth-Century Industrialist*, 1939.
Ashton, T. S., *An Economic History of England: The Eighteenth Century*, 1955.
Ashton, T. S., *Economic Fluctuations in England 1700–1800*, 1959.
Ashton, T. S., and Sykes, J., *The Coal Industry of the Eighteenth Century*, 1929.
Ashton, T. S., *The Industrial Revolution, 1760–1830*, 1948.
Ashworth, W., 'Changes in Industrial Structure', *Yorkshire Bulletin of Economic and Social Research*, 1965.

Baines, Edward, *History of the Cotton Manufacture*, 1835.
Baines, Edward, 'The Woollen Manufacture of England with Special Reference to the Leeds Clothing District'. Paper read before the British Association for the Advancement of Science, 1858. Reprinted in *Yorkshire Past and Present*, by Thomas Baines, 1877.
Banks, Sir Josiah, *The Propriety of Allowing Qualified Exportation of Wool*, 1782.
Barnes, D. G., *A History of the English Corn Laws*, 1930
Bauer, P. T., and Yamey, B. S., 'Economic Progress and Occupational Distribution', *Economic Journal*, 1951.
Beeke, H., *Observations on the Produce of the Income Tax and its Proportion to the whole Income of Great Britain*, 1800.
Bell, Benjamin, *Essays on Agriculture*, 1802.
Bell, Lowthian, I., *The Iron Trade of the United Kingdom*, 1882.
Briggs, Asa, *The Age of Improvement*, 1959.
Bellerby, J. R., 'The Distribution of Manpower in Agriculture and Industry 1851–1951', *The Farm Economist*, 1958.
Bernal, J. D., *Science in History*, 1954.
Bevan, G. P., *British Manufacturing Industries*, 1876.
Beveridge, Sir William, *Prices and Wages in England from the Twelfth to the Nineteenth Century*, vol. I, 1939.

Bischoff, James, *A Comprehensive History of the Woollen and Worsted Manufacturers and the Natural and Commercial History of Sheep*, 2 vols., 1842.

Blaug, M., 'The Productivity of Capital in the Lancashire Cotton Industry during the Nineteenth Century', *Economic History Review*, 1961.

Board of Agriculture and Fisheries, *Production of Wool in Great Britain in 1905 and 1906*, 1907.

Board of Trade, *Report on Wholesale and Retail Prices*, 1903.

Booth, Charles, 'Occupations of the People of the United Kingdom, 1801–81', *Journal of the Statistical Society*, 1886.

Bourne, Stephen, *Trade, Population and Food*, 1880.

Bowley, A. L., 'Comparison of the Changes in Wages in France, the United States and the United Kingdom from 1840 to 1891', *Economic Journal*, 1898.

Bowley, A. L., 'The Amount and Distribution of Income (other than wages) below the Income Tax Limit', *Journal of the Royal Statistical Society*, 1910.

Bowley, A. L., 'The Statistics of Wages in the United Kingdom during the Nineteenth Century', *Journal of the Royal Statistical Society*. Agricultural Wages, 1898–1900; Building Trades, 1900; Printers, 1900; Worsted and Woollen Manufacturers of the West Riding of Yorkshire, 1902.

Bowley, A. L., *Wages and Incomes since 1860*, 1937.

Bowley, A. L., and Wood, G. H., 'The Statistics of Wages in the United Kingdom during the Nineteenth Century: Engineering and Shipbuilding', *Journal of the Royal Statistical Society*, 1905–6.

Bradley, R., *Complete Body of Husbandry*, 1727.

Brewster, D., *Edinburgh Encyclopedia*, 1830.

British Iron and Steel Federation, *Statistics of the Iron and Steel Industries*, 1936.

Brooke, E. H., *Chronology of the Tinplate Works of Great Britain*, 1944.

Brown, E. H. Phelps, and Handfield Jones, S. J., 'The Climacteric of the 1890's: A Study in the Expanding Economy', *Oxford Economic Papers*, 1952.

Brown, E. H. Phelps, and Hart, P. E., 'The Share of Wages in National Income', *Economic Journal*, 1952.

Brownlee, John, 'The Health of London in the Eighteenth Century', *Proceedings of the Royal Society of Medicine*, 1925.

Brownlee, John, 'History of Birth and Death Rates in England and Wales', *Public Health*, 1916.

Buer, M. C., *Health, Wealth and Population in the Early Days of the Industrial Revolution*, 1926.

Burn, D. L., *The Economic History of Steel Making, 1867–1939*, 1940.

Burnham, T. H., and Hoskins, G. O., *Iron and Steel in Britain, 1870–1930*, 1943.

Caird, James, *English Agriculture*, 1851.

Caird, James, *The Landed Interest and the Supply of Food*, 1879.

Cairncross, A. K., *Home and Foreign Investment 1870–1913*, 1953.

Campion, H., *Public and Private Property in Great Britain*, 1939.

Carter, Alice, 'Dutch Investment 1738–1800', *Economica*, 1953.

Cary, John, *Inland Navigation*, 1795.

Cathcart, Earl, 'Wool in Relation to Science with Practice', *Journal of the Agricultural Society of England*, 1875.

Central Statistical Office, *National Income and Expenditure 1959*, 1959.

Chambers, J. D., 'Enclosure and Labour Supply in the Industrial Revolution', *Economic History Review*, 1953.

Chambers, J. D., 'The Vale of Trent 1760–1800', *Economic History Review*, Supplement No. 3, 1957.

Chapman, Agatha L., and Knight, Rose, *Wages and Salaries in the United Kingdom, 1920–1938*, 1953.

Chapman, Robert, *The Topographical Picture of Glasgow in its Ancient and Modern State*, 1820.

Clapham, J. H., *An Economic History of Modern Britain*, 3 vols., 1939.

Clark, G. N., *Guide to English Commercial Statistics 1696–1782*, 1938.

Coats, A. W., 'Changing Attitudes to Labour in the Mid-Eighteenth Century' *Economic History Review*, 1958.

Cole, W. A., 'Trends in Eighteenth-Century Smuggling', *Economic History Review*, 1958.

Coleman, D. C., 'Industrial Growth and Industrial Revolutions', *Economica*, 1956.

Coleman, D. C., 'Labour in the English Economy of the Seventeenth Century' *Economic History Review*, 1956.

Coleman, D. C., *The British Paper Industry, 1495–1860*, 1958.

Colquhoun, Patrick, *Treatise on Indigence*, 1806.

Colquhoun, Patrick, *Treatise on the Wealth, Power and Resources of the British Empire*, 1815 (2nd ed.).

Committee on Industry and Trade, *Survey of Textile Industries*, 1928.

Connell, K. H., *The Population of Ireland 1750–1845*, 1950.

Coontz, S. H., *Population Theories and the Economic Interpretation*, 1957.

Coppock, D. J., 'The Climacteric of the 1890's: A Critical Note', *Manchester School of Economic and Social Studies*, 1956.

Court, W. H. B., *The Rise of the Midland Industries, 1600–1838*, 1938.

Curtler, W. H. R., *A Short History of British Agriculture*, 1909.

Davis, Ralph, 'English Foreign Trade, 1660–1700', *Economic History Review*, 1954.

Davis, Ralph, 'The Rise of Protection in England, 1669–1786', *Economic History Review*, 1966.

Deane, Phyllis, 'The Implications of Early National Income Estimates for the Measurement of Long-Term Economic Growth in the United Kingdom', *Economic Development and Cultural Change*, 1955.

Deane, Phyllis, 'Contemporary Estimates of National Income in the Nineteenth Century', *Economic History Reveiw*, 1956 and 1957.

Deane, Phyllis, 'The Industrial Revolution and Economic Growth: The Evidence of Early British National Income Estimates', *Economic Development and Cultural Change*, 1957.

Deane, Phyllis, 'The Output of the British Woollen Industry in the Eighteenth Century', *Journal of Economic History*, 1957.

Deane, Phyllis, 'Capital Formation in Britain before the Railway Age,' *Economic Development and Cultural Change*, 1961.

Dobb, M. H., *Studies in the Development of Capitalism*, 1946.

Douglas, P. H., 'An Estimate of the Growth of Capital in the United Kingdom, 1865–1909', *Journal of Economic and Business History*, 1930.

Dundee Trade Report Association, *Statistics of the Linen Trade*, 1855.

Edwards, R. D., and Williams, T., *The Great Famine. Studies in Irish History*, 1957.

Ellison, T., *The Cotton Trade of Great Britain*, 1886.

Ernle, Lord, *English Farming Past and Present*, 1936.

Farey, J., *General View of the Agriculture and Minerals of Derbyshire*, 1815.

Feinstein, Charles, 'Income and Investment in the United Kingdom, 1856–1914', *Economic Journal*, June 1961.

Fenn, Charles, *A Compendium of the English and Foreign Funds, etc.*, 1837.

Fisher, A. G. B., 'A Note on Tertiary Production', *Economic Journal*, 1952.

Fisher, F. J., 'The Development of the London Food Market, 1540–1640', *Economic History Review*, 1935.

Flinn, M. W., 'Revisions in Economic History, XVII, The Growth of the English Iron Industry, 1660–1760', *Economic History Review*, 1958.

Forbes. U. A., and Ashford, W. H. R., *Our Waterways*, 1906.

Francis, J., *A History of the English Railway, 1820–45*, 2 vols., 1845.

Fussell, G. E., 'Population and Wheat Production in the Eighteenth Century', *History Teachers' Miscellany*, 1929.

Fussell, G. E., 'The Size of English Cattle in the Eighteenth Century', *Agricultural History*, 1929.

Fussell, G. E., and Goodman, Constance, 'Eighteenth-Century Estimates of British Sheep and Wool Production', *Agricultural History*, 1930.

Gayer, Arthur, Rostow, W. W., and Schwartz, Anna J., *The Growth and Fluctuations of the British Economy, 1790–1850*, 2 vols., 1953.

Geary, R. C., 'The Future Population of Saorstat Eireann and some Observations on Population Statistics', *Journal of the Statistical and Social Inquiry Society of Ireland*, 1935–36.

George, M. D., 'Some Causes of the Increase of Population in the Eighteenth Century as Illustrated by London', *Economic Journal*, 1922.

Giffen, R., *Growth of Capital*, 1889.

Gilboy, E. W., 'The Cost of Living and Real Wages in the Eighteenth Century', *Review of Economic Statistics*, 1936.

Gilboy, Elizabeth W., *Wages in Eighteenth-Century England*, 1934.

Gill, Conrad, *The Rise of the Irish Linen Industry*, 1925.

Gill, Conrad, *History of Birmingham*, 1951.

Glass, D. V., and Eversley, D. E. C., *Population in History*, 1965.

Gonner, E. C. K., 'The Population of England in the Eighteenth Century', *Journal of the Royal Statistical Society*, 1913.

Gregson, Matthew, *Portfolio of Fragments Relative to the History and Antiquities of the County Palatine and the Duchy of Lancaster*, 1817.

Talbot Griffith, G., *Population Problems of the Age of Malthus*, 1926.

Grimshaw, T. W., 'A Statistical Survey of Ireland', *Journal of the Statistical Society of Ireland*, 1888.

Habakkuk, H. J., 'English Population in the Eighteenth Century', *Economic History Review*, 1953.

Habakkuk, H. J., 'Essays in Bibliography and Criticism: The Eighteenth Century', *Economic History Review*, 1956.

Hamilton, Archibald, 'On Wool Supply', *Journal of the Statistical Society*, 1870.

Hamilton, H., *The English Brass and Copper Industries to 1800*, 1926.

Hammond, Barbara, 'Urban Death Rates in the Early Nineteenth Century', *Economic History*, 1928.

Hecht, J. J., *The Domestic Servant Class in Eighteenth-Century England*, 1956.

Hobsbawm, E. J., 'The British Standard of Living, 1790–1850', *Economic History Review*, 1957.

Hoffmann, W. G., *British Industry 1700–1950*, translated by W. O. Henderson and W. G. Chaloner, 1955.

Holzman, James M., *The Nabobs in England*, New York, 1926.

Hooper, Frederic, *Statistics Relating to the City of Bradford and the Woollen and Worsted Trades of the United Kingdom*, 1898, and issued annually thereafter by the Bradford Chamber of Commerce.

Hope-Jones, A., *Income Tax in the Napoleonic Wars*, 1939.

Houghton, J., *Husbandry and Trade Improved*, 1727.

Horner, John, *The Linen Trade of Europe during the Spinning-Wheel Period*, 1920.

Imlah, A. H., *Economic Elements in the Pax Britannica*, Cambridge, Mass., 1958.

Isserlis, L., 'Tramp Shipping Cargoes and Freights', *Journal of the Royal Statistical Society*, 1938.

Jackman, W. T., *The Development of Transportation in Modern England*, 2 vols., 1916.

Jacob, Giles, *The Country Gentleman's Vade Mecum*, 1717.

James, John, *History of the Worsted Manufacture in England*, 1857.

Jeans, J. S., *The Jubilee Memorial of the Railway System*, 1875.

Jefferys, J. B., and Walters, Dorothy, 'National Income and Expenditure of the United Kingdom', *Income and Wealth Series V*, 1956.

Jenkin, A. K. H., *The Cornish Miner*, 1927.

John, A. H., 'War and the English Economy, 1700–1763', *Economic History Review*, 1955.

Johnson, E. R., and others, *History of the Domestic and Foreign Commerce of the United States*, Washington, 1915.

Jones, J. H., 'The Present Position of the British Coal Trade', *Journal of the Royal Statistical Society*, 1930.

Jubb, Samuel, *The History of the Shoddy Trade*, 1860.

Kahn, H. R., 'The Distinction between Wages and Salaries', *Scottish Journal of Political Economy*, 1956.

Kalecki, M., *Theory of Economic Dynamics*, 1954.

Kelsall, R. K., *Wage Regulation under the Statute of Artificers*, 1938.

Keynes, J. M., 'Relative Movements in Real Wages and Output', *Economic Journal*, 1939.

King, Gregory, (a) 'Natural and Political Observations and Conclusions upon the State and Condition of England', (b) 'Of the Naval Trade of England 1688 and the National Profit then arising thereby', both published in *Two Tracts by Gregory King*, edited by George E. Barnett, Baltimore, 1936.

Krause, J. T., 'Changes in English Fertility and Mortality, 1781–1850', *Economic History Review*, 1958.

Lauderdale, James, Earl, *An Inquiry into the Nature and Origins of Public Wealth and into the Measurement of and Causes of its Increase*, 1804.

Lemon, Sir Charles, 'Statistics of the Copper Mines of Cornwall', *Journal of the Statistical Society*, 1838.

Lenfant, J. H., 'Great Britain's Capital Formation, 1865–1914', *Economica*, 1951.

Lewin, H. G., *Early British Railways*, 1925.

Lewis, W. Arthur, *The Theory of Economic Growth*, 1955.

Lewis, W. Arthur, 'International Competition in Manufactures', *American Economic Review Papers and Proceedings*, 1957.

Leyton, W. I., 'Changes in the Wages of Domestic Servants during Fifty Years', *Journal of the Royal Statistical Society*, 1908.

Lipson, E., *Economic History of England*, 1947.

Lomax, K. S., 'Production and Productivity Movements in the United Kingdom since 1900', *Journal of the Royal Statistical Society*, 1959.

Lord, John, *Capital and Steampower 1750–1800*, 1923.

Lover of his Country, *A Short Essay upon Trade in General but more enlarged on that relating to the woollen manufacturers of Great Britain and Ireland, etc., etc.*, 1741.

Lowe, Joseph, *The Present State of England*, 1822.

Luccock, John, *The Nature and Properties of Wool*, 1809.

McCulloch, J. R., *A Statistical Account of the British Empire*, 1837.

McKeown, Thomas, and Brown, R. G., 'Medical Evidence related to English Population Changes in the Eighteenth Century', *Population Studies*, 1955.

Macpherson, D., *Annals of Commerce*, 4 vols., 1805.

Malthus, T. R., *Principles of Political Economy*, 1836.

Mantoux, P., *The Industrial Revolution in the Eighteenth Century*, 1928.

Marshall, T. H., 'The Population Problem during the Industrial Revolution: A Note on the Present State of the Controversy', and 'The Population of England and Wales from the Industrial Revolution to the World War'. Both reprinted in E. M. Carus-Wilson, *Essays in Economic History*, 1954.

Massie, James, *A Computation of the Money that hath been Exorbitantly Raised, etc.*, 1760.

Mathias, Peter, 'The Social Structure of the Eighteenth Century; a Calculation by Joseph Massie', *Economic History Review*, 1957.

Maywald, K., 'The Construction Costs and the Value of the Merchant Fleet', *Scottish Journal of Political Economy*, 1956.

Meade, R., *The Coal and Iron Industries of the United Kingdom*, 1882.

Meek, R. L., 'Adam Smith and the Classical Concept of Profit', *Scottish Journal of Political Economy*, 1954.

Merttens, F., 'The Hours and Cost of Labour in the Cotton Industry at Home and Abroad', *Transactions of the Manchester Statistical Society*, 1893–4.

Middleton, J., *View of the Agriculture of Middlesex*, 1807.

Minchinton, W. E., *The British Tinplate Industry*, 1957.

Ministry of Agriculture and Fisheries, *The Agricultural Output and Food Supplies of Great Britain*, 1929.

Mingay, G. E., 'The Agricultural Depression, 1730–1750', *Economic History Review*, 1956.

Mitchell, B. R., 'The Coming of the Railway Age and United Kingdom Economic Growth', *Journal of Economic History*, 1964.

Mortimer, Jacob, *The Whole Art of Husbandry*, 1707.

Mullett, C. F., 'The Cattle Distemper in Mid-Eighteenth Century England', *Agricultural History*, 1946.

Mushet, David, *Papers on Iron and Steel*, 1840.

Mussson, A. E., and Robinson, E., 'The Early Growth of Steampower', *Economic History Review*, 1959.

Nef, J. U., *The Rise of the British Coal Industry*, 2 vols., 1932.

Nef, J. U., 'The Industrial Revolution Reconsidered', *Journal of Economic History*, 1943.

Newton, Mary, and Jeffery, James, 'Internal Migration', *General Register Office Studies on Medical and Population Subjects*, No. 5, 1951.

O'Brien, P. K., 'British Income and Property in the Early Nineteenth Century', *Economic History Review*, 1959.

Oddy, J. Jepson, *European Commerce*, 1805.

Pares, R., 'The London Sugar Market, 1740–1769', *Economic History Review*, 1956.

Pares, R., *War and Trade in the West Indies*, 1936.

Parker, R. A. C., 'Coke of Norfolk and the Agrarian Revolution', *Economic History Review*, 1955.

Pebrer, Pablo, *Taxation, Expenditure, Power, Statistics and Debt of the whole British Empire*, 1833.

Play, F. Le, *Description des Procédés Métallurgiques*, Paris, 1848.

Plot, Robert, *Natural History of Staffordshire*, 1686.

Poole, G. Braithwaite, *Statistics of Commerce*, 1852.

Porter, G. R., *Progress of the Nation*, 1847.

Porter, G. R., 'Treatise on the Silk Manufacture', in *The Cabinet Cyclopedia*, edited by Dionysius Lardner, 1831.

Prest, A. R., 'National Income of the United Kingdom 1870–1946', *Economic Journal*, 1948.

Prest, A. R., and Adams, A. A., *Consumers' Expenditure in the United Kingdom 1900–1919*, 1954.

Price-Williams, R., 'The Coal Question', *Journal of the Royal Statistical Society*, 1889.

Priestley, J., *Historical Account of Navigable Rivers, Canals and Railways of Great Britain*, 1831.

Ragatz, L. J., *The Fall of the Planter Class in the British Caribbean, 1763–1833*, New York, 1928.
Razzell, P. E., 'Population Change in Eighteenth Century England. A Reinterpretation', *Economic History Review*, 1965.
Redford, A., *Labour Migration in England*, 1926.
Rickman, John (ed.), *Life of Thomas Telford*, 1938.
Roepke, Howard G., 'Movements of the British Iron and Steel Industry, 1720–1951', *Illinois Studies in the Social Sciences*, Urbana, 1956.
Rogers, J. Thorold, *History of Agriculture and Prices in England*, 7 vols., 1866–1902.
Rostow, W. W., *The Stages of Economic Growth*, 1960.
Rousseaux, Paul, *Les Mouvements de Fond de l'Economie Anglaise 1800–1913*, Louvain, 1938.

Salaman, R. N., *The History and Social Influence of the Potato*, 1949.
Salt, Samuel, *Statistics and Calculations*, 1845.
Schubert, H. R., *History of the British Iron and Steel Industry*, 1957.
Schumpeter, E. B., *English Overseas Trade Statistics, 1697–1808*, 1960.
Schumpeter, E. B., 'English Prices and Public Finance 1660–1822', *Review of Economic Statistics*, 1938.
Scott, W. R., *The Constitution and Finance of English, Scottish and Irish Joint-Stock Companies to 1720*, 3 vols., 1911.
Scrivenor, H., *History of the Iron Trade*, 1854.
Sheridan, R. B., 'The Wealth of Jamaica in the Eighteenth Century', *Economic History Review*, 1965.
Sinclair, Sir John, *General Report of the Agricultural State and Political Circumstances of Scotland*. Drawn up for the consideration of the Board of Agriculture and Internal Improvement, Edinburgh, 1814. In 3 vols. plus 2 vols. of appendices. Extracts from these have been published elsewhere in various sources, e.g. *The Pamphleteer*, 1817.
Sinclair, Sir John, *Analysis of the Statistical Account of Scotland, with a General View of the History of that Country and Discussions on some Important Branches of Political Economy*, 1825.
Singer, Charles, Holmyard, E. J., Hall, A. R., and Williams, Trevor, *A History of Technology*, 4 vols., 1959.
Slater, Gilbert, *The English Peasantry and the Enclosure of Common Fields*, 1907.
Smith, Charles, *Three Tracts on the Corn Trade and the Corn Laws*, 1766.
Smith, J., *Memoirs of Wool*, 2 vols., 1757.
Solow, Robert, 'A Skeptical Note on the Constancy of Relative Shares', *American Economic Review*, 1958.
Stamp, J. C., *British Incomes and Property*, 1916.
Steel, W. L., *The History of the London and Northwestern Railway*, 1914.
Stephenson, Robert, *Observations on the Present State of the Linen Trade of Ireland*, 1784.

Taylor, F. D. W., 'United Kingdom Numbers in Agriculture', *The Farm Economist*, 1955.
Thomas, Brinley, *Migration and Economic Growth*, 1954.
Thorp, W. L., *Business Annals*, New York, 1926.
Tooke, Thomas, and Newmarch, W., *History of Prices 1793–1856*, 6 vols., 1838–1857.

Wadsworth, A. P., and Mann, J. L., *The Cotton Trade and Industrial Lancashire 1600–1780*, 1931.
Warden, A. J., *The Linen Trade Ancient and Modern*, 1864.
Welton, Thomas, 'On the Distribution of Population in England and Wales', *Journal of the Royal Statistical Society*, 1900.

Wheeler, James, *Manchester, its Political, Social and Commercial History*, 1836.

Whishaw, F., *The Railways of Great Britain and Ireland*, 1840.

Whittam, William, *England's Cotton Industry*. Report published by U.S. Department of Commerce and Labour, Bureau of Manufactures, 1907.

Williams, R. Price, 'On the Increase of Population in England and Wales', *Journal of the Statistical Society*, 1880.

Wissett, R., *A Compendium of East Indian Affairs*, 1802.

Wood, G. H., 'Factory Legislation Considered with Reference to the Wages, etc. of Operatives Protected thereby', *Journal of the Royal Statistical Society*, 1902.

Wood, G. H., 'The Course of Average Wages between 1790 and 1860', *The Economic Journal*, 1899.

Wood, George H., 'Real Wages and the Standard of Comfort since 1850', *Journal of the Royal Statistical Society*, 1909.

Wood, G. H., 'The Statistics of Wages in the United Kingdom during the Nineteenth Century: The Cotton Industry', *Journal of the Royal Statistical Society*, 1910.

Young, Arthur, *Political Arithmetic*, 1774–9.

Young, G. M., *Early Victorian England*, 1953.

Youngson, A. J., *Possibilities of Economic Progress*, 1959.

INDEX

References to tables and figures are given in italics

AFRICA, 86, *87*
Agriculture, 62–75
  capital, *271*, 273, *274*, *306*
  contribution to national income, 62, 77,
    155–7, 160–*1*, 162, *166*, 168, 174–*5*, *178*,
    180, 290, *291–2*, *298*, *299*
  employment incomes, 151–2, *257*
  index of output, 76, *78*
  investment, 90, 94–5, 261, 272, 304
  labour productivity, 75
  numbers in, 3, 62, 75, 137, 141, *142*, *143*–
    4, 145, *147*, 211
  prices, 79, 89–95, 280
  real product, *170*, *172*
  wages, 20, 21, 27
  Board of Agriculture, 194
America, North, 34, 38, 86, *87*
American War of Independence, 30, 34, 45,
  46, 47, 49, 85, 88, 261
Amiens, Peace of, 323
Anglesey, Isle of, 56–7
Arkwright's water-frame, 183
Armed forces, 102, 138
  pay, 243, *245*
Ashton, T. S., 40, 72, 90, 96, 137
Australasia, 38
Austrian Succession, War of, 48, 49, 85, 310

BAINES, EDWARD, 198
Balance of Payments, 33–8
Bank of England, 260
Barley, 63, 64
  yields, 66–7
Barna, T., 270
Bath, 112
Bedfordshire, 75n., 102, *103*, *108*, 110n.,
  112, *115*, *131*
Beeke, H., 158, 160, 270, 272, 304
Beer, *51*, 57
  See also brewing industry
Behrens, Sir Jacob, 198
Bell, Benjamin, 158, 160
Bellerby, J. R., 144, 165, 168, *298*, 301
Berkshire, *103*, *108*, *115*, *131*, 132
Beveridge, Lord, 13
Birmingham, 7, 120–1
Birth rate, 7, 122–35, 286, 287–8
Boer War, 268
Booth, Charles, 140
Bowley, A. L., 20, 21, 22–5, 148–9, 159, 241,
  245, 246, 250, 268, 300
Bradford Chamber of Commerce, 193, 194,
  197, 198
Brewing industry, 61
  See also beer
Bridgewater Canal, 237

Bristol, 7, 105n., 132n.
British Association, 22, 23
Brown, E. H. Phelps, 38, 241, 264, 275, 283
Brownlee, John, 5, 65, 77, 99, 100, 101, 102,
  106, 107, 124, 130, 155
Buckinghamshire, *103*, *108*, 112, *115*, *131*
Building industry, 58
  contribution to national income, *175*, *299*
  numbers in, *143*, *147*
  wages, 18, *19*–21, 26
Burn, D. L., 229

CAIRNCROSS, A. K., 10, 117, 264, 267
Cambridgeshire, 75n., *103*, 105, *108*, *115*,
  131
Campion, H., 274, *306*
Canada, 86n.
Canals, 97n., 238, 261, 262, 304
Capital
  consumption, 265, *307*
  formation, 3, 259–77, *303–9*
  —, government, 268, *313*
  growth, 268–*9*
  structure, 269–73, *274*, 275–6, 304, *305–6*,
    307
  See also investment
Capital-output ratio, *274*–7, *306*
Cattle
  numbers, 69
  plague, 70, 72, 74
  sales, 70–*2*
  size, 69–70
Central Statistical Office, 174, 242, 264, 307
Chapman, Agatha L., 151, 177, 243
Chemical industry
  contribution to national income, *175*, *178*,
    298, *299*
  exports, *31*
  numbers in, *146*
Cheshire, *103*, 104, *108*, 110n., 113n., 114,
  115, 129, *131*
Civil War, American, 188
Civil War, English, 60
Clapham, J. H., 215, 217
Cleveland, 228
Clothing and dress industries, *146*
Coal industry, 55, 59, 214–20
  coastal shipments, *51*, 55n., 59, 60, 6 ,
    215, 219
  contribution to national income, 218, 220
  exports, *31*, *59*, *216*
  investment, 263
  markets, 218–20
  output, *216*
  prices, *84*, 217–18
  wages, 20

Cobden Treaty, 209
Coleman, D. C., 58
Colonies
  British trade with, 34, 86–8
  investment in, 34–5
Colquhoun, Patrick, 3, 149, 158–9, 160, 184, 208, 252–3, 256, 272–3, 300
Committee on Industry and Trade, 193
Companies, joint-stock, 1
Connell, K. H., 5, 9n.
Copper and brass industries, 56–7, 58–9
  exports, 58–9
Copper-mining, 56, 61, 214
  Cornish output, 51
Coppock, D, J., 283
Corn Laws, 90, 92
Cornish Metal Company, 57
Cornwall, 51, 56–7, 58n., 103, 108, 115, 131
Cort, Henry, 221, 261
Cotton famine, 188, 204
Cotton industry, 50–2, 182–92, 293–5
  contribution to national income, 163, 184, 188, 191, 293, 294
  effect on other textile industries, 53, 54–5, 212–13
  exports, 30, 31–2, 59, 185, 187, 295
  imports of raw cotton, 51, 163, 184, 185, 187, 295
  inventions, 183
  investment, 190, 262, 263, 295
  labour force, 26, 27, 189–90, 191, 294
  mechanisation, 189, 190–1
  output, 185, 187, 212
  profits, 188–9, 295
  wages, 26, 27, 186, 187, 188–9, 295
Crompton's mule, 183
Cumberland, 103, 105, 108, 114, 115, 117, 131, 228
Customs duties, 2, 45, 88

Dairy Produce, imports of, 32, 74
Darby, Abraham, 61
Death rate, *see* mortality
Derbyshire, 103, 105, 108, 110, 114, 115, 117, 131
Devonshire, 100, 101–2, 103, 108, 115, 131, 132n.
Directors' fees, 254–5
Docks and harbours, investment in, 236, 262
Domestic service
  incomes, 1, 152, 175, 177, 178, 179, 299
  numbers in, 141, 142, 143, 147
Dorset, 103, 109, 115, 131
Douglas, P. H., 264
Dublin, 24
Dundee, 206
Durham, County, 103, 104, 105, 109, 113, 115, 131, 132

East India Company, 316n.
East Indies, 42, 87
Ecton, Staffordshire, 56n.
Eden, Sir F. M., 20, 42, 184, 328

Edinburgh, 7, 12
Electrical industry, exports, 31
Ellison, T., 183, 186, 187, 189, 203–4
Employees, 247–8, 303
Employers, 247–8
  insurance contributions, 243, 245
Enclosures, 75, 95, 161, 261, 272, 276–7, 304
Essex, 103, 108, 111, 115, 128, 131
Europe, Continental, 34, 86, 87, 188n.
Exports, 2, 28, 46, 47–9, 58–60, 86–8, 319–21
  at 1796–8 prices, 43–4, 316
  commodity composition, 30–2, 59
  geographical distribution, 34, 86, 87
  growth rates, 311
  'invisible', 34, 35–7
  official valuations, 42
  percentages of national income, 28–9, 33, 309–10
  prices, 84, 85, 162, 317
  world, 33

Factory Acts, 201, 211
Farr, William, 99, 100, 124
Feinstein, C. H., 264, 265, 281, 307
Finlaison, population estimates by, 62–3
Food imports, 32–3
France, 38n., 208–9
Francis, J., 229, 230
Fussell, G. E., 62–3, 69

Gasworks, 273
Gayer, A. D., 14–15, 16, 25
Giffen, R., 273, 274, 305
Gilboy, Elizabeth W., 13–14, 18, 19–20, 21, 91
Gin drinking, 93, 127, 134, 288
Glasgow, 7, 8
Glass and earthenware exports, 31
Glass industry, 51, 58
Gloucestershire, 103, 105, 109, 112, 113, 115, 131, 132
Gold discoveries, 17
Gonner, E. C. K., 100, 101, 104, 105
Government
  capital formation, 268, 313
  contribution to national income, 156, 158, 161, 162, 175, 177, 178, 179, 299
  employees' incomes, 153, 257, 294
  expenditure, 2, 3, 77, 78, 268
  output index, 76–7, 78
Grain
  consumption, 62–5
  exports, 42n., 65, 93, 94
  imports, 32, 65, 94
  output, 62–8, 74–5
  prices, 66
Greenwich Hospital, 71n., 217, 218
Griffith, G. Talbot, 99, 100, 106, 124

Habakkuk, H. J., 90, 98, 286
Hamilton, Archibald, 193, 197

Hampshire, *103*, *109*, 110n., 112, *115*, *131*
Hargreaves' spinning jenny, 183
Hart, P. E., 241
Harvests, 14, 66, 79
    economic effects of variations in, 89–95
Hemp products, 206
Herefordshire, 75n., *103*, *108*, 114, *115*, *131*, 133
Hertfordshire, *103*, *108*, 112, *115*, *131*
Hides and skins, *72*, 73–4
Hoffmann, W. G., 40–1, 79, 161–2, 296
Holkham, Norfolk, 69n.
Holland, 38
Hope-Jones, A., 323
Hubbard, 194, 195
Hume, David, 253
Hunt, Robert, 214
Huntingdonshire, 75n., *103*, *108*, *115*, *131*, 132

IMLAH, A. H., 35, 235, 265, 296, 297, 311
Immigration, Irish, 11, 172, 283
Imports, 2, 34, *46–7*, 48–9, 86–8, *319–21*
    at 1796–8 prices, *44*, 315–16
    commodity composition, 32–*3*
    estimates of, c.i.f., 47, 318–19, *319–21*
    geographical distribution, 34, *87*
    net, *46*, 47, *48*, 50
    official valuations, 42–3
    percentages of national income, 29, 309–10, 311n.
    prices, *84*, 85, 88, 91n., *317*
Income, national, 2, 3, 38, 159–60, 164–5, *166*, *175*, *178*, *274*, 278–85, *311*, 313, *328*, *329–33*
    contemporary estimates, 41, 81–2, 155–9, 164, 250–1, 251–3, 278–9, 290–1
    factor composition, 241–58, 299–303
    See also national output and product
Income tax, 34, 159–60, 164, 323–8
Incomes
    employment, 148–53, 241–58, 300, *301*–3
    mixed, 252, 299–300
    See also self-employed
India, 86n.
Industrial Revolution, 40
Industry
    contribution to national income, *156*, 157, *161*, 162, *166*, 168, 169, 174, 177–8, 180, 181, 290, *291*, 292, 299
    distribution of labour force, *146*
    employment incomes, 151, *152*, *257*
    growth, 40–1, 50–62, 162, *170*, 171, 172–3, 296–7, 299
    numbers in, 141–*2*, *143*, 144, 145, *147*
    index of output, 76, 77, *78*, 79, 280
    percentage of output exported, 42, 312
    prices, 91n., 162
Investment
    domestic, 2, *266*, 267, 269, 303, *308*
    foreign, in Britain, 34
    overseas, by Britain, 2, 34, *36*, 37, *266*, 267, 269, *271*, 273–4, 275, 303, *306*, *308*

Investment—*cont.*
    overseas, income from, 34–5, *36*, 37, *166*, 168–9, *175*, 176–7, *178*, 179, 180, 293
    See also capital formation
Ireland, 74, 86, 151, 168, 173–4, 248, 249, 256, 281, 283, 284
    cotton industry, 202
    labour force, 146–7
    linen industry, 201–2, 203, 204, 205, 206
    population, 5–*6*, 8, 9, 11–12, 172
    railways, 231
    textile industries, 137
    wages, *23*–4, 25, 27
    wool clip, 194
    woollen industry, 201
Irish Free State, 174
Iron and steel industry, 55, 58, 221–9
    contribution to national income, 223, 225–*6*
    exports, *31*, 32, 58, *59*, 221–2, *225*
    imports, *51*
    investment, 227–9, 262, 263, 273
    output, *225*
    prices, *84*, 222
    wages, 20
Iron-mining, 214, 220, 227
Irving, Thomas, 43, 44, 315, 316
Irving, William, 222
Isserlis, L., 239

JAMAICA, 89
James I, King, 60
James, John, 198
Jefferys, James B., 174, 243, 245, 246, 264, 281
John, King, 60
Jubb, Samuel, 197
Jute industry, 206–7

KALECKI, M., 242
Kay's flying shuttle, 183n.
Kent, *19*, *103*, 104, *109*, 111, *115*, *131*
Keynes, J. M., 241–2
King, Gregory, 1, 3, 28, 34, 35, 38, 67, 68, 69–70, 77, 82, 100, 137, 155–8, 252, 254, 256, 259, 263, 270, 279, 290, 300, 303
King's Lynn, 132n.
Knight, Rose, 151, 177, 243
Krause, J. T., 124–6, 130, 286

LABOUR
    changing attitudes towards, 93–4
    child, 139–40, 189–*90*, 211, 294
    female, 139–40, 189–*90*, 211, 294
    force, 27, 136–48, 191
    scarcity and technical innovation, 96–7
    supply and population growth, 89, 93, 96
    Ministry of Labour, 16, 268
    See also wages and employment incomes
Lancashire, 18–*19*, 20, 50, 56, *103*, 104, 105, *109*, 113–16, 119, 121, 129–30, *131*, 133, 228, 286, 287
Land, investment in, *271*–2, 273, 304
Lead-mining, 214

Leather industry, 57, 58n., 62
  See also hides and skins
Leeds, 120, 122
Leicestershire, *103, 109, 115, 131*, 133
Lincolnshire, 75n., *103*, 105, *108, 115, 131*
Linen industry, 52–3, 59–60, 201–6
  contribution to national income, 203, 205
  exports, *31, 59*–60, 205–6
  mechanisation, 203, 205, 206
  numbers in, 205
  output, *204, 212*
  raw material imports, *51, 204*
Liverpool, 119, 121
Lomax, K. S., 296, 299, 296–7
London, 3, 7, 8, *10*, 12, 18–*19*, 20, 21, 63, 72,
    97, 104, 111, 112, 113, *115*, 118, 120,
    121, *126, 127*–8, 130, 133, 134, 217, 287,
    288–9
  Coal Exchange, 217
  coal imports, *51*, 55n., 59, 215, 219
  Docks, 236
  Great Fire of, 260
  Great Plague of, 260
Louis XIV, King of France, 60, 91
Lowe, Joseph, 15–16, 164
Luccock, Sir John, 71, 194, 197

McCulloch, J. R., 195, 198, 209–10
Machinery exports, *31*
Macpherson, D., 53, 207, 321
Malt, 63, 64
Manchester, 8, 119, 120–1, 238
Mantoux, Paul, 45, 49
Marx, Karl, 98
Massie, Joseph, 82, 254, 279
Maywald, K., 264, 265, 270, 274, 308
Meat
  imports, 32–3, 74
  production, 68–75
Middlesex, 100,101,*103*,*109*,111,*115*,128,*131*
Middleton Tyas, Yorkshire, 56n.
Migration
  external, *10*, 11, 99, 289–90
  internal, *10*–11, 106–22, 287, 289
  See also immigration, Irish
Mining industry, 214–20
  contribution to national income, *175, 178*,
    220, 298, *299*
  employment incomes, *257*
  numbers in, *143*, 144, 145, *147*, 220
  wages, 20
  See also coal industry, copper-mining, etc.
Monmouthshire, *103*, 104, 107, *109*, 113,
    115, 131, 133
Mortality, 6–7, 122–35, 286, 287, 288
  infant, 7
Motor industry, 179, 240
Mulhall, M. G., 69

Napoleonic Wars, 14, 15–16, 17, 24, 27,
    30–1, 75, 96, 124–5, 127, 153, 168, 180,
    227, 268, 283, 291, 294
National Debt, 294
Navigation Acts, 86

Navy, Royal, 69, 222
Nef, J. U., 40, 55, 59
Newcastle-on-Tyne, 217
Newcomen's steam engine. 56, 61, 96
Nonconformity, 125n., 130
Norfolk, *103, 108, 115, 131*, 132
Northamptonshire, *103, 109, 115, 131*
Northumberland, *103*, 104, 105, *109*, 113,
    115, 131, 132
Norwich, 7, 132n.
Nottinghamshire, *103, 109, 115, 131*, 133

Oats, 63, 64
  yields, 66–7
Oddy, J. Jepson, 53
Output, national, 75–82, 280–1
Oxford Agricultural Economics Research
    Institute, 165, 298, 301
Oxfordshire, *19, 103, 108, 115, 131*, 132n.

Paper Industry, 58, *146*
Paris, Peace of (1763), 86n.
Pebrer, Pablo, 272–3, 304
Personal service industries, *142*, 143
Pewter, 56n.
Pitt, William (the Younger), 34, 45, 89, 158,
    160, 323
Population, 5–12, 98–135, 285–90
  and economic growth, 89–97
  England and Wales, 5–*6*, 65
  Great Britain, 5, 7, *8*, 9, 11
  Ireland, 5–*6*, *8*, 9, 11–12, 172, 174
  rural, 3, 9–11
  United Kingdom, *6*, *8*
  urban, 7–8, 9–11, 119–22
Porter, G. R., 209, 210
Portsmouth, 112
Power steam, 171, 191, 206, 210–1, 215, 218,
    226, 230, 251–3, 273, 283, 306
Prest, A. R., 174, 241, 243, 245, 246, 281
Prices, 12–18, 90–1, 95, 279, 281–2, *Fig. 7 at
    end of book*
  See also agriculture, exports, imports, in-
    dustry, etc.
Printed goods, *54*–5
Product, national
  industrial structure, 154–81, 290–9
  disposition, *266, 332*–3
  See also national income and output
Production, Censuses of, 173, 177, 198, 199,
    206, 210, 218, 220

Railway Industry, 229–34, 295–6
  contribution to national income, *176*, 180
  investment, *231, 232, 233*, 261, 263, *271*,
    273, 306
  numbers in, 231–2
  output, *233*–4
  traffic receipts, *177, 232, 233*
Raw material imports, 32, *33*
Redfern, P., 269–70, 307
Re-exports, 32, 35, 45–*6*, 309n., *317, 319*–21
  at 1796–8 prices, *44*, 50, 315
  geographical distribution, *87*
  official valuations, 42

Rents, *2*, 241, *247–8*, 251, 300, *301*
  arrears, 92, 95
  dwelling, *156*, *161*, 162, *166*, 169, *175*, 177, *178*, *291*, 292, *299*, 301
  restrictions, 301
Rhodesia and Nyasaland, Federation of, 256n.
Ribble, River, 119
Rickman, John, 5, 99–104, 122, 138
Roads, 97n., 236–8, 261, 304
Roses, Wars of, 38
Rostow, W. W., 14–15, 16, 25, 40, 260–1, 263, 280
Rousseaux, P., 16, 170, 282
Russia, 86
Rutland, 75n., *103*, 105, *108*, 110n., 114, *115*, *131*
Rye, 63
  yields, 66–7

SALARIES, 243, *245*, 246 303n.
Salt, Samuel, 216
Sankey Brook, 237
Schubert, H. R., 221
Schumpeter, Elizabeth B., 13–14, 316, 317, 318, 319
Schwartz, Anna J., 14–15, 16, 25
Scotland, 256, 281
  iron industry, 228
  jute industry, 206
  linen industry, *51*, 52–3, 60, 202, 203, 205, 206, 214
  overseas trade, 43n., 316, 319
  population, 5–*6*
  railways, 231
  wages, 27
  wool clip, 195
Self-employed
  decline of, 247
  numbers of, 149–50, *248*
  share of national income, 254
  See also mixed incomes
Service industries, 76–7, 78, 141, *156*, *161*, 162, *166*
  public and professional, *142*, *143*, 145, *147*, *152*
  domestic and personal, 141, *142*, *143*, 145, *166*, 211, 293
  See also domestic service, government employees, personal services
Seven Years War, 45, 85
Sheep
  numbers, 68, 73, 194, *195*
  sales, 70–*2*
Sheffield, 120, 122
Shipbuilding industry, 26, *234–6*
Shipping earnings, 34, *36*, *37*, 177, 179, *234*, 235, 296
Shoddy, 197
Shropshire, *103*, 107, *109*, 114, *115*, 121, *131*
Silk industry, 53–4, 207–11
  exports, *31*, *59*
  imports, *51*, 207, 208, 210
  output, *210*, *212*

Sinclair, Sir John, 5, 69–70
Smith, Adam, 90, 94, 98, 253
Smith, Charles, 63–5
Smithfield market, 69, 70–2
Smuggling, 44–5, 50
Soap industry, 57, 58n., *72*
Solow, R. M., 302
Somerset, *103*, *109*, *115*, *131*
Southampton, 112n.
Spanish Succession, War of, 49, 85, 88, 310
Staffordshire, *103*, 104, *109*, 113–14, *115*, 119, 120, 121–2, *131*, 133, 286, 287
Stamp, J. C., 245, 246, 249
Stephenson, Robert, 202
Stockton and Darlington Railway, 229, 230
Stone, J. R. N., 243
Stubs, Peter, 137
Suffolk, *103*, *108*, *115*, *131*
Sunderland, 217
Surrey, *103*, 104, *109*, 111, *115*, 128, *131*
Sussex, *103*, *108*, 114, *115*, *131*, 132

TALLOW
  candles, 57–8, *72–3*
  imports, *72*, 73
Textile industries, 163, 211–14
  contribution to national income, 163, 174–6, 212, 213, 214, 293
  exports, 31, 295
  imports, 32
  numbers in, 146, 211
  output, *212*, *213*
Thomas, Brinley, 289
Thorp, W. L., 171
Timber, *see* wood
Tin
  consumption, *51*, 56n.
  exports, *59*
  mining, 56, 214
  output, *51*, 56, 60
Tin-plate, 56n., 61
Tooke, Thomas, 43, 315
Toynbee, Arnold, 40
Trade
  contribution to national income, *175*, *178*, *299*
  employment incomes, *257*
  numbers in, *143*, 144, *147*
  overseas, 28–33, 41–50, 60–1, 83–8, 161–2, 180, 309–12, 315–22
  terms of, 48–9, 60, 83–5, 86–8, *319–21*
  Board of Trade, 151, 193, 194, 195, 196
  See also balance of payments, exports, imports and re-exports
Tramp-shipping freights, 240
Transport, 97n., 229, 238–40, 296
  contribution to national income, *175*, 176, *178*, 239, 240, *299*
  employment incomes, *257*
  investment, 239, 263, 274, 276, 277
  See also canals, railways, roads, etc.

UNEMPLOYMENT, 27, 150, 250
Union, Act of (1707), 321n.
United States of America, 33, 38
Urbanisation, 7–11, 99, 120–2, 261
Utrecht, Treaty of, 85

VEHICLES, EXPORTS OF, *31*

WAGES, 18–28, 91
    share of national income, 243, *245*, 246–7
Wages and salaries, *2*, 241–2
    industrial distribution, *152*, *257*
    share of national income, *247*, 251
    See also employment incomes
Walters, Dorothy, 174, 243, 245, 246, 264, 281
Warden, A. J., 203
Warwickshire, *103*, 104, *109*, 113–14, *115*, 119, 120, 121–2, *131*, 133, 286, 287
Waterloo, Battle of, 215, 218
Watt, James, 218, 221
Weber, B., 275
West Indies, 34, 86–8
Westminster School and Abbey, 71n.
Westmorland, *103*, 105, *109*, 114, *115*, 117, *131*
Wheat
    bread, consumption of, 62–3, 66
    output and yields, 62, 66–7
    prices, *91*
Whitney's cotton gin, 183
Wight, Isle of, 112n.
Williams, R. Price, 10
Wiltshire, *103*, *108*, *115*, *131*
Winchester, 112n.
    College, 13, 71
Wolverhampton, 120n.

Wood, G. H., 22–6, 248–9, 159, 187, 245, 250, 268, 300
Wood
    imports, *51*, 58
    industries, *146*, *175*
Wool
    imports, 69, 197
    production, 68–9, 197
Woollen and worsted industries, 52, 61, 77, 192–201
    contribution to national income, 199–200, 293–4
    exports, 30, *31*, 42–3, *59*, *196*, 295, *322*
    investment, 263
    mechanisation, *200*–1
    numbers in, 137, 201
    output, 184, *196*, *212*
    wages, 26
Worcester, *103*, 105, *109*, 110n., *115*, 121, *131*, 133
World War, First, 16, 37, 245, 246–7, 251, 257, 269, 284–5, 298
World War, Second, 16, 37, 153n., 243, 246, 247, 251, 257, 284–5, 298

YARMOUTH, GREAT, 132n.
Yorkshire
    East Riding, 102, *103*, 104, *109*, 110n., 113–14, *115*, 122, *131*
    North Riding, *103*, *109*, 113, 114, *115*, 117, *131*
    West Riding, 52, *103*, 104, 107, *109*, 113–14, *115*, 119, 121, 122, 129–30, *131*, 286, 287

YOUNG, ARTHUR, 20, 69, 77, 82, 155–8, 207, 279, 290